Antique Trader®

Furniture
PRICE GUIDE

Published by
Antique Trader Books, A Division of

krause publications

700 East State Street • Iola, WI 54990-0001
715/445-2214 • FAX: 715/445-4087   www.krause.com

Please, call or write us for our free catalog of antiques and collectibles publications.
Our toll-free number to place an order or obtain a free catalog is 800-258-0929 or
please use our regular business telephone, 715-445-2214.

Library of Congress Catalog Number: 2001091077
ISBN: 0-87349-225-0

Printed in the United States of America

TABLE OF CONTENTS

INTRODUCTION

It was in 1997 that Antique Trader Books published its first Furniture Price Guide and we are now proud to introduce an all new and greatly expanded edition of the comprehensive guide. Our focus continues to be on antique furniture from the 18th through the early 20th centuries, however, as the market has continued to evolve you'll find that we have worked to include a broader selection of collectible furniture up through the mid-20th century. American-made furniture pieces comprise a large majority of the listings included here but in order to reflect the full gamut of the furniture marketplace we also provide a selection of English, French, German and other European and even Oriental furniture.

As with all our price guides we have strived to provide the most accurate and detailed descriptions of each item listed and this volume is especially rich in illustrations, with some 1,200 black and white photographs included. In addition a special 16 page color supplement highlights some of the most interesting and exciting pieces we have listed here.

Since we would like this book to serve as a good general reference to furniture as well as simply a pricing guide we have added several special features including a special section of sketches to help you identify the various components of most furniture pieces, a timeline chart to major furniture styles, a select Bibliography of furniture books and two helpful Appendices, one listing major auction houses which deal in furniture and then a carefully illlustrated chart with "Stylisitic Guidlines" to American and English furniture.

I must express my sincere gratitude to Mark Moran, the Contributing Editor, who worked diligently to gather a tremendous selection of illustrations and descriptions of furniture through several sources. His efforts and dedication to producing the finest guide possible is greatly appreciated by my staff and myself as I know it will be by our readers. You will find a fine overview of the furniture marketplace today in Mark's special feature, "Antique Furniture in the New Millennium."

We also must acknowledge our debt to a large number of dealers and auction houses who generously shared information and photographs from their sales held in recent years. We list them below in alphabetical order:

Albrecht Auction Service, Vassar, Michigan; Alderfers, Hatfield, Pennsylvania; Jay Anderson Antiques, Wabasha, Minnesota; Charlton Hall Galleries, Columbia, South Carolina; Christie's, New York, New York; Copake Country Auctions, Copake, New York; Craftsman Auctions, Pittsfield, Massachusetts; DeFina Auctions, Austenburg, Ohio; William Doyle Galleries, New York, New York; DuMouchelles, Detroit, Michigan; John Fountaine Gallery, Pittsfield, Massachusetts; Garth's Auctions, Delaware, Ohio; Green Valley Auctions, Mt. Crawford, Virginia; Gene Harris Antique Auction Center, Marshalltown, Iowa; Michael Ivankovich Antiques & Auctions, Doylestown, Pennsylvania; Greg Kowles, Winona, Minnesota; Jackson's Auctioneers & Appraisers, Cedar Falls, Iowa; Northeast Auctions, Portsmouth, New Hampshire; Pettigrew Auctions, Colorado Springs, Colorado; David Rago Arts & Crafts, Lambertville, New Jersey; Skinner, Inc., Bolton, Massachusetts; Slawinski Auction Company, Felton, California; Sotheby's, New York, New York; and Treadway Gallery, Cincinnati, Ohio.

It is my hope that our efforts will provide you with the most comprehensive, detailed, accurate and well-illustrated pricing guide to the wide world of antique furniture and that it will serve all our readers well whether they are collectors, dealers, appraisers or simply students of American material culture. We always welcome letters from our readers and will do our best to reply if you have questions about this volume.

Kyle Husfloen, Editor

Please note: Though listings have been double-checked and every effort has been made to insure accuracy, neither the compilers, editors nor publisher can assume responsibility for any losses that might be incurred as a result of consulting this guide, or of errors, typographical or otherwise.

ON THE COVER: Left to right: a Victorian Renaissance Revival marble-topped walnut chest of drawers, $1,500 - $2,500, courtesy of Greg Kowles, Winona, Minnesota; a Victorian Rococo rosewood side chair, one of a set of four, $528, courtesy of Garth's Auctions, Delaware, Ohio.; a one-door country-style grain-painted corner cupboard, $2,500 - $3,500, courtesy of Garth's Auctions, Delaware, Ohio.

Antique Furniture in the New Millennium

By Mark Moran

The antiques marketplace has changed dramatically since this price guide was last updated eight years ago, and depending on who you talk to, the Internet and the cell phone have either been the trade's savior or its curse. Consider this:

Only a decade ago, the average dealer in Fond du Lac or Flagstaff, Bakersfield or Bangor had to rely on word of mouth, an ad in the regional trade paper, or the luck of a drop-in customer to sell merchandise that was unusual, eclectic or just plain odd. And good furniture—no matter how creatively presented or reasonably priced—is still the hardest sell of all.

And the retail customer—not the seasoned collector, but the average buyer seeking an accent piece or the right accessory—was limited by regional tastes and local bias: Refinished oak or old paint? Classic influences or country primitive? Victorian formal or folk-art funky?

The Internet has given buyers and sellers a global reach, but not all have embraced its influence. Some antique malls and shops have actually put up signs trumpeting "We don't sell on eBay!" They think this is something to be proud of, but when the market changes in such a profound way, those who ignore opportunities presented by technology are left to wonder why other dealers are thriving and the tech-fearing are not.

And the cell phone has reached to even the most remote and bucolic auction site, meaning the out-of-the-way farm sale with a rare painted kas, or the minor-league estate sale with the overlooked gem of a landscape are less likely to be the province of a select few, and more likely the target of the sharp-eyed (and sharp-eared) collector or dealer with unlimited roaming capabilities.

The book you are holding represents a meeting of minds on the question of antique sales in a high-tech world.

On the one hand, it offers hundreds of detailed photos and descriptions of furniture from virtually every stylistic era from the 17th to the 20th centuries, and the prices range from less than $200 to more than $30,000. So it's an excellent traditional guide for the beginning collector trying to get a handle on what's out there, and what fits best in their lives.

On the other hand, its scope represents an opportunity for a new generation of buyer to establish a collecting legacy in a marketplace where regional price differences are breaking down but still linger. This means that with the click of a mouse or the chirp of a cell phone (and this guide close at hand), even the most stay-at-home shopper can come up with just the right table, chair, chest or bed at a price that is hundreds or even thousands of dollars less than the prevailing rate in certain areas of the country.

The best advice for antique collectors remains unchanged by technology: Learn all you can from a variety of sources, take a chance now and then if your checkbook permits, and buy the best available pieces within your budget. And while you're out there shopping, whether it's on the road or on the 'net, remember that no one can have all the answers on price, style and rarity, but by tapping into the resources in print, online and from personal contacts, anyone can build a collection to be proud of.

This book would not have been possible without access to the resources of Jay Anderson Antiques in Wabasha, Minnesota.

I am especially indebted to my good friend Greg Kowles of Country Comfort Antiques in Winona, Minnesota, who generously gave of his time, knowledge and coffee.

Dedication: For Catherine

Mark Moran

FURNITURE DATING CHART

AMERICAN FURNITURE
Pilgrim Century – 1620-1700
William & Mary – 1685-1720
Queen Anne – 1720-50
Chippendale – 1750-85
Federal – 1785-1820
Hepplewhite – 1785-1800
Sheraton – 1800-20
Classical (American Empire) – 1815-40
Victorian – 1840-1900
Early Victorian – 1840-50
Gothic Revival – 1840-90
Rococo (Louis XV) – 1845-70
Renaissance Revival – 1860-85
Louis XVI – 1865-75
Eastlake – 1870-95
Jacobean & Turkish Revival – 1870-90
Aesthetic Movement – 1880-1900
Art Nouveau – 1895-1918
Turn-of-the Century
    (Early 20th Century) – 1895-1910
Mission-style
    (Arts & Crafts movement) – 1900-15
Colonial Revival – 1890-1930
Art Deco – 1925-40
Modernist or Mid-Century – 1945-70

ENGLISH FURNITURE
Jacobean – Mid-17th Century
William & Mary – 1689-1702
Queen Anne – 1702-14
George I – 1714-27
George II – 1727-60
George III – 1760-1820
Regency – 1811-20
George IV – 1820-30
William IV – 1830-37
Victorian – 1837-1901
Edwardian – 1901-10

FRENCH FURNITURE
Louis XV – 1715-74
Louis XVI – 1774-93
Empire – 1804-15
Louis Philippe – 1830-48
Napoleon III
    (Second Empire) – 1848-70
Art Nouveau – 1895-1910
Art Deco – 1925-35

Germanic Furniture
Since the country of Germany did not exist before 1870, furniture from the various Germanic states and the Austro-Hungarian Empire is generally termed simply "Germanic." From the 17th century onward furniture from these regions tended to follow the stylistic trends established in France and England. General terms are used for such early furniture usually classifying it as "Baroque," "Rococo" or a similar broad stylistic term. Germanic furniture dating from the first half of the 19th century is today usually referred to as Biedermeier, a style closely related to French Empire and English Regency.

AMERICAN FURNITURE TERMS

CHAIRS

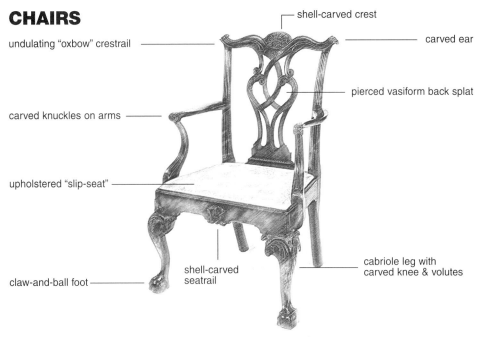

shell-carved crest

carved ear

undulating "oxbow" crestrail

pierced vasiform back splat

carved knuckles on arms

upholstered "slip-seat"

claw-and-ball foot

shell-carved seatrail

cabriole leg with carved knee & volutes

Chippendale Armchair

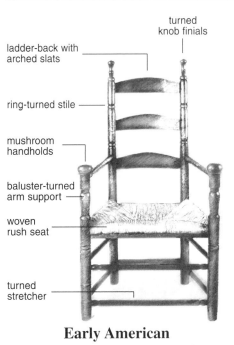

turned knob finials

ladder-back with arched slats

ring-turned stile

mushroom handholds

baluster-turned arm support

woven rush seat

turned stretcher

Early American "Ladder-back" Armchair

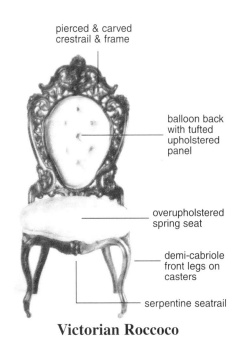

pierced & carved crestrail & frame

balloon back with tufted upholstered panel

overupholstered spring seat

demi-cabriole front legs on casters

serpentine seatrail

Victorian Roccoco Side Chair

CHESTS & TABLES

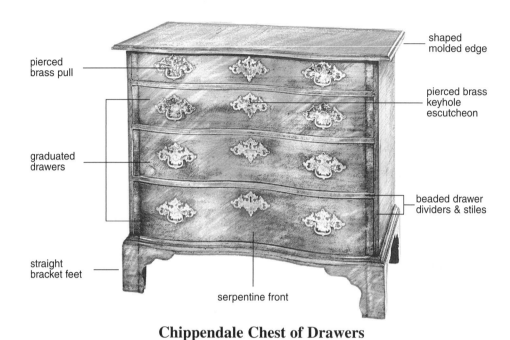

pierced
brass pull

shaped
molded edge

pierced brass
keyhole
escutcheon

graduated
drawers

beaded drawer
dividers & stiles

straight
bracket feet

serpentine front

Chippendale Chest of Drawers

leather-covered
top with tack trim

corbel

mortise & tenon
through-construction

medial shelf

Mission Oak Library Table

FURNITURE PEDIMENTS & SKIRTS

Classic Pediment

Plain Skirt

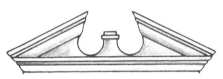

Broken Arch Pediment

Arched Skirt

**Bonnet Top with
Urn & Flame Finial**

Valanced Skirt

**Bonnet Top with Rosettes &
Three Urn & Flame Finials**

Scalloped Skirt

FURNITURE FEET

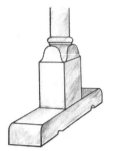

Trestle Foot

Pad Foot

Block Foot

Slipper Foot

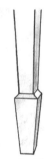

Spade Foot

Snake Foot

Tapered or Plain Foot

Spanish Foot

FURNITURE FEET

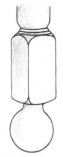

Ball Foot

Trifid Foot

Bun Foot

Hoof Foot

Turnip Foot

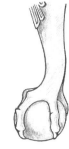

Claw-and-Ball Foot

Arrow or Peg Foot

Paw Foot

Bedroom Suites

Art Deco: stepped vanity, five-drawer chest of drawers, bedside table, double bed & bench; bird's-eye maple, simple classic squared design w/narrow curved metal pulls & large upright round off-center mirror on dressing table, dated & marked "1936 - Triangle Brand - Crane & McMahon," the set (ILLUS. of part bottom of page)... **$288**

Gilbert Rhode Bedroom Chests

Art Deco: tall chest of drawers, a chest of drawers w/mirror, a bed & a nightstand; blonde finished hardwood, the tall chest & chest of drawers w/mirror each w/rectangular tops above stacks of long graduated drawers w/catalin pulls, the round mirror supported on a curved tubular metal angled arm, looped tubular metal legs, the bed w/a curvilinear footboard, round nightstand, signed by designer Gilbert Rhode, manufactured by Herman Miller, Zeeland, Michigan, ca. 1933, tall chest 47" h., the set (ILLUS. of part)......... **4,888**

Jacobean Revival: a tall chest of drawers, a dresser w/mirror, a dressing table w/mirror, a double bed, stool & non-matching side chair; mahogany veneer & burled mahogany veneer, the tall chest w/a rectangular top w/molded edges above a long drawer w/a central raised burl panel flanked by carved scrolls & ring pulls w/quarter-round corner turnings above a stepped-back & inset stack of three long burl veneered drawers flanked by ring- and knob-turned outset posts on a rectangular top w/molded edges over a lower case w/two long burl veneered drawers trimmed w/a continuous raised rectangular banding & w/four ring pulls, half-round ring-turned side colonettes above the apron w/double beaded bands centered by a scroll-carved scalloped central section, raised on ring- and double-knob-turned front legs on casters, other pieces w/similar decoration, by the Continental Furniture Company, ca. 1920s, the set **550**

Louis XV-XVI-Style: double bed, a pair of five-drawer tall side cabinets, a lady's work table, a lady's dressing table, a nightstand, a guerdon, two armchairs, a side chair & footstool; bronze-mounted tulipwood, overall decorated patterned

Art Deco Bedroom Suite

veneered panels w/gilt-bronze mounts in the form of shells, foliage, laurel branches & putto, the bed signed "Linke," France, early 20th c., the footstool associated, the set... **29,500**

Modern style: bed, nightstand, tall chest of drawers & chest of drawers w/mirror; all in a wheat finish, the chests w/rectangular tops w/rounded edges over cases fitted w/five or four long graduated drawers w/central low arched long wood pulls, the shorter dresser fitted at the top w/a large rectangular mirror w/rounded top corners, chests on short rounded feet, matching bed & nightstand, attributed to Heywood Wakefield, ca. 1955, tall chest 46 1/2" h., the set (ILLUS. of part bottom this page) **978**

Modern Style Bedroom Furniture

Modern style: double bed, large & small chest of drawers & nightstand; molded plywood, each piece w/a simple rounded box form, the chests w/flush-front drawers w/incised finger grip bands, on bent-

wood band supports, color-enhanced reddish brown finish, decal mark of Plymodern Furniture, Plymold Corporation, Lawrence, Massachusetts, late 1940s - early 1950s, minor wear, large chest 42" h., the set (ILLUS. of large chest & nightstand)... **805**

Modern style: two single beds, two wardrobes, a nightstand, a dressing table, two benches & a blanket chest; painted beech, the beds & stand w/rectangular frames enclosing vertical slats w/cross-form framing, the two-door wardrobe w/one door composed of slats & the other w/a mirror above a long lower drawer, the dressing table & stool w/slatted base end sections, designed by Bruno Emmel, by A. Siegl, Vienna, early 20th c., the set..... **13,800**

Aesthetic Movement Vanity

Victorian Aesthetic Movement: bed, chest of drawers w/mirror, night table, side chair, vanity & side table; ebonized & gilt-

Heywood Wakefield Bedroom Suite

decorated, each piece w/a high rounded flat crestrail continuing to form a framework around the mirrored pieces & ornately decorated w/delicate gilt florals, the drawers & panels on each piece also decorated w/delicate gilt fern leaf or floral vine decorations, ca. 1875, the set (ILLUS. of vanity) **4,600**

Chest from Aesthetic Movement Set

Victorian Aesthetic Movement: chest of drawers w/mirror, two-door cupboard, commode, full-size bed; walnut & burl walnut, each piece w/a tall crown-form crest w/a pediment crest above a deeply carved rectangular panel of flowering vines flanked by arched brackets on a paneled rail between incised uprights, the chest of drawers w/a tall rectangular mirror flanked by small handkerchief drawers raised on turned colonettes above the rectangular white marble top over a case w/three long fppaneled & burl veneered drawers w/angular brass pulls & round wood keyhole escutcheons, side stiles w/blocked & incised decoration, commode & cupboard also w/white marble tops, ca. 1870, chest of drawers 24 x 55 1/2", 87 3/4" h., the set (ILLUS. of chest of drawers) **7,475**

Victorian Aesthetic Movement: double bed, chest of drawers w/mirror & washstand; cherry & mahogany, the highbacked bed w/a high, wide squared headboard w/a shaped crestrail carved w/scrolls & leaves above oblong panels w/further detailed leafy scroll carving, reeded pilaster stiles, a matching lower footboard & original siderails, the chest w/a tall superstructure frame carved to match the headboard & enclosing a large swiveling beveled mirror, the case w/a row of three small drawers over two long drawers on a molded base w/simple bracket feet, the washstand w/a door, two open side compartments & one drawer w/a mismatched, undersized marble top, ca. 1890, bed 61" w., 80" h., the set (some wear & edge damage) **4,125**

Fine Eastlake Half-tester Bed

Victorian Eastlake substyle: a high-back half-tester bed & tall chest of drawers; walnut & burl walnut, the bed w/a rectangular half-tester canopy w/flaring molded cornice above a scallop-cut & scroll-cut front, raised on curved & pierced spindled brackets on the side stiles of the headboard, headboard w/a scroll-carved crown crest above a scroll-carved band & burl panel over narrow burl panel & an arch-topped wide lower burl panels, spiral-turned side stiles, the lower footboard w/a gently arched crestrail over scroll carving & a wide burl panel, scroll-cut top corner ears & spiral-turned side stiles, original side rails, refinished, ca. 1880, w/a matching marble-topped chest of drawers, bed 60" w., 10' h., 2 pcs. (ILLUS. of bed) **10,500**

Victorian Eastlake substyle: chest of drawers & washstand; walnut & burl walnut, each w/a flat crestrail decorated w/a carved scalloped band flanked by carved corner posts on the tall reeded uprights flanking a large square or rectangular swiveling beveled mirror, the chest w/a reddish brown rectangular marble top above a stack of three long burl-veneered drawers w/pierced brass pulls & a molded apron, the washstand w/a high galleried reddish brown marble splashback on the marble top over a case w/two short burl-veneered drawers beside a paneled, burled door over the molded base, ca. 1880, chest 20 x 44", 76 1/2" h., 2 pcs... **1,100**

Victorian Eastlake substyle: highback double bed & marble top dresser; the bed w/a high crowned crest w/a central rondel & bar crest above a geometrically-pierced crestrail w/a sawtooth-cut lower border overhanging a set-back narrow horizontal frieze band carved w/stylized foliate designs & flanked below by short

Fine Eastlake Bed & Chest of Drawers

spindled & scroll-cut galleries above the set-back headboard w/a pair of geometrically-cut square panels flanking a long central burl panel all above lower plain panels, the dresser w/a matching crestrail above a tall rectangular mirror swinging between tall upright & lower candle shelves over floral-carved panels above the rectangular red marble top over a case w/a row of three short drawers over two long drawers all w/angular

brass pulls, molded base, ca. 1880, the pr. (ILLUS.).. **7,000**

Unusual Victorian Faux Bamboo Bed

Victorian faux bamboo style: two twin beds, dressing table, nightstand, chest of drawers & side cabinet; pine, each piece w/peaked crestrails & side posts all w/faux bamboo turnings enclosing bamboo-bordered panels & applied trim, ca. 1890, bed 35 x 73", the set (ILLUS. of one bed).. **9,600**
Victorian Golden Oak substyle: dresser, double bed & commode; the dresser w/a large rectangular mirror in a frame w/scroll-carved cresting & rounded corners swiveling between turned uprights & a scrolled crestboard above the molded rectangular serpentine top over a conforming case w/a pair of drawers over two long drawers; the matching medium-height headboard w/a large scroll-carved

Golden Oak Bedroom Suite

central cartouche, the commode w/a long bowed drawer over two small drawers beside a single paneled door, all on casters, ca. 1890-1900, the set (ILLUS. bottom of previous page) **1,000**

Ornate Moorish Revival Armoire

Victorian Moorish Revival: armoire, single bed & bedside table w/marble top; walnut, burl walnut & parcel-gilt, each piece w/elaborate pierced & carved decoration, the armoire w/an arched & pierced scroll-carved crest above a latticework crestrail between turned corner finials over a plain frieze band on scalloped rounded arched & turned columns above & flanking the set-back paneled doors w/a top rondel, large center panel & ornately parcel-gilt lower panel, a long raised-panel drawer across the bottom, molded base on bun feet, last quarter 19th c., armoire 23 x 51", 76 1/2" h., the set (ILLUS. of armoire) **4,025**

Large Renaissance Revival Chest

Victorian Renaissance Revival: bed, chest of drawers w/mirror, side chest &

cabinet; walnut & burl walnut, each w/a wide arched & ornately scroll-carved crestrail above a carved frieze band, the chest of drawers w/a large rectangular swivel mirror w/gently arched top frame, case pieces w/rectangular pink marble tops w/serpentine fronts above conforming veneered drawers, ca. 1885, bed 63" w., 88" h., the set (ILLUS. of chest of drawers) **17,920**

Outstanding Renaissance Revival Bed

Victorian Renaissance Revival: bed, tall chest of drawers, dressing table & bureau; gilt-incised walnut, each piece w/a massive arched crestrail centered by a large block over curved brackets & topped by a large urn-form finial, large tapering turned finials at each top corner, delicate gilt-incised banding & scrolls, the tall bed w/a lower footboard w/a heavy turned crestrail over turned & reeded sideposts & a shaped rectangular panel, bed siderails w/original velvet padding, ca. 1880, bed 56 1/2 x 73", 77" h., the set (ILLUS. of bed) **23,750**

Victorian Renaissance Revival: double bed & chest of drawers; walnut, the chest w/a white marble top below a tall swiveling mirror w/carved applied arched pediment, glove boxes on the top, the case w/three long drawers w/burl veneer raised panels & carved pulls, matching high back bed, ca. 1875-80, chest 21 x 44", 90" h., 2 pcs **1,650**

Victorian Renaissance Revival substyle: double bed, chest of drawers w/mirror & washstand; walnut & burl walnut, the bed w/a high back topped by a pointed arch shell and scroll-carved crest above a burl panel flanked by rondels & turned corner finials above a wide burl panel flanked by side colonettes above a narrow burl band & corner finials above a plain panel, matching lower footboard, the tall chest w/a similar crest above a long rectangular swiveling mirror above a white marble top over three long drawers, the washstand w/a white marble top w/small shelf above a case w/a long drawer over a pair of doors all trimmed w/burl, ca. 1885, 3 pcs. (ILLUS. bottom next page).. **6,700**

Victorian Renaissance Revival: walnut & burl walnut, each piece w/a high arched pedimented top centered by a large arched scroll-carved cartouche above a frieze band w/raised burl panels, the chest of drawers w/a tall rectangular round-topped mirror flanked by shaped sides fitted w/two small candleshelves & trimmed w/burl panels & side scrolls, a stepped top w/a square white marble top w/molded edges above two small drawers flanking the central well w/a white marble top, two long bottom drawers w/pairs of raised burl panels, deep molded base, brass & black teardrop pulls, ca. 1875, bed 54" w., 7' 8" h., four pieces (ILLUS. of chest of drawers)................... **11,2007**

Renaissance Revival Bedroom Suite

Beds

Fine Anglo-Indian Carved Tester Bed

Anglo-Indian tall-poster tester bed, rosewood-like wood, the rectangular deep ogee & serpentine tester frame raised on ring-, knob- and paneled-rod-turned posts, the headboard w/an ornately pierced & scroll-carved design, caned mattress support, three-quarter size, ca. 1835, 90" h. (ILLUS.) **$950**

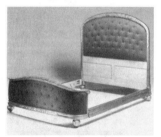

French Art Deco Bed

Art Deco bed, giltwood & upholstery, the high arched headboard & lower footboard carved w/narrow borders of flowerheads enclosing black silk tufted upholstery, joined by molded rails, in the manner of Paul Follot, France, ca. 1925, chips to gilding, 56" w. (ILLUS.) **2,070**

French Art Deco Palmwood Bed

Art Deco bed, palmwood, the upright thick rectangular headboard joined by low molded siderails continuing into the curved lower footboard on a quarter-round heavy bracket, France, ca. 1930s, veneer losses, 55" w. (ILLUS.) **2,875**

Majorelle Art Nouveau Bed

Art Nouveau bed, Les Lilas patt., carved mahogany, the high headboard w/shaped crestrail w/rounded corners over panels of carved lilacs above a wide veneered panel over a rail & four small veneered panels, the conforming lower footboard w/carved corners & two large veneered panels, shaped low feet, designed by Louis Majorelle, France, ca. 1900, 65 x 85", 61" h. (ILLUS.) **4,600**

Chippendale Revival Twin Bed

Chippendale Revival style twin beds, mahogany & mahogany veneer, the high headboard w/a broken scroll crest w/carved florettes flanking a central urn & flame finial, tall reeded turned & tapering headposts w/acorn finials, the footboard w/matching posts & a serpentined arch top w/gadrooned edging, gadrooned band on footboard rail, headboard w/turned tapering legs w/knob feet, footboard w/claw-and-ball feet, refinished, ca. 1920s, 48" w., 56" h. headboard, pr. (ILLUS. of one) **1,400**

Classical Country-style Painted Bed

Classical country-style low-poster bed, the wide scrolled head- and footboards flanked by ball-topped ring-turned posts ending in ring-turned tapering legs, overall graining simulating rosewood highlighted w/gilt stenciling & striping, old surface, probably northern New England, 1825-35, minor height loss, 52 1/4 x 79", 46 1/2" h. (ILLUS.) **1,495**

Classical Tiger Stripe Maple Bed

Classical country-style low-poster bed, tiger stripe maple, four boldly baluster-, ring- and urn-turned posts continuing to turned tapering legs, a scroll-cut headboard, the footboard w/a baluster- and ring-turned blanket rail above a lower flat rail, old refinish, New England, ca. 1830, side rails replaced, 52 x 81 1/2", 46" h. (ILLUS.) **1,840**

Classical country-style low-poster rope bed, curly maple, head- and footposts w/ball-turned finials above an urn over a tapering turned post continuing to a long block over the ring-turned tapering legs, a high rolled headboard w/ball terminals, the footboard w/a ball- and rod-turned blanket bar above a lower flat rail, refinished, includes original rails & bolts, first half 19th c., 54 x 72", 54" h. **935**

Classical country-style rope bed, cherry, boldly turned baluster-, ring- and rod-turned head- and footposts w/large ball finials & baluster- and ring-turned legs, the wide headboard w/scrolling crest arched in the center below a turned horizontal rod w/double-ball knobs at each end, the footboard w/a narrow shaped board above the pegged rails, cleaned down to old mellow finish, found in Ohio, first half 19th c., original rails, 51 x 76 1/4", 59 3/4" h. **1,210**

Classical Revival Poster Bed

Classical Revival four-poster bed, mahogany & mahogany veneer, each square corner post topped by ring-turned & leaf-carved sections w/pineapple finials, wide veneered head- and footboard w/round crestrails w/pointed, reeded end finials, short turned tapering legs, original finish & wood casters, three-quarter size, late 19th c., 50" w., 5' 6" h. (ILLUS.) **1,000**

Classical 'sleigh' bed, carved mahogany, high outscrolled ends w/rosette terminals & veneered crests, reeded edges continuing to a long narrow reeded seatrail w/leaf-carved blocks above the squared acanthus leaf carved legs raised on casters, probably New England, first quarter 19th c., 59 1/2 x 102", footboard 34 3/4" h., headboard 41 1/2" h. **4,025**

Classical 'sleigh' bed, carved mahogany, twin sized, reverse-scrolling head- and footboards on flowerhead- and leaf-carved supports, joined by gadrooned wide side rails on leaf-carved paw feet, New York, first half 19th c. **5,100**

Fine Classical Tall-poster Bed

Classical tall-poster bed, mahogany & mahogany veneer, a high arched headboard w/a cartouche carved at the top flanked by long S-scrolls over a shaped raised panel & a rectangular panel w/cut corners flanked by the tall headposts composed of four clustered round posts above the heavy square legs w/chamfered corners, joined by shaped side & end rails to matching footposts, ca. 1830-40, 108" h. (ILLUS.)...................................... **4,800**

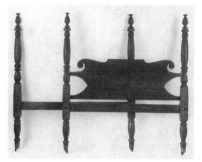

Early Classical Tall-poster Bed

Classical tall-poster bed, mahogany, the head- and footposts w/pineapple-carved finials on leaf spiral & ring-carved posts ending in vase- and ring-turned legs w/brass cuffs & casters, the headposts joined by a scrolled & shaped headboard, old refinish, New England, ca. 1820, imperfections, 49 1/4 x 72", 60" h. (ILLUS.) .. **2,875**

Classical Tall-poster Bed

Classical tall-poster bed, stained poplar, the flat-topped scroll-cut headboard flanked by tall hexagonal posts tapering to a paneled pointed top w/mushroom finial, original siderails w/knobs for ropes, footboard w/matching posts & a low shaped upper rail, turned tapering legs w/bun feet, original dark finish, ca. 1830, 58" w., 7' 6" h. (ILLUS.) **1,600**

Classical Tall-poster Tester Bed

Classical tall-poster tester bed, cherry, the four vase- and ring-turned posts continuing to block- and vase-turned legs & joined by a straight tester frame & a scroll-cut headboard, old refinish, New England, ca. 1825, 45 x 70", 90" h. (ILLUS.).. **1,955**

Country style rope bed, maple & curly maple, cannon ball-style, the even well-turned head- and footposts w/baluster- and ring-turnings & large ball finials, headboard w/cut-out ends w/shaped corners, footboard w/turned blanket bar, original rails 69" l., 51 1/2" w. **770**

Country-style child's bed, cherry, rectangular w/deep board sides gently down-curved between the head- and footboards w/slightly scrolled crests between turned ball corner finials w/ivory buttons, baluster- and ring-turned legs w/peg feet, pegged construction w/chip-carved detail at the posts, original finish, Zoar, Ohio, 19th c., 25 x 43", 30" h. (minor age splits).. **2,420**

Early Low-poster Rope Bed

Country-style low-poster bed, painted, a rounded headboard between square posts w/button finials joined by original hinged side rails to the footposts w/matching finials & joined by a heavy end rail, on ring- and baluster-turned legs w/a pair of fold-down legs where the side rails hinge, original red paint, rails drilled for roping, New England, early 19th c., very minor imperfections, 49 3/4 x 74", 35 1/2" h. (ILLUS.)... **805**

Early Low-poster Bed

Country-style low-poster bed, painted pine & maple, the pointed headboard between blocked stiles w/flattened knob-turned finials & swelled turned & tapering legs, original side rails w/rope holes & low footposts w/flattened knob-turned finials over the corner blocks on swelled turned & tapering legs, old red paint, Pennsylvania, early 19th c., 52 x 80", headboard 34 1/2" h. (ILLUS.)......................... **575**

Country-style low-poster bed, tiger stripe maple, ball tops above ring-turned posts which flank a shaped headboard, similar ring-turned legs on casters, old surface, side rails w/angle irons, New England, second quarter 19th c., 49 x 75 1/2", 50 1/4" h. (minor height loss)...................... **1,610**

Country-style low-poster "folding" bed, painted wood, turned headposts flanking a shaped headboard, joined to the footposts by jointed rails fitted for roping & folding, old Spanish brown paint, New England, early 19th c., 52 3/4 x 77 1/2", 33 1/2" h. (imperfections) **690**

Country-style low-poster rope bed, poplar, heavy ring- and block-turned even head- and footposts w/ring- and ball-turned finials w/a mushroom cap, wide shaped headboard & lower matching footboard, posts joined by heavy round rails w/turned rope knobs, old refinish w/some wear & white stain, original rails, first half 19th c., 55 x 72", 43 1/2" h. **220**

Early 'Pencil-post' Tester Bed

Country-style 'pencil-post' bed, birch, four slender octagonal tapering posts continuing to square legs joined by a molded peaked headboard & flat tester frame, side & end rails drilled for roping, probably New England, early 19th c., old surface, 51 x 71", 81" h. (ILLUS.) **2,300**

Country-style tall-poster tester bed, maple, the vase- and ring-turned reeded footposts joined to the hexagonal tapering headposts w/a simple arched headboard, straight tester frame, old refinish, minor imperfections, probably New England, early 19th c., 46 x 72", 83" h. **2,300**

Federal country-style tall-poster tester bed, maple & birch, an arched tester frame above the tapering pencil headposts flanking a low arched headboard & joined by rails to reeded vase-, cup- and ring-turned footposts, on casters, New England, early 19th c., 53 1/2 x 75", overall 78 1/4" h... **1,380**

Federal tall-poster bed, carved mahogany, the square tapering birch headposts flank an arched pine headboard, the reeded tapering footposts w/tobacco leaf carving & reeded legs ending in turned feet, w/rails & flat tester, probably Southern U.S., early 19th c., 56 3/4 x 79 1/2", 83 1/2" h. (restoration, patches)................. **4,025**

Massachusetts Federal Bed

Federal tall-poster bed, carved mahogany, the square tapering tall headposts centering a scroll-cut pine headboard, the footposts w/waterleaf-carved tapering reeded posts on swag- and leaf-carved urn-form supports on square tapering legs, all legs w/spade feet, w/flat tester, headboard possibly replaced, North Shore Massachusetts, ca. 1795, 59 x 80", 92" h. (ILLUS.) **5,750**

Federal tall-poster bed, carved mahogany, the tapering reeded footposts w/vase- and ring-turning continuing to square tapering spade-footed legs, the simple square tapering headposts joined by a plain rectangular headboard, original side rails, probably Massachusetts, ca. 1810-15,   50 x 70",   89 1/2" h... **2,070**

Federal tall-poster bed, carved mahogany, the vase- and ring-turned footposts carved w/pineapples above a reeded swelled post w/carved sheaves of wheat continuing to acanthus leaves & carved palmettes on vase- and ring-turned legs, the headposts also vase- and ring-turned but uncarved, all joined by a flat tester frame, 54 x 72", 87" h. **12,650**

Federal tall-poster bed, carved mahogany veneer, the reeded turned posts w/leaf carving above turnings punctuated w/neoclassical beading over carved Gothic arches & leaves on figured mahogany veneer dies above the ring-turned tapering legs, old refinish, Salem, Massachusetts, 1820-30, 55 3/4 x 58", 79" h. (height loss).. **6,325**

Federal tall-poster bed, painted, the vase- and ring-turned & reeded footposts joined to the simple turned headposts & shaped pine headboard w/an arched canopy frame, ring- and baluster-turned legs, old red stain, New England, ca. 1820, 48 x 69", 75" h. (minor imperfections) **2,645**

Federal tall-poster canopy field bed, maple, a low peaked headboard flanked by simple slender turned & tapering posts, the footposts w/ring- and baluster-turned posts & square tapering legs, w/an arched serpentine canopy frame, late 18th - early 19th c., 58 1/2" w., 68" h. **2,000**

Federal tall-poster tester bed, carved mahogany, the arched canopy surmounting four ring-turned & waterleaf-carved posts w/square-sectioned corner supports mounted w/ormolu medallions joined by straight rails, on ring-turned & compressed-ball legs, school of Samuel McIntire, Salem, Massachusetts, ca. 1800, 56 x 80", 80" h. **4,025**

Federal tall-poster tester bed, figured maple & pine, the arched tester above baluster-turned posts centering an arched headboard on tapering turned legs w/round spade feet, matching footposts, old   dry   surface,   probably Massachusetts, ca.   1810,   52 x 78", 70" h. **7,800**

Federal tall-poster tester bed, mahogany veneer, the mahogany veneered flat tester w/central rectangular tablets & ovolo corners above spiral- and leaf-carved footposts & turned red-painted headposts flanking a scrolled headboard, ring- and knob-turned legs, Salem Massachusetts, early 19th c., 52 x 76 1/2", 89" h. (some old refinish & height loss)...... **4,888**

Federal-Style bed, carved cherry, the knop finial above a rectangular tester over reeded, ring- and baluster-turned footposts & headposts centering an arched headboard, on square tapering legs w/spade feet, 20th c., 62 1/2 x 87 1/4", 82" h. **1,840**

Federal-Style Child's Bed

Federal-Style child's tall-poster tester bed, maple, the arched canopy frame w/small center urn finial raised on a tester frame on tall slender tapering corner posts of the high spindle-sided rails, raised on baluster- and ring-turned tapering legs on casters, original finish, ca. 1920s, 24 x 48", 5' h. (ILLUS.) **800**

French Empire-Style bed, mahogany w/ormolu trim, the rectangular headboard w/flat crest & end ears above stiles w/long palmette ormolu mounts flanking the large central raised panel border, the lower footboard matching, long siderails w/downcurved top & decorated at each end w/triangular scrolling ormolu mounts, France, early 20th c., 52 x 82", 46" h. (wear, some missing pieces of ormolu) **495**

Mission Style (Arts & Crafts movement) double bed, oak, tall square corner posts, the headboard w/rails flanking the seven slats, matching but slightly lower footboard, wide side rails, fine original finish, L. & J.G. Stickley, Model No. 84, 58" w., 54" h. **7,150**

Gustav Stickley Bed

Mission Style (Arts & Crafts movement) double bed, the headboard & slightly shorter footboard each w/a narrow invert-

ed V-top crestrail flanked by tall square tapering posts, five wide slats in each w/a wide lower rail, original finish, branded signature mark of Gustav Stickley, original side rails, 59 x 78" (ILLUS.).. **8,800**
Mission-style (Arts & Crafts movement) three-quarters bed, oak, tall tapering corner posts on the head- & slightly lower footboard, each w/six vertical slats, original side rails, original finish, mark of L. & J.G. Stickley, 51 3/4 x 84 3/4", 54" h. **3,300**

George Nelson "Thin Edge" Bed

Modern style "Thin Edge" bed, walnut, the wood frame w/an upright canted caned headboard, resting on a white-painted tubular steel frame & legs, metal tag marked "Herman Miller - George Nelson Design," ca. 1959, 58 x 82 1/4", 33 1/2" h. (ILLUS.) **8,740**

Ornate Early Brass Bed

Turn-of-the-century bed, brass, elaborately scrolled head- and footboards w/foliate detail, ca. 1900, one small spindle missing, 61" w., 64" h. (ILLUS.) **2,200**
Turn-of-the-Century brass bed, the high headboard w/a straight bar crestrail joined to ring-turned tall cylindrical stiles w/ball caps & pointed ring-turned finials, the headboard composed of a latticework of ball- and ring-turned vertical & horizontal bars centered by a panel w/a large C-form cartouche, matching lower footboard, on casters, polished, 55 x 72", 67 1/2" h. (one finial missing) **1,100**
Victorian Aesthetic Movement substyle bed, walnut & burl walnut, the high square headboard w/a slightly stepped crestrail w/the wider central panel carved w/a stylized blossom & leafy twigs flanked by low side panels w/a carved trellis design all above a triple-arch border over three large burl walnut rectangular panels flanked by narrow pilasters & blocks, a matching lower footboard w/a flat crestrail, ca. 1880, 67" w., 79" h. **3,360**

Victorian Golden Oak Double Bed

Victorian Golden Oak bed, the high headboard w/a scroll- and shell-carved center crest above a leaf-carved frieze band flanked by carved ears over rectangular panels, the lower footboard w/a heavy rounded crestrail over a wide panel, refinished, ca. 1910, full size, headboard 72" h. (ILLUS.) **800**
Victorian Renaissance Revival bed, carved walnut & burl walnut, the very high headboard topped by a high central canopy-style crest w/a large carved maiden's bust above an arched & scroll-carved crestrail over a sawtooth border band over a recessed arched burl panel flanked by balusters all flanked by lower peaked side crests & blocked corners w/turned urn finials, the wide triple-panel lower section w/arched top moldings, the low arched footboard w/a molded railing over arched burl panels over a triple-arch panel & rectangular burl panels along the bottom, ca. 1875, 66" w., 96" h. **2,800**

Tall Renaissance Revival Bed

Victorian Renaissance Revival bed, walnut & burl walnut, tall-back style, the very tall headboard w/an arched & molded pediment crest centered by a tall leaf- and scroll-carved finial & scroll & burl panel trim above projecting blocks over slender turned columns & shaped sides flanking a tall raised panel flanked by shorter side panels w/corner blocks w/turned finials, the lower footboard w/a flat top rail over rectangular, round & arched raised burl panels, canted blocked corners w/turned columns, old refinish, ca. 1875, 58" w., 8' h. (ILLUS.) **3,500**

Victorian Renaissance Revival double bed, walnut, highback headboard w/an arched scroll-pierced & pointed crestrail on an arched molding over a pair of large oval panels w/half-round raised molding across the top & a raised rondel above, the flattened stiles topped by spearpoint finials, curved corners, low arched footboard centered by a large raised bull's-eye rondel, ca. 1870, original side rails, refinished, 61 x 72", 83" h. (repairs to crestrail)... **770**

Fine Victorian Rococo Bed

Victorian Rococo, mahogany & mahogany veneer tall-poster style, monumental round headposts w/squatty flame-turned finials above the high arched headboard w/a shell- and fruit-carved crest over scrolled borders & two raised triangular panels above a large inset rectangular panel w/a rosette at each corner, gadrooned turning at the base of each post, the low footboard w/short round posts w/pointed gadrooned caps & bands above long Gothic arch panels flanking the low arched & scroll-carved footrail w/a central rosette & oval banding, old dark finish, some reconstruction, minor veneer damage, original rails, ca. 1850, 63" w., headposts 101" h. (ILLUS.)............. **6,875**

Large Rosewood Rococo Bed

Victorian Rococo, rosewood, the very high & wide headboard w/an arched & leaf-carved crestrail above a large lacy scroll-framed cartouche over long lobed recessed panels all flanked by tall paneled headposts w/urn-turned finials, the low footboard w/matching low posts flanking an arched central panel w/a leafy scroll-carved center design, ca. 1850-60, 63" w., 87" h. (ILLUS.)................................. **3,360**

Record-breaking Belter Patented Bed

Victorian Rococo bed, laminated rosewood, the tall serpentine & arched headboard crowned by an ornately pierce-carved crest w/a basket of fruit crest flanked by leafy scrolls & figures of putti, the headboard dropping down & continuing into serpentine deep carved side rails joining the lower serpentine footboard w/rounded corners & a cartouche-carved crest, patented by John Henry Belter, ca. 1850s, record for 19th c. American furniture (ILLUS.)... **101,750**

Fine Victorian Rococo Tester Bed

Victorian Rococo tester bed, rosewood, the high arched & paneled headboard w/a pierced floral- and scroll-carved arched crest flanked by heavy paneled stiles & slender reeded tapering posts, the low gently arched & paneled footboard flanked by heavy paneled stiles & tall slender reeded posts, wide cornice-form tester frame w/rounded corners, ca. 1850 (ILLUS.)... **13,500**

Benches

Art Deco Bench

Art Deco bench, mahogany, the reeded curved backrail continuing to half arms above an upholstered oblong seat w/fluted apron raised on square tapering & slightly curved legs joined by an H-stretcher, ca. 1930, 17 x 35 1/2", 21" h. (ILLUS.) **$1,680**

Arts & Crafts hall bench, oak, the high rectangular back w/a slightly arched crestrail above the inset back panel w/an arched top, flat open end arms w/rounded grips raised on rectangular stile front legs, long rectangular seat lifting to a storage compartment, medium brown finish, early 20th c., 17 3/4 x 38 1/2", 36 1/2" h. (minor abrasions & losses, newer finish, joint separations, crack) **403**

Bench, painted pine, the overhanging rectangular seat on shaped supports & arched cut-out feet joined by a straight skirt, vestiges of original salmon paint, probably Pennsylvania, ca. 1840, 11 3/4 x 77 3/4", 19 3/4" h **2,760**

Bucket (or water) bench, country-style, painted, a superstructure w/a narrow shelf w/a high three-quarters gallery above a row of three small drawers w/cast-iron finger pulls, shaped tapering tall sides above the wide rectangular lower shelf over a case w/a pair of paneled cupboard doors w/cast-iron thumb latches, slender bracket feet, old yellow repaint over earlier colors, pulls overpainted, 19th c., 17 1/4 x 42", 48" h. **4,400**

Bucket (or water) bench, country-style, painted pine, a two-board rectangular top w/a rounded front corner at one end overhanging & raised on one-board ends w/bootjack feet, joined by a lower one-board open shelf, old red paint, square nail construction, Pennsylvania, 19th c., 16 x 48", 27 1/2" h. (minor damage to foot finish) **660**

Bucket (or water) bench, country-style, painted poplar, a narrow upper shelf raised on tall shaped & incurved supports above a wide lower open shelf w/an apron & bootjack ends joined by a beaded through-tenon cross stretcher, square nail construction, various colors of old paint, 37" w., 33 1/4" h. (some later round nails) **1,155**

Bucket (or water) bench, country-style, poplar, the tall superstructure w/a rectangular top above a closed back w/a single shelf above a projecting rectangular well above a long deep dovetailed drawer above the closed back & lower shelf, one-board ends, worn red finish, 19th c., 21 3/4 x 42", 59 1/2" h. (some edge damage, feet worn down & w/some dry rot) **2,420**

Bucket (or water) bench, painted pine, a low backrail w/notched corners on a long rectangular board top w/chamfered front corners over an apron w/chamfered ends, raised on tall inset one-board legs w/low arched cut-outs, old worn & weathered grey paint, 19th c., 15 x 52", 31 3/4" h. (some edge damage) **363**

Bucket (or water) bench, painted pine, a narrow rectangular top shelf above incurved upper sides above two wider lower shelves above bootjack legs, traces of red paint, 19th c., 12 x 32", 37" h. (minor edge damage) **495**

Early Painted Bucket Bench

Bucket (or water) bench, painted pine, a rectangular top w/chamfered edges above an apron w/a pair of drawers w/turned wood knobs above two long open shelves, bootjack ends, old surface w/remains of old red paint, possibly New England, early 19th c., minor imperfections, 18 x 55 1/2", 40" h. (ILLUS.) **4,025**

Bucket (or water) bench, painted pine, rectangular top overhanging shaped supports & cut-out arched feet joined by a shaped skirt, red wash finish, New England, early 19th c., 10 3/4 x 41", 17 3/4" h. (surface imperfections) **978**

Bucket (or water) bench, painted pine, the rectangular top w/beaded & shaped sides joining cut-out splayed mortised ends to the beaded front stretcher, painted blue over earlier red, probably Pennsylvania, early 19th c., 10 1/2 x 40 1/4", 16" h. **863**

Bucket (or water) bench, painted poplar, two narrow top shelves w/a closed back & low pointed crestrail & gallery above curved-out wide sides flanking two wider open shelves w/a narrow apron across the bottom, old red painted finish, square nail construction, bootjack ends, 19th c., 12 3/4 x 43 3/4", 51 1/2" h. (one thin support missing at back) **2,200**

Bucket (or water) bench, painted wood, a rectangular top on a dovetailed case w/three mortised shelves, incised molded ends on case & shelves, bootjack feet, two-board back, old red wash, 19th c., 12 1/2 x 42", 49 1/2" h. **605**

Bucket (or water) bench, painted wood, the shallow shelf above a projecting lower shelf joined by cut-out sides & double-arch cut-out feet, probably New England, early 19th c., 10 1/2 x 28", 26" h. (imperfections) **3,738**

Cobbler's bench, painted pine, the thick rectangular top w/a three-quarters gallery & an open compartment at one end, the case w/a long drawer & small slot above an enclosed kneehole opening beside a stack of three deep drawers above an open compartment, a columnar-turned post attached to the left end, wooden knobs, old worn green paint, very worn from use, late 19th c., 17 x 43", 35 1/2" h. **550**

Cobbler's bench, pine, rectangular top w/a large square lid over a compartment at one end beside three small compartments w/sliding lids over shallower wells & above a row of small square drawers w/wood knobs along the bottom of the case, raised on slightly outset slender square tapering legs, w/a shoe pattern cut-out from a newspaper dated 1829, old refinish, 14 x 36", 20" h. **1,815**

Country-style bench, painted pine, long rectangular plank top flanked by narrow side aprons, raised on high shaped bootjack ends w/angled support braces to seat, layers of old worn paint, 12 1/2 x 54", 19" h. (wear, edge damage) **248**

Country-style bench, painted poplar, mortised construction, long narrow board top above narrow beaded aprons w/shaped ends, wide shaped bootjack legs, green repaint & scrubbed top, 19th c., 13 1/2 x 39", 18 1/2" h. (age cracks) **358**

Country-style bench, pine, long board seat w/rounded ends above deep side aprons w/shaped ends, bootjack plank legs joined by a medial shelf, refinished, 19th c., 10 1/2 x 28 3/4", 17 1/4" h. (edge damage) **275**

Country-style bench, stained pine, long narrow rectangular top above narrow rounded side aprons & bootjack feet, square nail construction, embossed "C--an.Dom" on end, 19th c., 9 x 31 1/2", 8" h. (one later nail added) **495**

Golden Oak Hall Bench

Hall bench, Victorian Golden Oak substyle, a wide crestrail w/a serpentine top edge above long carved scrolls over a row of five slender turned spindles, flat back stiles w/curved ears above the shaped open arms on incurved arm supports flanking the rectangular lift-lid seat over a deep well, simple cabriole legs, refinished, ca. 1900, 16 x 30", 32" h. (ILLUS.) **450**

Kneeling bench, painted wood, narrow long top on low base, grey-painted graining on a putty-colored ground, 19th c., 6 x 28 3/4", 7 1/2" h. (wear) **1,840**

Kneeling bench, poplar, a long narrow board top w/a narrow apron raised on three arched bootjack legs, old brown finish, 7 x 76 3/4" **220**

Kneeling bench, walnut, a narrow long rectangular top above a rounded-end apron, on short bootjack legs mortised through the top, old patina, late 19th c., 5 1/2 x 36" **275**

Mission-style (Arts & Crafts movement) bench, oak, rectangular bench seat flanked by high side rails w/five narrow slats, joined by through-tenons, lower horizontal stretcher, medium brown finish, early 20th c., 17 x 26 3/4", 28" h. (edge wear, scratches) **575**

Modern-style bench, upholstery & chrome, the wide rectangular upholstered top composed of two reupholstered cushions in green wool raised on a chrome frame w/short square end legs joined by a square stretcher, designed by George Nelson, manufactured by Herman Miller, ca. 1950s, 30 x 60", 15" h. **1,320**

George Nelson Modern Style Bench

Modern-style bench, a rectangular long seat composed of solid maple slats raised on three ebonized wood trapezoidal open legs, designed by George Nelson, produced by Herman Miller, ca. 1956, 72" l., 14" h. (ILLUS.) **1,568**

Koloman Moser Bench

Modern-style bench, Koloman Moser, beechwood & bronze, arched bentwood frame continuing to paneled sides, enclosing an upholstered seat, all raised on bronze feet, stained brown, J. & J. Kohn, Model No. 412, ca. 1902, 21" w., 26" h. (ILLUS.) **5,175**

Park bench, cast-iron & wood, the long wooden slat back & seat joining the pierced scrolled iron arms above pierced ends of squirrels among leafy vines on short legs of gargoyles ending in paw feet, painted green, George Smith and Co., Glasgow, Scotland, late 19th c., 31 x 98", 33" h. (ILLUS.) **2,070**

Regency-Style Bench

Regency-Style bench, walnut, a long serpentine-edged upholstered top in green striped silk over a foliage-carved & shell-pierced apron, raised on six cabriole legs

ending in scrolled toes, joined by stretchers, Europe, late 19th c., 17 x 45 1/2", 17" h. (ILLUS.) **1,840**

Classical Window Bench

Window bench, Classical style, mahogany veneer, the up-curving seat flanked by scrolled ends above four outscrolled legs, New York, 1815-25, old refinish, some veneer cracking & loss, 14 x 39 1/2", 23 5/8" h. (ILLUS.) **3,450**

George III Window Bench

Window bench, upholstered mahogany, the long upholstered rectangular seat w/raised rolled end arms, raised on six square molded legs joined by stretchers, on casters, George III era, England, late 18th c., 18 3/4 x 51", 26" h (ILLUS.) **6,900**

Window bench, Classical style, carved mahogany veneer, upholstered seat above a veneered rail on leaf-carved cyma-curved ends joined by a ring-turned medial stretcher, old surface, Boston, 1835-45, 16 1/4 x 48", 17 1/2" h. (imperfections) **2,185**

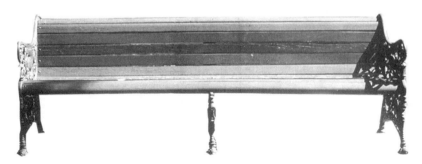

Long Wood & Iron Park Bench

Bookcases

Art Nouveau bookcase, carved mahogany, a gently arched top w/outset leaf- and whiplash-carved corners above an arrangement w/a flat long shelf above a stepped shelf unit over a compartmented section over a bottom section w/a square central paneled door flanked by two upright slots on each side, gently tapering sides & curved & molded feet, Diot, France, ca. 1900, 14 x 36 1/2", 79" h. **$2,875**

English Arts & Crafts Bookcase

Arts & Crafts bookcase, oak & leaded glass, a rectangular top w/molded edges above a frieze band & narrow molding over a pair of tall glazed cupboard doors w/upper panels of geometrically-glazed panels of striated green & colorless glass, opening to four wooden shelves, molded apron w/rounded block front feet on casters, England, late 19th c., wear, 14 1/4 x 40", 58 1/4" h. (ILLUS.) **805**

Arts & Crafts Oak Bookcase

Arts & Crafts bookcase, quarter-sawn oak, the rectangular top w/rounded cornice above a pair of tall doors w/oblong geometrically-glazed upper panels over tall plain glass panels opening to three shelves, flat base raised on front paw feet on casters, refinished, ca. 1900, 15 x 40", 5' 2" h. (ILLUS.) **1,400**

Unusual Oak Stacking Bookcase

Arts & Crafts bookcase, stacking-type, oak, five square stacked compartments each w/a geometrically glazed lift-front door resting on a raised molded base & fitted w/a round-fronted top cornice, early 20th c. (ILLUS.) **2,800**

Arts & Crafts bookcase, oak, a thin rectangular top overhanging a wide case w/three tall sliding doors each w/a top arched leaded-glass panel w/organic loops & scrolls above a single tall rectangular panel, opening to eight adjustable shelves, slightly shaped apron, original dark finish, metal tag of the Paine Furniture Co., missing backsplash, early 20th c., 14 x 60", 59" h. **2,420**

Biedermeier bookcase, maple & part-ebonized, the later high rounded arch cresting over an open shelf & a long narrow frieze drawer above a case fitted w/two tall glazed cupboard doors flanked by free-standing columns, on a shaped plinth, Europe, ca. 1820, 19 x 45", 81" h. .. **4,600**

Cherry Chippendale Bookcase

Chippendale bookcase, cherry, the flat rectangular top w/a flared cornice above a pair of large 12-pane glazed cupboard doors w/molded muntins opening to four shelves above a pair of long thumb-molded drawers w/replaced butterfly brasses, molded base on scroll-cut ogee bracket feet, old refinish, New England, ca. 1790, restored, 13 x 58 1/2", 62 1/2" h. (ILLUS.) **4,313**

Large Classical Style Bookcase

Classical bookcase, mahogany & crotchgrain mahogany veneer, two-part construction: the upper section w/a rectangular top w/rounded corners on the wide flaring coved cornice lifting off of the case w/a pair of tall 4-pane glazed doors w/double raised panels in the lower half, flowerheads carved at center of door mullions, opening to three shelves, on a shaped apron & bracket feet, ca. 1840, 18 x 62", 83 1/2" h. (ILLUS.) **3,900**

Tall Classical Mahogany Bookcase

Classical bookcase, mahogany, three-part construction: the top section w/a rectangular top & scroll-carved crest above a plain frieze centered & flanked by inlaid rectangular reserves above a conforming case fitted w/a pair of 9-pane glazed doors opening to a single shelf; the middle section w/a pair of tall 12-pane glazed cupboard doors opening to four shelves; the lower section w/a case fitted w/a pair of cockbeaded short drawers above two

similar drawers over an applied reeded molding centering an incised diamond plaque above a shaped skirt, on ring- and inverted baluster-turned legs, possibly Portsmouth, New Hampshire, 1825-45, 15 1/2 x 63", 114" h. (ILLUS.) **6,900**

Fine Classical Mahogany Bookcase

Classical bookcase, parcel-gilt mahogany & mahogany veneer, two-part construction: the upper section w/a rectangular top over a wide flattened flaring cornice over a deep veneered frieze band above a pair of glazed cupboard doors flanked by large carved parcel-gilt scrolls at the top & base sides above a row of three small round-fronted drawers; the lower section w/a projecting rectangular top above a long arched frieze drawer, raised on heavy scrolled legs carved at the front w/acanthus leaf, the sides w/grapevines & ending in large paw feet, above an incurved lower shelf raised on foliate-carved toupie feet, possibly Philadelphia, ca. 1830, 22 1/2 x 43", 5' 11 1/2" h. (ILLUS.) **9,200**

Classical Revival Mahogany Bookcase

Classical Revival bookcase, mahogany & mahogany veneer, the long rectangular top w/flat ogee cornice end sections flanking a central scroll-carved cornice section carved w/a baby's face, above a three-door case w/tall glazed doors opening to wooden shelves, molded base raised on carved paw feet on casters, refinished, ca. 1900, 18 x 54", 5' 10" h. (ILLUS.)... **2,600**

Country-style bookcase, decorated hardwood, a rectangular top above a tall case w/a pair of 2-pane cupboard doors w/a small pane above a tall pane, square stile legs on casters, the front frame decorated overall w/a burnt-wood narrow grapevine decoration against a checkered ground, dark red stain, late 19th - early 20th c., 16 1/2 x 40 1/2", 61" h. **495**

Early 20th century bookcase, oak, stacking lawyer's-type, four-section, a flat lift-off cornice w/rounded front edge above a long lift-front section w/a geometrically-leaded door above another long section w/a plain glazed lift-front door over a deeper section w/plain glazed lift-front door, the bottom projecting section much taller w/a plain glazed lift-front door, all on a ogee-front molded base, labeled "Globe Wernicke Co. Cincinnati, O.," ca. 1900, 19 x 34", 67" h...................................... **798**

Early 20th century bookcase, oak, the rectangular top w/narrow molded edges above a frieze band w/a half-round horizontal colonette above the tall glazed door opening to four shelves, raised on simple bracket feet, ca. 1910, 13 x 26", 56" h.. **316**

Unusual Oak Stacking Bookcase

rounded base rail, refinished, ca. 1910, 18 x 32", 4' 10" h. (ILLUS.) **1,200**

Quarter-sawn Oak Stacking Bookcase

Early 20th century bookcase, quarter-sawn oak, four-section stacking lawyer's-type, the rectangular top w/a flared rounded cornice above a two-pane glazed lift-front door over three lower stacked sections on a flat flared base, brass knobs, original dark finish, ca. 1910, 16 x 44", 4' 2" h. (ILLUS.) **1,400**

Early 20th century bookcase, quarter-sawn oak, lawyer's stacking-type, four-section, each rectangular section w/a rectangular glass lift-front door, curved top edge molding, raised on short cabriole front legs, ca. 1900, marked "Macey," 12 x 34", 59" h. **748**

Early 20th century bookcase, quarter-sawn oak, lawyer's stacking-type, three sections, the top w/a rectangular top & plain frieze band above the lift-front glazed door above two additional lift-front sections on a rectangular base w/short square stile legs, labeled "Macey," early 20th c., 11 1/2 x 34", 47" h. (ILLUS.)............. **330**

Early Oak Stacking Bookcase

Early 20th century bookcase, oak, three-section stacking lawyer's-type, a rectangular top w/rounded front corners & a dentil molding above a long lift-front glass door flanked by reeded columns stacking on two lower matching sections, deep molded base w/a long drawer w/brass bail pulls flanked by shaped sides & a molded flat bottom, original dark finish, possibly by Globe Wernecke, ca. 1900, 12 x 34", 42" h. (ILLUS.)............................. **1,200**

Early 20th century bookcase, quarter-sawn oak, four-section stacking lawyer's-type, the rectangular top w/a flared rounded cornice above the top section w/a leaded glass lift-front door above two matching sections w/plain glass lift-front doors set on the stepped-out bottom section w/a large glass lift-front door on a flat

Lawyer's Stacking-Type Oak Bookcase

Early 20th century bookcase, quarter-sawn oak, lawyer's stacking-type, three sections w/a flat three-quarter gallery on the rectangular top over the three sections w/a glazed lift-front door, raised on an aproned base w/short square legs, marked "Globe-Wernicke," old mellow finish, ca. 1910, 11 1/2 x 34", 53" h. **550**

Three-stack Lawyer's Bookcase

Early 20th century bookcase, quarter-sawn oak, three-section stacking lawyer's-type, the top section w/a rounded cornice over a lift-front door w/geometrically-leaded clear glass, the two lower sections w/lift-front glazed doors, base section w/a narrow ogee-front long drawer, labeled by the Macey Stacking Bookcase Co., refinished, ca. 1910, 13 x 36", 42" h. (ILLUS.) **950**

Federal Cherry Bookcase on Chest

Federal bookcase, cherry, two-part construction: the upper section w/a rectangular top over a flaring reeded cornice above a pair of 6-pane glazed doors opening to two shelves; the lower stepped-out section w/four long graduated drawers w/replaced clear blown glass pulls & inlaid diamond-form escutcheons, backboards marked "Canfield," short ring- and knob-turned legs, early 19th c., repairs, feet replaced, old finish, top 14 1/2 x 25", 83" h. (ILLUS.) **2,640**

Fine Federal Bookcase

Federal bookcase, inlaid mahogany, two-part construction: the upper section w/a rectangular top & molded swan's-neck crest w/openwork foliate designs centering a turned urn finial on a plinth inlaid w/oval foliage above a cove-molded cornice w/geometric band inlay over a frieze band & a pair of tall g7eometrically glazed cupboard doors w/incurved inlaid muntins centered by églomisé rectangular portrait medallions of George & Martha Washington, signed "by Kennedy, Balt.," the lower case w/a rectangular top over four long beaded graduated drawers w/string inlay over an inlaid band & scalloped apron continuing to tall French feet, the bookcase section w/a lift-top secret compartment behind the cornice, ca. 1800, 38 1/4" w., 88" h. (ILLUS.) **9,775**

Federal Revival Stacking Bookcase

Federal Revival bookcase, mahogany & mahogany veneer, two-part, each half composed of four rectangular stacking sections w/glazed lift-front doors, raised on five slender square tapering legs, made by Macey's Stacking Bookcase Company, original finish, ca. 1910, 14 x 50", 4' 6" h. (ILLUS.) **1,200**

George III Breakfront Bookcase

George III bookcase, mahogany, two-part breakfront-type: the upper section w/a removable paterae-mounted cornice above four tall multi-paned glazed doors w/Gothic arch-top panes opening to three shelves; the lower section w/mid-molding & conforming stepped-out central section w/a pair of paneled cupboard doors flanked by paneled end doors opening to shelves, on low bracket feet, England, ca. 1800, 19 x 77", 86" h. (ILLUS.) **10,350**

Georgian-Style Mahogany Bookcase

Georgian-Style bookcase, mahogany, three-door design, a rectangular top above an Chinese trellis-carved frieze band above the three tall glazed doors w/serpentine edged glazed panels over short matching blind panels, flanked by canted front corners w/garland-carved bands above reeded bands, molded base on scroll-cut bracket feet, England, ca. 1920, 18 x 72", 5' 4" h. (ILLUS.) **2,000**

Fine Gothic Revival Bookcase

Gothic Revival bookcase, mahogany & mahogany veneer, the rectangular top w/rounded front corners on the deep coved cornice above a pair of tall glazed doors w/arched mullions at the top, opening to four shelves, on a shaped bracket base, ca. 1840, 15 x 52", 83" h. (ILLUS.) .. **5,700**

Late Victorian Bookcase-Curio Cabinet

Late Victorian bookcase, stained maple, the serpentine scroll-carved crestrail above the rectangular top w/a bowed central section above a conforming case w/a pair of frosted glass small cupboard doors w/oval molding flanking a central bowed glazed cupboard door, all above a tall, wide glazed cupboard door w/a scroll-carved serpentine top opening to three adjustable wood shelves, shaped apron & simple bracket feet, original finish, ca. 1890s, 16 x 38", 5' 10" h. (ILLUS.) **2,000**

Mission-style (Arts & Crafts movement) bookcase, oak, a rectangular top on a four-shelf case, four D-shaped cut-outs on each canted side board, arched aprons at top & toe board, dark brown fin-

Mission Oak Bookcase

ish, stains, joint separation, early 20th c., 14 1/2 x 16 3/4", 43 3/4" h. (ILLUS.).. **1,495**

L. & J.G. Stickley Mission Bookcase

Mission-style (Arts & Crafts movement) bookcase, oak, a rectangular top w/a low gallery w/double pegged through-tenons above a pair of tall 12-pane glazed cupboard doors opening to shelves, copper plate pulls, double pegged through-tenon base, red Handcraft decal of L. & J.G. Stickley, Model No. 645, ca. 1910, 12 1/2 x 53", 55 1/2" h. (ILLUS.)...................................... **6,900**

Mission-style (Arts & Crafts movement) bookcase, oak, a rectangular top w/a shaped gallery above a case w/a single tall 6-pane glazed cupboard door opening to shelves, raised on stile legs, branded mark of L. & J.G. Stickley, ca. 1910, 11 x 22", 50" h. (refinished)........................ **4,312**

L. & J.G. Stickley Mission Bookcase

Mission-style (Arts & Crafts movement) bookcase, oak, a rectangular top w/three-quarters gallery w/through-tenons above a pair of tall 8-pane glazed doors opening to shelves, flat base w/through-tenons, hammered copper pulls, labeled "The Work of L. & J.G. Stickley," Model No. 643, ca. 1912, 12 1/8 x 36 1/2", 55 1/2" h. (ILLUS.) **6,900**

Mission-Style One-Door Bookcase

Mission-style (Arts & Crafts movement) bookcase, oak, quarter-sawn oak w/mortise-and-tenon construction, the rectangular top above a single tall 12-pane glazed cupboard door opening to three shelves, square stile legs on wooden casters, original finish, ca. 1910, 16 x 28", 56" h. (ILLUS.) **1,100**

Mission-style (Arts & Crafts movement) bookcase, oak, rectangular case w/overhanging top above double doors each w/eight small square leaded glass panes over pairs of tall narrow panes, flanked by a column w/capital at each side, above an arched apron, designed by Harvey Ellis, partial Craftsman paper label of Gustav Stickley, Model No. 73, ca. 1904, 14 1/8 x 54", 58" h.............. **15,525**

Mission-style (Arts & Crafts movement) bookcase, oak, rectangular top w/corbel support over two doors w/curved shaped top of two short over two long window panels, the interior fitted w/eight half-shelves, copper ring pulls, caned panels on the lower front & side, Lifetime Furniture Co., Grand Rapids, Michigan, early 20th c., 12 1/2 x 46 1/2", 57 1/2" h. (damage to caning, wear) **1,955**

Mission-style (Arts & Crafts movement) bookcase, oak, a rectangular narrow top w/a low galleried top w/keyed tenon ends above a case w/three tall 12-pane glazed cupboard doors opening to shelves, flat apron, lower keyed tenons & low arched end openings, original hammered copper hardware, fine original finish, "Handcraft" decal mark, L. & J.G. Stickley, Model No. 647, 12 x 73", 55" h.................................... **17,600**

Mission-style (Arts & Crafts movement) bookcase, oak, a three-quarters galleried top w/gently arched ends & keyed through-tenons on the top above a case w/a pair of tall 8-pane glazed doors opening to shelves, keyed through-tenons on the base, original iron hardware, cleaned finish, unsigned Gustav Stickley Model No. 718, 13 x 47", 56" h............................. **6,600**

Gustav Stickley Bookcase

Mission-style (Arts & Crafts movement) bookcase, oak, a rectangular top w/a low three-quarters gallery w/gently arched end board w/flush tenons, the case w/a pair of tall 8-pane glazed cupboard doors opening to shelves, original iron hardware, branded mark & paper label of Gustav Stickley, Model No. 717, recent finish, 13 x 48", 56" h. (ILLUS.)........... **5,225**

Mission-style (Arts & Crafts movement) bookcase, oak, a low three-quarter gallery top above three inset tall doors, each w/a geometrically leaded-glass top panel above a single long rectangular glass panel opening to shelves, new square hammered-copper pulls, decal mark of the Charles Limbert Furniture Co., 12 x 54", 57 1/2" h. (some touch-ups to original finish) **1,100**

Stickley Brothers Bookcase

Mission-style (Arts & Crafts movement) bookcase, oak, a rectangular long top w/arch-centered backsplash & round-topped corner stiles framing the long case w/three doors, each door w/a narrow panel of two rows of caramel slag-glass squares above pairs of plain glass tall narrow panels opening to adjustable shelves, original copper hardware, fine original finish, unsigned Stickley Brothers, 12 x 59", 60" h. (ILLUS.)...................... **5,225**

Neoclassical bookcase, kingwood & tulipwood parquetry, rectangular galleried top w/canted corners above a long drawer above a pair of tall glazed cupboard doors

opening to three shelves, raised on square tapered legs ending in flattened balls, ivory pulls & escutcheons, Baltic region, first quarter 19th c., 16 1/4 x 33 1/4", 57 1/2" h. (minor losses) **2,300**

Regency-Style "breakfront" bookcase, rosewood, a rectangular top w/a stepped-out wide central section w/a flaring molded cornice, the narrow stepped-back side sections each w/six open adjustable shelves, the center w/additional open adjustable shelves above & below a reeded medial band, molded plinth base, England, late 19th - early 20th c., 100" w., 100" h............................. **7,763**

Victorian Aesthetic Substyle Bookcase

Victorian Aesthetic Movement bookcase, carved & figured walnut, the pitched pediment above a pierced gallery & a reverse-breakfront frieze on columnar supports surmounted by figural masks, centering a pair of tall glazed doors w/adjustable wooden shelves on a conformingly-shaped plinth, decorated overall w/incised gilt designs, probably New York City, ca. 1870, missing central finial, 17 x 72", 104" h. (ILLUS.) **8,400**

Aesthetic Movement Oak Bookcase

Victorian Aesthetic Movement bookcase, quarter-sawn oak, the rectangular top w/a low three-quarters gallery centered by a low arched crest carved w/acorns & oak leaves above a square central paneled door carved w/a spray of oak leaves &

acorns flanked by open side compartments backed by rectangular beveled mirrors & arched framing w/ring- and baluster-turned corner supports above a case w/three tall glazed cupboard doors opening to three shelves, a row of three drawers w/stamped brass pulls across the bottom, molded base on casters, refinished, ca. 1895, 18 x 60", 6' h. (ILLUS.) **3,500**

Aesthetic Carved Breakfront Bookcase

Victorian Aesthetic Movement substyle 'breakfront' bookcase, walnut & burl walnut, the taller central projecting section w/a rectangular top & arched crestrail w/a scroll-carved crest & a band of carved scrolls above a dentil-carved cornice over a tall beveled glass door topped by a narrow rectangular panel carved w/a globe map flanked by olive branches opening to four wood shelves above the stepped-out base w/a burl-veneered drawer, the lower side cases w/a rectangular top w/a pierced-carved gallery composed of stylized leafy blossoms raised on a turned corner spindle over an open shelf w/a burled back panel over a scallop-cut & zigzag-incised frieze a opening to three shelves above a projecting base & a veneered drawer, brass ring pulls on drawers, molded base, refinished, ca. 1880s, 18 3/4 x 68", 6' 2" h. (ILLUS.) **9,500**

Fine Baroque Revival Bookcase

Victorian Baroque Revival bookcase, mahogany & mahogany veneer, the rectangular top w/a narrow beaded flared

cornice above a wide frieze band ornately carved w/leafy scrolls above a pair of wide single pane glazed doors flanked by reeded slender pilasters, two ornately scroll-carved drawers at the bottom w/lion head pulls, molded base raised on large paw feet on casters, refinished, ca. 1890, 18 x 50", 5' h. (ILLUS.) **2,800**

Victorian Baroque-Style Bookcase

Victorian Baroque-Style bookcase, carved ebonized wood, an ornately pierce-carved arched crest w/a pair of half-lion scrolling-tailed beasts flanking & supporting a central shield w/a carved lion above the molded rounded arch cornice above a single tall geometrically-glazed cupboard door w/orange-tinted glass flanked by scroll-carved caryatids on blocks flanking a long dragon-carved drawer, resting on a molded platform supported by two heavy shaped front legs ending in large paw feet, flat rear legs, probably Europe, late 19th c., 17 1/2 x 40 1/2", 99" h. (ILLUS.) **1,210**

Victorian Classical Double Bookcase

Victorian Classical bookcase, walnut, the rectangular top w/a deep coved cornice above a pair of tall 4-pane glazed doors w/pierced scroll-carved top corner brackets opening to adjustable shelves over the stepped-out base w/a pair of drawers w/black pear-shaped drop pulls, deep flat molded base, refinished, ca. 1850-70, 20 x 48", 6' 8" h. (ILLUS.) **1,800**

Victorian Country-style Tall Bookcase

Victorian country-style bookcase, walnut, the rectangular top w/a deep stepped & flaring cornice above a pair of 4-pane arch-topped doors w/solid lower panels opening to five adjustable shelves, the stepped-out lower section w/a single long paneled drawer w/wood knob pulls, slightly scalloped apron & simple bracket feet, demountable, refinished, ca. 1850, 18 x 45", 7' h. (ILLUS.)................................ **2,500**

Fine Golden Oak Double Bookcase

Victorian Golden Oak bookcase, quarter-sawn oak, a long low crestrail w/rounded ends above the rectangular top w/narrow carved frieze band above a long open compartment w/spindled end panels & two long narrow beveled mirrors above a scroll-carved band over a pair of tall glazed cupboard doors opening to two adjustable shelves, deep molded base on thin square feet, refinished, ca. 1900, 18 x 60", 68" h. (ILLUS.)............................. **3,300**

Victorian Golden Oak bookcase, quarter-sawn oak, the superstructure w/a low crestrail w/a small center swag carving above a narrow rectangular shelf raised on pierced & leaf-carved front supports & backed by a rectangular beveled mirror, the rectangular top above an incised band of wavy carving centered above the

Golden Oak Bookcase with Top Shelf

pair of tall glazed cupboard doors opening to four wooden shelves, gently carved apron on original porcelain casters, refinished, ca. 1905, 18 x 40", 5' 10" h. (ILLUS.)... **950**

Golden Oak Bookcase

Victorian Golden Oak bookcase, the narrow rectangular top w/a high three-quarter gallery w/a central rolled crest bar above a rounded cornice band over a pair of large single-pane glazed doors opening to eight adjustable shelves, flared molded base on simple bracket feet, ca. 1900-10, 14 x 49", 64" h. (ILLUS.) **633**

Victorian Breakfront Bookcase

Victorian Renaissance Revival book-case, oak, a tall breakfront style in three sections, the taller end sections w/rectangular tops & flared & dentil-carved cornices above tall glazed cupboard doors opening to shelves above a deep paneled drawer at the base, the protruding central section w/a scroll-cut crest above a stepped-down rectangular top w/beaded cornice above a tall glazed cupboard door above a paneled drawer, conforming blocked base w/beaded band trim, stamped brass pulls w/bails on drawers, ca. 1880-90, 16 x 75", 69" h. (ILLUS.).. **3,025**

Large Oak Breakfront Bookcase

Victorian Renaissance Revival book-case, oak, breakfront-style, the high central section w/a rectangular top & deep widely flaring cornice supported on carved brackets & half-round spindles over a tall arched & glazed cupboard door w/raised panels at the top corners & at the bottom opening to shelves, the stepped-back side sections each w/a rectangular top w/a deep widely flaring cornice above a plain frieze band over a tall narrow three-paneled door, the stepped-out base w/a group of four drawers w/metal pulls, a heavy flaring base molding on compressed bun feet, original finish, late quarter 19th c., 24 x 64", 7' 4" h. (ILLUS.)... **3,000**

European Victorian Bookcase

Victorian Renaissance Revival book-case, stained walnut, two-part construction: the upper section w/a rectangular top & deep flared cornice above a pair of tall glazed cupboard doors w/molded trim opening to a shelf; the lower stepped-out section w/a molded frieze band above a pair of circular-paneled cupboard doors on a plinth base, decorated throughout w/roundels & incised designs, Europe, probably Russian, late 19th c., 23 x 57", 87" h. (ILLUS.) **2,400**

Victorian Renaissance Revival book-case, walnut, a rectangular top w/a long low arched crestrail centered by a large crown cornice above a blocked panel & w/scalloped upright ears at each end, above a stepped frieze band above a pair of large two-pane glazed cupboard doors opening to four shelves & flanked by narrow paneled edges all above a slightly stepped-out lower section w/a pair of long line-incised drawers, flat molded base band, ca. 1880, 15 x 60", 93" h. **2,744**

Breakfront Renaissance Bookcase

Victorian Renaissance Revival book-case, walnut & burl walnut, breakfront style, the tall central projecting section w/a high crest topped by a broken-scroll crestrail centered by a high carved flame-form finial above deep molding over an arched panel centered by a large relief-carved bust of a woman w/a floral wreath in her hair all above a tall arched glazed door opening to adjustable shelves, the lower side cabinets w/broken-scroll crests on molded flaring cornices above burl frieze panels over the arched glazed cupboard doors opening to adjustable shelves, three drawers across the base each w/a raised burl panel & pairs of brass loop & bar pulls, deep molded flat base, refinished, ca. 1870, 22 x 72", 8' 5" h. (ILLUS.) **9,000**

Victorian Renaissance Revival book-case, walnut & burl walnut, breakfront-style, the top w/a band of applied dentil blocks & a stepped-out central section above a pair of very tall single-pane glazed cupboard doors opening to shelves & flanked by ring- and columnar-turned colo-

Victorian Breakfront Bookcase

nettes flanked by narrow glazed panels & another pair of colonettes beside the two tall stepped-back glazed side panels w/two further colonettes at the front corners, resting on a low rectangular bottom section w/a molded top over a long burl-fronted central drawer flanked by shorter side drawers, molded plinth base, ca. 1880, 96" h. (ILLUS.)... **4,675**

Renaissance Revival Bookcase

Victorian Renaissance Revival bookcase, walnut & burl walnut, the rectangular top w/a narrow molded & flaring cornice above a frieze band w/decorative blocks of burl walnut over a pair of tall glazed doors opening to four adjustable shelves flanked by ring- and post-turned colonettes w/blocked capitals & bases above a molded medial rail above a pair of burl veneered paneled bottom drawers w/replaced glass pulls, molded plinth base, ca. 1880, top 16 x 53 1/4", 64 1/4" h. (ILLUS.) **1,375**

Fine Renaissance Revival Bookcase

Victorian Renaissance Revival bookcase, walnut & burl walnut, three-door breakfront-style, the tallest central section w/a rectangular top w/rounded front corners over a deep stepped cornice & dentil-carved band over a burl veneer band above a tall glazed cupboard door opening to four shelves flanked by turned & reeded colonettes down the front, the shorter & slightly stepped-back matching side sections with matching cornices & details, burl panels across the conforming base, ca. 1875 (ILLUS.)....................... **4,100**

Renaissance Revival Bookcase

Victorian Renaissance Revival bookcase, walnut & burl walnut, two-part construction: the top section w/a rectangular top w/a flaring stepped cornice above a paneled frieze band w/burl panels & a center roundel above a pair of tall arched glazed doors w/triangular burl panels at the top corners & flanked by leaf-carved drops & raised burl panels down the sides, opening to three shelves; the lower stepped-out section w/a pair of deep drawers w/long shaped raised burl panels & black pear-shaped pulls flanked by burl panels, deep molded plinth base, ca. 1875, 20 x 42", 64" h. (ILLUS.) **2,000**

Fine Renaissance Revival Bookcase

Victorian Renaissance Revival bookcase, walnut w/ebonized panels, breakfront-style, two-part construction: the stepped rectangular top fitted w/an ornate scroll-cut crest w/incised scrolls & ebonized panels flanked by turned corner finials, the stepped-out central section w/an ebonized frieze band over the tall arched glazed door w/ebonized banding opening to shelves flanked by two matching shorter set-back doors flanked by chamfered front corners; the lower stepped-out base section w/three conforming drawers w/ebonized panels on a molded plinth base w/chamfered front corners, ca. 1875, originally from important Iowa mansion, 16 x 101", 114" h. (ILLUS.) **11,500**

Renaissance-Style Oak Bookcase

Victorian Renaissance-Style bookcase, carved oak, a rectangular top w/a deep flaring carved cornice above a wide frieze band w/ornate scroll carving centered by a cartouche above a molded rail over a pair of tall glazed cupboard doors w/arched panes enclosed w/narrow gadrooned molding & flanked by carved fruiting vines down the sides, a wide flaring mid-molding above a pair of paneled cupboard doors w/square beaded molding enclosing carved scrolled grape clusters flanked by further fruiting vines at the sides, deep flaring carved base molding, original finish, Europe, last quarter 19th c., 22 x 40", 6' 2" h. (ILLUS.)...................... **2,500**

Victorian Rococo bookcase, carved rosewood, two-part construction: the upper section w/an arched top w/a high ornate pierced, scroll-carved crest above a floral-carved frieze band & blocked corners above a pair of tall glazed arched doors w/delicate scroll-carved edging flanked by outset corner blocks w/bold leaf-, scroll- and floral carving & w/a pair of narrow drawers just below the doors; the stepped-out lower section w/conforming blocked corners & a pair of narrow drawers w/oval banding above a pair of paneled cupboard

Ornate Victorian Rococo Bookcase

doors w/delicate scroll-trimmed edging, molded serpentine apron, leaf- and scroll-carved blocked front corners above compressed bulbous feet, ca. 1850-60, 25 x 52", 95" h. (ILLUS.)................................ **4,140**

Late Victorian Oak Bookcase

Victorian turn-of-the-century bookcase, oak, a rectangular top w/a narrow flared cornice above a tall case w/a pair of large glazed doors w/inset rectangular panels at the bottom above a deep molded flat base, beaded board pine back, opens to five adjustable shelves, short section of molding missing at the side, ca. 1900, 18 x 68", 83" h. (ILLUS.) **1,045**

Bureaux Plat

Unique Egyptian Revival Bureau Plat

Egyptian Revival bureau plat, parcel-gilt & ebonized wood, the rectangular top w/beveled & gilt-trimmed border above an ornate apron w/three drawers decorated w/grotesque masks, spread-winged bird & lotus motifs & raised on curved figural legs carved & decorated to resemble a pharoah's casket, legs joined by a long slender X-stretcher mounted by a pair of recumbent Egyptian figures, early 20th c., 40 x 57 1/2", 31" h. (ILLUS.).. **$18,000**

Empire-Style Bureau Plat

Empire-Style bureau plat, gilt-bronze mounted mahogany, the rectangular top w/inset tooled leather writing surface, above an apron w/a center long drawer flanked by two short drawers all w/ormolu mounts including an urn flanked by classic lions & scrolled keyhole escutcheons, each corner block w/an ormolu lyre mount, raised on tapering round legs surmounted by a winged classical bust & terminating in a lion's paw ormolu mount, France, late 19th c., 29 1/2 x 47 1/2", 29" h. (ILLUS.)............................ **11,500**

Louis XV-Style bureau plat, gilt-bronze mounted fruitwood, the rectangular top inset w/a leather writing surface & w/gilt-bronze rounded corner mounts above the scalloped veneered apron w/a long center drawer flanked by shorter, deeper drawers all w/gilt-bronze bail pulls & shield-form keyhole escutcheons as well as scrolled feather gilt-bronze edge mounts & mask & scroll corner mounts above the simple cabriole legs ending in gilt-bronze lion's paw feet, France, late 19th c., 37 x 74", 32" h............................... **11,500**

Fine Louis XV-Style Bureau Plat

Louis XV-Style bureau plat, gilt-bronze mounted tulipwood parquetry, the rectangular top w/a gilt-tooled leather inset writing surface framed by a gilt-bronze border above the apron w/three shaped frieze drawers w/parquetry designs & scrolling gilt-bronze mounts, the central one recessed & opposing faux drawers, the sides fitted w/bacchic masks, raised on cabriole legs headed by female busts & ending in paw-form sabots, France, late 19th c., 69" l., 31" h. (ILLUS.) **5,750**

Louis XV-Style bureau plat, gilt-bronze mounted tulipwood, the rectangular top inset w/an embossed leather writing surface above shaped metal-mounted border over an apron w/three drawers, the central drawer recessed, complete on all sides, the reverse w/false opening drawers, raised on slightly shaped cabriole legs w/soldier bust caryatids at the top & fitted w/sabots at the foot, by Conquet, France, after a model by Charles Cressent, late 19th c., 39 3/4 x 81", 31" h. **23,750**

Rare Louis XV-Style Bureau Plat

Louis XV-Style bureau plat, gilt-bronze mounted tulipwood, the rectangular top w/ormolu edging above three frieze drawers w/ormolu banding & scrolled pulls raised on slender simple cabriole legs topped w/ormolu helmeted male busts & ending in scrolled sabot, further mounts & banding at each end, France, late 19th c., 47" l., 31" h. (ILLUS.) **11,400**

Louis XV-Style bureau plat, gilt-bronze mounted tulipwood, the shaped rectangular top w/a gilt-tooled leather inset writing surface within a gilt-bronze band above a shaped apron w/two deep round-edged drawers flanking a long shallower central drawer on one side opposed by matching faux drawers each w/scrolled bronze mounts, on cabriole legs headed by pierced foliate-cast *chutes* & ending in scrolled *sabots*, France, late 19th c., 48" l., 31" h. **6,900**

Louis XV-Style bureau plat, ormolu-mounted tulipwood parquetry, rectangular top w/rounded leaf-cast corners, the apron fitted w/three drawers opposed by sham drawers, on cabriole legs, covered w/foliate & gilt mask mounts, early 20th c., 32 x 70", 30" h. **2,760**

Louis XV-Style Bureau Plat

Louis XV-Style bureau plat, tulipwood marquetry, the rectangular top w/serpentine edges w/ormolu banding above a conforming apron inlaid w/banding & veneered designs & fitted on one side w/three drawers w/scrolled ormolu pulls & corner mounts, each cabriole leg headed by a large scrolled ormolu mount & metal-capped feet, France, late 19th c. (ILLUS.)... **6,000**

Louis XVI-Style Bureau Plat

Louis XVI-Style bureau plat, gilt-bronze mounted mahogany, the rectangular molded top w/an inset leather writing surface above a central pull-out writing surface over the kneehole & flanked by two small paneled drawers on each side, raised on turned tapering stop-fluted legs ending in toupie feet, France, late 19th c., 25 3/4 x 43 1/2", 29 3/4" h. (ILLUS.) **2,645**

Marquetry Bureau Plat

Marquetry bureau plat, rectangular top w/tooled leather border enclosing a central writing panel inlaid in various woods w/berries & leafage, above conforming inlaid apron w/two drawers, all raised on twist-carved legs, ca. 1900, 31 1/2 x 31 1/2 x 48" (ILLUS.) **6,900**

Napoleon III-Style Bureau Plat

Napoleon III-Style bureau plat, ebonized & gilt-trimmed wood, the rectangular top w/gilt tooled leather writing surface above a shaped apron w/a narrow long central drawer flanked by shorter, deeper end drawers, all w/gilt banding & gilt-bronze banding, pulls & leafy scroll mounts, on tapering reeded legs headed by gilt leaf clusters & gilt-bronze corner block mounts & terminating in gilt-bronze capped feet, late 19th c., 32 x 60", 30" h... **6,900**

Cabinets

Cellarette (wine cabinet), Federal, inlaid mahogany, rectangular top w/inlaid stringing & crossbanding above a shield-form inlaid keyhole escutcheon set on a molded frame above square casters, the top opening to a compartmented baize-lined interior containing eleven colorless blown glass decanters, old surface, possibly New England, ca. 1790-1810, 18 1/4" w., 22" h. (minor imperfections) ... **$8,050**

Small Art Deco China Cabinet

China cabinet, Art Deco style, burl walnut veneer, a stepped & triple-arched top above a conforming case w/a pair of 2-pane tall glazed central doors opening to two long glass shelves flanked by two glazed side panels, on a deep serpentine apron, electrified, ca. 1930s, 11 1/4 x 44 1/2", 50" h. (ILLUS.) **546**

Attractive Arts & Crafts China Cabinet

China cabinet, Arts & Crafts style, oak, a wide peaked crestrail flanked by open side rails on the rectangular top w/a pointed front edge above the conforming case w/a pair of tall glazed doors w/a diamond lattice panel at the top of each above a long plain glass pane, opening to five wooden shelves, matching glazed sides, peaked narrow apron & slender square tapering stile legs on small casters, ca. 1910, 15 x 37", 67" h. (ILLUS.)... **952**

China cabinet, Arts & Crafts style, oak, the rectangular top w/a low arched backsplash above a pair of tall glazed cupboard doors opening to six adjustable shelves, flat apron, short stile legs, silver-washed hammered copper hardware, fine original reddish brown finish, remnants of a paper label from a Grand Rapids maker, 13 x 45 1/2", 55 1/4" h. **1,760**

Unique Arts & Crafts China Cabinet

China cabinet, Arts & Crafts style, oak, the rectangular top w/an upright stepped & paneled crestboard w/metal mounts above a case w/a pair of glazed cupboard doors w/a pair of small panes flanking a central pane overlaid w/a pierced stylized spearpoint copper ornament above two tall narrow panes all above a pair of small square paneled doors flanking a stack of four small drawers at the bottom, long spearpoint copper strap hinges & inset pulls, matching glazed sides, short stile legs joined by sleigh feet on casters, metal tag marked "From Alexander H. Revel & Co. Chicago, Ill.," Model No. 8646, Stickley Brothers, ca. 1908, 18 x 48", 75 1/4" h. (ILLUS.)... **14,100**

Classical Revival China Cabinet

China cabinet, Classical Revival style, oak, a low flat crestrail on the D-form top above a conforming case w/a long curved glass center door flanked by curved glass sides & opening to four wooden shelves w/the top shelf backed by a rectangular mirror, conforming base on two C-scroll front legs & two square back legs all on casters, ca. 1910, 16 x 36", 60" h. (ILLUS.)............................... **532**

China cabinet, Federal-Style, inlaid mahogany & mahogany veneer, two-part construction: the upper section w/a rectangular top w/a molded cornice above a wide frieze band over two long 8-pane glazed doors opening to two shelves; the lower section w/a mid-molding above a case w/three long graduated drawers w/banded inlay & cast round ring pulls, shaped bracket feet, 20th c., 16 x 36", 69 1/4" h... **1,100**

China cabinet, late Victorian Classical Revival style, oak, the wide D-form top over a deep carved & molded cornice above glazed curved sides & a wide curved tall center door flanked by carved caryatids above tall blocked pilasters, molded base on four bold paw feet, mirrored interior back, four glass shelves, ca. 1890, 50" w., 66" h. **2,800**

China cabinet, late Victorian, mahogany veneer, D-form w/a stepped-out center section w/scroll-topped flat pilasters flanking the curved glass door & ending in heavy C-scroll feet, curved glass sides, encloses four wooden shelves w/a rectangular mirror behind the top shelf, on casters, dark finish, ca. 1900, 17 1/4 x 40", 61 1/2" h. (bottom drilled for electric line).. **688**

Finely Finished Oak China Cabinet

China cabinet, late Victorian, oak, half-round form w/rounded molded side cornices flanking a central serpentine cornice w/scrolled leaf carving & w/carved outset blocks above a conforming case w/free-standing ring-turned & reeded slender columns separating the curved center door & side panels, conforming base molding on short reeded cabriole legs w/paw feet, ca. 1900 (ILLUS.) **2,500**

China Cabinet with Carved Lion Heads

China cabinet, late Victorian, oak, the half-round top w/outset front corners above curved glass sides & a curved glass door w/carved lion heads topping the front framework, pair of stylized cabriole legs in the front & simple curved legs at the rear, ca. 1900 (ILLUS.)............................... **1,600**

China cabinet, late Victorian, oak, the half-round top w/outset front corners above curved glass sides & a curved glass door flanked by tall columns topped w/carved blocks, conforming base w/short cabriole front legs ending in claw-and-ball feet on casters, ca. 1900 .... **2,000**

Ornate Rococo-style China Cabinet

China cabinet, late Victorian Rococo-style, mahogany, the half-round case w/a high wide arched molded crestrail centered by a high scroll-carved crest above a tall arched glazed cupboard door flanked by curved glass sides all enclosing three glass shelves, conforming base w/scroll-carved apron, on short front cabriole legs w/claw-and-ball feet (ILLUS.)...................... **9,000**

Harvey Ellis-Designed Cabinet

China cabinet, Mission-style (Arts & Crafts movement), oak, a rectangular top overhanging a case w/a tall glazed cupboard door w/an arched top rail & a metal plate & ring pull, arched apron, designed by Harvey Ellis, produced by Gustav

Stickley, ca. 1904, 15 1/4 x 36", 60" h. (ILLUS.).. **8,625**

China cabinet, Mission-style (Arts & Crafts movement), oak, a rectangular top slightly overhanging tall case w/a tall single glazed door opening to three wooden shelves, chamfered back, arched apron, hammered copper V-pull on door, fine original finish & glass, unmarked Gustav Stickley, 15 x 35 3/4", 59 3/4" h. **18,700**

China cabinet, Mission-style (Arts & Crafts movement), oak, a rectangular top w/a top rail & front side stiles flanking a pair of tall glazed doors opening to interior fitted for shelves, glazed side panels, stiles continue to form legs, slightly arched front apron, unmarked, early 20th c., 14 x 45", 59" h. **575**

Strickley Brothers China Cabinet

China cabinet, Mission-style (Arts & Crafts movement), oak, a rectangular top w/a narrow crestrail above a case w/a pair of tall glazed cupboard doors w/gently arched tops, a small panel above a tall lower panel, 3-pane glazed sides, three interior shelves w/the top shelf backed by a mirror, flat apron, square stile legs, branded mark & Quaint tag of the Stickley Brothers, ca. 1914 (ILLUS.).................. **2,875**

China cabinet, Victorian Golden Oak period, side-by-side design, a long crestrail w/a small carved & pointed center crest above a long narrow shelf w/a round bar along the front edge & supported on C-scroll carved uprights on the long top backed by a narrow beveled mirror w/rounded ends, one side of the case w/a tall curved glass door opening to four shelves beside the half w/a pair of small cupboard doors w/asymmetrical leaded glass panels above a wide hinged slant front a scroll-carved design opening to a fitted desk interior above a stack of three curve-fronted drawers w/brass bail pulls, double-lobed base molding raised on

Oak Side-by-Side China Cabinet

short cabriole front legs ending in claw-and-ball feet, refinished, ca. 1900, 20 x 40", 6' 10" h. (ILLUS.) **1,750**

China cabinet, Victorian Golden Oak style, a demi-lune top above a conforming case w/a curved top frieze centered at the front by a straight rounded bar above a long single pane glazed door flanked by carved lions on monopodia over half-round columns, curved glass sides, opening to three wooden shelves, narrow molded apron raised on four short cabriole legs ending in paw feet, lions w/added "jeweled" eyes, ca. 1900, 14 x 39 3/4", 65" h. **1,073**

Ornate Golden Oak China Cabinet

China cabinet, Victorian Golden Oak style, the high crestrail centered by a pointed scroll-carved crest over leafy scrolls & rounded carved corners over the half-round top w/blocked projections at the front & a deep cornice above slender tall turned & leaf-carved columns flanking the wide curved glass center door, curved glass sides, four interior wooden shelves against a mirror back, molded conforming apron raised on four short cabriole legs w/paw feet, refinished, ca. 1895, 20 x 48", 5' 10" h. (ILLUS.) **3,000**

China cabinet, Victorian Golden Oak sub-style, quarter-sawn oak, the tall case w/a rectangular top & stepped cornice w/a thin zipper-carved edge band & cut-out scrolls above a central oval beveled mirror flanked by scroll clusters & above a shelf w/a pierced scroll gallery, each side w/a tall narrow cabinet door w/very large ornately scrolled strapwork hinges above & below a glass pane opening to shelves, the central section w/a pair of smaller tall glazed doors opening to shelves & carved bands above & below, over two long central drawers, the base section w/a beaded medial band above a pair of long drawers w/scroll-carved trim over the low serpentine apron w/a pierced oval scroll-carved panel & scroll-carved feet, old finish, ca. 1900, 14 x 58", 75 1/2" h. **1,513**

Fine Golden Oak China Cabinet

China cabinet, Victorian Golden Oak, the half-round top w/a high pointed & ornately scroll-carved crest above a pair of projecting tall reeded columns dividing the curved front glass door from the curved glass sides, molded conforming base raised on front paw feet on casters, encloses four wooden shelves w/a mirrored back at the top shelf, refinished, ca. 1895, 20 x 44", 70" h. (ILLUS.) **3,400**

Golden Oak China Cabinet

China cabinet, Victorian Golden Oak, the high arched crestrail w/rounded corners & applied scroll trim centering an oblong mirror over the D-form top w/flattened front edge above a long flat glazed center door & curved glass sides opening to three wooden shelves, conforming base raised on four simple cabriole legs on casters, ca. 1900, 13 x 34", 72" h. (ILLUS.)........................ **784**

Fine Limbert China Cabinet

China cabinet, Mission-style (Arts & Crafts movement), oak, a high gently arched crestrail w/a plate rail above the rectangular top overhanging a tall case w/molded corbels under each corner above a pair of tall glazed doors w/a small rectangular pane over a tall pane & original copper strap hinges, a long drawer across the bottom w/original copper hardware, original shelves, original finish, branded Limbert company signature, Model No. 1468, 17 x 48", 62" h. (ILLUS.).................... **4,950**

China cabinet, Mission-style (Arts & Crafts movement), oak, a high rounded crestboard above the trapezoidal top w/a projecting center above a pair of tall doors w/four square panes above a large single pane, glazed sides, arched aprons, five heavy stile legs, original copper pulls, refinished, branded mark of the Charles Limbert Co., Model No. 428, 19 x 40", 63" h.. **4,675**

China cabinet, Mission-style (Arts & Crafts movement), oak, a rectangular top w/a low three-quarters gallery w/gently arched ends above a pair of tall 8-pane glazed cupboard doors opening to shelves, 8-pane glazed sides, raised on sides w/arched cut-out feet, original brass hardware, lightly cleaned original finish, branded & paper label marks of Gustav Stickley, Model No. 815, minor distress to the top, 15 x 42", 64" h............. **8,800**

China cabinet, Mission-style (Arts & Crafts style), oak, the rectangular top w/a plate rail rack above a tall case w/a pair of 8-pane glazed doors opening to shelves, 4-pane side panels, original copper hardware, original finish, Stickley Brothers, illegible model number, 17 x 42", 64" h. **3,575**

Turn-of-the-century China Cabinet

China cabinet, late Victorian, oak, D-form top above deep cornice over conforming case w/long curved glass sides flanking a tall flat glazed door opening to four wooden shelves & a mirror in the upper half, molded base on four bun feet, ca. 1900, 15 x 48", 65" h. (ILLUS.) **1,093**

Ornate Oak China Cabinet

China cabinet, late Victorian, carved oak, D-form serpentine top w/outset half-round projections above a leafy scroll-carved cornice above a conforming case w/the top projections over tall reeded & carved columns headed by carved lions' heads w/"jeweled" eyes, over pilasters on each side of the tall curved glass central door, all flanked by curved glass sides, molded base on two large paw front feet & two plain back feet, four interior shelves, ca. 1900, 20 x 49", 70 3/4" h. (ILLUS.)... **2,090**

China cabinet, late Victorian, oak, D-form top w/a high mirrored back crest w/a flat top & leafy scroll-carved rounded corners, the front w/a flat crest over a curved glass tall door opening to four shelves & flanked by slender columns headed by narrow carved lion head monopeds w/"jeweled" eyes & ending in short cabriole front legs w/paw feet, curved glass sides, outswept square back legs, original alligatored finish, ca. 1900, 15 3/4 x 38 1/2", 72 5/8" h. (ILLUS. top next page).. **1,045**

China Cabinet with Mirrored Crest

Corner cabinet, Mission-style (Arts & Crafts movement), oak, a low gallery on the top above a pair of two cupboard doors each w/two tall panes of glass opening to shelves above a small central drawer over two paneled cupboard doors w/metal hardware, fine original dark finish, branded mark of Gustav Stickley, early 20th c., 29 x 41", 72 1/4" h. **27,500**

Chippendale Revival Curio Cabinet

Curio cabinet, Chippendale Revival style, mahogany, two-part construction: the very tall upper section w/a broken-scroll pediment w/pierced lattice carving & a small central platform finial above a cornice w/a dentil molding over a lattice-carved frieze band above the very tall geometrically-glazed cupboard doors opening to shelves; the stepped-out lower section w/a rectangular top w/molded edge above a long deep drawer w/lattice-carved border banding flanked by lattice-carved side stiles, narrow serpentine apron raised on slender carved cabriole legs ending in scroll feet on pegs, original finish, ca. 1890s, 20 x 34", 7' 6" h. (ILLUS.) **1,800**

Louis-XV Style Giltwood Curio Cabinet

Curio cabinet, Louis XV-Style, giltwood, a tan marble rectangular top w/rounded corners above a conforming case w/a wide frieze band of ornate leafy scrolls above a wide single-pane glazed door flanked by half-nude caryatids & scrolls at the front corners & glass side panels, the deep apron w/a center scroll drop, short demi-cabriole legs w/scroll-carved knees, two interior shelves, Europe, ca. 1900, 16 x 28", 42" h. (ILLUS.) **1,800**

Delicate Louis XV-Style Curio Cabinet

Curio cabinet, Louis XV-Style, walnut, two-part construction: the upper section w/an arched & scroll-trimmed cornice above a three-section case w/tall slender side doors w/tall oblong mirrors w/scrolled borders above a rounded scroll reserve flanking the slightly outset central cabinet section w/a glazed door w/delicate scrolling wood overlay opening to three shelves; the stepped-out lower section w/pierced lattice & scroll-carved apron raised on four slender & gently backswept cabriole legs joined at the base w/an arched & scrolled X-stretcher, France, late 19th - early 20th c., 16 x 43", 75" h. (ILLUS.).. **2,475**

Display cabinet, Victorian Aesthetic Movement substyle, ebonized wood, the arched top w/gallery above an inset panel over a galleried shelf, a central beveled glass cabinet door enclosing shelves & flanked by shelves above a drawer, on stylized feet, last quarter 19th c., 11 x 44", 79" h. (lacking inset panel, minor losses) **978**

Early 20th Century Filing Cabinet

Filing cabinet, early 20th century, oak, a rectangular flat top above a stack of four deep square drawers w/brass rectangular name tag holders & simple curved pulls, flat base, refinished, ca. 1900-20, 16 1/2 x 25", 51 1/2" h. (ILLUS.) **358**

Filing cabinet, Mission-style (Arts & Crafts movement), oak, stacking-type, four rectangular panel-fronted drawers w/brass name plate holders & loop handles vertically arranged on short square legs, paneled sides, ca. 1910, 15 x 24", 60" h. **288**

Mission Oak Gun Cabinet

Gun cabinet, Mission-style (Arts & Crafts movement), oak, a rectangular top w/a high three-quarters gallery above a tall 2-pane glazed door w/metal pull opening to a rack for rifles above a single drawer at the bottom, arched front apron, original finish & key, brass tag marked "Yeager Gun Cabinet - Allentown Pa - USA.," 14 x 23", 70 1/2" h. (ILLUS.)...................... **1,650**

Hanging wall cabinet, Victorian Aesthetic Movement substyle, cherry, the crestrail w/an arched & scroll-cut central crest flanked by pointed end crests above a narrow shelf over a small cabinet w/a beveled glass door w/a cut-out top band flanked by open side shelves w/slender columns supporting the ends of the upper shelf, the right side of cabinet shelf extended & w/a low scroll-cut back, the lower section below the cabinet w/a paneled backboard w/scalloped rim, original finish, ca. 1890, 8 x 26", 24" h. (small glued edge break) **440**

Early Labeled Hoosier Cabinet

Kitchen cabinet, early 20th century Hoosier-style, oak, the superstructure w/a rectangular top above a pair of paneled cupboard doors beside a wide door opening to a bin compartment above a high tambour-front storage area w/metal funnel-form bins flanking a hanging spice rack above a row of storage jars, the lower section w/a rectangular white porcelain-covered metal work surface above a pair of thin pull-out work shelves above a wide rectangular door beside a stack of three graduated drawers, square tapering legs on casters, original paper door inserts, repairs & strips of wood in tambour doors reinstalled, marked "Hoosier," ca. 1900, 22 x 41", 72" h. (ILLUS.) **825**

Kitchen cabinet, early 20th century Hoosier-type, pine, the upper section w/a rectangular top above a pair of glazed cupboard doors beside an arrangement of four small drawers, the bottom one w/a

Pine Hoosier-style Kitchen Cabinet

bin bottom, all overhanging a high opening w/curved sides on the stepped-out
zinc-covered rectangular work surface
above a pair of deep drawers flanking a
pair of short drawers above a pair of paneled cupboard doors beside a deep pull-
out bin drawer, six short bracketed feet
on casters, ca. 1900, 25 1/2 x 41", 65" h.
(ILLUS.) **600**

Liquor cabinet, Arts & Crafts style, oak,
rectangular top w/the front half hinged to
open to a copper-lined compartment over
a single narrow drawer over a tall flat
cupboard door opening to a shelf & fitted
compartment, metal pulls, square stile
legs, early 20th c., 17 1/4 x 23 1/2",
43" h. (one replaced pull) **2,415**

Classical Revival Music Cabinet

Music cabinet, Classical Revival style, mahogany veneer, a rounded crestrail w/a
scroll-carved center finial above the rect-

angular top over a case w/a round-fronted veneered drawer w/round brass pulls
& a brass keyhole escutcheon above a
flat paneled door w/fine crotch-grained
veneering & a brass knob, gadrooned
base band, raised on short cabriole legs
ending in carved paw feet, refinished, ca.
1910, 14 x 22", 42" h. (ILLUS.) **650**

Gustav Stickley Music Cabinet

Music cabinet, Mission-style (Arts & Crafts
movement), oak, a rectangular top w/a
stepped three-quarters gallery above a
tall narrow paneled door w/a rectangular
plate & ring pull, flat apron, branded mark
of Gustav Stickley, Model No. 70w, ca.
1912, 16 x 20", 46" h. (ILLUS.) **7,475**

Classical Revival Music Cabinet

Music cabinet, Victorian Classical Revival
substyle, mahogany, a high top crest w/a
flat crestrail w/delicate center carving &
curved scroll-carved ends enclosing an
oblong beveled mirror, the rectangular

top over a scroll-carved frieze band above a pair of tall cupboard doors w/rectangular beveled mirrors w/notched corners & ormolu sunburst mounts at each corner, quarter-round reeded columns at side, sides w/ormolu capitals & bases, narrow apron w/small carved center drop, raised on ring-turned & tapering feet w/ormolu tips, ca. 1890, 16 x 28", 4' h. (ILLUS.) **1,900**

Art Deco Side Cabinet

plinth base, repairs, losses to veneer, France, ca. 1930, 19 1/2 x 58", 39 1/2" h. (ILLUS.)... **2,070**

Louis XV-Style Curio-Music Cabinet

Music & curio cabinet, Louis XV-Style, Vernis Martin finish, a rectangular glass top w/serpentine front banded w/brass above a conforming case, a low mirror-backed curio display section w/glass on three sides & trimmed w/brass banding above a medial brass band above a single wide door centered by a rectangular allegorical painted panel w/brass banding & a scalloped apron, brass-banded side panels, raised on simple cabriole legs w/brass mounts, early 20th c., 15 x 20", 36" h. (ILLUS.)................................ **750**

Sewing cabinet, Mission-style (Arts & Crafts movememt), oak, a square top flanked by wide drop leaves above the deep apron w/a stack of two short drawers w/original copper ring pulls, square stile legs, cleaned original finish, some restoration to the top, unsigned Gustav Stickley, Model No. 630, 18" sq., 28" h...... **1,210**

Side cabinet, Art Deco, bronze-mounted satinwood marquetry, rectangular top w/serpentine front above a pair of long cupboard doors opening to drawers & flanked by columnar stiles, raised on short cabriole feet & a serpentine apron, the doors w/central vertical bands of stylized marquetry florals, Jules Leleu, France, 1940s, 20 x 45", 58" h. (finish brittle, small losses to veneer).................... **3,162**

Side cabinet, Art Deco, chrome-mounted rosewood & burlwood, a narrow stepped rectangular black marble top w/wide central section w/a pair of flat cupboard doors in light wood flanked by graduated stacks of four drawers each, all on a high

Decorated Arts & Crafts Cabinet

Side cabinet, Arts & Crafts style, oak, a rectangular top above a paneled long door w/a wooden latch & pyrographic picture of a peasant woman carrying a basket, each side trimmed w/three narrow slats, door opens to single shelf, square stile legs project at top corners, early 20th c., minor wear, 13 3/4 x 19 1/2", 42 1/2" h. (ILLUS.).. **978**

Chinese Coromandel Side Cabinet

Side cabinet, Coromandel-type, lacquered, the rectangular top above a pair of tall paneled doors each incised & lacquered w/Chinese figures in interiors, landscapes & pavilions, birds & flowers in side panels & delicate floral border bands, raised on bracket feet, China, 19th c., 16 x 30", 46" h. (ILLUS.)................ **1,955**

Modern Style Fornasetti Cabinet

Side cabinet, Modern style, transfer-printed decoration, rectangular top w/a black & white printed copy of scrolls & figured designs above a case covered w/a continuous print of a building w/a classical facade, two doors in the case, on tapering brass legs, Piero Fornasetti design, ca. 1950s, 13 3/4 x 27 1/2", 24 3/4" h. (ILLUS.).. **5,175**

Napoleon III Decorated Side Cabinet

Side cabinet, Napoleon III, gilt-bronze mounted marquetry-inlaid, a rectangular top w/outset rounded corners & a slightly outset central section above a conforming frieze band w/gilt classical banded designs above a conforming case w/the central cupboard door painted w/a panel depicting 18th-century lovers in a landscape, some damages, France, late 19th c., 17 x 52", 42 1/2" h. (ILLUS.)................. **3,220**

Side cabinet, Neoclassical Revival style, painted wood, a tall flat rectangular superstructure w/upper painted panel of 17th c. figures in a landscape above a large nearly square mirror bordered by molded bow & leafy vines

Neoclassical Revival Side Cabinet

flanked by tall slender panels w/molded clusters of trophies at the top & a classical urn at the bottom, all above the rectangular top w/molded edge above a cupboard w/a pair of flat flush cupboard doors painted w/a continuous oval landscape reserve w/delicate leafy scrolls above & below & flanked by narrow painted side panels, on short square legs, pale green ground w/gilt & polychrome painting, France, superstructure 19th c., base 20th c., wear, edge damage & paint touch-up, 12 x 48", 94 1/2" h. (ILLUS.)...... **1,650**

Gothic Revival Side Cabinet

Side cabinet, Victorian Gothic Revival substyle, a rectangular white marble top w/molded edges & rounded corners above a frieze w/a pair of narrow drawers framed by Gothic arch molding above a pair of cupboard doors also w/Gothic arch molding, scalloped apron & bracket feet on casters, marble top may be of later date, stenciled mark in drawers, C.A. Baudouine, New York City, ca. 1840, 21 x 45", 36 1/2" h. (ILLUS.)....................... **3,300**

Side cabinet, Victorian Renaissance Revival substyle, bronze-mounted & marquetry inlaid rosewood, a small stepped platform on the long top w/projecting central section w/incurved sides above a conforming case w/an ornate inlaid frieze band above a

Fine Renaissance Revival Cabinet

central arch-paneled door w/ornate swags & scrolls enclosing a large round bronze plaque depicting Cupid & Psyche w/a satyr infant, the curved side panels w/ornate inlaid floral & geometric reserves, turned columnar posts at front corners & sides above the conforming plinth base on disk feet, America, ca. 1870, 20 x 56", 48" h. (ILLUS.)... **5,175**

Side cabinet, Victorian Renaissance Revival substyle, marquetry inlaid tulipwood, mahogany & parcel-gilt, the rectangular top w/outset corners centering an inlaid foliate & scrolling top above parcel-gilt molded edge over a conforming case fitted w/two paneled short drawers above two doors, each w/astragal-shaped insert panel w/inlaid scrolls & diamonds centering a scrolled gilt foliate handle & base flanked by foliate scrolled sides, on a molded base, ca. 1875, 22 x 48", 36" h. **2,760**

Renaissance Revival Side Cabinet

Side cabinet, Victorian Renaissance Revival substyle, walnut, marquetry & parcel-gilt, the angular shaped top w/a removable statuary stand above an incised frieze band over a central cabinet door w/swag-framed & molded panel decorated w/an ornate floral & ribbon marquetry design flanked by reeded pilasters & angled side panels, all on a molded flaring conforming base w/shaped feet, ca. 1880, minor damage, 22 x 50 1/4", 51 3/4" h. (ILLUS.)... **3,738**

Victorian Rococo Side Cabinet

Side cabinet, Victorian Rococo substyle, carved rosewood, a white marble D-form top w/serpentine front edge above a conforming case w/a stack of four serpentine molded & fruit-carved drawers w/turned wood knobs flanked by quarter-round top drawers over quarter-round side cabinet doors w/large boldly carved fruit & nut clusters, conforming scroll- and cartouche-carved apron, New York City, ca. 1850-60, 21 x 52", 37 1/2" h. (ILLUS.)....... **2,530**

Fine Baroque Revival Silver Cabinet

Silver cabinet, Baroque Revival style, figured walnut veneer, the arched top w/a small medallion crest over the molded crestrail above the case w/a wide center door w/an upper arched & glazed panel w/scrolling grillwork over a veneered panel flanked by narrow side panels inset w/oval glass panes w/cut starburst designs, the lower section w/a deep midmolding over a case w/a single wide, deep drawer w/three arched panels in the front trimmed w/burl, burl banding & scrolls & w/brass teardrop pulls, raised & carved vertical dividers, a molded carved bottom molding w/a carved center drop raised on four legs w/bulbous reeded & gadrooned turnings above an incurved medial shelf on bun feet, original dark finish, ca. 1930, 20 x 42", 6' 4" h. (ILLUS.)................................. **950**

Colonial Revival Silver Cabinet

Silver cabinet, Colonial Revival style, walnut & walnut veneer, two-part construction: the upper section w/a rectangular top over a pair of large arch-topped molding-trimmed doors centered by a scroll-carved panel & fitted w/a large scrolled brass keyplate; the lower section w/a mid-molding above a narrow block-veneered band & a pierced & scroll-carved apron, raised on cabriole legs w/scroll-carved returns & ending in Spanish feet, joined by a serpentine scrolled stretcher, original finish, ca. 1920s, 19 x 44", 5' 6" h. (ILLUS.)................................... **800**

Smoker's cabinet, Mission-style (Arts & Crafts movement), oak, overhanging rectangular top above a single drawer & cabinet w/an arched apron, red decal mark of Gustav Stickley, Model No. 89, ca. 1910, 15 x 20 1/8", 29" h. **3,450**

Speciman cabinet, Federal style, mahogany, a rectangular top above a case w/two stacks of nine long narrow cockbeaded drawers fitted w/a locking mechanism & flanked by reeded stiles, on short tapering turned legs w/knob feet, Philadelphia, ca. 1815, 22 x 42 1/2", 38 1/2" h. (shrinkage cracks, top warpage) **9,775**

Fine Cherry Spool Cabinet

Spool cabinet, cherry, a rectangular top w/molded edges above a case of six long shallow drawers w/incised line trim & simple bail pulls, on a flat molded base, label for the Willimantic Linen Company,

back displaying the original lithograph logo of a winking owl against a full moon, late 19th c., 20 x 26", 20" h. (ILLUS.)......... **1,018**

Unusual Victorian Spool Cabinet

Spool cabinet, late Victorian, walnut, the rectangular top w/a deep molded cornice above a gently slanting front w/seven narrow glass-fronted drawers w/metal pulls above three long narrow bottom drawers w/wooden pulls & traces of original advertising, paneled sides, deep molded base, original finish, ca. 1880-90, 16 x 20", 24" h. (ILLUS.) **950**

Victorian Spool Cabinet-Display Case

Spool cabinet, Victorian Eastlake substyle, walnut, a rectangular top wa foliate-carved cornice above a large single-pane cupboard door opening to three display shelves over a slightly stepped-out lower case w/four long line-incised spool drawers w/inset brass pulls, molded flat base, ca. 1890 (ILLUS.) **1,000**

Clark's Walnut Spool Cabinet

Spool cabinet, Victorian Eastlake substyle, walnut, the rectangular top w/molded edge above a case w/six long shallow drawers each w/an inset panel w/black wording, carved & molded front side stiles, molded flat base, cast-brass hinged pulls, reads "Clark's - White - O.N.T. - Sole Agent - George A. Clark - Fast Black," some wear to glass panels, wood refinished, ca. 1880s, 18 x 22", 22" h. (ILLUS.).............................. **1,200**

Fine Clark's Walnut Spool Cabinet

Spool cabinet, walnut, rectangular top w/molded edges above a case w/six long narrow drawers w/teardrop pulls, each w/a red etched-glass panel w/wording, flat molded base, panels read "Clark's - Spool Cotton - O.N.T. - Sole Agent - George A. Clark - On White Spools," refinished, late 19th c., 16 x 22", 20" h. (ILLUS.)....................................... **2,200**

Massive Baroque Revival China Cabinet

Step-back wall china cabinet, Victorian Baroque Revival substyle, carved oak, two-part construction: the upper section w/a rectangular top w/blocked ends centered by an arched & scroll-carved crest centered by a carved finial over an oval button & flanked by urn-form corner finials above the stepped & carved cornice over a wide frieze band w/ornate carved scrolls over a pair of glazed cupboard doors w/beaded edging flanked by slender reeded & carved colonettes above a beaded base band all raised on figural lion-carved supports flanking a recessed panel-carved back; the projecting lower section w/a carved border above a pair of gadroon-carved drawers w/brass ring pulls above a pair of cupboard doors w/raised beaded border bands enclosing oval raised panels enclosing finely carved trophy designs & surrounded by a leaf sprig at each corner, slender turned colonettes down the sides, on a flaring carved & blocked base on bun feet, original finish, Europe, ca. 1880, 22 x 50", 8' h. (ILLUS.)................................ **3,000**

Vice cabinet, Mission-style (Arts & Crafts movement), oak, a thick rectangular top above a deep apron w/a long drawer front over a pair of small drawer fronts over another long drawer front, four of the six fronts being false to hide a wine rack & a compartment accessible from a swiveling top, original dark finish, early 20th c., 12 x 20", 29" h. **715**

Vitrine cabinet, Empire-Style, gilt-bronze mounted mahogany, the D-form red marble top w/a flat central section above a conforming frieze band mounted w/gilt-bronze griffins, sheaves of wheat & palmettes above a conforming case w/the wide flat glazed central door opening to glass shelves & flanked by gilt-bronze-mounted flat pilasters above a wide lower panel w/a large gilt-bronze mount of Apollo driving his chariot, the curved glass sides above lower panels w/gilt-bronze wreath mounts, molded apron on short peg feet, Antoine Krieger, Paris, early 20th c., 18 1/2 x 51", 72" h................ **9,000**

Vitrine cabinet, Louis VX-Style, ormolu-mounted mahogany & mahogany veneer, a rectangular marble top above a frieze band & raised center panel w/ormolu leaf sprigs flanked at the corners by ormolu cherub head mounts all above a wide single pane glazed door w/ormolu inner banding & an arched bottom rim opening to two glass shelves & a silk-lined back, the lower door w/a burl panel mounted w/a large ormolu leaf cluster, the short curved apron w/a long leafy ormolu mount flanked by cabriole legs w/long leafy scroll ormolu mounts at the knees, glass sides, early 20th c., 14 x 28", 65" h. **3,410**

Vitrine cabinet, Louis XV-Style, decorated giltwood w/ormolu trim, the oblong top w/rounded ends & peaked front corners above a conforming frame w/a wide bowed front door & curved glass ends & back enclosing two oval glass shelves, conforming narrow flared apron, on simple slender cabriole legs w/ormolu mounts at the knees & feet, original gold w/h.p. floral trim, beveled glass insert in the top, early 20th c., 21 x 27", 4' 2 1/2" h......................... **1,265**

Ornate Louis XV-Style Vitrine Cabinet

Vitrine cabinet, Louis XV-Style, gilt-bronze, kingwood & marquetry, the rectangular top w/rounded & molded edges fitted w/a low pierced brass three-quarters gallery above a floral swag marquetry frieze band above the tall bow-fronted glazed door w/notched top corners above a large rectangular lower panel w/ornate scrolling marquetry designs flanked by corner stiles w/starburst inlay & shaped glazed sides above conforming inlaid lower panels, scrolled ormolu mount on front apron, on slender cabriole legs w/brass mounts at the knees & feet, paper label for Paines Furniture Co., late 19th c., 17 x 28", 61" h. (ILLUS.)................. **2,645**

Outstanding Louis XV-Style Vitrine

Vitrine cabinet, Louis XV-Style, gilt-bronze mounted abalone & inlaid wood, two-part construction: the top section w/a high curved & arched cornice fitted w/pierced gilt-bronze scrolled crest & female terms at the corners above a curved & arched glazed cabinet door & rounded glazed sides all w/gilt-bronze trim, the conforming base w/gilt-bronze scrolls & a narrow inlaid panel; the conforming slightly stepped-out lower section w/serpentine edges above a pair of curved cupboard doors inlaid w/mother-of-pearl flowers & foliage within foliate-scrolled borders, the slender cabriole legs headed by foliate-cast female term mounts continuing down to leaf sabots & joined by a shaped stretcher shelf, France, ca. 1900, 34 1/4" w., 79" h. (ILLUS.) **10,200**

Louis XV-Style Inlaid Vitrine

Vitrine cabinet, Louis XV-Style, mahogany veneer, the arched & molded crestrail centered by a large upright scroll-carved crest above a conforming frieze band w/delicate raised molding enclosing herringbone inlay above a pair of tall beveled glass glazed cupboard doors w/scroll carving at the top & opening to shelves above a drawer insert, molded sides above a serpentined bottom rail over the conforming apron centered by a scroll-carved cartouche, on demi-cabriole front legs ending in scroll & peg feet, Europe, late 19th c., demountable, top 22 x 55", 99" h. (ILLUS.) **2,255**

Vitrine cabinet, Louis XV-Style, simulated painted rosewood finish w/ormolu mounts, a demi-lune top w/a crestrail dramatically arched at the front & fitted w/ormolu leafy scroll edge trim & a wreath mount above the conforming case w/a curved glass center door flanked by curved glass sides all trimmed w/ormolu banding & separated by pendant ormolu drops, the lower door & side panels w/further round ormolu medallions, serpentine apron & four slender cabriole legs w/ormolu knee & foot mounts, opening to two glass shelves, early 20th c., 13 1/2 x 26 1/2", 62 1/4" h. **715**

French Vernis Martin Vitrine Cabinet

Vitrine cabinet, Louis XV-style, *vernis martin* decoration, the high arched crestrail centered by a gilt-bronze pierced scroll crest above a figural decorated frieze band over the tall curved-front glaze door w/a bombé base decorated w/a large *vernis martin* decorated figural panel, the sides w/narrow glazed panels above the bombé base panels w/further painted decoration, short outswept legs, overall gilt-bronze mounts, France, late 19th - early 20th c., 17 x 32", 75" h. (ILLUS.)....... **1,870**

Vitrine cabinet, Louis XV-Style "Vernis Martin" style, a D-form top above a glazed center door flanked by curved glass sides all w/lower painted figural panels, short shaped legs, Europe, late 19th c., 15 x 28", 56" h.................................... **977**

Vitrine cabinet, Louis XV-Style, walnut, a rectangular red marble top atop the tall case w/a tall door w/a rectangular beveled glass front within a serpentine framework above a lower rectangular panel w/serpentine edges & ornate scroll carving, molded chamfered corner bands, scroll-carved serpentine apron & simple cabriole legs w/scroll carving & scroll & peg feet, France, late 19th - early 20th c., 15 1/2 x 32", 61" h. **2,310**

Louis XVI-Style Round Vitrine

Vitrine cabinet, Louis XVI-Style, gilt-metal mounted mahogany, round marble top w/a low pierced gilt-metal gallery above a conforming case w/four curved sides, two forming doors, doors w/thin gilt-metal banded trim w/further trim on the narrow rounded apron, raised on simple cabriole legs ending in sabots, France, late 19th to early 20th c., 25 3/4" d., 59" h. (ILLUS.)...... **3,738**

Louis XVI-Style Vitrine Cabinet

Vitrine cabinet, Louis XVI-Style, Vernis Martin finish, the oblong marble top w/serpentine edges mounted w/a pierced brass gallery above a frieze band of looping scrolls above a serpentine-fronted door w/a large glass panel above a lower Vernis Martin panel painted w/a romantic scene of an 18th c. couple in a landscape, the bowed glass sides above similar painted panels, raised on simple squared cabriole legs w/gilt-brass mounts, original finish, ca. 1920s, 18 x 30", 5' 4" h. (ILLUS.)............................ **1,500**

One of Two Victorian Vitrine Cabinets

Vitrine cabinets, Victorian, ormolu-mounted inlaid satinwood, each w/oblong crossbanded molded top w/canted corners above glazed sides & a glazed door, the door w/an arched pane below a delicate inlaid leafy swag band, raised on a deep molded base w/bead-trimmed disk-topped peg feet, Europe, late 19th c., 10 x 28", 29 1/2" h., pr. (ILLUS. of one)..... **5,980**

Chairs

Adirondack-style Painted Armchair

Adirondack-style armchairs, composed of hickory sticks, the rectangular back frame enclosing seven spindles above the open round arms on curved supports continuing down to form front legs, woven splint seat, double front & side rungs, crackled white over earlier green paint, possibly New York state, early 20th c., 38 3/4" h., pr. (ILLUS. of one)...................... **$805**

Art Deco Upholstered Armchair

Art Deco armchair, carved parcel-gilt mahogany & upholstery, the narrow gently arched gilt-trimmed crestrail above the upholstered back flanked by downswept closed upholstered arms w/carved hand rests atop tapering round front reeded legs, cushion seat, attributed to Sue et Mare, France, ca. 1925 (ILLUS.)................. **4,600**

French Art Deco Armchair

Art Deco armchair, oak & tubular steel, the low thick upholstered back flanked by heavy plank arms above the deep upholstered seat on a shaped tubular steel framework, grey plaid fabric, France, ca. 1930s (ILLUS.).. **2,875**

French Art Deco Club-style Armchair

Art Deco armchairs, club-style, upholstered, an arched flat-topped upholstered back flanked by deep curved-top upholstered closed arms, the upholstered seat on a deep front seatrail, in Bachausen upholstery in shades of silvery taupe & black, raised on narrow Macassar ebony bases, France, ca. 1930, pr. (ILLUS. of one)....................................... **3,450**

Art Deco Rattan Armchairs

Art Deco armchairs, rattan, the rounded upright back frame w/vertical rattan spindles continuing to the wide arched arms w/rattan spindles continuing to the apron composed of further spindles, gold Naugahyde back & seat cushions, made by Heywood-Wakefield, ca. 1935, 30" h., pr. (ILLUS.)....................................... **805**

Art Deco armchairs, upholstered mahogany, a sloped upholstered backrest flanked by shaped plank arms centering a loose seat cushion raised on reeded round feet, attributed to Dominique, France, ca. 1925, pr. (upholstery distressed)... **6,325**

Art Deco Club chair, upholstered & ebonized wood, of rectangular outline w/a square upholstered backrest flanked by padded arms centering a loose seat cushion, raised on short block feet, possibly designed by Donald Desky, American, 1930s (upholstery distressed, finish scuffed).. **690**

Art Deco Club chairs, walnut & leather-upholstered, the high lobed upholstered back continuing to the rounded arms centering a high tight seat raised on short feet on casters, upholstered in pale bluish grey leather upholstery, England, 1930s, pr. (wear at edges) **1,380**

Ruhlmann Art Deco Desk Chair

Art Deco desk chair, upholstered rosewood, the arched upholstered back sloping down to raised closed arms above a round deep upholstered seat, raised on a round rosewood frame above a central pivoting mechanism, further raised on four arched tapering wide flat legs, mustard yellow leather upholstery, branded "Ruhlmann B.," Emile-Jacques Ruhlmann, France, ca. 1926 (ILLUS.)............. **29,900**

Art Deco 'Zig-Zag' Chair

Art Deco 'Zig-Zag' chair, elm, flat boards forming an angular seat, designed by Gerrit Reitvelt in 1934, produced by De Groenekan, Holland (ILLUS.) **4,600**

Art Nouveau armchair, carved mahogany, the arched pierced crestrail carved w/clematis blossoms & leaves fanned above a solid center panel flanked by up-

holstered back panels, the top continuing to molded & carved wing arms flanking the upholstered seat above a serpentine & scroll-carved apron above slightly canted squared legs, modern blue suede upholstery, Louis Majorelle, France, ca. 1900.. **7,475**

Art Nouveau Armchair

Art Nouveau armchair, fruitwood marquetry w/backsplat inlaid in various woods w/chestnuts & leafage, flanked by twist-carved spindles & molded arms above upholstered seat, raised on twist-carved front legs, Majorelle, France, ca. 1900 (ILLUS.)... **3,450**

Italian Art Nouveau Armchair

Art Nouveau armchairs, walnut, a molded serpentine crestrail over an arched upholstered panel above a pierced & foliage- and whiplash-carved back flanked by carved & scrolled open arms on curved arm supports over the over-upholstered seat, simple molded cabriole front legs, Italy, ca. 1900, pr. (ILLUS. of one).... **1,380**

Arts & Crafts armchair, oak, a wide gently curved crestrail above a back w/a pair of slender slats flanking a wide center slat w/two square cut-outs all resting on a lower back rail, flat open arms on flat front stile legs w/narrow tapering rectangular cut-outs, new black leather seat cushion, wide flat low stretchers, original finish, Limbert branded mark, 38 1/2" h. (small repair to rear leg) **4,675**

Arts & Crafts chairs, oak, each w/a square-topped back stile flanking a shaped crestrail pierced w/a heart flanked by scrolls above three slender slats, shaped open arms, upholstered seat, squared tapering front legs, medium brown finish, England, early 20th c., two armchairs & four side chairs, 42 1/4" h., set of 6 (some wear) **3,565**

Arts & Crafts Inlaid Rocking Chair

Arts & Crafts rocking chair w/arms, inlaid oak, a wide gently arched crestrail & flat lower rail flanking two plain slats & a shaped center splat w/Art Nouveau style looping foliate inlay, tapering stiles w/rounded tops, flat open arms on shaped armrests forming front legs, floral upholstered seat, flat stretchers, mortised rockers, medium brown finish, ca. 1910, 35" h. (ILLUS.) **1,035**

Arts & Crafts side chair, ebony-inlaid oak, the arched crestrail decorated w/three ebony-inlaid squares on chair back w/a woven cane center panel, shaped back posts inlaid w/ebony squares connected w/a narrow band, woven cane seat, offset stretchers w/single slats, medium brown finish, branded Charles Limbert mark, ca. 1915, 38 1/2" h. (minor wear) **1,093**

Bentwood armchair, beech, Modern style, the U-form backrail angling down to form open arms, a rectangular upholstered back panel above the upholstered seat, slender square front & canted rear legs each w/a ball mount at the corner & connected to the U-form base, design attributed to Kolomon Moser, produced by J. & J. Kohn, Vienna, Austria, Model No. 725 BF, ca. 1902 .... **4,025**

Bentwood armchair, the U-shaped frame w/armrests centering a diamond-shaped element, the seat w/a sphere beneath each corner, U-form base rail, traces of the paper label of J. & J. Kohn, Austria,

designed by Josef Hoffmann, Model No. 728/3F, ca. 1907, 30 1/2" h. **978**

Early Thonet Bentwood Side Chairs

Bentwood side chairs, a high tapering bentwood back frame enclosing a wide upper cross rail w/three holes above three slender spindles to a thin lower rail above the caned seat in a bentwood frame forming the front legs joined by a high flat stretcher, a forked downswept bentwood stretcher at each side of the base, Thonet, Austria, late 19th c., paint restoration, 38 1/2" h., pr. (ILLUS.) **575**

Biedermeier-Style Side Chairs

Biedermeier-Style side chairs, fruitwood & part-ebonized, wide arched & shaped crest above a small ebonized wreath on a shaped lower back rail flanked by simple stiles, overupholstered seat on gently curved square tapering legs, Europe, late 19th c., 32 1/2" h., set of four (ILLUS. of two) **3,335**

Boston rocking chair w/arms, painted & decorated, the wide rounded crestrail above six tall spindles & simple turned stiles above the S-scroll arms on a spindle & turned canted arm support, deep S-scroll seat, knob- and rod-turned front legs w/a knob-turned front stretcher, plain turned side & back stretchers, worn original red & black graining w/yellow striping w/fruit in colored bronze powder on the crest, early 19th c., 39 1/2" h. (rockers worn) **220**

Early Campeche Lolling Chair

Campeche armchair, lolling-type, walnut, tall back w/rolled flat crestrail flanked by stiles continuing down to upcurved seat, small truncated wings at top sides, flat S-scroll open arms on shaped arm supports, inverted-U legs joined by squared & shaped cross-stretchers, old webbing, Southern United States, first half 19th c. (ILLUS.).. **8,338**

Chippendale Armchair with Wingback

Chippendale armchair w/wingback, upholstered mahogany, the serpentine crest above the curving wings & outwardly scrolling arms flanking a cushioned seat & upholstered apron, on square molded legs joined by square molded stretchers to the raking rear legs, old surface, surface imperfections, New England, 1780-1800, 48 1/2" h. (ILLUS.)........ **7,475**

Cherry Chippendale Side Chair

Chippendale country-style side chair, cherry, serpentine crestrail w/flared ears over a loop-pierced splat between raked stiles, upholstered slip seat on square beaded legs, old surface, crewel-worked seat cover in golds & blues, Connecticut, 1770-1800, imperfections, 37 3/4" h. (ILLUS.)... **690**

Country Chippendale Side Chair

Chippendale country-style side chair, stained wood, the gently arched crestrail w/short molded ears above a heart- and geometrically-pieced splat above the upholstered slip seat on square legs w/molded outside edges joined by square molded stretchers, old dark stain, Concord, Massachusetts, last quarter 18th c., imperfections, 39" h. (ILLUS.)........... **805**

Chippendale country-style side chair, tiger stripe maple, serpentine crestrail w/raked molded ears above a pierced splat, old rush seat & block- and vase-turned front legs joined by a turned stretcher, old refinish, Connecticut River Valley, 39" h. (imperfections)........................ **863**

Walnut Chippendale Side Chair

Chippendale country-style side chairs, walnut, the oxbow crestrail above a scroll-carved solid back splat flanked by slightly curved stiles above the upholstered slip seat, square legs joined by flat box stretchers, Pennsylvania, late 18th c., set of 4 (ILLUS. of one).......................... **9,900**

Chippendale "ladder-back" side chairs, carved mahogany, a serpentine crestrail pierced w/a central circle & scrolls & w/a beaded edge above three matching slats between the raked molded stiles over the trapezoidal upholstered slip seat, on square beaded legs joined by box stretchers, old refinish, probably Philadelphia, ca. 1780, 37 1/2" h., pr. (minor imperfections) **1,725**

Irish Chippendale Revival Armchair

Chippendale Revival armchair, carved mahogany, the scroll-carved serpentine crestrail centered by a shell carving above the ornate pierced & scroll-carved splat, shaped open arms ending in curled hand grips above the scroll-carved incurved supports, wide overupholstered seat w/a serpentine seatrail carved w/gadrooning, cabriole front legs w/shell- and scroll-carved knees & ending in raised scroll feet, original finish, Irish, ca. 1910, 39" h. (ILLUS.)... **1,000**

Philadelphia Chippendale Chair

Chippendale side chair, carved mahogany, serpentine crestrail w/decorated carved scrolls & flaring ears above a lattice-carved back splat between carved canted stiles over the molded upholstered slip seat accented by pierced brackets & flanked by square molded legs, old refinish, Philadelphia, 1770-85, imperfections (ILLUS.) **2,185**

Massachusetts Chippendale Chair

Chippendale side chair, carved mahogany, the bow-shaped crestrail ending in scrolled terminals above a pierced & scroll-carved splat flanked by outward flaring stiles above a trapezoidal slip seat, front cabriole legs ending in pad feet on platforms, joined by turned stretchers to the raked chamfered rear legs, old finish, Boston or Salem, Massachusetts, ca. 1770, minor imperfections, 37 3/4" h. (ILLUS.)........................ **7,475**

Chippendale side chair, carved mahogany, the serpentine crestrail w/foliate-carved scrolled ears above a pierce-carved interlaced Gothic splat flanked by molded stiles over a trapezoidal seat & conforming slipseat on cabriole front legs ending in ball-and-claw feet, Philadelphia, ca. 1770, 38 1/4" h. **8,625**

Carved Mahogany Chippendale Chair

Chippendale side chair, carved mahogany, the serpentine crestrail w/leaf carving & molded ears above the carved pierced scrolled splat flanked by raked stiles joined to the frontal cabriole legs ending in pad feet w/block-turned stretchers, old refinish, missing returns, other imperfections, Massachusetts, ca. 1780, 37 1/2" h. (ILLUS.)..................................... **1,380**

Chippendale side chair, carved mahogany, the shaped crestrail w/carved leafage above a pierced splat flanked by raked stiles on a trapezoidal overupholstered seat, on cabriole front legs w/acanthus leaf & scroll carving & ending in claw-and-ball feet, chamfered canted rear

Fine Carved Chippendale Side Chair

legs, block-, baluster- and ring-turned stretchers, old refinish, some imperfections, attributed to Sewall Short, Newburyport, Massachusetts, 1760-80, 37" h. (ILLUS.).. **3,738**

Fine Boston Chippendale Side Chair

Chippendale side chair, carved mahogany, the shaped leaf- and volute-carved crestrail above a pierced strapwork splat & overupholstered seat on acanthus-carved cabriole legs joined by block- and baluster-turned stretchers & ending in claw-and-ball feet, old surface w/dark brown color, Boston, Massachusetts, ca. 1770, 37" h. (ILLUS.) **4,600**

Carved Chippendale Side Chair

Chippendale side chair, carved mahogany, the shaped leaf-, scroll- and ruffle-carved crestrail flanked by leaf-carved ears above a pierced strapwork splat, gadrooned shoe & trapezoidal slip seat flanked by wavy stiles, the shaped molded seat frame below on leaf-, bellflower-, and scroll-carved cabriole legs ending in scroll feet, possibly Southern United States, crack to crest at juncture w/splat, 1740-70, 38 1/2" h. (ILLUS.)....................... **4,025**

Massachusetts Chippendale Chair

Chippendale side chair, carved walnut, serpentine crestrail w/raked ears above the pierced splat w/C-scrolls & lattice over the upholstered compass slip seat over cabriole front legs ending in high pad feet, raking rear legs, old refinish, restoration to stiles, Boston or Salem, Massachusetts, 1760-80, 38 1/2" h. (ILLUS.) **2,185**

Chippendale "Ladder-back" Side Chair

Chippendale side chair, mahogany, four serpentine pierced horizontal splats above an overupholstered seat & stop-fluted front legs joined to the raking rear legs by square stretchers, old dark surface, Rhode Island, 1775-1810, minor imperfections, 36 1/2" h. (ILLUS.).............. **1,150**
Chippendale side chair, mahogany, the serpentine crest w/molded ears above a pierced strapwork splat, the overupholstered seat raised on angular cabriole legs joined by turned stretchers & ending in pad feet, New England, third quarter 18th c. **1,092**

Boston Chippendale Side Chair

Chippendale side chair, mahogany, the serpentine crestrail centering a foliate-carved device & ending in scrolled-carved ears above the pierced carved intertwining splat flanked by raked stiles, trapezoidal overupholstered seat on cockbeaded square legs joined by flat stretchers, old refinish, minor imperfections, Boston, Massachusetts, ca. 1780, 37" h. (ILLUS.).. **8,625**

New Hampshire Chippendale Chair

Chippendale side chair, mahogany, the serpentine crestrails w/central piercing & beaded edge above a scrolled pierced splat flanked by gently outswept stiles over the overupholstered seat, on square molded legs joined by square stretchers, old surface, minor repairs, attributed to Robert Harrold, 1765-75, Portsmouth, New Hampshire, 37" h. (ILLUS.)................ **1,955**

Chippendale side chair, the serpentine crestrail w/scrolled-back ears & a central carved shell above a vasiform splat & raked stiles joined to the molded trapezoidal slip seat centering a shell-carved seatrail on front cabriole legs ending in claw-and-ball feet, old finish, Philadelphia, 1760-80, 40" h. (minor repairs, losses) **6,325**

Chippendale side chair, walnut, the serpentine crestrail ending in shaped terminals above a heart-pierced vasiform splat, chamfered raked stiles & a trapezoidal slip seat on frontal cabriole legs ending in pad feet on platforms, New-

bury, Massachusetts, ca. 1760-80, 37 1/2" h. (minor imperfections)................ **1,955**

Chippendale side chair, carved mahogany, the ox yoke crestrail w/upswept molded ears above a scroll-pierced vasiform splat & raked stiles over the trapezoidal slip seat, front cabriole legs ending in pad feet on platforms, raked chamfered rear legs, Massachusetts, ca. 1780, old refinish, 37" h. **1,725**

Chippendale side chair, carved mahogany, a serpentine crestrail w/molded ears above a pierced Gothic design splat, molded seatrails w/upholstered seat, cabriole front legs ending in claw-and-ball feet, baluster- and block-turned stretchers joining front legs to rear chamfered raked legs, old refinish, Massachusetts, 1755-90, 36 1/8" h. (minor surface abrasions) **4,255**

Chippendale Mahogany Side Chair

Chippendale side chairs, carved mahogany, the serpentine crest above an ornate scroll-pierced splat & raked stiles over a trapezoidal slip seat on frontal cabriole legs w/carved scrolled returns & ending in claw-and-ball feet, raked square rear legs, old refinish, possibly North Carolina, ca. 1760-80, 40 3/4" h., pr. (ILLUS. of one) **5,750**

Fine Chippendale Side Chair

Chippendale side chairs, carved mahogany, the serpentine crestrail w/a central carved shell w/flanking chip-carved & raking molded ears above the strapwork design pierced splat in scrolls over the trapezoidal upholstered slip seat on molded frame above cabriole front legs w/arris knees & ending in ball-and-claw feet, joined by turned stretchers to the raking square rear legs, old refinish, Boston - Salem, Massachusetts, 1750-1800, imperfections, 37 1/2" h., pr. (ILLUS. of one) **27,600**

Boston Chippendale Side Chair

Chippendale side chairs, carved mahogany, the serpentine crestrail w/scroll-carved ears above a slender vase-form pierced splat w/carved scrolls flanking floral devices on a molded shoe, trapezoidal slip seat on straight molded frame joining square chamfered legs & molded box stretchers, missing brackets, other minor imperfections, attributed to George Bright, Boston, ca. 1760-90, 36 1/4" h., pr. (ILLUS. of one) **3,450**

Chippendale side chairs, mahogany, a cyma-curved crestrail w/raked terminals & a central carved fan over a scroll- and bar-pierced splat on a molded shoe over the trapezoidal upholstered slip seat in molded seatrails, square front legs w/beaded edges joined by an H-stretcher & a single rear stretcher, old surface, Massachusetts, 18th c., 37 3/4" h., pr. **8,625**

Chippendale side chairs, transitional-style, painted & decorated wood, the serpentine oxbow crestrail w/outswept ears centered by a lunette over the vase-form loop-pierced splat over the upholstered slip seat, on square tapering legs joined by flat stretchers, later black paint w/gilt band trim, Newport, Rhode Island, or Connecticut, 1765-90, 37 3/4" h., pr. (repair to a foot) **2,645**

Chippendale-Style Armchair

Chippendale transitional-style armchair, mahogany, the simple ox yoke crestrail w/rounded corners continuing into the inward curving stiles flanking the simple solid vasiform splat, shaped open arms w/scroll-carved hand grips on incurved arm supports, wide needlepoint-covered slip seat, plain curved seatrail over cabriole front legs w/acanthus leaf-carved knees & ending in heavy claw-and-ball feet, canted square rear legs joined to front legs w/a block- and reel-turned H-stretcher, old finish, late 19th - early 20th c., minor wear, 43 3/4" h. (ILLUS.) **275**

Queen Anne Chippendale-Style Chair

Chippendale transitional-style side chair, carved mahogany, the arched crestrail w/rounded corners centered by ornate leafy scroll section centering a flowerhead above the spooned solid vasiform splat, the tapering curved stiles above the upholstered balloon-form slip seat, curved plain seatrail above cabriole front legs ending in claw-and-ball feet, square canted rear legs w/spade feet, old finish, Centennial era, late 19th - early 20th c., 40" h. (ILLUS.) **358**

Chippendale Wingchair

Chippendale wing armchair, walnut, the arched upholstered back flanked by slightly flared serpentined upholstered wings above rolled upholstered arms above the wide cushion seat, square molded legs joined by box stretchers, late 18th c. (ILLUS.) **3,850**

Chippendale-Style armchair, mahogany, the serpentine crestrail w/carved leafy scrolls above a pierced leafy scroll-carved vasiform splat flanked by molded stiles, serpentine open arms w/scroll-carved handholds on incurved arm supports flanking the wide overupholstered seat w/a thin gadroon-carved seatrail, cabriole front legs w/leafy scroll-carved knees & ending in claw-and-ball feet, canted square rear legs, old dark finish, early 20th c., 37 1/2" h. (repairs, seat reupholstered) **330**

Chippendale-Style chairs, carved mahogany, the scalloped crest w/shell-carved center & carved ears above a Gothic-style pierced splat, two w/S-scroll arms w/carved hand grips on incurved leaf-carved supports, upholstered slip seat, arched apron on cabriole front legs w/flower- and acanthus leaf-carved knees & ending in heavy ball-and-claw feet, 20th c., two armchairs & ten side chairs, 40 1/4" h., the set (edge wear, one w/damage at knee & upholstery stain) **4,400**

Chippendale-Style Child's Armchair

Chippendale-Style child's armchair, mahogany, the arched crestrail over a slender pierced vase-form splat & gently flared stiles, shaped open arms on incurved arm supports above the seat frame, raised on cabriole front legs w/claw-and-ball feet, original finish, ca. 1920, no seat, 14 x 16", 30" h. (ILLUS.) **150**

Chippendale-Style child's wingchair, tall upholstered back w/arched crest above narrow curved wings over the rolled upholstered arms & overupholstered seat, square mahogany legs w/side stretchers, worn floral upholstery, early 20th c., 29" h. (cross-stretcher missing, leg chips) **660**

Chippendale-Style corner chair, a back-scrolled crestrail on a U-form even rail ending in shaped arms w/scrolled hand-

holds above two scroll-bordered vase-form splats pierced w/a central spade design & alternating w/three ring-turned columnar spindles above the square upholstered slip seat, cabriole legs w/scrolled returns & ending in claw-and-ball feet joined by a turned cross-stretcher, old dark finish, early 20th c., 33 1/2" h. (one arm w/age crack) **330**

Chippendale-Style dining chairs, walnut, a serpentine crestrail centering a carved shell flanked by scrolled ears above a pierced vasiform splat over a trapezoidal slip seat above a shaped seatrail centering a carved shell, on cabriole legs w/ball-and-claw feet, two armchairs w/downscrolling arms w/hand holds over shaped arm supports, four side chairs, in the Philadelphia manner, 20th c., the set .. **4,025**

Chippendale-Style side chair, cherry, double-scrolled crestrail above a solid vasiform splat over a balloon-shaped slip seat above a conforming seatrail w/carved shell, on cabriole legs w/scrolled acanthus-carved knees & returns, ending in ball-and-claw feet, in the Philadelphia manner, 20th c., 41 1/4" h. **920**

Chippendale-Style side chair, mahogany, the serpentine crestrail w/carved swags above the ornately pierced looping splat flanked by the square slightly flaring stiles above the overupholstered seat, cabriole front legs w/leafy scroll-carved knees & ending in claw-and-ball feet, square canted rear legs, Centennial-type, old refinishing, late 19th c., 38" h. **440**

Chippendale-Style side chairs, hardwood w/old brown finish, ladder-back style w/four pierced ribbon-form back slats flanked by molded stiles above the upholstered slip seat w/needlepoint upholstery, square molded legs joined by an H-stretcher, early 20th c., 37" h., set of 8 ...... **1,144**

Chippendale-Style side chairs, mahogany, Gothic-style w/a carved ox yoke crestrail above a pierced Gothic arch & loop-carved splat flanked by outcurved stiles, upholstered slip seat above the shell-carved seatrail, cabriole front legs w/shell-carved knees & ball-and-claw feet, early 20th century w/manufacturer's number "406," 40" h., pr. (seats reupholstered) **605**

Chippendale-Style side chairs, mahogany, the relief-carved serpentine crestrail above a pierced looped scrolling splat flanked by molded stiles, overupholstered seat, square molded legs joined by box stretchers, varnished finish, 20th c., 36" h., set of 6 (minor foot wear) .. **1,430**

Chippendale-Style wing chair, the tall upholstered back w/a serpentine crest flanked by slightly curved upholstered wings above the rolled upholstered arms, cushion seat above the upholstered seatrail, on mahogany cabriole front legs w/leafy scroll-carved returns & ending in claw-and-ball feet, reupholstered, 20th c., 41" h. **385**

Chippendale-Style Wingchair

Chippendale-Style wing-back armchair, mahogany, the high arched upholstered back flanked by flared wings above the out-scrolled upholstered arms above the cushion seat, cabriole front legs w/shell-carved knees & ending in claw-and-ball feet, squared canted rear legs, old dark finish, early 20th c., 45" h. (ILLUS.) **440**

Fine Classical Mahogany Armchair

Classical armchair, mahogany & mahogany veneer, the wide rounded crestrail above a wide urn-form splat flanked by stiles joined to the open scroll-carved arms above the upholstered seat, veneered seatrail above the modified cabriole front legs & square stile rear legs, refinished, ca. 1840, 35" h. (ILLUS.) **250**

Classical Children's Side Chairs

Classical children's side chairs, mahogany, a paneled rectangular concave crestrail above a lower horizontal splat joining the raked stiles, upholstered slip seat, on sabre legs, refinished, probably Boston, ca. 1820, 28" h., pr. (ILLUS.) **546**

Decorated Pennsylvania Rocker

Classical country-style rocking chair w/arms, the wide crestrail w/rounded ends above a wide bootjack-form splat flanked by tapering stiles, heavy scrolled arms over a single spindle, wide shaped plank seat, turned & canted front legs joined by a turned front stretcher, on long rockers, original green paint w/black & grey striping & stenciled & free-hand floral & fruit decoration w/grapes, strawberries, etc. in black, red, gold & green, gilt trim on crestrail, Pennsylvania, mid-19th c., some wear, 42 1/2" h. (ILLUS.) **715**

Classical country-style side chair, curly maple, a wide curved & rolled crestrail attached to tapering curved stiles above a lower curved rail over the replaced paper rush seat, front sabre legs joined by a flat stretcher, turned side & back stretchers, ca. 1830, 34 1/4" h. **248**

Large Classical Revival Armchair

Classical Revival armchair, carved oak, the wide square upholstered back flanked by large boldly carved seated winged lions forming the arms, a wide spring-upholstered seat above a leaf-carved seat frame raised on canted front legs ending in large paw feet, square tapering rear legs, leather upholstery, refinished, American-made, ca. 1880-90, 40" h. (ILLUS.) **5,500**

Classical side chairs, brass-inlaid & carved mahogany, a horizontal reverse-scrolling crest board above a pierced flowerhead- and leaf-carved lower rail, upholstered slip seat, on sabre legs, rich patina, nice old finish, New York City, ca. 1810, 32" h., set of 4 .... **5,175**

Classical side chairs, carved mahogany, a scrolled tablet crestrail centering two carved cornucopia above shaped molded stiles joined by a lower rail over a trapezoidal caned seat, front sabre legs w/hairy hoof feet, New York City, 1810-15, 32 1/2" h., pr. **1,265**

Baltimore Classical Side Chairs

Classical side chairs, carved mahogany, gently curving & rolled veneered crestrail above a leaf-carved & pierced splat, upholstered slipseat over a flat veneered seatrail between ring-, knob- and reeded rod-turned tapering legs w/pad feet, Baltimore, 1815-20, imperfections, 34 1/2" h., set of 4 (ILLUS. of two) **805**

Classical side chairs, carved tiger stripe maple, the scroll & acanthus leaf carved tablet crest above a pierced acanthus leaf & scroll-carved splat & shaped stiles continuing to trapezoidal cane seats on flaring vase- and ring-turned front legs joined to the raked back legs by turned stretchers, old finish, probably New England, ca. 1825, 32 1/2" h., set of 4 .... **2,645**

Classical side chairs, grain-painted, a curved horizontal crestrail atop stiles flanking a flat lower rail above the caned seat, on klismos-type legs, original graining in imitation of rosewood w/gold accent striping, northern New England, ca. 1825-35, 33" h., set of 6 (imperfections) **1,380**

Fine Boston Classical Side Chairs

Classical side chairs, mahogany & mahogany veneer, the concave veneered crestrails w/leaf-carved terminals atop shaped stiles joined by scroll-carved slats above the upholstered slip seats & molded seatrail, incurved front legs & outswept rear legs, old refinish, very minor imperfections, Boston, 1825-35, set of 4 (ILLUS. of two) **2,300**

Classical side chairs, tiger stripe maple, stepped rectangular curved crestrail above angular-cut vase-form splat above the seat w/curving front rail, on flat Grecian legs, refinished, one branded "A.G. Case," Norwich, Connecticut area, 1830-50, 33 1/2" h., set of 6 (caned seats missing, other imperfections) **3,105**

Early "Banister-back" Armchair

Country style "banister-back" armchair, painted, the carved stag horn form crestrail over four split banisters on a stayrail flanked by baluster-, knob- and rod-turned stiles w/knob finials, shaped scrolling arms on baluster-turned arm supports over the woven rush seat on ring- and rod-turned front legs joined by two baluster-turned front stretchers & plain double side stretchers, old black paint, Portsmouth, New Hampshire area, ca. 1725-75, imperfections, 43 3/4" h. (ILLUS.) **2,990**

Country style "banister-back" side chair, carved & painted, the scroll-carved & pierced crestrail above four ring- and baluster-turned split banisters flanked by ring-, column- and block-turned stiles w/ball finials over a trapezoidal rush seat, on baluster-, block- and ring-turned legs joined by ring- & bulbous-turned front stretcher & box stretchers, on baluster-turned feet, painted black, New England, mid-18th c., 41 3/4" h. (loss of height) **805**

Woven Splint Armchairs

Country-style armchairs, stained maple, the squared back panel of tightly woven splint between projecting backswept stiles w/long shaped open arms on baluster-turned arm supports continuing down to form side braces, tightly woven splint seat, simple turned legs w/plain turned double front & side & rear stretchers, splints partially distressed, minor chips to feet, back of stiles worn, late 19th - early 20th c., 34 1/2" h., pr. (ILLUS.) **805**

Country-style "arrow-back" side chairs, decorated, wide crestrail above four curved arrow slats between the curved tapering stiles, shaped saddle seat on bamboo-turned legs joined by a turned front stretcher & plain turned side stretchers, original red decoration, the crestrail w/yellow & green foliage, usual stretcher wear, early 19th c., 35" h., set of 4 .... **2,970**

Country-style "banister-back" side chair, carved maple, the tall back w/baluster- and knob-turned stiles & ball finials above a fan-carved crestrail above four split-balusters continuing to a lower rail w/an arched pendant, the woven splint seat on baluster-, ring- and rod-turned legs joined by two swelled front stretchers & simple turned side & back stretchers, traces of dark green stain, probably New Hampshire, second half 18th c., 44 1/2" h. (reduced in height) **4,600**

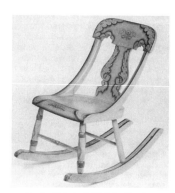

Early Painted Child's Rocker

Country-style child's armless rocking chair, painted & decorated, the wide rounded crestrail above a vasiform splat flanked by curved stiles joined to the wide plank seat, ring-turned front legs & stretcher, long rockers, a mustard yellow ground paint w/yellow, red, green & black accents & leafy scroll & floral decoration on the crestrail & splat, original surface, very minor imperfections, Pennsylvania, mid-19th c., 32" h. (ILLUS.) **748**

Country-style Child's Rocking Chair

Country-style child's rocking chair w/arms, painted & decorated, a flat crestrail above five plain spindles flanked by simple turned stiles over the turned open arms, original woven splint seat, plain turned legs & double turned stretchers at the front & sides, original red paint w/black striping, mid-19th c., 15 x 16", 27" h. (ILLUS.) **200**

Country-style "ladder-back" armchair, maple & ash, four arched slats joining knob- and rod-turned stiles w/knob finials over long scrolled arms on baluster- and knob-turned arm supports continuing into turned front legs, woven splint seat, double knob-turned front stretchers & plain double side stretchers, old painted surface, restored, probably Massachusetts, early 18th c., 45 1/2" h. (ILLUS top next page.) **546**

Early "Ladder-Back" Armchair

Country-style "ladder-back" armchair, maple, the tall turned stiles w/turned ball finials joined by reverse-graduated arched slats, shaped open arms w/scrolled handholds on baluster- and ring-turned arm supports above the rush seat, rod- and ball-turned front legs w/ball feet joined by a double ball & ring-turned front stretcher & plain turned side & back stretchers, old refinish, Delaware River Valley, 18th c., 46 1/2" h. (slight imperfections)... **9,200**

New England "Ladder-back" Armchair

Country-style "ladder-back" armchair, painted birch & hickory, four arched back slats between sausage-turned stiles w/knob finials flanked by shaped arms w/fluted terminals, baluster-turned arm supports above the woven rush seat, ring- and rod-turned front legs joined by two ring-turned stretchers, double plain side stretchers, old yellow & red paint, losses to paint, height reduced, formerly fitted w/rockers, New England, 1700-40, 41 1/4" h. (ILLUS.)... **920**

Early 18th Century "Ladder-back" Chair

Country-style "ladder-back" armchair, pine & ash, the tall back w/four arched graduated slats between tall ring- and rod-turned stiles w/triple-knob finials above simple rod arms w/rod-turned front supports & button finials continuing to form front legs, woven rush seat, simple double stretchers at the front & sides, remnants of old red paint, Scituate or Marshfield, Massachusetts, early 18th c., imperfections, height loss, 43 3/4" h. (ILLUS.)... **2,875**

Country-style "ladder-back" child's rocking chair w/arms, the back w/three arched slats between simple turned stiles w/knob finials, flat shaped arms on turned arm supports continuing into the turned front legs, woven splint seat, old dry red surface, 25 1/4" h. (minor seat damage)... **275**

Country-style "ladder-back" highchair, simple turned back stiles w/vase- and ring-turned finials, the back rails composed of shaped horizontal slats, the arms fitted w/cylindrical hand-holds, the cylinder & ring-turned stiles & arm supports joined by stretchers, old surface, New England, late 18th c., 37 1/2" h. (imperfections, missing front seatrail)................. **374**

Country-style "ladder-back" weaver's chair, hardwood, the tall back w/two arched slats between slender turned stiles w/button finials, stiles continue down to form very tall back legs & matched tall front legs supporting a woven splint seat, a high simple turned front stretcher above a lower ring-turned stretcher, plain turned double side stretchers, button-and-peg feet, old natural finish, 19th c., overall 38" h. (joints need regluing) **770**

Danish Modern dining chairs, teak, each w/a swelled arched crestrail curving to form a U-form rail w/slender flattened open arms all supported on four slightly canted turned & swelled supports flanking the caned seat, designed by Hans Wegner, each branded "Johannes Hansen Copenhagen Denmark," ca. 1949, set of 12 28,750

Danish Modern rocking chair w/arms, teak, a curved crestrail & arms on tapering squared stile legs joined by slender arched seatrails, on rockers, woven rust-colored back & seat cushions, foil label of M. Nissan, Denmark, 28" h. 173

Early 20th century armchair, mahogany-finished hardwood, the wide arched crestrail carved w/a grotesque Old Man of the North face over a grouping of five baluster- and knob-turned slender spindles all between slender stiles & shaped open arms ending in scrolled grips over incurved arm supports, the wide shaped seat raised on cabriole front legs ending in claw-and-ball feet & square canted rear legs joined by swelled box stretchers, old dark worn finish, ca. 1900, 36 1/2" h. 193

Early Pressed-back Side Chair

Early 20th century 'pressed-back' side chairs, oak, the wide crest w/rounded corners pressed at the sides w/large C-scrolls flanking a central fanned design above knob- and rod-turned stiles flanking ten slender baluster-, ring- and rod-turned spindles, wide shaped plank seat, ring- and rod-turned front legs joined by two turned stretchers, plain side & rear stretchers & legs, some edge damage, age cracks, one crest incomplete, ca. 1900, set of 6 (ILLUS. of one) 561

Early American "banister-back" armchair, painted, the double arched & scalloped crestrail flanked by ring- and baluster-turned stiles flanking four half-round banisters & attached to serpentine arms above ring-turned front legs ending in knob feet, old black paint, Connecticut, 1725-75, 49" h. (imperfections) 6,900

Early "Ladder-back" Armchair

Early American country-style "ladder-back" armchair, probably maple, the tall back w/five arched slats between turned stiles w/oblong finials, the shaped open arms w/baluster-turned arm supports continuing to the front legs & flanking the replaced woven rush seat, double knob- and baluster-turned stretchers in the front & simple turned stretchers at the sides & back, original dark finish, ca. 1820, 46" h. (ILLUS.) 350

Early American "ladder-back" child's highchair, maple, the tall back stiles forming rear legs & back & ending in turned knob finials above three arched slats in the back above serpentine open arms on baluster-turned arm supports continuing into front tall turned legs, replaced paper rush seat, front rungs worn from use, refinished, 35" h. (age cracks, chips on finial) 468

Early American "ladder-back" side chair, maple, tall simple turned back stiles w/pointed knob finials flanking five arched slats, woven rush seat, baluster- and rod-turned front legs joined by a double-knob and ring-turned stretcher, double plain side stretchers & one at the back, found in Bucks County, Pennsylvania, reputed to have belonged to an early Quaker, old refinishing & rush seat, late 18th - early 19th c., 43 3/4" h. 605

Early American "ladder-back" side chair, painted, the tall back w/four reverse-graduated arched slats between slender ring- and rod-turned stiles w/knob finials, replaced rush seat on baluster-, knob- and rod-turned front legs joined by a double-knob turned high stretcher, plain turned double side & a single back stretcher, old black repaint, late 18th - early 19th c., 43" h. 825

Egyptian Revival armchair, painted hardwood, the square back w/an upholstered panel below the wide rectangular crestrail decorated w/a winged half-serpent ornament & flanked by slender open arms w/carved wings & curved supports above the overupholstered seat on a flat seatrail & turned front legs ending in carved paw feet, old worn red & green repaint w/gilding, early 20th c., 36 3/4" h. **605**

Federal Leather & Wood Armchair

Federal armchair, mahogany, butternut & leather, the ring-turned slender crestrail above the raking leather-upholstered back, downward scrolling open arms on urn-shaped arm supports on a wide leather-upholstered seat over ring- and baluster-turned tapering front legs on peg feet, square back stile legs, original surface & leather, minor imperfections, possibly Portsmouth, New Hampshire, early 19th c., 40" h. (ILLUS.)........................ **1,150**

Early Painted Boston Rocker

Federal country-style "Boston" rocker, painted & decorated, the high back w/a curved crestrail centered by a rectangular plaque decorated w/stenciled grapes & vines, raised on simple stiles flanking the seven slender back spindles, shaped open arms on a bamboo-turned spindle & arm support, wide S-scroll seat raised on canted knob- and ring-turned front legs

joined by a turned front stretcher & bamboo-turned side & back stretchers & legs on rockers, original mustard yellow paint & decoration, ca. 1830, 46" h. (ILLUS.)........ **375**

Federal "lolling" armchair, mahogany, the tall upholstered back w/a serpentine crest above molded open serpentine arms on slightly molded & incurved arm supports joining an overupholstered seat on molded square front legs joined by square stretchers to the raking rear legs, muslin underupholstery, Massachusetts, 1785-1800, 43 1/4" h. (minor imperfections).................. **4,255**

Federal side chair, carved mahogany, shield-shaped back w/a beaded frame w/fan carving on molded stiles & joined to the overupholstered shaped seat, on square tapering molded legs joined by flat stretchers, old refinish, Massachusetts or Rhode Island, ca. 1790, 27 1/4" h. (minor imperfections).................. **2,645**

Salem Federal Side Chair

Federal side chair, carved mahogany, the back w/an arched crestrail centered by a narrow tablet w/carved swags & draping on a star-punched background above thin latticework splats carved w/Neoclassical design, overupholstered seat w/serpentine front seatrail over molded tapering front legs joined to canted rear legs by square stretchers, old refinish, minor repairs, Salem, Massachusetts, 1790-1800, 35 1/2" h. (ILLUS.) **863**

Federal side chair, mahogany, the shield-form back w/fanned & pierced splat carved at the center w/sheaf of wheat & raised above the overupholstered seat on square tapering legs, old refinishing, late 18th - early 19th c., 36 3/4" h. (minor repairs) **495**

Federal side chairs, carved mahogany, a gently arched & stepped crestrail on a square back w/Neoclassical carving on the tablet & beaded edges above reeded & carved criss-cross splats on a curved beaded stay rail over the overupholstered seat w/bowed front seatrail, on square tapering front legs ending in spade feet joined by square stretchers to the raking rear legs, old surface, Salem,

Massachusetts, ca. 1800, 35" h., set of 4
(very minor imperfections).......................... **6,900**

Part of Federal Shield-back Chair Set

Federal side chairs, carved mahogany,
shield-back style, the arched & molded
crestrail & molded stiles above a carved
kylix splat w/festoons draped from flanking carved rosettes, above a pierced
splat terminating in a carved lunette at its
base above the molded rear seatrail &
overupholstered seat w/serpentine front,
square tapering front & canted rear legs
joined by flat stretchers, seats w/old
black horsehair, old surface, Rhode Island or Salem, Massachusetts, ca. 1795,
four side chairs & matching armchair,
armchair w/arm restoration, 37 3/4" h.,
the set (ILLUS. of two) **23,000**

New York Shield-back Federal Chair

Federal side chairs, carved mahogany,
shield-back style w/serpentine molded
arched crestrail above a pierced splat
carved w/swags, plumes & feathers, the
overupholstered seat below on square
tapering molded front legs & gently canted rear legs, one w/repair to crest &
patches to back of splat, other w/cracks
to splat, New York, ca. 1795, 40" h., pr.
(ILLUS. of one).. **5,175**
Federal side chairs, mahogany, arched
molded crestrails continuing to shaped
stiles flanking vasiform pierced carved
splats over the trapezoidal slip seat, on
square beaded tapering front legs joined to
the raked rear legs by square stretchers,
New England, ca. 1790, refinished, minor
imperfections, 37 1/4" h., pr. (ILLUS.) **2,990**

Federal Mahogany Side Chairs

Federal wing-back armchair, upholstered
mahogany, the arched crestrail & rounded upholstered back & wings above
rolled upholstered arms over the tight upholstered seat on frontal ring- and baluster-turned legs w/peg feet, square back
legs, old refinish, New England, early
19th c., 46" h. (imperfections) **1,725**
Federal-Style armchair, mahogany, the
squared upholstered back w/rounded
corners above padded open arms on incurved molded arm supports, overupholstered curved seat, square tapering legs
ending in spade feet, old dark finish, early
20th c., 35 1/2" h. **303**
Federal-Style side chair, mahogany,
shield-shaped back w/a vase-form
pierced splat centered by Prince of
Wales Plumes, raised above an overupholstered seat w/blue needlepoint
w/roses, square tapering legs joined by
flat stretchers, legs w/line inlay & banded
cuffs, late 19th - early 20th c., 37" h.............. **220**
George III-Style dining chairs, mahogany,
ribbon-back style, each w/a back composed of four gently arched & pierced ribbon slats, upholstered seat, square
molded legs joined by stretchers, England, late 19th c., 37 1/2" h., set of 8
(restorations) **3,738**

Hitchcock Decorated Side Chair

Hitchcock fancy side chairs, painted & decorated, the turned crestrail above a wide horizontal splat stenciled w/a fox hunting scene flanked by raised stiles w/further stenciled decoration above the rush seat, ring- and knob-turned raked front legs joined by a ring- and knob-turned front stretcher & plain side & back stretchers, gilt & polychrome trim, Hitchcocksville, Connecticut, ca. 1825-30, imperfections, 33 1/2" h., pr. (ILLUS. of one) **1,150**

Hitchcock side chair, child's, painted & decorated, a rolled crest above a rectangular splat above the woven rush seat & ring-turned legs, black-painted ground, some of it wood-grained, & gold-leaf decoration, Hitchcocksville, Connecticut, early 19th c., 21" h. (minor surface imperfections) **863**

Hitchcock side chairs, rosewood-grained surface w/the original gilt decoration including an urn centering the cornucopiaform splat, old rush seat, ring-turned legs, original surface, Hitchcocksville, Connecticut, 1830s, 35 1/2" h., set of 4 ..... **1,265**

Hunzinger 'patent' platform rocker, ebonized hardwood, the tall back w/bobbin-turned stiles joined by cross rails supporting a large needlework panel raised above the padded arms on bobbin-turned arm supports & w/cross-braces & curved underarm supports over the needlepoint-upholstered seat, bobbin-turned frame support on the slender platform base, ca. 1880 .... **1,600**

French Provincial-Style Armchair

Louis XV Provincial-Style armchair, carved hardwood, the arched serpentine crestrail w/leaf carving continuing to oblong back frame w/serpentine carved medial rail, slender curved open arms on incurved arm supports over the woven rush seat, curved front seatrail w/scalloped rim, simple cabriole front legs w/scroll-carved stretchers, plain turned side & back stretchers, worn brown finish, France, late 19th - early 20th c., 37 1/4" h. (ILLUS.) **138**

Louis XV Revival Upholstered Armchair

Louis XV Revival armchair, mahogany, the oval medallion back w/figural needlepoint upholstery w/brass tack trim, arched & shaped padded open arms on carved incurved arms over the wide needlepoint-upholstered spring seat w/brass tack trim, serpentine seatrail w/shell and scroll carving, carved cabriole front legs ending in scroll feet on pegs, original finish, ca. 1920s, 38" h. (ILLUS.) **650**

Louis XV Revival armchair w/wingback, the narrow walnut gently arched crestrail centered by a scroll-carved boss & continuing to form the framing of the rounded, tapering side wings continuing to the padded arms w/carved grips, incurved carved arm supports flank the upholstered back, wings & spring seat, gently serpentined seatrail carved w/a central leafy scroll & border scrolls, simple cabriole legs w/carved knees ending in scroll & peg feet, France, late 19th - early 20th c., reupholstered, 42 1/2" h. (some frame damage) **440**

Louis XV-Style armchair, carved hardwood, the rectangular upholstered back panel w/serpentine sides & a gently arched crestrail carved w/rococo scrolls above open shaped padded arms & raised above the overupholstered seat w/a curved seatrail w/scroll carving & carved simple cabriole front legs ending in peg feet, antique white highlights, platinum satin upholstery w/gold bees, early 20th c., 37 1/2" h. **523**

Unusual Louis XV-Style Hooded Chair

Louis XV-Style hooded armchair, white gesso on wood frame, the arched shell-form paneled & upholstered top above a tall upholstered back & side wings over low padded closed arms, cushion seat above serpentine seatrail continuing to demi-cabriole front legs, original paint & gilt highlights, ca. 1920s, 32" w., 4' 6" h. (ILLUS.) **800**

Louis XV-Style open-arm armchair, the squared back frame w/serpentine edges & arched crest w/floral carving & molded edges enclosing a petit-point upholstery panel of a man in 18th c. attire walking in a garden, padded open molded & serpentine arms above the spring seat w/further petit-point upholstery in a floral design, serpentine front seatrail w/carved central floral reserve, molded cabriole legs w/peg feet, early 20th c., 37 1/2" h. (some stitches missing) **385**

Mission Oak Armless Rocker

Mission-style (Arts & Crafts movememt) rocking chair without arms, oak, a flat gently curved crestrail above four slender slats between square stiles, upholstered spring cushion seat, gently arched aprons join square legs on rockers, attributed to L. & J.G. Stickley, ca. 1912, minor wear, 33 3/4" h. (ILLUS.) **374**

Mission-style (Arts & Crafts movement) armchair, oak, the tall back w/heavy stiles joined by four wide gently curved slats, flat arms over five slats, upholstered cushion seat, deep flat apron, branded mark of Gustav Stickley, Model No. 324, ca. 1901, 42 3/8" h. **2,185**

Mission-style (Arts & Crafts movement) armchair, oak, a wide gently curved upper & lower rail flanking the three wide slats between square stiles above flat shaped arms above front stile legs w/corbels, recovered drop-in leather cushion seat, wide box stretchers, original finish, branded mark of Charles Limbert Co., Model No. 931, 24 x 28", 37" h. **880**

Mission-style (Arts & Crafts movement) armchair, oak, a wide gently curved crestrail w/a square cut-out at each end between the square stiles & a single lower slat, flat curved arms above square stile legs w/top corbels, high flat front stretcher & low flat stretchers at the side & back, original finish, branded mark of the Limbert Furniture Co., 38" h. (torn original woven rush seat) **990**

Mission-style (Arts & Crafts movement) armchair, oak, a wide peaked crestrail above five narrow slats between the narrow stiles, flat shaped arms on slender square front stile legs, drop-in re-covered leather cushion seat, "The Work of..." mark of L. & J.G. Stickley, Model No. 810, 39" h. **440**

Gustav Stickley Armchair

Mission-style (Arts & Crafts movement) armchair, oak, a top & lower back rail flanking three wide slats between the slender square back stiles over flat shaped arms on square front leg stiles w/corbels under the arms, replaced upholstered seat, recent finish, unsigned Gustav Stickley, Model No. 340, 41" h. (ILLUS.) **605**

Mission-style (Arts & Crafts movement) cube chair, oak, a wide crestrail above two vertical slats flanked by low stiles projecting slightly above the thick rectangular arms each over two slats, through-tenons on apron rails, deep drop-in spring seat, original dark finish, decal mark of Ritter Craft, 25 3/4 x 27", 32" h. **605**

Mission-style (Arts & Crafts movement) desk chair, oak, the back w/three vertical slats between upper & lower rails & square stiles forming rear legs, single high flat front & rear stretchers & double side stretchers, original finish, branded mark of L. & J.G. Stickley, 36" h. (re-covered leather seat) **413**

Mission-style (Arts & Crafts movement) dining chairs, oak, each w/a gently curved top rail over a narrower lower rail between the square stiles, square seatrail on square legs joined by flat stretchers, no seats, L. & J.G. Stickley, refinished, ca. 1920, 36" h., set of 4 (ILLUS. top next page) **2,000**

Set of Mission Oak Dining Chairs

Mission-style (Arts & Crafts movement) dining chairs, oak, the rectangular back w/stiles & rails enclosing three vertical slats raised above the cushion seat, square tapering legs joined by high flat stretchers, Gustav Stickley Model No. 353, after 1909, 39 1/4" h., set of 6 .... **2,760**

Mission-style (Arts & Crafts movement) dining chairs, oak, each w/a narrow curved crestrail above a single back splat flanked by slender square stiles & a lower rail raised above the trapezoidal seat w/replaced inset tacked-in seat inserts, square legs w/box stretchers, original dark finish, branded mark of the Charles Limbert Furniture Co., six side chairs Model No. 911 & two armchairs Model No. 613, 37" h., set of 8 .... **3,080**

Mission-style (Arts & Crafts movement) dining chairs, oak, the heavy ladder-back w/three horizontal slats between square stiles above the woven rush seat, wide flat front & rear stretchers & small double side stretchers, original finish, faint signature of Gustav Stickley, Model No. 349, 37" h., set of 4 (two seats replaced) **3,300**

Mission-style (Arts & Crafts movement) Morris chair, a slatted adjustable back above wide flat arms on heavy square stile legs w/underarm corbels flanking five slats, wide front apron, new dark finish, paper label of J.M. Young, 37" h. (loose seat & back cushions) **3,300**

Mission-style (Arts & Crafts movement) Morris chair, the adjustable back w/a wide curved top slat above three lower slats between the heavy stiles, wide flat shaped arms above pairs of slats & stile legs w/corbels, wide lower side stretchers, original sling cushion seat, recent finish, unsigned Gustav Stickley, Model No. 2341, 30 x 34", 39" h. **3,575**

Mission-style (Arts & Crafts movement) Morris rocking chair w/arms, oak, the adjustable back w/horizontal slats above wide flat shaped arms on front leg supports w/corbels, recovered original back & seat cushions, recoated original finish, unsigned L. & J.G. Stickley, 40" h. **1,045**

Mission-style (Arts & Crafts movement) rocking chair w/arms, oak, a curved crestrail over five back slats, shaped arms w/through-tenons & long corbel supports, two side slats on each side, medium brown finish, spring cushion

seat, early 20th c., 35" h. (needs upholstering, minor wear) **403**

Mission-style (Arts & Crafts movement) rocking chair w/arms, oak, a curved crestrail over four vertical slats, shaped flat arms over a single slat w/cut-out, arched seatrail, square legs on rockers, original finish, branded Charles Limbert mark, Model No. 644, 39" h. (no seat) **1,093**

Harden & Co. Mission Rocker

Mission-style (Arts & Crafts movement) rocking chair w/arms, oak, a wide curved crestrail over four narrow & one wide vertical slats flanked by square stiles, flat shaped open arms on front leg supports w/side corbels, spring cushion leather seat, paper label of Harden and Co., early 20th c., some stains & roughness, 37" h. (ILLUS.) **518**

Mission-style (Arts & Crafts movement) rocking chair w/arms, oak, double flat & gently curved crestrails above five vertical slats between the square back stiles, flat gently arched arms over rails flanking vertical slats on each side, wide flat seatrail, new brown leather drop-in cushion spring seat, fine original finish, unmarked Harden Co., 36" h. (shallow gouging, crack in one crestrail) **1,045**

Mission-style (Arts & Crafts movement) rocking chair w/arms, oak, the tall back composed of five slats between the square stiles, flat shaped arms above vertical slats & front corbels on the stile legs, deep apron, on rockers, branded signature mark of Gustav Stickley, Model No. 323, 29 x 33", 40" h. (replaced cushions, one rocker replaced) **1,870**

Mission-style (Arts & Crafts movement) rocking chair without arms, oak, the tall rectangular back w/three slats below the crestrail, each inlaid w/a stylized pewter & wood floral design, raised above the drop-in leather seat above arched aprons & square legs joined by box stretchers, designed by Harvey Ellis, Gustav Stickley Model No. 337, ca. 1912, 33 3/4" h...... **6,325**

Mission-style (Arts & Crafts movement) sewing rocker, oak, an H-style back w/a single wide slat notched at the top & bottom, above a drop-in seat w/original Japan leather, mint original finish, branded Gustav Stickley mark, 34" h. (ILLUS.) **413**

Gustav Stickley Sewing Rocker

Mission-style (Arts & Crafts movement) side chair, oak, a back w/tall square stiles flanking a leather-covered panel w/tack trim, raised above the leather-covered seat, square slender legs joined by a wide flat front stretcher & narrow flat side stretchers, small red decal mark of Gustav Stickley, Model No. 380, ca. 1904-07, 39 1/2" h. **2,300**

Mission-style (Arts & Crafts movement) side chairs, oak, a flat crestrail & lower rail supporting three vertical slats above the planked seat, square slender legs joined by wide flat box stretchers, L. & J.G. Stickley Model No. 940, ca. 1915, set of 8... **2,070**

Arne Jacobsen "Ant" Chairs

Modern style "ant" chairs, molded plywood, the back & seat in a continuous shaped form of walnut-veneered plywood, on three bent & painted tube-steel legs, designed by Arne Jacobsen, manufactured by Fritz Hansen, impressed "FH/Denmark," ca. 1952, 30" h., set of 4 (ILLUS.) **1,150**

Wright-designed Modern Armchair

Modern style armchair, wood & upholstery, deep upholstered sides w/a rolled crest & large back cushion above the wide cushion seat over a deep flat upholstered seatrail,

wood base frame on short squared legs, green velvet upholstery, designed by Frank Lloyd Wright, manufactured by Heritage Henredon, Style No. 1483, ca. 1955, 29 1/2 x 33 1/2", 27" h. (ILLUS.)...................... **748**

Eames Armchair & Ottoman

Modern style armchair & ottoman, bent & laminated wood & leather, the chair w/a high oblong leather-upholstered & tufted crest panel above an upholstered lower back & wide seat flanked by curved padded arms all within a bent & laminated wood frame swiveling on a five-arm footed base, matching upholstered ottoman on a four-arm base, designed by Charles & Ray Eames, manufactured by Herman Miller, ca. 1956, some wear & abrasions, chair 32" h., 2 pcs. (ILLUS.)........................ **1,265**

Eames Armchair & Ottoman

Modern style armchair & ottoman, molded wood & leather, the armchair w/a high wide rectangular black leather-upholstered back rest above a lower upholstered back flanked by rolled arms & a deep upholstered seat w/a molded rosewood veneer shell raised on a five-prong aluminum base, the large leather-upholstered ottoman of matching construction, designed by Charles & Ray Eames, ca. 1956, wear to leather, 33" h., 2 pcs. (ILLUS.)........................... **748**

Andre Arbus Armchair

Modern style armchairs, hardwood, the upright rectangular upholstered back flanked by shaped tapering open arms on incurved arm supports above the upholstered seat, on square tapering legs, designed by Andre Arbus, ca. 1945, pr. (ILLUS. of one)... **2,070**

Norman Cherner Plywood Chair

Modern style chairs, molded plywood, a wedge-shaped back tapering sharply & continuing to the rounded seat, raised on slender tapering legs, molded walnut arms on the armchair, designed by Norman Cherner, ca. 1960, made by Plycraft, Lawrence, Massachusetts, one armchair & three side chairs, repair to one leg, wear, nicks, 31" h., the set (ILLUS. of side chair) **920**

Eames "DCW" Side Chairs

Modern style "DCW" side chairs, walnut plywood, wide curved back panel on curved support over the dished wide curved seat, arched tapering canted legs, designed by Charles Eames, w/paper label, ca. 1950s, 28" h., pr. (ILLUS.)....... **546**

Modern style music room side chairs, bentwood, a tall narrow bentwood back frame enclosing an oval upholstered back panel raised above the shaped rectangular upholstered seat, raised on tapering legs set w/spherical brackets in the front, designed by Josef Hoffmann, original label & branded factory mark of J. and J. Kohn, Austria, ca. 1904, pr. (ILLUS.).......................... **575**

Hoffmann Music Room Side Chairs

Modern style rocking chair w/arms, fiberglass, metal & wood, the molded fiberglass U-form seat w/arched back & rolled arms in salmon raised on slender black wire struts w/curved birch rockers, designed by Charles Eames, label of Herman Miller Co., ca. 1950, 27" h.................. **1,540**

Saarinen "Womb" Chair & Ottoman

Modern style "Womb" armchair & ottoman, upholstered, the deep rounded & cupped form w/rolled arms enclosing two cushions raised on a tubular steel frame & legs, together w/a matching ottoman, avocado green wool upholstery, manufacturer's tag of Knoll Associates, New York, designed by Eero Saarinen, introduced in 1948, wear to upholstery edges, chair 36" h., 2 pcs. (ILLUS.)........................ **1,380**

Neoclassical Revival Painted Armchair

Neoclassical Revival armchair, painted & decorated, a gently rolled needlepoint-upholstered back flanked by wing-carved stiles continuing into leafy scroll arms terminating in large blossom medallions flanking the wide upholstered seat w/an incurved seatrail, ring-turned & reeded tapering front legs, reeded tapering rear legs, painted white & gold, original surface, ca. 1920s, 36" h. (ILLUS.)............... **800**

Nutting-signed Carver armchair, hardwood, 17th c. style, Model No. 464............... **963**

Nutting-signed Child's Windsor Chair

Nutting-signed child's "fan-back" Windsor armchair, the serpentine crest w/scrolled ends raised on seven tall spindles above a U-form central rail ending in shaped arms & above numerous turned swelled spindles, on baluster- and knob-turned canted arm supports, on a deeply shaped saddle seat, on canted baluster-, ring- and rod-turned legs joined by a swelled H-stretcher, labeled "Wallace Nutting, Saugus, Mass.," early 20th c., surface imperfections, dark stain, 27" h. (ILLUS.).. **1,380**

Nutting-signed Windsor bow-back side chair, the bowed backrail over eight slender swelled spindles & a pair of brace spindles behind, shaped saddle seat, canted baluster-, ring- and rod-turned legs, original finial, paper label reading "Wallace Nutting," branded "301," early 20th c., 38 1/4" h... **550**

Nutting-signed Windsor comb-back armchair, Pennsylvania-style, Model No. 412 .... **1,045**

Nutting-signed Windsor continuous-arm armchair, the rounded crestrail continuing down to slender flattened arms & fitted at the top w/a slender scrolled comb crest on four short spindles, eleven slender swelled spindles in the back & a pair of brace spindles behind, baluster- and ring-turned canted arm supports, shaped saddle seat, canted baluster-, ring- and rod-turned legs joined by a swelled H-stretcher, branded & paper label reading "Wallace Nutting 402," early 20th c., 44 3/4" h... **825**

Nutting-signed Windsor "sack-back" armchair, hardwood, Model No. 408............ **935**

Ornately Carved Chinese Armchairs

Oriental armchairs, carved dark hardwood, one w/a cartouche-form back panel ornately carved w/scrolls w/the heavy curved open arms w/figural handgrips, the wide seat w/deep scroll-carved apron raised on heavy dot-incised cabriole legs w/scroll feet, the other w/the pierced back panel carved w/entwined dragons w/the arms formed by their necks & the heads forming the handgrips, the wide seat above a deep scroll-carved apron & heavy cabriole legs w/dot-incised bands & scroll feet, China, late quarter 19th c., each 34" h., group of two, each (ILLUS.) **800**

Oriental armchair, carved teak, the square back w/a gently arched crest above the pierce-carved panel centering a figural reserve surrounded by long dragons & clouds w/the dragon heads facing each other at the crest, heavy plain back stiles & bottom rail above pierce-carved arms above the wide seat w/curved, scroll-incised seatrail, simple cabriole front legs ending in paw feet, w/brocade cushion, China, 20th c., 42" h....... **457**

Pilgrim Century "Carver" armchair, turned maple, the baluster- and rod-turned stiles topped w/ball finials w/two turned rails centering three turned spindles, the turned front posts w/ball finials above the rush seat, plain turned box stretchers, old dry finish, dark brown color, Rhode Island, 1670-1700, 39 1/2" h. (feet worn, chips throughout, right arm & right stretcher probably replaced)............... **7,475**

Pilgrim Century "Great Chair," turned & joined oak, the flame & ring finials above turned & incised stiles centering a double-baluster & ring-turned crest over three tapering spindles, all above cylindrical open arms & bun-turned hand grips over turned front post legs over a trapezoidal rush seat, on cylindrical legs joined by double box stretchers, Plymouth County, Massachusetts, 1715-30, 38 3/4" h.. **8,050**

Pilgrim Century "Great Chair," turned & painted, the knob- and rod-turned stiles w/knob finials joining three flattened-arch slats & shaped flat open arms ending in a knob handrest above the knob- and rod-turned front legs, simple turned double rungs in from sides & single rung at back, woven rush seat, old red paint, southern New England, late 17th c., 43" h. (imperfections).. **4,025**

Pilgrim Century highchair, turned & painted maple & chestnut, the turned beaker-form back finials on sausage-turned tall rear stiles centering two pointed-arch slats, open arms w/front tall sausage-turned arm supports & legs w/ball finials flanking the plank seat, all joined by box stretchers, New England, probably Rhode Island, 1700-30, 35 3/4" h. (formerly fitted w/a rush seat) **4,312**

Prairie School Oak Side Chair

Prairie School side chairs, inlaid oak, a tall slender flat back w/angled top corners above an inlaid geometric design, board plank seat mortised through to the back & on square legs w/Mackmurdo feet, some veneer loss to top of one back, original finish, early 20th c., 41" h., pr. (ILLUS. of one) **1,760**

New England Queen Anne Armchair

Queen Anne armchair, maple, the yoked crestrail over a vasiform splat & molded stay-rail flanked by raked stiles joining scrolling molded arms on baluster-, block- and ring-turned supports continuing to front legs, joined by a bulbous turned front stretcher & square side & back stretchers to the raked rear legs,

vestiges of old red stain, New England, ca. 1740-60, minor imperfections, 40 3/4" h. (ILLUS.) **9,200**

Queen Anne corner armchair, maple, the curved shaped crest continuing to form arms on curved armrests over three ring-turned tapering stiles centered by twin trapezoidal splats, the trapezoidal slip-seat on front cabriole leg ending in a pad foot, New England, 18th c........................... **1,500**

Queen Anne corner armchair, walnut, the low shaped crest on a U-form flattened crestrail ending in outscrolled grips on vase- and ring-turned supports flanking two vasiform splats, the slip seat on a shaped seat frame on a frontal cabriole leg ending in a pad foot, remaining simple turned legs w/tiny pad feet, all joined by block- and vase-turned cross-stretchers, old surface, Boston, ca. 1740-60 (imperfections)... **6,900**

Queen Anne corner armchair, walnut, the shaped low crest continuing to scrolled hand holds above three ring- and rod-turned stiles & two vase-form splats on molded shoes, the slip compass seat on a frontal cabriole leg ending in a pad foot, three straight turned tapering back legs ending in pad feet (one damaged), all joined by cut-out seat frame above block-, rod- and ring-turned cross stretchers, old surface, Boston, 1752-60, 30" h. (imperfections)... **43,700**

Queen Anne Corner Chair

Queen Anne corner armchair, walnut, U-form crestrail w/raised center continuing to form flat scrolled arms above two wide scroll-cut vase-form splats & three ring-, rod- and knob-turned spindles, upholstered compass seat, front cabriole leg ending in pad foot & three simple turned legs w/pad feet, block-, rod- and baluster-turned cross-stretchers, old refinish, restored, southern New England, 18th c., 29 5/8" h. (ILLUS.)....................................... **2,990**

Queen Anne corner chair, carved & figured mahogany, the shaped U-form crest above a shaped scrolled crestrail on three ring-turned supports centering two solid vase-form splats, balloon-form seat on four cabriole legs w/a shell-carved knee on the front leg, ending in pad feet, English or Irish, 18th c., 32 1/2" h.............. **4,025**

Queen Anne Corner Commode Chair

Queen Anne corner commode chair, maple, U-form back crestrail w/raised center section & continuing to scrolled arms over two slender vase-form splats & three ring- and rod-turned spindles over the upholstered molded seat, deep scalloped aprons, cabriole frontal leg w/deep pad foot, turned & swelled side & back legs, old refinish, minor imperfections, New England, 18th c., 31" h. (ILLUS.) **2,070**

Country Queen Anne Armchair

Queen Anne country-style armchair, painted, a double-arched crestrail centered by carved scrolls above the vasiform splat & molded stiles, long shaped & molded open arms ending in scrolled hand grips raised on ring-, knob- and baluster-turned arm supports, woven rush seat, block-, ring- and knob-turned front legs joined by a ball-turned front stretcher, double turned side stretchers to the square canted rear legs, old black repaint, New Hampshire, mid-18th c. (ILLUS.) **4,125**

Country Queen Anne Painted Chair

Queen Anne country-style side chair, carved & painted, the arched & carved crestrail above a tall vasiform splat & molded raked stiles, the rush seat on block-, baluster- and ring-turned front legs joined by bulbous turned front & side stretchers, retains old burnt sienna & dark brown paint w/yellow pinstriping, New England, 18th c., 41" h. (ILLUS.) **1,495**

Queen Anne country-style side chair, cherry & ash, the shaped crestrail above a vase-form splat on an arched stay rail flanked by baluster- and ring-turned stiles, the rush seat on baluster- and ring-turned tapering legs ending in pad feet on platforms, joined by bulbous turned front stretchers & plain turned double side stretchers, old refinish, attributed to Jacob Smith, New York, 18th c., 41 1/2" h. **748**

Queen Anne country-style side chair, grain-painted, the yoked crestrail above a vasiform splat & raked stiles joined by a lower rail above the woven rush seat, on block-, vase- and ring-turned front legs ending in carved Spanish feet joined by a bulbous turned front stretcher & side stretchers, old brown grained painting, New England, second half 18th c., worn, 39 3/4" h. **920**

Country Queen Anne Side Chair

Queen Anne country-style side chair, painted hardwood, the oxbow crestrail above a vase-form splat flanked by baluster- and ring-turned stiles over the replaced woven seat, simple turned front legs joined by a worn baluster-turned front stretcher & plain side & rear stretchers, old finish, possibly original black paint, 1750-80, 40" h. (ILLUS.) **200-400**

Queen Anne country-style side chair, painted maple, the ox yoke crest w/rounded corners above tall flat stiles flanking a vase-form splat to a lower rail, woven splint seat w/old light green paint, old dry red paint, 18th c., 42 1/4" h. **1,045**

Queen Anne country-style side chair, painted, slighted curved crestrail above tall knob- and baluster-turned stiles flanking the vasiform splat, replaced rush seat, ring- and rod-turned tapering front legs ending in raised pad feet, double-knob turned front stretcher, plain turned side & back stretchers, old alligatored red

& black repaint, attributed to Samuel Durand, Milford, Connecticut, 18th c., 40 3/4" h. **880**

Queen Anne side chair, carved cherry, the bow-form crestrail w/curved & curled ears on slightly canted flat stiles flanking the vasiform splat & shaped upholstered slip seat within arched rails, on cabriole front legs & square canted rear legs joined by baluster- and block-turned stretcher & ending in pad feet, old & possibly original finish, Massachusetts, 1730-50, 39" h. **2,587**

Queen Anne side chair, maple, the spooned crestrail above a vasiform splat & raked chamfered stiles joined to the trapezoidal slip seat by a scrolled frame, on two front cabriole legs ending in pad feet, raked rear square legs joined by block-, baluster- and ring-turned stretchers, refinished, imperfections, Massachusetts, 18th c., 40" h. **2,070**

New Hampshire Queen Anne Chair

Queen Anne side chair, maple, the yoked crestrail above a solid vase-form splat flanked by molded stiles over a trapezoidal rush seat above a shaped front skirt, on cabriole front legs ending in padded disk feet joined by ring- and baluster-turned front stretcher & side flat stretchers, canted square rear legs, restorations to stretchers, New Hampshire, 1740-60, 42 1/4" h. (ILLUS.) **2,070**

Queen Anne Maple Side Chair

Queen Anne side chair, maple, the yoked crestrail over a vasiform splat & molded shoe flanked by raked & chamfered stiles, the overupholstered balloon seat on frontal cabriole legs ending in pad feet, joined to the rear shaped & raked legs by block-, baluster- and ring-turned stretchers,   old   refinish, Massachusetts, ca. 1740-60, minor restorations (ILLUS.) **4,313**

Queen Anne side chair, painted & carved, the yoked crestrail w/beaded edges continuing to raked beaded stiles flanking the vasiform splat over a trapezoidal needlework slip seat, scalloped front seatrail on front arris cabriole legs ending in squared arris pad feet & squared & chamfered back legs joined by block-, vase- and ring-turned H-form stretchers & swelled rear stretcher, old red stain w/black accents, Connecticut River Valley, ca. 1740-60, partial MFA exhibition label on rear leg, 41 3/4" h. (imperfections) **2,300**

Early Painted Queen Anne Chair

Queen Anne side chair, painted, transitional style w/a carved yoked crestrail over a vasiform splat flanked by molded raked stiles above an overupholstered seat w/a cyma-curved skirt & a medial stretcher w/ball- and reel-turnings flanked by black- and baluster-turned front legs ending in Spanish feet, joined to the rear raked legs by square stretchers, old black paint w/gilt highlights, Portsmouth, New Hampshire, 1735-50, 40" h. (ILLUS.) **3,738**

Queen Anne side chair, painted, the yoked crestrail above a vasiform splat & raked stiles joined to the rush seat by block-, vase- and ring-turned legs on Spanish feet w/a double-knob turned front stretcher & square side stretchers, old surface, Massachusetts, 18th c., 41" h. **1,150**

Queen Anne side chair, walnut, the double arched crestrail w/a central carved shell above a vasiform splat flanked by gently canted stiles, an upholstered balloon-shaped seat overupholstered above the front cabriole legs ending in padded disk feet & joined by block- and baluster-turned H-stretchers to the canted turned rear legs, old surface, Boston, 1740-65, 40 1/2" h. (imperfections) **8,050**

Queen Anne side chair, walnut, the serpentine crestrail w/upturned ears above a vasiform splat, raked stiles, molded seatrails frame the upholstered seat, front cabriole legs ending in pad feet, joined to rear legs w/block- and vase-turned stretchers, old refinish, die-branded under front seatrail "F. Shaw," Massachusetts, 18th c., 37 1/4" h. (restored, imperfections)................. **805**

Queen Anne Walnut Side Chair

Queen Anne side chairs, carved walnut, shaped crestrail w/volute-carved ears above a pierced beaker-form splat, upholstered slip seat over scalloped front apron & cabriole front legs ending in trifid feet, turned & canted rear legs, chocolate brown color, old finish, Mid-Atlantic States, ca. 1740, 40" h., pr. (ILLUS. of one)... **10,925**

Queen Anne side chairs, walnut, the serpentine crestrail above a simple vaseform splat on molded shoes flanked by gently raked stiles, upholstered slip seat on cabriole front legs ending in pad feet on platforms joined to the chamfered rear legs by cut-out seatrails & block- and vase-turned stretchers, refinished, Massachusetts, ca. 1740-60, 38" h., pr. (minor restoration) **8,625**

Queen Anne-Style Rocking Chair

Queen Anne-Style rocking chair w/arms, mahogany & mahogany veneer, the

rounded back w/a looping pierced vaseform splat w/carved leaf trim, shaped & curved open arms above the upholstered spring seat, curved seatrail raised on cabriole front legs w/scroll feet & square rear legs on rockers, reupholstered, original finish, early 20th c., 38" h. (ILLUS.) **450**

Queen Anne-Style side chair, mahogany, the tall back w/an ox yoke crestrail w/rounded corners & tall spooned stiles flanking the tall solid vasiform splat, trapezoidal upholstered slip seat, slightly shaped front seatrail on cabriole front legs w/scroll-cut returns & ending in pad feet, canted square rear legs, old worn finish, early 20th c., 44" h................................ **83**

Queen Anne-Style wing chair, the high upholstered back flanked by rounded tapering wings above outrolled upholstered arms, cushion seat over the upholstered seatrail, simple cabriole front legs ending in pad feet, square canted rear legs, modern reproduction w/striped velvet upholstery, 46" h. **248**

Ornate Rococo Revival Corner Chair

Rococo Revival corner chair, carved giltwood, the U-form crestrail ornately carved w/a full-relief reclining classical woman beside a shield & scrolls, the drapery-wrapped rail continuing to full figure arm supports carved as classical woman, a central back splat flanked by relief-carved serpents, deep round upholstered spring seat, round carved seatrail w/a large scroll-carved central drop, on gently curved front legs trimmed w/beading & raised on peg feet, remnant of original upholstery, probably French, ca. 1890, 32" h. (ILLUS.) **1,800**

Roman-Style armchair, carved mahogany, a wide arched & heavily scroll-carved back rail w/a grotesque face between blocked carved stiles w/high inscrolled ears above the open serpentine arms above the wide U-form seat raised on four S-scroll supports resting on a heavy block X-form base w/carved toes on casters, dark reddish brown original finish, paper label for Stomps - Burkhart, Dayton Furniture Company, early 20th c., 37 3/4" h. (crack in support board beneath the seat)... **330**

Rustic Child's Rocking Chair

Rustic style child's rocking armchair, the high bent-twig arched back entwined w/large twig loops flanking a central board slat above the looped twig arms above the plank seat w/twig edging on canted legs w/a twig stretcher above the wide rockers, New York state, ca. 1900, old dark natural surface (ILLUS.) **230**

Salem-type rocking chair w/arms, child's, painted & decorated, the flat crestrail w/round corners decorated w/painted flowers & leaves above canted turned stiles flanking four slender spindles, S-shaped arms on canted, turned arm supports & one spindle over the deeply S-shaped seat, turned front legs joined by turned rung above inset rockers, old blue w/striping & polychrome crest, New England, mid-19th c., 24 3/4" h. (surface imperfections) **316**

Victorian Aesthetic Movement Armchair

Victorian Aesthetic Movement corner armchairs, ebonized & parcel-gilt, flat crestrails forming square corner w/each back section centered by a panel of gilt stenciled stylized birds & geometric designs flanked by short ring-turned spindles all raised above the overupholstered seat on a line-incised gilt-trimmed seatrail on chamfered legs ending in casters, Kimbel and Cabus, New York, New York, ca. 1870s, 27 1/2" h., pr. (ILLUS. of one) **4,485**

Baroque Revival Armchair

Victorian Baroque Revival armchair, carved mahogany, a flat pierce-carved crestrail flanked by squared, pointed finials above the wide upholstered back, scrolled open arms ending in carved faces above the carved square tapering armrests above the wide upholstered seat, ring-, ball- and block-turned legs on low blocked feet, legs joined by a turned H-stretcher, original finish, late 19th c., 42" h. (ILLUS.) **650**

Italian Baroque-Style Grotto Armchair

Victorian Baroque Revival armchair, walnut, a grotto-style chair w/the high back & wide seat carved as large shells w/figural dolphin-form arms, on curved coral-form legs, Italy, ca. 1880 (ILLUS.) **1,500**

Victorian Baroque Revival Armchair

Victorian Baroque Revival armchair, walnut, the tall back ornately pierce-carved w/an arched scroll-carved crestrail above a wide pierced scroll- and lattice-carved splat flanked by slender turned stiles above the heavy scrolled & molded arms on curved supports, wide overupholstered seat on spiral-turned front legs joined by a high arched & pierced scrolling stretchers, turned H-stretchers join all the legs, ca. 1900 (ILLUS.) **920**

Ornate Baroque Revival Dining Chairs

Victorian Baroque Revival dining chairs, carved hardwood, each w/a tall narrow back w/an ornately carved framework, the high arched crest centered by a carved animal head surrounded by pierced leafy scrolls & continuing down to form the carved framework around a narrow tufted upholstered back panel, flanked by spiral-turned stiles capped w/urn finials & raised above the overupholstered seat, block-, baluster- and ring-turned front legs joined by a spiral-turned front stretcher w/turned H-stretcher connecting all the legs, the armchairs w/padded rests & carved dog head hand grips, four side chairs & two armchairs, late 19th c., the set (ILLUS. of two) **6,325**

Victorian Baroque Revival dining chairs, carved oak, the arched crestrail carved w/fruit & flowers & centered by a cut-out handhold above a square upholstered back panel raised above the square seat w/inset upholstered panel within a carved seat frame, carved apron, raised on block- and knob-turned front legs joined by a spiral-twist stretcher w/spiral-turned rear legs & turned H-stretcher, original dark finish, late 19th c., 18" h., 34" h., set of 8 (back & seat panels probably originally caned) **800**

Victorian Baroque Revival rocking chair w/arms, carved fruitwood, unique highly carved design, the back w/a diamond-shaped panel topped by a high pierced scroll-carved crest w/a figural putto at one side flanked by heavy curved arms w/scroll-carved grips resting on pierce-carved sides composed of large leafy scrolls w/large figural caryatids forming

Unique Ornate Baroque-Style Rocker

the arm supports & front legs, the heavy curved rockers w/carved scrolls at the rear tips & figural busts over scrolls at the front tips, made for the Chicago Columbian Exposition of 1893, deaccessioned by the Chicago Museum of Science and Industry, probably Italian, 36 x 52", 4' h. (ILLUS.) **10,000**

Morris Chair with Dolphin Stretcher

Victorian Baroque-Style Morris armchair, quarter-sawn oak, the tall upholstered back pad resting on an adjustable reclining back frame flanked by wide arched arms over turned spindles & reeded urn-form arm supports flanking the wide cushion seat, seatrail w/heavy paneled corner blocks over legs w/reeded knobs connected by long slender dolphin-forms carved as the stretcher, original finish, old upholstery, ca. 1900, 44" h. (ILLUS.) **850**

Victorian Baroque-style Morris chair, mahogany, the upright adjustable rectangular back frame above wide flat arms over boldly carved figural arm supports w/large winged griffin heads on bold scrolls & arched carved front legs ending in padded paw feet, curved back arm supports on down-scrolled back legs, upholstered back & seat cushions, on casters, ca. 1890 .... **1,904**

Unique Classical Revival Armchair

Victorian Classical Revival armchair, oak & walnut, the tall back w/a fan-carved rounded crestrail above a pierce-carved back w/a lyre-form splat carved w/bold scrolls, the back stiles w/square knob finials above narrow shaped side wings above the wide flat arms w/scrolled hand grips raised on a flat armrest, the long caned trapezoidal seat lifting to expose a hole for a chamber pot, deep apron, simple turned front legs on casters, original finish, last quarter 19th c., 40" h. (ILLUS.)..... **250**

Victorian Balloon-back Side Chairs

Victorian country-style "ballon-back" side chairs, painted & decorated, a rounded back rail w/tapering stiles centered by a vase-form splat, shaped plank seat on ring- and rod-turned front legs joined by a turned stretcher, plain turned rear legs & plain turned side & rear stretchers, the crestrail decorated w/a stenciled basket of fruit above the splat stenciled w/an eagle & shield w/"Union," gilt vine stenciled border, stiles, seat & legs w/yellow & salmon striping, Pennsylvania, ca. 1860, some paint wear, 33 1/2" h., pr. (ILLUS.) **460**

Victorian country-style "balloon-back" side chairs, painted & decorated, the arched rounded backrail w/a gently scalloped crest above a wide vertical splat, the shaped plank seat on slightly canted knob-turned front legs joined by a knob-turned front stretcher, original black over red ground w/white scrolled trim, fruit &

foliage on crest & splat, some initialed under seat "W.F.H., Trenton, O.," restorations w/small areas of touch-up, 33" h., set of 4 .... **770**

Victorian country-style highchair, painted & decorated, a wide gently arched crestrail w/upturned ends w/a black ground decorated w/red striping & stenciled fruit & foliage in shades of bronze powder, raised on canted knob- and rod-turned stiles joined by an arched lower rail over three knob- and rod-turned spindles, bentwood seat guards on the round plank seat, raised on tall tapering knob- and rod-turned legs w/a knob-turned worn front footrest stretcher & plain turned stretchers at the sides & back, overall black ground w/painted trim, mid-19th c., 35 3/4" h... **413**

Oak Highchair-Stroller Combination

Victorian Golden Oak child's highchair, convertible-type, a wide rounded crestrail w/a lower pressed arched design over six slender turned spindles & baluster-turned stiles flanked by arms on turned spindles & arm supports & a swing-up rectangular feeding tray, square seat w/padded center fitted at the front w/a footrest & raised on tall flatted cross-form hinged legs on iron wheels which lower the seat to form a stroller, refinished, ca. 1900, highchair 40" h. (ILLUS.)...................... **500**

Ornate Golden Oak Rocking Chair

Victorian Golden Oak rocking chair w/arms, quarter-sawn oak, the tall back w/two scalloped crestrails joined by a central roundel & a row of tiny spindles, the upper rail w/stylized lion-carved ears, over a slender center carved vase-form splat flanked by slender bead-turned spindles all flanked by knob- and rod-turned stiles, shaped flat arms over knob-turned spindles & arm rests above a shaped round pressed composition seat (not shown), ring- and knob-turned front legs joined by double turned stretchers, refinished, ca. 1890s, 45" h. (ILLUS.) **350**

Gothic Revival Armchair

Victorian Gothic Revival hall armchair, walnut, the tall back w/a Gothic arch-pointed crest w/spire finial over carved rails & a panel w/pierced trefoils, a diamond & a raised ring band over the tall arched upholstered back panels flanked by free-standing squared stiles & low padded three-quarter arms on curved supports, upholstered seat on front seatrail w/raised burl panels, ring-, rod- and knob-turned front legs on casters, 19th c., 70" h. (ILLUS.) **518**

Fine Gothic Revival Armchair

Victorian Gothic Revival armchair, carved rosewood, the arched Gothic-carved crestrail above tall oblong molding flanked by open arms w/carved scrolled terminals & curved arm supports over the spring-upholstered serpentine & cyma-curved seat & seatrail, front demi-cabrole legs, 1850-60, possibly New York City, surface imperfections, 41 1/2" h. (ILLUS.) **3,335**

Victorian Gothic Revival armchair, carved walnut, the tall back w/a high pointed & pierced crestrail tapering to a point & enclosing an open quatrefoil over a pair of Gothic arch openings between ring- and rod-turned stiles w/ring- and knob-turned pointed finials, a large upholstered oval back medallion rests on a lower rail w/pierced trefoils at the lower corners & pointed drops below, straight square open arms end in large knob grips above baluster- and ring-turned supports flanking the upholstered seat, scalloped seatrail between corner blocks above the knob-, ring- and rod-turned legs w/knob feet on casters, old worn finish, old worn leathered black cloth upholstery, mid-19th c., 52 1/2" h. **413**

Victorian Gothic Revival Side Chairs

Victorian Gothic Revival side chairs, mahogany & mahogany veneer, rounded & peaked molded crestrail over a veneered panel above four slender ring- and baluster-turned spindles forming five Gothic arches, the lower rail raised above the upholstered slip seat, simple flattened cabriole front legs & canted rear legs, ca. 1850, 32" h., set of 10 (ILLUS. of two) **1,380**

Victorian Neo-Grec Armchair

Victorian Neo-Grec armchairs, ebonized & gilt-trimmed hardwood, the canted & back-scrolled crest w/upholstered central panel above a frame enclosing seven short turned spindles flanked by conforming gilt-incised stiles leading to downscrolling upholstered arms & arched, gilt-incised armrests over similarly incised downscrolling side rails flanking the rectangular upholstered seat, on a carved & gilt-incised curule-form base joined by a turned stretcher, on casters, American, ca. 1870, 34 1/4" h., pr. (ILLUS. of one)... **3,680**

rounded, curved & spiral-turned open arms above the upholstered seat on spiral-turned supports & spiral-turned stretchers on the platform base, old finish, illegible paper label, attributed to George Hunzinger, ca. 1880s, 41 1/2" h. (ILLUS.)... **660**

John Jelliff Renaissance Armchairs

Victorian Renaissance Revival armchairs, walnut & burl walnut, the arched back panel w/a carved crestrail composed of turned rods flanking a central roundel & w/projecting turned corner ears, a tufted upholstered panel above the lower back rail centered by another roundel, open padded arms w/the arm supports carved as ladies' heads, the wide upholstered seat w/a bowed seatrail above a conforming apron w/burl trim, knob- and ring-turned tapering front legs on casters, by John Jelliff, Newark, New Jersey, new upholstery, original finish, ca. 1875, 38" h., pr. (ILLUS.).......... **3,000**

Late Victorian "Patent" Platform Rocker

Victorian "patent" platform rocking chair w/arms, walnut, the high arched back w/a padded headrest above an upholstered oval central medallion between the spiral-turned stiles w/rounded top corners & supported by slender spindles,

Fancy Victorian Child's Rocker

Victorian Renaissance Revival child's rocker without arms, walnut, a scroll-carved crestrail w/fanned center crest above the oval caned back panel w/scroll-cut bottom frame & raised on stiles w/serpentine skirt guards flanking the rounded caned seat, ring-turned front legs & front stretcher w/plain turned side & rear stretchers, on long rockers, 30" h. (ILLUS.) **336**

Rare Branch-carved Hall Chair

Victorian Renaissance Revival hall chair, carved walnut, the tall pierced back ornately carved w/a pointed palmette crest above entwined leafy oak branches w/large acorns, above the flat trapezoidal seat w/molded edges above a curved apron carved w/crossed oak leaves & acorns, raised on ring- and rod-turned reeded legs w/knob feet, by Mitchell and Rammelsberg of Cincinnati, Ohio, 18 x 20", 4' h. (ILLUS.) **5,000**

Victorian Renaissance Revival Chair

Victorian Renaissance Revival side chairs, carved rosewood, the tall upholstered back w/a high scroll- and architectural-carved crestrail centered by a

carved maidenhead above incurved stiles over the serpentine upholstered seat on a conforming seatrail w/central carved drop, on boldly turned & tapering trumpet legs on casters, red silk upholstery, attributed to John Jelliff, ca. 1870, 38 1/2" h., pr. (ILLUS. of one) **978**

Victorian Rococo Rosewood Armchair

Victorian Rococo armchair, carved rosewood, the tall shaped & upholstered balloon back w/a high pierced & scroll-carved crest joined to pierce-carved scrolls down the sides above the padded open arms w/incurved & leaf-carved arm supports, wide upholstered spring seat w/a serpentine seatrail w/a scroll-carved apron, raised on demi-cabriole front legs & canted square rear legs all on porcelain casters, original finish, ca. 1850-60, 44" h. (ILLUS.) **1,600**

Rococo Carved Rosewood Armchair

Victorian Rococo armchair, carved rosewood, the tall upholstered balloon back w/a high arched & pierce-carved crest w/bold fruit & floral carving on the molded frame raised above the upholstered spring seat flanked by padded shaped open arms w/incurved supports, serpentine seatrail w/nut-carved center, on demi-cabriole front legs on original casters, refinished, new upholstery, ca. 1860, 44" h. (ILLUS.) **1,200**

"Stanton Hall" Pattern Chairs

Victorian Rococo armchair, laminated carved rosewood, the high balloon back w/a raised arched crestrail w/gadroon-carved border flanking a central carved painted crest all above pierce-carved rail continuing to flaring pierce-carved back stiles flanking the waisted oblong upholstered back panel raised on open arched supports & flanked by padded open arms on molded incurved arm supports flanking the deep, wide upholstered seat w/serpentine front seatrail w/carved banding & central cartouche, demi-cabriole front legs, curved & canted rear legs, "Stanton Hall" patt., attributed to J. & J. Meeks, New York, ca. 1855, old needlepoint upholstery, minor age cracks, 43 3/4" h. (ILLUS. center) **3,410**

Victorian Rococo Open-arm Armchair

Victorian Rococo armchair, mahogany, the tall upholstered balloon back w/a molded frame & pierced scroll-carved crest, shaped & padded open arms on incurved arm supports flanking the wide

upholstered seat w/a serpentine molded seatrail continuing to the demi-cabriole front legs on casters, old refinish, newer upholstery, ca. 1870, 44" h. (ILLUS.) **650**

Victorian Rococo armchair, walnut, the waisted upholstered balloon back w/a low arched leaf- and rose-carved crest above the finger-molded frame, padded curved open arms raised on incurved molded arm supports over the upholstered spring seat, serpentine seatrail w/a carved central medallion, demi-cabriole front legs w/rose & leaf carving at the knees & raised on casters, old worn refinishing, ca. 1860, 43" h. (repairs to frame) **358**

Belter "Rosalie" Pattern Armchairs

Victorian Rococo armchairs, carved & laminated rosewood, a tall shaped upholstered balloon back w/an ornately floral-carved crest, base of back also scroll-carved, shaped & molded open arms above the upholstered spring seat w/a serpentine seatrail w/floral carving, on demi-cabriole front legs on casters, "Rosalie" patt., John Henry Belter, New York, ca. 1855, old, possibly original upholstery, original finish, 47" h., pr. (ILLUS.) **9,500**

Rococo Carved Rosewood Armchairs

Victorian Rococo armchairs, carved laminated rosewood, the tall balloon back w/an arched crestrail topped by a carved band of realistic florals, the crestrail continuing to long S-scroll side rails flanking the waisted upholstered back panels raised on leaf-carved panels over the wide upholstered seat flanked by open curved & carved arms, serpentine seatrail w/central carved leaf & flower band, demi-cabriole front legs w/floral-carved knees, curved & canted square rear legs all on casters, rust colored damask upholstery, probably New York City, ca. 1850s, 43 1/4" h., pr. (ILLUS.) **6,038**

Unusual Iron-framed Victorian Rocker

Victorian Rococo platform rocking chair, upholstered iron & wood, the openwork scrolling iron framework w/a high padded headrest above the tall shaped upholstered back flanked by serpentine padded arms rests on iron scroll supports, a squared upholstered seat raised on high curved iron spring supports raised on long slender wooden rails, old reupholstery, original painted surface, repaired headrest, ca. 1850-60, 46" h. (ILLUS.) **550**

Victorian Rococo 'Lincoln' Rocker

Victorian Rococo rocking chair w/arms, carved walnut, so-called 'Lincoln' or 'Grecian' style, tall upholstered balloon back w/a rounded crestrail carved w/a fruit- and nut-carved crest above the molded

waisted frame over the padded ornately scroll-carved open arms above the upholstered spring seat, scroll-carved serpentine seatrail on short tapering legs on rockers, refinished, ca. 1860, 46" h. (ILLUS.) **650**

Victorian Rococo rocking chair w/arms, Grecian-style w/high balloon back w/walnut thumb-molded frame around the upholstered back, open padded arms above the upholstered spring seat, serpentine veneered seatrail above shaped front legs on long rockers, ca. 1860 .... **358**

Victorian Rococo Rocking Chair

Victorian Rococo rocking chair w/arms, the large shaped balloon-back w/a fruit-carved crest enclosing a needlepoint upholstery panel above curved padded open arms on incurved molded arm supports, wide needlepoint upholstered seat w/a serpentine seatrail & demi-cabriole front legs, on rockers, ca. 1860s, 38" h. (ILLUS.) **650**

Unique Rococo 'Grecian' Rocker

Victorian Rococo rocking chair w/arms, walnut, so-called 'Grecian' or 'Lincoln' style, the tall upholstered & shaped back w/a curved crestrail carved w/fruits & flowers & continuing to form sides of back & the padded scrolled arms on S-scroll arm supports, wide upholstered rolled seat raised on a long double-S-scrolls resting on the long serpentine rockers, refinished, old velvet upholstery, ca. 1850-70, 42" h. (ILLUS.) **450**

Victorian Rococo side chair, carved & laminated rosewood, a tall waisted balloon back w/an arched floral-carved crest above the upholstered back panel, over-upholstered spring seat w/a serpentine finger-molded seatrail above demi-cabriole front legs on casters & outswept rear legs on casters, "Rosalie" patt. by John H. Belter, ca. 1855, 37" h. **1,680**

Baudouine-style Rococo Side Chair

Victorian Rococo side chair, carved & laminated rosewood, an oblong tufted upholstered back panel framed w/an elaborately pierce-carved arched framewood tapering down to arched skirt guards on the high upholstered spring seat w/a serpentine seatrail decorated w/a center shell carving, raised on cabriole front legs w/shell-carved knees & ending in scroll feet on casters, original finish, upholstery, attributed to Charles A. Baudouine, New York City, 40" h. (ILLUS.)... **2,400**

Victorian Rococo side chair, carved laminated rosewood, high arched crestrail w/gadroon-carved rails flanking a carved pointed central cartouche all over a scrolling pierce-carved rail continuing down to pierce-carved wide side rails flanking the waisted tufted upholstered back panel raised on scrolls over the round deep upholstered seat on a mold-carved round seatrail w/central carved cartouche, demi-cabriole front legs on casters, canted rear legs, slightly worn velvet upholstery, minor age cracks, "Stanton Hall" patt., attributed to J. & J. Meeks, New York, ca. 1855, 41" h. (ILLUS. left with armchair)........................... **1,760**

Victorian Rococo side chair, carved laminated rosewood, high arched crestrail w/gadroon-carved rails flanking a carved pointed central cartouche all over a scrolling pierce-carved rail continuing down to pierce-carved wide side rails flanking the waisted tufted upholstered back panel raised on scrolls over the round deep upholstered seat on a mold-carved round seatrail w/central carved cartouche, demi-cabriole front legs on casters, canted rear legs, colorful floral brocade upholstery, minor age cracks, "Stanton Hall" patt., attributed to J. & J. Meeks, New York, ca. 1855, 40 1/2" h. (ILLUS. right with armchair) **1,870**

Belter Carved Rosewood Side Chair

Victorian Rococo side chair, carved & laminated rosewood, the tall back framework composed of large carved C-scrolls enclosing pierce-carved grapevines & w/a carved floral crest all centered by a small round upholstered panel, the deep overupholstered spring seat on a serpentine seatrail w/floral carving & cabriole front legs w/floral-carved knees, on casters, original finish, reupholstered, John Henry Belter, ca. 1855, 40" h. (ILLUS.) **3,800**

Belter "Rosalie" Pattern Side Chair

Victorian Rococo side chair, carved & laminated rosewood, the tall balloon back w/a tufted upholstered panel within a scroll-carved frame topped by an arched fruit & blossom-carved crest, the wide upholstered spring seat w/a serpentine seatrail carved w/a central floral cluster, raised on demi-cabriole front legs w/carved knees & casters, "Rosalie" patt. by J.H. Belter, New York City, ca. 1855, original finish, old reupholstery, 40" h. (ILLUS.) **2,400**

Victorian Rococo side chair, mahogany, the open balloon-back w/a rounded & stepped crest carved w/a floral band, the incurved stiles joined by a lower pierced scroll-carved rail above the overupholstered spring seat, cabriole front legs ending in scroll & peg feet, old finish, newer grey & brown brocade upholstery, ca. 1855, 34 1/2" h. **204**

Set of Meeks Rosewood Side Chairs

Victorian Rococo side chairs, carved & laminated rosewood, a balloon-form tufted upholstered back panel framed by an ornate pierce-carved frame w/a peaked crestrail w/a center cartouche flanked by ropetwist-carved scroll bands continuing to further scroll carving down the sides to the lower rail & skirt guards, wide rounded upholstered spring seat, serpentine seatrail w/central carved cartouche, raised on demi-cabriole front legs, "Stanton Hall" patt. by J. & J.W. Meeks, New York City, ca. 1855, original finish, old but not original upholstery, 40" h., set of 3 (ILLUS.) **4,500**

Meeks-style Rosewood Slipper Chair

the short carved & shaped front legs, attributed to J. & J.W. Meeks, New York City, ca. 1855, old reupholstery, original finish, ca. 1855, 42" h. (ILLUS.) **1,600**

Rare Labeled Belter Side Chairs

Victorian Rococo side chairs, carved laminated rosewood, the high arched & pierced floral-carved crestrail w/an arched floral-carved crest, top rail continuing halfway down the sides to large carved C-scrolls over S-scroll rails flanking further pierce-carved florals, oval upholstered back panel & upholstered seat w/serpentine seatrail w/ornate floral clusters in the center & at the corners above the demi-cabriole front legs on casters, square curved & canted rear legs on casters, labeled by John Henry Belter, New York, ca. 1855, pr. (ILLUS.) . **31,900**

Victorian Rococo slipper chair, carved & laminated rosewood, the tall balloon-form wood back ornately pierce-carved w/tight scrolls & grape clusters below a high arched & rope twist-carved crest, the deep upholstered spring seat on a narrow seatrail w/a carved front medallion between

Ornate Victorian Rococo Slipper Chair

Victorian Rococo slipper chair, carved walnut, the tall pierce-carved back w/an arched crestrail carved w/scrolls & a central fruit cluster above a hairpin-shaped molding enclosing a large pierced leafy scroll design, slender ring-turned back stiles above low scrolled skirt guards flanking the balloon-form upholstered seat, ring- and knob-turned front legs on casters, refinished, ca. 1850-60, 38" h. (ILLUS.)............ **450**

Fine Rococo Slipper Chair

Victorian Rococo slipper chair, pierce-carved laminated rosewood, the tall serpentine-framed back w/a floral-carved crest above ornate looping vines & a central grape cluster, rounded upholstered spring seat on a conforming seatrail w/a carved front border, raised on slender tapering squared legs w/carved knees, attributed to Meeks of New York, ca. 1850-60, refinished, 40" h. (ILLUS.) **1,200**

"Rosalie with Grapes" Pattern Armchair

Victorian Rococo substyle armchair, carved & laminated rosewood, the tall balloon back w/a tapering oval upholstered panel framed w/a wide arched crest of ornate floral & grape carving & long scroll-carved sides above the curved & molded open arms on incurved arm supports above the wide upholstered seat w/a serpentine seatrail, raised on demi-cabriole front legs w/floral-carved knees & raised on casters, canted square rear legs on casters, by John H. Belter, New York City, "Rosalie with Grapes" patt., ca. 1855 (ILLUS.)......... **4,480**

Victorian Rococo Side Chair

Victorian Rococo substyle side chairs, carved rosewood, an oval back w/a finger-carved frame w/a carved floral crest enclosing the upholstered panel, raised above the overupholstered spring demi-seat w/a serpentine seatrail w/finger-carving continuing into demi-cabriole front legs on casters, reupholstered in red floral damask, ca. 1860, 39" h., repairs, set of 4 (ILLUS of one).......................... **528**

Victorian Roman-style Armchair

Victorian Roman-style chairs, mahogany & mahogany veneer, armchair & matching rocker, each w/a large oval back panel w/delicate scroll-carved borders suspended between heavy carved stiles topped by carved lion's head w/"jeweled" eyes, heavy shaped open arms on U-form supports enclosing the solid curved seat, wide scroll-carved seatrail continuing to flattened cabriole legs ending in large paw feet, old dark finish, one arm support w/glued break, ca. 1900, armchair 42" h., pr. (ILLUS. of armchair) **550**

Victorian Steer Horn Armchair

Victorian steer horn armchair, the high arched tufted upholstered back framed by curved steer horns continuing down to flank the deep upholstered seat, on arched outswept steer horn legs, original worn upholstery, on casters, ca. 1870, 36 1/2" h. (ILLUS.)....................................... **1,035**

Victorian stick-style novelty folding chair, the back & front legs formed from a single forked tree branch w/the upper back squared off & fitted w/a short crossbar above etched designs of people, animals, flowers, birds & inscriptions above the small rectangular seat supported by a hinged carved third support leg, marked "Liberty Indiana, March 1892," made by Hosea Hayden, 30" h. (ILLUS.)................. **13,750**

Unique Victorian Folk Art Folding Chair

Wicker corner chair, a flat rolled crestrail of tightly woven wicker above back panels w/bands of fine diamond lattice weaving above & below a narrow central band w/short vertical strips, a tightly woven cane quarter-round seat above a double band looped wicker apron, three front & one rear wrapped legs, old burgundy painted finish, early 20th c., 28" h. (minor scuffs) **248**

Wicker rocking chair w/arms, a high rounded arch back w/a rolled wide tightly woven border continuing down to form rounded arms, the back w/a large woven wheel-form center panel over a lacy scroll lower section, loosely scrolled arm supports, oblong woven seat above a lattice woven front apron & double turned side & back rungs, on rockers, ca. 1890....... **392**

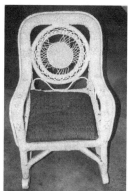

Wicker Child's Rocking Chair

Wicker rocking chair w/arms, child's, an arched & rounded tightly woven crestrail continuing down to form the rounded arms, the back w/a round medallion w/delicate weaving (damaged) above the padded seat, wrapped legs & angled braces on rockers, ca. 1910 (ILLUS.)............ **110**

Wicker rocking chair w/arms, the high arched serpentine back w/wide bands of tightly woven wicker centered by a tall ta-

pering oblong delicately scrolled wicker central panel, the rolled crestrail continues down to form wide rolled arms over lattice panels, rounded seat over ornately scrolled apron on rockers, ca. 1880-90 .... **784**

Fancy Victorian Wicker Rocker

Wicker rocking chair w/arms, the tall back w/a tall pointed center crest composed of ornate tight cane scrolls above curved bands of lattice weaving above the ornately caned back panel, all flanked by very tall pointed stiles, ornate looping scroll arms & ornate scrolls under the back panels, later upholstered seat cushion, each leg w/ornate scrolled cane corner brackets, original natural finish, ca. 1890, 46" h. (ILLUS.)................................. **504**

William & Mary-Style armchair, walnut, the tall back w/an arched & pierced scroll-carved crestrail above a pierced scroll-carved framework centering an oval caned panel, free-standing ropetwist-turned stiles w/knob finials above long shaped open arms ending in scrolled hand grips, wide upholstered seat above a narrow flat carved seatrail on ropetwist- and block-turned front legs joined by an arched, pierced & scroll-carved wide flat stretcher, the front & rear legs joined by a ropetwist-turned H-stretcher, old finish, late 19th - early 20th c., 50" h. (minor edge damage)...................... **275**

William & Mary-Style Side Chair

William & Mary-Style side chair, walnut, the tall back w/arched & pierced scroll-carved crestrails above a back panel framed w/further scroll carving centered by an oval caned panel, free-standing twist-turned stiles w/knob-turned finials above the wide upholstered seat above a narrow scroll-carved seatrail above twist- and block-turned legs joined by a wide arched & scroll-pierced front stretcher, the four legs joined by a ropetwist-turned H-stretcher, old finish, early 20th c., seat originally caned, 46 1/2" h. (ILLUS.) **248**

William & Mary-Style wingchair, upholstered mahogany, the tall upholstered back w/a round top flanked by tall rolled wings over the upholstered rolled arms & upholstered seat, the turnip-, block- and ball-turned front legs joined by a high, wide arched pierced scrolled front stretcher, turned H-stretcher joins the legs, dark green velvet upholstery, Kittinger, 20th c., 49 1/2" h. **715**

Windsor "arrow-back" armchair, painted, a flat curved crestrail between two tapering curved stiles flanking three curved arrow back slats, turned rod open arms w/canted bamboo-turned arm supports & a single arrow splat, wide rounded shaped plank seat, canted bamboo-turned legs joined by a flattened front stretcher & bamboo-turned side & back stretchers, old worn mustard yellow paint, first half 19th c., 32" h. **275**

Windsor "Arrow-back" Highchair

Windsor "arrow-back" highchair, painted, a stepped crestrail raised on back-swept tapering stiles flanking three long curved arrow slats over simple turned arms on bamboo-turned spindles over the thick shaped plank seat, tall canted swelled bamboo-turned legs w/a front footrest over a high turned swelled stretcher & matching rear stretcher, lower side stretchers, early red paint, very minor surface imperfections, New England, 1820-30, 36" h. (ILLUS.) **2,875**

Windsor "arrow-back" side chairs, painted & stenciled, each w/a gently curved rectangular crestrail between tapering curved stiles flanking four arrow slats, shaped incised plank seat on bamboo-

turned splayed legs joined by a front shaped & decorated stretcher & plain round side & back stretchers, original yellow ground decorated on the crestrail w/roses & green leaves, first half 19th c., 33 3/4" h., set of 5 .... **5,750**

Bamboo-turned Windsor Side Chairs

Windsor "bamboo-turned" side chairs, painted & decorated, the flat crestrail above four swelled bamboo-turned spindles between bamboo-turned stiles over a shaped saddle seat, canted bamboo-turned legs joined by box stretchers, yellow ground w/green & red stenciled leaf & berry decoration on the crestrail & green accents, New England, ca. 1820-30, some repaint, 33 1/4" h., set of 4 (ILLUS. of two).. **863**

Painted Birdcage Windsor Side Chair

Windsor "birdcage" side chairs, painted, the birdcage crestrail w/three short over seven long spindles flanked by turned stiles on a shaped, incised saddle seat, four splayed bamboo-turned legs joined by matching stretchers, overall old red paint w/yellow accents & yellow seat, the stiles w/leaf decoration, New England, ca. 1810, seats repainted, 34 1/4" h., pr. (ILLUS. of one) **1,850**

Windsor "birdcage" side chairs, painted, the double bamboo-turned crestrails &

curved stiles enclosing three short spindles above seven long spindles joining the shaped & incised seat on splayed bamboo-turned legs & stretchers, old brown paint, underside inscribed in chalk "N. Tuck," New England, ca. 1800, 34" h., set of 6 .... **6,325**

Windsor "birdcage" side chairs, the back w/two simple turned horizontal crestrails joined by three short spindles above seven simple turned long spindles all flanked by canted bamboo-turned stiles, oblong-shaped plank seat on canted bamboo-turned legs joined by bamboo-turned box stretchers, old refinishing, first half 19th c., 33 1/2" h., pr. **275**

Windsor "bow-back" armchair, painted, the bowed crestrail above seven spindles, shaped arms on two spindles & a canted bamboo-turned arm support, slightly shaped plank seat on canted bamboo-turned legs joined by a bamboo-turned H-stretcher, old alligatored black paint over earlier colors, illegible signature, Pennsylvania, late 18th - early 19th c., 36" h. (repaired crack in seat) **935**

Windsor Child's Armchair

Windsor "bow-back" child's armchair, maple & ash, the bowed crestrail over five slender spindles & joined to shaped arms over a spindle & canted arm supports, shaped saddle seat raised on canted bamboo-turned legs joined by a bamboo-turned H-stretcher, New England, early 19th c., refinished, repairs, 22 1/3" h. (ILLUS.) **1,265**

Windsor "bow-back" side chair, a bowed & reeded back rail above nine slender swelled spindles, shaped saddle seat on canted bamboo-turned legs joined by a bamboo-turned H-stretcher, old dark finish, branded mark of Ebenezer Tracey, Lisbon, Connecticut, late 18th - early 19th c., 35 1/2" h. (well made repairs) **880**

Windsor "bow-back" side chair, hardwood, the bowed crestrail over seven turned tapering spindles on a shaped saddle seat over bamboo-turned canted legs joined by a double-swelled H-stretcher, old dark varnish stain over white paint, late 18th - early 19th c., 33 3/4" h. (some variation in spindles) **193**

Windsor "bow-back" side chair, maple & ash, the bowed beaded crestrail over nine tapering bamboo-turned spindles & an incised saddle seat, bamboo-turned splayed legs joined by swelled & bamboo-turned H-stretcher, refinished, branded "S.J. Tuck," Boston, 1790, 38" h. **1,093**

Windsor "bow-back" side chair, painted, slender arched backrail above seven slender turned spindles over the shaped saddle seat, canted bamboo-turned legs joined by a swelled H-stretcher, old worn black paint, late 18th - early 19th c., 38" h. **358**

Windsor "bow-back" side chair, painted, the bowed crestrail above eight swelled spindles & a shaped saddle seat w/a pair of swelled back brace spindles, on splayed ring- and baluster-turned legs joined by a swelled H-stretcher, old green over early dark green, New England, ca. 1780, 35 1/2" h. **748**

Windsor "bow-back" side chairs, painted, the rounded molded back rail above seven bamboo-turned spindles, shaped saddle seat on canted bamboo-turned legs joined by a bamboo-turned H-stretcher, old red repaint over white, attributed to the Boston area, late 18th - early 19th c., 37 3/4 & 38" h., pr. **1,430**

Windsor Child's Rocking Chair

Windsor child's rocking armchair, painted & decorated, rectangular tablet crestrail decorated w/colored florals & leaves raised on simple turned stiles joined by a narrow medial rail & flanked by simple turned open arms over the thick shaped saddle seat, ring-turned front legs & plain turned rear legs w/simple turned stretchers, mounted on heavy, long rockers, greenish yellow ground w/striped decoration in olive green & black, minor damage, Pennsylvania, mid-19th c., 18" h. (ILLUS.) **3,450**

Windsor "comb-back" armchair, the serpentine crestrail w/carved rounded ears above nine spindles over a shaped rail ending in curved arms on baluster- and ring-turned arm supports & numerous short spindles, wide D-form shaped seat, baluster- and ring-turned canted legs w/ball feet joined by a ball-and-bobbin-turned H-stretcher, Pennsylvania, 1770-90, dark finish, 44" h. **2,070**

Windsor "comb-back" rocking chair w/arms, painted, a curved rectangular small crest raised on five bamboo-turned curved spindles above the plain crestrail between canted stiles & above five bamboo-turned spindles, S-scroll arms on canted, bamboo-turned arm supports, wide thick plank seat, canted bamboo-turned legs joined by stretchers, inset rockers, old dark greenish black repaint w/yellow striping & crest w/date of 1769 & a "C" on the comb, found in Vermont, late 18th - early 19th c., 44" h. **770**

Painted Windsor Comb-back Rocker

Windsor "comb-back" rocking chair w/arms, painted & decorated pine & maple, the tall comb w/a rectangular crestrail over five slender spindles above the shaped back crestrail flanked by rabbit-ear curved stiles flanking five tall slender spindles, S-scroll arms on a spindle & canted arm support over the wide dished plank seat, simple turned canted legs on inset rockers, original painted & stenciled decoration w/blossoms & leaves on the crestrails against a dark brown ground, ca. 1830, 46" h. (ILLUS.) **450**

Windsor "comb-back" writing-arm armchair, the arched comb-back crest on six tall plain spindles above the shaped arm rail w/scroll arm terminals & an oblong writing surface over a thin drawer, turned spindles under the arm rail, baluster- and ring-turned canted arm supports, wide saddle seat over a deep suspended drawer, on canted baluster- and ring-turned legs joined by a swelled H-stretcher, old refinish, attributed to Ebenezer Tracy, Lisbon, Connecticut, ca. 1770-80, 46" h. (restorations) **5,175**

Windsor "combed arrow-back" rocking chair w/arms, painted, the comb-back above the rectangular crest & four arrow-form slats flanked by raked stiles & scrolled arms on bamboo-turned supports over the shaped seat, splayed turned legs on rockers joined by stretchers, original yellow & green foliate decoration on a mottled brown & black ground, New England, ca. 1830, 38" h. (imperfections) **633**

Windsor "continuous arm" brace-back armchair, chestnut & maple, the arched crestrail w/beaded edge continues down to form arms w/shaped hand holds above turned spindles & canted balus-

Signed Continous Arm Windsor

ter-turned arm supports, a shaped saddle seat w/two forked brace spindles to the top of the back, raised on canted baluster- and ring-turned legs joined by a swelled H-stretcher, branded "E.B. Tracy," Lisbon, Connecticut, 1780-1803, 37" h. (ILLUS.) **1,093**

Painted Continuous Arm Windsor

Windsor "continuous-arm" armchair, painted, the arched crestrail continuing to flat arms & hand holds above seven spindles & baluster- and ring-turned canted arm supports, shaped saddle seat on bamboo-turned canted legs joined by a swelled H-stretcher, old salmon red paint, attributed to Ebenezer Tracy, Jr., New London County, Connecticut, ca. 1800, 35 1/2" h. (ILLUS.) **3,105**

Windsor "continuous-arm" armchair, painted, the arched slender crestrail continuing down to form flat arms, the back w/seven slender swelled spindles w/two short spindles & a canted baluster- and ring-turned arm support under each arm, a shaped saddle seat on four canted baluster- and ring-turned legs joined by a swelled H-stretcher, green paint, probably Pennsylvania, late 18th - early 19th c., 39" h. (repairs) **978**

Windsor "continuous-arm" armchairs, each w/a molded bowed back continuing down to slender shaped arms, seven slender bamboo-turned back spindles & two short spindles under each arm w/a canted baluster- and ring-turned arm support, wide shaped saddle seat on canted bamboo-turned legs joined by a swelled H-stretcher, old brown finish, size varies so possibly a lady's & gentleman's set, attributed to Connecticut, possibly by Beriah Green, Windham County, 37" & 39 3/4" h., pr. **5,225**

Windsor "continuous-arm" brace-back armchair, painted, the incised arched crestrail curving down & ending in shaped hand grips enclosing twelve spindles & two splayed rear braces, on ring- and baluster-turned canted arm supports, shaped saddle seat, canted ring-, baluster- and rod-turned legs joined by a swelled H-stretcher, painted green, late 18th c., 37" h. **633**

Windsor "continuous-arm" brace-back armchair, painted, the slender arched crestrail curving down to form slender arms w/scrolled grips above numerous slender turned spindles & canted baluster- and ring-turned arm supports, shaped saddle seat, on canted baluster-, ring- and rod-turned tapering legs joined by a swelled H-stretcher, old black paint, New York, school of W. MacBride, 18th c. ... **2,500**

Windsor Continuous-Arm Armchair

Windsor "continuous-arm" brace-back armchair, painted, the slender molded crestrail continuing down to form narrow arms above six tall slender swelled spindles & two under-arm spindles & canted baluster-turned arm supports, the shaped saddle seat w/a back projection supporting a pair of flared brace spindles, on baluster- and rod-turned tapering canted legs joined by a swelled H-stretcher, old black over early paint, imperfections, underside left arm repair, branded "E. Swan," Elisha Swan, Stonington, Connecticut, 1755-1807, 39" h. (ILLUS.) **2,760**

Windsor "fan-back" armchair, ash & maple, the shaped crestrail above eight tall spindles & a U-form central rail continuing to form shaped arms on baluster- and ring-turned arm supports & six additional short spindles, wide shaped saddle seat, splayed baluster- and ring-turned legs joined by a swelled H-stretcher, refinished, New England, ca. 1790, 46" h. **3,738**

Windsor "fan-back" armchair, painted, a long serpentine crestrail w/scroll-carved terminals above nine tall spindles, a medial armrail ending in scrolled carved hand holds on baluster- and ring-turned

Fine Windsor Fan-back Armchair

arm supports, shaped saddle seat, canted baluster-, ring- and rod-turned legs joined by a swelled H-stretcher, New England, ca. 1780, 43 1/2" h. (ILLUS.) **5,463**

Windsor "fan-back" armchair, a narrow serpentine crestrail supported by six short spindles on a U-form medial rail continuing to form shaped arms ending in shaped handholds w/canted baluster-turned arm supports & above eleven turned spindles, wide carved saddle seat on four canted baluster- and ring-turned legs joined by a swelled H-stretcher, three old coats of red paint, New England, ca. 1790, 31" h. (minor imperfections).. **6,325**

Windsor "fan-back" rocking armchair, serpentine crestrail w/downscrolling ear volutes above ring- and baluster-turned & blocked stiles centered by nine tapering spindles over shaped arms terminating in downscrolling knuckled hand holds above ring- and baluster-turned arm supports over a shaped plank seat, on ring- and baluster-turned legs joined by a baluster-turned H-stretcher, shaped rockers, early 19th c., 39" h. **1,610**

Windsor "fan-back" side chair, painted, a serpentine crestrail above a back w/seven slender turned spindles between canted baluster- and ring-turned stiles, shaped saddle seat w/incised band at back, on canted baluster- and ring-turned legs joined by a swelled H-stretcher, old worn black paint over traces of earlier red, attributed to Connecticut or Rhode Island, late 18th c., 33 1/4" h. (age cracks in seat) **1,980**

Windsor "fan-back" side chair, painted, the serpentine crestrail above five slender tapering spindles flanked by baluster- and knob-turned stiles, a shaped plank seat w/pommel & bulbous turned splayed legs joined by swelled H-stretchers, original green paint, southern New Hampshire or northern Massachusetts, ca. 1790, 35 1/4" h. (minor paint loss)............. **2,070**

Windsor "fan-back" side chair, painted, the serpentine crestrail over nine spindles flanked by ring- and baluster-turned canted stiles over the shaped saddle seat on canted baluster- and ring-turned legs joined by a swelled H-stretcher, old green paint, Connecticut, 1790-1810, 40" h. (paint wear & loss) **3,450**

Windsor "fan-back" side chairs, a cupid's-bow shaped crestrail above six
swelled spindles flanked by baluster- and
ring-turned canted stiles & a pair of projecting back braces, the shaped saddle
seat raised on canted baluster-, ring- and
rod-turned legs joined by a swelled H-
stretcher, 18th c., pr. **3,100**
Windsor "fan-back" side chairs, painted,
shaped crest & shaped incised seats
above turned, splayed legs joined by medial stretchers, old black paint, New England, early 19th c., 35 7/8" h., pr. (im-
perfections) **1,035**
Windsor "fan-back" writing-arm arm-
chair, painted, a small shaped crestrail
above five tall slender spindles above the
U-form mid-rail continuing at one side to
form a wide writing surface w/two small
drawers beneath, numerous slender
swelled spindles from mid-rail to wide
shaped seat over a small drawer, raised
on canted bamboo-turned legs joined by
a bamboo-turned H-stretcher, old black
paint, New England, early 19th c.,
42 1/2" h. (restoration to drawers) **4,025**
Windsor low-back writing-arm armchair,
country-style, a curved shaped crestrail
continuing to form arms ending in knuckled armrests & a wide teardrop-shaped
writing surface at one side above a small
bowed drawer all raised on simple bamboo-turned spindles, a wide shaped
plank seat on canted bamboo-turned
legs joined by turned box stretchers,
overall worn black paint, Vermont, late
18th - early 19th c. **5,200**
Windsor "rabbit-ear" side chairs, painted
& decorated, a wide gently curved top
crestrail over two thin lower rails over four
short turned spindles above the seat all
between backswept tapering rabbit-ear
stiles, rounded thick plank seat on canted
bamboo-turned legs joined by box
stretchers, yellow painted ground w/sten-
ciled fruit & leaf designs in green & raw
umber w/gilt highlights on the crestrail,
dark striping, old repaint, New
England, ca. 1830-40, 33 1/2" h., set of 6
(imperfections) **3,220**
Windsor "rod-back" child's side chairs,
painted, a curved crestrail above seven
bamboo-turned spindles & a shaped saddle seat over bamboo-turned canted legs
joined by stretchers, painted dark red,
New England, ca. 1790, 28" h., pr. (minor
imperfections).. **633**
Windsor "rod-back" side chairs, painted
& grained, double crestrails over raked
incised spindles, incised saddle seat on
splayed, turned legs, old repaint w/gold
striping & brown graining on the seats,
New England, early 19th c., 33" h., pr.
(surface imperfections) **920**
Windsor "sack-back" armchair, grain-
painted, the wide bowed crestrail over
seven spindles continuing through the
medial rail that extends to form scrolled
arms on a spindle & a baluster- and ring-

Grain-painted Sack-back Windsor

turned canted arm support, wide oblong-
shaped saddle seat, on canted ring- and
baluster-turned legs joined by a swelled
H-stretcher, later rosewood graining &
yellow outlining, old surface, minor repairs, southern New England, late 18th
c., 38" h. (ILLUS.) **1,495**
Windsor "sack-back" armchair, painted,
the bowed crestrail above seven slender
spindles continuing through a medial rail
forming flat arms w/carved hand grips, a
spindle under each arm & canted balus-
ter- and ring-turned arm supports, wide
shaped seat on canted baluster-, ring-
and rod-turned legs joined by a swelled
H-stretcher, black repaint, late 18th c.,
38 1/4" h. (old break in bow crest).............. **2,860**

Early Sack-back Windsor Armchair

Windsor "sack-back" armchair, painted,
the bowed crestrail over seven spindles
continuing through the medial rail that extends to form narrow shaped arms over
spindle & baluster- and ring-turned canted
arm supports, wide oblong saddle seat, on
slightly splayed ring- and baluster-turned
tapering legs joined by a swelled H-
stretcher, old green paint over earlier
black, imperfections, southeastern New
England, ca. 1780, 38 1/2" h. (ILLUS.) **3,335**
Windsor "sack-back" armchair, painted,
the bowed crestrail over seven spindles
joining shaped arms w/vase- and ring-
turned canted supports, the shaped & incised seat on splayed vase- and ring-
turned legs joined by swelled H-form
stretchers, old worn black over green
paint, New England, ca. 1790, 39" h. (im-
perfections)... **14,950**

Windsor "sack-back" armchair, the arched crestrail on a U-form medial rail ending in shaped hand-holds on canted baluster-turned arm supports & nine spindles across the back, on a thick shaped seat w/incising & pommel on ring-turned splayed legs joined by swelled stretchers, old refinish, New England, 1790-1810, 38" h. **1,495**

Windsor "sack-back" armchair, the bowed crestrail above eight spindles continuing through a curved medial rail ending in shaped arms above a plain spindle & a baluster- and knob-turned canted arm support, wide shaped seat on canted ring-, baluster- and rod-turned legs joined by a knob-turned H-stretcher, painted salmon red & black over earlier green, New England, ca. 1780, 37 1/2" h. (loss to feet)... **1,840**

Windsor Sack-back Armchair

Windsor "sack-back" armchair, the bowed crestrail over seven spindles continuing through the U-form medial rail forming the arms w/scrolled hand grips above canted baluster- and ring-turned arm supports, shaped saddle seat on canted baluster- and ring-turned legs joined by a swelled H-stretcher, late 18th c. (ILLUS.)............................. **2,860**

Windsor "step-down" side chairs, shaped stepped crestrail over seven bamboo-turned spindles & raked stiles over the shaped seat, on splayed bamboo-turned legs joined by turned box stretchers, old refinish, later painted decoration, New England, ca. 1810, 33" h., set of 6 (some repairs)................................ **1,150**

Windsor "step-down" side chairs, the narrow stepped crestrail above backswept & tapering stiles & seven slender spindles above the wide shaped saddle seat, on canted swelled & turned legs joined by box stretchers, decorated w/the original yellow ground paint w/freehand gold & green decoration on the crestrail w/light brown front seatrail & leg decoration, highlighted w/brown striping, original surface, Farmington, Maine, ca. 1820, 35" h., set of 4 (very minor imperfections) **9,200**

Windsor-Style "arrow-back" side chairs, a flat crestrail between tapering rabbit ear stiles flanking the arrow slats above the shaped saddle seat, raised on canted bamboo-turned legs w/an arrow form

stretcher & plain turned side & back stretchers, old worn dark brown finish, branded label of L. & J.G. Stickley, "Stickley - Fayetteville - Syracuse," New York, early 20th c., 34 3/4" h., set of 6 .... **825**

Windsor-Style "birdcage" side chair, painted, double slender turned crestrails joined by three short spindles above seven long spindles between slightly canted stiles, shaped saddle seat on canted baluster- and ring-turned legs joined by a turned & swelled H-stretcher, worn yellow repaint, old but not period, laminated seat w/painted-over paper label, 35 1/2" h. **275**

Windsor-Style "bow-back" braced side chairs, painted, the bowed & molded backrail over eight slender rod-, knob- and baluster-turned spindles w/two matching brace spindles at the back, shaped saddle seat on canted baluster- and ring-turned legs joined by a swelled H-stretcher & a single swelled rear stretcher, original dark finish w/wear, labeled "Phoenix Chair Company," Sheboygan, Wisconsin," early 20th c., 36" h., set of 4 .... **495**

Windsor-Style "fan-back" armchair, a long serpentine crest raised on nine slender spindles above a curved medial rail continuing to form out-scrolled flat arms w/scroll handgrips above numerous slender swelled spindles, wide shaped saddle seat & canted baluster- and ring-turned arm supports & pair of back brace spindles to the base of the upper crest, canted baluster-, ring- and tapering rod-turned legs joined by a swelled H-stretcher, original dark finish, early 20th c., labeled "Simonds," 44 3/4" h. **330**

Windsor-Style "fan-back" side chair, maple, the arched crestrail w/lobed ears above nine spindles over a shaped plank seat, on ring- and baluster-turned legs joined by a swelled H-stretcher, late 19th - early 20th c., 39 1/4" h. **575**

Windsor-Style Rocking Chair

Windsor-Style rocking chair w/arms, oak, a narrow serpentine scroll-carved crestrail above a back w/eight tall baluster-turned spindles & stiles backed by turned brace spindles, shaped arms on baluster-turned spindles & canted arm supports, wide shaped seat, slightly canted baluster- and knob-turned legs joined by a turned H-stretcher, refinished, ca. 1900, 44" h. (ILLUS.) **450**

Chests &
Chests of Drawers

Apothecary chest, country-style, painted pine, the rectangular top w/a high three-quarters gallery above the tall case w/rows of 49 small square drawers w/small brass pulls above a single long drawer across the bottom, bootjack feet, old penciled or ink labels, original bluish grey paint, New England, early 19th c., 9 x 37 3/4", 57 1/2" h. **$24,200**

Victorian Oak Apothecary Chest

Apothecary chest, oak, a long rectangular top w/a molded edge over a case of drawers w/four small graduated drawers arranged in eight rows, each drawer w/cast-metal pulls, deep molded base, paneled ends, original finish, late 19th c., 22 x 76", 36" h. (ILLUS.) **2,400**

Apothecary chest, painted & decorated pine, a rectangular top on the dovetailed case enclosing 64 small square numbered drawers w/small knobs above a row of three deep drawers across the bottom, grain-painted overall in light brown on tan to resemble mahogany, probably New England, early 19th c., 14 1/4 x 43", 39" h. (imperfections) **10,925**

Apothecary chest, painted pine, a rectangular top above a short open compartment across the top of the tall case containing rows of 20 large drawers over a lower section of 16 graduated small drawers, various wood & brass knobs & remnants of labels, square nail construction, old worn brown & tan grained repaint, 19th c., 15 1/2 x 48 1/4", 66" h. **3,520**

Apothecary chest, painted poplar, a narrow rectangular top above a case w/21 graduated drawers w/turned wood knobs arranged as two rows of six above a row of five over a row of four all above long narrow hinged panel door at the base, old worn greenish black paint, late 19th c., 9 3/4 x 35", 26 1/4" h. (mismatched knobs, backboards replaced) **1,045**

Apothecary chest, poplar, a rectangular top above a case w/three stacks of six small rectangular drawers above a single long drawer across the bottom, square nail con-struction, old finish, 7 x 21", 24 1/2"h. (some damage on back boards) **1,045**

Early Apothecary-style Chest

Apothecary chest, stained wood, rectangular top slightly overhanging tall case of 48 square drawers w/turned wood pulls & beveled edges, sizes & lettering on most drawers, wire nail construction, bootjack ends, old black stain, probably used by a cobbler or saddle maker, 19th c., minor edge chips, 13 x 42 1/2", 62" h. (ILLUS.) .. **4,070**

Apothecary chest, pine & walnut, a rectangular walnut top over a case enclosing 32 small square drawers w/white porcelain knobs over two rows of 12 slightly larger drawers w/large porcelain knobs, wire nail construction, refinished, 14 1/4 x 36 3/4", 21 3/4" h. (top board added) **1,375**

Apothecary chest, hardwood w/old dark stain, a rectangular top above a tall case w/six rows of three small drawers each, simple bail pulls, a single paneled long drawer at the bottom flanked by two small square panels, molded apron & short square stile legs w/corner brackets, faint Chinese characters on each drawer, China, late 19th - early 20th c., 22 x 32", 40" h. **770**

Art Deco Cedar Chest

Art Deco cedar chest, red cedar-lined w/mixed rosed & mahogany exterior veneering, a low stepped crestrail centered by a built-in electric clock & w/small hanky drawers over the rectangular top lifting above a deep well, the front w/elaborate light & dark veneering w/incised angular line detail above a pair of long bottom drawers w/yellow Bakelite pulls, on square legs on a trestle base, refinished, ca. 1930s, 20 x 44", 30" h. (ILLUS.)...................... **400**

Art Deco Mahogany Chest of Drawers

Art Deco chest of drawers, mahogany, a rectangular raised-panel mahogany top over a case w/three long canted & zigzag drawers w/square patinated metal pulls, matching sides, the whole supported on tapered angular legs in a lighter shade of mahogany matching the band around the top, scratches, wear, ca. 1935, 20 x 30 1/2", 35 1/2" h. (ILLUS.) **1,840**

Art Deco chests of drawers, aluminum, rectangular top over a case w/three long drawers w/"porthole" handles & original salmon vinyl drawer facing, ca. 1930s, 19 x 43", 34" h., pr. **1,650**

Chippendale Child's Blanket Chest

Blanket chest, child's, Chippendale country-style, painted pine, six-board construction, a hinged rectangular top w/molded edges above a dovetailed case on a molded base w/scroll-cut bracket feet, original mustard yellow & brown grain paint to resemble exotic wood, probably New England, late 18th c., repairs, 12 x 20 1/2", 14" h. (ILLUS.) **1,850**

Blanket chest, country-style, painted & decorated pine, the rectangular hinged top w/molded edges opening to a well w/a lidded till, the dovetailed case w/a base molding above shaped dovetailed bracket feet, original brown over salmon squiggled band decoration w/black paint on the feet, script signature within the decoration on the front panel reads "James Mortlane, 1850," 17 1/2 x 38", 22 3/4" h. (wear, repairs to feet, hinges replaced)........................ **715**

Blanket chest, country-style, painted & decorated poplar, a rectangular hinged top w/molded edges opening to a deep well, dovetailed case w/applied moldings & a pair of narrow bottom drawers above the narrow curved apron & bracket feet, original red paint w/black & yellow trim & gold-stenciled decoration including foliage, flowers & "Jeremias Wever, 1859, Mf. by C.C.B.," drawer divider a cut-out small panel w/heart & circles in black over yellow, old round glass drawer pulls, replaced inlaid escutcheons, Soap Hollow, Pennsylvania, 22 3/4 x 49 1/2", 28 1/2" h. (minor repairs to feet, some edge damage & wear) **11,000**

Blanket chest, country-style, painted pine, a rectangular hinged top opening to a deep well in the plain case above a flush long drawer at the bottom, arched bootjack feet, old grey paint, possibly Long Island, 18th c., 19 x 39", 33 1/2" h................ **2,300**

Blanket chest, country-style, painted pine, a rectangular top w/molded edges opening to a well w/a lidded till, the front w/four small rectangular panels each centered by an applied finger-carved rectangle & all painted dark green, band of four plain square large panels painted deep red, the dividing stiles w/brown-grained yellow paint resembling curly maple, molded base band in dark green on bracket feet in dark red, found in Johnstown, Pennsylvania area, 21 x 48 1/2", 25" h. (minor edge damage, one front foot facing w/damage)... **4,400**

Blanket chest, country-style, painted pine, rectangular hinged lid w/molded edges opening to a well w/a lidded till & wrought-iron strap hinges & beartrap lock w/key, the dovetailed case decorated w/original vinegar graining faded to an olive & mustard yellow, molded base & black scroll-cut bracket feet, penciled inscription in lid, late 18th - early 19th c., 18 x 40", 22 3/4" h. **3,300**

Blanket chest, Federal country-style, painted pine, six-board construction, hinged rectangular top w/molded edges opening to a well w/lidded till above the dovetailed case w/metal ring end handles, molded base on shaped bracket feet, early red paint, New York State or Pennsylvania, early 19th c., 21 1/2 x 48", 24 1/2" h. (imperfections)... **1,093**

Blanket chest, painted & decorated, a rectangular hinged top w/applied molding opening to a well w/till & a dovetailed case w/a molded base & double-scallop apron & bracket feet, overall greyish blue paint decorated w/yellow, red & blue rosettes, pinwheels & geometric designs around a double scrolling foliate vine above three painted reserve-enclosed inscriptions "DUR - MUR - 1819," Indiana, 22 3/4 x 52 1/2", 27 3/4" h. **9,200**

Fancy Paint-decorated Blanket Chest

Blanket chest, painted & decorated pine, a rectangular hinged top w/original geometric patterned sponged painting to resemble inlay, the front w/similar sponging w/a large diamond panel within a rectangular panel, bail end handles, flat molded base, mid-19th c., 18 x 40", 20" h. (ILLUS.) **400**

Blanket chest, painted & decorated pine, the rectangular one-board hinged lid w/mortise & tenon breadboard ends opening to a well w/a till & two small drawers, dovetailed case painted on the front w/three arched panels w/bold stylized bouquets of flowers on a light ground in each panel, molded base on scroll-cut bracket feet, wrought-iron hinges w/replaced screws, several old repaints, Pennsylvania, late 18th - early 19th c., 18 3/4 x 49", 24 1/4" h. (lock missing, age cracks, edge damage) **1,375**

Blanket chest, painted & decorated poplar, Sonnenberg-type, rectangular hinged top w/molded edges opening to a well w/a lidded till, dovetailed base w/bottom flat molding, simple bracket feet, decorated w/original dark red paint ground w/yellow stripe-edged reserves w/polychrome floral designs on the front panel, yellow striping & a compass star in red & yellow on the top, 19th c., 19 3/8 x 37 5/8", 23 1/4" h. **10,450**

Paint-decorated Blanket Chest

Blanket chest, painted poplar, six-board dovetailed construction, the rectangular

top opening to a deep well on the dovetailed case w/a molded base & scroll-cut bracket feet, old salmon orange paint in a dappled brown pattern, probably Pennsylvania, early 19th c., paint worn, imperfections, 48" l., 24 1/2" h. (ILLUS.) **1,150**

Blanket chest, painted, six-board construction, the rectangular top w/molded edge above a well w/lidded till, on a molded base w/shaped bracket feet, original blue paint, Connecticut, late 18th c., 17 x 42", 23 1/2" h. (very minor paint wear) **2,070**

Blanket chest, pine, six-board construction, rectangular top over a case w/canted front & back, bound in wrought iron w/carrying end handles, old reddish brown paint, Mohawk-Hudson River Valley, New York, late 18th c., 16 x 48", 16" h. **460**

Blanket chest, poplar, a rectangular hinged lid w/molded edges opening to a deep well w/lidded till, dovetailed case w/molded base & scroll-cut bracket feet, old dark brown finish, early 19th c., 14 1/2 x 28 3/4", 18 1/2" h. (lid rehinged, till lid repaired) **660**

Blanket chest, country-style, painted & decorated, six-board construction, the rectangular molded & hinged top opening to a well w/a till & drawer above a dovetailed case w/a molded base on bracket feet, the exterior painted mustard yellow to resemble tiger stripe or bird's-eye maple, brass keyhole escutcheon, lettered in black on the back "G.H.C.," possibly New England, early 19th c., 14 3/4 x 32", 16 1/8" h. (repairs) **431**

Blanket chest, Chippendale country-style, painted & decorated pine, a hinged rectangular top w/molded edges & original bright-cut strap hinges opening to a well & till, the case decorated w/tombstone & diamond panels, flowers & dated "1771," the sides similarly painted, the molded base below hung w/a central pendant on straight bracket feet, Pennsylvania, 22 x 51", 20" h. (top decoration worn, feet shortened) **1,265**

Blanket chest, country-style, painted & decorated poplar, rectangular top w/molded edges & wrought-iron strap hinges opening to a well w/lidded till, the dovetailed case w/a molded base & scroll-cut bracket feet, decorated w/original red graining, early 19th c., 19 1/2 x 45", 23" h. (some foot repair) **1,210**

Blanket chest, country-style, painted & decorated pine, six-board dovetailed construction, the rectangular hinged top w/molded edges opening to a well w/a lidded till, base molding, raised on short, heavy ring- and knob-turned legs, original red vinegar graining on a yellow ground, feet in black, lock w/key, 19th c., 19 3/4 x 43 1/2", 24 1/2" h. **935**

Blanket chest, country-style, painted pine, six-board dovetailed construction, the rectangular top w/molded edge hinged above a deep well above a molded base raised on bracket feet, original red paint, New England, ca. 1780, 19 x 43 3/4", 26" h. (minor imperfections) **690**

Blanket chest, Chippendale country-style, walnut, a rectangular hinged lid w/molded edges opening to a well w/till, dovetailed case w/original brass butterfly keyhole escutcheon, a mid-molding above a lower row of three drawers each w/butterfly pulls above the molded base on ogee bracket feet, wrought-iron bear-trap lock, mellow finish, Pennsylvania, attributed to Chester County, late 18th - early 19th c., 24 1/4 x 55", 29" h. (slight warp in lid) **4,950**

Blanket chest, country-style, painted & decorated poplar, a rectangular lid w/molded edges opening to a well w/a lidded till w/secret compartment over a dovetailed case w/two small drawers at the bottom above a base molding & scroll-cut bracket feet, the sides decorated w/original brown graining & green painted trim & stenciled decoration in gold, white & green including fruit, flowers, lyres & foliage w/"D.R. 1857," similar to the Soap Hollow School, Pennsylvania, 20 3/4 x 46 3/4", 29 1/2" h. (back feet repaired, other minor repair) **3,025**

Early Massachusetts Blanket Chest

Blanket chest, painted pine, rectangular hinged top w/molded edges opening to a well w/a lidded, molded till, a single long drawer across the bottom w/old replaced pressed glass pulls, molded base band on shaped bracket feet, old green over old red paint, paint wear on top, western Massachusetts, 18th c., 17 x 45", 31 5/8" h. (ILLUS.) **2,645**

Blanket chest, country-style, painted & decorated six-board style, the rectangular hinges opening to a deep well, solid board ends w/high arched bootjack legs, overall putty-grained finish in quarter-round and half-round designs, New England, 19th c., 39" l. **1,700**

Carpenter's chest, pine, thick rectangular hinged lid opening to a fitted interior, dovetailed case w/thick top & base molding, rope end handles, refinished, 19th c., 38" l. (edge damage, age cracks) **330**

Chippendale blanket chest, walnut, rectangular hinged top w/molded edges opening to a well w/lidded till & two secret drawers, the dovetailed case w/two bottom drawers w/simple bail pulls, molded base on ogee bracket feet, old finish, original brasses, wrought-iron strap hinges, Pennsylvania, late 18th c., 23 1/2 x 51 1/2", 28" h. (lock missing, minor age cracks in top, small repairs to feet) **7,260**

Chippendale "block-front" chest of drawers, mahogany, the rectangular thumbmolded top w/a double-blocked front edge above a conforming case of four long blocked drawers on a molded base, raised on scroll-cut bracket feet, old refinish, replaced butterfly brasses, Boston, 1750-90, 19 1/4 x 33", 29 1/4" h. (rear foot missing) **46,000**

Chippendale "Block-front" Chest

Chippendale "block-front" chest of drawers, mahogany, the rectangular top w/serpentine front w/molded edge overhanging a conforming cockbeaded case w/four graduated block-front drawers, molded base, pointed central apron drop & shaped bracket feet, old but not original brasses, restored, Boston, ca. 1770, 19 x 33", 30" h. (ILLUS.) **19,550**

Chippendale "bow-front" chest of drawers, mahogany, the rectangular top w/molded edges & bowed front overhanging a conforming case w/four long graduated cockbeaded drawers w/butterfly brasses & keyhole escutcheons, molded base on short cabriole legs w/ball-and-claw feet & scroll-curved brackets, Massachusetts, ca. 1780, 22 x 37 3/4", 34 1/2" h. (brasses replaced, imperfections) **5,463**

Chippendale Birch Chest of Drawers

Chippendale chest of drawers, birch, rectangular top slightly overhanging a case w/four long graduated cockbeaded drawers w/butterfly pulls & keyhole escutcheons, molded base on tall scroll-cut bracket feet, old refinish, replaced brasses, minor imperfections, Massachusetts, ca. 1770-80, 17 1/4 x 36", 34" h. (ILLUS.) **6,785**

Cherry Chippendale Chest of Drawers

Chippendale chest of drawers, cherry, a rectangular top w/molded edge widely overhanging a case w/four long graduated beaded drawers w/simple bail pulls, molded base on scroll-cut bracket feet, appears to retain original brasses, two foot facings replaced, New England, probably Connecticut, ca. 1790, 20 1/4 x 31", 31 1/2" h. (ILLUS.) **4,025**

Fine Chippendale Chest of Drawers

Chippendale chest of drawers, cherry, a rectangular top w/molded edges & serpentine front above a conforming case w/four long graduated cockbeaded drawers w/butterfly pulls & keyhole escutcheons, molded base on scroll-cut ogee bracket feet, Hartford, Connecticut, ca. 1770-80, 22 1/2 x 34", 32 1/2" h. (ILLUS.) **17,250**

Chippendale chest of drawers, cherry, rectangular top w/deep flaring molded cornice above a case w/a pair of short thumb-molded drawers over four long graduated thumb-molded drawers all w/butterfly brasses & keyhole escutcheons, molded base on tall scroll-cut ogee feet, old refinish, probably Rhode Island, ca. 1770-80, 18 1/2 x 36 1/2", 42" h. (replaced brasses, restoration) **2,415**

Mahogany Chippendale Chest

Chippendale chest of drawers, mahogany, the rectangular molded top above a case of four long graduated thumb-molded drawers w/butterfly pulls & keyhole escutcheons on a molded base w/carved claw-and-ball front feet & ogee bracket rear feet, old replaced brasses, refinished, imperfections, possibly Pennsylvania, ca. 1760-80, 21 x 36", 32 1/2" h. (ILLUS.)..................................... **9,200**

Chippendale chest of drawers, walnut, rectangular top w/molded edges above a pair of molded overlapping drawers above three long overlapping graduated drawers all w/simple bail pulls & brass keyhole escutcheons, molded base on ogee bracket feet w/scroll-cut returns, the front corners w/reeded quarter columns, late 18th c., 20 3/4 x 37", 37 1/2" h. (old worn finish, feet & brasses replaced, other restoration)... **3,025**

Chippendale chest-on-chest, cherry, two-part construction: the upper section w/a deep flared molded cornice above a case w/a row of three small drawers over a pair of drawers above three long thumb-molded graduated drawers all w/butterfly pulls & keyhole escutcheons; the lower section w/a mid-molding above a case w/three long graduated drawers, both cases flanked by fluted quarter columns, on a molded base w/ogee bracket feet, Delaware River Valley, ca 1770-90, 20 1/2 x 40", 78 3/4" h. (replaced brasses, restoration, imperfections).................. **12,650**

Chippendale chest-on-chest, maple, two-part construction: the upper section w/a rectangular top & deep cove molding above a case of five long graduated drawers w/simple bail pulls; lower section w/a mid-molding above a slightly stepped-out case of four long graduated drawers w/simple bail pulls, brass oval keyhole escutcheons, base molding above the apron w/a carved central drop & scroll-carved bracket feet, old pulls, refinished, possibly Massachusetts or New Hampshire, ca. 1760-80, 18 1/2 x 36", 76" h. (minor repairs) **14,950**

Chippendale chest-on-chest, maple, two-part construction: the upper section w/a rectangular top w/a flaring coved cornice above a pair of thumb-molded drawers over a stack of four long graduated thumb-molded drawers; the lower section w/a mid-molding over four long graduated thumb-molded drawers, probably original brass butterfly pulls & keyhole escutcheons, molded base, tall shaped bracket feet, old refinish, possibly Torrington, Connecticut, ca. 1760-80, 17 1/4 x 36", 71" h. (imperfections)........... **14,950**

Chippendale country-style blanket chest, painted & decorated poplar, rectangular hinged top w/molded edges opening to a well w/a lidded till & two secret drawers, the dovetailed case w/a molded base on ogee bracket feet, original stylized painted decoration w/green swirls & a diagonal wavy band across the front on a white ground, red shows as ground under lip & small places, dark green feet, good wear, Pennsylvania, late 18th - early 19th c., 21 x 49 1/4", 28" h. **6,050**

Country Chippendale Blanket Chest

Chippendale country-style blanket chest, pine, a rectangular hinged top w/molded edges opening to a deep well w/a lidded till above the dovetailed case, two cockbeaded drawers at the bottom above a base molded & scroll-cut bracket feet, original brass pulls, old refinish, ca. 1775, 21 x 46", 24" h. (ILLUS.)................... **1,500**

Chippendale country-style chest of drawers, maple & birch, a rectangular top slightly overhanging a case of four long reverse-graduated drawers w/incised beading & diamond inlaid escutcheons, molded base on tall bracket feet, replaced oval brass pulls, varnish over old red wash, New England, ca. 1790, 17 x 40", 38 3/4" h. (minor restoration) **2,185**

Chippendale country-style chest of drawers, maple, rectangular top w/narrow molded cornice above a case of five long graduated thumb-molded drawers, base molding on scroll-cut bracket feet & a central drop pendant, refinished, New England, ca. 1780, 17 x 36 1/2", 41 1/2" h. (replaced bail pulls, repairs)....... **1,610**

Chippendale country-style chest of drawers, painted & decorated pine & curly maple, rectangular top w/deep coved cornice above a case w/four long overlapping dovetailed drawers w/simple bail pulls, one-board ends, scroll-cut bracket feet, original red flame graining, backboards signed "L.L. 1807 - P.P.H.G.—(grained) 1847," replaced brasses, 22 x 39 1/4", 42 1/2" h. **6,050**

Chippendale country-style chest of drawers, tiger stripe maple, rectangular

top w/molded edge above a case of four long thumb-molded graduated drawers w/butterfly pulls, molded base on dovetailed bracket feet, old refinish, southern New England, ca. 1780, 38 1/2" h. (replaced brasses, minor imperfections) **2,990**

Chippendale country-style tall chest of drawers, cherry, a rectangular top w/a flaring coved cornice above a case of six beaded long graduated drawers w/simple turned wood knobs & brass keyhole escutcheons, molded base on bracket feet, old refinish, possibly Worcester County, Massachusetts, ca. 1790, 17 x 37 1/4", 53 1/4" h. (replaced pulls)... **11,500**

Chippendale country-style tall chest of drawers, cherry & maple, the rectangular top w/a deep coved cornice above a case w/five long graduated thumb-molded drawers, base molding on tall bracket feet, old refinish, New England, ca. 1780, 19 3/4 x 39 1/2", 49" h. (replaced oval brasses & keyhole escutcheons, imperfections) **3,105**

Connecticut Chippendale Chest

Chippendale "serpentine-front" chest of drawers, cherry, rectangular top w/a molded edge & serpentine front overhanging a case of four long graduated beaded drawers w/oval pulls flanked by fluted quarter-columns, the molded base on heavy ogee scroll-cut bracket feet, repair to front left foot & both rear feet, Connecticut, ca. 1780, 23 x 41", 37 3/4" h. (ILLUS.)....................................... **6,325**

Chippendale "serpentine-front" chest of drawers, mahogany, the rectangular top w/serpentine sides & molded edges overhanging a conforming case w/three long cockbeaded graduated drawers w/replaced butterfly brasses & keyhole escutcheons, molded base on four scroll-cut short cabriole legs ending in ball-and claw feet, Boston, ca. 1760-80, old refinish, 20 x 36", 32 1/4" h. **34,500**

Chippendale tall chest of drawers, cherry, a rectangular top w/a deep flaring stepped cornice above a case w/seven long graduated thumb-molded drawers w/simple bail pulls & oval keyhole escutcheons, molded base on tall bracket feet, old red-stained finish, Rhode Island, late 18th c., 19 1/2 x 36 3/4", 62 1/2" h. (minor imperfections) **7,475**

Chippendale tall chest of drawers, cherry & maple, a rectangular top above a deep coved cornice over a case w/a top central deep fan-carved drawer flanked by a stack of two small drawers on each side above six long graduated drawers, molded base on tall scroll-cut bracket feet, oval brass pulls appear to be original, old finish, probably Connecticut, 18th c., added casters, 18 x 37", 62 3/4" h. (minor restoration)... **46,000**

Chippendale tall chest of drawers, cherry, rectangular top w/deep flaring cornice above a row of three small drawers over a pair of drawers above five long graduated cockbeaded drawers, reeded quarter-columns down the front sides, molded base, scroll-cut tall ogee bracket feet, old replaced round brass pulls in original holes, attributed to New Jersey, late 18th - early 19th c., old refinish, 22 x 42 3/8", 5' 9 1/4" h. (minor glued breaks in some foot facings, small chips on drawer edges) **10,725**

Chippendale tall chest of drawers, cherry, rectangular top w/deep molded cornice above a case w/six long graduated thumb-molded drawers, molded base on tall scroll-cut bracket feet, round brass pulls, New England, 1770-80, 19 1/2 x 38 1/2", 56" h. **6,900**

Chippendale Tall Chest of Drawers

Chippendale tall chest of drawers, maple, a rectangular top w/a coved cornice above a case of six long thumb-molded drawers w/butterfly pulls & keyhole escutcheons, molded base above scroll-carved apron w/central drop & tall bracket feet, original brasses, refinished, New Hampshire, late 18th c., 18 x 36 3/4", 58" h. (ILLUS.)... **6,613**

Chippendale tall chest of drawers, maple, a rectangular top w/a narrow cornice above a case w/a pair of drawers above four long graduated drawers all w/butterfly brasses & keyhole escutcheons, molded base on scroll-cut tall bracket feet, wood w/some curl & old brown finish, late 18th c. **9,900**

Chippendale tall chest of drawers, maple, a rectangular top w/deep molded coved cornice above a pair of thumb-molded drawers over four long graduated thumb-molded drawers all w/butterfly pulls & keyhole escutcheons, base molding on scroll-cut bracket feet, old refinish, most brasses appear original, probably Massachusetts, ca. 1770-80, 18 x 36 3/4", 44 1/2" h. **4,025**

Chippendale tall chest of drawers, maple, the rectangular top w/a deep flaring molded cornice above a case w/a pair of drawers over five long thumb-molded drawers all w/butterfly brasses & keyhole escutcheons, molded base on high scroll-cut bracket feet & central pendant, original brasses, old refinish, Connecticut, ca. 1760-80, 16 1/2 x 36", 58" h. (very minor imperfections)............... **9,200**

Chippendale tall chest of drawers, tiger stripe maple, rectangular top above a deep flaring stepped cornice over a case w/a pair of drawers above a stack of five long graduated thumb-molded drawers w/simple bail pulls & brass keyhole escutcheons, molded base raised on shaped bracket feet, original brasses, refinished, southwestern Massachusetts or Rhode Island, late 18th c., 19 1/4 x 38", 53" h. (very minor imperfections)............... **8,050**

Chippendale tall chest of drawers, tiger stripe maple, rectangular top w/a deep stepped cornice above a case of seven long graduated thumb-molded drawers w/replaced butterfly brasses, refinished, southeastern New England, ca. 1780, 22 x 36", 64" h. (restored) **3,220**

Chippendale tall chest of drawers, walnut, a rectangular top w/molded flaring cornice above a case w/a row of three small drawers over a pair of drawers above four long graduated drawers all w/oval brasses, molded base on scroll-cut bracket feet, old finish, late 18th - early 19th c., 24 3/8 x 43", 58 5/8" h. (replaced brasses, some corner repair on upper drawer, some edge damage) **4,400**

Tall Chippendale Chest over Drawers

Chippendale tall chest over drawers, painted pine, a rectangular molded hinged top opening to a deep well in a case w/two false long drawer fronts over four long working thumb-molded graduated drawers, molded base on tall bracket feet, simple bail brasses appear to be original, minor imperfections, painted red, New England, late 18th c., 18 x 36", 52 1/2" h. (ILLUS.)... **4,888**

Chippendale-Style Blanket Chest

Chippendale-Style blanket chest, pine, rectangular hinged top opening to a deep well over a single long drawer w/turned wood knobs, the front centered by a carved fan, dovetail & square nail construction, single-board sides, bracket feet, refinished, ca. 1900, 17 x 40", 28" h. (ILLUS.).. **450**

Chippendale-Style chest of drawers, mahogany, rectangular top w/molded edges above a conforming case fitted w/four long graduated drawers flanked by fluted chamfered corners over a molded base, on ball-and-claw feet w/scroll-carved returns, 20th c., 21 1/2 x 37 1/2", 35" h. **1,725**

Chippendale-Style Serpentine Chest

Chippendale-Style "serpentine-front" chest of drawers, mahogany & mahogany veneer, the rectangular molded top w/serpentine front edge above a conforming case w/four long graduated cockbeaded drawers w/oval brass pulls & keyhole escutcheons, molded base on scroll-cut ogee bracket feet, early 20th c. w/some old parts, 21 x 38", 33 1/2" h. (ILLUS.) **770**

Chippendale-Style "serpentine-front" chest of drawers, mahogany, the rectangular top & serpentine front w/canted corners above a conforming case w/four long graduated cockbeaded drawers flanked by stop-fluted canted corners, on ogee bracket feet, in the Philadelphia manner, 20th c., 34 3/4" h. **2,070**

Fine Chippedale-Style Tall Chest

Chippendale-Style tall chest of drawers, carved mahogany, a rectangular top w/a gadrooned cornice above a case w/a pair of drawers carved w/grotesque masks & scrolls above two stacks of four small, deep leafy scroll-carved drawers w/pierced butterfly pulls flanked by a central stack of four concave-fronted drawers, the top one w/carved scrolls & a fanned design, gadrooned base band on four leaf-carved cabriole legs ending in square pad feet, R.J. Horner Co., late 19th c. (ILLUS.)... **1,000**

Classical (American Empire) country-style chest of drawers, birch, a high crestboard w/a flat top & scroll-cut & rounded corners above a pair of small handkerchief drawers w/small replaced round brasses, the rectangular top above a single long, deep stepped-out drawer above ring-, rod- and block-turned columns flanking three long setback drawers, ring-turned tapering legs w/ball feet, replaced butterfly brasses, old mellow refinishing, first half 19th c., 17 3/4 x 37", overall 48 1/4" h... **935**

Classical Mahogany Butler's Chest

Classical butler's chest, mahogany & mahogany veneer, a rectangular black marble top w/rounded front corners above an ogee-fronted false drawer folding down to form a writing surface & enclosing a fitted interior above three long working drawers w/original panel-cut glass pulls, deep molded base on corner block feet, French polish finish, ca. 1840, 18 x 42", 38" h. (ILLUS.).. **1,800**

Classical Mahogany Chest of Drawers

Classical chest of drawers, carved mahogany & mahogany veneer, a flat-topped scroll-ended top backboard above a row of three short drawers stepped back on the rectangular top over a pair of overhanging deep drawers above three long drawers flanked by columns w/a carved pineapple over leaf bands & a spiral-carved section, molded conforming base on heavy knob-, ring- and baluster-turned tapering legs, replaced early glass pulls, refinished, imperfections, North Shore Massachusetts, ca. 1825, 22 x 42 3/4", 45" h. (ILLUS.).. **978**

Paw-footed Classical Chest

Classical chest of drawers, carved mahogany & mahogany veneer, the rectangular top over a long drawer overhanging a case w/three long drawers flanked by carved free-standing columns on a molded base, simple turned wooden knobs, acanthus-carved heavy paw front feet & turned rear feet, old refinish, minor imperfections, possibly Pennsylvania, ca. 1825, 23 1/2 x 45 1/2", 47" h. (ILLUS.) **920**

Classical chest of drawers, curly maple & cherry, a rectangular cherry top over a cherry frame w/a long deep curly maple drawer flanked by inlaid curly maple side reserves & overhanging three long grad-

uated curly maple lower drawers flanked by half-round ring- and spiral-twist-turned columns, ring- and baluster-turned legs w/button feet, replaced round brasses w/rings, signed on back "Jacob Kinney - Weston, Ohio," first half 19th c., 21 3/4 x 43 3/4", 49 7/8" h. (age cracks in top, refinished) **1,375**

Classical Stenciled Chest of Drawers

Classical chest of drawers w/mirror, mahogany & stenciled mahogany veneer, a rectangular black-painted & foliate-stenciled mirror frame supported between S-scroll acanthus-carved supports above the stepped-back top w/three small drawers w/stenciled trim above the projecting top over a long convex top drawer w/central fruit cluster stenciling projecting above two long drawers w/star-inlaid wood drawer pulls flanked by free-standing stencil-decorated columns continuing to knob-turned feet, minor imperfections, possibly New York, ca. 1825, 22 1/2 x 36 1/2", 63" h. (ILLUS.) **2,990**

Classical Child's Chest of Drawers

Classical child's country-style chest of drawers, painted & decorated, the rectangular top fitted w/an arched crestboard w/a pair of small handkerchief drawers above a long deep drawer projecting over two long drawers flanked by serpentine side pilasters & C-scroll front feet, decorated overall w/original brown & red painted w/gold & olive band linear trim, original turned wood pulls, New England, 1835-45, very minor surface imperfections, 14 1/8 x 22", 27 1/4" h. (ILLUS.).......... **748**

Classical country-style chest of drawers, cherry & poplar w/old cherry red finish, a rectangular top above a pair of deep overhanging drawers over ring-turned columns flanking a lower case w/three long graduated drawers, simple turned wood pulls, on ring- and knob-turned feet, ca. 1840, 21 x 43 1/8", 47 1/4" h. **605**

Classical country-style chest of drawers, cherry, rectangular top above a pair of deep beaded drawers above three long graduated beaded drawers, all w/simple turned wood knobs, scalloped apron, ring- and baluster-turned short legs w/knob feet, paneled sides, first half 19th c., 19 1/4 x 40 1/2", 48" h. (minor damage to drawer edges) **935**

Classical Country-style Chest

Classical country-style chest of drawers, figured maple & walnut, a low scroll-end-ed backsplash on the rectangular top overhanging a pair of narrow drawers flanked by projecting blocks above a stack of three reverse-graduated long drawers w/Rockingham glazed pottery knobs, scalloped corner brackets on base, refinished, ca. 1840-50, 18 x 38", 45" h. (ILLUS.).. **450**

Classical country-style chest of drawers, painted & decorated birch & maple, a tall rectangular backboard w/molded edges above the rectangular top over a stepped-out long drawer w/turned wood knobs above three long set-back drawers w/wood knobs flanked by engaged columns raised on baluster- and ring-turned legs w/ball feet, original red paint & faux graining on the drawers simulating mahogany, original pulls, Barre, Vermont area, ca. 1830s, 19 1/4 x 43", 39 1/2" h. ... **2,415**

Classical country-style chest of drawers, tiger stripe maple, a scroll-cut crestrail w/block ends on the rectangular top over a case w/three small shallow projecting drawers over a long deep drawer above three long graduated drawers all

w/turned wood knobs, short turned legs w/knob feet, paneled ends, old finish, probably Pennsylvania, ca. 1830, 19 1/2 x 46", 49 1/2" h. **2,185**

Curly Maple Classical Tall Chest

Classical country-style tall chest of drawers, curly maple, a rectangular top over a pair of drawers over four long graduated drawers flanked by baluster- and ring-turned free-standing columns, molded base on heavy turned ovoid front feet on casters, first half 19th c. (ILLUS.)...... **715**

Classical Revival Mirrored Chest

Classical Revival chest of drawers, mahogany & mahogany veneer, princess-style, the tall mirrored back composed of a oblong central beveled mirror w/a palmette-carved finial & scroll-topped support posts flanked by shorter hinged oblong beveled mirrors w/scroll-carved outer ears over scroll-carved bands on the drop-well base w/a curve-fronted small drawer on each side of the well over two long serpentine-front drawers, all w/simple brass bail pulls, serpentine apron w/a small scroll-carved center drop raised on short cabriole front legs on casters, refinished, ca. 1910, 20 x 42", 6' 4" h. (ILLUS.) **1,200**

Classical Tall Chest of Drawers

Classical tall chest of drawers, tiger stripe maple & cherry, the rectangular top above a case w/a pair of narrow cockbeaded drawers above a long deep drawer w/a walnut-veneered border flanked by sawtooth-carved panels slightly projecting above four long graduated cockbeaded drawers flanked by ring- and rod-turned engaged columns continuing to turned feet, simple turned wood pulls, old refinish, minor imperfections, Pennsylvania or Ohio, ca. 1825, 22 x 42 3/4", 56" h. (ILLUS.) **2,760**

Tall Bird's-eye Maple Lingerie Chest

Colonial Revival tall lingerie chest of drawers, bird's-eye maple veneer, a large arched crescent-form mirror swiveling between slender columnar supports w/urn finials above the rectangular top w/serpentine edges over a conforming serpentine case w/two small drawers beside a small cupboard door above four long graduated drawers all w/pierced brass pulls, serpentine apron & simple short cabriole front legs, early 20th c., 27" w., 5' 9" h. (ILLUS.) **1,400**

Danish Modern chest of drawers, walnut & cherry, two-part construction: the upper section w/a rectangular top above a pair

Danish Modern Chest of Drawers

of flat cupboard doors opening to divided compartments & raised above the lower section; the lower section w/a rectangular top over a stack of four flat long drawers framed by outset turned legs joined by curved cross braces, Scandinavia, ca. 1960, wear, 23 x 44", 48" h. (ILLUS.) **517**

Early Pennsylvania Dower Chest

Dower chest, painted & decorated, a rectangular top w/molded edges opening to a well, the front decorated w/a large arch-topped rectangular panel centered by a large spread-winged eagle w/shield & banner in its beak, pinwheels, compass stars & tulips around the bird, in dark shades of umber, black, red & yellow within a red & white border, the background w/a finely sponged black & brown ground, black base molding & scroll-cut bracket feet, light surface cleaning, several spurs replaced, Center County, Pennsylvania, ca. 1814 (ILLUS.) **12,500**

Dower chest, painted & decorated pine, the rectangular hinged white pine top w/molded edge & strap hinges opens to a well in the dovetailed case, molded base w/worn bracket feet, the front decorated w/three painted arches each w/a small urn w/a large bouquet of flowers in blue, red, yellow & brown on a white ground outlined in red, paint appears original, attributed to Christian Selzer, Lebanon County, Pennsylvania, late 18th c., 22 1/4 x 51 1/2", 23" h. (height loss, other imperfections)... **6,325**

Dower chest, painted poplar, rectangular hinged top w/molded edges opening to an interior w/a till, dovetailed case w/a lower molding over two thumb-molded drawers on a molded base w/bracket feet, old light blue paint, replaced brasses, Pennsylvania, ca. 1780, 22 x 48", 26 1/2" h. (minor imperfections)................. **1,725**

Dower chest, walnut, a rectangular hinged top w/molded edge opening to a well w/till, dovetailed case above a heavy molding over a pair of base drawers above a molded base on scroll-cut bracket feet, old refinish, replaced brass pulls, Berks County, Pennsylvania, 1780s, 23 1/4 x 50 3/4", 31" h. (imperfections)...... **1,380**

Ornate Tall Rococo Revival Chest

Early 20th century tall chest of drawers, mahogany veneer, Rococo Revival style, two-piece construction: an oblong serpentine-sided beveled mirror in a conforming frame w/a scroll-carved crest swiveling between two S-scroll carved uprights on the rectangular lift-off molded top w/rounded corners above a tall bombé case w/a pair of narrow top drawers w/two pairs of small wood pulls each above four long graduated drawers w/two pairs of small wood knobs each, serpentine scroll-carved apron & cabriole legs ending in scroll & peg feet on casters, ca. 1900 (ILLUS.) **1,815**

Fine Late Victorian Tall Chest

Early 20th century tall chest of drawers, mahogany veneer, Rococo-style w/a large cartouche-form beveled mirror in a molded conforming frame w/an ornate scroll-carved crest & tilting between ornate scroll-carved S-form uprights on the

rectangular molded top w/serpentine front above a conforming case w/two curved-front small upper drawers flanking a wide curved-front door above three conforming long drawers all w/scroll brass pulls, scroll-carved apron w/central cartouche in front, raised on scroll-carved legs w/paw feet on casters, ca. 1890-1900 (ILLUS.)... **1,750**

Fine Federal "Bow-front" Chest

Federal "bow-front" chest of drawers, cherry & bird's-eye maple veneer, a rectangular top w/bowed front over a case of four long graduated cockbeaded drawers outlined in cross-banded mahogany around bird's-eye maple, scalloped apron & tall slender French feet, replaced oval brasses, old surface w/minor veneer patching, attributed to Eliphalet Briggs, Keene, New Hampshire, ca. 1810, 20 1/2 x 39 3/4", 38 1/2" h. (ILLUS.) **9,775**

Federal "Bow-front" Chest of Drawers

Federal "bow-front" chest of drawers, mahogany, a rectangular top w/molded edges & a bowed front above a conforming case w/four long graduated cockbeaded drawers w/oval pulls, molded base on slightly canted bracket feet, patches & repairs to feet, New England, ca. 1795, 24 x 42", 33 1/2" h. (ILLUS.).......................... **3,737**
Federal "bow-front" chest of drawers, mahogany & bird's-eye maple veneer, the rectangular top w/bowed front & inlaid edge above a conforming case w/four long cockbeaded drawers veneered w/bird's-eye maple surrounded by cross-banded mahogany veneer, scroll-cut apron continuing into tall curved French feet, oval brasses appear original, old refinish, probably New Hampshire, early 19th c., 22 x 39 3/4", 37" h. (minor imperfections)..... **9,775**
Federal "bow-front" chest of drawers, mahogany, rectangular top w/a curved front edge overhanging a conforming case of four long cockbeaded graduated drawers w/round brasses, valanced skirt & tall

slender flaring French feet, brasses appear to be original, old refinish, probably Massachusetts, ca. 1800, 19 3/4 x 40", 38 1/2" h. (imperfections) **3,738**

Federal "bow-front" chest of drawers, cherry, a rectangular top w/bowed front above a conforming case w/four long cockbeaded graduated drawers w/oval brasses & keyhole escutcheons, veneered cyma-curved front apron, tall French feet, original brasses, old refinish, New England, early 19th c., 21 3/8 x 41 1/2", 37" h. (surface imperfections) **2,875**

Federal Bird's-eye Maple Chest

Federal chest of drawers, birch & bird's-eye maple veneer, a rectangular top w/reeded edges above a case w/four long reverse-graduated beaded drawers w/oval pulls & brass keyhole escutcheons, flat base, raised on baluster- and ring-turned legs w/peg feet, brasses appear to be original, old refinish, imperfections, New England, 1815-25, 19 x 40 1/2", 38" h. (ILLUS.) **2,415**

Federal Cherry Chest of Drawers

Federal chest of drawers, cherry, the rectangular top slightly overhanging a case w/four long graduated cockbeaded drawers w/round brass pulls & brass keyhole escutcheons, serpentine apron continuing into tall French feet, old pulls, old finish, southeastern New England, ca. 1800-10, 19 x 36 3/4", 36 1/2" h. (ILLUS.) **4,600**

Federal Curly Maple Chest of Drawers

Federal chest of drawers, curly maple & curly maple veneer, a rectangular top above a case of four long graduated cockbeaded drawers w/oval pulls, valanced apron w/center blocked drop, tall slender French feet, brasses appear to be original, old finish, imperfections, southern New England, ca. 1790, 18 x 39 3/4" h., 37" h. (ILLUS.) **4,888**

Federal chest of drawers, inlaid cherry, rectangular top w/string inlaid edges overhanging a case w/four long graduated drawers w/mahogany veneer bordered by stringing & interrupted line inlay, on tall splayed French feet joined by an inlaid valanced skirt, apparently original oval brasses, old refinish, possibly Connecticut, ca. 1800, 18 3/4 x 39 1/4", 36 3/4" h. (minor imperfections) **5,750**

Federal chest of drawers, inlaid cherry, rectangular top w/string-inlaid edges slightly overhanging a case w/four long graduated cockbeaded drawers above a double-scallop apron & flaring slender French feet, New England, ca. 1800, 19 3/4 x 42", 38" h (replaced oval brasses, refinished) **2,990**

Federal chest of drawers, mahogany & figured mahogany veneer, the rectangular top over a case of four cockbeaded long graduated drawers & replaced oval brasses & keyhole escutcheons, deeply scalloped apron & tall flaring French feet, early 19th c., 20 x 42 1/2", 41" h. (age cracks in top & ends, minor veneer repair) **2,750**

Federal chest of drawers, mahogany & mahogany veneer, a rectangular top w/reeded edges above a case of four cockbeaded long graduated drawers w/pairs of original oval brass pulls, deeply scalloped apron raised on tall French feet, early 19th c., 20 3/8 x 41 3/4", 37 3/4" h. (age cracks in top, refinished, restorations) **1,375**

Federal chest of drawers, painted cherry, rectangular top w/ovolo corners above a case of four long cockbeaded graduated drawers w/oval brass pulls & keyhole escutcheons flanked by quarter-engaged baluster- and ring-turned reeded posts continuing to turned legs, old red-painted surface, New England, ca. 1815-20 (replaced brasses, minor imperfections) **3,220**

Federal chest of drawers, wavy birch, a rectangular top w/beaded edges slightly overhanging the case w/four long beaded drawers w/simple bail pulls & brass keyhole escutcheons, shaped apron above tall tapering French feet, old refinish w/remnants of red paint, original brasses, New Hampshire, early 19th c., 18 x 39 1/2", 38" h. (minor imperfections).. **1,840**

Federal Mahogany Chest-on-Chest

Federal chest-on-chest, inlaid mahogany & mahogany veneer, two-part construction: the upper section w/a rectangular top & widely flaring stepped cornice over a wide line-inlaid frieze band above a pair of drawers over three long graduated drawers w/inlaid ivory diamond keyhole escutcheons & simple turned wood pulls; the lower section w/a mid-molding over a case w/three long graduated drawers matching upper drawers, curved apron & high simple bracket feet, old finish w/original painted side decoration, section of side molding missing, several veneer chips & puttied repairs, late 18th - early 19th c., 24 x 44", 80" h. (ILLUS.)............... **3,740**

Federal country-style chest of drawers, birch & flame-grained birch, a rectangular top w/reeded edges above a case w/four long flame birch drawers w/beaded edging & simple turned wood pulls, on ring- and baluster-turned legs, refinished, early 19th c., 18 3/4 x 41 1/4", 34 3/4" h. (minor damage to rear foot)............................. **1,320**

Federal Country-style Cherry Chest

Federal country-style chest of drawers, cherry, a rectangular top above a case w/four long graduated drawers w/old replaced oval brasses, scalloped apron & tall French feet, old refinish, Connecticut, early 19th c., 18 x 40", 42" h. (ILLUS.) **1,100**

Federal Country Chest of Drawers

Federal country-style chest of drawers, cherry, a rectangular top above a pair of very deep drawers w/simple turned wood knobs above three long graduated drawers w/wood knobs, ring- and baluster-turned legs w/knob feet, old dark finish on case & drawer frames, drawer fronts cleaned down to red stain, mid-19th c., top 19 1/2 x 41", 45 1/4" h. (ILLUS.) **935**

Federal country-style chest of drawers, cherry, rectangular top w/banded inlay around the edges above a case of four long graduated beaded drawers w/replaced round brasses, a band of inlay above the scrolled apron above ring- and baluster-turned legs w/knob feet, attributed to Stark County, Ohio, early 19th c., old soft finish, 19 1/4 x 41", 45 3/4" h........ **3,575**

Federal country-style chest of drawers, cherry, rectangular top w/ovolo corners overhanging a case w/four long graduated scratch-beaded drawers flanked by reeded quarter engaged columns ending in turned tapering legs, original turned wooden pulls, old refinish, Massachusetts, 1820-30, 21 x 43 1/8", 39 1/4" h....... **1,150**

Federal country-style chest of drawers, painted & decorated basswood, rectangular top above a case of four long graduated thumb-molded drawers above a curved apron & simple cut-out feet, original painted decoration simulating exotic wood bordered by stringing & crossbanding in shades of tan & light brown, original oval brasses, signed "Henry Davist...Readsboro Feb... 1815 $7.50," Vermont, 19 x 41", 42" h. **7,475**

Federal country-style chest of drawers, painted & decorated maple & birch, rectangular top above a case of four long graduated drawers w/old replaced round brasses, serpentine apron & tall bracket feet, old black & brown grain decoration over an earlier red, 17 1/2 x 37", 34 1/2" h. (minor age cracks) **1,980**

Federal country-style chest of drawers, painted & decorated pine & poplar, the crestrail across the top cut w/pairs of incurved repeating scrolls flanking a central tab above the rectangular top over a tall case w/a pair of narrow drawers over four long graduated drawers, paneled ends, on short ring- and baluster-turned legs w/knob & peg feet, original overall red graining w/ebonized trim, yellow striping & gold-stenciled flowers, birds & a label on the rail under the top drawers reading "Manufactured by John Sala," end panels in dark blackish brown w/gold stenciled flowers, bird in flowering tree & "G.W. 1852," clear pressed glass drawer pulls, Soap Hollow, Pennsylvania, 20 1/2 x 38 1/2", 46 3/4" h. **16,500**

Decorated Ohio Federal Chest

Federal country-style chest of drawers, painted & decorated poplar, a low scroll-cut crestrail on the rectangular top above a narrow projecting frieze board over a long deep top drawer & three long graduated drawers all flanked by turned half-round columns, ring-turned feet, original red graining on a yellow ground w/ebonized detail, replaced oval brasses, attributed to North Jackson, Trumbull County, Ohio, early 19th c., 20 1/2 x 41 3/4", overall 53 1/2" h. (ILLUS.) **7,150**

Federal country-style chest of drawers, painted pine, rectangular top slightly overhanging the case w/a deep thumb-molded long drawer over three graduated matching drawers all w/pairs of simple turned wood knobs, serpentine apron continuing into simple bracket feet, red & black graining simulating mahogany, New England, early 19th c., 17 1/4 x 39 1/2", 41" h. (replaced pulls, imperfections).. **1,265**

Federal country-style chest of drawers, walnut, rectangular top over a case w/four long graduated beaded drawers w/diamond-form inlaid keyhole escutcheons, short ring-turned legs w/knob feet, paneled ends, old worn refinishing, early 19th c., 20 1/2 x 42, 43" h. (some edge damage, replaced pressed glass pulls, one missing) **715**

Federal Birch & Cherry Chest

Federal country-style chest of drawers, wavy birch & grained cherry, the double-arched & scroll-cut top splashboard above a rectangular top w/ovolo front corners over ring-turned colonettes flanking four long graduated drawers w/oval brass pulls, raised on ring- and baluster-turned legs w/knob feet, old refinish, North Shore, Massachusetts, early 19th c., replaced brasses, imperfections, 17 1/2 x 39 1/2", 49" h. (ILLUS.) **1,380**

Federal country-style chest of drawers, cherry, a rectangular top above a case of four long dovetailed graduated drawers w/simple turned wood knobs, scalloped apron, simple turned feet, paneled ends, refinished, early 19th c., 19 3/4 x 40 3/4", 39 1/2" h... **770**

Federal Cherry Sugar Chest

Federal country-style sugar chest, cherry, a rectangular hinged top w/molded edges opening to a deep divided interior well above a pair of small drawers, baluster- and ring-turned legs w/peg feet, paneled sides, oval drawer brasses, early 19th c., 16 1/2 x 35 1/2", 35" h. (ILLUS.)... **6,050**

Federal country-style sugar chest, cherry, a rectangular hinged bin lid above a deep divided interior well, one-board sides & ends, rod- and ring-turned short legs w/peg feet, mellow refinishing, Southern U.S., first half 19th c., 19 1/2 x 30", 29 1/4" h. (pieced repairs) ... **1,375**

Federal country-style tall chest of drawers, curly maple veneer & cherry, a rectangular top w/a deep coved cornice above a case w/a row of three small cockbeaded drawers above a stack of five long graduated beaded drawers, simple turned curly maple knobs, drawers w/curly maple veneer & frame & ring- and knob-turned legs in cherry, inlaid shield-shaped keyhole escutcheons replaced, refinished, early 19th c., 21 1/2 x 42 3/4", 67" h. (some edge damage, replaced knobs, minor repair) **4,345**

Federal Birch Tall Chest of Drawers

Federal tall chest of drawers, birch, a rectangular top w/a flaring molded cornice above a case of six long thumb-molded drawers w/oval brasses, molded base on simple bracket feet, original brasses, refinished, Concord, New Hampshire, late 18th - early 19th c., 16 1/4 x 35 3/4" h., 54 3/4" h. (ILLUS.) **4,255**

Federal tall chest of drawers, cherry, a rectangular top w/a deep coved cornice above a case w/a row of drawers w/two larger flanking a small central one above five long graduated drawers w/oval brasses & keyhole escutcheons, drawers flanked by reeded quarter columns down the sides, molded base on scroll-cut bracket feet, old mellow refinish, original brasses, early 19th c., top 23 x 42 1/2", 63 3/4" h. (minor edge damage) **6,050**

Federal Walnut & Cherry Tall Chest

Federal tall chest of drawers, cherry & walnut, the rectangular top w/a wide flat flaring cornice above a band of inlay over a row of three drawers over a stack of five cockbeaded graduated long drawers w/oval brasses & oval keyhole escutcheons, old finish, double-paneled sides, scroll-cut ogee bracket feet, replaced brasses, 21 1/2 x 41 1/2", 65" h. (ILLUS.).. **6,050**

Federal tall chest of drawers, curly maple & cherry, rectangular top above a wide coved cornice over a narrow diamond-inlaid frieze band above a row of three drawers over five long graduated beaded drawers w/replaced oval eagle brasses, a wide diamond-inlaid band across the bottom, scroll-cut bracket feet, refinished, minor restorations, late 18th - early 19th c., 22 1/2 x 45 1/2", 5' 2 3/4" h. **4,400**

Federal tall chest of drawers, inlaid cherry, a rectangular top w/a deep coved cornice w/a dart-inlaid band above a case w/a row of three small drawers above five long graduated cockbeaded drawers w/oval brass pulls & diamond-inlaid keyhole escutcheons, inlaid lambrequin corners, herringbone inlaid band across the base, short bracket feet, old refinish, probably Pennsylvania, ca. 1790-1800, 21 x 40 1/2", 60 3/4" h. (replaced brasses, loss of height) **3,450**

Fine Inlaid Federal Tall Chest

Federal tall chest of drawers, inlaid walnut, rectangular top w/a wide coved cornice above a narrow diamond-inlaid frieze band above a row of three small drawers over five long graduated drawers all w/line-inlaid oval bands, oval brasses & diamond-form inlaid keyhole escutcheons, narrow inlaid banding down front stiles, veneered band around the base, on tall French feet, soft rubbed-out finish, Pennsylvania, late 18th - early 19th c., 24 3/4 x 46", 66 1/2" h. (ILLUS.) ... **6,325**

Federal-Style "serpentine-front" chest of drawers, inlaid mahogany, a rectangular top w/serpentine front above a conforming case w/a pull-out serving shelf above four long graduated drawers w/crotch-grain veneering & cross-banding, on a serpentine apron & bracket feet, manufacturered by Baker Furniture, 20th c., 20 3/4 x 35", 35 1/4" h. (minor wear) **1,210**

French Provincial-Style Tall Chest

French Provincial-Style tall chest of drawers, inlaid walnut, a rectangular top w/serpentine ends above a tall case w/six long graduated drawers w/oblong panels centered by light wood leafy scroll inlays, paneled sides, serpentine apron, simple cabriole legs ending in scroll feet, keys used to pull open each drawer, original finish, ca. 1920s, 18 x 36", 5' h. (ILLUS.)...... **600**

George III-Style Chest of Drawers

George III-Style "bow-front" chest of drawers, inlaid satinwood, rectangular top w/bowed front over a case w/four long graduated bowed drawers w/inlaid banding over the serpentine apron continuing to tall French feet, oval brass & metal keyhole escutcheons, small veneer losses, England, ca. 1900, 20 1/2 x 33", 33" h. (ILLUS.) **4,600**

Georgian-Style Chest on Chest

Georgian-Style chest on chest, mahogany & mahogany veneer, two-part construction: the upper section w/a rectangular top w/cut front corners over a narrow cornice above three long deep drawers flanked by chamfered reeded edges; the lower section w/a mid-molding over two long, deep drawers, all w/butterfly brasses & keyhole escutcheons, molded base & serpentine apron on simple bracket feet, England, late 19th - early 20th c. (ILLUS.).. **800**

Hardware chest, poplar, a thin rectangular top & sides enclosing stacks of 35 small drawers w/tiny knobs, old brown finish, wire nail construction w/plywood back, some drawers w/worn tape labels, 5 1/4 x 16 3/8", 16 3/8" h................................. **330**

Decorative Immigrant's Chest

Immigant chest, painted & decorated, heavy rectangular slightly domed top w/braced ends opening to a deep well, deep dovetailed case decorated on the front w/red & yellow scrolls & swags with a name & date of 1828, the top w/original forest green ground w/red & black trim & polychrome florals similar to the front, scalloped wrought-iron brackets, bands & lockplate, w/partial paper label for Royal Mail Steamers, w/original key, Scandinavian, early 19th c., 20 x 40", 23" h. (ILLUS.)............. **770**

Late Victorian Marble-topped Chest

Late Victorian chest of drawers, walnut & walnut veneer, the tall superstructure w/a serpentine scallop-carved crestrail above a burl band flanked by large rounded leafy scrolls at the corners above a molded rail over a veneer band & scroll trim above line-incised supports flanking the swiveling rectangular beveled mirror w/a serpentine top, all resting on the rectangular rouge marble top overhanging a slightly bowed case w/a row of three drawers over two long drawers all w/stamped brass pulls, scroll-carved curved apron on carved feet, ca. 1890s, original hardware & finish, 22 x 42", 6' 2" h. (ILLUS.).................. **850**

Louis XV-Style chest of drawers, fruitwood, a rectangular top w/serpentine cove-molded border on three front sides, a pair of narrow long drawers in the front of this border above the wide bombé case w/swelled sides & front w/two long drawers carved w/incised oblong panels, paneled ends & cartouche-carved front corners, serpentine flared apron on molded cabriole legs ending in short peg feet, antique finish, 20th c., 19 x 45 1/2", 33 1/4" h. **578**

Rare G. Stickley Chest of Drawers

Mission-style (Arts & Crafts movement) chest of drawers, oak, a low crestrail above the rectangular top above a case w/a pair of short drawers over four long drawers, vertical pull plates on drawers form two bands up the front, paneled end w/cut-out feet, branded mark of Gustav Stickley, Model No. 906, ca. 1912, 21 x 41", 48" h. (ILLUS.)........................... **13,800**

Fine Gustav Stickley Tall Chest

Mission-style (Arts & Crafts movement) tall chest of drawers, oak, a low crestboard above the tall case w/slightly bowed side stiles & three pairs of small drawers over three long graduated drawers all w/turned wood knobs, arched apron, designed by Harvey Ellis, red decal mark of Gustav Stickley, Model No. 913, lightly cleaned original finish, slight veneer split, 20 x 36", 51" h. (ILLUS.)........ **7,700**

Gustav Stickley Tall Chest of Drawers

Mission-style (Arts & Crafts movement) tall chest of drawers, a low splashboard on the rectangular top overhanging a tall case w/two stacks of three small drawers above three long graduated drawers, hammered copper pulls, bowed side stiles & arched apron, fine original finish, red decal of Gustav Stickley, Model No. 913, minor stains on top, 20 1/4 x 36", 50 1/2" h. (ILLUS.)...................................... **9,350**

Modern style chest of drawers, hardwood, rectangular top over a case w/five plain graduated long drawers w/recessed handles, platform base, light finish, metal tag mark of Dunbar, Berne, Indiana, post-World War II, 18 x 28", 31 1/4" h. (scratches, wear)... **863**

Heywood-Wakefield Vanity Chest

Modern style vanity chest, maple, a large, tall upright rectangular back mirror w/rounded corners at one end above a glass shelf & open compartment, a case w/three graduated drawers at the other end, each w/tapering applied finger grip pulls, short block feet, wheat colored finish, round branded mark of Heywood-Wakefield, ca. 1950s, light wear, 13 1/4 x 53 3/4", base 24" h. (ILLUS.).......... **345**

Country Chippendale Mule Chest

Mule chest (box chest w/one or more drawers below a storage compartment), Chippendale country-style, pine & poplar, the hinged cotter-pine rectangular top opening to a deep well above a two long base drawers w/batwing pulls & keyhole escutcheons, molded base w/bracket feet, old refinish, late 18th c., 18 x 48", 42" h. (ILLUS.)................................ **650**

Mule chest (box chest w/one or more drawers below a storage compartment), Classical country-style, painted & decorated pine, a rectangular hinged top w/molded edges opening to a deep well faced w/two false drawers above two matching working drawers all w/turned wood knobs, on bulbous baluster- and ring-turned legs, original reddish brown graining in imitation of flame figured wood w/line inlay, black feet, found in New Hampshire, first half 19th c., 18 3/4 x 40", 40" h. (minor edge damage) **1,650**

Mule chest (box chest w/one or more drawers below a storage compartment), country-style, painted & decorated pine, a rectangular hinged top opening to a very deep well above two long reverse-graduated bottom drawers, on tall bootjack legs, overall old red paint w/sponged black dot band graining, mismatched Rockingham glazed pottery drawer pulls, 17 1/4 x 38 1/4", 42 3/4" h. (old replaced hinges, batten on lid renailed) **2,090**

Mule chest (box chest w/one or more drawers below a storage compartment), country-style, painted pine, six-board construction, rectangular hinged top w/molded edges opening to a well, a long bottom nailed drawer w/round brasses, curved apron & bracket feet, original brown flame graining, 19th c., 19 1/2 x 49", 33 1/4" h. (one front foot split & nailed, edge damage) **550**

Mule chest (box chest w/one or more drawers below a storage compartment), Federal country-style, painted, a rectangular top w/molded edge lifting above a deep well faced with two mock

drawers w/round metal knobs above two long working drawers w/knobs, high cutout bracket feet, old red paint, ca. 1820, 19 x 38", 38" h. **4,888**

Mule chest (box chest w/one or more drawers below a storage compartment), Federal country-style, painted pine, a hinged rectangular top w/molded edges opening to a well w/two false long drawer fronts w/oval brasses above two long matching working drawers, original greyish blue vinegar graining on a greyish olive ground w/black & yellow edge striping, shaped apron on high tapering feet, bottom signed "Daniel," attributed to Essex, Massachusetts, early 19th c., 19 3/8 x 42 3/4", 41 3/4" h. **7,700**

Mule chest (box chest w/one or more drawers below a storage compartment), Federal country-style, painted pine, a rectangular top w/molded edges opening to a deep well w/interior compartment fitted w/iron lock & hinges, two long graduated dovetailed drawers at the bottom above the scalloped apron & high bracket feet, old red repaint, early 19th c., 17 1/2 x 36", 35 1/4" h. (replaced oval drawer brasses, minor age cracks) **2,585**

Fine Decorated Pine Mule Chest

Mule chest (box chest w/one or more drawers below a storage compartment), painted & decorated pine, a rectangular molded top opening to a deep well above two long drawers at the bottom, each w/replaced round brass pulls, high shaped bracket feet, original putty wood graining in red, green & yellow w/umber tones, very minor surface imperfections, northern New England, ca. 1830, 17 5/8 x 38", 36 1/2" h. (ILLUS.).... **16,100**

Early Painted Mule Chest

Mule chest (box chest w/one or more drawers below a storage compartment), painted pine, a rectangular hinged top opening to a deep well w/two false drawers at the front above two working drawers, all w/simple butterfly pulls & keyhole escutcheons, molded base on bootjack end legs, repainted greyish brown, probably Massachusetts, early 18th c., replaced brasses, 18 x 39 1/2", 37" h. (ILLUS.) **1,150**

Early Painted Mule Chest

Mule chest (box chest w/one or more drawers below a storage compartment), painted pine & poplar, the rectangular hinged top w/molded edges opening above a deep well, the front w/two false-front drawers w/round brass knobs above two long working drawers, on simple bracket feet, old mustard yellow paint over original red, replaced pulls, New England, early 19th c., 18 x 38", 42" h. (ILLUS.) **650**

Grain-painted Early Mule Chest

Mule chest (box chest w/one or more drawers below a storage compartment), painted pine, rectangular top w/molded edges opening to a deep well above a single long drawer across the bottom, on high arched & shaped bracket feet, original turned wood knobs, original red & yellow painting simulating tiger stripe maple, old dry surface, minor surface scratches on top, Rhode Island, 1830-40, 20 x 39 3/4", 36" h. (ILLUS.) **2,070**

Mule chest (box chest w/one or more drawers below a storage compartment), painted pine, rectangular hinged top w/molded edges opens to a well above two thumb-molded drawers on a straight front skirt w/side shaping, early hinges, old red paint, New England, late 18th c., 18 1/2 x 43 3/4", 41 1/4" h. (replaced pulls, minor imperfections) **1,840**

Mule chest (box chest w/one or more drawers below a storage compartment), painted pine, rectangular hinged top w/molded edge opening to a deep well above a pair of long drawers below, original grain painting resembling mahogany w/two banded false drawers at the top over the two working drawers, four oval brasses at the top & two each on the working drawers, molded band w/simple bracket feet w/painted banding, old repaint, early 19th c., 17 1/2 x 21 1/2", 44 1/2" h. (repairs to feet, scratches on side) **825**

Chinese Chest of Drawers

Oriental chest of drawers, brass-bound mahogany & camphorwood, two-part construction: the upper section w/a rectangular top of a pair of small drawers above a deep long drawer; the lower section w/two long reverse-graduated drawers, fitted w/brass inset handles & end handles, on small tapering turned feet, refinished, minor imperfections, China, mid-19th c., 19 3/4 x 38 3/4", 34 1/2" h. (ILLUS.) **4,025**

Pilgrim Century blanket chest, oak & pine, joined construction, the overhanging thumb-molded hinged white pine top above a three-paneled front w/applied moldings over a long drawer flanked by shadow molded stiles, recessed panel sides, the drawer w/stippled inscription "1707 HI," interior open till, old dark stained surface, New Haven Colony, Connecticut, 1680-1740, minor imperfections, 19 1/4 x 43", 31 1/2" h. (ILLUS. top next column) **9,775**

Early Pilgrim Century Joined Chest

Pilgrim Century chest of drawers, painted oak, cedar & yellow pine, a rectangular top w/applied molding above a case of four long drawers each w/molded fronts & chamfered mitered borders & separated by applied horizontal moldings, the sides w/two recessed vertical molded panels above a single horizontal panel, deep cove-molded base on turned ball feet, old red paint, southeastern New England, ca. 1700, 20 1/2 x 37 3/4", 35" h. (minor imperfections) **26,450**

Fine Pilgrim Century Chest of Drawers

Pilgrim Century chest of drawers, painted oak, cedar & yellow pine, joined construction, the rectangular top w/applied molded edges above a case of four long drawers each w/molded fronts & chamfered mitered borders & separated by applied horizontal moldings, the sides w/two recessed vertical molded panels above a single horizontal panel on a base w/applied moldings & four turned ball feet, old red paint, old replaced feet, southeastern New England, ca. 1700, 20 1/2 x 37 3/4", 35" h. (ILLUS.) **13,800**

Pilgrim Century chest over drawer, pine, a rectangular molded top w/pintle hinges above a single-arch molded base centering a panel w/carved initials "MG" & a single long drawer w/teardrop pulls, on turned ball front feet & square rear feet, pierced brass keyhole oval escutcheons, Massachusetts, early 18th c., apparently original hardware, 18 1/2 x 42", 32 3/4" h. (imperfections) **4,600**

Queen Anne blanket chest over drawers, pine, rectangular hinged top w/molded edges opening to a well above a pair of faux short drawers & a long faux drawer above two lower working long drawers, all w/teardrop pulls, molded base & wide bracket feet w/valanced sides, remains of bluish green paint, Mid-Atlantic States, 14 1/2 x 21 1/2" (replaced brasses, restorations) **2,070**

Queen Anne chest of drawers, figured walnut, a rectangular molded top w/notched corners overhanging a case w/a pair of short drawers over three long graduated drawers flanked by fluted chamfered corner columns, the molded base on ogee bracket feet, appears to retain original rare openwork brass butterfly pulls & keyhole escutcheons, Pennsylvania, 1750-60, 22 x 36 1/2", 34 1/2" h. (patched to back of top where mirror was fitted, half of front left foot replaced) **13,800**

Queen Anne chest of drawers, maple, a rectangular top w/a deep molded edge above a case w/a pair of drawers above four long graduated cockbeaded drawers each w/butterfly brasses & keyhole escutcheons, molded base on shaped bracket feet, refinished, replaced brasses, New England, late 18th c., 19 x 41", 46" h. (imperfections) **2,070**

Queen Anne Chest of Drawers

Queen Anne chest of drawers, stained wood, rectangular top above a case w/four long graduated drawers w/small turned wood pulls, molded base on high arched bracket feet, old dark brown stain, imperfections, New England, mid-18th c., 16 1/4 x 38", 40 1/2" h. (ILLUS.) **2,990**

Queen Anne chest-on-frame, carved & painted pine & maple, two-part construction: the upper section w/a rectangular top w/a widely flaring & stepped cornice above a band of dentil molding over a case w/two pairs of small drawers flanking a deep fan-carved central drawer w/incised scallops & overlapping lunettes, over a stack of four long graduated drawers, all w/simple bail pulls; the lower section w/a molded top above a deeply scalloped apron raised on short angled cabriole legs ending in pad feet, New Hampshire, 18th c., 36" w., 56" h. **2,500**

Queen Anne chest-on-frame, maple, two-part construction: the upper section w/a rectangular top w/a deep stepped cornice above a case of four long graduated thumb-molded drawers w/butterfly brasses & keyhole escutcheons; the lower section w/a mid-molding above a single long narrow drawer over the apron w/two drop pendants flanking a small central carved fan, cabriole legs ending in high pad feet, old refinished surface, Newburyport, 1750-80, 15 1/2 x 36", 56 1/2" h. (replaced brasses, imperfections) **8,050**

Queen Anne country-style chest of drawers, cherry, rectangular top w/deep molded cornice above a case w/four long overlapping graduated dovetailed drawers w/pierced butterfly brasses & keyhole escutcheons, molded base w/apron w/central drop & high bracket feet, cleaned down to old red, attributed to Pennsylvania, 18th c., 17 3/4 x 38", 44" h. (one front foot ended out, some edge damage, minor repair to drawer lip, backboards old replacements) **2,255**

Queen Anne country-style chest of drawers, stained birch & butternut, rectangular top w/deep ogee cornice above a pair of thumb-molded drawers over three long drawers all w/turned wood knobs, molded base on bracket feet, old red surface, replaced pulls, Connecticut, 18th c., 18 3/4 x 36 3/4", 40 1/4" h. (minor losses) **2,645**

Queen Anne Chest over Drawers

Queen Anne country-style chest over drawers, the rectangular hinged molded top opening above a deep well w/a cast front w/a pair of short over one long false drawers above two working long drawers, applied base molding above the scroll-cut arched apron, old refinish, imperfections, probably Connecticut, mid-18th c., 17 1/2 x 35 1/2", 45" h. (ILLUS.) ... **2,070**

Queen Anne mule chest (box chest w/one or more drawers below a storage compartment), painted pine, a rectangular top w/molded edges opening to a deep well w/a case front of three thumb-molded graduated false drawers over two working drawers, molded base on simple high bracket feet centering a small shaped pendant, replaced butterfly pulls, old dark brown paint, minor imperfections, probably Massachusetts, mid-18th c., 17 1/4 x 36 1/2", 46 1/2" h. (ILLUS.) **3,738**

Queen Anne Mule Chest

Queen Anne tall chest of drawers, carved & painted, a rectangular top w/a deep stepped projecting cornice above a case of five long graduated drawers w/simple rounded butterfly pulls & oval keyhole escutcheons, molded base w/carved beading & dog-tooth carving, raised on short bandy cabriole legs ending in pad feet, old red paint, New Hampshire, Dunlap School, 18th c., 35 3/4" w., 48" h. **40,000**

Queen Anne Tall Chest of Drawers

Queen Anne tall chest of drawers, maple, the rectangular top w/flaring stepped cornice over a pair of small drawers over four long graduated drawers, molded base on simple shaped bracket feet, appears to retain most of the original brasses, numerous chips & patches to drawer lips, one inch missing on left rear foot, New England, 1740-60, 19 1/2 x 39", 45 1/4" h. (ILLUS.) **2,300**

Queen Anne tall chest of drawers, tiger stripe maple, the rectangular top w/a narrow flared cornice above a case w/a row of four small thumb-molded drawers over a pair of drawers above four long graduated drawers all w/butterfly brasses & keyhole escutcheons, molded base on tall bracket feet, replaced brasses, old refinish, southeastern New England, ca. 1750, 18 x 34 3/4", 49 1/2" h. (minor imperfections) **21,850**

Queen Anne-Style chest-on-frame, walnut & burl walnut veneer, the rectangular top above a case w/four long graduated dovetailed drawers w/brass teardrop pulls set onto a molded frame w/arched apron & short cabriole front legs ending in duck feet, England, first half 20th c., 19 1/4 x 33 1/2", 38 1/2" h. **825**

Sheraton country-style chest of drawers, walnut, rectangular top above a case w/a pair of small beaded drawers above three long graduated beaded drawers, simple turned wood knobs, old varnish finish, baluster- and ring-turned short legs w/knob feet, early 19th c., 20 x 41 1/4", 47" h. **770**

Spice chest, country-style, oak & bird's-eye maple, rectangular top w/molded edges over a square nailed case w/two ranks of four deep drawers each w/turned wood knobs, cut-out end legs, maple drawer fronts, 7 1/2 x 14 1/2", 17 3/4" h. **385**

Early Southern Sugar Chest

Sugar chest, cherry, a rectangular hinged lid above a deep dovetailed well divided into three compartments, a long bottom drawer w/two turned wood knobs, on baluster-, ring- and knob-turned legs w/knob feet, drawer bottom w/scraps of the "Weekly Courier Journal, Louisville" from the 1880s, refinished, age crack in lid, minor edge damage on feet, Southern, 19th c., 19 1/4 x 27 3/4", 40" h. (ILLUS.) **4,675**

Sugar chest, cherry & poplar, a rectangular hinged top w/molded edges opening to a deep well above a small drawer beside a long drawer over a pair of matching drawers over a single long bottom drawer, knob-turned feet, paneled ends, refinished, found in Kentucky, 15 3/4 x 37 1/4", 29 3/4" h. (restorations, old alterations to drawers, turned pulls replaced) **2,420**

Early Virginia Sugar Chest

Sugar chest, Federal country-style, walnut, a hinged rectangular top opening to a deep well above a single long drawer at the bottom w/simple turned wood pulls, square tapering legs, Shenandoah Valley, Virginia, first half 19th c. (ILLUS.) **2,000**

Sugar chest on frame, walnut, the chest w/a rectangular hinged breadboard top opening to a deep well in the dovetailed case, the lower section w/a deep apron w/a single long dovetailed drawer w/two small turned wood knobs, on ring- and baluster-turned legs w/peg feet, refinished, Kentucky, early 19th c., 15 1/2 x 24", 34 1/4" h. (chest missing in-

terior dividers, mid-molding missing, lid reworked) **3,245**

Victorian country-style chest of drawers, Renaissance Revival substyle, walnut, a tall oval mirror swiveling between a pierced "wishbone" frame on a short pedestal above the rectangular top over a case w/long drawer w/a raised panel & carved leaf pulls slightly overhanging three matching long lower drawers, bracket front feet, ca. 1875, 18 x 41", base, 43" h. plus mirror **489**

Victorian country-style chest of drawers, Renaissance Revival substyle, walnut, an arched & scalloped crestboard above a narrow rectangular shelf above a pair of shallow handkerchief drawers w/turned wood knobs & quarter-round turnings at the corners, the rectangular top w/molded edges above a case w/chamfered front corners & half-round bobbin-turned drops at the top corners above four long graduated drawers w/turned wood knobs, half-round bobbin turnings at the bottom front corners flanking the scroll-cut bracket feet, refinished, ca. 1870, 18 x 39 1/2", overall 50 3/4" h. **605**

Victorian country-style child's chest of drawers, walnut, an arched & shaped splashback on the rectangular top above a case w/a pair of small drawers above two long drawers, simple turned wood knobs, scalloped apron, simple bracket feet, old varnish finish, ca. 1870, 7 1/2 x 12 3/4", 12 1/2" h. plus splashback.............................. **550**

Tall Eastlake Chest of Drawers

Victorian Eastlake chest of drawers, walnut, a rectangular mirror w/a molded frame & scroll-carved crestrail tilting between plain uprights beside a pair of small handkerchief drawers on the rectangular molded top above the tall case w/a pair of molded drawers beside a small paneled door over three long molded drawers, all drawers w/incised leafy scrolls, molded base on knob & peg feet on casters, paneled sides, ca. 1880 (ILLUS.) **975**

Decorative Eastlake Chest of Drawers

Victorian Eastlake chest of drawers, walnut & burl walnut, the superstructure w/a crestrail composed of small carved open arches above a narrow panel w/line-incised scrolls flanked by reeded corner blocks above reeded supports flanking the large rectangular swiveling mirror w/a notch-cut framework above a lower panel carved w/stylized blossoms, the rectangular top w/molded edge above a case of three long line-incised & blossom-carved drawers w/brass pulls, blocks & reeded base side stiles, on casters, some original hardware, refinished, ca. 1885, 20 x 40", 6' 4" h. (ILLUS.) **650**

Victorian Eastlake Cottage-style Chest

Victorian Eastlake Cottage-style chest of drawers, painted & decorated pine, the superstructure w/a notch-cut crestboard w/peaked center & incised & gilt-trimmed lines & florettes over a gilt-banded frame enclosing a rectangular swivel mirror over decorated panels & a narrow open shelf flanked by shaped side uprights w/gilt-trimmed line-incised florals & loops, the rectangular top w/molded edge w/further gilt trim over a case of four long graduated drawers painted w/a large round continuous reserve decorated w/a lakeside landscape, the reserve surrounded by a rectangular gilt band frame w/angled corners & further stylized gilt florals, on original brown & orange comb-grained ground accented w/black, the top in olive green w/a rose & gold floral design, original round ring pulls & paint, on casters, ca. 1880-90, height loss, 18 3/4 x 38", 76" h. (ILLUS.) **978**

Victorian Empire Revival chest of drawers, mahogany veneer, a large rectangular mirror w/rounded wide frame swiveling between S-scroll uprights above the rectangular top w/a pair of long, narrow round-fronted drawers w/small brass ring pulls above a bombé swelled lower case of three long drawers, each w/stamped brass pulls, rounded baseboard on short claw-and-ball front legs on casters, ca. 1890s, 27 x 48", 72" h. **403**

Golden Oak Chest with Tall Mirror

Victorian Golden Oak chest of drawers, the left side w/a tall rectangular beveled mirror swiveling within a simple rectangular framework w/a scroll-carved crestrail, the top right side w/a low carved arched crestrail above a square shelf over a raised panel square door above a stack of two small drawers all above two long bottom drawers w/stamped brass pulls, serpentine apron, on casters, refinished, ca. 1900-10, 20 x 40", 6' 4" h. (ILLUS.) **750**

Golden Oak Chest of Drawers

Victorian Golden Oak chest of drawers, the top mounted w/a large squared mirror w/rounded corners within a framework w/a high arched & scroll-carved crestrail & shaped sides & rounded bottom corners swiveling between tall scrolled uprights w/scroll carving across the base, the rectangular top w/a serpentine front over a conforming case w/a pair of drawers over two long drawers, all w/pierced brass pulls, simple cabriole front legs & square rear legs, on casters, ca. 1900, 20 x 44", 82" h. (ILLUS.)................................ **403**

Golden Oak "Highboy" Chest

Victorian Golden Oak "highboy" chest of drawers, oak, a rectangular top w/molded edges mounted w/a simple wishbone upright support holding an oblong serpentine-framed beveled swiveling mirror, the tall case w/a pair of small serpentine-front drawers over four long drawers, simple turned wood pulls, scalloped apron & short shaped front legs & square rear legs, on casters, ca. 1900, 19 x 34", 66" h. (ILLUS.)... **259**

Victorian Golden Oak "Highboy" Chest

Victorian Golden Oak "highboy" chest of drawers, the rectangular top w/molded edges & incurved sides mounted w/an oblong cartouche-form beveled mirror in

conforming scroll-carved frame swiveling between wishbone uprights w/scroll carving along the bottom, the tall case w/a pair of drawers over four long drawers, all w/pierced brass pulls, scroll-carved apron & leaf-carved front cabriole legs & square back legs, excellent condition, ca. 1900 (ILLUS.)... **850**

Golden Oak "Side-by-Side" Chest

Victorian Golden Oak "side-by-side" chest of drawers, a tall narrow rectangular beveled mirror on one side swiveling within a framework w/an arched & scroll-carved crestrail, beside a short scroll-carved top crest over a stack of two small drawers over a small paneled cupboard door, all on a rectangular top w/molded edges over two long drawers, stamped brass pulls, ca. 1900, possibly missing feet (ILLUS.) **150-300**

Marble-topped Renaissance Chest

Victorian Renaissance Revival chest of drawers, carved walnut, the tall superstructure w/a tall arched beveled mirror frame w/a tall leaf-carved finial flanked by scrolls, the whole swiveling between slender uprights w/two small graduated open shelves at each side above narrow open panels & side finials, the rectangular white marble top w/molded edge set w/two narrow stepped hanky boxes w/hinged lift lids, the case w/a long drawer w/a raised oval molding & leaf-carved pulls flanked by rounded front corners projecting slightly over two lower matching long drawers, deep molded flat base, original finish, ca. 1860, 20 x 40", 6' 8" h. (ILLUS.).................. **2,500**

Pine Renaissance Revival Chest

Victorian Renaissance Revival chest of drawers, pine w/walnut stain, the arched superstructure enclosing an arch-topped swiveling mirror flanked by shaped sides w/small candle shelves above small handkerchief drawers on the rectangular top w/molded edges, the case w/four long graduated drawers w/raised oval bands & carved leaf pulls, low serpentine apron & bracket feet on casters, ca. 1870, 17 x 39", 71" h. (ILLUS.)...................... **495**

Victorian Renaissance Revival chest of drawers, walnut, an inset rectangular white marble top within a molded border w/rounded corners above a case w/two long drawers each w/raised oval band molding enclosing elongated four-point mounts for pulls & small round keyhole escutcheons, molded plinth base on casters, ca. 1875-80, old finish, 21 1/4 x 45 1/2", 32" h. **440**

Fine Renaissance Revival Chest

Victorian Renaissance Revival chest of drawers, walnut & burl walnut, drop-well style, the tall superstructure w/a tall pedimented crest w/carved palmette & scrolls above an arched molded crestrail over a frieze band w/two raised burl panels flanked by scroll-carved brackets on the side panels w/narrow raised burl panels above small candle shelves & tall S-scroll carved brackets all centering a tall mirror, raised side sections w/rectangular white marble tops w/molded edges above stacks of two small drawers flanking the white marble-topped drop well above two long lower drawers w/double raised burl panels centered by cartouche-form carvings & fitted w/brass & wood pulls, canted front corners on base, deep molded flat apron, old refinish, ca. 1870s, 22 x 44", 7' 6" h. (ILLUS.) **1,800**

Renaissance Revival Walnut Chest

Victorian Renaissance Revival chest of drawers, walnut & burl walnut, the tall superstructure w/a scroll-carved crowned pediment over angled molded rails over a frieze w/burl raised panels over a tall arch-topped mirror flanked by sides w/raised burl panels, rounded candle shelves & curved base brackets over a stepped white marble top w/two small drawers flanking a marble-topped well over two long drawers each w/two oblong raised burl panels, stamped brass pulls, molded base on casters, ca. 1880, 21 x 43", 88" h. (ILLUS.) **661**

William & Mary chest over drawer, child's, painted pine, a rectangular hinged top w/molded edges opening to a deep well, half-round edge moldings down the corners & above the long base drawer molded to resemble two small drawers, front & sides w/a red painted wash & brown freehand designs of concentric rings, demilune & meandering vines, the drawer painted salmon, red, & brown, single arch molding in black, possibly coastal Massachusetts, early 18th c., 17 1/8 x 28", 19" h. (minor imperfections)........................ **9,200**

Cradles

Bentwood, the arched bentwood matching head- and footrail above simple turned spindles w/the side composed of seven turned spindles between turned rails, a slat rail bottom, suspended & swinging between simple turned uprights w/knob finials raised on shaped & arched shoe feet w/a central drop w/two long rod stretchers from end to end, ivory fittings, late 19th - early 20th c., 41" l., 39" h. **$440**

Bentwood Cradle on Frame

Bentwood cradle on frame, the oblong shell-form bentwood crib suspended within a sinuous bentwood frame surmounted by a shepherd's crook at one end, probably Austria, ca. 1905, wear, 30 x 55", 76" h. (ILLUS.) **1,380**

Country-style Painted Cradle

Country-style, painted pine, rectangular deep mortised frame w/paneled side slats w/double almond-shaped cut-outs, hooded end, found in Amish country, old worn black paint, 19th c., 31" l. (ILLUS.) **880**

Country-style low cradle on rockers, painted poplar, arched angled head- and footboards w/heart-form cut-out above tapering paneled ends, headboard w/shaped rim brackets on the rounded edge rail over the canted paneled sides, turned knob finials at each corner, beveled into deep scroll-shaped rockers, old worn red paint w/blue sponged panels & white trim, 19th c., 36" l. (rockers restored) **413**

Deep cradle on rockers, Pilgrim Century, joined & paneled oak, the high paneled headboard stepping to deep paneled sides & a paneled footboard, turned corner finials, on wide solid rockers, refinished, New England, late 17th - early 18th c., minor imperfections, 20 x 39", 30 1/2" h. (ILLUS.) **1,840**

Pilgrim Century Oak Cradle

Hooded cradle on rockers, mahogany, top board of hood w/flame veneer over the enclosed headboard & gently canted sides, shaped dovetailed footboard, Chippendale-style brasses on ends, mortised rockers w/scrolled ends, old dark finish, found in Michigan, 18 x 40", 26 1/2" h. (renailing w/veneer repair, empty holes in base) **330**

Low cradle on rockers, cherry w/soft old worn finish, rectangular w/nearly straight sides & slightly shaped top edges, corner posts w/turned acorn finials, low wide rockers, two hanging knobs on each side, heart cut-outs in head- and footboards, 16 x 35", 20" h. (some edge damage) **275**

Low cradle on rockers, painted walnut, rectangular w/slightly canted dovetailed sides & gently arched head- and footboards, the sides composed of three panels in a mortised & pinned frame, top of headboard shows holes possibly for removable hood, old worn red & black paint, 19th c., 39" l. **275**

Rustic style, twig-constructed sides on a rocker base, unsigned, early 20th c., 22 x 33", 22" h. **55**

Victorian Eastlake Cradle

Victorian Eastlake substyle, walnut, the head- and footboards w/openwork panels at the top w/a flat crestrail flanked by block- and knob-turned stiles w/knob finials above a central pierce-carved wheel device & slender spokes, flat siderails above numerous simple turned spindles, on curved supports rocking on the platform base w/outswept legs on casters, original finish, ca. 1885, 20 x 38", 36" h. (ILLUS.) **450**

Cupboards

Chimney cupboard, poplar, rectangular flat top above a very tall narrow case w/a long two-panel door opening to four shelves above a single panel lower door opening to two shelves, dark stain on the front, unfinished on sides, 13 3/4 x 20 1/4", 92" h. **$1,100**

rectangle, the side panels w/an arched open top compartment above a tall narrow door w/a tall glazed panel, three interior shelves, raised on simple turned ovoid legs, ca. 1930s, 34 x 71 1/4", 71 1/2" h. (ILLUS.)... **2,300**

China Cupboard with Upper Door

China cupboard, Victorian Golden Oak, quarter-sawn oak, a half-round top w/a small scroll-carved crest above a short rectangular bowed glazed door flanked by open shelves backed by small squared beveled mirrors above the half-round case w/a tall glazed bowed center door flanked by curved sides, four wooden shelves & a mirrored back in the upper half, narrow molded base on two short cabriole front legs w/paw feet & shaped rear legs, refinished, ca. 1900, 18 x 48", 6' 4" h. (ILLUS.)... **2,500**

Demilune Inlaid Corner Cupboard

Corner cupboard, Baroque Revival style, inlaid mahogany, the high arched & molded top centered by a large oval cartouche above the demi-lune case w/a dentil molding above a pair of tall cupboard doors w/thin decorative molded panels centered by ribbon bow inlay & an inlaid oval w/flower-filled urn & flanked by blocked pilasters, a heavy mid-molding above a shorter pair of matching cupboard doors flanked by serpentine heavy pilasters ending in heavy carved paw feet, second half 19th c., Europe., requires some restoration (ILLUS.)............... **8,800**

Exotic Art Deco Corner Cupboard

Corner cupboard, Art Deco, mahogany w/exotic veneers, a central flat rectangular top flanked by squared angled ends above a conforming case w/a central pair of tall cupboard doors w/light panels of triangular veneer centering a small dark

Tall Chippendale Corner Cupboard

Corner cupboard, Chippendale architectural-type, curly maple, one-piece construction, the top w/a broken-scroll pediment w/starburst-carved scroll ends & ball-and-flame-turned finials above a pair of tall arched two-panel cupboard doors w/a short arched panel above a tall rectangular panel above a mid-molding over a pair of paneled cupboard doors, molded base on ogee bracket feet, old refinishing, feet, finials & ends of scrolls replaced, late 18th c., 44 1/2" w., 99 1/2" h. (ILLUS.)..................... **10,450**

Chippendale Cherry Corner Cupboard

Corner cupboard, Chippendale, carved cherry, two-part construction: the upper section w/a scrolled molded pediment flanking a fluted keystone w/flame finial above a wide arched door w/geometric glazing flanked by reeded columns, opening to three serpentine-shaped painted shelves; the slightly projecting lower section w/a pair of paneled cupboard doors opening to single shelf flanked by reeded columns, scalloped apron on simple bracket feet, old refinish, hardware changes, minor patching, probably Pennsylvania, early 19th c., 17 3/4 x 41 1/2", 95" h. (ILLUS.) **9,200**

Chippendale Poplar Corner Cupboard

Corner cupboard, Chippendale, poplar, two-part construction: the top section w/a flat top & deep stepped cornice over a wide arched molding w/central keystone above a pair of geometrically glazed cupboard doors opening to two serpentine

shelves w/plate rail & spoon cut-outs; the slightly stepped-out lower section w/a pair of raised panel doors w/H-hinges opening to a single shelf, serpentine apron & simple bracket feet, old surface, imperfections, Pennsylvania, late 18th - early 19th c., 25 1/2 x 51", 67" h. (ILLUS.)................... **3,680**

Corner cupboard, Chippendale style, walnut, two-part construction: the upper section w/a deep stepped flaring cornice above a large 12-pane glazed cupboard door opening to three shaped shelves; the lower section w/a mid-molding over a wide four-panel hinged door raised on a molded base on ogee bracket feet, old refinish, Chester County, Pennsylvania, ca. 1780, 22 1/2 x 44", 84 1/4" h. (replaced brass H-hinges & ring pulls, minor imperfections).... **14,950**

Chippendale Walnut Corner Cupboard

Corner cupboard, Chippendale, walnut, two-piece construction: the upper section w/a broken-scroll molded cornice centered by a block & urn-form finial above an arched molding continuing down to reeded pilasters flanking the arched geometrically-glazed cupboard door opening to three shelves; the lower section w/a mid-molding over a pair of short paneled cupboard doors flanked by reeded pilasters, blocked & scroll-cut base, late 18th c. (ILLUS.)......... **6,500**

English Chippendale-Style Cupboard

Corner cupboard, Chippendale-Style, mahogany, two-part construction: the upper section w/a flat top & narrow molded cornice over a lattice-carved frieze band over a tall single geometrically glazed door opening to three shaped shelves; the stepped-out lower section w/a wide single geometrically glazed door opening to a single shaped shelf, molded base & bracket feet, England, early 20th c., 28" w., 72 1/4" h. (ILLUS.).............................. **715**

Corner cupboard, Classical country-style, painted & decorated pine & poplar, two-part construction: the upper section w/a stepped & molded flaring cornice above a single large 12-pane glazed door flanked by wood-grained sides imitating mahogany; the lower section w/a mid-molding above a pair of small flush drawers over a pair of paneled doors all flanked by wide side panels & decorated overall w/mahogany wood graining, molded base on bun front feet, Rupp of Yorktown, Pennsylvania, first half 19th c., top 47 1/2" w., overall 86 3/4" h. (replaced hardware, some edge & surface wear) **8,800**

One-piece Cherry Corner Cupboard

Corner cupboard, country-style, cherry & poplar, one-piece construction, the top w/a wide coved cornice above a pair of two-panel doors w/simple wood knobs above a mid-molding over two single panel cupboard doors, molded base w/deeply scalloped apron & bracket feet, cleaned down to traces of old red, edge damage, repairs, top 44 1/2" w., 76" h. (ILLUS.)...................... **1,430**

Corner cupboard, country-style, cherry & poplar, two-piece construction: the upper section w/a stepped coved cornice above a pair of 6-pane glazed cupboard doors; the lower section w/a long center drawer above a pair of paneled cupboard doors, flat apron & simple cut-out feet, mismatched cast-iron thumb latches w/porcelain knobs, mid-19th c., refinished, 58" w., 83 1/2" h. (one end of cornice w/nailed repair)... **2,640**

Corner cupboard, country-style, cherry, two-part construction: the upper section w/a flat flared cornice above a pair of tall 6-pane glazed cupboard doors opening

to two shelves; the lower section w/a single central drawer above a pair of paneled cupboard doors, flat apron w/simple cut-out feet, cast-iron thumb latches w/brass knobs, interior w/modern blue paint, refinished, mid-19th c., 48 1/4" w., 82 3/4" h. **3,630**

Tall Slender Corner Cupboard

Corner cupboard, country-style, painted pine, one-piece construction, the top & sides framed by a wide molding flanking a tall upper geometrically-glazed cupboard door opening to three shelves above a tall double-panel cupboard door, serpentine apron, old green repaint, interior painted red, early 19th c., repairs, border molding replaced, 27" w., 87 1/2" h. (ILLUS.)...................................... **1,155**

Exceptional Country Corner Cupboard

Corner cupboard, country-style, painted pine, two-part construction: the upper section w/a deep coved cornice above a tall 12-pane glazed cupboard door opening to shelves; the lower section w/a mid-molding over a pair of overlapping drawers above a pair of paneled cupboard doors, serpentine apron & high bracket feet, worn original white paint w/vinegar graining in red & yellow ochre, dark grey on apron & feet, one pane replaced, some edge damage & replaced brass knobs, 48 1/2" w., 7' 8 1/2" h. (ILLUS.).... **19,250**

Corner cupboard, country-style, painted poplar, one-piece construction, the flat top w/narrow molded cornice above a long cupboard door divided into a cross panel at the top above two parallel panels, a shorter two-panel lower door, scalloped apron w/bracket feet, distressed two-tone orange repaint, 19th c., 34 1/4" w., 81" h. **1,045**

Early Barrel-back Corner Cupboard

Corner cupboard, country-style, pine, barrel-back style, one-piece construction, a flat molded deep cornice above a tall raised panel cupboard door opening to three shaped shelves, a smaller raised panel cupboard door below, framed by applied moldings, original wrought-iron butterfly hinges, old natural color, minor imperfections, New England, late 18th c., 20 1/2 x 46", 93 1/2" h. (ILLUS.) **3,450**

Corner cupboard, country-style, pine, one-piece construction, the flat top w/molded edge above a central 6-pane glazed cupboard door over a four-panel cupboard door all flanked on each side by four narrow rectangular panels, flat apron & low cut-out feet, side molding at each side, old refinish, missing front bracket, New England, ca. 1800, 22 x 48", 84" h. **3,450**

Corner cupboard, country-style, poplar, one-piece construction, the flat top w/a narrow molded cornice above a tall narrow paneled door w/wood knob above a shorter paneled door, simple cut-out feet, old dark cherry finish, wide front stiles, 19th c., 45 1/2" w., 74" h. **1,210**

One-piece Walnut Corner Cupboard

Corner cupboard, country-style, walnut, one-piece construction, the flat top w/a deep stepped & coved cornice above a herringbone-cut band above reeded banding framing a pair of tall two-panel cupboard doors over a mid-molding & a pair of shorter paneled cupboard doors over the shaped apron & bracket feet, refinished, backboards partially patched & renailed, repairs, hinges replaced, found in Kentucky, mid-19th c., top 49 1/2" w., 88 3/4" h. (ILLUS.) **1,980**

Corner cupboard, country-style, walnut, two-piece construction: the upper section w/a deep coved cornice above a pair of tall 8-pane glazed cupboard doors opening to three shelves; the lower section w/a mid-molding above a pair of drawers w/wooden knobs above a pair of paneled cupboard doors w/original brass thumb latches, molded base w/short bracket feet, old finish, late blue paint on the interior, 19th c., 59 1/2" w., 84" h. (feet worn down, one end of cornice incomplete, panes incomplete) **3,960**

Yellow Pine Corner Cupboard

Corner cupboard, country-style, yellow pine, one-piece construction, the flat molded cornice above an arched opening w/three shaped shelves above two raised panel cupboard doors, all framed by an applied molding, wrought-iron hinges appear to be original, blue, green & yellow wash, Shenandoah Valley, Virginia, late 18th c., repairs, 22 x 41", 89 1/2" h. (ILLUS.) **2,990**

Fine Federal Walnut Corner Cupboard

Corner cupboard, Federal, carved walnut, two-part construction: the upper section w/a flat top & deep coved cornice over a narrow tiger stripe maple frieze band over a raised arched molding w/center keystone & serrated inner edge continuing down to tall pilasters flanking the tall arched geometrically glazed cupboard door opening to three shelves; the lower section w/a mid-molding over a pair of drawers above a pair of paneled cupboard doors w/H-hinges, flat molded apron on scroll-cut bracket feet, old refinish, imperfections, probably New Jersey, early 19th c., 22 x 44", 94 1/4" h. (ILLUS.)..................... **8,625**

Corner cupboard, Federal, cherry, one-piece construction, the top w/a deep ogee & molded cornice w/a dentil-carved band above a pair of tall 8-pane glazed cupboard doors flanked by reeded side panels & opening to three shelves, a wide medial band above a pair of paneled cupboard doors also flanked by reeded side panels, molded base over a small central apron scallop & tall simple bracket feet, old mellow finish, found in Ohio, early 19th c., 21 x 53", 90 1/2" h. (stress cracks in back foot w/added support, few pieces of dentil molding missing)........................... **8,250**

Corner cupboard, Federal, cherry, one-piece construction, the top w/a deep stepped & cove-molded cornice above a case w/a tall single 12-pane glazed cupboard door w/original brass ring pull & opening to three butterfly shelves, a medial band above a pair of raised-panel cupboard doors w/a wooden knob, scalloped apron & simple bracket feet, good old dark finish, early 19th c., 22 1/2 x 46", 91 3/4" h. (some plate rails missing or replaced)... **6,600**

Federal Cherry Corner Cupboard

Corner cupboard, Federal, cherry & tiger stripe maple inlaid, the flat top w/a coved cornice over a narrow arched band w/center block continuing down to two blocks over narrow inlaid tiger stripe maple bands all flanking the arched open front w/three shaped shelves above a

slightly stepped-out lower section w/a single raised double-panel door flanked by narrow tiger stripe bands & opening to a single shelf, flat molded base, Mid-Atlantic States, early 19th c., restored, 20 x 41 1/2", 89" h. (ILLUS.)...................... **1,610**

Large Inlaid Federal Corner Cupboard

Corner cupboard, Federal, cherry, two-part construction: the upper section w/a flat top over a deep coved cornice over a reeded frieze band over a tall 12-pane glazed cupboard door opening to three shelves; the lower section w/mid-molding over a pair of small paneled cupboard doors centered by inlaid rings, molded base on shaped bracket feet, old finish, feet replaced, minor repairs, found in Tennessee, early 19th c., 49 1/2" w., 89 3/4" h. (ILLUS.)...................................... **5,225**

Corner cupboard, Federal, cherry, two-piece construction: the upper section w/a wide flaring flat cornice above a single wide 12-pane glazed door w/three top panes rounded at the top, opening to three shelves; the lower section w/a mid-molding over a pair of drawers w/small brass knob pulls over a pair of paneled doors w/brass turnbuckle, molded base, high curved bracket feet, beaded backboards w/square nails, early 19th c., 23 x 47", 89 1/4" h...................................... **7,425**

Country Federal Corner Cupboard

Corner cupboard, Federal country-style, cherry, one-piece construction, a flat top w/a widely flaring deep coved cornice over a dentil band above a pair of tall double raised-panel doors opening to shelves over a pair of shorter raised panel cupboard doors, deeply scalloped apron & bracket feet, old worn refinishing, repairs, edge damage & wear, early 19th c., 52 1/2" w., 85" h. (ILLUS.) **1,045**

Federal One-piece Corner Cupboard

Corner cupboard, Federal country-style, cherry, one-piece construction, a flat top w/cove-molded cornice over a pair of tall 8-pane cupboard doors opening to three shelves over a pair of small drawers over a pair of wide paneled cupboard doors, curved apron & simple bracket feet, minor edge damage & age cracks, one pane w/corner crack, old refinishing, first quarter 19th c., 53 3/4" w., 88 3/4" h. (ILLUS.) **2,970**

Federal Cherry Corner Cupboard

Corner cupboard, Federal country-style, cherry, one-piece construction, the flat deep coved cornice above a pair of tall 8-pane glazed cupboard doors opening to three shelves above a pair of paneled cupboard doors, serpentine apron & simple bracket feet, old mellow refinishing, two panes cracked, back feet replaced, piece of cornice missing, early 19th c., 48" w., 80 3/4" h. (ILLUS.) **2,640**

Early Ohio Cherry Corner Cupboard

Corner cupboard, Federal country-style, cherry, one-piece construction, the flat flaring cornice above a wide 9-pane glazed cupboard door w/brass thumb latch above a mid-molding over a pair of raised-panel cupboard doors, serpentine apron & simple bracket feet, found in Ohio, early 19th c., top 44 3/4" w., 76 1/2" h. (ILLUS.) **4,620**

Tall Inlaid Walnut Corner Cupboard

Corner cupboard, Federal country-style corner cupboard, inlaid walnut, one-piece construction, the flat top w/a narrow coved cornice above a pair of tall paneled cupboard doors flanked by leafy vining inlay down the stiles above a central board w/line inlays over a pair of shorter cupboard doors w/string inlay above a low scalloped apron flanked by line inlay, inlaid diamond keyhole escutcheons, refinished, repairs, hinges replaced, door edges restored, backboards renailed, found in Kentucky, early 19th c., top 47" w., 85" h. (ILLUS.) **2,090**

Fine Curly Maple Corner Cupboard

Corner cupboard, Federal country-style, curly maple, two-part construction: the upper section w/a flat top over a coved cornice above a pair of tall 8-pane glazed cupboard doors opening to three shelves; the lower section w/a mid-molding above a pair of paneled cupboard doors w/small knobs, flat apron on shaped bracket feet, old refinishing, replaced hardware, minor edge damage & restoration, early 19th c., 49" w., 83" h. (ILLUS.) **7,920**

Inlaid Federal Corner Cupboard

Corner cupboard, Federal country-style, inlaid cherry, one-piece construction, the top w/a deep coved cornice above a narrow inlaid band above a pair of tall paneled cupboard doors above a narrow inlaid medial band over a pair of shorter paneled cupboard doors above a narrow inlaid band over the scalloped apron w/a

central fan-inlaid drop, simple bracket feet, each door w/inlaid rectangular banding in the panel, early 19th c., feet replaced, repairs, 45 1/4" w., 82 1/4" h. (ILLUS.) **3,300**

Virginia Federal Corner Cupboard

Corner cupboard, Federal country-style, inlaid walnut, the flat top w/a coved cornice above a frieze band w/geometric inlay over a pair of tall 8-pane glazed cupboard doors opening to three shelves above a mid-molding over a pair of cupboard doors w/tombstone-form line inlay, narrow molded base on scroll-cut bracket feet, Shenandoah Valley, Virginia, early 19th c. (ILLUS.) **4,000**

Painted Two-piece Corner Cupboard

Corner cupboard, Federal country-style, painted pine, two-piece construction: the upper section w/a coved cornice over a carved geometric band above reeded stiles flanking a pair of tall double-paneled cupboard doors w/a small panel over a tall panel & opening to serpentine shelves w/spoon cut-outs; the lower section w/a mid-molding over a single long drawer over a pair of paneled cupboard doors all flanked by reeded stiles, molded base & simple bracket feet, old worn dark blue repaint over earlier cream, possibly Hackensack, New Jersey area, early 19th c., top 45" w., 84 3/4" h. (ILLUS.)..... **15,400**

Painted Federal Corner Cupboard

Corner cupboard, Federal country-style, painted poplar, one-piece construction, the flat top over a deep stepped cornice over a pair of tall paneled doors w/double incised vertical bands & cast-iron latch over a pair of shorter matching doors, flat apron & plain bracket feet, worn blue paint, Pennsylvania, ca. 1830, 43" w., 69 1/2" h. (ILLUS.).. **5,175**

Grain-painted Corner Cupboard

Corner cupboard, Federal country-style, painted walnut, one-piece construction, a deep coved cornice above a single wide 9-pane glazed cupboard door opening to two shelves above a mid-molding over a pair of tall paneled cupboard doors,

molded base on bracket feet, old brown grained repaint, brass knob on lower door may be original, early 19th c., top 25 3/4 x 48 1/4", 79" h. (ILLUS.) **4,675**

Early Dark Pine Corner Cupboard

Corner cupboard, Federal country-style, pine, one-piece construction, the deep stepped & flaring cornice above a dentil-carved band above narrow raised molding framing the single wide 9-pane glazed cupboard door opening to two shelves, a mid-molding above a pair of double-panel cupboard doors, molded base on simple bracket feet, old dark varnish finish, rose-head nail construction, hinged & back foot replaced, some re-nailing, pads added on front feet, late 18th - early 19th c., top 27 x 50", 81" h. (ILLUS.).. **5,500**

Pennsylvania Pine Corner Cupboard

Corner cupboard, Federal country-style, pine, one-piece construction, the thick

stepped cornice above a pair of tall narrow 2-pane glazed cupboard doors
w/early brass latch & ring pulls & opening
to shelves above a mid-molding over a
pair of short paneled cupboard doors,
molded base & simple bracket feet, two
small sections of molding replaced, original red finish, Pennsylvania, early 19th
c., top 23 1/2 x 47 1/2", 78" h. (ILLUS.) **3,300**
Corner cupboard, Federal country-style,
pine & poplar, two-piece construction:
the upper section w/a cove-molded cornice above a pair of 8-pane glazed doors
opening to three shelves; the lower section w/a mid-molding above a pair of
small drawers over two paneled cupboard doors, molded base & simple cut-
out apron, old yellowish brown grained
repaint, first half 19th c., 54" w.,
90 1/2" h. **2,750**

Federal Country Corner Cupboard

Corner cupboard, Federal country-style,
pine, two-part construction: the upper
section w/a flat top over a deep stepped
flaring cornice above a single wide 16-
pane glazed cupboard door opening to
three shelves; the lower section projecting above two cupboard doors w/cock-
beaded panels, flat base w/applied molding, old refinish, replaced hardware,
imperfections, New England, early 19th
c., 29 1/2 x 57", 88 3/4" h. (ILLUS.) **1,725**
Corner cupboard, Federal country-style,
pine, two-piece construction: the upper
section w/a deep flaring & stepped cornice above a pair of tall, narrow 8-pane
glazed cupboard doors w/molded
muntins & wooden knob opening to
three shelves; the lower section w/a
mid-molding over a single cockbeaded
drawer w/two wooden knobs above a
pair of cross-form paneled cupboard
doors w/brass latch, molded base on
scroll-cut ogee bracket feet, Middle Atlantic states, early 19th c., restoration,
21 1/2 x 48 1/2", 87" h. **2,415**

Corner cupboard, Federal country-style,
poplar, two-piece construction: the upper
section w/a high broken-arch scrolled
crest w/three replaced baluster-turned
finials & a center block w/rosette over a
short half-round turned bar above the
large arched cupboard door w/15 panes
of glass opening to three shelves cut-out
for spoons flanked by long half-round
ring-, knob- and baluster-turned pilasters; the lower section w/a pair of drawers
w/turned wood knobs above a pair of
paneled cupboard doors flanked by
shorter ring-, knob- and baluster-turned
pilasters, molded base w/low shaped
bracket feet, mellow finish, pulls replaced, minor restoration to waist molding, Pennsylvania, early 19th c.,
24 x 44 1/2", 90 1/2" h. **5,610**

Federal Tulipwood Corner Cupboard

Corner cupboard, Federal country-style,
tulipwood, two-part construction: the upper section w/a flat top over a deep coved
cornice over a wide tall 12-pane glazed
door w/the three upper panes forming
Gothic arches, opening to three shelves;
the lower section w/a paneled central
drawer flanked by small recessed panels
above a pair of paneled cupboard doors
w/H-hinges opening to a shelf, serpentine apron continuing to bracket feet, old
refinish, some imperfections, probably
Pennsylvania, ca. 1830, 19 x 41",
84 3/4" h. (ILLUS.)..................................... **3,910**
Corner cupboard, Federal, poplar, two-
part construction: the upper section w/a
deep molded cornice above a large 12-
pane glazed door w/the three top panes
arched, opening to three shelves; the
lower section w/a mid-molding over a
case w/a pair of small drawers flanking a
longer center drawer all above a pair of
paneled cupboard doors, flat base raised
on heavy cylindrical feet, old cherry finish, early 19th c., 40 1/2" w., 80 3/4" h.
(feet ended out, replaced brasses includ-
ing H-hinges)... **2,750**
Corner cupboard, Federal, tiger stripe ma-
ple, one-piece construction, the flat top
w/a molded cornice above a pair of tall 8-

pane glazed cupboard doors opening to a three-shelved interior above a pair of recessed panel doors opening to a simple shelf, scalloped apron & short bracket feet, old surface, Middle Atlantic States, 1820, 54" w., 91" h. (height loss) **8,625**

Corner cupboard, Federal, walnut, one-piece construction, the top w/a deep coved cornice above a tall solid cupboard door w/a raised tombstone panel above a lower rectangular raised panel door, wrought-iron surface hinges, molded base w/bracket feet, dovetailed case w/rosehead nail construction, old finish, attributed to James Gheen, Piedmont, North Carolina, late 18th c., top 18 5/8 x 41", 83" h. (feet ended out, front bracket replaced) **9,625**

Federal-Style Corner Cupboard

Corner cupboard, Federal-Style corner cupboard, poplar, one-piece construction, the flat top w/a deep stepped cornice above a tall cross-framed four-panel door above a lower shorter double-panel door w/overall thin fluting, scalloped apron & simple bracket feet, simple turned wood knobs, wear, late 19th c., 22 x 38", 84" h. (ILLUS.) **1,092**

French Neoclassical Corner Cupboard

Corner cupboard, Neoclassical style, barrel-front hanging-type, mahogany & satinwood inlay, the quarter-round top w/a molded cornice above a pair of tall curved cupboard doors w/a center almond-shaped

pinwheel inlay & banded border inlay, on a narrow flat base molding, French polished finish not original, France, ca. 1830, 20 x 26", 44" h. (ILLUS.)................................... **850**

Hanging cupboard, country-style, pine, a narrow rectangular top w/a peaked front edge & molded crest above a pair of canted hinged doors w/molded arched glazed panels opening to three shelves, on a conforming molded base, old refinish w/vestiges of green & red paint, probably New England, late 18th c., 7 x 25", 23" h. (imperfections).................................. **2,645**

Hanging cupboard, country-style, walnut, a rectangular top w/molded cornice over a narrow dentil-carved band over the single beaded panel cupboard door within a beaded frame, molded flat base, old finish, Ohio, early 19th c., 13 3/4 x 20 1/2", 25 3/4" h... **1,760**

Gothic Revival Wall Cupboard

Hanging cupboard, Gothic Revival style, walnut, the top composed of three tall pointed pierce-carved flat Gothic spires w/a taller central spire above a narrow arched mirror framed by molding, above a pair of small square drawers over two long drawers, Gothic arch-cut front apron & back panel, old dark finish, replaced clear glass knobs, 19th c., 7 1/4 x 15 3/4", 37 1/4" h. (ILLUS.)................ **385**

European Hanging Cupboard

Hanging cupboard, painted, a rectangular top w/a flaring coved cornice over a single paneled door w/scrolled brass keyhole escutcheon, molded base, old dark green paint bordered by red, probably lacks interior drawers, other imperfections, probably northern Europe, last half 18th c., 8 x 16", 17" h. (ILLUS.) **1,495**

Hanging cupboard, painted cherry & ash, a rectangular top w/molded edges above a tall single door w/two raised panels above a small set-back shelf across the bottom, dovetailed case, brass pull, old mustard yellow repaint, 19th c., 11 1/4 x 25", 42" h. (small glue repair on lower back) **990**

Hanging cupboard, painted & decorated pine, rectangular top above a case w/a single wide board door w/wooden thumb latch, old red & black graining, found in Maine, 19th c., 11 3/4 x 24 3/4", 39" h. (some edge damage, interior shelves replaced) **303**

Hanging cupboard, painted pine, rectangular top w/molded border framing a hinged door w/two vertical recessed panels opening to a shelved interior, original red grain-painted surface, New England, early 19th c., 6 1/2 x 16 1/4", 23" h. (minor imperfections) **1,840**

Hanging cupboard, painted poplar, a rectangular top w/a narrow widely flaring cornice over a dovetailed case w/a single paneled door opening to an interior fitted w/vertical pigeonholes, a narrow drawer across the bottom, flat molded base, original dark red paint, 19th c., 12 x 23", 26" h. (latch missing, old chips on top interior of cornice) **880**

Country Pine Hanging Cupboard

Hanging cupboard, pine, a rectangular top w/a wide flaring & stepped cornice above a single wide paneled door centered by a raised diamond device & metal latch above a narrow base drawer w/simple wood knob, refinished w/traces of old green paint, early 20th c., 10 x 20", 24" h. (ILLUS.) **200**

Pine Hanging Wall Cupboard

Hanging cupboard, pine, the rectangular top w/a flaring cornice above a conform-

ing case w/a paneled door opening to a shelved interior, over a molding above a shelf w/shaped sides, red-stained, 19th c., 9 1/4 x 20", 25 1/2" h. (ILLUS.) **978**

Hutch cupboard, country-style, painted, a flat rectangular top above slightly sloping front framed by molded boards around the two-shelf open upper section above the stepped-out lower section w/a pair of tall flat cupboard doors w/wooden thumb latches, painted red, New England, late 18th - early 19th c., 35" w., 70" h. **2,800**

Early Painted Hutch Cupboard

Hutch cupboard, painted pine, one-piece construction, the flat rectangular top w/a narrow front molded cornice above a large open hutch front w/two shelves flanked by wide side boards above a single flat lower door w/H-hinges opening to three shelves, old bluish grey paint, New England, late 18th - early 19th c., replaced hinges, imperfections, 18 x 47 3/4", 72 1/2" h. (ILLUS.) **2,645**

Slant-front Hutch Cupboard

Hutch cupboard, pine, slant-front style, a flat rectangular overhanging top above a cockbeaded open front w/three shelves above a tall raised panel door w/wrought-iron HL hinges, flat base, old refinish, replaced door, New England, 18th c., 12 3/4 x 29 1/2", 93" h. (ILLUS.) **1,610**

Hutch cupboard, pine, slant-front style, the flat rectangular top w/a stepped cornice above narrow back-slanting boards framing the open front w/two shelves, the stepped-out lower section w/wide side

Early Pine Hutch Cupboard

boards flanking the narrow tall raised panel door w/small wood knob, flat base, old refinish, imperfections, top doors missing, New England, late 18th c., 18 x 37 1/2", 73" h. (ILLUS.) **2,300**

Primitive Hutch Cupboard

Hutch cupboard, poplar, one-piece construction, the wide flat top above wide flat boards framing the open front w/two shelves above the stepped-out lower section w/wide side boards flanking the narrow crude flat cupboard door, one-board sides w/bootjack feet, old dark reddish brown finish, age cracks, top probably cut down, 19th c., 18 x 42", 71 1/2" h **1,430**

Nutting Pine Hutch Cupboard

Hutch cupboard, Wallace Nuttting-signed, pine, one-piece construction, the rectan-

gular top w/a wide stepped cornice above a scallop-cut open top enclosing two shaped shelves above the stepped out lower case w/a single flat cupboard door w/HL hinges, Model No. 923 Pine Scrolled Cupboard, early 20th c. (ILLUS.).. **4,290**

Jelly cupboard, cherry, the rectangular top w/a low three-quarters gallery above a pair of tall two-panel cupboard doors, the upper panels fitted w/added punched tin panels, scalloped apron & slender bracket feet, refinished, first half 19th c., 20 1/4 x 41 1/4", 51" h. (ILLUS. top next column) **880**

Jelly Cupboard with Tin Panels

Jelly cupboard country-style, cherry & poplar w/flame veneer, a rectangular top above a pair of flat drawers w/flame veneer over a pair of tall paneled cupboard doors opening to three shelves, flat apron & shaped bracket feet, mid-19th c., 18 1/2 x 46 3/4", 59" h. (drawer pulls removed & holes filled in, slight warp to top, backboards renailed) **1,485**

Paint-decorated Jelly Cupboard

Jelly cupboard, country-style, painted & decorated pine & poplar, the rectangular top w/a three-quarters gallery w/rounded ends above a pair of molded drawers w/large wood knobs overhanging a pair of baluster- and acorn-turned short side drops above a pair of tall paneled doors, scalloped apron & ring- and knob-turned feet, old brownish yellow wood graining w/burl design on drawers & door panels, Pennsylvania, mid-19th c., 24 1/2 x 46 3/4", overall 58 3/4" h. (ILLUS.) **495**

Jelly cupboard, country-style, painted & decorated poplar & pine, a high peaked crestrail w/molded top above the rectangular top above a pair of deep drawers w/replaced porcelain knobs overhanging the lower case w/a pair of tall paneled cupboard doors, molded base & tapering ring-turned feet, old comb graining w/chamfered designs on drawers & tops & bottoms of doors, 19th c., 21 x 45", 55 3/4" h. (replaced cast-iron door latches) **1,430**

Old Grain-painted Jelly Cupboard

Jelly cupboard, country-style, painted pine, rectangular top w/flared, stepped cornice above a pair of tall paneled cupboard doors opening to shelves, molded base w/simple bracket feet, original reddish brown grained decoration w/crosshatch design on door & side panels, back w/'T' & rose head nails, feet w/worn black paint, one shelf missing, glued repairs on feet, early 19th c., 17 x 45", 66" h. (ILLUS.) **5,390**

Jelly cupboard, country-style, poplar, a rectangular top above a case w/two tall doors w/three pierced tin panels decorated w/a large center diamond & circle & smaller corner circles, a long nailed drawer across the bottom, three tin panels in each side, square stile legs, side tins w/embossed label "G.F. Co.," backboards w/old painted inscriptions, refinished, 19th c., 14 1/4 x 40", 50" h. **853**

Jelly cupboard, country-style, poplar, the rectangular top w/a high three-quarters gallery above a pair of drawers w/simple wood pulls above a pair of tall paneled cupboard doors w/a cast-iron latch w/porcelain knob, scalloped apron, square nail

Country-style Jelly Cupboard

construction, original finish, ca. 1870, 20 x 42", 4' 10" h. (ILLUS.) **600**

Federal Country-style Jelly Cupboard

Jelly cupboard, Federal country-style, cherry, a rectangular top above a pair of cockbeaded drawers w/turned wood knobs over a long rectangular 2-pane glazed cupboard door, paneled ends, molded base on simple short turned legs w/knob feet, Pennsylvania or Ohio, ca. 1830s, refinished, imperfections, 13 1/2 x 28" , 25" h. (ILLUS.) **1,840**

Grain-painted Federal Jelly Cupboard

Jelly cupboard, Federal country-style, painted & decorated, a rectangular top w/a narrow coved cornice above a case w/a pair of drawers w/oval brasses above a pair of tall paneled cupboard doors, serpentine apron & tall French feet, fine overall reddish brown grain painting imitating mahogany, early 19th c. (ILLUS.) **7,150**

Jelly cupboard, painted, a high peaked crestboard on the rectangular top over a pair of drawers over a pair of tall paneled doors w/iron latches, simple bracket feet & bootjack ends, old dry mustard yellow paint, found in Berks County, Pennsylvania, 19th c., 17 x 44 1/2", 4' 10 1/4" h......... **3,630**

Jelly cupboard, painted & decorated pine & poplar, a rectangular top w/an arched & shaped crestboard above the tall narrow case w/a single drawer w/porcelain knobs above a molding over a single tall paneled cupboard door w/a chamfered surround & opening to four shelves, small bracket feet, old mustard combed & grained decoration over early red, Pennsylvania, 21 x 25 1/2", 5' 11 1/2" h.............. **1,210**

Fine Decorated Jelly Cupboard

Jelly cupboard, painted & decorated pine, the rectangular top over a deep coved cornice above a tall narrow paneled & molding-trimmed central door w/original brass thumb latch flanked by tall narrow molding-trimmed side panels, wide double-arched apron, original overall red flame graining, minor damage, 19th c., 16 1/2 x 48 1/4", 63" h. (ILLUS.) **4,620**

Jelly cupboard, painted & decorated, rectangular top w/a thick stepped cornice above a case w/a pair of tall double-paneled cupboard doors opening to three interior shelves, original cast-iron & brass latches, old mustard yellow over tan grained repaint w/an orangish red on the cornice, Ohio, 19th c., 15 1/2 x 51", 59" h., 4' 11" h. (areas of wear, one rear foot ended out, chip on front foot) **1,650**

Jelly cupboard, painted pine, low three-quarters gallery on the rectangular top above a case w/a pair of drawers over a single long drawer above a pair of tall paneled cupboard doors, flat apron & simple tapered front stile feet, old repaint w/olive graining on a yellowish ground,

19th c., 16 1/2 x 43", overall 53 1/2" h.(wear, one gallery end repaired) **1,705**

Jelly cupboard, painted pine & poplar, plain rectangular top above a wide tall board & batten door flanked by wide front boards, old yellowish brown graining, 19th c., 15 x 42", 40 1/2" h.............. **550**

Jelly cupboard, painted pine & poplar, rectangular top w/high three-quarter gallery w/shaped ends, a pair of drawers w/old replaced wooden knobs above a pair of tall paneled cupboard doors w/old brass latches, one-board ends w/cut-out feet, found in Smoketown, Pennsylvania, old yellow graining over red, 19th c., 13 x 40", overall 47 1/2" h. **3,960**

Jelly cupboard, painted poplar, a rectangular top w/a low crestrail above a case w/a long drawer w/two turned wood knobs above a pair of tall paneled cupboard doors w/a turned wood knob, two punched tin panels w/a heart & leaf design on each side, scalloped apron, square stile legs, old brown repaint, attributed to Ohio, 19th c., 16 1/2 x 40 1/4", 52 1/2" h. plus crest (minor edge damage).............. **1,045**

Painted Jelly Cupboard with Gallery

Jelly cupboard, painted poplar, the rectangular top w/a low three-quarters gallery above a case w/a pair of drawers w/porcelain knobs above a pair of tall paneled doors w/porcelain knobs & cast-iron latch, scroll-cut apron & bracket feet, yellow grained decoration over earlier red & black, square nail construction, minor edge wear, first half 19th c., 19 x 42 1/2", 51" h. (ILLUS.) **1,540**

Jelly cupboard, painted walnut & poplar, the rectangular top w/a low three-quarters gallery above a pair of drawers over a pair of tall two-panel cupboard doors w/a longer panel over a shorter panel, flat apron, one-board sides, short stile legs, old red paint, 19th c., 16 x 44 1/2", 53 1/2" h. plus gallery **990**

Jelly cupboard, pine, a rectangular top fitted w/a shaped backsplash over two short drawers over a pair of paneled doors, raised on elongated tapering legs, 19th c., 22 1/2 x 51 1/2", 48 1/2" h. **1,624**

Pine Jelly Cupboard

Jelly cupboard, pine, a rectangular top w/beaded edges overhanging a case w/a pair of tall raised & molding-trimmed double-paneled doors w/wood turn latch & replaced brass thumb latch, slightly scalloped apron & low bracket feet, refinished, strip between doors added, age cracks in top, 19th c., 18 x 43 1/2", 42 1/2" h. (ILLUS.).. **605**

Country-style Victorian Jelly Cupboard

Jelly cupboard, Victorian country-style, butternut & walnut, a serpentine crestrail on the rectangular top above a pair of drawers over a pair of tall doors w/oblong panels w/pointed ends, a low double-arch apron & bracket feet, pegged construction, refinished, mid-19th c., 18 x 42", 4' 6" h. (ILLUS.) **750**

Jelly cupboard, walnut, a rectangular top above a pair of long drawers w/white porcelain knobs above a pair of tall double-paneled cupboard doors, the side panels of tin punched w/pots of flowers, on short square stile legs, old worn finish, attributed to Wythe County, Virginia, mid-19th c., 17 1/4 x 50", 47" h. (rust & damage to tin).... **1,155**

Jelly cupboard, walnut, country-style, a rectangular top w/a narrow coved cornice above a pair of tall narrow flat doors opening to five shelves, flat molded base, nice mellow color, Zoar, Ohio, 19th c., 16 x 39 1/2", 55" h. **1,210**

Kitchen cupboard, Golden Oak, two-piece construction: the upper section w/a rectangular top w/stepped cornice above a pair

Golden Oak Kitchen Cupboard

of single-pane glazed doors opening to two shelves above a row of drawers w/a long drawer flanked by two small drawers; the lower section w/a cylinder front w/a pull-out work shelf over a tall paneled-front fold-down flour bin beside a square double-paneled door over a drawer, scrolled bracket feet, on casters, ca. 1900, 21 x 37 1/2", 83" h. (ILLUS.)........................ **1,320**

Hoosier-style Kitchen Cupboard

Kitchen cupboard, Hoosier-style, oak, the central projecting cupboard section w/a rectangular top above a pair of paneled & geometrically-glazed cupboard doors above a pull-down door opening to fitted kitchen accessories over a projecting white porcelain work surface above a pair of drawers over a pair of cupboard doors, flanked by tall three-panel set-back cupboard doors, original finish, ca. 1930, 28 x 84", 6' h. (ILLUS.) **1,200**

Kitchen cupboard, late Victorian, ash, two-part construction: the upper section w/a rectangular top & high arched, shaped & scroll-carved front crest above a pair of rectangular glazed cupboard doors w/serpentine top molding opening to two shelves & above a narrow scalloped border band & shaped sides flanking an

Late Victorian Kitchen Cupboard

open pie shelf; the lower section w/a rectangular top w/molded edge over a pair of drawers w/stamped brass pulls over a pair of double-paneled doors, simple apron & bracket feet, carved wood keyhole escutcheons, refinished, ca. 1900, 20 x 42", 7' 2" h. (ILLUS.) **1,600**

Old Glass-doored Kitchen Cupboard

Kitchen cupboard, oak & pine, two-part construction: the upper section w/a rectangular top over two wide square frosted glass doors w/etched geometric designs opening to a shelf over a row of three small drawers, the center w/a curved-down bottom over incurved sides & a narrow shelf; the lower section w/a wide rectangular top overhanging a case w/a central pull-out work shelf over a large paneled door beside a drawer over a smaller paneled door, flat apron, square stile legs, ca. 1910, 26 x 45", 70" h. (ILLUS.) **345**

Fine Cherry Chippendale Linen Press

Linen press, Chippendale, cherry, two-part construction: the upper section w/a rectangular top w/deep flaring cornice over a pair of tall paneled cupboard doors w/serpentine top molding & opening to three shelves; the lower slightly projecting section includes three long thumb-molded graduated drawers, molded base on scroll-cut bracket feet, old oval brasses, old refinish, repairs, imperfections, probably Pennsylvania, late 18th c., 19 1/2 x 47", 80" h. (ILLUS.) **6,325**

Country Chippendale Linen Press

Linen press, Chippendale country-style, painted poplar, the rectangular top w/a deep cove-molded cornice above a pair of tall double raised-panel doors w/a short panel above a tall panel & hung w/H-hinges above two long drawers w/butterfly brasses & keyhole escutcheons, molded base on high bracket feet, old red finish, late 18th - early 19th c., repairs, foot facings & cornice replaced, top 17 x 45 1/2", 73" h. (ILLUS.) **4,400**
Linen press, Chippendale, figured maple, two-part construction: the upper section w/a stepped rectangular top molded above two arched paneled cupboard doors opening to two shelves flanked by fluted stiles;

Chippendale Maple Linen Press

the lower section fitted w/a mid-molding over a pair of drawers over two long drawers, molded base on bracket feet, repairs to feet, right side of cornice repairs, New York or New Jersey, ca. 1780, 23 x 56", 78" h. (ILLUS.)... **9,775**

Early New Jersey Linen Press

Linen press, Chippendale, gumwood, two-part construction: the upper section w/a rectangular top above a narrow cornice w/a dentil-carved band above a frieze band w/blind fretwork over a pair of tall cupboard doors w/arched panels flanked by reeded pilasters & opening to three shelves; the lower section w/a mid-molding over a case w/three long graduated drawers over a molded base & simple bracket feet, replaced brasses, refinished, repairs, attributed to Matthew Egerton, New Brunswick, New Jersey, late 18th c., 17 3/4 x 48", 84" h. (ILLUS.) .. **5,175**

Linen press, Classical, carved walnut veneer, the rectangular top above a plain frieze band over two tall recessed three-panel doors flanked by wide carved & fluted flat columns on molded bases above four front ring-turned legs w/knob feet, the front doors open to an interior of shelves & drawers, the central ones small & veneered, the recessed panel

Fine Classical Linen Press

sides open to an interior w/wooden pegs, old surface, minor imperfections, probably Philadelphia, ca. 1830, 24 x 84", 87 1/2" h. (ILLUS.)..................................... **10,925**

Linen press, Federal country-style, painted & decorated pine & poplar, one-piece construction, rectangular top above a pair of tall paneled cupboard doors w/ring pulls opening to a repainted bluish grey interior w/four shelves above a stepped-out lower case w/three long graduated drawers w/ring pulls, French feet, original brown over tan grain painting w/dark brown painted border detail simulating band inlay on drawers & doors, attributed to Maine, early 19th c., base 14 3/8 x 49", 81 3/4" h. **4,400**

Inlaid Federal Linen Press

Linen press, Federal, inlaid mahogany, two-part construction: the upper section w/a swan's-neck pediment centering an acorn finial on a conch shell-inlaid support, the field-paneled cupboard doors below each centering a patera inlaid w/a spread-winged eagle clutching a shield beneath two rows of stars; the lower section w/a mid-molding over four long cock-beaded graduated drawers w/oval brasses, scalloped apron & slender tall French feet, front left foot restored, rear foot repaired, finial of later date, repairs at upper hinges, partially illegible inscription on the top of the lower section "My — Sa-Iyer (?) 1810, 1810," New York, ca. 1810, 21 x 46 1/4", 93" h. (ILLUS.) **12,650**

Linen press, Federal, mahogany, mahogany veneer & ebony inlay, three-part construction: the rectangular top w/a removable deep cornice arched at the top w/a molded cornice & ball finials at each corner, the frieze band inlaid w/ebony banding, the central section w/a pair of tall molded-panel doors opening to five pull-out shelves; the lower section w/a mid-molding above a case w/a pair of small drawers above three long graduated drawers all w/turned wood knobs, scalloped apron & tall French feet, attributed to New York, early 19th c., 22 x 48", 88" h. (repairs to cornice, center finial missing) **8,800**

Federal Mahogany Linen Press

Linen press, Federal, mahogany & mahogany veneer, two-part construction: the upper section w/a rectangular top over a flared, stepped cornice above a pair of large paneled cupboard doors opening to three adjustable shelves; the stepped-out lower section w/two long faux drawers folding down to form desk writing surface above a pair of paneled cupboard doors, molded base & scroll-cut backet feet, labeled "Thomas Burling," New York, ca. 1830-40, old refinish, replaced pulls, lower case of different origin, 23 1/2 x 49", 88 1/2" h. (ILLUS.) **1,840**

Linen press, Victorian country-style, painted walnut & pine, two-piece construction: the upper section w/a rectangular top w/a widely flaring deep cornice above a pair of tall paneled cupboard doors w/cast-iron thumb latch opening to two shelves; the flush lower section w/a pair of drawers above two long graduated drawers all

Scarce Early Pewter Cupboard

w/turned wood knobs, gently scalloped apron & low block feet, old brown over mustard yellow grained decoration, originally made as one piece, 21 x 47 1/2", 71" h. (small sections of cornice missing).... **1,540**

Linen press, Victorian, oak, two-part construction: the upper section w/a rectangular top & overhanging cornice above a pair of cupboard doors w/large recessed & gently pointed panels & opening to later shelves, the sides w/knob- and spiral-turned columns; the lower section w/a mid-molding over two pairs of short drawers over a single long drawer at the bottom, molded base on scroll-cut bracket feet, England, mid-19th c., 21 x 53 1/4", 79" h. **4,600**

Pewter cupboard, Chippendale country-style, pine & poplar, two-part construction: the upper section w/a rectangular top over a deep molded cornice above a pair of 9-pane glazed cupboard doors opening to two shelves over an open pie shelf w/shaped projecting ends; the lower section w/a stepped-out rectangular top over a row of three small drawers w/wooden knobs over a pair of paneled cupboard doors w/wooden turn latches & knobs, molded base on short bracket feet, old refinish, imperfections & repairs, probably Pennsylvania, late 18th c., 21 x 56 3/4", 86" h. (ILLUS.)........................ **5,463**

Simple Painted Pewter Cupboard

Pewter cupboard, country-style, painted pine, one-piece construction, the flat rectangular top above an open hutch top w/three shelves above a stepped-out top over a case w/a narrow tall one-board door flanked by wide side boards, simple angle-cut feet, red paint, some old reconstruction, 19 x 38 1/4", 71 1/2" h. (ILLUS.) **2,090**

Early Painted Pewter Cupboard

Pewter cupboard, country-style, painted pine, one-piece construction, the flat rectangular top above two wide side boards flanking an open two-shelved compartment, the stepped-out lower section w/a pair of flat board doors flanked by wide side boards, worn old sage green paint over red, shelves somewhat altered, some edge damage & renailing, 19th c., 17 x 49", 73" h. (ILLUS.) **2,200**

Early Ohio Pewter Cupboard

Pewter cupboard, country-style, poplar, one-piece construction, a rectangular top w/a widely flaring stepped cornice above a tall beaded open hutch w/three shelves above a stepped-out lower case w/a single cupboard door w/four raised panels, old red finish, attributed to Ohio, cornice replaced, early 19th c., top 14 x 39 1/4", 79" h. (ILLUS.) **3,960**

Pewter cupboard, painted pine, one-piece construction, a rectangular top w/a very deep flaring stepped cornice above wide side boards flanking a tall narrow open compartment w/two incurved shelves & scallop-cut sides & top above a tall narrow raised-panel lower door w/wood thumb latch, molded base w/short scroll-cut bracket feet, old red repaint on exterior, areas of old dry blue on interior, case w/wooden peg & rosehead nail construction, top 18 3/4 x 39 1/2", 79 3/4" h. (wear, age cracks, insect damage, base reshaped) **2,750**

Pewter cupboard, pine, one-piece construction, the flat rectangular top w/narrow molding across cornice & down the front sides framing the open three-shelf cupboard w/plate rails, the slightly stepped-out lower section w/a pair of paneled cupboard doors, flat base, old nut brown finish, 19th c., 13 1/4 x 41 3/4", 70 1/2" h. (bottom rail under doors replaced, feet worn down, repairs, backboards renailed) **1,650**

Early Pine Pewter Cupboard

Pewter cupboard, pine, rectangular top over a narrow scalloped apron over a tall two-shelf open section w/two wide backboards & one-board sides w/upper scallops, the lower projecting section w/a pair of plain flat doors w/replaced hardware, flat apron w/simple bracket feet, refinished, ca. 1830, 21 x 42", 6' 8" h. (ILLUS.) **1,200**

Pie safe, cherry, a rectangular top w/a low three-quarter gallery above a pair of tall three-panel doors each w/a punched-tin panel decorated w/a central diamond framed by four punched circles, one door w/wood knob, a long drawer w/two wood knobs at the base, raised on ring-, rod- and knob-turned tapering legs, three matching tin panels on each end, refinished, 19th c., 18 x 42", overall 60" h. (considerable foot restoration, gallery replaced) **1,045**

Fine Cherry & Tin Pie Safe

Pie safe, cherry & punched tin, a rectangular top above a pair of drawers w/simple turned knobs above a pair of large cupboard doors each w/four large rectangular punched tin panels decorated w/a central pinwheel w/fanned leaf devices in each corner, flat base, baluster- and ring-turned legs w/peg feet, old worn brown finish w/traces of oilcloth, two punched tin panels on each end, found in east Tennessee, mid-19th c., 18 3/4 x 53", 49" h. (ILLUS.)..... **5,225**

Early Pie Safe with Punched Tin

Pie safe, country-style, hardwoods, the rectangular top w/a low shaped three-quarters gallery above a tall case w/a pair of two three-panel doors w/pierced tin inserts w/scrolling designs above a pair of deep drawers at the bottom, turned & tapering legs w/knob & peg feet, three pierced tins on each side, mid-19th c. (ILLUS.) **1,450**

Pie safe, grain-painted wood, a rectangular flat top slightly overhanging the case w/a single screened door flanked by narrow screened panels, pair of narrow screened panels on each side, raised on tall stile legs, overall grain-painted finish, 19th c., 35" w., 48" h. **850**

Pie safe, hanging-type, pine & tin, a flat rectangular top above a frame of four square projecting stiles framing a single front door w/a long pierced tin panel decorated w/a central circle w/star & quarter-round circles in each corner, the door flanked by narrow side tin panels w/pierced half-circle designs, tin sides w/similar pierced designs, old red finish, 19th ., 20 x 30", 34 1/2" h. **935**

Pie safe, painted cherry, a rectangular top above a pair of dovetailed drawers over a pair of tall cupboard doors each fitted w/six side-by-side punched tin panels forming continuous patterns of central rings enclosing four hearts & half-round & quarter-round corner rings w/hearts alternating w/a large rounded pinwheel in each panel, side tin panels w/pinwheel & birds designs, a flat apron & round ring-turned legs w/knob feet, old green repaint, square nail & peg construction, 24 1/2 x 58", 64" h. (door hinges, pulls & turn buckles old replacements) **4,675**

Single-door Cherry Pie Safe

Pie safe, painted cherry, the flat rectangular top above a single very wide door w/raised molding around two long pierced tin panels w/stars & hex signs & further decorated w/thin reeded bands, matching pierced tin side panels, heavy tapering ring-turned feet, old red paint, probably New Jersey, early 19th c., imperfections, 31 1/4" w., 46 1/4" h. (ILLUS.) **633**

Pie safe, painted & decorated, a rectangular top w/a high triple-arched & shaped backrail, the case w/a pair of large cupboard doors w/wide bottom & top moldings enclosing screen panels & opening to two shelves, simple bracket feet, small Rockingham glazed door pulls, old brown over mustard yellow graining, 19th c., 18 x 61",

50 1/2" h. (one rear foot & shelf missing, some pieces of molding missing) **1,320**

Pie safe, painted poplar, a rectangular top above a pair of tall cupboard doors each fitted w/three pierced tin panels decorated w/a large five-point star within a circle in the center against an urn device in background, two small stars in the upper panel corners & two larger ones in the lower corners, three tin panels down each side, on tall square stile legs, old black repaint, white porcelain door knob, tins mounted backward, 19th c., 17 x 41 1/2", 59" h. (one side tin starting to deteriorate, one door w/small half moon edge cut-out) **2,090**

Pie safe, painted poplar, a rectangular top w/a low three-quarters gallery above the tall case w/a pair of tall doors each w/three pierced tin panels, three matching tin panels on each side, flat apron, tall rectangular stile legs, the tin panels pierced w/a large central diamond enclosing a sunburst & w/a half-circle on each edge, old bluish green repaint, 15 1/4 x 36 1/2", 52 1/2" h. plus replaced gallery (tin panels w/some rust & damage).................................... **743**

Pie safe, painted poplar, rectangular top above a pair of drawers w/small wooden knobs over a pair of tall three-panel doors each tin panel w/a pierced floral design, one-board ends, tall slightly tapering stile legs, old grey repaint, 19th c., 17 x 42 1/2", 57 3/4" h. **770**

Tall Painted Poplar Pie Safe

Pie safe, painted poplar, the flat rectangular top above a tall case w/a pair of tall three-panel cupboard doors w/three pierced tin inserts in a circle & diamond design above a central long drawer over a pair of paneled doors at the bottom, flat stile legs, old black paint, bookjack ends, light stains at sides, first half 19th c., 16 x 41 3/4", 84 1/2" h. (ILLUS.) **1,980**

Painted Poplar Pie Safe

Pie safe, painted poplar, the rectangular top above a pair of tall three-panel cupboard doors, a punched tin in each panel in a circle & star design, one door w/simple wooden knob, a single long drawer across the bottom w/two wooden knobs, three panels on each side w/punched-tin panels, tall stile legs, old blue paint over other colors, 19th c., 17 1/2 x 39 3/4", 59" h. (ILLUS.) **1,540**

Pie safe, painted poplar & walnut, a rectangular top above a tall case w/a long narrow dovetailed drawer w/small knobs above a pair of tall three-panel cupboard doors w/star pattern punched tin panels, slender stile legs, old paint w/a top layer of green, found in Missouri, 19th c., 16 1/2 x 38 1/2", 54" h. (some damage to tins) **440**

Tall Painted Walnut Stepback Pie Safe

Pie safe, painted walnut, one-piece construction, a rectangular top w/a thick molded cornice above a pair of tall three-panel cupboard doors each w/three pierced tin panels decorated w/tulips & leaves above a pair of drawers, the stepped-out lower section w/a pair of two-panel cupboard doors w/matching pierced tin panels, old light blue repaint, one-board sides, edge & rodent damage, tin rusted, holes drilled in bottom case, first half 19th c., 19 1/2 x 40", 79 1/4" h. (ILLUS.)...................................... **2,200**

Pie safe, painted wood, a flat rectangular top above a pair of tall three-panel doors each w/a punched tin panel in a tulip & vase design, three matching tin panels down each side, raised on short stile legs, painted white, 19th c., 41 1/2" w., 45" h. **850**

Early Screened Pie Safe

Pie safe, pine, a rectangular top above a single long drawer w/two recessed panels over a pair of four-panel screened cupboard doors all flanked by reeded stiles, opening to three shelves, old refinish w/some red color remaining, New Jersey, early 19th c., imperfections, 44" w., 54" h. (ILLUS.).. **2,645**

Pie safe, pine country-style, mortise & tenon construction, a flat rectangular top above a pair of tall doors each w/two upper rectangular openings for screening above a lower solid panel, matching configuration on the sides, on tall slender square tapering stile legs, mid-19th c., 17 x 45", 77" h. (screen missing in panels) **523**

Pie safe, pine & poplar, rectangular top above a single long drawer over a pair of tall doors each w/three star punched tin panels on each side, stile legs, 19th c., 17 1/4 x 43", 57 3/4" h. (refinished) **605**

Poplar & Punched Tin Pie Safe

Pie safe, poplar & punched tin, a flat rectangular top above a pair of tall paneled cupboard doors w/three punched tin panels each decorated w/a large central star in a circle flanked by four small stars, a long narrow drawer across the bottom, one-board ends, tightly scallop-cut apron, square stile legs, refinished, 19th c., 15 x 40 3/4", 49" h. (ILLUS.)........................ **1,375**

Pie safe, walnut, a rectangular top w/a flared cove-molded cornice above a mortised & pinned case w/a pair of tall three-panel doors each w/a punched tin panel decorated w/a large pinwheel & quarter-round circles in each corner, three matching panels on each side, tall simple turned legs, old gold repaint on tins, 19th c., 19 3/4 x 44 1/4", 57" h. (some damage to side tins) **1,540**

Side cupboard, cherry, a rectangular top w/chamfered front corners & narrow molded cornice above a conforming case w/a long raised panel door w/a central raised diamond, wrought-iron rattail hinges w/leaf finials, long bottom drawer w/wooden knob, molded flat base, Zoar, Ohio, early 19th c., (old mellow refinishing, missing feet, small chip off base molding, top lip of drawer damaged)......... **3,575**

Side cupboard, painted pine, rectangular top w/flat molded cornice above two doors w/raised panels opening to two shelves, on a flat base w/applied moldings, brasses appear to be original, old brown varnished surface, New England, early 19th c., 10 x 36", 23 1/2" h. (imperfections) **920**

Step-back hutch cupboard, walnut, one-piece construction, a rectangular top w/narrow molded cornice above an open-front case w/three shelves above a stepped-out lower case w/a pair of paneled cupboard doors w/a thumb latch & porcelain knob, scalloped apron & slender bracket feet, mellow old finish, 19th c., 11 1/2 x 40 1/2" top, 76" h. **1,760**

Step-back wall cupboard, butternut w/old dark brown finish, two-part construction: the upper section w/a rectangular top w/a deep flaring cornice above a pair of tall double-paneled cupboard doors opening to shelves, the top one w/cut-out for spoons; the stepped-out lower section w/a pair of flush drawers above a pair of paneled cupboard doors, on short double knob-turned feet, found in Cairo, Ohio, mid-19th c., 13 x 49 1/4", 80" h. (most hardware removed)...................................... **1,980**

Step-back wall cupboard, cherry, one-piece construction, the rectangular top w/a narrow flared cornice above a pair of tall double-paneled doors opening to shelves above the slightly projecting lower section w/a pair of paneled shorter doors, flat apron & simple bracket feet, refinished w/traces of old paint, possibly Kentucky, mid-19th c., 13 3/8 x 31 1/8", 81 1/2" h. (some edge damage, filled holes from insect damage, replaced hinges).................... **1,430**

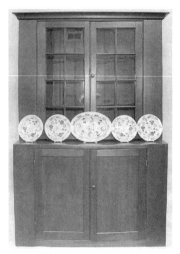

Cherry & Poplar Step-back Cupboard

Step-back wall cupboard, country-style, cherry & poplar, two-piece construction: the upper section w/a rectangular top over a simple coved cornice above a pair of 8-pane glazed cupboard doors opening to three shelves & flanked by wide side boards; the stepped-out lower section w/a pair of tall paneled cupboard doors flanked by wide side boards, flat base, repairs, cut-down w/pie shelf removed, cornice replaced, old finish, mid-19th c., top 15 1/4 x 57", 79 3/4" h. (ILLUS.)................... **1,513**

Cherry Step-back Wall Cupboard

Step-back wall cupboard, country-style, cherry, two-part construction: the upper section w/a rectangular top w/a wide flat & flaring cornice over a pair of tall 6-pane glazed cupboard doors opening to two shelves over a low open pie shelf; the stepped-out lower section w/a pair of shallow drawers w/wood knobs over a pair of paneled doors w/a keyhole & wooden knob, flat apron & curved bracket feet, original brass latch in top, replaced wooden pulls, old refinishing, 19th c., 15 1/2 x 54 1/4", 83 3/4" h. (ILLUS.) **3,960**

Tall Step-back Cherry Wall Cupboard

Step-back wall cupboard, country-style, cherry, two-piece construction: the upper section w/a rectangular top w/a coved cornice over a dentil-carved frieze band above a pair of very tall two-panel cupboard doors w/a smaller square panel over a tall rectangular panel above a pair of short drawers w/simple turned wood knobs; the stepped-out lower section w/a pair of paneled cupboard doors over the serpentine apron, refinished, repairs to hinge rails & one upper door w/replaced surface-mounted hinges, replaced pulls, minor edge damage, mid-19th c., top 14 x 45 3/4", 87" h. (ILLUS.)...................... **1,980**

Flame-painted Step-back Cupboard

Step-back wall cupboard, country-style, painted & decorated pine & poplar, two-piece construction: the upper section w/a rectangular top over a deep coved cornice above a pair of tall cupboard doors w/three horizontal panels over an open pie shelf w/shaped ends; the stepped-out lower section w/a rectangular top over a row of three round-fronted drawers above a pair of cupboard doors w/two horizontal panels each, flat apron & short bracket feet, one-board ends, original red flame-graining on yellow ground w/solid red door panels, mismatched latches & replaced pulls, mid-19th c., 13 x 57 3/4", 84" h. (ILLUS.)... **6,875**

Step-back wall cupboard, country-style, painted & decorated walnut, two-piece construction: the upper section w/a rectangular top & deep flaring coved cornice above a pair of 3-pane glazed cupboard doors opening to two shelves above an open pie shelf w/shaped sides; the stepped-out lower case w/a pair of drawers w/turned knobs above a pair of paneled cupboard doors w/a cast-iron latch w/porcelain knob, gently scalloped apron & short bracket feet, reddish brown over tan grained repaint, 19th c., 18 1/2 x 49", 85 1/4" h... **1,925**

Step-back wall cupboard, country-style, painted pine, one-piece construction, a rectangular top w/a narrow molded cornice above a pair of long plain flush doors opening to three shelves above three low compartments on the projecting lower case w/another pair of plain doors opening to three shelves, flat base, interior painted red, exterior painted light blue, New England, early 19th c. (surface losses & repairs) **2,990**

Step-back wall cupboard, country-style, painted pine, one-piece construction, the rectangular top w/a widely flaring coved cornice above a pair of tall paneled doors separated by a paneled center stile, the stepped-out base w/a pair of shorter paneled doors separated by a paneled center stile, molded base w/finely scroll-cut apron, old red paint w/red comb graining at one end, trim picked out in green, old replaced cast-iron thumb latches w/brass knobs, first half 19th c., 18 x 55", 75" h...... **2,475**

Painted Step-back Wall Cupboard

Step-back wall cupboard, country-style, painted pine, one-piece construction, the rectangular top w/a widely flaring

stepped cornice over a frieze band w/molding above a pair of paneled cupboard doors w/molding-trimmed panels & simple wood knobs above the stepped-out lower section over two very small drawers over another pair of matching paneled doors, molded base w/simply cut-out apron, old blue paint over a lighter blue, found in northern Maine, edge wear & damage, 19th c., toop 20 x 62 1/4", 78 1/2" h. (ILLUS.)....................................... **6,050**

Painted Pennsylvania Cupboard

Step-back wall cupboard, country-style, painted pine, two-part construction: the upper section w/a rectangular top over a shallow widely flaring stepped cornice over a deep frieze above a pair of 6-pane glazed cupboard doors opening to two shelves over a low pie shelf w/shaped end brackets; the lower stepped-out section w/a row of three drawers w/turned wood knobs over a pair of double-paneled cupboard doors w/wood knobs & a wooden thumb latch, molded apron on heavy ball feet, yellow paint of later date, chips to cornice, missing right side of mid-molding, Pennsylvania, ca. 1830, 18 x 54", 88" h. (ILLUS.) **7,475**

Step-back wall cupboard, country-style, painted poplar, two-piece construction: the upper section w/a flared & stepped cornice above a pair of 3-pane glazed cupboard doors opening to two shelves above an arched pie shelf; the lower stepped-out section w/a pair of flush drawers over a pair of paneled cupboard doors, gently scalloped apron & low bracket feet, old yellowish brown steel comb-graining on a white ground, brass thumb latch on botton doors, cast-iron latch on upper doors, worn paint, some edge damage, top 13 1/2 x 49", 82 1/2" h. **1,045**

Step-back wall cupboard, country-style, painted poplar, two-piece construction: the upper section w/a rectangular top w/a wide flat & flaring cornice over a pair of tall 2-pane glazed cupboard doors opening to two shelves; the stepped-out lower section w/a single long shallow drawer over a pair of cupboard doors, flat apron & simple cut-out bracket feet, dark red repaint w/yellow interior & yellow line banding on drawer & lower doors, 17 3/4 x 39 1/2", 81 1/2" h. **1,540**

Early Pine Step-back Wall Cupboard

Step-back wall cupboard, country-style, pine, one-piece construction, the flat rectangular top above a molded edging across the top & down the sides flanking a pair of tall double-paneled doors w/a small square panel over a long rectangular panel over a deep pie shelf, the stepped-out lower section w/further molded edging & a pair of tall paneled doors w/small turned wood knobs, flat base, two shelves in top & three in bottom, old refinish, New England, 1790-1810, 21 x 37 1/2", 86" h. (ILLUS.) **2,990**

Poplar & Curly Maple Wall Cupboard

Step-back wall cupboard, country-style, poplar w/some curly maple, two-part construction: the upper section w/a rectangular top over a deep coved cornice above a pair of tall 3-pane glazed cupboard doors opening to two shelves over a low open pie shelf; the lower stepped-out section w/a pair of drawers w/turned wood knobs over a pair of paneled cupboard doors w/a replaced brass thumb latch, tightly scalloped apron on low bracket feet, pieced cornice repair, 19th c., 14 x 45 1/2", 81" h. (ILLUS.) **1,595**

Step-back wall cupboard, country-style, poplar & walnut, two-part construction: the upper section w/a flaring ogee cornice w/rounded corners above a pair of tall 8-pane glazed cupboard doors opening to three shelves; the stepped-out lower section w/a rectangular top w/molded edges & rounded front corners above an ogee frieze w/a pair of longer drawers flanking a central small drawer all w/simple turned wood knobs above a pair of paneled cupboard doors flanked by rounded front corners, low lightly scalloped apron, refinished, second half 19th c., 19 3/4 x 50 1/2", 81 1/2" h. **825**

Step-back wall cupboard, country-style, walnut, butternut & oak, two-piece construction: the upper section w/a rectangular top & deep stepped cornice above a pair of large single-pane glazed cupboard doors w/molded edging w/rounded corners, opening to two shelves & plate racks above an open pie shelf; the stepped-out lower section w/a row of three molded drawers w/cast-iron finger grip pulls above a pair of double-panel cupboard doors each w/a cast-iron thumb latch w/white porcelain knob, flat apron on slender curved bracket feet, old varnish finish, Ohio Amish, second half 19th c., 19 1/4 x 51 3/4", 80 1/2" h. **1,320**

Nice Walnut Step-back Cupboard

Step-back wall cupboard, country-style, walnut, one-piece construction, a rectangular top w/a wide flat & flaring cornice above a pair of 6-pane glazed cupboard doors w/original brass latch opening to two shelves, the stepped-out lower section over a pair of shallow drawers w/small wood knobs over a pair of paneled cupboard doors w/a brass latch, gently scalloped apron on bracket feet w/casters, knobs missing on latches, light blue interior repaint, minor foot damage, old varnish finish, mid-19th c., 16 3/4 x 50 1/2", 81 1/4" h. (ILLUS.) **1,980**

Step-back wall cupboard, country-style, walnut, one-piece construction, a rectangular top w/a deep coved cornice above a pair of tall 6-pane glazed cupboard doors opening to shelves, the stepped-out lower section w/a pair of paneled cupboard doors, shaped apron w/simple bracket feet, some edge damage, cornice renailed, worn old finish, top 14 3/4 x 46 3/4", 80 1/4" h. **2,090**

Tall Walnut Step-back Wall Cupboard

Step-back wall cupboard, country-style, walnut, two-piece construction: the upper section w/a rectangular top w/a simple coved cornice above a pair of tall 8-pane glazed cupboard doors opening to shelves above the open pie shelf w/shaped sides; the lower stepped-out section w/a rectangular top over a row of three drawers above a pair of paneled cupboard doors flanking a narrow central panel, short turned tapering legs w/knob feet, old worn finish, original brass swivel latches on doors, brass knobs replaced, base w/old shipping label "Vandalia RR Co.," mid-19th c., top 13 1/2 x 54", 93 1/4" h. (ILLUS.) **4,400**

Painted Step-back Wall Cupboard

Step-back wall cupboard, Federal country-style, painted, two-part construction: the upper section w/a flat rectangular top above a pair of tall narrow raised panel doors opening to four shelves above an open pie shelf; the stepped-out lower section w/a pair of raised panel cupboard doors opening to two shelves, small wood knobs & wood thumb latches, old blue paint, New England, early 19th c., imperfections, 17 x 36 1/2", 80 1/2" h. (ILLUS.).. **7,475**

Step-back wall cupboard, Federal country-style, walnut, one-piece construction, a rectangular top w/a molded cornice above a pair of tall 4-pane glazed cupboard doors opening to two shelves above the projecting base w/a pair of paneled cupboard doors, scallop-cut apron & narrow feet, old refinish, probably Pennsylvania or Ohio, early 19th c., 16 x 35 3/4", 62" h. **2,415**

Mid-Atlantic Federal Cupboard

Step-back wall cupboard, Federal, maple, two-part construction: the upper section w/a rectangular top & deep flared cornice above two 6-pane glazed cupboard doors flanking a 3-panel central panel above a tall pie shelf w/scalloped sides; the stepped-out lower section w/a pair of narrow long drawers flanking a small central drawer over a pair of paneled cupboard doors, molded base w/serpentine apron & simple bracket feet, Mid-Atlantic States, early 19th c., H-hinges on upper doors, 17 1/2 x 57 1/2", 84" h. (ILLUS.) **6,325**

Step-back wall cupboard, Federal, pine, two-part construction: the upper section w/a rectangular top & deep flaring stepped cornice above a reeded frieze band over a pair of 6-pane glazed cupboard doors flanked by reeded pilasters & opening to shaped shelves; the stepped-out lower section w/a long central drawer w/two

Early Hackensack Wall Cupboard

panels of molding flanked by small square drawers above a pair of recessed panel doors flanked by narrow molded side panels, molded base, bootjack feet at sides, old refinish, minor imperfections, Hackensack, New Jersey, ca. 1800-10, 51" w., 84" h. (ILLUS.) **6,900**

Step-back wall cupboard, Federal style, pine, two-part construction: the upper section w/a rectangular top w/a deep stepped flaring cornice over a patterned diagonally-reeded frieze band above a pair of 6-pane glazed doors w/arched top panes & molded muntins all flanked by paneled & reeded pilasters; the lower section w/a mid-molding on the projecting top over a long molded central drawer flanked by small square end drawers above a pair of double-molded cupboard doors flanked by tall narrow molded panels, molded base on slender arched feet, old brass pulls, old refinish, probably Hackensack, New Jersey, ca. 1810, 19 x 50 3/4", 85" h. **10,350**

Step-back wall cupboard, Georgian, walnut, two-piece construction: the upper section w/a rectangular top over a narrow flared cornice & a carved dentil band above a pair of 6-pane glazed cupboard doors flanking three central fixed panes all flanked by side rails w/a carved paterae panel above a row of three small raised rectangular panels over an open pie shelf w/scroll-cut brackets; the projecting lower section w/a pair of drawers w/small wood knobs flanked by horizontally incised rectangular panels over a pair of raised panel cupboard doors flanked by long narrow raised panels, molded base on scroll-cut bracket feet, old dark varnish finish, Canada, early 19th c., 12 1/2 x 63", 85 1/4" h. (restoration to top, back replaced by plywood) **4,400**

Step-back wall cupboard, Neoclassical, inlaid mahogany, two-part construction: the upper section w/a pair of flat-topped rectangular cupboards w/a single-pane glazed door opening to two shelves & mounted at the upper corners w/ormolu bosses flanking the central set-back rectangular tall mirror w/a gently arched top & molded crestrail w/an ormolu shell & leafy branch mount, the lower section w/a light rectangular marble top above a case w/a pair of banded drawers w/simple pulls above a pair of banded cupboard doors w/central oval floral urn inlays, leafy sprig ormolu mounts at each upper corner, flat molded apron on simple baluster-turned legs, France, early 20th c., 20 3/4 x 55", 75 1/2" h. **1,265**

Simple Painted Pine Cupboard

Step-back wall cupboard, painted pine, one-piece construction, a rectangular top w/a narrow cornice above a pair of tall flat cupboard doors opening to three shelves above a short section of three open compartments above the stepped-out lower case w/a pair of flat cupboard doors, painted light blue, interior painted red, New England, early 19th c., surface losses & repairs (ILLUS.) **2,990**

Step-back wall cupboard, painted pine, one-piece construction, the rectangular flat top above a pair of narrow flat board-and-batten doors w/small wood knobs & thumbpieces, the stepped-out lower section w/a matching pair of tall narrow flat doors, flat apron w/angled cut-out feet, old apple green repaint over earlier red, found in New Hampshire, 19th c., 22 3/4 x 43", 79" h. (chip in one front foot) **1,100**

Step-back wall cupboard, painted pine, one-piece construction, the rectangular top w/a flared molded cornice above a pair of tall paneled doors w/steel thumb latch, the stepped-out lower section w/a long nailed drawer w/iron pull above a pair of paneled cupboard doors, very narrow arched apron, old green repaint, second half 19th c., 17 3/4 x 35 3/4", 59 1/2" h. **990**

Early Pennsylvania Painted Cupboard

Step-back wall cupboard, painted pine, two-part construction: the upper section w/a rectangular top & deep flaring cornice above a pair of 6-pane glazed cupboard doors opening to three shelves w/plate grooves & spoon rack above a low open pie shelf; the stepped-out lower section w/a row of three drawers above a pair of paneled cupboard doors, molded base & simple bracket feet, later off-white paint, replaced hardware, Pennsylvania, late 18th c., imperfections, 17 1/2 x 52", 84" h. (ILLUS.).. **9,775**

Painted One-piece Cupboard

Step-back wall cupboard, painted poplar, one-piece construction, the rectangular top w/a narrow flat cornice above a pair of 6-pane glazed cupboard doors opening to two shelves above a stepped-out lower section w/a pair of paneled cupboard doors, gently curved apron & angled bracket feet, old brown repaint, interior w/old

worn yellow paint, first half 19th c., repairs, top 12 1/4 x 50 1/2", 76" h. (ILLUS.).................. **880**

Painted Step-back Wall Cupboard

Step-back wall cupboard, painted wood, two-part construction: the upper section w/a flat rectangular top above a pair of tall narrow raised paneled doors, opening to interior shelves above a pie shelf; the lower stepped-out section w/a pair of raised panel cupboard doors, old blue paint, New England, early 19th c., imperfections, 16 x 36 1/2"., 80 h. (ILLUS.)....... **7,475**

Step-back wall cupboard, pine, two-part construction: the upper section w/a rectangular top w/narrow molded cornice over a pair of short paneled doors, the stepped-out lower section w/a pair of tall paneled doors, simple cut-out feet, old refinishing w/nut brown color, 19th c., 17 1/2 x 48 1/2", 75" h. **1,089**

Step-back wall cupboard, pine, two-piece construction w/dry sink base; the upper section w/a rectangular top over a deep coved cornice above a pair of tall paneled doors w/replaced brass thumb latches over a high open section w/three paneled sides; lower section w/a top dry sink well w/molded edges over a case w/three short graduated raised-panel drawers beside a small paneled door, molded base, dovetailed & nailed construction, refinished, 19th c., base 18 1/4 x 41 1/2", overall 87 1/2" h.. **1,650**

Step-back wall cupboard, Victorian Baroque Revival substyle, carved oak, two-part construction: the upper section w/a rectangular top w/a high ornately-cut crestrail centered by a carved grotesque mask of Bacchus clenching grapevines in his teeth which scroll across the front of the crestrail, above a deep stepped & flaring cornice above a frieze band carved w/grapevine & centered by a scroll-carved mount, all above a pair of tall glazed cupboard doors w/narrow beaded molding flanked by fruit- and leaf-carved side rails, the stepped-out lower section w/a molded edge above a pair of

Ornately Carved Baroque Cupboard

drawers carved w/scrolling grapevines over a pair of paneled cupboard doors bordered by beaded molding & carved in bold relief w/figural tavern scenes, further fruit & leaf carving down the sides, carved flaring flat base molding on bun feet, refinished, Europe, late 19th c., 22 x 44", 8' 4" h. (ILLUS.) **3,400**

Step-back wall cupboard, Victorian country-style, painted & decorated pine, two-part construction: the upper section w/a rectangular top w/a very widely flaring stepped cornice above a case w/two single-pane glazed cupboard doors w/arched tops opening to two shelves; the lower case w/a molding around the upper case & the stepped-out lower case w/a molded edge above a single drawer w/two turned wood knobs above a pair of arch-topped paneled cupboard doors, thick molded flat base, old black over brown grained decoration, mid-19th c., 17 3/4 x 35 1/2", 71 1/4" h. (edge wear, one pane cracked) **1,100**

Victorian Country Step-back Cupboard

Step-back wall cupboard, Victorian country-style, pine, two-piece construction: the upper section w/a rectangular top w/angled front corners over a deep stepped & flaring cornice over a frieze band of carved arrowhead devices separated by three half-round drop spindles over a pair of 4-pane glazed cupboard doors w/thumb latches & small half-round spindles applied to dividing rails above a pair of small drawers w/raised panels separated w/applied low pyramidal blocks; the stepped-out lower section w/a pair of double-paneled cupboard doors w/a small button in the center of each panel & cast-iron latches, flanked at the sides by chamfered corners w/half-round applied spindles, flat molded apron on bracket feet, refinished, ca. 1860, 23 x 58", 7' 1" h. (ILLUS.) **4,500**

Late Victorian Step-back Cupboard

Step-back wall cupboard, Victorian country-style, stained maple, two-part construction: the upper section w/a rectangular top w/a flared cornice above a pair of tall 3-pane glazed cupboard doors opening to two shelves; the stepped-out lower section w/a pair of narrow drawers over a pair of paneled doors, apron w/small center drop, simple bracket feet, cleaned down to original stain, second half 19th c., 20 x 42", 6' 10" h. (ILLUS.) **1,000**

Step-back wall cupboard, Victorian country-style, walnut, two-part construction: the upper section w/a rectangular top & deep flaring flat cornice above a pair of tall paneled cupboard doors w/cast-iron latches w/porcelain knobs above a pie shelf w/shaped sides; the lower stepped-out section w/a pair of drawers w/porcelain knobs over a pair of paneled cupboard doors w/cast-iron latches, simple bracket feet, mellow finish, 19th c., 18 x 45", 85 1/2" h. (one knob missing, right door swollen) **2,090**

Fancy Oak Step-back Wall Cupboard

Step-back wall cupboard, Victorian Golden Oak substyle, two-part construction: the upper section w/a high serpentine & scroll-carved front crestrail above a egg-and-dart molding above a pair of glazed cupboard doors w/shaped tops trimmed w/carved scrolls & opening to two shelves; the lower section w/a rectangular support shelf raised on S-scroll brackets & a paneled back on the rectangular top w/molded edges above a pair of drawers w/stamped brass pulls over a single long drawer all flanked by sunbursts & diamond carving above a pair of large paneled cupboard doors w/bold scroll-carved designs, serpentine apron & bracket feet, refinished, ca. 1900, 18 x 42", 7' 8" h. (ILLUS.) **3,600**

Step-back wall cupboard, Victorian-Style, mahogany, two-part construction: the upper section w/a rectangular top above a deep flaring ogee cornice above a pair of tall glazed cupboard doors topped w/a band of applied pierced scroll carving across the top & scroll-carved drops at the front corners; the stepped-out lower section w/a rectangular top over a pair of flush-fronted drawers over a pair of raised panel cupboard doors w/a band of applied pierced scroll carving across the top & flanked by scroll-carved drops at the sides, molded flat plinth base, early 20th c., 12 1/2 x 42 1/2", 86 1/2" h................ **935**

Step-back wall cupboard, walnut, two-part construction: the upper section w/an overhanging flared & stepped cornice above a pair of 6-pane glazed cupboard doors opening to two shelves fitted w/spoon racks, flanked by wide fluted pilasters over the open pie shelf; the stepped-out lower section w/fluted side pilasters flanking a row of three small drawers each separated by a fluted block above a pair of wide paneled cupboard doors centered by another fluted pilaster, molded base on straight bracket feet, old finish, Pennsylvania, 1750-70, 19 1/2 x 63 1/2", 90" h. (patch on

left side of cornice, strips added to base of upper section) **20,700**

Step-back wall cupboards, walnut & poplar, two-piece construction: the upper section w/a rectangular top over a flat angled cornice over a pair of very tall paneled doors over a low pie shelf; the lower stepped-out section w/a pair of drawers w/wooden knobs over a pair of paneled cupboard doors, simple bracket feet, bootjack sides, old refinish, mid-19th c., 19 x 45", 85 3/4" h. (chip on rear foot, one end of cornice replaced) **1,870**

European Baroque Revival Cupboard

Wall cupboard, Baroque Revival style, oak, rectangular raised-center top w/wide stepped & flaring cornice over a wide frieze band centered by a wide carved scrolled cartouche over a molding above a pair of tall set-back cupboard doors w/leafy scroll-carved panels over arched tops & three tall narrow panels of beveled glass in each door over a square stepped panel, the doors flanked by bold stepped-out spiral-turned columns w/top & base capitals over a pair of small drawers at the bottom on a molded base w/short bracket feet, old dark finish, repairs, back reinforced w/plywood, Europe, late 19th c., 22 1/2 x 56", 83 1/4" h. (ILLUS.) **660**

Wall Cupboard with Paneled Doors

Wall cupboard, cherry, one-piece construction, a rectangular top w/a widely flaring shaped cornice above a pair of tall double-paneled cupboard doors above a pair of drawers over another pair of shorter double-paneled cupboard doors, shaped apron & simple bracket feet, old refinishing, 19th c., 19 1/4 x 47 3/4", 80 3/4" h. (ILLUS.) **2,200**

Eighteenth Century Wall Cupboard

Wall cupboard, Chippendale country-style, painted pine, one-piece construction, a rectangular top w/narrow flared cornice above a pair of tall narrow doors each w/two narrow raised panels & mounted w/H-hinges, molded base w/short bracket feet, opens to five shelves, old tan over green paint, hinges appear to be original, probably Rhode Island, late 18th c., imperfections, 10 1/2 x 41 3/4", 75 3/4" h. (ILLUS.) **6,900**

Country Chippendale Pine Cupboard

Wall cupboard, Chippendale country-style, pine, a rectangular top w/a narrow cornice above a pair of tall cupboard doors

each w/four raised panels & hung w/H-hinges, molded base & scroll-cut bracket feet, opening to three shelves, old refinish, restored, late 18th c., 20 3/4 x 42", 69" h. (ILLUS.) **2,990**

Unique Classical Open Cupboard

Wall cupboard, Classical, painted & decorated, a rectangular top w/flared & stepped cornice above a tall open compartment w/seven shelves flanked by tall tapering pilasters w/carved, scrolled Ionic capitals, painted to resemble rosewood, probably New England, ca. 1820-30, minor imperfections, 11 1/2 x 32", 65 1/2" h. (ILLUS.) **5,463**

Wall cupboard, country-style, cherry, a flat rectangular top w/no cornice above a pair of tall paneled doors w/original brass thumb latches w/porcelain knobs above a lower pair of shorter paneled doors w/matching latches, flat bottom, refinished, mid-19th c., 16 1/2 x 46 1/2", 83 3/4" h. (porcelain knobs damaged, minor edge damage) **990**

Short Cherry Wall Cupboard

Wall cupboard, country-style, cherry, one-piece construction, a rectangular top above a single 4-pane glazed cupboard door above a raised-panel cupboard door both flanked by wide side boards, old brass hardware & latches, refinished, scalloped apron, 19th c., top 13 1/2 x 32", 54 1/2" h. (ILLUS.) **1,870**

Walnut One-piece Wall Cupboard

Wall cupboard, country-style, one-piece construction, a flat rectangular top above a band of reeded molding continuing down each side & flanking a tall 12-pane glazed cupboard door above a pair of flat lower cupboard doors, flat base, old dark brown finish over red, hinges replaced, old alterations, 19th c., 47" w., 83" h. (ILLUS.).. **1,650**

Red-painted Pine Wall Cupboard

Wall cupboard, country-style, painted pine, one-piece construction, rectangular flat top over a single wide raised double-paneled door w/latch & simple wood knob opening to three painted shelves over a medial rail & a short two-panel lower door opening to one shelf, shaped apron w/short bracket feet, original red exterior paint, repainted interior, hardware changes, minor height & cornice loss, old scraping to original red, New England, early 19th c., 19 1/4 x 43 1/2", 81" h. (ILLUS.)..... **1,093**

Simple Painted Pine Cupboard

Wall cupboard, country-style, painted pine, one-piece construction, the rectangular top w/a molded cornice over a tall narrow raised panel door opening to three full shelves & one contoured shelf over a similar shorter door opening to a single shelf, tall wide solid board front sides, hardware losses & changes, repainted chrome yellow, restoration, probably New York state, early 19th c., 19 x 36", 81" h. (ILLUS.) **978**

Wall cupboard, country-style, painted pine, one-piece construction, the rectangular top w/a narrow coved cornice above a large tall door w/two raised panels, opening to five shelves w/plate grooves, simple curving cut-out front feet & cut-out side feet, original powder blue painted surface, possibly New Hampshire, early 19th c., 12 1/2 x 36 3/4", 75 1/2" h. (very minor imperfections) **34,500**

Wall cupboard, country-style, painted pine & poplar, one-piece construction, a flat plain top w/no molding above a tall narrow flat one-board door above a shorter flat one-board door w/wide side boards flanking them, cast-iron thumb latches, worn old layers of greenish grey & olive tan paint, 19th c., 14 1/4 x 36 1/2", 74 3/4" h. **1,128**

Early Canadian Painted Cupboard

Wall cupboard, country-style, painted pine, rectangular top w/a deep stepped cornice over a pair of wide & tall raised double-paneled doors w/wooden thumb latches at the top, molded base on tall scroll-cut bracket feet, paneled sides, painted blue, restoration, Canada, late 18th c., 21 1/4 x 53 1/2", 71 1/2" h. (ILLUS.) **1,725**

Wall cupboard, country-style, painted pine, the rectangular top w/a deep flaring stepped cornice above a tall narrow case w/two double raised-panel cupboard doors opening to six shelves, molded base on bracket feet, remnants of red paint, New England, late 18th c., 18 1/4 x 38", 79 1/2" h. **4,830**

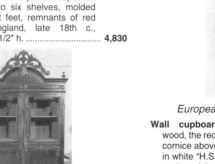

European Wall Cupboard

Wall cupboard, country-style, painted pine, the rectangular top w/a high arched central section topped by a tall pierced & scrolling crest over flattened side cornices w/turned finials at the front corners, raised panel narrow frieze panels alternating w/rondels over a pair of tall cupboard doors w/single-pane glazed sections w/raised molding borders w/outset corners over matching solid panels in the lower section all opening to wooden shelves, a pair of drawers at the base above a flat apron on heavy ring- and peg-turned legs, old dark painted finish, damage & repairs, Europe, second half 19th c., 16 x 39", 73" h. (ILLUS.) **605**

Early Painted Wall Cupboard

Wall cupboard, country-style, painted, rectangular top w/a narrow stepped molding over a wide frieze board w/wooden thumb latch above a pair of tall paneled doors w/a turned wood knob, flat wide apron on slender baluster-turned legs on knob and peg feet, opens to unpainted interior w/two shelves, bluish green worn paint, all original condition & surfaces, Pennsylvania or Ohio, 1835-45, 14 1/8 x 36 1/4", 59 1/4" h. (ILLUS.) **4,600**

European Painted Wall Cupboard

Wall cupboard, country-style, painted wood, the rectangular top w/a flat molded cornice above a projecting frieze initialed in white "H.S.F. 1833," over two paneled cupboard doors w/applied molded panels & wrought-iron hinges separated by a mid-molding on a low cut-out base, original red paint, probably Northern Europe, 14 3/4 x 34", 69" h. (ILLUS.) **3,335**

Early Pine Wall Cupboard

Wall cupboard, country-style, pine, a rectangular top w/a narrow coved cornice above a single narrow tall two-panel door flanked by wide side rails, low shaped bracket feet, shelved interior, old natural surface, interior w/red wash, New England, early 19th c., minor imperfections, 42 x 42 3/4", 78" h. (ILLUS.) **1,265**

Unusual Early Pine Wall Cupboard

Wall cupboard, country-style, pine, one-piece construction, the rectangular top w/stepped-out front corners over a deep conforming flaring cornice above a pair of sliding triple-paneled tall doors enclosing three shelves above a gadrooned molding & a single four-panel hinged door, all flanked by paneled pilasters w/molded capitals & bases, old refinish, remnants of bluish green paint, minor imperfections, southeastern New England, 18th c., 19 1/2 x 37 1/2", 78" h. (ILLUS.) **9,775**

Compact Walnut Wall Cupboard

Wall cupboard, country-style, walnut, one-piece construction, a rectangular top w/a deep flaring ogee cornice above a pair of tall two-panel cupboard doors w/a cast-iron thumb latch above a row of three drawers w/a long central drawer, each w/a cast-iron grip pull over a pair of shorter paneled cupboard doors w/a cast-iron thumb latch, low scalloped apron, second half 19th c., small-sized (ILLUS.) **770**

Walnut One-piece Wall Cupboard

Wall cupboard, country-style, walnut, one-piece construction, the rectangular top w/a thick slightly overhanging cornice over a single wide double-paneled door w/a brass thumb latch over a medial band & a slightly shorter matching lower door, flat base, old finish, 19th c., 18 x 44", 76 3/4" h. (ILLUS.) **1,375**

Wall cupboard, Federal country-style, cherry, one-piece construction, the rectangular top w/a flaring stepped cornice over a pair of tall paneled cupboard doors opening to three shelves above a lower shorter pair of cupboard doors, scalloped apron, cut-out feet, old worn soft patina, 19th c., 17 1/2 x 46", 76 3/4" h. **2,915**

Fancy Federal Pine Wall Cupboard

Wall cupboard, Federal, pine, one-piece construction, the rectangular top w/deep stepped cornice & blocked corners above a conforming case w/a pair of tall geometrically-glazed cupboard doors flanked by wide reeded pilasters & opening to interior reeded columns & arched top shelved unit above a mid-molding over a pair of paneled cupboard doors above further reeded pilasters ending in a blocked deep base, old mellow refinishing, base molding replaced, some height loss & restoration, early 19th c., 15 x 42 1/2", 76" h. (ILLUS.)........................ **2,750**

Gothic Revival Oak Wall Cupboard

Wall cupboard, late Victorian Gothic Revival, quarter-sawn oak, a high ornately pierce-carved crest centered by a chalice overflowing w/grapevines continuing down the side of the crest, the flaring cre-strail w/sawtooth carving above a single glazed door w/carved trefoils in the upper corners above a glazed arched panel w/Gothic arch muntins centered by a carved rose wreath, sawtooth bands down the sides & at the base above a single drawer w/a wooden knob, simple molded base, probably used for storing wine & hosts in a Roman Catholic church, original finish, ca. 1900, 12 x 21", 34" h. (ILLUS.)... **950**

Wall cupboard, mahoganized poplar, a long rectangular top w/a stepped flared cornice above a case w/a pair of tall double-raised paneled doors w/H-hinges flanked by wide matching side panels, a single long drawer below the doors, molded base on simple bracket feet, appears to retain original wrought-iron hinges, Pennsylvania, second half 18th c., 20 x 61", 78" h... **1,800**

Unique Decorated Southern Cupboard

Wall cupboard, painted & decorated poplar, one-piece construction, the top w/a high upright front cornice board deeply cut in a zigzag design above molded bands over a pair of tall double-panel cupboard doors w/wide molded framing & side stiles, the top panels in blue & tan paint in a design of undulating stripes & a recumbent stag, the lower panels w/further stripes, molded base w/deep zigzag cut apron, molded block feet, framing painted black, opens to two shelves, found in Georgia, one foot replaced, 14 3/4 x 45", 84" h. (ILLUS.) **4,070**

Wall cupboard, painted & decorated, the rectangular top w/a coved molding above a pair of tall paneled doors w/knobs opening to two interior shelves above another longer pair of paneled doors opening to shelves, the molded base on ogee bracket feet, decorated overall w/burnt-orange & mustard yellow combed painted decoration, probably Pennsylvania, 19th c., 21 1/4 x 41 1/2", 72 1/2" h............ **12,650**

Tall Narrow Painted Wall Cupboard

Wall cupboard, painted pine, a flat rectangular top above a single tall door w/two raised panels opening to five shelves, original bright blue paint, New England, early 19th c., some surface imperfections, 14 1/2 x 28", 79 3/4" h. (ILLUS.) **5,520**

Painted New England Wall Cupboard

Wall cupboard, painted pine, a rectangular thick top above a pair of tall double-panel cupboard doors opening to three shelves, deeply scalloped apron & simple bracket feet, old Spanish brown paint, New England, mid-19th c., height loss, surface imperfections, 18 x 48", 60" h. (ILLUS.)........... **2,300**

Wall cupboard, painted pine, one-piece construction, rectangular top w/narrow molding above a case w/a flush long board & batten door above a slightly short matching door w/wooden thumb latch, cleaned down to old red, flat base, 19th c., 16 1/2 x 37", 76 1/4" h. (minor edge damage)... **1,650**

Wall cupboard, painted pine, one-piece construction, the rectangular top w/a molded cornice above a raised-panel cupboard door above a matching door both above a long drawer at the bottom, one-board sides w/cut-out feet, cut-out front feet, old grey paint w/good history of earlier colors, interior w/modern paint, found in Rhode Island, 21 1/2 x 38 1/2", 73" h. (rehinged w/"H" hinge & turned) **5,775**

Simple Painted Wall Cupboard

Wall cupboard, painted pine, plain rectangular top above a pair of tall plain doors opening to an interior of numbered shelves, some of which are also labeled, flat base, old light green paint, interior unpainted,

New Lebanon, New York area, possibly Shaker, 19th c., some shelves missing, 7 1/2 x 23 3/4", 40 1/2" h. (ILLUS.) **1,610**

Wall cupboard, painted pine, the rectangular top w/a peaked front crest w/molding above a tall door w/a forty-two opening lattice grill above two lower panels, wide flat front side boards & flat baseboard, opens to incomplete shelves, old worn red paint over orange, attributed to Wisconsin, 19th c., 19 x 42", 74 3/4" h. (hinge replaced, porcelain knob added, some edge damage & age cracks) **880**

Painted Poplar Wall Cupboard

Wall cupboard, painted poplar, a flat rectangular top above a single tall narrow flat door flanked by wide side boards continuing down to form shaped bracket feet, opens to single shelf & closet, old red & grain-painted surface, probably New England, first half 19th c., base reshaped, 17 1/4 x 37", 76 1/4" h. (ILLUS.) **920**

Wall cupboard, painted poplar, one-piece construction, rectangular top w/molded cornice above a stack of two paneled cupboard doors flanked by wide board side stiles forming simple bracket feet, cast-iron turn latches, worn old yellow graining, wear, one front foot w/edge damage, 19th c., 19 3/4 x 40", 72" h. (ILLUS.) **3,080**

Grained Poplar Wall Cupboard

Wall cupboard, pine, a pair of glazed cupboard doors opening to a single shelf above a pair of recessed-panel doors opening to six shelves, refinished, New England, mid-19th c., 17 3/4 x 39", 81 3/4" h. (some height loss, one pane missing) **1,840**

Simple Pine Wall Cupboard

Wall cupboard, pine, one-piece construction, rectangular top w/narrow coved cornice above a single tall narrow two-panel door flanked by wide side boards forming simple bracket feet, opening to shelves, old natural surface, interior w/red wash, New England, early 19th c., minor imperfections, 42" w., 78" h. (ILLUS.) **1,265**

Wall cupboard, walnut, rectangular top above a pair of short square ornately pierce-carved doors each w/a central floral- or bird-carved cartouche framed by pierced scroll bands above a pair of tall flat cupboard doors w/flat oval two-part central latch, serpentine apron carved w/slender facing dragons, on slender square stile legs, old finish, China, late 19th - early 20th c., 18 x 38", 60 3/4" h. **660**

Late European Welsh Cupboard

Welsh cupboard, pine & poplar, two-part construction: the upper section w/a rectangular top w/a deep flared cornice above a large three-shelved open compartment w/a scalloped top rail & sides; the stepped-out lower section w/a fold-out work surface above a case w/a row of three drawers over a square cupboard door beside two long drawers all w/turned wood knobs, flat base w/narrow molding, raised on bun feet on pegs, waxed finish, Europe, ca. 1910, 24 x 60", 6' 10" h. (ILLUS.) **1,400**

Desks

McArthur Art Deco Desk

Art Deco desk, aluminum tubing & black lacquered wood, the rectangular black lacquered top w/a central raised support w/a tubular light, raised on anodized tubular frame w/a kneehole opening on the right & an open black lacquered shelf over two yellow lacquered drawers on the left, drawers w/aluminum arched pulls, designed by Warren McArthur, made by McArthur Industries, 1930s, repainted, 24 x 44", 29" h. (ILLUS.) **$5,225**

Thonet Art Deco Desk

Art Deco desk, painted wood & tubular steel, the elevated rectangular wood top above an asymetical arrangement of three short drawers on the right side, supported on a continuous tubular steel frame, attributed to Marcel Breuer, produced by Thonet, Austria, ca. 1930, 30 x 54", 30" h. (ILLUS.) **2,070**

Fine Art Deco Walnut Desk

Art Deco desk, walnut & ivory, the rectangular top w/rounded corners & inset front section decorated w/veneer panels & inlaid banding above the shallow case w/a pair of small drawers w/square ivory pulls on each side of a long central drawer over a thin pull-out slide, outset slender rounded tapering legs w/light stripe inlay, designed by Joubert et Petit, produced by D.I.M., France, ca. 1925, 43 1/2" l., 32" h. (ILLUS.) **14,950**

"Bonheur du Jour" Desk

Art Nouveau "bonheur du jour" desk, fruitwood marquetry, central upright case w/fall front opening to an interior fitted w/shelves, pigeonholes, pen tray & glass Waterman inkwell, above a writing plateau w/drawer below, all inlaid w/various woods w/stylized poppies & leafage, the whole raised on tapering legs carved w/poppies, signed in marquetry "Gallé/Nancy," ca. 1900, 21 x 28 1/2 x 46" (ILLUS.) **5,750**

Unusual Oak Art Nouveau Desk

Art Nouveau desk, oak, a rectangular top w/rounded corners above a single apron drawer over a wide arched kneehole w/serpentine sides & line-incised scrolls, each end w/two narrow open shelves, scratches, roughness, ca. 1900, 29 3/4 x 47 1/4", 28 1/2" h. (ILLUS.) **518**

Art Nouveau writing desk, fruitwood parquetry, the rectangular top inlaid in various woods w/a large butterfly amid blossoms & chestnut leaves, the apron w/a single long drawer, raised on slender buttressed slightly flaring molded legs, signed in marquetry "Gallé," France, ca. 1900, 26 x 41", 31" h. **4,312**

Unique Carved Burmese Desk

Burmese desk, carved hardwood, the superstructure w/a high undulating pierce-carved central crestrail over two openings w/pierced arched crests & center small columns over a rectangular surface fronted by a sloped writing surface, all flanked on each side w/a tall narrow rectangular cupboard w/scallop-carved crest above a pierce-carved door, all on a rectangular top w/carved rim over a central kneehole opening w/pierced arched bracket flanked by two ranks of three ornately carved drawers all on square carved short stile legs joined by a back stretcher, Burma, late 19th c., 28 x 56", 51" h. (ILLUS.)............................... **1,840**

Chippendale country-style slant-front desk, birch, a narrow rectangular top above a wide hinged slant lid opening to a two-stepped interior w/open valanced compartments above smaller drawers & a central opening, all above a case of four long graduated drawers w/butterfly brasses & keyhole escutcheons, molded base on scroll-cut bracket feet, refinished, northern New England, mid- to late 18th c., 18 x 39", 43" h. (replaced brasses, imperfections) **3,105**

Chippendale country-style slant-front desk, painted maple & pine, a narrow rectangular top above the wide hinged slant front opening to an interior fitted w/four narrow drawers flanking a square center drawer over two long low arcaded slots, the case w/four long graduated drawers w/butterfly pulls, molded base on scroll-cut bracket feet, old red finish, 18th c., 18 1/2 x 37", 41 3/4" h. (replaced brasses) **12,100**

Chippendale Revival Slant-front Desk

Chippendale Revival slant-front desk, quarter-sawn oak, the narrow rectangular top w/a low wood & brass beaded gallery over the wide hinged slant front w/a large shell-carved center design & scroll-carved corners opening to a fitted interior above a case w/pull-out slide supports flanking a long drawer over three long drawers all w/stamped brass pulls & keyhole escutcheons, quarter-round spiral-turned columns at the sides, gadrooned base band on scroll-carved claw-and-ball feet, original hardware & finish, late 19th - early 20th c., 20 x 34", 40" h. (ILLUS.).... **2,500**

Chippendale slant front desk, curly maple, a narrow rectangular top above a wide hinged slant front opening to an interior fitted w/a row of small drawers above a row w/two drawers centering a pigeonhole above arcaded & plain pigeonholes, the case w/three long thumb-molded graduated drawers w/butterfly brasses, molded base on scroll-cut bracket feet, old refinish, Massachusetts or New Hampshire, late 18th c., replaced brasses, 17 1/2 x 36", 43 1/2" h. (imperfections) **3,335**

Chippendale slant front 'reverse serpentine' desk, carved mahogany, narrow rectangular top above the wide hinged slant front opening to a stepped interior of small drawers, the central one w/shaping on a case w/four long graduated scratch-beaded conforming drawers above a conforming molded base w/central drop & front ball-and-claw feet & shaped bracket rear feet, old refinish, Massachusetts, 18th c., 22 x 42", 44 1/2" h. (repairs).................... **5,175**

Chippendale slant-front desk, birch, a narrow rectangular top over a wide hinged slant top opening to a shaped interior of ten compartments & small drawers, the cockbeaded case w/four long graduated drawers on a molded base w/scroll-cut bracket feet, probably Massachusetts, ca. 1780, 21 1/4 x 40", 44 1/4" h. (old refinish, imperfections) **1,955**

Chippendale slant-front desk, carved maple & cherry, a narrow rectangular top above a hinged molded slant lid opening to an interior fitted w/a central fan-carved drawer flanked by document drawers &

Chippendale Slant-Front Desk

six pigeonholes above four short drawers, the case below w/four long graduated drawers above a central apron pendant, scroll-cut bracket feet, repairs to feet, New England, probably New Hampshire, ca. 1780, 17 1/2 x 35", 41 3/4" h. (ILLUS.) **6,900**

Chippendale slant-front desk, curly maple, a narrow rectangular top above the hinged slant front opening to an interior fitted w/six valanced pigeonholes & five short drawers w/a central fan-carved prospect door, the case w/four long graduated drawers w/butterfly pulls & keyhole escutcheons on a molded base w/central drop pendant & scroll-cut bracket feet, New England, ca. 1780, 18 1/2 x 36", 42" h. (valances of later date, prospect door possibly reworked, repairs to feet) **7,475**

Chippendale Slant-front Desk

Chippendale slant-front desk, figured mahogany, a narrow top above a wide hinged slant front opening to an interior fitted w/six slots over four small drawers centered by a bowed center prospect door, the case w/pull-out slide supports flanking a long drawer over three long

graduated drawers w/simple bail pulls, molded base on high bracket feet, replaced hardware, refinished, late 18th c., 18 x 38", 38" h. (ILLUS.) **2,000**

Chippendale slant-front desk, mahogany, a narrow top above a wide hinged slant lid opening to an interior fitted w/a central concave fan-carved prospect door opening to three concave drawers flanked by baluster-fronted document drawers, three valanced compartments, blocked drawers & a fan-carved drawer above two concave drawers, the case w/four long graduated thumb-molded drawers w/butterfly pulls & small brass keyhole escutcheons, molded base w/scroll-cut bracket feet, old finish, Boston, ca. 1770-80, 19 1/2 x 39 1/2", 42 1/2" h. (brasses replaced, imperfections) **27,600**

Chippendale slant-front desk, tiger stripe maple, a narrow rectangular top above a wide hinged slant front opening to a two-stepped interior of valanced compartments over small drawers, the central one flanked by document drawers & tiger stripe maple columns w/capitals & bases over a molded step above three additional small drawers over the case w/four long graduated thumb-molded drawers w/butterfly pulls, molded base w/bracket feet & central drop, old refinish, New England, mid-18th c., 19 1/2 x 34", 44 1/4" h. (some replaced brasses) **6,325**

Chippendale-Style Block-front Desk

Chippendale-Style block-front desk, mahogany, rectangular top w/molded edge above a case w/a long blocked top drawer over two racks of three blocked drawers on each side of the kneehole w/a scalloped top & a recessed cupboard door, molded base raised on claw-and-ball feet, Centennial-type, late 19th c., 20 x 36", 30" h. (ILLUS.) **1,500**

Chippendale-Style block-front slant-front desk, mahogany, a narrow top above a winged slant lid opening to an interior fitted w/three shell-carved arches above stacks of small drawers separated by arched pigeonholes over small drawers, the case w/four long block-front

Chippendale-Style Block-Front Desk

drawers each w/brass butterfly pulls & keyhole escutcheons, labeled "Museum Reproduction, Authorized by Edison Institute, Dearborn, Mich., Colonial Mfg. Co. Zeeland, Mich.," old finish, early 20th c., minor wear & edge damage, 22 1/4 x 40 1/2", 43 1/4" h. (ILLUS.)........... **1,375**

Chippendale-Style slant-front desk, mahogany, a narrow rectangular top above a wide hinged slant front opening to a fitted interior above a double-serpentine fronted case w/four long graduated drawers w/butterfly brass & keyhole escutcheons, molded conforming base on short front cabriole legs w/claw-and-ball feet, marked "Maddow Colonial, Jamestown, NY," ca. 1920s, refinished, 16 x 28 1/2", 40" h... **440**

Classical Butler's Desk

Classical butler's desk, carved mahogany & mahogany veneer, the rectangular top above a drawer opening to a writing surface & a bird's-eye maple interior of eight drawers & six valanced pigeonholes, the case w/three recessed long drawers w/flanking free-standing columns w/acanthus carved Corinthian capitals, on a stepped plinth base & large ball-turned feet on casters, replaced brasses, old feet, possibly New England, ca. 1825, imperfections, 22 x 45", 48" h. (ILLUS.).............. **920**

Classical lady's desk, carved & veneered mahogany, the rectangular top w/hinged desk box & fitted interior of three drawers above a recessed case of two long drawers w/turned wood knobs flanked by free-standing columns on square plinths continuing to baluster- and ring-turned legs, old refinish, minor imperfections, New England, ca. 1825, 19 1/2 x 36 1/2", 36" h. (ILLUS.).. **863**

Classical Lady's Desk

Colonial Revival Lady's Desk

Colonial Revival lady's writing desk, quarter-sawn oak, the scalloped & scroll-carved crestrail over a narrow shelf above the wide hinged slant front decorated w/applied delicate scrolling & opening to a fitted interior w/pigeonholes, small drawers & the fold-down writing surface, the serpentine lower case w/a long conforming top drawer over a pair of small drawers flanking the bracket-trimmed kneehole opening, raised on slender simple cabriole front legs, original pierced brass hardware, refinished, ca. 1910, 18 x 32", 44" h. (ILLUS.).. **1,200**

Early Painted Pine Country Desk

Country-style desk, painted pine, a narrow rectangular top above an interior fitted w/stacks of 16 small & larger drawers w/porcelain knobs flanked by curved sides above the pull-out writing surface over a case w/a pair of small drawers over two long drawers, painted old red, New England, early 19th c., imperfections, 19 x 36", 48" h. (ILLUS.) **5,750**

Early Cherry Desk on Stand

Country-style desk on stand, cherry, a narrow galleried top shelf above a hinged slanted lift lid w/applied edge molding opening to a compartmented interior set into a base w/a long thumb-molded drawer & flat apron raised on four tall slender square beaded legs joined by box stretchers, original brown paint, central Massachusetts, ca. 1800, 19 x 30 3/4", 47 1/2" h. (ILLUS.) **3,220**

Country-style fall-front desk, walnut, a rectangular top above a large flat hinged fall-front opening to form a writing surface w/an interior composed of pigeonholes & letter slots w/two small drawers & a secret compartment, the lower case w/two long drawers each w/two turned wood knobs & a keyhole, simple bracket feet, old finish, 19th c., 17 x 37", 44 3/4" h. **605**

Country-style Plantation Desk

Country-style 'plantation' desk, butternut, two-part construction: the tall upper section w/a rectangular top w/deep stepped & flaring cornice above an open-fronted case w/32 pigeonholes above vertical slots flanking a galleried central compartment over a pair of drawers; the stepped-out lower section w/a rectangular top over a single long drawer w/carved pulls, on ring-, knob- and baluster-turned legs w/knob feet, long oval raised molding at the sides of the upper case, ca. 1860-70, 26 x 38", 6' 8" h. (ILLUS.) **750**

Country-style school master's desk, walnut, a low three-quarters gallery around a narrow shelf above the wide hinged slant top w/edge molding opening to a deep well, on rod- and ring-turned legs w/ball and peg feet, old soft finish, 19th c., 26 x 41", 38" h. **495**

Country-style 'stand-up' desk, pine, rectangular hinged top opening to a well fitted w/eight dovetailed small drawers & six pigeonholes, above three long dovetailed drawers w/simple turned wood knobs, brass keyhole escutcheons, raised on simple turned legs, possibly Shaker, refinished, 19th c., 17 3/4 x 33", 45 1/2" h. (one escutcheon missing, age cracks in ends) **2,255**

Early New England 'Stand-up' Desk

Country-style 'stand-up' desk, stained pine, the rectangular top w/a wide slightly sloped hinged lid opening to an interior fitted w/four open compartments, raised on slender turned legs joined by a square H-stretcher, peg feet, old red stain, New England, early 19th c., surface imperfections, 17 3/4 x 30", 44" h. (ILLUS.) **1,380**

Danish Modern Teak Desk

Danish Modern desk, teak, a narrow rectangular top above a wide fall-front opening to interior compartments & two small drawers above a stepped-out lower case w/three long drawers w/wooden pulls, raised on four tapering cylindrical legs, paper label, designed by Mogensen Designs, Finland, retailed by Design Research, Cambridge, Massachusetts, late 1940s - early 1950s, 18 x 39 1/4", 47 1/2" h. (ILLUS.) **690**

Empire Revival partner's desk, carved mahogany, a wide rectangular top w/a gadrooned border above a molded apron w/carved corner panels & each side fitted w/two long drawers, one working & one false, above small drawers flanking the kneehole opening, one drawer working & the other false, raised on pairs of heavy carved pineapple-form supports resting on rectangular blocks raised on gadrooned large paw feet joined by a turned leaf-carved heavy stretcher, old dark finish, late 19th - early 20th c., 33 x 54", 29 1/4" h. (one lock & a few brasses missing) **1,045**

Federal butler's desk, inlaid mahogany, the rectangular top w/inlaid edge of crossbanding & stringing above a cockbeaded inlaid drawer w/hinged front opening to a desk interior of four drawers & nine small valanced compartments, above a case w/three long graduated drawers all w/ring pulls, on an inlaid base of flaring French feet joined by a valanced skirt, old refinish, ca. 1800, 21 x 41", 43" h. (replaced brasses, imperfections) **2,990**

Federal Butler's Desk

Federal butler's desk, inlaid mahogany, the rectangular top w/string-inlaid edge above a case w/a deep drawer w/two inlaid ovals set in mitered panels bordered by stringing & opening to an interior of a fold-out writing surface & central prospect door inlaid w/an urn of flowers bordered by stringing, flanked by document drawers w/inlay of simulated pilasters & three small drawers above four valanced compartments, the lower case w/three long graduated band inlaid drawers on a serpentine apron & slender French feet, replaced oval brasses, imperfections, 21 x 46", 44" h. (ILLUS.) **2,530**

Federal country-style schoolmaster's desk, walnut & poplar, a low three-quarters gallery around a narrow top shelf

above the wide hinged slant lid opening to an interior fitted w/pigeonholes, four dovetailed drawers & a center door, raised on ring- and rod-turned tapering legs w/baluster-turned feet, old red exterior finish, interior w/black painted trim, found in northeast Ohio, first half 19th c., 27 x 29 1/2", 38" h. **743**

Federal country-style slant-front desk, cherry, a narrow rectangular top above the wide hinged slant front opening to a well w/four dovetailed small drawers & a hidden central compartment, the deep apron w/an inlaid diamond keyhole escutcheon at the front, on ring-, knob- and spiral-turned rod legs w/short peg feet, mellow refinishing, first half 19th c., 23 3/4 x 32 3/4", 35 1/2" h. (hinges replaced) **825**

Federal Lady's Desk on Turned Legs

Federal lady's desk, carved mahogany & mahogany veneer, the rectangular box top opening to an interior of three drawers & a writing surface on a base w/a single long drawer w/two round brass pulls raised on ring-, knob- and spiral-turned legs ending in disk & peg feet on casters, old finish, probably Massachusetts, ca. 1825, minor imperfections, 19 1/2 x 29 1/2", 37 3/4" h. (ILLUS.) **1,093**

Fine Federal Lady's Desk

Federal lady's desk, mahogany & mahogany veneer, two-part construction: the upper section w/a rectangular top w/a narrow molded cornice over a pair of beaded & veneered cupboard doors enclosing three shaped document drawers flanked by two short drawers above three valanced compartments; the lower projecting section w/a fold-out writing surface above a case w/three long cockbeaded & veneered drawers, scalloped apron & ring- and baluster-turned legs w/peg feet, old pressed glass pulls, old refinish, imperfections, Massachusetts, ca. 1810, 32 3/4 x 39 1/2", 53" h. (ILLUS.)... **3,220**

Federal Lady's "Tambour-front" Desk

Federal lady's "tambour-front" desk, inlaid mahogany, two-part construction: the upper section w/a rectangular top above a pair of tambour sliding doors opening to four short drawers & two valanced pigeonholes flanking a central door opening to two short drawers & a valanced pigeonhole; the lower projecting section w/a hinged writing flap above two long drawers w/oval brasses & inlaid dies, on square double-tapering line-, bellflower-, dot- and lozenge-inlaid legs ending in crossbanded cuts, appears to retain original brasses, Boston, Massachusetts, ca. 1795, losses to inlay, patches to veneer, repair to one front leg, 20 x 36 1/2", 43" h. (ILLUS.) **4,312**

Federal "oxbow" slant-front desk, mahogany & birch, a narrow top above the wide hinged slant front opening to an interior of seven small drawers w/inlaid stringing above seven valanced compartments, the cockbeaded case w/four graduated long serpentine-front drawers w/oval brasses, on a conforming base w/bracket feet, old brasses, probably Massachusetts, ca. 1780, 19 1/2 x 40", 43 1/2" h. (refinished)................................. **4,025**

Federal "oxbow" slant-front desk, mahogany & mahogany veneer, a narrow rectangular top above a wide hinged slant front opening to an interior of five drawers & nine valanced compartments, the case w/four long graduated double-serpentine drawers w/oval brasses & keyhole escutcheons, curved apron & flaring French feet, old brasses, old refinish, probably Massachusetts, ca. 1790-1810, 42" w., 44" h. (imperfections)............ **4,600**

Federal slant-front desk, cherry, a narrow rectangular top above a wide hinged slant-front w/breadboard ends opening to a stepped interior of a central drawer flanked by eight valanced compartments above five short drawers & two shallow drawers, the case w/four long graduated drawers above a valanced apron & slender French feet, New England, ca. 1800, 15 x 40", 44" h. (replaced butterfly brasses, refinished, imperfections)...................... **4,880**

Federal slant-front desk, cherry, a narrow rectangular top above the wide hinged slant lid opening to an interior fitted w/three small pigeonholes over two narrow drawers on each side of a square center door flanked by letter drawers, the case w/four cock-beaded long graduated drawers, deeply scalloped apron & tall French feet, replaced oval brasses, old mellow refinishing, early 19th c., 19 x 41 1/2", 46" h. (old pieced repairs) **3,025**

Federal slant-front desk, cherry, a narrow rectangular top above the wide hinged slant front opening to an interior fitted w/a central prospect door in front of two concave carved drawers flanked by three valanced compartments & two drawers, the lower case w/four long graduated cockbeaded drawers w/oval brasses, scalloped apron & tall flared French feet, old finish, New England, ca. 1800, 40 3/4" w., 42 3/4" h. (imperfections) **3,450**

Federal slant-front desk, inlaid mahogany veneer, a narrow rectangular top above a hinged slant front opening to an interior fitted w/two groups of four small drawers over arcaded pigeonholes flanking a center prospect door, the lower case w/four long drawers w/banded veneer & stringing inlay, oval brasses & keyhole escutcheons, curved apron & French feet, old surface, original brasses, New York state, early 19th c., 21 1/2 x 41 1/2", 44" h. (veneer cracking, loss & patching, other surface imperfections) **2,530**

Federal slant-front desk, mahogany & mahogany veneer, narrow rectangular top above a wide hinged slant lid opening to an interior w/seven small drawers & seven valanced compartments, the case w/four long graduated veneered drawers w/inlaid edges & oval brasses, molded base on tall inlaid bracket feet, old refinish, New England, ca. 1790, 19 x 39 3/4", 43 1/2" h. (old replaced brasses, imperfections) **2,875**

Federal slant-front desk, stained maple, a narrow rectangular top above a wide hinged slant front opening to an interior fitted w/valanced compartments & small beaded drawers over a case w/four long graduated drawers w/oval brasses above the scalloped apron & tall French feet, old dark red stain, original brasses, New England, early 19th c., 20 x 39 1/2", 44" h..... **4,313**

Federal Slant-front Walnut Desk

Federal slant-front desk, walnut, a narrow rectangular top above a wide hinged slant front opening to a fitted interior, the case w/slide supports flanking a long top drawer over three long drawers all w/old replaced butterfly brasses, gently arched narrow apron on short French feet, old refinish, late 18th - early 19th c., 19 x 40", 40" h. (ILLUS.)... **1,800**

Federal slant-front desk, wavy birch, a narrow top above a wide hinged slant lid opening to a valanced multi-drawer interior w/pigeonholes over a case w/four long graduated cockbeaded drawers w/simple bail pulls, serpentine apron over simple French feet, old refinish, southern New England, ca. 1780-1800, 19 1/2 x 39 1/4", 43 1/2" h. (replaced brasses, minor imperfections) **2,530**

Federal "tambour" desk, inlaid mahogany, two-part construction: the upper section w/a stepped-back rectangular top above a row of two long drawers flanking a short center drawer all above twin tambour doors flanking a small plain prospect door all opening to an arrangement of drawers & valanced pigeonholes; the lower section stepped-out w/a fold-down writing surface over a case of three long graduated drawers flanked by banded stiles & raised on ring- and rod-turned tapering cylindrical legs w/peg feet, probably Newburyport, Massachusetts, early 19th c., 21 1/2 x 40 3/4", 52" h. **4,140**

Federal-Style lady's writing desk, inlaid mahogany & flame veneer, a narrow rectangular top above an upper case w/a pair of end doors flanking a pair of small drawers over two long drawers all w/line inlay & round brass pulls, the projecting lower section w/a fold-out hinged writing surface above an apron w/pull-out supports flanking a long line-inlaid drawer w/oval brasses, slender square tapering legs joined by an H-stretcher, labeled "Williams - Kemp Furniture, Grand Rapids, Mich.," 20th c., 16 x 28", 38 3/4" h. **825**

Federal-Style writing desk, inlaid mahogany, a rectangular top above a pair of long drawers w/inlaid border banding above a central arched kneehole opening w/applied fans at corner brackets flanked by two smaller inlaid drawers, round brass pulls, worn blonde finish, 20th c., 30 x 48", 28 3/4" h. **220**

Fine Classical Revival Desk, mahogany & mahogany veneer, a superstructure w/a center raised rectangular two-door compartment flanked by leaf-carved pilasters further flanked by stacks of three convex drawers, all on the rectangular top w/a pull-out writing surface above a long narrow round-fronted drawer over two smaller round-fronted drawers flanking the kneehole, carved acanthus leaf carving at the sides, raised on four turned & leaf-carved supports on blocks joined by a turned & carved H-stretcher, on large paw feet, late 19th c., 22 x 44", 45" h. (ILLUS.) **1,950**

George III-Style Partner's Desk

George III-Style partner's desk, mahogany, the rectangular molded top inset w/gilt-tooled burgundy leather, above an apron fitted w/three drawers on each side, raised on cabriole legs w/scroll-carved knees & ending in claw-and-ball feet, England, early 20th c., 36 x 61 1/2", 31" h. (ILLUS.) **3,220**

George III-Style pedestal desk, mahogany, the rectangular molded top inset w/gilt-tooled green leather, above a long center drawer over the kneehole flanked by two stacks of four small drawers each, deep molded plinth base on casters, England, ca. 1900, 28 1/2 x 54", 29 1/2" h. (wear, lower drawers loose within case) **1,610**

Georgian-Style "kidney-shaped" desk, mahogany veneer, the oblong gently curved top w/a long central drawer over the kneehole opening flanked by stacks of five graduated drawers all w/banded veneer trim & oval brasses, the back of the case w/open book shelves, refinished, probably England, early 20th c., 23 x 48", 29 1/2" h. **605**

Walnut Roll-top Desk

Fine Classical Revival Desk

Late Victorian 'roll-top' desk, walnut, a narrow rectangular top over the S-roll scroll opening to an interior fitted w/pigeonholes & small drawers above the writing surface, an edge molding over the kneehole opening beside a band of five small drawers w/leaf-carved pulls, paneled sides at top & bottom sides, molded base, refinished, last quarter 19th c., 30 x 48", 48" h. (ILLUS.).............................. **2,400**

Louis XV-Style "Bonheur du Jour"

Louis XV-Style "bonheur du jour" desk, gilt-bronze mounted marquetry, the upper section w/a central tall solid door set w/an oval "Sevres" porcelain plaque surrounded by gilt-metal banding & crossbanded veneer & a gilt-lattice crest, flanked by two lower sections each w/three small drawers above the projecting serpentine base w/gilt-metal banding above a serpentine veneered apron w/long drawer w/a writing surface all raised on slender veneered cabriole legs w/gilt-metal knee mounts & "sabots," France, late 19th c., 22 x 36", 44" h. (ILLUS.)... **4,312**

Louis XV-Style Cylinder-front Desk

Louis XV-Style 'cylinder-front' desk, gilt-bronze mounted mahogany, a rectangular top w/a low gilt-metal gallery above three narrow drawers w/gilt-bronze pulls & mounts above the wide cylinder front w/gilt-bronze scroll banding opening to a slide-out inset leather writing surface, all above a heavy gilt-bronze border over the apron w/a long central drawer w/gilt-bronze mounts flanked on one side by two small drawers & on the other by a sin-

gle deep drawer each w/scrolling gilt-bronze mounts, on simple cabriole legs w/long gilt-bronze scroll mounts down the legs ending in feet w/"sabots," France, late 19th c., 30 x 64", 48" h. (ILLUS.)....... **13,800**

Louis XV-Style desk, mahogany, the rectangular top w/a superstructure containing drawers & pigeonholes, the apron w/three drawers, raised on twisted columnar legs, France, 19th c., 24 x 49", 36" h......................... **862**

Louis XVI-Style desk, gilt bronze-mounted mahogany, the rectangular top w/inset tooled leather writing surface above a conforming case w/a single center drawer over a kneehole opening flanked by two stacks of three drawers each, France, late 19th c., 34 1/2 x 72", 31" h. ... **3,162**

Mission Oak Writing Desk

Mission-style (Arts & Crafts movement) desk, oak, a rectangular top w/through corner posts above a narrow central drawer w/turned wood pulls flanked by slatted end book compartments joined by a flat wide medial shelf, unsigned, ca. 1916, 28 x 48", 29" h. (ILLUS.) **805**

Mission-style (Arts & Crafts movement) desk, a rectangular top slightly overhanging an apron w/a long flush central drawer over the kneehole opening flanked on each side by a stack of two deep drawers w/original copper hardware, through-tenon construction & paneled sides & back, square legs, original finish, branded mark of L. & J.G. Stickley, Model No. 501, 30 x 48", 30" h. **2,090**

Mission-style (Arts & Crafts movement) desk, a rectangular top above a case w/a long flush drawer over the central kneehole opening flanked on one side by a stack of three small drawers & on the other side w/a single small drawer over a false-double-fronted file drawer, pull-out writing shelves, original dry finish, "Handcraft" decal of L. & J.G. Stickley, Model No. 615, 32 x 60", 30" h. (some refinishing on the top).. **4,400**

Mission-style (Arts & Crafts movement) partner's desk, oak, a wide rectangular top supported by eight square legs inset into the top, four on each side of the central kneehole opening, each side w/a pair of small deep drawers flanking the kneehole opening & each w/a square, pointed pull, applied X-design on the sides, the legs ending in shaped Mackmurdo feet, original dark finish, attributed to McHugh, 37 x 56", 29" h. (one knob replaced)......... **1,430**

Lifetime Mission Slant Front Desk

Mission-style (Arts & Crafts movement) slant front desk, oak, a low crestrail on a narrow top shelf over the wide hinged slant front opening to a fitted interior including drawers above a deep apron w/a pair of small, deep drawers flanking a small, arched central kneehole drawer, square legs extending above the top of the front edge, low side stretchers joined by a narrow medial shelf stretcher, new dark finish, foil decal of the Lifetime Furniture Company, 16 x 31 1/2", 44 1/2" h. (ILLUS.) **1,045**

Stickley Brothers Slant Front Desk

Mission-style (Arts & Crafts movement) slant front desk, a narrow rectangular top w/pointed rear stiles above a wide hinged slant top w/long copper strap hinges, opening to a fitted interior above a long drawer above the kneehole opening, slender square legs joined by short double end stretchers & a single rear stretcher, on slightly arched shoe feet, cleaned original finish, unsigned Stickley Brothers, Model No. 6516, 15 x 30", 47" h. (ILLUS.)... **2,090**

Mission-style (Arts & Crafts movement) slant front desk, oak, a narrow top w/a high three-quarters gallery above the wide hinged slant front w/original pointed copper strap hinges opening to a fitted interior above a pair of short drawers over

a long drawer above a pair of flat cupboard doors w/long pointed copper strap hinges, original hardware, flush tenons at sides, fine original finish, early red decal mark of Gustav Stickley, Model No. 550, ca. 1902, minor separation on one side, 14 x 33", 48" h. **12,100**

Modernist Heywood-Wakefield Desk

Modern style desk, light hardwood, a rectangular top w/a gently bowed front above a single long comforming drawer over two stacks of two deep drawers flanking the kneehole opening, each drawer w/a long low arched grip pull, on small rounded block feet, Heywood-Wakefield Co., Model No. C3978W w/wheat finish, ca. 1950, 21 x 46", 30" h. (ILLUS.) **400-800**

Modern Style Oak Desk

Modern style desk, oak, rectangular top w/cream-colored laminated surface & curved face front w/a long center drawer flanked by a shallow & deep drawer w/curved finger grips, raised on slender square tapering gently curved legs, light finish, metal tag of Dunbar Company, Berne, Indiana, mid-20th c., wear, stains, scratches, 21 x 50", 29 1/4" h. (ILLUS.) **460**

Herman Miller 1950s Desk

Modern style desk, walnut & brass, a demi-lune shaped top above a conforming case w/a three-slot compartment above a stack of two drawers w/round brass pulls & open side compartment to the left of the kneehole, raised on cylindrical brass legs, design attributed to Gilbert Rhode, manufactured by Herman Miller, Zeeland, Michigan, ca. 1950s, minor wear, 24 x 45 1/2", 29 1/4" h. (ILLUS.) **1,150**

Modern Style Desk & Chair

Modern style desk & chair, maple, the desk w/a rectangular top over a central kneehole flanked on each side by a bank of two curved-front drawers w/horizontal wood pulls, raised on turned canted legs, an accompanying side chair w/a wide curved wooden back above an upholstered slip seat on a curved-front seatrail on slender square tapering legs, by Heywood-Wakefield, ca. 1950s, desk 22 x 50", 29 1/4" h., 2 pcs. (ILLUS.) **403**

Plantation desk, country-style, painted poplar, two-part construction: the upper section w/a rectangular top w/a flat flared cornice above a single wide 6-pane glazed cupboard door opening to a shelf above a high arched base opening; the widely stepped-out lower section w/a long front hinged drop leaf w/rounded corners, raised on square tapering legs, old worn red finish, 19th c., base 17 1/2 x 36 1/4", 66 1/2" h. **550**

Queen Anne Child's Slant-front Desk

Queen Ann child's slant-front desk, cherry & tiger stripe maple, a narrow rectangular top above the hinged slant-front opening to an interior fitted w/pigeon-

holes, the case w/two graduated long drawers w/butterfly pulls & keyhole escutcheons, molded base w/simple bracket feet, engraved brasses appear to be original, New England, mid-18th c., height loss, other imperfections, 19" w., 20 3/4" h. (ILLUS.) **9,200**

Queen Anne child's slant-front desk, maple, narrow rectangular top above a wide hinged slant front opening to a compartmented interior above a case w/two long thumb-molded drawers w/butterfly pulls & keyhole escutcheons, molded base & scroll-cut bracket feet, old refinish, New England, ca. 1750, 11 1/2 x 19 1/4", 20" h. (brasses probably replaced, restored) **2,530**

Queen Anne desk, inlaid walnut, a rectangular top w/molded edges & stringed inlay outlining above a case w/a single long drawer above two banks of small square drawers flanking the kneehole opening w/a recessed raised panel door opening to a shelf & pulls forward, banded inlay in each drawer front, butterfly brasses, molded base, simple curved bracket feet, Boston, 1735-60, 31 1/2 x 33 3/4", 30 1/2" h. (repairs) **25,300**

Queen Anne slant front desk, maple, a narrow top above a wide hinged slant front opening to an interior of valanced compartments above small drawers, the end drawers separated by scrolled dividers, above a case of three long thumb-molded drawers on a molded base w/bracket feet & central drop pendant, old darkened surface, probably northern Maine, 18th c., 17 1/2 x 35 1/2", 40 1/4" h. (imperfections) **5,175**

Queen Anne slant-front desk, maple, a narrow rectangular top above a wide hinged slant lid opening to an interior of valanced compartments separated by scrolled dividers & small drawers, above a case of four long graduated thumb-molded drawers w/butterfly pulls, molded base w/short cabriole legs ending in square pad feet, original brasses, early surface, Norwich, Connecticut area, 1730-50, 18 1/4 x 33 3/4", 41" h. **6,325**

Queen Anne Table-top Desk

Queen Anne table-top desk, a narrow rectangular top above a hinged & molded slant-front opening to an interior of valanced compartments above two drawers & a well, the dovetailed shallow case w/pull-out trunnels on a molded base w/central shaped pendant & simple bracket feet, refinished, restoration, Pennsylvania, ca. 1740-60, 14 1/4 x 23 1/2", 16 1/2" h. (ILLUS.)............... **2,530**

Queen Anne-Style Child's Desk

Queen Anne-Style child's desk on frame, curly maple, two-part construction: the upper section w/a narrow rectangular top over a hinged slant-lid opening to a block-and fan-carved interior w/three graduated drawers below; the lower section w/a mid-molding over one long drawer above a scroll-cut apron on cabriole legs ending in pad feet, butterfly pulls, probably 19th c., 15 x 25 3/4", 38 1/2" h. (ILLUS.) **6,900**

Queen Anne-Style Desk on Stand

Queen Anne-Style desk on stand, parcel-gilt red-japanned wood, two part construction: the upper section w/a narrow rectangular top over a hinged slant-lid opening to an interior w/pigeonholes & three small drawers over two long cock-beaded drawers w/teardrop pulls; on a base w/a mid-molding above a narrow apron w/central drop all raised on tall cabriole legs ending in pad feet, decorated overall w/chinoiserie scenes & designs, probably 19th c., chips, 16 1/4 x 21 1/2", 37" h. (ILLUS.)... **2,300**

Queen Anne-Style Library Desk

Queen Anne-Style library desk, oak, a wide rectangular top w/molded edge above a deep bowed band w/a long conforming drawer w/bail pulls at the front above the kneehole opening, above an incurved band w/a small drawer on each side of the kneehole, raised on heavy cabriole legs ending in paw feet, ca. 1900, 28 x 45", 30" h. (ILLUS.) **863**

Dutch Rococo-Style Lady's Desk

Rococo-Style lady's slant-lid desk, mahogany & floral marquetry, a narrow rectangular top above a wide hinged slant-lid opening to a fitted writing compartment above a slightly inset small central drawer over the kneehole opening flanked by double small square drawers on each side, simple cabriole legs ending in "sabots," Holland, third quarter 19th c., together w/a Neoclassical-style mahogany & floral marquetry side chair, desk 18 1/2 x 29 1/2", 37 1/2" h., 2 pcs. (ILLUS. of desk).. **1,840**

Schoolmaster's desk, country-style, walnut, a narrow top w/low three-quarters gallery above a wide hinged slant-top w/breadboard ends opening to pigeonholes, on tall square tapering legs, refinished, 19th c., 24 1/2 x 36 1/2", overall 36" h. (edges of lid & front rail ended out)...... **275**

Schoolmaster's desk on frame, poplar, two-part construction: the upper section w/a narrow top shelf w/a three-quarters gallery above a wide hinged sloping lid opening to the dovetailed case w/ten pigeonholes; the lower section w/a single long drawer w/two wooden knobs raised on baluster- and ring-turned legs w/knob feet joined by flat box stretchers, original red wash, 19th c., 26 1/2 x 39", 47 1/2" h. (base wobbly).. **660**

Victorian Aesthetic Movement captain's desk, walnut & burl walnut, the superstructure w/a high peaked center crest topped by a short spindled gallery over a sloped shingle-like 'roof' projecting above a band of ebonized scallops & flanked by small open shelves w/scallop-cut aprons raised on block- and ring-turned columnar supports flanking a projecting small central compartment w/a beveled mirror in the door flanked by side panels decorated w/incised & ebonized geometric incised lines, a wide hinged slope front writing surface opening to a fitted well above a line-

Aesthetic Movement Captain's Desk

incised & ebonized front apron projecting above the lower case & supported by ring-, knob- and rob-turned slender spindles flanking a pair of paneled doors decorated w/burl & gilt-incised line decoration, original finish, ca. 1880, 22 x 30", 4' 2" h. (ILLUS.) ... **2,000**

Baroque Desk on Griffin Supports

Victorian Baroque Revival partner's desk, mahogany, the rectangular top w/molded edges & rounded corners above a case w/an upper rounded border w/three drawers on each side & carved overall w/ornate baroque scrolls, a lower pair of matched end drawers on each side flanking the arched kneehole openings, raised at each corner on large carved figural winged griffins on a long cross-form stretcher w/egg-and-dart-carved incurved sides, on gadroon-carved block feet, original finish, attributed to J. R. Horner, New York City, ca. 1880, 30 x 60", 30" h. (ILLUS.) **12,500**

Ornate Baroque Revival Partner's Desk

Victorian Baroque Revival partner's desk, oak & oak veneer, the long oval top w/molded flaring edges above rounded end sections each w/a pair of drawers centering ornately scroll-carved curved doors centering on each side a long scroll-carved drawer over the kneehole opening, raised on a scroll-carved apron & four heavy animal paw legs on casters, late 19th c. (ILLUS.) **3,575**

Victorian Cylinder-front Desk

Victorian 'cylinder-front' desk, Renaissance Revival substyle, walnut, a narrow molded top above the high cylinder-front w/recessed burl panels opening to an interior fitted w/large pigeonholes over small drawers above a mid-molding over the lower case w/an arched central long drawer over a paneled kneehole opening flanked by a pair of projecting drawers w/recessed burl panels above stacks of three drawers w/recessed burl panels flanked by molded & shaped blocks, paneled base ends, plinth base, right side w/side-lock false drawer, kneehole w/false privacy panel w/locking door, ca. 1880, 31 x 48", 56" h. (ILLUS.) **2,588**

Victorian "Davenport" desk, mahogany, the upper section w/a leather-lined slanted writing surface opening to three drawers & one false drawer front releasing one at the right, above the lower case fitted w/five drawers on one side opposing false drawers, raised on carved turned feet on casters, second quarter 19th c., England, 20 x 22", 30" h. (wear) **805**

Country Eastlake Captain's Desk

Victorian Eastlake country-style captain's desk, walnut, the superstructure w/an arched, pierced & scroll-cut crestrail flanked by pointed side rails over the narrow shelf above a lower open shelf flanked by pierced, arched sides above a small line-inlaid drawer flanking an open compartment, the slant-front case w/a wide lid opening to a well & w/a small candle shelf to one side, raised on pierce-carved cross-form supports joined by a ring- and baluster-turned cross stretcher w/a small turned finial, original finish, ca. 1875-85, 24 x 30", 42" h. (ILLUS.) 650

Wooton Patent Cylinder Top Desk

Victorian 'patent' desk, Renaissance Revival substyle, walnut & burl walnut, a low spindled three-quarters gallery w/a central paneled crest above a sawtooth-cut frieze band over a cylinder front opening to an interior fitted w/pigeonholes & small drawers over the writing surface over a row of three narrow drawers, the lower case w/two rotary swing-out compartments fitted w/drawers & letter slots flanking the central kneehole opening, signed by The Wooton Desk Company, Indianapolis, Indiana, ca. 1875, 29 x 53", 62" h. (ILLUS.).. 15,120

Wooton Patent Secretary-Desk

Victorian 'patent' desk, Renaissance Revival substyle, walnut & ebonized wood, the high arched & scroll-carved crest w/turned finial flanked by similar ornament above a shaped & veneered gallery over a molded shelf above an outset rectangular case w/projecting quarter-round upper section fitted w/two conforming & paneled doors embellished w/applied ornament & each w/a molded metal plaque, the first

w/flip door & inscribed "Letters" & fitted on the reverse w/various shelves & the second inscribed "Manufactured by - The Wooton Desk Co. - Indianapolis Ind. - Pat. Oct. 6 1874" & fitted on the reverse w/forty small cardboard removable drawers opening to an elaborately compartmented interior comprised of variously sized pigeonholes & drawers w/fall-front & leather-lined writing surface, all above a shaped skirt, on paired downscrolling legs fitted w/casters, 31 x 42 1/2" closed, 72" h. (ILLUS.) 21,850

Wooton Patent Secretary - Desk

Victorian plantation desk, walnut & mahogany veneer, two-part construction: the upper section w/a rectangular top w/flaring stepped cornice above a wide veneered frieze band over a full-width two-panel fall-front hinged lid opening to a fitted interior; the lower stepped-out section w/a rectangular top over a single long veneered drawer w/replaced brasses, raised on four ring-, knob- and block-turned legs w/ball feet, mid-19th c., 21 1/2 x 34", 59 1/4" h. (restoration) (ILLUS. open)... 770

Victorian substyle 'patent' desk, walnut, burl walnut & burl bird's-eye maple, a rectangular top w/a high blocked & pierced carved gallery above a pair of rounded wide swing-out doors fitted w/either pigeonholes or paper slots flanking the central case w/a fold-down writing surface & numerous veneered small drawers & slots, deep molded base w/long molded shoe feet on casters, Wooton Patent Secretary, Standard grade, ca. 1876 15,000-20,000

Wooton Standard Grade Desk

Victorian 'patent' desk, walnut & walnut veneer, Standard Grade, a paneled & spindled top gallery above the curved, paneled & hinged double door case opening to an ornately fitted desk interior, on block feet on casters, Wooton Desk Company, ca. 1880 (ILLUS.) **12,000**

William & Mary Desk on Frame

William & Mary desk on frame, tulipwood & oak, two-part construction: the upper section w/a narrow rectangular top over a hinged raised-panel fall-front opening to an interior of four compartments, three drawers & a well w/sliding closure above a double arched deep molded front; the lower section w/a mid-molding above a wide molded rectangular top overhanging a deep apron w/a long drawer w/brass teardrop pulls & a diamond-form keyhole escutcheon over the valanced apron, knob- and trumpet-turned legs on shaped flat cross stretchers over turned 'turnip' feet, replaced brasses, old refinish, minor imperfections, probably Connecticut, early 18th c., 15 x 24 3/4", 42 1/2" h. (ILLUS.)........................ **17,250**

William & Mary slant-front desk, maple, a narrow top above a wide hinged slant lid opening to an interior fitted w/valanced pigeonholes & seven short drawers centering a blocked hinged prospect door above a well, the lower case w/a pair of short drawers w/butterfly pulls & keyhole escutcheons above a pair of long drawers w/similar pulls, molded base raised on large ball feet, probably New York area, 1710-30 (formerly painted white, several valances replaced) **40,250**

William & Mary Slant-front Desk

William & Mary slant-front desk, walnut veneer, a narrow rectangular top above a wide hinged slant front opening to a valanced interior w/two document drawers w/columns above four drawers w/burl veneer & a well below, a double-arch molded case of two short drawers & two long drawers, the case w/a pair of short drawers above two long drawers each w/butterfly brasses & keyhole escutcheons, molded base on large turned turnip feet, old refinish, replaced brasses, restored, probably Connecticut, early 18th c., 19 1/2 x 34", 40 1/2" h. (ILLUS.) **5,175**

William & Mary-Style writing desk, oak, rectangular top w/molded edges above a case w/a central long drawer w/angular border molding forming a long panel over the kneehole opening flanked by two stacks of three drawers each decorated w/similar molding & panels, each drawer w/a brass teardrop pull, raised on eight baluster-, ring- and block-turned legs joined by low ball-turned stretchers, on ball feet, old finish, early 20th c., 27 3/4 x 59", 31" h. (one piece of drawer molding missing)... **495**

Dining Room Suites

Art Deco: dining table & eight dining chairs; mahogany & rosewood, the table w/a rectangular canted-corner top w/draw-ends raised on tapering splayed legs ending in brass sabots, two armchairs & six side chairs each w/a curved backrest above a leather seat raised on tapering legs, France, ca. 1925, table 42 x 75", 29" h., the set (chair restoration) **$8,625**

Art Deco Dining Suite

Art Deco: dining table & six side chairs; thuya & mahogany, the table w/a rectangular top w/cut corners in veneer over an eight-paneled cone-shaped pedestal on a short waisted band above the flared paneled base, each chair w/an angular arched crestrail above a tapering splat, upholstered seat on slender square tapering legs, faux suede seats in navy blue, Europe, ca. 1938, minor wear, table 49 x 59", 31 1/2" h. (ILLUS.) **4,600**

Art Deco Walnut Dining Room Suite

Art Deco: draw-leaf dining table & eight chairs; walnut & wrought iron, the table w/a rectangular top w/parquetry & raised on four legs inset w/leather panels conjoined by a wood & wrought-iron stretcher, raised on plinths, the chairs w/tall leather-upholsterd back panels & seats on square legs joined by high slender stretchers, ironwork impressed "J. Gallix," France, ca. 1935-40, table open 39 1/4 x 120", 29 1/2" h., the set (ILLUS.).. **5,750**

Art Deco: extension table & four dining chairs; the table in painted wood w/a black rectangular top over a narrow pale green apron on slender tapering square black ends & square open central supports in black & green, the chairs w/a painted black curved crestrail raised on green tubular-metal stiles continuing down & looping to form legs, upholstered

seats, designed by Pierre Chareau, France, ca. 1928, w/four table leaves, table 16 1/4 x 58 1/2", 38" h., the set **13,800**

Art Deco Maple Dinette Set

Art Deco: table & four side chairs; decorated maple, the extension dinette table w/a rectangular top w/cut corners above a reeded apron raised on U-shaped end & central supports w/reeded edges on a trestle-form base w/outswept reeded feet, each chair w/a stepped crest centered by a hand hole above a stencilled American eagle & shield design, shaped seat on square tapering & blocked front legs & slender square back stile legs joined by stretchers, National Chair Co., Boston, Massachusetts, ca. 1938, finish wear, table 42" w., chairs 34" h., the set (ILLUS.) **345**

German Art Deco Dining Room Suite

Art Deco: table, two armchairs & four side chairs; exotic wood veneer, the table w/an oval expandable top above a deep apron on four slight incurved square tapering legs, the chairs also of exotic wood w/lattice-style backs & legs matching the table, upholstered seats, Germany, ca. 1930, veneer loss, table, 45 x 55", chairs 34 1/2" h., the set (ILLUS. of part) **460**

Fine Classical Revival Dining Suite

Classical Revival: round expandable table, sideboard, wall mirror, eight side chairs & two armchairs; mahogany & mahogany veneer, the table w/a carved edge & deep apron above a central support & four heavy scroll-carved legs on a cross-form plinth, the sideboard w/a high scroll-carved backboard above the rectangular top over an arrangement of drawers & doors, each chair w/a wide shaped crestrail over a wide scalloped splat, scroll-cut front legs w/low H-stretchers, ca. 1900, the set (ILLUS.) **12,075**

Danish Modern Dining Suite

Danish Modern: extension dining table, two armchairs & four side chairs; walnut, the oval topped table w/three leaves raised on tapering cylindrical legs, each chair w/an upholstered back panel in a simple turned walnut frame w/a cushion-form seat, all in original green upholstery, minor upholstery wear, laminate loss on skirt, Denmark, ca. 1955, chairs 30" h., table 42 x 60", 28 1/2" h., the set (ILLUS.) **575**

Jacobean Revival: refractory dining table, six chairs, a court-style cupboard & a sideboard; oak, ornate turned & paneled details w/turned legs, in the 17th c. style, ca. 1920s, the set **3,410**

Modern style: dining table & eight chairs; hardwood, the table w/a long plain rectangular top & apron & square post legs, each chair w/a round-cornered crestrail above square canted rear & front legs w/an upholstered seat cushion, the arm-

Edward Wormley Dining Room Suite

chairs w/scrolled open arms, designed by Edward Wormley, labeled by the Dunbar Company, ca. 1950s, table 41 7/8 x 72", 30 1/2" h., the set (ILLUS.) **4,887**

Victorian Golden Oak substyle: round-top extension dining table & six side chairs; quarter-sawn oak, the table top opening to hold four leaves above a heavy round ring-turned split pedestal w/four curved legs ending in paw feet on casters, side chairs w/flat slightly curved crestrail above a simple vase-form splat above the seat w/upholstered insert, simple cabriole front legs ending in paw feet, ca. 1900, table 48" d., 30" h., the set **1,540**

William & Mary Revival: dining table, eight chairs & side cabinet; walnut & walnut veneer, the expandable table w/a rectangular top w/rounded corners & molded edges above a scroll-carved border raised on ornate pierced & carved corner legs & squared cross stretchers to the central baluster-turned supports, the high-backed chairs w/pierced & scroll-carved crestrails above the oblong serpentine frame enclosing the upholstered panel above the upholstered slip seat in a serpentine frame w/carved scrolls at front apron & carved cabriole front legs ending in trifid feet, turned rear legs & scrolled & carved flattened H-stretcher, Century Furniture Co., Grand Rapids, Michigan, ca. 1910-30 (ILLUS. of part) **12,000**

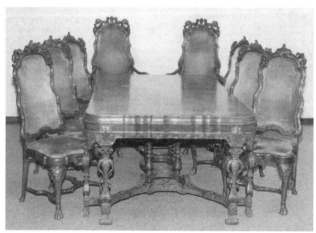

William & Mary Revival Dining Suite

Dry Sinks

Grain-painted Country Dry Sink

Painted & decorated poplar, rectangular well top w/a raised backboard w/curved ends above a pair of drawers w/turned wood knobs over a pair of paneled doors w/the original cast-iron thumb latch w/porcelain knob, one-board ends, cut-out feet, original dark brown graining, 19th c., 17 1/4 x 41", 34" h. plus crest (ILLUS.)...... **$1,045**

Early New England Painted Dry Sink

Painted pine, a low backsplash over the deep rectangular well over a pair of flat cupboard doors w/wood knobs, shaped bracket feet, old red paint, New England, early 19th c., imperfections, 17 1/2 x 42", 30" h. (ILLUS.).. 633

Painted pine, the rectangular well top w/upright board edging above a case w/a pair of narrow flush-mounted single-board doors, old goldenrod repaint, 19th c., 47 3/4" l., 28 1/2" h. (one bottom board loose, feet gone) 770

Painted pine & birch, rectangular well top projecting over a case w/a single cupboard door, old salmon-colored paint, 19th c., 34" l... 1,500

Painted Child's Dry Sink

Painted pine & poplar, child's size, the superstructure w/a shaped & pointed crest-

board over a narrow shelf & two short doors w/old replaced blue glass panels over a set-back narrow shelf above a rectangular well & work surface over a small drawer, the lower case w/a pair of paneled cupboard doors, simple bracket feet, original brown paint, wire nail construction, white porcelain pulls, late 19th c., 13 x 28", 34" h. (ILLUS.) 660

Dry Sink with Lift-top

Painted pine & poplar, the rectangular top w/a low backsplash above a long hinged lift-top over a well on the right end next to a smaller work surface over a small drawer, two paneled cupboard doors below, on turned knob feet, old red paint, some paint touch up, door pulls & thumb latches replaced, minor repair to one foot, 19th c., top 21 1/2 x 49", 36 1/2" h. (ILLUS.)............. 1,210

Painted poplar, a high board back w/a narrow top shelf above down-curved sides to the rectangular top well beside a small work shelf at one end over a small drawer, the lower case w/a pair of large paneled cupboard doors w/old cast-iron thumb latches w/brass knobs, old green repaint, 19th c., probably old conversion from cupboard, 18 1/4 x 43 1/2", 52" h. (drawer knob replaced, some edge damage)............... 770

Painted poplar, a shallow rectangular well beside a small rectangular working surface over a single smaller drawer w/a turned wood knob above the case w/a pair of paneled rectangular cupboard doors w/cast-iron latch, curved bracket feet, w/old zinc liner, dry-scraped to original putty-white color, 19th c., 18 3/4 x 48 1/4", 32" h. (chip on one rear foot & along top edge of drawer) 1,375

Painted poplar & chestnut, two-piece construction: the upper section w/a rectangular top over a pair of raised panel cupboard doors raised high above the lower case; the lower section w/a rectangular well w/a small work shelf at one end above a small drawer w/turned wood knob, two raised panel cupboard doors below, simple low bracket feet, old dark brown paint & brown feathering over yellow on door panels, attributed to the Ohio Amish, 19th c., base 19 1/4 x 44 1/2", 68" h. (two repairs in well)............................ 2,200

Painted poplar & pine, a superstructure w/a narrow rectangular top over a pair of small drawers flanking a long central compartment, the lower rectangular well above a case w/a pair of paneled cupboard doors w/cast-iron latches w/knobs, shaped bracket feet, worn comb-grained decoration, 19th c., 18 3/4 x 48", 50 1/2" h. **2,090**

Painted walnut, a long rectangular top well w/a high splashback & stepped sides above a case w/a pair of doors w/raised double panels flanking a small square central drawer over a rectangular small raised panel, shaped bracket feet, old black paint & traces of dark blue & red on splashback, 19th c., 22 1/4 x 54 1/4", 33" h. (crack in drawer front)....................... **3,300**

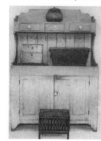

Fine High-back Dry Sink

Painted walnut & ash, high-back style, the superstructure w/a high stepped crestboard w/shaped sides flanking a narrow shelf over a row of three small drawers raised above incurved sides & the long well, the base w/a pair of double-paneled cupboard doors, simple bracket feet, beaded backboards, old grey paint, chips on drawers & glued repair, 19th c., 17 3/4 x 48", 68" h. (ILLUS.) **5,775**

Painted wood, rectangular top w/shallow well above a case w/a pair of shallow drawers w/turned wood knobs above a pair of paneled cupboard doors w/a cast-iron thumb latch w/porcelain knob, low arched apron, original dark brown paint, one-board ends, found in Ohio, 19th c., 17 1/2 x 42", 33 1/2" h. (surface wear, one foot ended out) **990**

Decorative Pine Dry Sink

Pine, a long rectangular shallow top well above a case w/headboard paneling in the sides & forming a diagonal panel in the two doors, cast-iron latches, narrow sawtooth-cut apron, warm patina, late 19th c., 19 x 44", 32" h. (ILLUS.) **633**

Pine, the rectangular splashboard w/shelf joining molded shaped sides above a cockbeaded case & a single cupboard door w/recessed panel, on cut-out arched base, old surface w/vestiges of red paint, possibly New England, early

19th c., 25 x 44 1/2", 41" h. (replaced hinges & hardware, other imperfections)... **1,035**

Large Hutch-style Dry Sink

Poplar, hutch-type, a narrow rectangular raised back section w/a row of four drawers above downswept sides flanking the long well w/a rectangular work surface at one end, the lower case w/a stack of three graduated drawers beside a pair of double-paneled cupboard doors w/cast-iron thumb latches w/porcelain knobs, flat base, short stile feet, old finish, replaced porcelain knobs, found in Ohio, late 19th c., 23 x 73 3/4", 50 1/2" h. (ILLUS.) **1,870**

Poplar, long rectangular well w/a small work shelf at one end above a smaller drawer, a wide two-panel door in the base flanked by wide side boards, square nail construction, scalloped apron, red stain finish, 19th c., 18 1/4 x 53 3/4", 34 1/2" h. (damage & repair to back feet, some edge damage)... **688**

Red-stained softwood, a rectangular shallow dry sink well above one-board ends w/crescent cut-out feet flanking a single open shelf, 19th c., 21 x 41", 32" h............ **1,100**

Softwood, a long rectangular hinged top opening to a shallow dovetailed well slightly overhanging a case w/a pair of drawers over a pair of simple paneled doors, simple turned wood knobs, flat apron, refinished, late 19th c. **358**

Simple Softwood Dry Sink

Softwood, a low three-quarters gallery above the shallow rectangular well over a pair of drawers over a pair of paneled cupboard doors, simple bracket feet, 19th c., 17 x 35 1/2", 35" h. (ILLUS.)............ **770**

Walnut & maple, a low splashback above the long rectangular well w/a small working surface at one end above a small drawer w/an oval facing & turned wood knob, two large double-paneled cupboard doors below, flat apron & short bracket feet, refinished, square nail construction, 19th c., 20 x 54 1/4", 34" h. **825**

Garden & Lawn

Cast iron unless otherwise noted.

Armchair, the arched back composed of entwined tree branches w/scattered leaves, arched twig arms, seat & legs w/twig end stretchers, dark green repaint, late 19th c., 29" h.. **$715**

Armchairs, the squared back w/two cross-bars flanking an openwork cast design of a classical urn issuing long leafy grape-vines, high shaped bar handles on in-curved arm supports above the seat composed of slender crossbars, X-form arched side legs joined by two bar stretchers, old dark green repaint, 19th c., 28 1/4" h., pr.. **3,025**

Planter, painted & decorated wood, a taper-ing square paneled form w/faceted carved finials painted in shades of green, the grain-painted sides w/green border outlined in yellow, early 19th c., 13 3/4" sq., 14" h. (minor paint wear)...................... **4,600**

Settee, a high triple-arch back composed of pierced looping scrolling flowering leafy vines curving to form arms w/shaped bird head arm supports above the D-form geometrically-pierced seat, on cabriole legs w/pierced leafy corner brackets, dark green repaint, seat labeled "Kramer Bros., Dayton, Ohio," 33 1/2" h. (old re-pair on back, one screw in leg needs re-placing)... **990**

Settee, a serpentine crest cast w/swags & floral clusters above the back composed of latticework arches flanked by scroll-topped arms over scrolled slats, the pierced seat above heavy scroll-cast ca-briole front legs, labeled "Mfg. by the Kramer Bros Fdy Co., Dayton, O," 19th c., old white repaint, 43 1/4" l. (break in top rail)... **605**

Settee, the arched back composed of en-twined tree branches w/scattered leaves, arched twig arms, seat & legs w/twig end stretchers, dark green repaint, late 19th c., 33" h. **1,540**

Small Branch-form Garden Settee

Settee, the arched back composed of open-work leafy entwined branches flanked by arched branch arms over the entwined branch seat, on branch-form legs joined by end stretchers, old blue repaint, 19th c., 35" l., 33" h. (ILLUS.)................................ **1,430**

Settee, the back w/an overall pierced de-sign of scrolling fern fronds continuing to form high arms & the pierced seat, arched end legs, painted white, 19th c., 53 1/2" l. **920**

Long Branch-form Garden Settee

Settee, the long back composed of entwined leafy branches flanked by arched branch arms over the openwork entwined branch seat, branch-form legs w/looped end stretchers, painted, 19th c., 50" l. (ILLUS.).. **2,160**

Garden Settee with Figural Medallions

Settee, the long cast-iron back w/sawtooth upper & lower borders & an arched cen-ter enclosing four small round pierced medallions w/various plant designs & a large central medallion w/a pierced de-sign of a dog among foliage, scrolled cast-iron arms w/round medallions w/birds flanking the long shaped wood plank seat, on a cast-iron trestle-form base w/arched legs, painted, ca. 1890, 50 1/2" l. (ILLUS.)... **1,265**

Settee, the serpentine crestrail cast w/or-nate scrolls above the back pierced w/rows of small arches flanked by ser-pentine stepped arms w/upright scroll supports, scroll-pierced seat above a scroll-cast seatrail & scrolling cabriole front legs, 19th c., worn dark green paint over earlier white, 45 1/2" l., 36" h. **633**

Settee, the serpentine crestrail w/heavy scrolls centered by a small classical bust above a band of delicate lacy scrolls over the high back composed of a wide band of interlacing ovals flanked by outswept scrolling half-arms above the oblong scroll-pierced seat w/a serpentine seatrail above a lacy scroll apron on scroll-cast cabriole front legs, dark green repaint, 19th c., 44 1/4" l., 32 1/2" h. (repaired break on one side of front leg)............ **990**

Settee, the serpentine ribbon- and flower-cast crestrail above a back composed of repeating rows of rounded arches flanked by downswept arms over scroll supports, openwork seat above a narrow scroll-cast apron & heavy scroll-cast cabriole front legs, old white repaint, second half 19th c., 46" l. **660**

Labeled Cast-Iron Garden Settee

Settee, triple-back design, the rectangular back w/a higher central panel topped by a sunburst crest over a band of rings flanked by lower matching crests, each panel w/ornate openwork scroll design flanked by simple scrolled end arms above the pierced criss-cross lattice seat above an apron of pierced rings & scrolled spearpoints, simple bar legs w/end stretchers, painted black, John McLean, New York, second half 19th c., repairs, 17 x 46", 36" h. (ILLUS.) **863**

Settee, triple-back style, a high central rectangular panel w/arched & floral scroll-pierced crest & ears above a leafy scroll-pierced panel flanked by two shorter matching panels, low rounded arms w/pierced scrolls above the pierced rectangular seat & front apron, on gently arched end legs joined by scroll stretchers, marked "Patd. May 17, 1895," old green repaint over white, 33" l., 38 1/4" h. (rust)... **605**

Settee, twig design, the gently arched back composed of entwined slender branches w/scattered leaves, arched branch arms & seat composed of straight twig branches, entwined branch legs, layers of old paint, 39" l., 32" h. **1,100**

Fine Rococo Revival Garden Settees

Settees, Rococo Revival style, the serpentine crest cast w/floral swags above a back of delicate openwork arches flanked by stepped scrolled arms on scrolled pierced supports above the ornately pierced seat, floral scroll apron & scroll-cast cabriole legs, old white repaint, New York City or Boston, third quarter 19th c., minor paint wear, 19 5/8 x 45 1/2", 35 3/4" h., pr. (ILLUS.).... **3,105**

Modern Style 1950s Garden Suite

Suite: a settee, two side chairs, two round drink tables & a square occasional table; Modern style, iron rod & metal lattice construction, the settee w/a long oblong back w/diamond lattice metal sheeting within a frame raised on curved metal supports above the narrow oblong matching seat w/upturned ends, double-bar curved legs & stretchers, matching chairs & tables w/matching latticework tops & curved metal bar bases, white, ca. 1955, settee 51 1/4" l., 31" h., the set (ILLUS. of part)....... **805**

Victorian Three-Piece Garden Suite

Suite: settee & two armchairs; each back composed of pierced lyre-form & scrolling panels w/a flat crest w/arched & pierced finial, crestrail continuing to scrolled arms above pierced scrolling panels over the pierced lattice seat, leafy scroll apron & simple cabriole legs joined by slender bar stretchers, painted white, late 19th - early 20th c., the set (ILLUS. in background) **1,200**

Hall Racks & Trees

Hall rack, Arts & Crafts, copper & metal, rectangular patinated lattice strapwork w/eight coat hooks, pierced copper riveted frame on beveled mirror, early 20th c., 48" w., 26 3/4" h. (missing rivet).................. **$489**

Early Aluminum Hall Rack

Hall rack, Modern style, anodized tubular aluminum frame w/rubber "doughnut" feet, multi-tube shaft & upturned hooks at top, manufactured by Warren McArthur Industries, ca. 1930s, 24" d., 67" h. (ILLUS.) **3,575**

Oak Hall Rack with Steer Horns

Hall rack, oak & steer horn, a large shield-shaped oak plaque mounted at the top w/large longhorn steer horns over another pair of smaller horns over a small diamond-shaped mirror above three lower upturned horns, original finish, late 19th c., 30" w. at horns, 36" h. (ILLUS.) **350**

Hall rack, Victorian Aesthetic Movement substyle, walnut, the tall superstructure w/an arched crestrail pierced w/leafy rondels & side arches above a molded rail over a panel of raised scrolling molding above a tall rectangular mirror flanked by wide pierced side panels w/metal coat hooks above a lower wide panel w/four rondel-carved corner panels alternating w/pierced spindled panels all centering a

larger central panel, shaped arms w/an umbrella bracket above a drip pan at one side, wide lift seat above a deep paneled base on turned feet, 15 x 33", 82" h. **886**

Carved Golden Oak Hall Rack

Hall rack, Victorian Golden Oak, wall-mounted, wide flat upper & lower quarter-sawn oak rails w/ornate leafy scroll carving joined to slender ring-turned side stiles w/knob finials & mounted w/three double brass hooks on each side, a central rectangular beveled mirror joined by short carved rails to the side stiles, refinished, ca. 1890, 44" l., 36" h. (ILLUS.)...... **650**

Art Deco Hall Tree

Hall tree, Art Deco, black enameled wood, upright rectangular form w/angle-cut top above staggered chrome hooks & a large rectangular tinted mirror w/cut corners above a small projecting drawer, a lower chrome bar rack above the bottom drip tray, on four large ball feet, slight wear, ca. 1930s, 7 3/4 x 33", 76" h. (ILLUS.) **489**

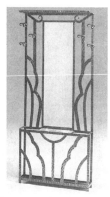

French Art Deco Hall Tree

Hall tree, Art Deco, marble-inset wrought iron, the rectangular upright framework composed of hammered bands, the rectangular hat rack above a beveled long mirror flanked by hooks above an inset marble shelf & umbrella stand w/a drip pan, wear, small dents, France, ca. 1925, 6 x 32", 74" h. (ILLUS.)...................... **5,750**

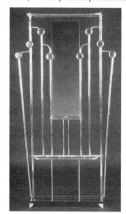

Art Deco Chromed Aluminum Hall Tree

Hall tree, Art Deco streamline-design, chromed aluminum, the tall rectangular open framework joined by round disk-shaped hat racks & curved brackets to slender uprights supporting at the center a tall narrow rectangular mirror, the outer uprights gently angled out, a narrow loop in the lower section forming an umbrella rack, design attributed to Jean Lucian, France, ca. 1935, 8 x 37 1/2", 70" h. (ILLUS.) **805**

Hall tree, Art Deco, wrought iron, rectangular outline w/an upper hat rack above coat hooks & a rectangular mirror flanked by half-round umbrella stands, decorated throughout w/hammering & pierced scrolls, France, ca. 1925, 13 x 37", 71" h... **2,875**

Hall tree, Arts & Crafts, oak, the scalloped crestrail centered by an incised cluster of stylized flowers above incised frieze

Arts & Crafts Oak Hall Tree

bands flanked by projecting shaped brackets flanking three turned bars above a backboard fitted w/hooks on the sides flanking two panels centering further rectangular designs of stylized flowers w/a tall rectangular beveled mirror in the center, all above a narrow horizontal panel above a small rectangular central cabinet w/a hinged lid above a tall paneled door w/a floral panel flanked by brass rounded side rails & quarter-round drip trays at the bottom, some wear, early 20th c., 39" w., 80" h. (ILLUS.)........................ **495**

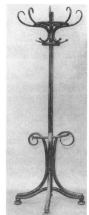

Tall Bentwood Hall Tree

Hall tree, bentwood, hickory, the top composed of a ring of long upturned S-scroll hooks joined by central rings & raised on a tall square shaft w/four long scroll braces joining the cross-form base on disk feet, worn original black paint, one hook repaired, one ball finial missing, ca. 1900, 74" h. (ILLUS.) **248**

Ornate Late Victorian Hall Tree

Hall tree, late Victorian, mahogany, the tall, wide squared back w/a narrow deep flaring crestrail above a beaded band over a wide section centered by a panel w/carved tight looping scrolls flanked by small open panels w/spindled insets all above a wide rectangular beveled mirror flanked by narrow stiles mounted w/brass hooks above two narrow open slots over a large double panel w/a each side carved w/a large seated winged griffin, scrolled open arms flanking the upholstered fixed seat, bobbin-turned front legs & square back legs joined by box stretchers, original dark finish, ca. 1880, 18 x 40", 7' 6" h. (ILLUS.) **2,000**

Large Mission Oak Hall Tree

Hall tree, Mission-style (Arts & Crafts movement), oak, the wide tall rectangular back w/a wide convex oak frame surrounding a large mirror & mounted with four ornate three-part brass coat racks w/long shaped flat backplates, all above a scroll-carved panel flanked by low shaped arms flanking a rectangular lift-top seat above the deep apron fitted w/scroll-cut applied brass corner binding, flaring molded base on bun feet, refinished, minor wear to mirror, early 20th c., 20 x 53", 92" h. (ILLUS.) **1,430**

Hall tree, turn-of-the-century, mahogany, a tall molded back w/a carved pediment centering a beveled mirror, mounted w/cast-metal coat & hat hooks, leading

down to scrolling hand rests, over a hinged seat, a molded front bottom panel, ending in reeded bun feet, ca. 1890, 20 x 36 1/2", 80" h. **644**

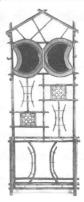

Victorian Bamboo Mirrored Hall Tree

Hall tree, Victorian bamboo, rattan & tile-inset tree, an openwork design of bamboo twigs above a pair of back-to-back wide crescent-form beveled mirrors over further curved & square bamboo w/tiles & woven rattan sections above the umbrella rack bottom framework, probably England, late 19th c., 9 1/2 x 32", 84" h. (ILLUS.) **978**

Two Late Victorian Hall Trees

Hall tree, Victorian Eastlake substyle, walnut, a tall slender form w/a scroll-cut crestrail on three small spindles between narrow stiles w/a projecting bar w/hooks at the left side & hooks down the right stile all flanking a small rectangular mirror over fanned spindles beside a tall row of short horizontal spindles above the backed rectangular seat flanked by slender turned open arms & spindled apron on turned legs joined by flat stretchers, ca. 1890, 14 x 20", 77" h. (ILLUS. right) **633**

Victorian Faux Bamboo Hall Tree

Hall tree, Victorian faux bamboo style, maple, the tall rectangular back composed of numerous turned faux bamboo crossbars joined by short turned spindles & supported by bamboo-turned side posts w/beehive-turned finials, mounted w/nine long S-scroll hat hooks & centered by a rectangular mirror, the lower section w/a narrow rectangular umbrella rack, ca. 1880, 9 x 35", 87" h. (ILLUS.) **5,040**

Massive Golden Oak Hall Tree

Hall tree, Victorian Golden Oak style, quarter-sawn oak, massive size w/the tall back topped by a carved fanned crest over

scrolls & flanked by scrolled corner ears above a wide half-round frame enclosing a large oval beveled mirror flanked by pairs of triple hooks above a wide central panel w/ornate leafy scrolls & a half-round horizontal column above the shaped flat arms on ring-turned columnar arm supports & front legs flanking the wide lift seat above a deep apron w/serpentine rim, squatty bun feet, refinished, ca. 1890s, 20 x 40", 7' h. (ILLUS.) **3,500**

Oak Hall Tree with Mirror over Roundel

Hall tree, Victorian Golden Oak style, quarter-sawn oak, the tall back w/a serpentine crestrail decorated w/carved scrolls above flat stiles flanking the large rectangular beveled mirror & mounted w/four double coat hooks on pointed brass mounts, the lower back w/a wide central panel carved w/spiky scrolls above an arched panel centered by a large roundel, arched open arms flanking the lift seat w/a deep apron decorated w/a band of wood buttons & scalloped apron & flanked by heavy square legs w/wood buttons above bun feet, refinished, ca. 1900, 18 x 30", 7' h. (ILLUS.) **1,450**
Hall tree, Victorian Golden Oak style, quarter-sawn oak, the tall back w/an arched crestrail centered w/a pointed scroll-carved finial & a wide band of raised scrolls above a tall rectangular beveled mirror w/scalloped top flanked by side columns on leaf scrolls, mounted w/four cast-brass coat hooks above a plain back panel flanked by shaped flat open arms over the rectangular hinged lift seat over a deep well & apron w/a serpentine edge, shaped arm supports form the front legs, refinished, ca. 1900, 20 x 28", 7' h. (ILLUS. top next page) **1,600**

Impressive Golden Oak Hall Tree

Oak Hall Tree with Glass Panel

Hall tree, Victorian Golden Oak style, the tall back composed of a diamond-shaped beveled glass panel within a wide flat frame w/scroll-carved rounded sections at each point, flanked by flattened stiles mounted w/four replaced cast-brass double hooks & joined by a flat vase-form panel joined by four shaped braces to the stiles, low open arms on S-scroll arm supports above the rectangular lift-seat over a deep apron w/scalloped edge, refinished, 1890s, 18 x 30", 6' 6" h. (ILLUS.) **1,250**

Hall tree, Victorian Golden Oak style, the tall back w/an arched scroll- and shell-carved crestrail over a wide oval frame mounted w/bronzed metal hooks surrounding the oval beveled mirror over flat stiles flanking a waisted & scroll-carved splat over the curved open arms on curved supports flanking the lift-top deep seat w/a scroll-carved apron & curved stile front legs, ca. 1900, 16 x 29", 82" h. (ILLUS. left)...................................... **661**

Hall tree, Victorian Golden Oak, the tall superstructure w/a high arched & scroll-

carved crest flanked by high scroll-carved ears above a rectangular mirror flanked by flat stiles mounted w/forked bronzed metal coat hooks w/the wide lower back panel w/bands of raised scroll carving, low open arms flanking the rectangular lift seat & boxed base w/scalloped apron & scrolled front feet, ca. 1900, 15 x 36", 83" h. **690**

Fine Renaissance Revival Hall Tree

Hall tree, Victorian Renaissance Revival substyle, walnut & burl walnut, the arched crestrail centered by a projecting crown-from center crest carved w/ornate scrolls above a burl panel flanked by roundels & small projecting corner ears, raised above a tall frame w/narrow burl panels enclosing an arched tall mirror, tall slender outside free-standing columns mounted w/coat pegs, U-form umbrella racks at the lower sides above a rectangular white marble shelf above a deep arched apron w/burl trim flanked by the round metal umbrella drip trays in heavy round frames, refinished, ca. 1870s, 18 x 46", 7' 6" h. (ILLUS.) **4,400**

Renaissance Revival Hall Tree

Hall tree, Victorian Renaissance Revival substyle, walnut & burl walnut, the tall back w/a large pedimented crest centered by a large carved cartouche medallion w/pointed finial & suspended drops flanked by delicate pierced carved devices & burl panels above the tall arch-topped rectangular mirror flanked by burl pilasters each mounted w/three brass coat hooks above a burl base panel centered by a raised diamond & flanked by round finials & C-form umbrella holders flanking a rectangular white marble shelf over a narrow burl-trimmed drawer hanging above an open lower platform w/metal shell-form drip trays at each round end, ca. 1870s, 54" w., 8' 4" h. (ILLUS.) **5,264**

Elaborate French Hall Tree

Hall tree, Victorian Rococo substyle, cast iron, the back formed as a tree wrapped w/a berried vine, the four tree branches issuing double-arm hooks, the back enclosing a hinged oval mirror, the whole topped w/three candle branches, the lower section w/branches forming an umbrella holder continuing to figures of French soldiers w/guns & a cannon, the base fitted w/removable drip trays, stamped "Alfred A. Charleville No. 29," France, third quarter 19th c., 85" h. (ILLUS.) **2,280**

Acanthus Leaf & Scroll-cast Hall Tree

Hall tree, Victorian Rococo substyle, cast iron, the tall top section composed of pierced acanthus leaf & S-scrolls w/six long scrolling coat hooks centered by a small oval mirror above a wide cast acanthus leaf-cast supported on scrolls above the oblong scroll-cast base fitted w/a drip tray, old dark finish, small break, umbrella holder ring needs to be reattached, ca. 1850, 13 x 28 1/2", 78" h. (ILLUS.) **1,100**

Fancy Victorian Cast-Iron Hall Tree

Hall tree, Victorian Rococo substyle, cast iron, the top w/an oblong lacy pierced scrolling floral design centering a small oval mirror & raised on a scroll-cast standard supporting an oblong loop for umbrellas above a leaf- and scroll-cast lower standard above the scroll-cast oblong base w/a drip tray, old black paint, signed "Greenwood Co. Patent 1852," umbrella loop w/welded break, 26" w., 74" h. (ILLUS.) **1,760**

Fine Victorian Cast-iron Hall Trees

Hall trees, Victorian, cast iron, tree-form w/the top cast as openwork leafy tree branches w/coat hooks centered by a small oval mirror, raised on a slender tree trunk-form pedestal w/an oval umbrella ring above the dished oblong base, patent-dated "Nov. 16 '59," second half 19th c., 73" h., pr. (ILLUS.) **2,875**

Highboys & Lowboys

HIGHBOYS

Connecticut Queen Anne Highboy

Chippendale "bonnet-top" highboy, cherry, two-part construction: the upper section w/a broken-scroll crown crest w/serpentine cove molding centering a shaped finial support above a case w/two shallow drawers flanking a deep fan-carved central drawer over four long graduated thumb-molded drawers; the lower case w/a mid-molding over a long narrow drawer over a row of three deep drawers, the center one w/a carved fan, skirt w/front & side shaping on cabriole legs ending in pad feet, some replaced butterfly brasses, refinished, New England, 18th c., 19 1/2 x 38", 84" h. (repairs, missing finials & pendants) **$37,950**

Chippendale country-style "flat-top" highboy, cherry, two-part construction: the upper section w/a rectangular top over a deep coved & molded cornice above two pairs of small drawers flanking a small square drawer w/a carved sunburst over a stack of four long graduated dovetailed drawers; the lower section w/a wide mid-molding over a narrow long drawer over two deep drawers flanking a short, narrow central drawer above a deeply scalloped apron w/a fan carving at the center, raised on scroll-carved cabriole legs ending in claw-and-ball feet, small simple brass drawer knobs, old soft finish, 19 x 37 1/4", overall 75" h. (legs possibly old replacements, drawer edge damage & repair, pulls incomplete) **4,620**

Chippendale "flat-top" highboy, walnut, two-part construction: the upper section w/a molded cornice above a rectangular case w/a row of three small drawers over a pair of drawers above three long graduated & thumb-molded drawers, all flanked by fluted quarter columns; the lower case w/a conforming mid-molding over a case fitted w/a long thumb-molded drawer flanked by similar fluted quarter columns above an elaborate scroll-cut apron, on shell-carved cabriole legs

w/ball-and-claw feet, Pennsylvania, 1750-60, 22 1/2 x 40 1/2", 63" h. **40,250**

Queen Anne "bonnet-top" highboy, cherry, two-part construction: the upper section w/a broken-scroll crest w/three tall slender urn-form finials above a deep fan-carved drawer flanked by short drawers above a stack of four long graduated drawers w/pierced butterfly brasses; the lower section w/a mid-molding over a long narrow drawer over a fan-carved center drawer flanked by smaller drawers, scalloped apron, simple cabriole legs ending in raised pad feet, Connecticut, late 18th c., some original brasses, old refinish, some reconstruction, 22 x 40", 7' h. (ILLUS.) **9,500**

Queen Anne "Flat-top" Highboy

Queen Anne "flat-top" highboy, carved maple, two-part construction: the upper section w/a flat rectangular top w/a flaring stepped cornice over a row of three drawers w/two larger flanking a small fan-carved center drawer over a stack of four long graduated drawers; the lower section w/a mid-molding over two long drawers over a long drawer disguised as three deep drawers, the center one fan-carved, scalloped apron, cabriole legs ending in pad feet, replaced mid-moldings, New Hampshire, 1740-60, 20 1/2 x 39 1/2", 77" h. (ILLUS.) **8,200**

Queen Anne "flat-top" highboy, cherry, two-part construction: the upper section w/a flat rectangular top w/a deep coved cornice above a case of five long graduated drawers; the lower section w/a mid-molding over a case w/a pair of deep drawers flanking a shallow central drawer all above the deep scalloped apron, simple cabriole legs w/raised pad feet, old refinish, old replaced brasses, Massachusetts, ca. 1750, 17 1/2 x 34 1/2", 64" h. (repairs) **19,500**

Queen Anne "flat-top" highboy, curly maple, two-part construction: the upper section w/a rectangular top over a deep flaring stepped coved cornice above five long thumb-molded graduated drawers w/butterfly brasses & keyhole escutch-

Fine Curly Maple Queen Anne Highboy

eons; the lower section w/a mid-molding over a long narrow drawer above a row of three deep drawers, the center one w/fan carving, shaped apron w/two turned acorn drops, cabriole legs ending in raised pad feet, old mellow finish, New Hampshire, 18th c., minor repair, original brasses, apron drops replaced, top 22 1/2 x 43", 73 1/4" h. (ILLUS.) **55,000**

Queen Anne "flat-top" highboy, figured maple, two-part construction: the upper section w/a rectangular flat top w/a deep widely flaring stepped cornice over a pair of thumb-molded drawers over a stack of four long graduated thumb-molded drawers; the lower section w/a medial band above a single long, narrow drawer over a pair of deep square drawers flanking a central short drawer all above a deeply scalloped apron w/two turned acorn drops, on cabriole legs ending in pad feet, appears to retain original butterfly brasses & keyhole escutcheons, Rhode Island, ca. 1740, 18 1/2 x 37", 70 1/2" h. (some drawer lip patches, replaced drops) **10,925**

Queen Anne "flat-top" highboy, figured maple, two-part construction: the upper section w/a rectangular top w/deep flaring & stepped cornice above a case w/a row of three small drawers above four long graduated thumb-molded drawers w/butterfly pulls & keyhole escutcheons; the lower section w/a mid-molding above a shallow long drawer over a pair of deep drawers flanking a central shallow drawer over a large shell-carved & scalloped apron w/acorn drops, cabriole legs w/padded disk feet, possibly by Major John Demeritt, Madbury, New Hampshire, 1770-1800, 20 1/2 x 40", 73" h. **17,250**

Queen Anne "flat-top" highboy, figured maple, two-part construction: upper section w/a rectangular top w/deep molded cornice above a row of three small drawers over a stack of four long graduated drawers; the lower section w/a mid-molding over two long drawers above a row of three deep drawers, the central one fan-carved, scalloped & scroll-cut apron above cabriole legs ending in pad feet, appears to retain original butterfly brasses & keyhole escutcheons, attributed to Major John Dunlap, New Hampshire, ca. 1760, 19 1/2 x 38 1/2", 77" h. (bottom drawer discolored) **9,775**

Queen Anne "flat-top" highboy, hardwood, two-part construction: the top section w/a rectangular top above a very deep flaring stepped cornice above a case w/a pair of dovetailed drawers over a stack of three long graduated drawers; the lower section w/a mid-molding above a pair of deep drawers flanking a shallow central drawer all above a scalloped apron w/two pointed turned drops, cabriole legs ending in pad feet, old dark red finish, old replaced batwing brasses, New England, first half 18th c., 20 x 37 1/2", 66" h. (restorations) **7,700**

Queen Anne "flat-top" highboy, maple & birch, two-part construction: the upper section w/a deep flared & molded cornice above a case w/five long graduated thumb-molded drawers w/butterfly brasses; the lower section w/a mid-molding above a long narrow drawer over a row of three deep drawers, the central one fan-carved, a valanced concave apron on cabriole legs ending in pad feet, apparently original brasses, old refinish, Massachusetts, ca. 1770, 19 x 38 1/4", 73 1/4" h. (repairs)..................... **10,350**

Queen Anne "flat-top" highboy, maple, two-part construction: the upper section w/a flat rectangular top w/a deep stepped flaring cornice above a case w/four long graduated drawers w/butterfly brasses & keyhole escutcheons; the lower section w/a mid-molding above a case w/a long narrow drawer above two deep drawers flanking a shallower central drawer w/fan-carving, scalloped apron, cabriole legs ending in raised pad feet, New England, mid-18th c., 19 x 38 1/4", 71 1/2" h. **4,313**

Queen Anne "flat-top" highboy, maple, two-part construction: the upper section w/a rectangular flat top w/a deep coved cornice above a pair of small drawers over a stack of four long thumb-molded drawers all w/butterfly brasses & keyhole escutcheons; the lower section w/a molded edge over a long drawer over a row of three drawers w/two small square drawers flanking a long center drawer, arched apron w/two drops, simple cabriole legs ending in pad feet, probably Massachusetts, ca. 1760, 21 x 38", 72" h. (imperfections)................................. **9,775**

Fine Queen Anne Maple Highboy

Fig. 1

Fig. 2

Fig. 3

Fig. 4

Fig. 5

Fig. 3 Early 20th century oak
stacking lawyer's bookcase with
leaded glass door, Macey Stacking
Bookcase Co. label $950
Courtesy of Greg Kowles, Winona, Minnesota.

Fig. 1 Late Victorian Golden Oak
double bookcase $3,300
Courtesy of Greg Kowles, Winona, Minnesota.

Fig. 2 Chippendale Revival mahogany &
mahogany veneer twin bed, one of a pair,
ca. 1920s, pr. $1,400
Courtesy of Greg Kowles, Winona, Minnesota.

Fig. 4 Tall-back Victorian
Renaissance Revival walnut &
burl walnut bed $3,500
Courtesy of Greg Kowles, Winona, Minnesota.

Fig. 5 Late Victorian Golden Oak
double bed, ca. 1900-10 . . . . $800
Courtesy of Greg Kowles, Winona, Minnesota.

Fig. 6

Fig. 7

Fig. 8

Fig. 9

Fig. 10

Fig. 6 Victorian Renaissance Revival
walnut & burl walnut bookcase,
ca. 1875 . . . . $2,000
Courtesy of Greg Kowles, Winona, Minnesota.

Fig. 7 Late Victorian curved-front
Golden Oak china cabinet $3,400
Courtesy of Greg Kowles, Winona, Minnesota.

Fig. 8 Late Victorian Golden Oak
combination highchair-stroller $500
Courtesy of Greg Kowles, Winona, Minnesota.

Fig. 9 Fine Classical style
mahogany & mahogany veneer
armchair, ca. 1835 . . . . $250
Courtesy of Greg Kowles, Winona, Minnesota.

Fig. 10 Late Victorian Golden Oak
adjustable piano stool with
spindled back $300
Courtesy of Greg Kowles, Winona, Minnesota.

Fig. 11

Fig. 12

Fig. 13

Fig. 14

Fig. 15

Fig. 11 Early American country-style 'ladder-back' armchair, original dark finish, early 19th century $350
Courtesy of Greg Kowles, Winona, Minnesota.

Fig. 12 One of a set of four Pennsylvania country Chippendale side chairs, late 18th century, the set. $9,900
Courtesy of Garth's Auctions, Delaware, Ohio.

Fig. 13 Fine Victorian Rococo slipper chair in pierce-carved & laminated rosewood, attributed to Meeks of New York, ca. 1855 . . . . $1,200
Courtesy of Greg Kowles, Winona, Minnesota.

Fig. 14 One of a set of four Victorian Rococo side chairs with rosewood frames, the set. $528
Courtesy of Garth's Auctions, Delaware, Ohio.

Fig. 15 Victorian Rococo walnut 'Lincoln' rocker, ca. 1860 . . . . $650
Courtesy of Greg Kowles, Winona, Minnesota.

Fig. 16

Fig. 17

Fig. 18

Fig. 19

Fig. 20

Fig. 21

Fig. 16 A pair of Victorian Renaissance
Revival walnut armchairs by John
Jelliff, Newark, New Jersey,
ca. 1875, pr. $3,000
Courtesy of Greg Kowles, Winona, Minnesota.

Fig. 17 Two ornately carved hardwood
armchairs from China, late 19th - early
20th century, each $800
Courtesy of Greg Kowles, Winona, Minnesota.

Fig. 18 Queen Anne Revival rocking chair
with arms, mahogany & mahogany veneer,
early 20th century. $450
Courtesy of Greg Kowles, Winona, Minnesota.

Fig. 19 Louis XV Revival needlework-
upholstered armchair, ca. 1920s $650
Courtesy of Greg Kowles, Winona, Minnesota.

Fig. 20 Elaborately carved late
Victorian armchair with new leather
upholstery, refinished. $5,500
Courtesy of Jay Anderson Antiques,
Wabasha, Minnesota.

Fig. 21 Unique elaborately carved
Baroque Revival style late Victorian
rocking chair, made for the Chicago
Columbian Exposition of 1893,
probably Italian $10,000
Courtesy of Jay Anderson Antiques,
Wabasha, Minnesota.

Fig. 23

Fig. 22

Fig. 24

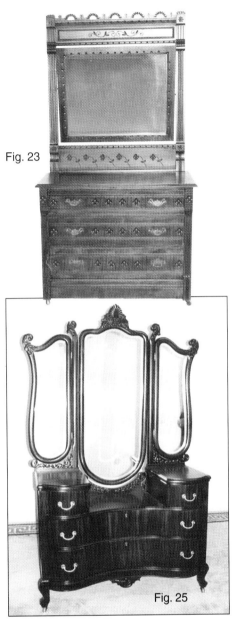

Fig. 25

Fig. 22 Victorian Renaissance Revival
walnut & burl walnut marble-topped
chest of drawers, ca. 1875 . . . . $1,800
Courtesy of Greg Kowles, Winona, Minnesota.

Fig. 23 Victorian Eastlake substyle
chest of drawers in walnut & burl
walnut, ca. 1885 . . . . $650
Courtesy of Greg Kowles, Winona, Minnesota.

Fig. 24 Late Victorian walnut &
walnut burl veneer marble-topped
chest of drawers, ca. 1890s $850
Courtesy of Greg Kowles, Winona, Minnesota.

Fig. 25 Unique Classical Revival
serpentine-front chest of drawers
in mahogany & mahogany
veneer, ca. 1910. . . . . $1,200
Courtesy of Greg Kowles, Winona, Minnesota.

Fig. 26 Late Victorian country-style
stained maple step-back
wall cupboard $1,000
Courtesy of Greg Kowles, Winona, Minnesota.

Fig. 27 Classical country-style chest of
drawers in figured maple & walnut,
ca. 1840-50. . . . . $450
Courtesy of Greg Kowles, Winona, Minnesota.

Fig. 28 Early American country-style
'mule' chest with old mustard yellow paint,
early 19th century. $650
Courtesy of Greg Kowles, Winona, Minnesota.

Fig. 29 Victorian country-style
butternut & walnut jelly cupboard,
mid-19th century $750
Courtesy of Greg Kowles, Winona, Minnesota.

Fig. 30 Late Victorian ash two-part
kitchen cupboard, ca. 1900. . . . . . . $1,600
Courtesy of Greg Kowles, Winona, Minnesota.

Fig. 31

Fig. 32

Fig. 33

Fig. 35

Fig. 34

Fig. 31 Chippendale Revival
oak slant-front desk, late 19th -
early 20th century $2,500
Courtesy of Greg Kowles, Winona, Minnesota.

Fig. 32 Fine Victorian Golden Oak
side-by-side china cabinet & desk
with leaded glass doors, ca. 1900 . . $1,750
Courtesy of Greg Kowles, Winona, Minnesota.

Fig. 33 Early 20th century Colonial Revival
oak lady's writing desk
with slant front. $1,200
Courtesy of Greg Kowles, Winona, Minnesota.

Fig. 34 Victorian Eastlake country-style
walnut captain's desk $650
Courtesy of Greg Kowles, Winona, Minnesota.

Fig. 35 Late 19th century ornately
carved European walnut cupboard
with mirror $1,760
Courtesy of Garth's Auctions, Delaware, Ohio.

Fig. 36

Fig. 37

Fig. 38

Fig. 39

Fig. 40

Fig. 36 Fine Classical Revival
mahogany & mahogany veneer
writing desk, late 19th - early
20th century. $1,950
Courtesy of Greg Kowles, Winona, Minnesota.

Fig. 37 Unique elaborately carved Victorian
Baroque Revival partner's
desk with large carved winged
griffin legs, attributed to J.R.
Horner, ca. 1880s. $12,500
Courtesy of Greg Kowles, Winona, Minnesota.

Fig. 38 Late Victorian small walnut
roll-top desk with S-scroll top $2,400
Courtesy of Greg Kowles, Winona, Minnesota.

Fig. 39 Victorian Renaissance
Revival "Wooton's Patent"
secretary-desk, Standard grade,
ca. 1876 . . . . $15,000-20,000
Courtesy of Greg Kowles, Winona, Minnesota.

Fig. 40 Victorian Aesthetic Movement
walnut & burl walnut captain's desk
with fine detailing $2,000
Courtesy of Greg Kowles, Winona, Minnesota.

Fig. 41 Victorian Golden Oak
hall tree with diamond-shaped
beveled mirror $1,250
Courtesy of Greg Kowles, Winona, Minnesota.

Fig. 42 Victorian Golden Oak hall
tree with a rectangular mirror &
simple details. $1,100
Courtesy of Greg Kowles, Winona, Minnesota.

Fig. 43 Late 19th - early 20th century
oak upright two-door icebox
with carved decoration $650
Courtesy of Greg Kowles, Winona, Minnesota.

Fig. 44 Victorian Golden Oak large
ornate hall tree with oval mirror. . . $3,500
Courtesy of Greg Kowles, Winona, Minnesota.

Fig. 45 Victorian Renaissance Revival
walnut & burl walnut hall tree
with marble shelf $4,400
Courtesy Jay Anderson Antiques,
Wabasha, Minnesota.

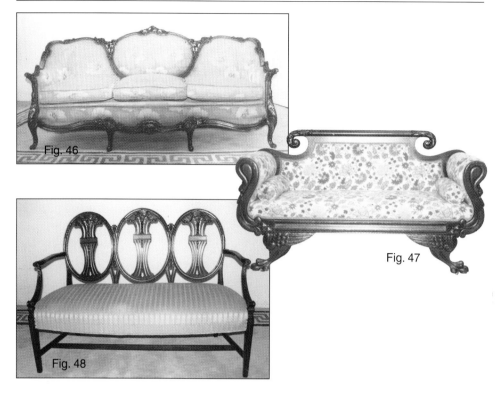

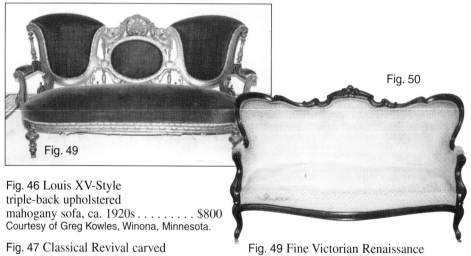

Fig. 46

Fig. 47

Fig. 48

Fig. 50

Fig. 49

Fig. 46 Louis XV-Style
triple-back upholstered
mahogany sofa, ca. 1920s $800
Courtesy of Greg Kowles, Winona, Minnesota.

Fig. 47 Classical Revival carved
mahogany sofa, ca. 1910 with
later upholstery $1,600
Courtesy of Greg Kowles, Winona, Minnesota.

Fig. 48 Federal Revival mahogany
triple-back settee, late 19th -
early 20th century $1,600
Courtesy of Greg Kowles, Winona, Minnesota.

Fig. 49 Fine Victorian Renaissance
Revival triple-back walnut
sofa, ca. 1875. . . . . $1,400
Courtesy of Greg Kowles, Winona, Minnesota.

Fig. 50 Victorian Rococo carved
mahogany sofa with simple details,
ca. 1860 . . . . $950
Courtesy of Greg Kowles, Winona, Minnesota.

Fig. 51

Fig. 52

Fig. 53

Fig. 54

Fig. 55

Fig. 51 Victorian Rococo upholstered
walnut recamier, ca. 1860 . . . . $950
Courtesy of Jay Anderson Antiques,
Wabasha, Minnesota.

Fig. 52 Federal mahogany
wall mirror, ca. 1820. . . . . $600
Courtesy of Greg Kowles, Winona, Minnesota.

Fig. 53 Ornate Empire Revival
ormolu-mounted mahogany cheval
mirror, ca. 1880 . . . . $3,000 to $3,500
Courtesy of Greg Kowles, Winona, Minnesota.

Fig. 54 Early Classical giltwood wall
mirror with reverse-painted panel
showing sailing ships, ca. 1825-30 . . $800
Courtesy of Greg Kowles, Winona, Minnesota.

Fig. 55 Large Victorian Aesthetic
Movement walnut-finished oak
pier mirror, original finish,
ca. 1885, 4' h. $450
Courtesy of Greg Kowles, Winona, Minnesota.

Fig. 56

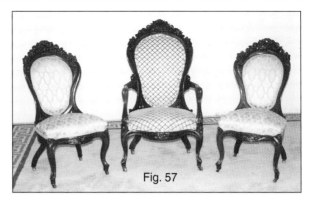

Fig. 57

Fig. 58

Fig. 59

Fig. 60

Fig. 56 Victorian Elizabethan
Revival mahogany firescreen with
needlepoint panel, ca. 1860. . . . . $750
Courtesy of Greg Kowles, Winona, Minnesota.

Fig. 57 Victorian Rococo John Belter
"Rosalie" pattern carved rosewood
parlor suite, three pieces $9,750
Courtesy of Greg Kowles, Winona, Minnesota.

Fig. 58 Elaborate triple-back
Victorian Renaissance Revival
walnut sofa, sold with a matching
armchair, two pieces $2,900
Courtesy of Greg Kowles, Winona, Minnesota.

Fig. 59 Victorian Aesthetic Movement
walnut firescreen with an finely
etched glass panel, ca. 1880 . . . . . . $850
Courtesy of Greg Kowles, Winona, Minnesota.

Fig. 60 William & Mary-Style
lowboy in cherry & mahogany,
late 19th - early 20th century $600
Courtesy of Greg Kowles, Winona, Minnesota.

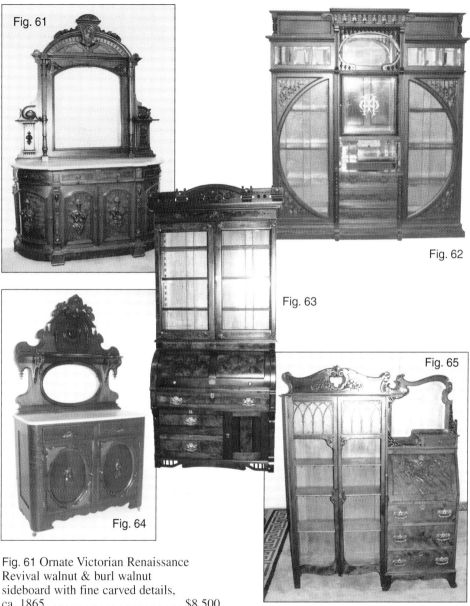

Fig. 61 Ornate Victorian Renaissance
Revival walnut & burl walnut
sideboard with fine carved details,
ca. 1865 . . . . $8,500
Courtesy of Greg Kowles, Winona, Minnesota.

Fig. 62 Victorian Aesthetic Movement
walnut secretary-bookcase,
original finish, ca. 1885 . . . . $7,500
Courtesy of Jay Anderson Antiques,
Wabasha, Minnesota.

Fig. 63 Victorian Eastlake substyle
walnut & burl walnut 'cylinder-front'
secretary-bookcase, ca. 1880 . . . . . $2,600
Courtesy of Greg Kowles, Winona, Minnesota.

Fig. 64 Victorian Renaissance
Revival walnut sideboard with
oval mirror & marble top $2,400
Courtesy of Greg Kowles, Winona, Minnesota.

Fig. 65 Late Victorian flame cherry
& birch side-by-side secretary-
bookcase with ornate carved
details, ca. 1890s $2,200
Courtesy of Greg Kowles, Winona, Minnesota.

Fig. 66

Fig. 67

Fig. 68

Fig. 69

Fig. 70

Fig. 66 A pair of Louis XV-Style nightstands with fine veneering & inlay, original finish, early 20th century, pr. $900
Courtesy of Greg Kowles, Winona, Minnesota.

Fig. 67 Victorian Aesthetic Movement cherry sideboard with elaborate superstructure, ca. 1880s $1,600
Courtesy of Jay Anderson Antiques, Wabasha, Minnesota.

Fig. 68 Victorian Renaissance Revival walnut marble top nightstand, ca. 1865-70. . . . . $800
Courtesy of Greg Kowles, Winona, Minnesota.

Fig. 69 Late Victorian Golden Oak small sideboard with oblong mirror & leaded glass door . . . . $1,750 to $2,000
Courtesy of Jay Anderson Antiques, Wabasha, Minnesota.

Fig. 70 Classical-Victorian transitional style mahogany & mahogany veneer server, ca. 1840s, ... $650
Courtesy of Greg Kowles, Winona, Minnesota.

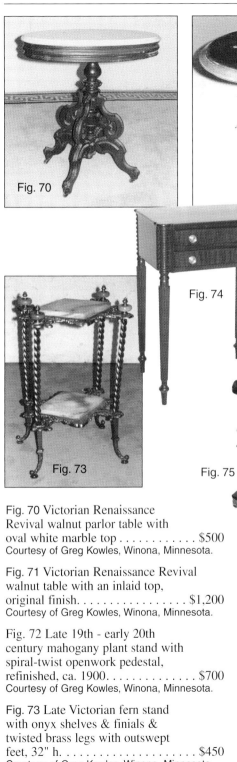
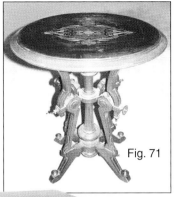

Fig. 70

Fig. 71

Fig. 72

Fig. 73

Fig. 74

Fig. 75

Fig. 76

Fig. 70 Victorian Renaissance
Revival walnut parlor table with
oval white marble top $500
Courtesy of Greg Kowles, Winona, Minnesota.

Fig. 71 Victorian Renaissance Revival
walnut table with an inlaid top,
original finish. $1,200
Courtesy of Greg Kowles, Winona, Minnesota.

Fig. 72 Late 19th - early 20th
century mahogany plant stand with
spiral-twist openwork pedestal,
refinished, ca. 1900. . . . . $700
Courtesy of Greg Kowles, Winona, Minnesota.

Fig. 73 Late Victorian fern stand
with onyx shelves & finials &
twisted brass legs with outswept
feet, 32" h. $450
Courtesy of Greg Kowles, Winona, Minnesota.

Fig. 74 Mahogany Federal-Style
two-drawer stand, refinished,
ca. 1920s $500
Courtesy of Greg Kowles, Winona, Minnesota.

Fig. 75 Modernist end table
modeled as a stack of large books,
carved wood with a painted gesso
finish, ca. 1950s-60s, 24" h. $350
Courtesy of Jay Anderson Antiques,
Wabasha, Minnesota.

Fig. 76 One of a pair of ornately
carved stained pine stands with
figural putti forming the pedestal,
Europe, 19th century, 38" h., pr. . . . $6,200
Courtesy of Jay Anderson Antiques,
Wabasha, Minnesota.

Fig. 77

Fig. 78

Fig. 79

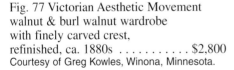

Fig. 80

Fig. 81

Fig. 82

Fig. 77 Victorian Aesthetic Movement
walnut & burl walnut wardrobe
with finely carved crest,
refinished, ca. 1880s $2,800
Courtesy of Greg Kowles, Winona, Minnesota.

Fig. 78 Victorian Baroque Revival
quarter-sawn oak library table with
ornate scroll carving & carved
caryatid legs with paw feet, late
19th century, 30 x 44", 36" h.. . . . $10,000
Courtesy of Jay Anderson Antiques,
Wabasha, Minnesota.

Fig. 79 Victorian Renaissance
Revival tall walnut & burl walnut
etagere with a marble shelf $4,500
Courtesy of Greg Kowles, Winona, Minnesota.

Fig. 80 Victorian Rococo armoire
in walnut with faux rosewood
graining, ca. 1860 . . . . $2,400
Courtesy of Greg Kowles, Winona, Minnesota.

Fig. 81 Late Victorian Golden Oak
wardrobe with scroll-carved
high crest. $2,500
Courtesy of Greg Kowles, Winona, Minnesota.

Fig. 82 Early 20th century
square-topped oak extension
dining table, original finish,
with four leaves, 48" w. $1,200
Courtesy of Greg Kowles, Winona, Minnesota.

Queen Anne "flat-top" highboy, maple,
two-part construction: the upper section
w/a rectangular top over a deep coved
cornice over a row of three drawers w/the
center one fan-carved over a stack of
four long graduated thumb-molded drawers; the lower section w/a mid-molding
over a long drawer over three deep drawers w/the center one fan-carved, scalloped apron & cabriole legs ending in pad
feet on platforms, the butterfly brasses
appear to be original, old refinish, minor
imperfections, Massachusetts, ca. 1760,
20 1/4 x 38 1/2", 74 1/2" h. (ILLUS.)........ **27,600**

Queen Anne Curly Maple Highboy

Queen Anne "flat-top" highboy, maple
w/curly maple facade, two-part construction: the upper section w/a rectangular top
above a deep flared coved cornice above
a pair of drawers flanking a small square
central drawer above four long thumb-
molded graduated drawers w/butterfly
pulls & keyhole escutcheons; the lower
section w/a mid-molding above a long narrow drawer above a pair of deep drawers
flanking a shallow central drawer, deeply
scalloped apron, cabriole legs ending in trifid feet, refinished, original brasses, base
reworked, some incomplete brass & one
missing escutcheon, mid-18th c., top
20 7/8 x 39", 70 1/4" h. (ILLUS.) **7,370**
Queen Anne "flat-top" highboy, walnut &
maple, two-part construction: the upper
section w/a flat high coved cornice above
two short & three long thumb-molded
drawers each w/butterfly pulls & keyhole
escutcheons; the lower section w/a mid-
molding over a narrow long drawer over a
row of three deep drawers, flat apron, cabriole legs ending in pad feet on platforms,
original brasses, old mellow surface,
Massachusetts, ca. 1740-60, 20 x 38",
70 3/4" h. (minor imperfections)................. **17,250**
Queen Anne "flat-top" highboy, walnut &
walnut veneer, two-part construction: the
upper section w/a rectangular top over a
deep stepped & flaring cornice w/a con-
cealed linen drawer above a pair of small
drawers over three long graduated drawers
all w/veneering & crossbanding; the lower
section w/a deep flaring mid-molding over
a pair of shallow drawers over a pair of
deep drawers flanking a shallow central

Fine Veneered Queen Anne Highboy

drawer above the highly arched & scalloped apron w/two acorn drops, on simple
cabriole legs ending in raised pad feet, old
engraved butterfly pulls & keyhole escutcheons, old refinish, minor restorations, probably Boston or Essex County, ca. 1730-50,
22 1/2 x 38 1/2", 72 1/4" h. (ILLUS.)........... **33,350**
Queen Anne "flat-top" highboy, cherry &
maple, two-part construction: the upper
section w/a rectangular flat top w/a deep
coved cornice over two pairs of small drawers flanking a deep fan-carved center
drawer over a stack of four long graduated
drawers; the lower section w/a mid-molding over a single long drawer over a row of
three drawers w/plain smaller square drawers flanking a central longer fan-carved
drawer, scalloped apron, cabriole legs ending in pad feet, refinished, 18th c., Massachusetts, 21 1/2 x 29", 79 3/4" h.(replaced
Ball & Ball butterfly brasses, repairs &
some replacements)...................................... **8,525**
Queen Anne-Style "bonnet-top" high-
boy, maple, two-part construction: the
upper section w/a broken swan's-neck
pediment centering & flanked by three
urn-turned finials above a case fitted
w/three thumb-molded short drawers, the
central drawer w/carved fan, over four
long graduated thumb-molded drawers;
the lower section w/a mid-molding above
three thumb-molded short drawers, the
central one w/a carved fan, over a
shaped skirt, on cabriole legs ending in
padded disk feet, in the New England
manner, 20th c., 19 1/2 x 36", 77" h.............. **920**
William & Mary "flat-top" highboy, maple
& pine, two-part construction: the upper
section w/a rectangular flat top w/narrow
flaring cornice over a row of three small
drawers over three long graduated drawers; the lower section w/a heavy mid-
molding over a case w/two deep drawers
flanking a shallow central drawer over a
triple-arched apron, raised on four trumpet-form front legs w/bun feet joined by
flat curved stretchers, grained in the late
19th c., original brasses & keyhole es-

Rare William & Mary Highboy

cutcheons, North Shore, Massachusetts, 1700-30, minor repairs to stretchers, 22 5/8 x 44", 63 1/2" h. (ILLUS.) **34,500**

Early William & Mary Highboy

William & Mary "flat-top" highboy, painted pine, two-part construction: the upper section w/a rectangular top w/a shallow flaring cornice over a pair of short drawers over three long graduated drawers; the lower section w/a widely flaring stepped mid-molding over a pair of deep drawers flanking a shallow central drawer above the deeply arched apron on trumpet-turned legs joined by flat stretchers & bun feet, teardrop brasses may be original, painted dark brown, restoration, southeastern New England, early 18th c., 18 x 33", 55" h. (ILLUS.)............................ **16,100**

William & Mary Reproduction Highboy

William & Mary-Style "flat-top" highboy, curly maple & curly maple veneer, two-part construction: the upper section w/a

rectangular top over a stepped flaring cornice over a case of four long graduated drawers w/butterfly brasses & keyhole escutcheons; the lower section w/a stepped mid-molding over a pair of deep drawers flanking shallow drawers above the deeply scalloped apron raised on four tall trumpet-turned front legs joined by flattened scalloped stretchers & raised on ball feet, two matching rear legs joined by flat scalloped side stretchers & a plain rear stretcher, hand-made reproduction, age crack in one end, 20th c., top 19 3/4 x 37", 65 3/4" h. (ILLUS.) **5,610**

LOWBOYS

Queen Anne Lowboy

Queen Anne lowboy, mahogany, a rectangular top w/molded edges above a single long drawer w/three large butterfly brasses over a row of three drawers w/the central one fan-carved, scalloped apron w/two teardrop drops, cabriole legs ending in pad feet, New England, 18th c., 20 x 30", 30" h. (ILLUS.) **4,600**

Queen Anne-Style lowboy, walnut, rectangular top w/narrow molded edges over a case w/a long narro[w drawer w/three butterfly brasses above a row of three small drawers each w/a butterfly brass, triple-arched apron w/blocked drops, angled cabriole legs ending in pad feet, hand-made reproduction by Bob Pusecker, 20th c., 18 3/4 x 35 1/2", 29 3/4" h. **385**

William & Mary-Style Lowboy

William & Mary-Style lowboy, cherry & mahogany, the rectangular top w/molded edge overhanging a case w/a pair of deep drawers flanking a shallow center drawer, deeply scalloped apron raised on four trumpet-form legs resting on a serpentine cross-stretcher on turned turnip feet, original brass teardrop pulls, original finish, ca. 1880, 20 x 30", 30" h. (ILLUS.)...... **600**

Ice Boxes

Rare Late Victorian Ice Box

Turn-of-the-century, cabinet-style, oak, the rectangular top w/molded edges above a beaded band flanked by carved lion heads at the top corners above a long rectangular upper mirrored door w/ornate scroll-carved frame & heavy brass hardware above a tall rectangular two-panel door w/ornate scroll carving & heavy brass hardware, spiral-carved front corner rails, egg-and-dart band above the molded base w/carved corner blocks, paneled sides, ca. 1900 (ILLUS.) **$1,750**

Oak Upright Ice Box

Turn-of-the-century, chest-style, oak, an upright form w/hinged rectangular lid to the ice compartment above a raised panel over a lower paneled cupboard door w/heavy brass hardware, deep molded flat base, ca. 1910-20, 18 x 27", 43" h. (ILLUS.).. **450**

Fine Golden Oak Ice Box

Victorian Golden Oak substyle, a rectangular top w/a deep flaring cornice above a two-panel upper door decorated w/carved scrolls above a tall double-paneled bottom drawer w/matching carving, original hardware, metal nameplate on the front, scroll-decorated apron & block feet, tin-lined, refinished, early 20th c., 18 x 24", 40" h. (ILLUS.) **650**

Love Seats, Sofas & Settees

Daybed, Art Deco, rosewood, upright slightly scrolled ends enclosing an upholstered seat above a shaped front apron trimmed w/ormolu, on heavy blocked canted short legs w/ormolu mounts, Jules LeLeu, France, ca. 1935, 85" l., 35" h. (ILLUS. bottom of page) **$8,050**

Daybed, child's, country-style, painted wood, the shaped back & side panels joining four square tapering posts, old red paint, New England, early 19th c., 22 1/4 x 39 1/2", 32" h. **1,380**

Daybed, Classical country-style, walnut, the scroll-carved serpentine crestrail above a solid back panel flanked by outscrolled end arms above the lift-top board seat pulling forward to form a double bed, outswept flat legs w/front center block supports, original finish, New England, ca. 1840-60, 28 x 80", 33" h. (ILLUS. bottom of page) **1,100**

Daybed, Federal country-style, painted & decorated, the triple-sectioned back w/turned top rails above a flat center rail & lower rail above rows of short spindles flanked by turned arms over spindles & w/baluster-turned arm supports, a hinged fold-out bed forming the seat w/a deep paneled apron, original yellow ground paint w/brown leaf & berry stencil decoration & striping, New England, early 19th c., replaced seat w/modern textile cover, 36 1/2" h. (ILLUS. bottom next page)........ **4,025**

Daybed, Mission-style (Arts & Crafts movement), oak, a low slanted back w/angled sides at one end, on a rectangular seat frame w/square post legs, branded Limbert mark, Model No. 850, early 20th c., 30 1/4 x 79 1/4", 24 3/4" h. **7,050**

Daybed, Mission-style (Arts & Crafts movement), oak, the upright even ends

French Art Deco Daybed

Classical Country-Style Daybed

w/heavy square stiles supporting wide flat upper & lower rails framing six wide slats, wide siderails pinned into end stiles, Gustav Stickley Model No. 220, after 1909, 35 1/2 x 84", 34" h. **3,450**

Daybed, Modern style, a rectangular seat & back frame in solid maple raised on V-form bent wire legs, fitted w/two checkered pattern rectangular back cushions & a single long seat cushion, designed by George Nelson, produced by Herman Miller, ca. 1956, 75" l., 26" h. (ILLUS. bottom this page)... **1,344**

Daybed, Victorian Renaissance Revival substyle, walnut, the back w/a pair of short scroll-framed hinged end panels pierced w/quatrefoils flanked by matching serpentine end arms w/similar pierced panels all above the deep rectangular rails w/raised panels & center roundels, back panels open allowing the framework to expand to form a full bed, refinished, ca. 1870, 32 x 76" l. closed, 32" h. (ILLUS. bottom this page).................... **700**

Daybed, Mission-style (Arts & Crafts movement), oak, the even ends w/heavy square posts flanking a wide top rail over

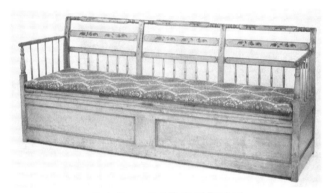

Early Decorated Federal Daybed

George Nelson Modern Daybed

Unusual Victorian Daybed

four vertical slats at each end, chamfered side rails & narrow lower stretchers, re-upholstered drop-in spring seat, original medium dark finish, branded L. & J. G. Stickley mark, 29 x 80", 28" h. **3,300**

Love seat, Art Deco, ébène-de-macasar & upholstery, the long narrow arched crestrail above a three-section upholstered back, narrow arm rails w/a raised upholstered central section above the closed arms, long cushion seat above a narrow gently curved seatrail, gently swelling arm supports continuing down to form the tapering front legs, tapering rear legs, branded mark of Emile-Jacques Ruhlmann, France, ca. 1925, 63" l. **43,125**

Love seat, Art Deco, stained beech, a narrow U-form crestrail over the conforming tightly upholstered back & deep upholstered seat flanked by reeded tapering front stile legs, spots on fabric, restorations, France, ca. 1925, 48" l. (ILLUS. bottom this page) **2,300**

Mammy's bench, country-style, painted & decorated, the long rectangular crestrail above numerous simple turned back spindles flanked by turned stiles & scrolled arms raised on a spindle & baluster- and knob-turned arm supports, S-scroll long seat w/a wide rectangular upright board insert w/rounded top corners at one end, ring-, knob- and baluster-turned front legs joined by a flat stretcher & plain turned rear legs w/a flat stretcher, on rockers, old black repaint w/well done free-hand & stencilled decoration including fruit & vining on the crest, pineapple & leaves on the seat insert & yellow flourish designs on arm supports, legs & stretchers, first half 19th c., 52" l., 30 1/2" h. (repairs where legs meet rockers, one arm w/pieced repairs) **523**

Méridienne, Classical, carved mahogany, the shaped crestrail carved w/a flowerhead above a conforming padded back, the outscrolled arms w/flowerhead termi-

French Art Deco Love Seat

Fine Classical Méridienne

nals continuing to elaborately-carved flowerheads, the rectangular upholstered seat
above conforming seatrail raised on legs
carved w/S-scrolls, foliage & fruit & ending
in paw feet, American, ca. 1820-30,
88 1/2" l. (ILLUS. bottom previous page) **5,520**
Méridienne, Victorian Rococo substyle,
carved & laminated rosewood, the high
arched upholstered curved back at one
end enclosed by a scroll-carved border
w/a fruit- and flower-carved crest, the oblong serpentine upholstered seat above
a conforming floral-carved seatrail, on
demi-cabriole legs on casters, John H.

Belter, New York, New York, ca. 1850,
42" l., 38" h. (ILLUS. bottom this page) **5,040**
Méridiennes, carved & painted wood, the
low arched & curved upholstered back at
one end enclosed by high pierce-carved
C-scrolls & ornate floral carvings continuing down the molded end arm, the upholstered oblong serpentine seat on a conforming seatrail w/further ornate leafy
scroll & blossom carving, on front demi-
cabriole legs ending in scrolls & square
rear legs all on casters, John H.
Belter, ca. 1855, 25" l., pr. (ILLUS. of one
bottom this page) **14,950**

Belter High-backed Méridienne

Carved & Painted Belter Méridienne

Recamier, Classical, brass-mounted carved mahogany & mahogany veneer, of box form, an upright squared end w/a heavy rounded crestrail along the arm & long back & terminating at each end w/a leaf-carved scroll, the closed upholstered arm & low back panel opposite the out-scrolled end w/cornucopia-carved support, long upholstered seat on a flat seatrail, the closed arm w/a columnar arm support w/brass-mounted capital & base, on heavy short legs w/a carved acanthus leaf cluster over a bulbous reeded knob foot, New York, ca. 1815, 34 x 86", 16" h. .. **8,400**

Recamier, Classical, mahogany, the molded & shaped back rail continuing to a leaf-carved scroll above the scrolled paneled arms w/concentric ringed bosses, above a paneled seatrail & carved paw feet on casters, Boston, old finish, ca. 1825, 65 1/8" l. (ILLUS. bottom this page)... **8,625**

Recamier, Empire-Style, gilt-bronze mounted mahogany, the low undulating back continuing to rolled arms terminating in carved swans' heads, above a simple rectangular upholstered seat w/straight seatrail mounted w/gilt-bronze winged lions, stars & scrolls, raised on figural legs headed by gilt winged lion heads & ending in paw feet, France, late 19th c., 72 1/2" l. (ILLUS. bottom this page) **4,888**

Recamier, Federal, mahogany, a narrow reeded downward curving crestrail above the upholstered back & joining a high & low scrolled end arm w/reeded scrolled framing continuing down to the reeded seatrail, on reeded sabre legs ending in brass paw feet w/casters, probably Boston, early 19th c., 76" l. **7,475**

Finely Carved Classical Recamier

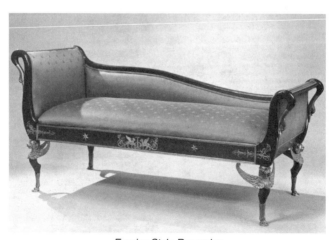

Empire-Style Recamier

Recamier, Regency, brass-inlaid beech-wood, a long low upholstered back w/serpentine molded crestrail ending in an inlaid brass pinwheel, the curved upholstered end arm w/a carved arm support, the long oblong seat w/a wide reeded seatrail decorated w/inlaid scrolling brass plaques above the heavy carved acanthus leaf legs on reeded knob feet on casters, long seat cushion & bolster pillow, England, second quarter 19th c., 76" l. (ILLUS. bottom this page).... **4,600**

Recamier, Victorian Rococo substyle, walnut, the high arched & rounded back w/a scroll-carved crestrail w/a pierced hand grip continuing down to form a short padded & closed side arm & a long low padded back rail, long oval upholstered seat on a finger-carved serpentine seatrail, raised on demi-cabriole legs w/porcelain casters, early reupholstery, ca. 1860, 24 x 68", 36" h. (ILLUS. bottom this page) **950**

Recamiers, Federal-Style, parcel-gilt & ebonized wood, the outscrolled open back rest formed w/turned & paneled slats above a long shaped arm over the narrow rectangular caned seat on slender knob- and ring-turned splayed legs joined by turned stretchers, decorated overall w/Classical designs in gold on black, some wear, ca. 1900, 76" l., pr. (ILLUS. of one bottom next page) **2,875**

English Regency Inlaid Recamier

Victorian Rococo Recamier

Settee, bentwood, beechwood, the shaped rectangular back composed of sinuous open curves & swirls above the long oval caned seat flanked by curled bentwood arms, on slender turned & gently curved legs joined by a high oval bentwood stretcher, designed by Joseph Hoffmann, fragmentary maker's paper label, Austria, ca. 1905, wear, 45" l. (ILLUS. bottom this page) **3,450**

Settee, child's Windsor arrow-back style, painted & decorated, the wide flat crestrail over eight plain spindles alternating w/two arrow slats, simple turned end arms over the incised plank seat, on simple turned raked legs w/a rectangular front stretcher & round side & back stretchers, original red paint w/yellow striping to simulate inlay on the crest which includes yellow & black leafage & highlights, all original form & decoration, New England, early 19th c., 9 x 25 3/4", 21 3/4" h. (ILLUS. top next page) **12,650**

Settee, Chippendale-Style, mahogany, the delicately carved slender triple-arch crestrail above delicate scroll- and swag-carved pierced splats, slender curved open-end arms on incurved arm supports, upholstered spring seat w/a thin serpentine seatrail, slender carved cabriole front legs & square canted rear legs, old finish, early 20th c., 42" l. (one back leg repaired) **770**

Federal-Style Decorated Recamier

Classic Austrian Bentwood Settee

Settee, Classical, carved mahogany, the upholstered double-shield-form back centered by a carved spread-winged eagle above a veneer panel, scrolled back stiles above the deep semi-overupholstered seat on a bolection-molded plinth & eagle-carved legs ending in paw feet, formerly fitted w/casters, probably New York City, ca. 1825, 72" l. (ILLUS. bottom this page) **6,325**

Settee, Classical-Style, mahogany, the bowed crestrail above an upholstered back w/molded outscrolled arm supports over a D-shaped overupholstered seat, on square tapering legs w/casters, 20th c., 35 x 61 1/2", 34 1/2" h. **1,150**

Settee, Edwardian, painted satinwood, the rectangular back frame w/a raised, paint-

ed central crest panel above a long rectangular caned panel flanked by pierced panels w/forked splats centered by a decorated oval medallion, a pierced lattice band along the bottom of the back, slender open downswept arms on molded supports above the caned seat w/a loose button cushion, raised on square tapering legs ending in spade feet, painted w/flowers & classical designs, England, ca. 1900 (repairs, chips) **3,120**

Settee, Federal country-style "fancy" type, a long flat crestrail w/downturned scroll ends above a triple back w/three decorated slats, S-scroll arms on ring- and knob-turned arm supports, long rush seat, four canted ring-, knob- and baluster-turned front legs & plain turned rear legs joined

Scarce Child's Windsor Settee

Finely Carved Classical Settee

by baluster- and ring-turned front stretchers, the front seatrail w/double-lobed pendants at the centers of each section, ground paint simulates rosewood w/gold stencil decoration of compotes of fruit & leafage on the crestrail & slats, old surface, New York, 1815-25, 76 3/4" l., 35 1/2" h. (losses, needed repairs) 920

Settee, Federal country-style, hardwood, six-section back, the wide crestrail w/six arched sections across the back above heavy stiles & sets of four slender spindles, divided by four slender open scrolled arms on simple turned supports, S-scrolled long plank seat, six pairs of canted turned tapering legs joined by long slat front & back stretchers, worn & weathered surface w/traces of old red paint, first half 19th c., 109" l. (front foot rest battered, renailed & partially replaced) 880

Settee, Federal country-style, painted & decorated, triple-back style, the long wide board crestrail divided into three sections, each w/a flat-topped center flanked by serpentine sections & ending in rounded corners, four back stiles dividing the three lower rails each above five baluster- and knob-turned short spindles, S-scroll arms on two baluster- and knob-turned spindles & a matching arm support, long shaped plank seat, four ring- and rod-turned front legs joined by simple turned stretchers, original painted decoration w/birds & fruit across the back panels in red, blue, green & tan, yellow line detail around borders, Pennsylvania, first half 19th c., 73" l., 35" h. (wear, repair to arms) 1,210

Settee, Federal country-style, turned & painted, triple-back style w/the divided

crestrail having a tablet at the center of each section above three slender cut-out medallion & urn-shaped spindles in each section joined to a lower rail & divided by four simple turned stiles, high end arms w/matching cut-out spindles above the long rush seat above eight simple turned legs, the front four joined by medallion-cut stretchers, original brown paint w/gilt & red highlighting the neoclassical elements, New England, 1810-20, 16 x 70", 33" h. (imperfections, one spindle missing) 2,070

Settee, Federal Revival style, triple-back form, the back composed of three oval sections enclosed pierced vase-form splats topped w/a carved urn & swags, shaped slender open arms on incurved arm supports above the wide overupholstered seat, raised on square tapering legs joined by a long H-stretcher, late 19th c., reupholstered in the 1920s, original finish, 22 x 58", 40" h. (ILLUS. bottom this page) 1,600

Settee, Louis XVI-Style, hardwood, long oval back w/gadroon-carved frame around central caning, open padded end arms w/carved incurved arm supports above the caned seat w/a fitted cushion, gadroon-carved seatrail, turned reeded legs w/peg feet, early 20th c., 46 1/2" l. 880

Settee, Queen Anne-Style, walnut, the triple-arched crest on the paneled upholstered back w/wood end stiles above open scrolled arms & curved supports above the overupholstered seat w/scalloped edge, simple cabriole front legs w/shell-carved knees ending in raised pad feet, dark mellow finish, early 20th c., 21 x 62", 42" h. (one front leg return replaced) 330

Federal Revival Triple-back Settee

Settee, Scandinavian-American country-style, painted pine, mortise & tenon construction, the wide scallop-cut crestrail above three rectangular panels w/slender spindles, high outscrolled end arms w/turned top rails over curved lower rails, the long rectangular hinged seat above a deep well, short square stile legs, original grey paint, ca. 1870, 21 x 80", 36" h. (ILLUS. bottom this page) **1,200**

Settee, Victorian Rococo substyle, walnut, the serpentine crestrail w/finger-carving curved down to form closed padded arms & curved arm supports, vertically tufted back, upholstered spring seat, serpentine finger-molded seatrail between demi-cabriole front legs on casters, light blue velvet upholstery, ca. 1860, repairs, 62 1/4" l. (ILLUS. bottom this page) **358**

Scandinavian-American Settee

Simple Victorian Rococo Settee

Settee, wicker, ornate late Victorian style, the high serpentine back w/ornate feather-like border scrolling above a shaped delicately woven back panel flanked on one end by a rolled arm & on the other by a high flattened arm, tightly woven seat w/rolled-under end above a seat apron composed of wicker heart-form designs, raised on wrapped outswept legs joined by a cross-stretcher, original varnished rattan, Heywood Brothers & Wakefield Company, Gardner, Massachusetts, 1898-1904, 41 1/4" l., 41" h. (ILLUS. bottom this page)................................. **4,025**

Settee, William & Mary-Style, mahogany, triple-back style, the back section w/a high arched & pierced scroll-carved crestrail above a scroll-carved frame enclosing an oval caned panel between freestanding rope-twist stiles w/knob finial, long shaped open end arms w/scroll-carved hand grips on rope-twist supports above the long upholstered seat on new plywood over the original caning, narrow carved seat rail raised on four rope-twist- and block-turned front legs joined by three wide arched & scroll-carved flat stretchers, long rope-twist H-stretcher joining front & rear legs, early 20th c., old dark finish, 66" l., 50" h. **715**

Settee, William & Mary-Style, oak, the high double-arched upholstered back flanked by shaped upholstered wings above the rolled upholstered arms, long cushion seat above the scalloped upholstered seatrail, raised on onion- and block-turned front legs & square canted rear legs joined by two sets of flattened double-arch stretchers, old worn finish, early 20th c., Europe, 60" l. **935**

Settee, Windsor "arrow-back" style, a long flat board crestrail above numerous arrow slats between the turned & tapering stiles & S-scroll arms over three turned spindles & a turned & canted arm support, long plank seat raised on four pairs of turned & tapering legs joined by horizontal front arrow stretchers & plain turned side & back stretchers, black repaint, first half 19th c., 78" l. **495**

Settee, Windsor "arrow-back" style, painted & decorated, the long flat crestrail divided into three sections w/four tapering stiles, seven arrow slats in each section, scrolled end arms above slender turned spindles & canted turned arm supports, long plank seat raised on eight ring-turned tapering legs joined by stretchers w/three central tablets & plain side & back stretchers, the crestrail w/gilt floral sprig decoration & banding on a dark ground, overall dark

Fine Early Wicker Settee

ground w/gold banding on slats & leaf bands on stretcher tablets, Pennsylvania, 1820-30, 178" l., 36" h. (some old repaint, minor imperfections) **1,093**

Settee, Windsor "birdcage" style, maple, ash & hickory, a long double-bar crestrail joined by six short spaced out spindles above a multi-spindled lower back w/bamboo-turned spindles flanked by bamboo-turned arms on two spindles & a canted arm support, the long plank seat raised on four gently canted bamboo-turned front legs & four rear legs all joined by long bamboo-turned stretchers, old finish, New England, early 19th c., 72" l., 31 1/2" h. (imperfections) **2,415**

Settee, Windsor "birdcage" style, maple & pine, a triple-section back w/a pair of upper crestrails in each section centered by a rectangular tablet & two tiny spindles above the lower back composed of numerous bamboo-turned spindles & bamboo-turned stiles, the bamboo-turned open arms w/two short spindles & a canted arm support above the long rectangular plank seat raised on eight bamboo-turned canted legs joined by bamboo-

turned stretchers, old refinish, imperfections, New England, ca. 1810, 78" l., 33" h. (ILLUS. bottom this page) **3,220**

Settee, Windsor country style, painted & decorated, the long flat crestrail between tapering stiles & a narrow medial rail over numerous short turned spindles, scrolled arms over turned spindles & a canted turned arm support, long plank seat raised on four canted ring-turned front legs joined by three baluster-turned front stretchers & four simple turned rear legs joined by simple turned stretchers, worn old red & brown graining w/yellow & orange striping & floral decoration on the crestrail & slat, crack in seat w/old underside bracing, repairs, early 19th c., 81" l. (ILLUS. bottom this page) **880**

Settee, Windsor country-style, bamboo-turned hickory & poplar, a long flat crestrail between turned & flattened stiles w/two other stiles dividing the back into three sections filled w/slender turned tapering spindles, scrolled end arms over turned, canted arm supports & four spindles, long thick plank seat raised on eight canted bamboo-turned legs joined by

Windsor "Birdcage" Style Settee

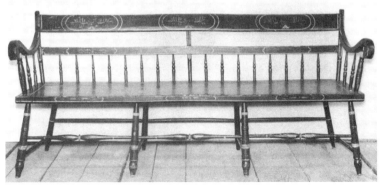

Windsor Country Settee

flattened front stretchers & turned rear stretchers, refinished, first half 19th c., 84" l. (age cracks in seat) **935**

Settee, Windsor country-style, painted & decorated, double-back form, a long wide crestrail cut-out to form two sections raised on three stiles above lower rails each over six short turned spindles, S-scroll arms over two spindles & a turned canted arm support, long plank seat raised on eight turned & canted legs joined by turned box stretchers, old brown paint w/yellow & blue striping & polychrome floral decoration on the crestrail, Pennsylvania, mid-19th c., overall wear, some surface & edge damage, revarnished, 71" l. (ILLUS. bottom this page) **1,100**

Settee, Windsor country-style, painted & decorated, the shaped triple-back crestrail raised on three stiles over a pair of long lower rails over numerous knob-turned short spindles, scrolled arms on two spindles & a canted turned arm support over the wide plank seat, raised on eight ring-turned tapering legs joined by turned box stretchers, worn original brown paint w/light green & cream-colored striping & h.p. rose decoration on the crest sections, stenciled label "E.D. Jeffries... Philadelphia, PA," plank seat worn, repaired break in one arm at post, first half 19th c., 73 1/2" l. (ILLUS. bottom this page) **1,430**

Settee, Windsor low-back style, the shaped crestrail continuing to downscrolled knuckled grips above twenty-one turned spindles flanked by ring- and baluster-turned arm supports over a long shaped plank seat, on six ring-, rod- and baluster-turned legs w/tapered ball feet joined by turned & swelled H-stretchers, old green

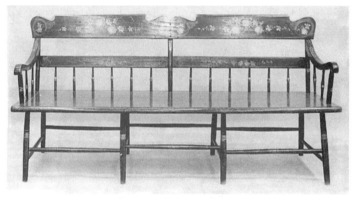

Decorated Windsor Settee

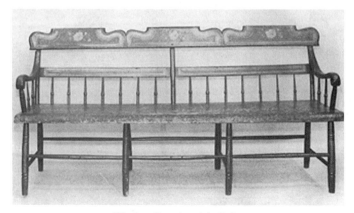

Windsor Country-style Settee

paint, Lancaster County, Pennsylvania, 1770-90, 18 1/2 x 45 1/2", 31" h.................. **2,990**

Settee, Mission-style (Arts & Crafts movement), oak, a wide V-back top rail above twelve vertical slats between the square stiles, flat shaped arms on square front stile legs w/corbels under the arms, recovered leather seat, wide flat front & rear stretchers & narrow double side stretchers, large red decal mark of Gustav Stickley, Model No.212, 24 x 48", 36" h. (ILLUS. bottom this page)................ **3,300**

Settees, Victorian Rococo substyle, mahogany, a long oval upholstered back w/a low arched pierced & floral-carved crest above open padded arms w/molded incurved arm supports, a long upholstered seat w/a serpentine seatrail carved w/scrolls in the center, raised on demi-cabriole front legs on casters, newer velvet upholstery,

Gustav Stickley Signed Settee

One of Two Victorian Rococo Settees

refinished, ca. 1865, 60" l., 38" h., pr. (ILLUS. of one bottom this page)................. **3,600**

Settle, child's early American country-style, painted pine, the tall back w/a flat top & three rectangular banded panels flanked by tall incurved narrow arms above the lift seat opening to a compartment, the lower front w/two rectangular banded panels, mortised construction w/rosehead nails, small worn feet & low arched aprons, old comb-grained repaint, 14 x 36", 37 1/2" h. (edge wear, one seat hinge damaged)... **2,475**

Settle, Jacobean, oak, the rectangular upright paneled back & scrolled open end arms above a rope seat, planked legs joined by box stretchers, England, late 17th c., 75" l., 41 1/2" h. **6,325**

Settle, painted pine, the high back constructed of beaded horizontal boards above the seat w/a hinged top over the deep straight front & cut-out feet, tall shaped arms formed by end boards, old red varnish over earlier blue paint, New England, early 19th c., imperfections, 16 x 42", 49" h. (ILLUS. bottom this page).......................... **18,400**

Settle, painted pine, the very tall flat curved back w/a narrow brace between the rounded wing sides continuing down to form sides w/small rounded hand grips, curved plank seat above lower narrow brace, old worn black & grey paint, late

Early High-back Painted Settle

18th - early 19th c., 50 1/2" w., 69" h. (wear, some edge damage) **4,125**

Settle, painted yellow pine, the low rectangular back flanked by downswept arms above a hinged long seat & straight deep apron, the sides w/exposed tenons on cut-out feet, old green over earlier white paint, probably Pennsylvania, early 19th c., 18 x 60 1/2", 34 1/2" h. (ILLUS. bottom this page) **2,415**

Settle, Mission-style (Arts & Crafts movement), oak, the tall solid paneled back w/rounded side wings w/oval cut-out continuing to form low side arms flanking the wide lift-seat w/a deep apron, cut-out low feet, through-tenon construction, recoated original finish, some distress to the sides, red decal mark of Gustav Stickley, Model No. 224, 22 x 48", 45" h. (ILLUS. bottom this page) **4,400**

Early Painted Pine Settle

Unusual Gustav Stickley Settle

Sofa, Art Deco, bent bamboo, the rectangular back & seat w/loose cushions flanked by arms formed w/concentric bands of bundled bamboo, ca. 1940s, 78" l. (small losses) **2,070**

Sofa, Baroque-Style, carved walnut, the simple rectangular back w/an elaborate surmounted crest in the form of a grotesque mask surrounded by foliate scrolls, flanked by winged female figures, Europe, late 19th c., 85" l. **3,737**

Sofa, Chippendale-Style, mahogany, camel-back design w/a serpentine upholstered crestrail above a canted back over outward scrolling arms above an overupholstered rectangular seat, on Marlborough legs joined by H-stretchers, 20th c., 30 x 90", 38" h. **2,760**

Sofa, Classical, carved mahogany, the crestrail w/a raised central rectangular panel flanked by scroll-carved sections & decorated w/water-leaf carving & veneered crossbanding, above the upholstered back flanked by high upright outscrolled reeded arms curving down to form the seatrail w/circular bosses flanking leaf-carved panels below the upholstered seat, on frontal hairy paw feet below carved eagle head & wing supports, leaf-carved turned rear feet, old refinish, on

casters, probably New York, ca. 1830, 21 1/4 x 82", 31 3/4" h. (imperfections)...... **1,955**

Sofa, Classical, carved mahogany, the long narrow rolled single paneled crestrail above out-scrolled arms w/reeded arm supports punctuated w/carved rosettes, upholstered back, arms & cushion seat, reeded seatrail w/flanking panels of foliate & leaf carving above reeded sabre legs on brass paw feet on casters, old surface, minor imperfections, attributed to the workship of Duncan Phyfe, New York City, 1815-25, 85" l. (ILLUS. bottom this page) **4,600**

Sofa, Classical, carved mahogany, the serpentine crestrail w/acanthus leaf carving & two rosettes centering a carved shell w/Prince-of-Wales feathers above an upholstered back w/outscrolling arms w/similar Prince-of-Wales feathers & acanthus leaf carving over a rectangular seat w/incised line seatrail, on ring-turned & spiral-carved legs w/casters, ca. 1830-40, 27 x 83", 33" h. **1,093**

Sofa, Classical, carved & veneered mahogany, a gently arched reeded crestrail w/scroll-carved terminals over the upholstered back & flanked by rolled arms w/applied carved frontal shells over the cushion seat & seatrail w/gadrooning on front egg-and-dart-carved feet on casters w/ring-turned rear feet, Baltimore or

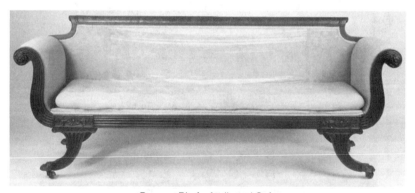

Duncan Phyfe-Attributed Sofa

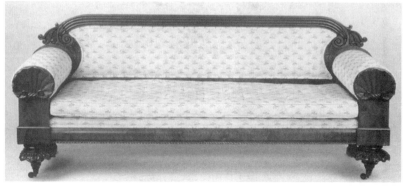

Attractive Classical Sofa

Philadelphia, ca. 1825-35, imperfections, 84" l. (ILLUS. bottom this page) **690**

Sofa, Classical, mahogany & mahogany veneer, the long straight round crestrail ending in leaf-carved downturned scroll ends above the long low upholstered back flanked by outswept S-scroll upholstered arms w/leaf- and scroll-carved arm supports, a long straight rounded seatrail raised on carved cornucopia brackets over the paw feet, original finish, old but not original upholstery, ca. 1830, 76" l., 36" h. (ILLUS. bottom this page)...... **2,400**

Sofa, Classical, mahogany & mahogany veneer, the raised crestrail w/rope-carved top & incurved ends above the uphol-

stered back flanked by out-scrolling arms w/floral & cornucopia-carved arm supports continuing to carved panels & a flat molded seatrail raised on figural dolphin-carved front legs & turned back legs, refinished, reupholstered, first quarter 19th c., 107" l. (ILLUS. bottom this page) **3,850**

Sofa, Classical, mahogany & mahogany veneer, the raised flat crestrail w/a rod crest ending in pineapple finials above serpentine leaf-carved rails over the long upholstered back flanked by wide rolled upholstered arms w/leaf-carved arm supports continuing to the seatrail, raised on carved cornucopias above flared paw feet on casters, old finish, reupholstered

Classical Mahogany Scroll-arm Sofa

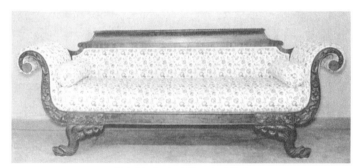

Dolphin-footed Classical Sofa

Carved Mahogany Classical Sofa

in gold velvet, ca. 1830-40, 77" l., 35" h. (ILLUS. bottom this page) **1,430**

Sofa, Classical, mahogany & mahogany veneer, the serpentine crestrail centered by a pierced scroll-carved crest over the tufted upholstered back flanked by outscrolled arms w/S-scroll carved arm supports above the long upholstered seat on a wide beaded & ogee seatrail joined by scrolled front legs on casters, reupholstered in striped velvet, ca. 1840-50, 84" l. (ILLUS. bottom this page) **385**

Sofa, Classical, mahogany veneer, a wide rolled flat veneered crestrail above a low

upholstered back flanked by wide gently rounded closed arms w/heavy S-scroll arm supports flanking the upholstered cushion seat, flat rounded seatrail between heavy C-scroll front feet, old finish, reupholstered, some edge wear, ca. 1835-45, 81 3/4" l. (ILLUS. bottom this page) **853**

Sofa, Classical Revival style, mahogany, the raised round rod crestbar w/carved curled-under ends above the shaped crestrail above the outscrolled rolled arms w/swan head carving above the long upholstered seat w/bolsters, ogee seatrail raised on winged paw front legs on cast-

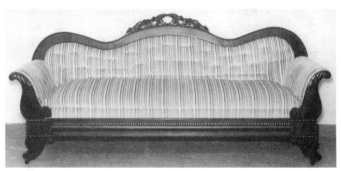

Late Classical Mahogany Sofa

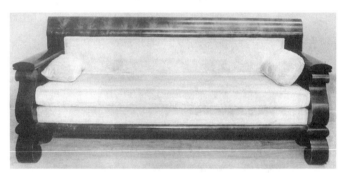

Heavy Classical Sofa

Classical Revival Mahogany Sofa

ers, original finish, ca. 1910, later upholstery, 68" l. (ILLUS. bottom this page) **1,600**

Sofa, Classical-Victorian transitional style,
carved mahogany & mahogany veneer,
the triple-arch crestrail w/high arched end
sections centered by a shell & leafy scroll
crest w/each end topped by a pierce-
carved scroll crest, crestrail curved down
around the upholstered back & arms &
terminates in heavy scroll-carved arms
on heavy scrolled front legs, molded serpentine seatrail, reupholstered, some
frame damage, ca. 1840, 92" l. (ILLUS.
bottom this page) **743**

Sofa, Danish Modern style, teak, a long
rectangular tack back frame joined to the
seat by two steel rods, slanted teak armrests similarly joined to seat, tapered
legs, repeating fan design on the salmon
-colored upholstered back, seat & arm
cushions, Hans Wegner, Denmark, ca.
1955, 82" l., 30 1/4" h...................................... **575**

Sofa, Federal, inlaid mahogany, the gently
arched upholstered back flanked by side
upholstered arms & molded armrests
w/vase- and ring-turned, reeded &
swelled posts, inlaid panels at the legs &
arm supports, the bowed seat frame join-

ing four front vase- and ring-turned reeded tapering legs ending in turned peg
feet, old finish, probably Boston or North
Shore, Massachusetts, ca. 1800-10,
25 x 80 1/2", 39" h. (imperfections) **17,250**

Sofa, Federal, inlaid mahogany, the long
slightly arched upholstered back continuing to downward sloping upholstered
sides & reeded arms on swelled vase-
and ring-turned reeded arm supports on
bird's-eye maple & string-inlaid panels
continuing to ring-turned tapering reeded
front legs, canted square rear legs, slight-
ing bowed upholstered front seatrail, old
surface, probably Massachusetts, ca.
1810-15, 25 x 78", 37 1/2" h. (imperfec-
tions).. **8,625**

Sofa, Federal, mahogany & mahogany veneer, the narrow flat reeded crestrail
above an upholstered back & downswept arm rails over closed arms & baluster-turned arm supports, a long cushion seat over the curved seatrail on four
turned & tapering front legs on brass
casters & four square tapering rear legs
on casters, old refinish, imperfections,
some height loss, Boston or North
Shore, Massachusetts, ca. 1815-20,

Classical-Victorian Transitional Sofa

Massachusetts Federal Sofa

13 x 76", 34 1/8" h. (ILLUS. bottom this page) **7,475**

Sofa, Federal, mahogany veneer, the upholstered back w/a flat crest above downswept upholstered arms w/curved, reeded & baluster-turned arm supports on veneered corner blocks, overupholstered seat, on four front tapering reeded legs w/swelled & turned feet, square rear legs, old surface, Massachusetts, ca. 1800, 76" l. (imperfections) **2,530**

Sofa, Federal-Style, carved mahogany, the narrow molded serpentine crestrail above an upholstered back flanked by rolled upholstered deep arms w/molded scrolled arm supports, a long cushion seat over the serpentine seatrail w/dentil carving raised on four reeded, turned & tapering front legs, late 19th c. (ILLUS. bottom this page) **1,792**

Sofa, Federal-Style, mahogany, long narrow crestrail carved w/three drapery- and floral-carved panels over the upholstered back flanked by scrolled closed arms on reeded turned & tapering arm supports & paneled corner blocks, flat seatrail on four reeded, turned & tapering legs w/peg feet, labeled "Hickory, N.C.," 20th c., 80" l. (ILLUS. bottom this page) **468**

Sofa, Federal-Style, mahogany & satinwood, a long narrow flat crestrail w/satinwood above the upholstered back flanked by downswept arms & upholstered ends, down-curved hand grips above reeded & baluster-turned arm supports flanking the long cushion seat, long flat satinwood seatrail raised on four ringturned tapering & reeded front legs w/peg feet, old pink satin upholstery, early 20th c., 66" l. (some veneer damage) **1,100**

Fine Federal-Style Sofa

Federal-Style Mahogany Sofa

Sofa, Louis XV-Style, carved mahogany, triple-back style, the oblong upholstered center medallion enclosed by narrow pierce-carved molding continuing around the arched serpentined upholstered side panels, serpentine arm rails continuing to incurved front arm support, three-cushion seat, serpentine apron w/a scroll-carved serpentine seatrail, on serpentine front legs ending in scroll feet, original finish & upholstery, ca. 1920s, 76" l., 36" h. (ILLUS. bottom this page) **800**

Sofa, Mission-style (Arts & Crafts movement), oak, a single wide back rail & even end arms w/five slats at each end flanking the original leather-covered drop-in spring seat w/some tears, original light finish, paper label & decal of Gustav Stickley, Model No. 225, 31 x 78", 29" h. (ILLUS. bottom this page) **4,950**

Sofa, Mission-style (Arts & Crafts movement), oak, a wide flat crestrail above twelve wide vertical slats between the square stiles, flat tapering arms raised on front leg supports w/corbels, wide flat apron, original drop-in spring cushion seat recovered in brown leather, refinished, unsigned L. & J. G. Stickley, 25 x 65", 36" h. **1,980**

Sofa, Mission-style (Arts & Crafts movement), oak, even-arm style w/wide flat top rails joined by heavy square corner leg stiles w/tapering tops, the back composed of 22 narrow & wider slats & each end w/seven slats, wide seatrail, two large recovered cushions, recent finish, unsigned L. & J.G. Stickley, probably the Onondaga Shop, 31 x 77", 39" h. **6,600**

Sofa, Mission-style (Arts & Crafts movement), oak, even-arm style, wide top rails above the low back & sides w/numerous wide slats, recovered seat cushions, through-tenon construction, original finish, faint red decal mark of Gustav Stickley, Model No. 208, 32 x 76", 29" h. **8,800**

Sofa, Mission-style (Arts & Crafts movement), oak, long crestrail w/downcurved top edge over seven wide back slats, shaped drop arms over two wide slats & long corbel supports, three-cushion seat, red decal mark of L. & J.G. Stickley, Model No. 263, ca. 1914, 69 1/2" l., 37" h. (replaced brown vinyl cushions & seat sup-

Louis XV-Style Upholstered Sofa

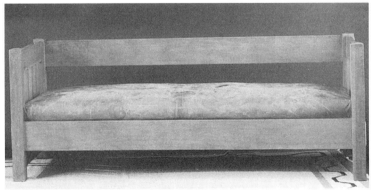

Gustav Stickley Model 225 Sofa

port, staining, wear, some joint separation) **6,900**

Sofa, Modern style "Sling" style, leather & chrome, a heavy gauge chrome tube steel framework supporting three leather back & seat cushions, on slender tubular steel legs, designed by George Nelson, manfactured by Herman Miller, ca. 1964, 31 1/2 x 86", 28 7/8" h. (ILLUS. bottom this page) **4,600**

Sofa, Queen Anne-Style, walnut, rectangular-framed upholstered back over out-scrolled arms, three loose cushions in seat, raised on cabriole front legs ending in pad feet, floral upholstery, England, early-20th c., 76 1/2" l., 39" h. **1,840**

Sofa, Victorian Baroque Revival style, carved mahogany, a wide flat crestrail ornately carved w/leafy scrolls flanking a central cartouche joining wide scroll-carved stiles above the upholstered back & padded rounded arms over upholstered sides & blocked columnar scroll-carved arm supports flanking the long upholstered seat, a gadroon-carved flat seatrail & heavy block front feet, ca. 1890-1900 (ILLUS. bottom this page) **2,500**

Sofa, Victorian Egyptian Revival substyle, ebonized & brass-mounted, the gently arched upholstered crest flanked by rails w/leaf-and-berry carving further flanked by brass-mounted lions' heads w/open jaws above an upholstered back over tufted arms above scrolled supports fronted by brass-mounted Egyptian busts over a partially overupholstered triple-lobed seatrail centered by a brass-mounted lion's head, on sabre legs w/brass-mounted hoof feet, the mounts

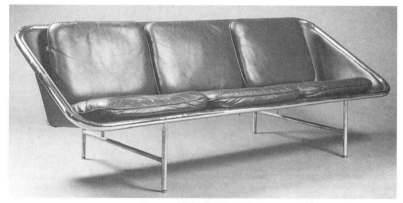

George Nelson "Sling" Sofa

Victorian Baroque Revival Sofa

stamped "PS," attributed to Pottier & Sty-
mus, New York City, ca. 1880, 72" l. **9,200**
Sofa, Victorian Renaissance Revival substyle, bronze-mounted rosewood & par-
cel gilt, triple-back style, the high rounded
end panels w/tufted upholstery & reeded
& carved stiles flank the lower long central section w/tufted upholstery below a
central arched crest carved w/leaves &
berries above a round medallion carved
w/a scene of Leda & the swan, low outswept upholstered arms w/arm supports
carved w/full-figural busts of children,
long upholstered spring seat w/gently
curved seatrail w/gilt line-incised decoration, reeded trumpet-turned front legs,
green velvet upholstery, ca. 1875, restoration, 72" l., 36 1/2" h. (ILLUS. bottom
this page) **6,900**
Sofa, Victorian Renaissance Revival sub-
style, carved, gilt & ormolu-mounted
rosewood, the carved, incised & gilt pediment crest centered w/a carved stylized
palmette cartouche over a swag w/cen-
tral applied ormolu rosette above an incised & gilt Greek key motif, all flanked
w/acanthus leaf carving over a parti-
tioned canted back w/ormolu rosettes
heading further Greek key designs centering & flanked by the upholstered back
& arms w/ormolu figural cherub head
hand rests & carved & gilt-incised arm
supports surrounding a trapezoidal partially overupholstered seat w/gilt & molded front rail centered w/gilt-incised scroll-
decorated pendant on Ionic gilt-incised
tapering colonettes, the center ones
headed w/ormolu rosettes, the side ones
w/gilt triglyphs, decorated w/ormolu cuffs
& fitted w/casters, New York, 1860-80,
28 1/2 x 74 1/2", 42 3/4" h. **2,990**

Exceptional Renaissance Revival Sofa

Fine Renaissance Revival Sofa

Sofa, Victorian Renaissance Revival sub-style, mahogany & burl veneer, a triple-panel tufted upholstered back w/the central arched panel topped w/a carved figural crest & leafy & drop carved decorations on the side back panels, upholstered curved half-arms w/figural carved arm supports flanking the upholstered seat over the scalloped & carved apron w/burl panels, raised on four trumpet-turned tapering front legs on casters, burgundy velvet upholstery, ca. 1875, 81" l., 53" h. (ILLUS. bottom previous page)... **2,200**

Sofa, Victorian Renaissance Revival sub-style, upholstered parcel-gilt walnut, the long back w/a low carved & scroll-ended center rail over upholstery joining high curved & upholstered end sections w/tufted upholstery backs each flanked by carved curved stiles w/large turned &

carved drops flanked by low rolled upholstered arms w/wide arm supports carved as figural Grecian lady heads, the long serpentine-fronted seat above a conforming seatrail w/burl walnut panels & incised gilt trim centered by three curved center drops & raised on four boldly carved & incised front trumpet-form legs on casters, attributed to John Jelliff, ca. 1870, 81" l. (ILLUS. bottom this page)....... **2,070**

Sofa, Victorian Renaissance Revival sub-style, walnut & burl walnut, triple-back style, the large central panel w/a rounded rectangular upholstered back below the arched crestrail topped w/a carved crown crest centered by the bust of a lady & flanked by square post finials, tapering blocked dividers between the squared upholstered side back panels w/carved bird head stile finials, the back panels raised on burl veneer panels & flanked by

Quality Renaissance Revival Sofa

Fine Renaissance Revival Sofa

curved upholstered arms w/carved lady head arm rests over the long upholstered spring seat, serpentine seatrail w/carved drops, raised on four block- and rod-turned legs w/peg feet, repairs, ca. 1875, 73" l. (ILLUS. bottom previous page) **1,320**

Sofa, Victorian Renaissance Revival sub-style, walnut & burl walnut, triple-back design, the central shaped & upholstered back panel topped by an ornate baluster-turned spindle & rondel pierced crest over a burl-trimmed rail curving down to ornately carved & pierced panels joining the outer flaring upholstered back panels w/carved frames above curved padded arms w/carved lady head hand grips over

curved supports, long oblong uphol-stered seat w/an incurved front seatrail w/burl panels, on knob- and ring-turned tapering legs on casters, attributed to John Jelliff, ca. 1875 (ILLUS. bottom this page) **1,600**

Sofa, Victorian Renaissance Revival sub-style, walnut, the triple-section back composed of two large U-form upholstered panels flanking a smaller upholstered oval center panel framed by pierced scroll and shell carving, padded open arms w/rolled arm supports above the long oval uphol-stered seat on a conforming molded se-atrail, tapering knob- and ring-turned front legs, original finish, ca. 1875, later velvet

Fine Renaissance Revival Sofa

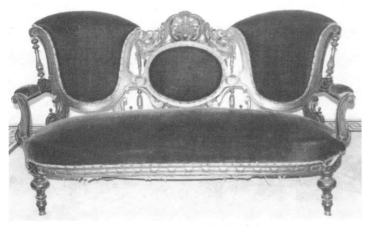

Unique Renaissance Revival Sofa

upholstery, 68" l. (ILLUS. bottom this page)... **1,400**

Sofa, Victorian Rococo substyle, carved laminated rosewood, the long triple-arch back w/a high, ornately pierce-carved crestrail centered by a very high arched flower- and scroll-carved crest over scrolling grapevines continuing to arched corners w/carved baskets of flowers w/vines continuing down to the padded closed arms all flanking the tufted upholstered back, double-serpentine seatrail carved w/fruit and flower clusters alternating w/twist-carved & reeded sections, on three front demi-cabriole legs on casters & two rear legs, by John Henry Belter, New York City, ca. 1855, record price, 93 1/2" l. **77,000**

Sofa, Victorian Rococo substyle, carved & laminated rosewood, the ornate arched & pierce-carved crestrail centered by a pointed rose crest over gadrooned bands & open scrolls continuing to curved pierce-carved corners continuing down & flanking the high tufted upholstered back, closed arms w/incurved carved arm supports continuing to the serpentine finger-carved seatrail & demi-cabriole front legs on casters, "Stanton Hall" patt. attributed to J. & J. Meeks, ca. 1855, age cracks, some edge damage, 65 1/2" l. (ILLUS. bottom this page).. **5,500**

Sofa, Victorian Rococo substyle, carved & laminated rosewood, the ornate arched & pierce-carved crestrail centered by a

Meeks' "Stanton Hall" Sofa

Meeks "Henry Ford" Pattern Sofa

pointed rose crest over gadrooned bands & open scrolls continuing to curved pierce-carved corners continuing down & flanking the high tufted upholstered back, closed arms w/incurved carved arm supports continuing to the serpentine finger-carved seatrail & demi-cabriole front legs on casters, "Henry Ford" patt. attributed to J. & J. Meeks, ca. 1855 (ILLUS. bottom previous page)................................... **13,200**

Sofa, Victorian Rococo substyle, carved mahogany, the arched & serpentine crestrail w/a carved center crest & rounded corners continuing down around the upholstered back to the padded closed arms w/molded curved arm supports flanking the long upholstered seat w/a serpentine seatrail raised on demi-cabriole front legs on casters, old upholstery, ca. 1860, 66" l. (ILLUS. bottom this page) **950**

Sofa, Victorian Rococo substyle 'medallion-back' style, walnut, the back w/a large oval tufted upholstered central back panel w/a leaf-carved crest & raised on wide pierced & scroll-carved panels joining it to the lower upholstered side panels curving around & faced w/scroll-carved arm supports, long upholstered seat on a gently shaped seatrail joined by demi-cabriole front legs on casters, reuphol-

Simple Victorian Rococo Sofa

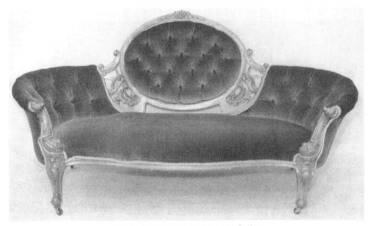

Victorian 'Medallion-back' Sofa

stered in dark blue velvet, ca. 1855-65, 74" l. (ILLUS. bottom this page) **880**

Sofa, Victorian Rococo substyle, walnut, triple-back style w/a large oval upholstered central panel flanked by oval upholstered panels each w/finger-carved frames & floral- and leaf-carved crests, raised above a long upholstered seat flanked by padded open arms on curved arm supports, serpentine molded & carved seatrail joined to demi-cabriole legs on casters, canted back legs w/casters, ca. 1860 (ILLUS. bottom this page) **1,680**

Sofas, Victorian Renaissance Revival substyle, carved rosewood, a long narrow gently arched crestrail centered by a carved cartouche w/shell & scrolls flanked by molded stiles headed by scroll-carved finials on floral-incised plinths w/carved drapery above the tufted upholstered back over padded arms on downswept arm supports above the long tufted upholstered seat w/a bowed seatrail trimmed w/raised banding centering an oval reserve above a shaped pendant, on tapering turned legs on casters, probably New York City, ca. 1875,

Triple-back Victorian Rococo Sofa

Renaissance Revival Rosewood Sofa

68 1/4" l., 44" h., pr. (ILLUS. of one bottom this page)... **5,750**

Tete-a-tete, early faux bamboo-style, painted wood, each corner bamboo-turned crestrail above four bamboo-turned spindles & matching lower rail, between bamboo-turned stiles continuing to form the six legs joined by double bamboo-turned stretchers, old black paint, probably Boston, early 19th c., minor imperfections,

17 1/2 x 37", 28" h. (ILLUS. bottom this page) **1,380**

Tete-a-tete, Golden Oak style, a pair of wide balloon-form opposing backs tapering to a pierced & leafy scroll-cut section above a shaped rectangular seat, backs joined by a central rail over spindles, curved end arms over turned spindles & arm supports, knob-turned edges joined by knob-turned stretchers, ca. 1900 (ILLUS. bottom this page)... **1,400**

Early Faux Bamboo Tete-a-Tete

Unusual Late Victorian Tete-a-Tete

Wagon seat, child's, ash or chestnut, double-back style, each back section w/two gently arched slats between the three turned, tapering stiles above open rod arms w/turned front supports forming the front end legs, short center leg, woven splint seat, old finish, 19th c., 23 1/4" w., 22 1/2" h. **660**

Wagon seat, maple & hickory, double-seat type, three back stiles w/pointed turned finials each separated by two gently arched slats, simple rod open arms to heavy front leg supports w/a mushroom grip, double woven splint seat, simple turned double rungs in front & at sides, old refinishing, pegged construction, 29 3/4" h. (some reweave & damage on seat)............................. **550**

Wagon seat, painted, double-seat style, each section of the low back w/two arched slats between the three heavy turned stiles w/pointed tips, open arms on turned arm supports continuing down to form the front legs, replaced woven rush seat, double rungs at the front & sides, original green paint, found in Brewster, Massachusetts, 19th c., 19 x 34 1/2", 30 3/4" h. (back feet ended-out)..................................... **935**

Wagon seat, painted pine, the rectangular seat flanked by side supports w/rounded tops & flaring bases joined by a single square stretcher, old orange wash finish, New England, early 19th c., 12 1/2 x 34 1/2", 30" h. (imperfections)...... **1,265**

Wagon seat, painted & turned wood, two pairs of arched slats joining three simple turned back stiles, double woven rush seat flanked by turned arms & turned handholds atop the turned, tapering front end legs, shorter center legs all joined by simple turned rungs, old brown paint over earlier grey, New England, late 18th c., 30" l., 15" h. **1,093**

Wagon seat, painted wood, primitive country-style, a narrow square crestrail & matching lower rail flanked by turned tapering back leg stiles & forming a two-section back w/seven slender turned spindles in each section, open turned arms above the two-part early splint seat above six heavy turned legs, original red paint, New England, mid-19th c., imperfections, 34 1/4" l., 17" h. (ILLUS.) **460**

Wagon seat, two-part back w/two slightly arched slats in each section between three simple heavy turned stiles, slender shaped open end arms raised on tapering supports continuing to form front legs, central front leg, woven splint seat, simple double rungs at front & sides, refinished, 19th c., 36 1/2" l. (seat old re-

Primitive Painted Wagon Seat

Mirrors

Art Nouveau wall mirror, carved hardwood, rectangular w/the wide flat crestrail centered by a large applied carved cluster of two pine cone-shaped fruits & leaves, curved sides w/pointed ears at the top & long carved vines forming the edges ending in large fruit & leaf clusters at each bottom corner, brass liner & rectangular beveled mirror, ca. 1900, 27 x 41" **$385**

Art Nouveau-Style Mirror

Art Nouveau-Style wall mirror, carved mahogany, the rectilinear form of pierced whiplashes w/gilded blossom clusters surrounding the conforming mirror, some age but not period, age cracks, old finish, 38 x 47 1/2" (ILLUS.) **715**

Unusual Figural Carved Wall Mirror

Baroque Revival wall mirror, carved pine, a large ornately carved winged dragon supports a large crescent moon-shaped mirror w/a large upright winged mermaid wrapped around the top, her tail w/flowers enclosing one side of the mirror, her large winged body w/her arms wide apart, original finish, Europe, last quarter 19th c., 24" w., 38" h. (ILLUS.) **2,500**

Chippendale wall mirror, carved mahogany, the arched & scroll-cut pediment flanked by shaped ears above a molded frame w/cusped upper corners enclosing a rectangular mirror, a scrolled pendant base w/scrolled ears, the backboard w/printed paper label of John Elliott, Jr., Philadelphia, 1796-1803, 32 3/4 x 45" **12,650**

Chippendale wall mirror, mahogany, arched & scroll-carved top w/curved corners above a rectangular molded frame enclosing the mirror, delicate scroll-carved projections at each corner & arched scroll-carved bottom panel, labeled "L.C. Lyman, Middletown, Connecticut," 15 1/4 x 24" **4,888**

Chippendale Wall Mirror

Chippendale wall mirror, mahogany & gilt gesso, the high arched & scroll-carved crestrail centered by a gilded round foliate device & ending in curved ears over the molded gilt-incised liner & gilt-incised scrolled base pendant, old refinish & regilding, England, late 18th c., 20 1/2 x 36" (ILLUS.) **1,265**

Fine Chippendale Mirror with Phoenix

Chippendale wall mirror, mahogany, the arched & scroll-cut crest centering a pierced & gilded carved phoenix flanked by scrolled ears above a rectangular & gilt-carved liner w/cusped upper corners enclosing a mirror, scroll-shaped base,

American or English, late 18th c., 20 1/4 x 36 1/2" (ILLUS.) **4,025**

Chippendale Mahogany Wall Mirror

Chippendale wall mirror, mahogany veneer & giltwood, the high arched scrolled & pierced crest w/a central gilded Hoho bird above a molded & parcel-gilt molding surrounding the mirror plate, deep scroll-cut pendant base, old surface, minor repairs, probably England, 18th c., 31 1/4" h. (ILLUS.) **1,093**

Chippendale wall mirror, parcel-gilt mahogany, the high arched & scroll-cut crest centered by a gilt-incised concave round shell above upward scrolled ears over the narrow rectangular molded frame & mirror plate w/gilt-incised liner, downward scrolled ears & arched & scroll-cut base apron, probably England, ca. 1790, 14 3/4 x 27" (old refinish) **633**

Chippendale wall mirror, walnut & giltwood, the wide arched crest ornately scroll-cut & centered by a round opening enclosing a giltwood foliate device, tall rectangular mirror plate w/rounded top corners & gilt incised liner, scroll-cut ears & apron at the bottom, old refinish, England, ca. 1750-70, 25 1/2" w., 45" h. (imperfections) **6,900**

English Chippendale Wall Mirror

Chippendale wall mirror, walnut & parcel-gilt, the high scroll-carved crest centered by a gilt feathered plume above a molded mirror frame w/rounded top corners, an inlaid gilt-incised liner, a scroll-carved bottom drop panel, England, late 18th c., refinished, imperfection, 24 3/4 x 43 1/4" (ILLUS.) **2,415**

Chippendale-Style Wall Mirror

Chippendale-Style wall mirror, curly maple, the high & elaborately scroll-cut crest flanked by ears above a rectangular molding enclosing the mirror, deep scroll-cut base drop & ears, old mellow finish, early 20th c., one ear cracked, one small piece missing, 21 x 45" (ILLUS.) **660**

Fine Classical Girandole Mirror

Classical girandole wall mirror, giltwood, a round coved & reeded frame enclosing a convex mirror flanked by candlearms & topped by a large spread-winged eagle on rockwork finial flanked by scrolling leaf

& blossom brackets, scrolling leaf & blossom base drop, original finish, ca. 1830, 22" w., 38" h. (ILLUS.) **2,000**

Classical overmantel mirror, gilt gesso, the egg-and-dart molded cornice above a frieze of oak leaves & acorns, the tri-part mirror glass outlined by black reeded liner w/rosettes at top frame corners, half-engaged ring-turned acanthus leaf columns, New England, ca. 1825, 55" l., 33" h. (regilding, imperfections).................. **1,265**

Classical overmantel mirror, gilt gesso, the molded cornice above a horizontal split baluster joined to the vertical split balusters by corner blocks & rosettes enclosing the three-part mirror, New England, ca. 1830, 59 3/4" l., 21 3/4" h. (some imperfections)...................................... **920**

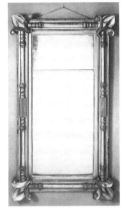

Classical Giltwood Pier Mirror

Classical pier mirror, giltwood, the rectangular divided mirror plate surrounded by flattened & partially reeded pilasters w/bold carved fleur-de-lis corner mounts, second quarter 19th c., 34 1/2 x 62" (ILLUS.)............ **2,300**

Fine Classical Shaving Mirror

Classical shaving mirror, mahogany & mahogany veneer, table-top, a flat crest cornice raised on half-round columnar

supports flanking the swiveling rectangular mirror w/rounded frame, above a rectangular top w/rounded front corners over two ogee-fronted drawers w/an ivory keyhole or tiny knob, original finish, ca. 1840, 10 x 16", 28" h. (ILLLUS.) **350**

Fine Convex Classical Wall Mirror

Classical wall mirror, giltwood & part-ebonized, a round convex mirror plate in a molded round frame set w/spherules, a tall crest carved w/a large spread-winged giltwood eagle on a pile of rocks, a half-round sunburst gilt base drop, possibly American, ca. 1825, repairs, 25" d., 44" h. (ILLUS.) **5,750**

Fine Classical Giltwood Wall Mirror

Classical wall mirror, giltwood, the long rectangular frame w/leafy scroll-carved corner brackets at the top & bottom, the frame w/half-round ring- and baluster-turned spindles, an upper reverse-painted tablet w/a scene of sailing ships above the original rectangular mirror plate, original surface, ca. 1830, 22 x 38" (ILLUS.)....... **800**

Classical wall mirror, mahogany & mahogany veneer, the flaring stepped cornice w/blocked ends above lyre-inlaid blocks flanking a wide veneer panel over the double mirror plate flanked by half-round ring-turned, leaf-carved & rope-twist columns above small bottom corner blocks w/rondels flanking a narrow veneer panel, ca. 1815-30, 25 1/4" w., 50 1/2" h. **715**

Classical wall mirror, painted & decorated wood, the rectangular narrow frame composed of knob- and rod-turned half-round columns painted in alternating black & gold w/corner blocks w/applied florettes, a tall rectangular mirror plate below an upper reverse-painted square glass plate decorated w/an elegant seated Empire period lady wearing a long dress, shawl & turban & framed w/large swagged draperies within a stenciled polychrome leaf border band, ca. 1830-40, 16 x 32" **578**

Early European Courting Mirror

Courting wall mirror, a wide rectangular molded frame w/a high stepped & rounded crest w/hanging hole, the framework encloses narrow panels of reverse-painted glass, the mirror plate w/a border of delicate scrolls, leaf sprigs & a small leaping stag at the bottom center, northern Europe, late 18th c., imperfections, 11 1/4 x 18 1/2" (ILLUS.) **3,738**

Danish Modern Wall Mirror

Danish Modern wall mirror, walnut, a flat crestrail above flaring shaped & molded narrow sides w/a narrow shelf below the tall mirror plate, Denmark, ca. 1955, 17 1/4" w., 24 3/4" h. (ILLUS.) **201**

Fine Empire Revival Cheval Mirror

Empire Revival cheval mirror, ormolu-mounted mahogany, a long oval narrow frame w/ormolu mounts enclosing a beveled mirror swiveling between tall square uprights w/urn-form finials & swelled scroll base bracket all decorated w/ormolu mounts, the uprights also w/heavy scrolled inner brackets w/ormolu mounts resting on the heavy bottom cross stretcher w/long ornate ormolu mounts, raised on heavy rectangular blocks raised on bun feet on casters, original finish, ca. 1880, 36" w., 6' 10" h. (ILLUS.) **3,000-3,500**

Federal country-style wall mirror, pine, molded flat top w/blocked corners above reeded side pilasters to lower corner blocks joined to a reeded lower rail, original upper reverse-painted glass panel showing the steam paddlewheeler "Ohio," good color, old refinished pine frame, early 19th c. (pieced cornice repairs) **605**

Federal Mahogany Dressing Mirror

Federal dressing mirror, mahogany & mahogany veneer, the shield-form mirror in a conforming veneered frame w/string-inlaid edges flanked by scrolled & incised supports w/ringed bosses at the terminals, on stepped & shaped trestle feet joined by incised shaped stretcher, old finish, imperfections, label of I. Richman, New York City, late 18th - early 19th c., 8 3/4 x 14", 21 1/4" h. (ILLUS.)............... 1,265

Federal Transitional Wall Mirror

Federal transitional-style wall mirror, carved walnut, a spread-winged eagle finial perched on a plume above a high arched & pierce-carved leafy scroll crest atop the oval molded frame set w/gilded wood buttons, a pierced leaf-carved band at the bottom, original finish, ca. 1840, 24 x 38" (ILLUS.) 1,000

Federal Decorated Wall Mirror

Federal wall mirror, gilt gesso, the flat molded crestrail w/stepped-out block

ends above a band of applied spherules above a large reverse-painted tablet showing a woman w/a spyglass surrounded by a silver leaf & white border, the rectangular mirror below, the sides w/half-round engaged turned columns, back w/label of James Todd, Portland, Maine, ca. 1825, tablet cracked (ILLUS.)...... 920

Federal wall mirror, giltwood, a narrow molded cornice over applied spherules & a rectangular narrow frame enclosing an upper églomisé tablet painted w/a large basket of fruit below swagged drapery above the rectangular mirror panel flanked by applied spiral rope carvings, square molded base, tablet, gilding & mirror appear to be original, Boston, 1810-20, 13 1/2 x 28 1/2" (imperfections).. 1,610

Federal wall mirror, giltwood, a narrow rectangular cornice w/stepped-out corners above a band of small spherules over an églomisé panel decorated w/a central almond-shaped reserve w/a basket of flowers surrounded by a diamond-lattice design & flanked by blocks w/small molded trophies, slender half-round pilasters down the sides flanking the mirror, narrow bottom rail w/corner blocks, probably English, early 19th c., 30 x 47" ... 1,840

Federal wall mirror, giltwood, a narrow rectangular projecting molded cornice w/fourteen spherules over a rectangular églomisé tablet showing an American & British ship battling within a marbleized border & above the rectangular mirror, all in a narrow molded frame flanked by ropetwist carving, old gilt surface & mirror, apparently original tablet, probably Massachusetts, ca. 1815, 21 1/4 x 32 1/4" (minor imperfections)......... 2,530

Federal wall mirror, giltwood, coved & molded crestrail w/stepped-out ends above a conforming frieze over a central panel w/a lozenge pattern flanked by molded engaged pilasters & molded base rail, probably Salem, Massachusetts, ca. 1807-08, 18 1/2 x 34 1/2" (regilding, replaced glass)... 1,725

Finely Decorated Federal Mirror

Federal wall mirror, giltwood & églomisé, stepped pedimented top suspending spherules over a tapering cornice above the rectangular églomisé panel painted white w/a gilt spread-winged eagle within a wreath & floral swags & bows, finely beaded side & bottom rails, attributed to Barnard Cermenati, probably Newburyport, Massachusetts, 1807-19, 19 1/2 x 36" (ILLUS.)..................... **3,335**

Federal Mirror with Rustic Panel

Federal wall mirror, giltwood & églomisé, stepped rectangular pediment crest suspending spherules above a conforming frieze band w/molded rosettes at each side over the églomisé panel painted w/a rustic landscape over the rectangular mirror plate all flanked by slender half-round reeded colonettes, molded flat base, probably Boston, early 19th c., original gilt, one spherule missing, restoration, 22 3/4 x 41 1/2" (ILLUS.)................. **1,265**

Federal wall mirror, giltwood & part-ebonized, a round molded frame mounted w/small spheres & a reeded inner band around the convex mirror, surmounted by a carved spread-winged eagle gazing to the right & flanked by scrolls, a gadrooned & ruffled leaf pendant at the bottom, American, ca. 1825, 28 x 42" (repairs to finial & apron)............................... **2,875**

Federal wall mirror, giltwood, the flaring flat pediment w/stepped-out ends above a band of acorn drops over a frieze band molded w/panels of paterae centering a floral basket panel above the two-part rectangular mirror flanked by ring- and baluster-turned pilasters w/molded classical scrolls w/a long central rope-twist section, ring- and rope-twist-turned lower rail, first quarter 19th c., 31 x 53"............... **4,313**

Federal wall mirror, inlaid mahogany & giltwood, the delicate swan's-neck cresting centered by a low giltwood urn issuing slender stemmed plants above a frieze panel w/a central eagle-inlaid oval above the molded rectangular mirror frame w/slender carved filets suspended from the upper corners, ornate scroll-cut lower corners & apron centered by an inlaid oval panel w/a seashell, late 18th to early 19th c., 59" h. **3,000**

Federal wall mirror, inlaid mahogany & parcel-gilt, the scrolled cresting w/rosette

terminals centering an urn of flowers above an oval inlaid conch shell, the rectangular string-inlaid frame w/gilt-incised borders & flanking fillets above scrolled pendant, refinished, New York, ca. 1800, 20 x 51" (regilding, imperfections).............. **9,775**

Federal Mahogany Wall Mirror

Federal wall mirror, mahogany, a flaring deep crestrail w/blocked ends above a central burl veneer panel flanked by blocks w/roundels above reeded panels over leaf-carved & rope twist pilasters flanking the two-section mirror, corner blocks at bottom w/roundels, original finish, ca. 1820, 18 x 42" (ILLUS.)................. **600**

Mahogany & Églomisé Federal Mirror

Federal wall mirror, mahogany & églomisé, a stepped pediment crest w/coved cornice over a plain conforming frieze band over the rectangular églomisé panel painted w/a landscape w/a Native American & tiger over the rectangular mirror plate all flanked by half-round reeded colonettes, stepped-out base molding w/corner blocks & rondels, early 19th c., 38" h. (ILLUS.)............................... **3,335**

Folk Art Court Jester Wall Mirror

Folk art wall mirror, polychrome decorated carved pine, figural, the body of a court jester-like man w/tall hat, long hair & pointed chin wrapping around the oval mirror plate as the frame, finely carved facial detail & delicately carved hands framing his face, legs crossed at the bottom, late-19th c., repair to right foot, minor losses, 12 x 21" (ILLUS.) **3,738**

George II Mahogany Mirror

George II wall mirror, parcel-gilt mahogany, the high arched & scroll-cut crest centered by a gilded spread-winged phoenix above a molded narrow frame & gilt liner w/scroll-cut apron below, patches to veneer, replacements, England, mid-18th c., 22 1/4 x 39 1/2" (ILLUS.) **1,380**

George III-Style Girandole Mirror

George III-Style girandole mirrors, giltwood, a round mirror plate within a molded frame surmounted by a spread-winged eagle & scrolling leafy vines, the similar apron fitted w/a pair of candle-arms, chips & losses, England, late 19th c., 20 x 34 1/2", pr. (ILLUS. of one) **4,312**

Ornate Neoclassical-Style Mirror

Neoclassical-Style wall mirror, carved mahogany, an oval frame carved w/resembled clustered, wrapped reeds w/a pair of figural carved kissing birds at the top above a floral-carved swag, suspended on a long forked branch w/a large bow at the top, further floral-carved swags along the lower frame, ca. 1920s, 22 x 40" (ILLUS.) **850**

Queen Anne country-style wall mirror, figured walnut veneer, a high scroll-cut arched crest w/inwardly curled ears above a rectangular narrow molded frame enclosing the old mirror replacement, old refinishing, 18th c., 11 x 20 1/2" (age cracks in veneer) **583**

Queen Anne wall mirror, a simple wide arched molded black-painted frame encloses a beveled-edge mirror w/an engraved stylized basket of flowers & vines across the bottom, probably New England, 18th c., 16 x 17 1/2" **690**

Etched Queen Anne Mirror

Queen Anne wall mirror, walnut, the shaped crest centering an upper mirror plate etched w/flowers issuing from a vase flanked by birds & smaller vases issuing flowers surmounted by a scrolling foliate border, a lower rectangular beveled mirror w/conforming frame, American or English, 1740-60, 17 x 35 1/4" (ILLUS.) **3,220**

Fine Regency Girandole Mirror

Regency girandole mirror, gilt gesso, the round convex mirror framed in a circular molding w/applied spherules & topped by a carved eagle on a rocky perch flanked by leafage, side candle sconces on leafy brackets, leafy-carved base bracket, probably England, ca. 1810, 20" w., 32 1/2" h. (ILLUS.) **9,200**

Ornate Rococo Revival Wall Mirror

Rococo Revival wall mirror, gilt gesso, the cartouche-form mirror in a conforming wide molded border w/an outer framework composed of bold ornate pierced leafy scrolls w/a fanned crest, ca. 1900, 16 x 24" (ILLUS.) **450**

Victorian Aesthetic Movement overmantel mirror, walnut & maple, a wide flat top rail centered by a pointed crest w/fanned finial & flanked by a pair of flat stiles at each end w/carved pointed finials above incised leafy bands, the stiles flanking side panels decorated w/Aesthetic floral designs, wide flat bottom rail, in the manner of Isaac Scott, ca. 1870, 60 1/4" l., 31" h. (ILLUS. bottom this page).................... **748**

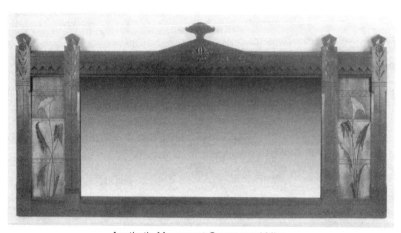

Aesthetic Movement Overmantel Mirror

Aesthetic Movement Pier Mirror

Victorian Aesthetic Movement pier mirror, oak w/walnut finish, the high crown crest w/an arched rail over a flared molding over a band of carved leafage above a band of carved balls flanked by rounded ears over a flaring crestrail above molded brackets flanking a frieze band inset w/three small diamond-shaped beveled mirrors above the tall rectangular beveled mirror flanked by baluster- and rod-turned side columns ending in blocks flanking the molded bottom rail, original finish, ca 1880-1890, 22" w., 4' h. (ILLUS.) **450**

Victorian Aesthetic Movement substyle cheval mirror, oak, a tall rectangular narrow reeded mirror frame topped by a half-round high pierced crest w/a band of circles & bars set w/two green 'jewels' above an arch of four small spindles, the mirror frame w/bulbous pointed corner finials & swiveling between tall slender columns w/small urn finials, raised on a trestle base w/a wide band of spindles joining the arched legs on casters, ca. 1880-90, 26" w., 73" h. **2,408**

Victorian Aesthetic Movement substyle pier mirror, walnut & burl walnut, tall narrow form, the top w/a dentil rail above a pierced & leafy scroll-carved crestrail flanked by pointed finials above a coved cornice w/zigzag incised band above carved blocks & long narrow burl panels down the sides, the base w/a stepped-out central block w/a square white marble top above a carved bracket panel flanked by raised panels carved w/drop clusters of leaves, molded conforming base, ca. 1890, carving picked out in gold paint, 29 3/4" w., 100" h. **660**

Victorian Aesthetic Movement substyle pier mirror, walnut, the tall superstructure w/a crown crestrail w/an arched & pierced center crest flanked by pierced stylized carved bands over a raised burl frieze band & shaped corner blocks above the tall rectangular mirror flanked by turned half-round colonettes, a narrow

white marble shelf below the mirror supported on a stepped-out shelved bracket w/a small drawer above bobbin spindles & curved bracket supports on slender turned front legs, solid backboard w/molded base, 11 x 23", 87" h. **633**

Victorian Eastlake Pier Mirror

Victorian Eastlake substyle pier mirror, carved walnut, the arched crest w/applied stepped molding over a leafy vine panel flanked by brackets w/turned finials above the slender side rails w/half-round colonettes halfway down above line-incised bands & blocked brackets on a rectangular marble shelf below the tall mirror plate, the base w/a central leaf cluster-carved panel flanked by curved brackets & turned spindles fronting the back panel & resting on a rectangular molded flat base, old finish, ca. 1880 28" w., 92" h. (ILLUS.) **1,155**

Victorian Faux Bamboo Cheval Mirror

Victorian faux bamboo cheval mirror, maple, a beveled tall rectangular mirror swiveling between faux bamboo stiles surmounted by a delicate pierced crest w/turned spindles centering roundels, a band of faux bamboo spindles across the bottom frame, outswept faux bamboo legs, late 19th c., 30 1/2 x 71" h. (ILLUS.).. **6,325**

Victorian Renaissance Revival overmantel mirror, giltwood, the crestrail carved w/a raised central female mask on an acanthus-topped shield flanked by husk swags, blocked top corners w/palmettes above a raised frieze molding over the large gently arched mirror flanked by block & columnar sides above a molded flat base, w/a marble support shelf, third quarter 19th c., 56" w., 79" h. (ILLUS. bottom this page).. **3,335**

Victorian Renaissance Revival wall mirror, walnut, the deep molded shadowbox frame w/a wide arched top & flat base, a scroll-carved crest centered by a carved leaf & cone cluster, scroll brackets at the bottom corners, gilt liner, ca. 1870, 24" w., 48" h. (ILLUS. top next column)........ **560**

Victorian Rococo substyle pier mirror, giltwood, the high pointed arch crest ornately pierce-carved w/rococo scrolls & a central trefoil above the tall rectangular

Renaissance Revival Wall Mirror

mirror plate w/rounded top, narrow molded side & base framed w/carved scrolls at the bottom corners, ca. 1850, 36 1/2" w., 94" h. (well done repairs & some regilding).. **1,155**

Fine Renaissance Revival Mirror

Parlor Suites

Art Deco: settee & two armchairs; carved giltwood & upholstery, arched crestrail on the settee above high rolled upholstered arms w/reeded arm supports continuing to form the front legs, barrel-back armchairs w/matching legs, cushion seats, molded seatrails, attributed to Paul Follot, France, ca. 1920s, settee 62" l. (ILLUS. bottom this page) **$31,625**

Art Deco: sofa & armchair; upholstered black lacquer & Lucite, the sofa w/a long gently rounded vertically-tufted back curving around to end in paneled arm supports consisting of alternating bands of lacquer & Lucite, long gently bowed cushion seat & seatrail, lacquer panel back frame & raised on molded lacquer seatrail, pale grey mohair upholstery, Kem Weber, ca. 1930s, sofa 78" l., the set (ILLUS. of sofa bottom this page) **3,450**

Art Deco: sofa & pair of club chairs; silvered & carved wood, each w/lobed upholstered back & seat flanked by uprights boldly carved w/curling feathers, American-made, ca. 1930s, sofa 84" l., 3 pcs. (chips).. **1,380**

Art Deco: sofa & two armchairs; fully upholstered, each w/a flared, squared back & outswept squared arms, raised on short sycamore legs w/bronze sabots, Jules Leleu, France, ca. 1930, the set **10,925**

Art Nouveau: settee, two armchairs & two side chairs; Fougères patt., carved mahogany, each piece w/a high back w/a

Rare Art Deco Parlor Suite

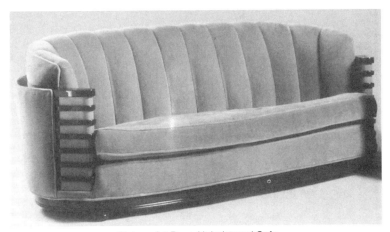

Unique Art Deco Upholstered Sofa

downcurved crestrail w/peaked corners pierce-carved w/a lattice leaf design & continuing down to form the back frame enclosing the upholstered back, the outswept closed arms w/curved lattice-carved arm supports continuing into the squared, gently curved front legs w/further carving, serpentine front seatrail, Louis Majorelle, France, ca. 1900, settee 55" l., the set.. **27,600**

Art Nouveau: two armchairs & two side chairs; carved mahogany, "Les Pins" patt., tall slightly tapering back frames carved at the crest w/pine cones & nee-dles above upholstered back panels, the armchairs w/curved closed arms over curved carved seatrails, gently outswept square legs, upholstered in tan leather, Louis Majorelle, France, ca. 1900, the set (ILLUS. of part)..................................... **10,350**

Bentwood: rocking chair w/arms, side chair & armchair; each w/a rounded rectangular back enclosing a horizontal backrail pierced w/circular cut-outs, above vertical slats & a D-shaped seat, the armchair & side chair branded "Thonet," Model No. 511, Austria, early 20th c., side chair 39" h., the set (ILLUS. below) **2,300**

Art Nouveau Armchair & Side Chair

Three-piece Thonet Bentwood Set

Bentwood: settee & two armchairs; each w/a flared back of continuous form w/rolled crestrail, the padded bentwood frame above a cushion seat, the legs joined by hoop stretcher, upholstered in camel-colored leather, attributed to Marcel Kammerer, for Thonet of Austria, ca. 1906, settee 68 1/4" l., the set (ILLUS. bottom of page) **5,875**

Biedermeier-Style: settee & two armchairs; inlaid fruitwood, each w/a shaped crestrail w/raised center & small inlaid bands over back stiles flanking numerous tiny short turned slender spindles raised on a lower rail, the settee w/outswept matching arms, deep upholstered seats over a flat seatrail w/small inlaid bands, on square tapering legs w/end sabre legs on the settee, Europe, late 19th c., settee

67" l. (ILLUS. of settee at bottom of page) **3,738**

Classical Revival Parlor Suite

Classical Revival: sofa, two armchairs, a lady's chair & a rocking chair w/arms; a heavy arched crestrail w/an ornate scroll-carved crest & arched scroll-carved lower panel above the wide upholstered back w/boldly carved stiles, heavy scrolled

Early Bentwood Parlor Suite

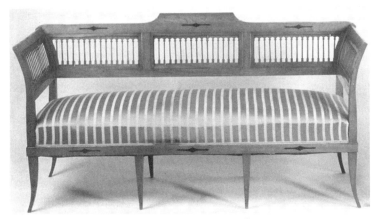

Biedermeier-Style Fruitwood Settee

open arms on incurved arm supports flanking the upholstered spring seat, serpentine seatrail, heavy cabriole legs ending in paw feet on casters, original finish, original upholstery, ca. 1890, sofa 54" l., the set (ILLUS.) **1,000**

Empire-Style: settee & a pair of open-arm armchairs; ormolu-mounted mahogany, each w/an upright squared panel back w/gently rolled stiles joined by a narrow crestrail w/ormolu mounts, downswept arms w/further mounts on incurved arm supports, upholstered back panel & seat, the seatrail w/a central long leaf spring mount & corner rosettes atop the square tapering legs w/ormolu paw feet, France, ca. 1890, settee 54 1/2" l., the set ... **6,463**

Empire-Style: settee & two armchairs; gilt-bronze mounted mahogany, each piece w/a square upholstered back within a conforming frame, the wide crestrail centered by gilt-bronze swans & scrolls continuing to padded arms w/round hand grips & further mounts raised on gilded swan-form supports enclosing the deep upholstered seat, flat seatrail w/long fern leaf mounts on turned front legs ending in gilt leaftips, heavy square rear legs, France, late 19th c., the set (ILLUS. bottom this page) **14,950**

Louis XV-Style: settee & four open-arm armchairs; giltwood, each w/a needlepoint upholstered back panel surrounded by a squared serpentine giltwood frame w/molded corner scrolls & central leafy floral bands & a central cluster, padded open arms w/leaf-molded incurved arm supports above the wide needlepoint upholstered seat, molded serpentine seatrail w/central floral clusters & simple cabriole legs w/leafy scroll feet, France, ca. 1880, settee 67" l., the set **15,275**

Louis XV-Style: sofa & two armchairs; giltwood, each w/a serpentine crestrail cen-

Empire-Style Parlor Suite

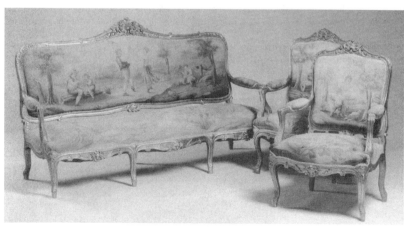

Louis XV-Style Parlor Suite

tered by a foliate-carved cartouche-shaped crest above the Aubusson landscape tapestry-upholstered back flanked by padded open arms on curved arm supports, tapestry upholstered wide seat on serpentine scroll- and cartouche-carved seatrails on demi-cabriole legs, France, late 19th c., sofa 68" l., the set (ILLUS. bottom previous page) **5,750**

Louis XVI-Style: canape, two open-arm armchairs & two chaise longues; grey-painted, each w/a narrow molded crestrail centered by a ribbon-carved crest above the foliate-carved rectangular back frame around the upholstered back flanked by downswept padded open arms on curved arm supports, wide upholstered spring seat above carved seatrails on knob-turned & tapering reeded legs w/peg feet, ecru silk print upholstery, France, early 20th c., canape 41" l., chairs 36 1/2" h., the set (ILLUS. of part bottom this page) **3,450**

Louis XVI-Style: settee & two open-arm armchairs; each w/a square upholstered back within a ribbon-tied & bead-carved frame continuing to leaf-carved scrolled padded arms flanking the upholstered seat, gently curved seatrail w/bead carving & round fluted foliate-carved legs headed by rosettes, upholstered in floral Aubusson tapestry panels, France, late 19th c., settee 50 3/4" l., the set **6,900**

Louis XVI-Style: settee, two open-arm armchairs, four side chairs; giltwood, each piece w/a molded oval medallion back w/a ribbon bow design & a ribbon bow top crest upholstered in floral needlepoint & raised on short stiles above wide rounded needlepoint spring seats, the arms w/upholstered pads & downswept carved arm supports, on reeded tapering round legs ending in peg feet, needlepoint w/red, white & pink roses w/yellow tulips & leaves on a cream ground, France, late 19th - early 20th c., the set (minor wear) **2,145**

Louis XVI-Style: settee & two open-arm armchairs; giltwood, each w/a raised tapestry upholstered back panel w/a gently arched crestrail w/twisted ribbon band centered by a small wreath crest above matching slightly canted side stiles, pad-

Louis XVI-Style Parlor Suite

Louis XVI-Style Giltwood Parlor Suite

ded gently curved arms on incurved leaf-carved arm supports above the wide tapestry upholstered seat, curved seatrail w/narrow roundel band, on turned & tapering reeded & carved legs, France, second half 19th c., settee 52" l., the set (ILLUS. bottom previous page) **8,500**

Victorian Eastlake Sofa & Armchair

Victorian Eastlake substyle: sofa & armchair; walnut, each w/an angular stepped & pierced crestrail, the sofa wtwo tufted upholstered panels separated by a scroll-carved panel w/short turned spindles, padded arms on angular blocked arm supports, gently curved seatrail w/angular short center drop, ring-turned tapering front legs on casters, original finish, ca. 1880s, sofa 60" l., 2 pcs. (ILLUS.) **1,000**

Victorian Egyptian Revival Armchair

Victorian Egyptian Revival: triple-back sofa, armchair & two side chairs; carved walnut, each gently arched crestrail set w/a patinated-metal plaque depicting classical figures & flanked by carved ears above the tapering tufted upholstered back panel, the arms terminating in carved Egyptian busts, curved seatrail centered by a half-round plaque, ring-turned & tapering front legs on casters, canted rear legs, third quarter 19th c., the set (ILLUS. of armchair) **6,038**

Victorian Golden Oak substyle: settee, low-arm chair & armchair; oak, each w/a low arched crestrail carved w/central scrolls framed by carved gadrooning above an upholstered back, shaped molded open arms ending in carved lions' heads on incurved arm supports, upholstered spring seat, flat molded seatrail, heavy cabriole front legs ending in large paw feet on casters, reupholstered in burgundy velvet, ca. 1900, settee 51" l., the set **1,650**

Victorian Renaissance Revival: pair of 64" l. settees, armchair, & four side chairs; walnut w/parcel-gilt & patinated metal mounts, the settee w/double oval-shaped upholstered back panels flanking a large central upright oval medallion w/a carved Grecian woman's profile, all matching frames carved w/elongated leaftips & acorn back finials, deep upholstered spring seats, tapering trumpet-form front legs on casters, incised gilt decoration, attributed to Pottier and Stymus, New York, 1865-75, the set **6,900**

Victorian Renaissance Revival: sofa, armchair & two side chairs; ormolu-mounted rosewood, the armchair w/carved & gilded crest above an upholstered back flanked by incised gilt column stiles headed by turned finials, padded arms fronted by applied ormolu putti & acanthus leaves above an overupholstered seat, on turned tapering front legs on casters, the sofa w/a three-part upholstered back w/an arched, gilt-trimmed crestrail flanked by ormolu female busts, side chairs similar to armchair, New York City, ca. 1880, sofa 72" l., the set **2,990**

Ornate Renaissance Revival Armchair

Victorian Renaissance Revival: sofa, gentleman's chair & lady's chair; carved & gilt-incised rosewood, oval tufted upholstered back medallions topped by a high peaked & pierce-carved crest of scrolls centering a bust, the high outswept stiles

ending in ornate turned ears, curved padded open arms w/female busts carved on
the arm supports, deep rounded upholstered seat on a conforming seatrail,
raised on tapering ring-turned front legs
on casters, canted rear legs on casters,
attributed to John Jelliff, ca. 1875, the set
(ILLUS. of gentleman's chair) **6,160**
Victorian Renaissance Revival: sofa &
three armchairs; carved walnut, each
piece w/a long narrow crestrail centered
by a high arched center crest carved at
the top w/a bust of a Classical woman
above a roundel & flanked by curved
pierced side swags, each rounded corner
carved w/a down-curved projecting scroll
w/drop, rectangular upholstered backs,
two chairs w/lower backs & one w/a tall
back, the long sofa back curving to form
rolled upholstered arms w/pendant-
carved arm supports, spring upholstered
seats on burl-paneled seatrails, raised on
turned trumpet-form front legs on cast-
ers, John Jelliff, ca. 1870, the set **3,920**

Victorian Renaissance Revival substyle:
sofa, armchair, two 'demi' side chairs &
center table; the center table w/a shaped
oval marble-inset top w/marquetry panel
all within a bronze figural-cast band
above an apron centered by marquetry
panels, raised on scrolled incurved supports headed by gilt-bronze Egyptian
heads ending in stylized hoof feet, the
seating pieces w/squared upholstered
backs, the sofa w/three tufted sections
centered by a carved bust medial finial,
outswept upholstered arms, the sofa
w/gilded child mask arm supports, ring-
and rod-turned tapering legs on casters,
possibly by Pottier and Stymus, New
York City, third quarter 19th c., the set
(ILLUS. of part bottom this page).............. **20,700**
Victorian Renaissance Revival substyle:
sofa & armchair; walnut, the triple-back
sofa w/tufted upholstered back panels below curved crestrails, the center section
w/a tall crown-form crest w/a carved classical mask, each section separated by a
ring-, rod- and block-turned column

Fine Renaissance Revival Suite

Renaissance Revival Sofa from Suite

w/pointed finial, upholstered closed arms w/curved & carved arm rests, a triple cushion seat on the sofa above a seatrail w/three burl panels above roundel drops, tapering ring-turned front legs on casters, matching armchair, ca. 1875, velvet upholstery ca. 1920, sofa 45" h., 80" l., the set (ILLUS. of sofa bottom previous page).. **2,900**

Choice Renaissance Revival Suite

Victorian Renaissance Revival substyle: sofa & two armchairs; carved walnut & burl walnut, the triple-back sofa w/a wide arched upholstered center panel w/an arched crestrail w/a scroll- and bar-carved finial centered by a face of a classical woman, the lower curved side panels divided from the center section by large ornate turned urns, curved padded open arms above the upholstered spring seat, three-section seatrail w/burl panels, raised on trumpet-form turned legs on casters, matching upholstered armchairs, original finish, old upholstery, ca. 1875, sofa 80" l., 44" h., 3 pcs. (ILLUS.).. **11,000**

Victorian Rococo substyle: gentleman's armchair & two side chairs; carved & laminated rosewood, each w/a tall upholstered balloon back w/an ornately floral-carved crestrail continuing to the molded back framework above the upholstered

seat, shaped & molded open arms on the armchair, serpentine front seatrail w/floral carving, raised on demi-cabriole front legs & canted rear legs all on casters, "Rosalie" patt., John Henry Belter, New York, New York, ca. 1855, armchair 44" h., the set (ILLUS. bottom this page).. **9,750**

Victorian Rococo Parlor Suite

Victorian Rococo substyle: sofa & armchair; carved walnut, the medallion-back sofa w/an arched grape-carved crest flanked by arched & rounded side rails continuing to low padded closed arms w/incurved molded arm supports, long seat w/gently swelled front on a conforming seatrail, molded demi-cabriole legs on casters, matching balloon-back open-arm armchair, original finish, old reupholstery, ca. 1865, settee 5" l., 2 pcs. (ILLUS.) **1,200**

Victorian Rococo substyle: sofa, armchair & slipper chair; carved rosewood, the serpentine-back sofa w/a high pierce-carved crestrail of ornate fruiting grapevines centered by a large fruit cluster center crest, rounded sides continuing down to the half-arms w/molded serpentine arm supports, serpentine seatrail w/molded &

Belter "Rosalie" Parlor Suite

leaf-carved reserves continuing into the demi-cabriole legs on casters, canted rear legs on casters, ca. 1855, 71" l., the set (ILLUS. of the sofa bottom this page). **17,250**

Victorian Rococo substyle: sofa & two side chairs; carved rosewood, the triple-back sofa w/a central crest of finely carved roses & other florals flanked by scroll-carved rails continuing down to form the arms, a molded serpentine seatrail ending in demi-cabriole front legs, matching side chairs w/front casters, John H. Belter, "Rosalie without Grapes patt., ca. 1855, the set (ILLUS. bottom this page) **7,000**

Victorian Rococo substyle: two sofas & three chairs; carved rosewood, the triple-back sofa w/a high fruit- and flower-carved center crest & smaller carved crests at each end continuing to spiral-carved side rails above the padded half-arms w/in-

One of a Pair of Rococo Sofas

curved spiral-carved arm supports, serpentine seatrail w/central carved reserve, demi-cabriole front legs on casters, canted rear legs on casters, ca. 1860, the set (ILLUS. of one sofa) **7,560**

Elaborate Victorian Rococo Sofa

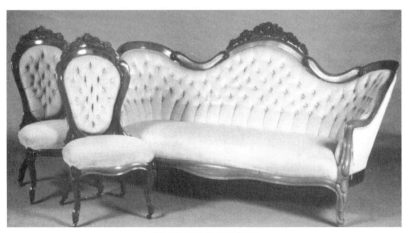

Fine Belter Parlor Suite

Screens

Firescreen, Art Deco, iron & mesh, in three parts, the arched central panel flanked by pivoting sloping side panels, each cast w/slender stylized hounds, the whole painted black, designed by William Hunt Diederich, ca. 1920s, 41" l., 26 1/2" h. **$6,325**

French Art Deco Firescreen

Firescreen, Art Deco, wrought iron, an upright square frame centered by a vining flowering plant composed of tightly scrolled leafy branches ending in blossoms, an outer border band of thin bars accented w/small C-scrolls & w/a large flowerhead in each corner, on short curved feet, in the manner of Paul Kiss, France, ca. 1925, 34" w., 40 1/2" h. (ILLUS.) **6,900**

Gallé-signed Inlaid Firescreen

Firescreen, Art Nouveau, marquetry fruitwood & mahogany, an upright rectangular panel w/a high arched & shaped top, decorated w/an inlaid design of a stalk of blooming irises on a variegated ground, set on a molded cross stretcher joining molded inverted-V end feet, signed in inlay "Gallé," leg repairs, France, ca. 1900, 22 x 33" (ILLUS.) **2,875**

Fine Early Classical Firescreen

Firescreen, Classical, carved rosewood veneer & grained giltwood, a central large rectangular black ground floral needlepoint panel set in a frame w/simulated brass inlay & flanked by faux rosewood columns w/brass capitals & bases above gilded acanthus leaves on curving legs ending in brass paw feet on casters, Boston, 1815, surface imperfections, 18 x 24", 38 1/4" h. (ILLUS.) **32,200**

Classical Mahogany Firescreen

Firescreen, Classical, mahogany, tiger stripe maple & mahogany veneer, the high rolled crestrail above the silk textile screen flanked by veneered columns w/brass capitals & bases above arched feet, repairs, Mid-Atlantic States, 1815-25, 13 x 26 1/4", 40 3/4" h. (ILLUS.) **1,610**

Firescreen, Edgar Brandt, wrought iron raised on strapwork legs, center panel wrought w/hunter holding bow & his prey, reserved against a field of stylized foliage, all within field of looping calligraphic devices, surrounded by a hammered frame, impressed "E. Brandt," early 20th c., 29 1/2" w., 38" h. **13,225**

Fine Aesthetic Movement Firescreen

Firescreen, Victorian Aesthetic Movement, brass & colored glass, the rectangular screen frame inset w/amber & topaz colored glass square tiles within a leaftip cast frame raised on foliate-scrolled supports joined by an arched pierced leafy vine stretcher, American-made, ca. 1890, 30 x 38" (ILLUS.) **12,650**

Victorian Aesthetic Firescreen

Firescreen, Victorian Aesthetic Movement substyle, walnut & glass, the rectangular wood framework w/an arched crest highlighted w/gilt incised lines & scrolls & w/a wide base band w/further gilt incised decoration, swiveling between slender reeded uprights w/gilt trim & turned finials, on outscrolled legs on shaped shoe feet, the framework enclosing a large blue & white etched glass panel w/Neoclassical designs, ca. 1875, original finish, 26" w., 44" h. (ILLUS.) **850**

Firescreen, Victorian Aesthetic Movement, ebonized wood, the high arched frame crestrail pierce-carved as leafy cattails flanked by the wings & heads of herons at the upper corners of the rectangular frame enclosing a needlepoint & beaded panel featuring a guardian angel carrying

Carved Aesthetic Movement Firescreen

a child above a bouquet of roses, the lower rail also pierce-carved w/cattails flanked by arched animal-form legs w/paw feet, last quarter 19th c., probably English, 51" h. (ILLUS.) **1,265**

Victorian Needlepoint Fire Screen

Firescreen, Victorian Elizabethan Revival substyle, mahogany & mahogany veneer, a large pierced & scroll-carved crest flanked by small urn finials on a flat veneered crestrail above the tall spool-turned supports flanking the large rectangular needlepoint panel w/a colorful parrot & flowers, raised on a trestle-form base w/spool-turned cross-stretcher connecting the scrolled outswept legs on casters, original finish, minor damage to needlepoint, ca. 1850-70, 18 x 24", 45" h. (ILLUS.) **750**

Folding screen, two-fold, lacquer & carved ivory, each panel decorated w/ivory birds, Japan, late 19th - early 20th c., each panel 30 1/2" w., 70" h. **575**

English Regency Folding Screen

Folding screen, three-fold, Regency style, walnut & ebonized wood, each walnut crossbanded & molded ebonized framework panel fitted w/a pleated green silk insert, England, second quarter 19th c., each panel 24 1/2" w., 53 1/2" h. (ILLUS.) .. **2,070**

Art Nouveau Style Screen

Folding screen, three-fold, Art Nouveau style, in the manner of René Lalique, stained leather & wood, each panel well carved & tooled w/flock of gulls & tree branches, beneath pine boughs abundant w/cones, above a field of flowers, stained & heightened w/gilt, all set within wood frame w/plaque stamped "Finnegan, Deansgate, Manchester," ca. 1900, 6' 1" x 5' 1/2" (ILLUS.).................................. **25,300**

Art Nouveau Pyrography Screen

Folding screen, three-fold, Art Nouveau, pyrographic-decorated oak, each oak-framed panel divided into three sections w/the top section pierced w/leafy landscape scenes above red, green & gilt-painted decoration of birds & cascading foliage, the reverse w/fabric, heavy wear to fabric, paint wear, American, early 20th c., 73" w., 63 1/4" h. (ILLUS.) **403**

Folding screen, three-fold, Arts & Crafts style, oak, top of each panel w/pyrography decoration depicting poppies & pods, colored in green, yellow & gold, early 20th c., 59 1/4" w., 68" h. (splitting, marring)................. **259**

Folding screen, three-fold, Edwardian style, painted satinwood, each panel decorated w/foliage & flowers, England, early 20th c., each panel 24" w., 70" h. **2,875**

Ornate Carved Baroque Revival Screen

Folding screen, three-fold, Baroque Revival style, walnut, the center panel pierced & carved w/a female caryatid beneath a pair of flowerheads, the lower section w/a standing female figure, all amid elaborate foliage, the side panels pierced & carved w/urns issuing flowers & foliage above the lower panel carved w/medallions, the central mythological mask-form crest flanked by cartouche crests, raised on opposing lion-form feet, late 19th c., each panel 21" w., 73 1/8" h. (ILLUS.) **3,450**

Rare Gustav Stickley Folding Screen

Folding screen, three-fold, Mission style, oak, each tall panel composed of three mortised long boards, side stiles continue down to form short legs, Gustav Stickley, early 20th c. (ILLUS.) **22,000**

Folding screen, four-fold, lacquered wood, each panel screen-printed in black & colors to resemble continuous open book shelves filled w/books & "objets d'art" on the obverse, each reverse panel w/a clustered trophy printed *en grisaille* against a mottled grey ground, Piero Fornasetti, unsigned, ca. 1960, 55" w., 52" h. **8,625**

Decorative Lacquered Wood Screen

Folding screen, four-fold, lacquered wood, the four panels depicting on one side a 'trompe l'oeil' decoration of book shelves w/books, pottery & various other objects, the other side depicting musical instruments, in browns, red, yellow, blue & black, designed by Piero Fornasetti, Italy, 1950s, each panel 13 3/4" w., 53 1/4" h. (ILLUS.) **9,200**

Louis XVI-Style Folding Screen

Folding screen, four-fold, Louis XVI-Style, giltwood, each panel w/a carved giltwood frame w/foliate-scrolled crest & a lower floral- and scroll-decorated silk panel, France, early 20th c., each panel 19" w., 65" h. (ILLUS.) **1,380**

Oriental Lacquer Landscape Screen

Folding screen, four-fold, inlaid lacquer, the four panels composing a continuous Chinese landscape composed of inlaid figures, buildings & accents w/gilt detailing, inlaid border band, China, ca. 1920s, open 60" w., 5' 10" h. (ILLUS.) **500**

Chinese Lacquer Folding Screen

Folding screen, four-fold, lacquered wood, the four panels decorated w/a continuous battle scene w/horses, riders, warriors & trees in colored hardstone, bone & ivory inlaid on the black lacquer ground, China, 72" h. (ILLUS.) **403**

Folding screen, four-fold, lacquer & cloth, each section w/a black lacquer frame w/gilt trim & a stepped crestrail above a rectangular panel painted w/a scene of an Oriental temple, each panel fitted w/printed fabric w/tall Chinese landscape scenes in browns, grey & salmon, China, late 19th - early 20th c., each panel 27" w., 74 1/2" h. **413**

Art Deco Folding Screen

Folding screen, four-fold, painted wood, Art Deco style, decorated as a continuous scene w/a tall Art Deco lady garbed in a huge fur-trimmed robe followed by a small fairy-winged footman in 18th c. attire, all against a stylized wooded landscape, muted colors of green, red & black, signed, ca. 1930, 116" l., 84" h. (ILLUS.) **1,725**

Green-japanned European Screen

Folding screen, four-fold, green-japanned & gilt-decorated wood, each panel w/three inset panels decorated w/Chinese figures or birds & foliage, Europe, 19th c., losses, retouching, splits to some panels., each panel 23" w., 90" h. (ILLUS.)........................ **2,587**

Piero Fornesetti Modern Screen

Folding screen, four-fold, Modern style, each panel w/a mottled cream-colored ground transfer-printed in black & white w/long detailed pendant Renaissance-style trophies, designed by Piero Fornesetti, Italy, ca. 1955, 56" w. (ILLUS.)......... **6,900**

Painted Leather Folding Screen

Folding screen, four-fold, painted leather, the panels painted as a continuous landscape w/an 18th c. hunting party on horses, early 20th c., minor damage (ILLUS.).. **1,380**

Folding screen, five-fold, gilt & black lacquer, each fold decorated on both sides w/a border above & below, centering a Chinese landscape including figures, raised on shallow feet, Chinese Export, 19th c., each panel 17 5/8" w., 70 3/4" h. (chips & repairs, missing hinges, now mounted w/hanging brackets) **2,530**

Folding screen, six-fold, molded ash plywood, the undulating panels joined by canvas hinges, designed by Charles Eames, manufactured by Herman Miller, ca. 1950, 60" w., 68" h. (some minor chips) **4,675**

Art Deco Eight-Panel Walnut Screen

Folding screen, eight-fold, Art Deco style, walnut & bronze, each narrow walnut panel enclosed in a wide bronze border band, attributed to Eugene Printz, France, ca. 1928, 99" l., 67 1/2" h. (ILLUS.)................. **23,000**

Pole screen, Louis XVI-style, gilt bronze-mounted mahogany, the standard set w/an oval pastel portrait of an 18th c. lady, mounted as a lamp, France, late 19th c., overall 54" h. **1,840**

Secretaries

French Art Deco Secretary

Art Deco secretary, fruitwood, a rectangular mirrored top w/molded edges above a case w/a heavy rounded molding enclosing an upper wide fall-front panel opening to a fitted interior above a medial band w/an undulating brass strap band above a pair of flat cupboard doors, looped brass pulls, raised on a flared platform base, France, ca. 1940, 17 1/2 x 31 1/2", 53" h. (ILLUS.).. **$8,625**

Unusual Arts & Crafts Secretary

Arts & Crafts secretary-bookcase, oak, a rectangular top w/a flaring cornice highlighted by a band of diamonds above a pair of geometrically glazed cupboard doors w/clear panes accented by green slag diamond-shaped panes, raised on incurved sides above the rectangular top over a pair of small drawers flanking the kneehole opening, large half-round cutouts at the lower sides & arched base cut-out, front stile legs w/through-tenon construction, original finish, probably English, early 20th c., 18 1/2 x 32", 5' 1/4" h. (ILLUS.) **2,310**

Country Chippendale Secretary

Chippendale country-style secretary-bookcase, butternut, two-part construction: the upper section w/a rectangular top w/a deep stepped cornice above a pair of tombstone-arched paneled cupboard doors w/H-hinges on the sides of the case above a pair of narrow drawers; the lower section w/a hinged slant front opening to an interior of valanced pigeonholes & a row of small drawers, the lower case w/four long graduated drawers, molded base on high bracket feet, old dark red finish, brasses replaced, pigeonhole valances replaced, feet w/nailed repairs, found in Vermont, late 18th c., top 11 3/4 x 36 1/4", 78 1/2" h. (ILLUS.) **11,550**

Fine Chippendale Secretary-Bookcase

Chippendale secretary-bookcase, cherry, two-part construction: the upper section w/a broken-scroll pediment centering a raised spiral-twist finial & flanked by two matching corner finials above a pair of fielded raised panel cupboard doors flanked by reeded pilasters, the interior w/concave shells over three serpentine shelves divided by a cyma-curved vertical board; the lower section w/a hinged slant front opening to a desk interior of valanced compartments & small drawers flanking a prospect door & columns w/a valanced compartment & two small drawers, all above four long graduated cockbeaded drawers on a molded base w/scroll-cut tall bracket feet, old replaced butterfly pulls & keyhole escutcheons, refinished, imperfections, Springfield - Longmeadow, Massachusetts, ca. 1780, 20 3/4 x 38", 7' 2 1/2" h. (ILLUS.).............. **79,500**

Chippendale Cherry Secretary

Chippendale secretary-bookcase, cherry, two-part construction: the upper section w/a rectangular top over a deep flared cornice above a pair of tall paneled cupboard doors; the lower section w/a hinged slant front opening to an interior w/a central prospect door w/two faux valanced compartments & drawer & three interior drawers flanked by four valanced compartments & two interior drawers, the lower case w/four long graduated drawers w/butterfly pulls & keyhole escutcheons, molded base on scroll-cut bracket feet, southeastern New England, ca. 1780, old brasses, refinished, restored, 18 x 40 1/4", 82" h. (ILLUS.) **2,760**

Chippendale secretary-bookcase, cherry, two-part construction: the upper section w/a rectangular top w/a deep coved cornice over a pair of tall paneled cupboard doors; the projecting lower section w/a rectangular top over a hinged slant-lid opening to a central prospect door flanked by valanced compartments & shallow

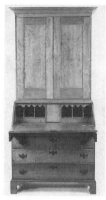

Chippendale Secretary-Bookcase

drawers, the lower case w/four long graduated thumb-molded drawers w/butterfly pulls & keyhole escutcheons, molded base w/scroll-cut bracket feet, replaced brasses, refinished, New England, ca. 1780, restored, 20 1/8 x 39 1/4", 86" h. (ILLUS.) **4,140**

Fine Classical "Secretaire à Abattant"

Classical *secretaire à abattant*, mahogany & mahogany veneer, the rectangular white marble top above a coved cornice over a wide frieze band over two veneered side columns w/Corinthian capitals & ending in large ebonized ball feet flanking the recessed central section w/a wide hinged fall-front opening to a writing surface & fitted interior over a pair of plain cupboard doors at the bottom, paneled sides, old refinish, imperfections, Boston, Massachusetts, 1820-25, 17 1/2 x 35", 57 1/2" h. (ILLUS.)...................................... **16,100**

Classical *secretaire à abattant*, marquetry, a rectangular top above a tall case w/a long narrow slightly projecting top drawer w/two knobs & a band of marquetry inlaid leafy blossoms & light banding flanked by light inlaid banded corner blocks above a wide rectangular flat hinged fall-front decorated w/a light wood central design of a compote of fruit framed by leafy scrolls & butterflies within an oval band framed by butterflies & a series of thin rectangular bands enclosed by leafy scroll corner designs & floral vines, the fall-front opening to a fitted interior above the lower case of three long drawers each w/matching marquetry designs of pairs of cornucopias issuing flora vines, the front sides w/light band inlaid columns on blocked feet, Holland, 19th c., 19 12 x 39", 56 1/2" h. **2,070**

Baltimore Classical Secretary

Classical secretary-bookcase, carved mahogany & mahogany veneer, two-part construction: the upper section w/a rectangular top w/a narrow cornice & frieze band over a pair of triple Gothic-arch glazed 6-pane doors opening to two shelves & flanked by free-standing columns; the lower section w/a wide cylinder-front opening to an interior fitted w/six small drawers over nine valanced compartments & a felt-lined writing surface above a pair of overhanging small drawers above two long graduated drawers flanked by short free-standing columns, original round brass & ring pulls, ring- and knob-turned feet on casters, early surface, imperfections, Baltimore, Maryland, ca. 1825-35, 24 x 46", 78 1/4" h. (ILLUS.) **2,070**

Classical secretary-bookcase, carved mahogany, two-part construction: the upper section w/a rectangular top w/a deep flaring stepped cornice over a plain frieze band above a pair of tall glazed doors fitted w/scroll- and leaf-carved mullions centered by rosettes & opening to a shelved interior; the stepped-out lower section w/a rectangular fold-down writing surface opening to an interior w/a row of three small shallow drawers above the case w/a pair of drawers overhanging a pair of raised-panel cupboard doors flanked by free-standing columns w/leaf and Ionic-carved capitals above a conforming base, on double ball-turned feet, attributed to Anthony H. Jenkins, Balti-

more, Maryland, ca. 1835-40, 25 1/4 x 41 1/4", 93 1/2" h. **9,200**

Classical Mahogany Secretary

Classical secretary-bookcase, figured mahogany veneer, two-part construction: the upper section w/a rectangular top & deep ogee cornice above a pair of Gothic arched glazed doors w/pairs of trefoil cutouts opening to shelves & w/a pair of narrow drawers below; the stepped-out lower section w/a fold-out writing surface above a case w/a slightly projecting long top drawer over two long drawers all w/simple wooden knobs, scalloped apron & bracket feet on casters, some edge & veneer damage, ca. 1840, 14 1/4 x 43 3/4", 82" h. (ILLUS.) **1,540**

Tall Classical Secretary-Bookcase

Classical secretary-bookcase, mahogany & mahogany veneer, two-part construction: the upper section w/a rectangular top & widely projecting flattened cornice over a plain frieze band above a pair of tall geometrically-glazed cupboard doors opening to shelves above a row of three small drawers; the projecting lower section w/a fold-out writing surface which lifts to a well w/two drawers & open compartments, false drawer facade flanked by pull-out supports above a pair of recessed paneled cupboard doors opening to shelves & flanked by S-scroll pilasters raised on heavy leaf- and paw-carved legs, replaced brasses, refinished, restoration, New England, 1825-35, 23 1/4 x 40", 81" h. (ILLUS.) **1,380**

Classical Mahogany Secretary-Bookcase

Classical secretary-bookcase, mahogany & mahogany veneer, two-part construction: the upper section w/a rectangular top & deep ogee cornice above a wide frieze band above a pair of tall geometrically-glazed cupboard doors w/Gothic arch top opening to three shelves above a pair of long drawers flanking a small central drawer; the lower section w/a stepped-out fold-out writing surface above a long ogee-front drawer overhanging two long flat drawers flanked by ring- and rod-turned colonettes on blocks above the heavy ring-turned tapering short legs, ca. 1840 (ILLUS.) **3,500**

Classical Rosewood Secretary

Classical secretary-bookcase, rosewood veneer, two-part construction: the rectangular top w/rounded front corners & a deep coved cornice above a beaded band over a pair of tall Gothic-arch glazed cupboard doors opening to three adjustable shelves over a row of three smaller drawers, the stepped-out lower case w/a hinged narrow fold-down writing surface opening to small satinwood-veneered drawers & valanced compartments over a pair of Gothic arch paneled & beaded cupboard doors on a molded base w/scroll-cut bracket feet, ivory escutcheons & tapered wooden pulls, old refinish, minor losses, New York City, ca. 1840s, 20 5/8 x 44", 94 1/4" h. (ILLUS.) **5,175**

Country-style secretary-bookcase, painted, a rectangular top w/a narrow molded cornice above a pair of tall plain flush doors opening to a painted interior w/three fixed shelves over a lower case w/a flat hinged drop lid opening to a desk interior of open compartments above a pair of plain lower cupboard doors opening to two shelves, old dark red paint on exterior, old mustard yellow paint on interior, New England, early 19th c., 14 3/8 x 48", 84 1/2" h. (imperfections)...... **1,380**

Unusual Secretary-Bookcase

Early 20th century secretary-bookcase, mahogany veneer, a long rectangular top above a dentil-carved cornice above the three-section case, each side w/a tall glazed cupboard door topped by a glazed panel w/ornate scrolling latticework flanking the center section w/a pair of small mirrored doors above an open mirror-backed shelf over the fold-down slant front w/applied scroll carving opening to a fitted interior all above stepped-out section w/a long flat-fronted drawer over three bow-fronted drawers all w/stamped brass & bail pulls, molded conforming base on four square tapering feet, original dark finish, ca. 1900, 20 x 60", 72" h. (ILLUS.).. **2,800**

Federal secretary, cherry, two-part construction: the upper section w/a rectangular top & narrow coved cornice above a pair of paneled cupboard doors opening to an interior of four drawers & five valanced compartments; the projecting lower section w/a fold-out writing surface & case of three long graduated drawers w/incised beading, curved inlaid apron & flared French feet, old finish, New England, ca. 1800-10, 22 x 42", 55" h. (replaced oval brasses, imperfections) **1,840**

Federal secretary, mahogany, bird's-eye maple & rosewood veneer, two-part construction: the upper section w/a rectangular top & narrow flared cornice above an inlaid three-panel frieze band above two veneered doors flanked by inlaid simulated columns; the stepped-out lower section w/a fold-out felt-lined writing surface above the case w/three long cockbeaded drawers outlined in bird's-eye maple inlay flanked by bird's-eye maple veneered edge panels over the ring-turned tapering legs w/peg feet, early surface, Gilman Clifford, Gilmanton, New Hampshire area, ca. 1810, 20 x 41 3/8", 57 1/2" h. (replaced brasses, some veneer loss) **9,775**

imperfections, New England, ca. 1820, 21 x 39", 80 1/2" h. (ILLUS.) **5,175**

Federal secretary-bookcase, inlaid bird's-eye maple, two-part construction: the upper section w/a scrolled gallery centering a satinwood & cockbeaded plinth & urn foliate-carved finial, flanked by corner reeded plinths & finials, above a cove molding & a veneered frieze centering a satinwood panel, over two-pane glazed doors w/reeded muntins & arched upper panes & inlaid satinwood panels bordered by mahogany banding & opening to two shelves above two short rectangular cockbeaded doors w/bird's-eye maple veneer & mahogany cross-banded border opening to a multi-drawer, valanced & compartmented interior; the lower section w/an inlaid fold-out writing surface & a case of three long graduated cockbeaded inlaid drawers w/butterfly pulls flanked by cockbeaded panels, the scroll-cut apron centered by a cockbeaded satinwood rectangular panel, raised on tapering baluster- and ring-turned legs, old refinish, New Hampshire, early 19th c., 20 x 40", 83 3/4" h. (replaced brasses, imperfections) **10,350**

Unusual Federal Secretary-Bookcase

Federal secretary-bookcase, cherry, cherry veneer & poplar, three-part construction: the top section w/a flat molded cornice above a pair of tall cupboard doors w/recessed reeded panels enclosing shelves above a mid-section w/two shorter doors w/recessed reeded panels enclosing compartmented four-drawer interior, the lower projecting base section w/a fold-out writing surface over a case w/a long drawer above a pair of small cupboard doors flanked by narrow bottle drawers & flanked by reeded pilasters, baluster- and ring-turned legs w/knob feet, replaced brasses, old refinish, minor

Fine Federal Secretary-Bookcase

Federal secretary-bookcase, inlaid walnut, two-part construction: the upper section w/a rectangular top over a flaring stepped cornice above a pair of tall geometrically-glazed cupboard doors opening to shelves; the lower projecting section w/a rectangular top above a hinged fall-front writing surface opening to an interior fitted w/seven drawers & pigeonholes, the lower case w/a pair of paneled doors w/circular inlaid bandings above a narrow inlaid band above the scalloped apron & flared French feet, found in Tennessee, attributed to Thomas Hope, minor veneer damage & minor repairs, early 19th c., top 12 1/4 x 43 3/4", 93 3/4" h. (ILLUS.)... **8,800**

Inscribed Federal Secretary

Federal secretary-bookcase, mahogany & mahogany veneer; two-part construction: the top section w/a shallow shaped gallery above a flat molded cornice & two diamond-glazed square doors opening to a small drawer & compartments flanking a square flat central door over a small drawer; the projecting lower section w/a fold-down writing surface above a pair of cockbeaded drawers over two long cockbeaded drawers all w/round brass pulls w/rings, square tapering legs w/inlaid cross-banding, old refinish, imperfections & some restoration, New England, inscribed "22 Geo. L. Deblois September 12th 1810," 20 x 37 1/8", 51 1/2" h. (ILLUS.) **2,990**

Federal Secretary-Bookcase

Federal secretary-bookcase, rosewood & birch-inlaid mahogany, two-part construction: the upper section w/a rectangular top w/narrow molded cornice & veneered frieze band over a pair of Gothic arch-glazed cupboard doors opening to two shelves, four short drawers & ten pigeonholes; the stepped-out lower section w/a cross-banded hinged writing flap opening to a tooled leather surface above four cockbeaded long graduated drawers w/oval brasses, band-inlaid apron w/central squared pendant, tall slender French feet, North Shore, Massachusetts, ca. 1810, 20 x 39 3/4", 65" h. (ILLUS.) **14,950**
Federal secretary-bookcase, walnut & walnut veneer, two-part construction: the upper section w/a delicate broken-scroll pediment centered by a block w/urn finial & flanked by corner urn finials above a pair of tall paneled cupboard doors; the lower section w/a wide hinged slant front

Fine Federal Walnut Secretary

opening to a compartment w/small drawers over pigeonholes, the case w/four long graduated drawers w/round brass pulls, molded base on cut-out bracket feet, late 18th - early 19th c. (ILLUS.) **20,900**

Rare Federal "Tambour" Secretary

Federal "tambour" secretary-bookcase, mahogany & mahogany veneer, two-part construction: the tall upper section w/a rectangular top w/a deep flared cornice over a carved dentil band above a pair of geometrically-glazed cupboard doors opening to shelves over a pair of sliding tambour doors opening to a figured maple interior; the lower stepped-out section w/a hinged writing surface over a case w/two long cockbeaded drawers w/oval pulls raised on tall square tapering legs joined by recessed box stretchers, probably New England, early 19th c., 40" w., 73" h. (ILLUS.) **5,750**

Federal-Style Secretary-Bookcase

Federal-Style country secretary-book-case, cherry, two-part construction: the upper section w/a rectangular top w/a narrow molded cornice over a pair of tall diamond-glazed doors opening to shelves; the stepped-out lower section w/a fold-out writing surface above an apron w/a single long drawer w/brass pulls, on slender ring- and rod-turned tapering legs, old refinish, mid-19th c., 23 x 36", 5' 4" h. (ILLUS.) **650**

Federal-Style secretary-bookcase, inlaid mahogany, two-part construction: the upper section w/a rectangular top w/cornice above a banded edge above a conforming case w/a line-inlaid frieze over molding above two tambour doors opening to reveal an interior fitted w/four drawers above six valanced pigeonholes centering a prospect door enclosing a valanced pigeonhole over a drawer, all flanked by inlaid pilasters w/Ionic capitals; the lower section w/molding surround above a line-inlaid rectangular hinged top opening to a writing surface over a conforming case fitted w/two line-inlaid graduated long drawers, on bellflower & line-inlaid square tapering legs, 20th c., 25 x 36", 47 1/4" h. **1,380**

Small George III-Style Secretary

George III-Style secretary-bookcase, mahogany, diminutive size, two-part construction: the upper section w/a broken-arch pediment above a pair of tall narrow geometrically-glazed cupboard doors opening to shelves; the lower section w/a wide hinged slant front opening to a fitted writing compartment above a case w/a pair of small square drawers flanking a longer center drawer over a pair of drawers above two long drawers at the bottom, all w/butterfly pulls & keyhole escutcheons, molded base on scroll-cut bracket feet, England, late 19th c., 19 1/2 x 27", 81" h. (ILLUS.) **4,313**

Ornate Late Victorian Secretary

Late Victorian secretary-bookcase, flame cherry & birch, side-by-side style, the left side w/a tall bookcase section w/a serpentine crestrail w/a pierced center opening & carved leafy scrolls above a pair of tall glazed cupboard doors each w/a frosted clear smaller upper pane w/Gothic arch grillwork above long glazed panels w/scroll-trimmed framing, the right side w/a serpentine crestrail over an asymmetrical beveled mirror over a shelf w/a small handkerchief drawer & pierced scroll trim above a hinged slant front decorated w/an ornate scroll-carved panel opening to a fitted interior above a stack of three graduated drawers w/stamped brass pulls, serpentine aprons & bracket feet, old refinish, ca. 1890s, 18 x 48", 5' 6" h. (ILLUS.) **2,200**

Queen Anne secretary on frame, cherry, three-part construction: the upper section w/a rectangular top w/a deep stepped molded cornice above a pair of tall raised paneled doors opening to shelves; the lower section w/a mid-molding over a hinged slant top opening to eight small drawers & twelve pigeonholes above four long graduated drawers on the separate molded stand w/short cabriole legs ending in pad feet w/peaked toes, New England, 18th c. & later, 19 x 36 1/2", 91" h... **4,600**

Queen Anne Secretary

Queen Anne secretary-bookcase, carved & figured maple, two-part construction: the upper section w/a broken swan's-neck pediment w/pinwheel terminals surmounted by three turned finials over a pinwheel-carved scrollboard above a pair of tall raised-panel cupboard doors w/tiny knobs & brass keyhole escutcheons opening to an interior fitted w/thirteen pigeonholes; the lower section w/a hinged slant front opening to an interior w/eight valanced pigeonholes & fifteen short drawers, the case w/four long cockbeaded graduated drawers w/butterfly pulls & keyhole escutcheons, molded base on scroll-cut bracket feet, repairs, eastern Connecticut, 1740-60, 18 x 36", 84" h. (ILLUS.) **43,125**

Queen Anne secretary-bookcase, carved & inlaid cherry, two-part construction: the upper section w/a swan's-neck pediment above a pair of raised panel 'tombstone' doors flanked by molded corners & similarly paneled sides opening to three shelves; the lower section w/a mid-molding over a hinged slant front w/a compass star inlay opening to an interior fitted w/eight valanced pigeonholes centering inlaid document drawers & a prospect door opening to three drawers, within an arrangement of five short drawers, the case w/four long graduated drawers w/pierced butterfly pulls & keyhole escutcheons, base molding adorned w/a shaped pendant, on short cabriole legs ending in claw-and-ball feet, Connecticut or New Hampshire, 1750-70, 18 x 36", 92" h. (repair to finial plinth, lacking one valance, one short drawer rebuilt, patches to drawer lips) **31,050**

Victorian Aesthetic Movement 'cylinder-front' secretary-bookcase, walnut & burl walnut, two-part construction: the upper section w/a very high stepped cornice w/a pierce-carved crest over a pierced panel carved w/crosses above three burl panels carved w/stylized leafy vines above the flaring cornice over a pair of tall single-pane glazed doors w/small up-

Aesthetic Cylinder-front Secretary

per corner brackets; the lower case w/a cylinder front w/two burled panels opening to a fitted interior w/pull-out writing surface above a pair of line-incised & burl-trimmed drawers over a small paneled square door beside two small drawers w/incised lines & burl trim, stamped brass pulls, deep molded base, refinished, ca. 1880s, 20 x 40", 8' 2" h. (ILLUS.) **2,800**

Victorian Aesthetic Fall-front Secretary

Victorian Aesthetic Movement fall-front secretary, mahogany, two-part construction: the upper section w/a rectangular top w/a widely flaring stepped cornice over a dentil-carved band above pairs of reeded & carved flat pilasters at the sides flanking the paneled & mirrored hinged fall-front opening to a fitted writing compartment; the stepped-out lower section w/a rectangular top & rounded front corners over a conforming dentil-carved cornice over a long drawer & raised panel cupboard door flanked by side panels topped by boldly carved putto heads, molded base on scroll-cut bracket feet, possibly Boston, last quarter 19th c., 19 1/2 x 39 3/4", 68 1/4" h. (ILLUS.).......... **2,300**

Fine Aesthetic Movement Secretary

Victorian Aesthetic Movement secretary, Modern Gothic-style, walnut, the top w/a flat crestrail over a gallery above two panels over a wide double-panel hinged writing surface w/heavy L-shaped brackets opening to a fitted compartment above a long drawer over a pair of recessed paneled doors w/angled metal brackets over two small drawers at the base, molded botton & blocked side stiles, ca. 1870, 20 1/4 x 36", 63 1/2" h. (ILLUS.)... **2,415**

Ornate Aesthetic Secretary-Bookcase

Victorian Aesthetic Movement secretary-bookcase, walnut, the tall case w/a projecting central section, the top sides w/paneled back rails & spindled supports flanking the taller central section w/a rectangular leaf-carved cornice enclosing a hidden drawer above an open compartment framed at the front by an oval railing

enclosing short spindles & backed by a rectangular mirror above a large glazed door w/gilt initials over a fold-down writing surface opening to a fitted interior above a stack of three burl-trimmed drawers, the side sections each w/a low top storage section w/three glass beveled panes above tall glazed cupboard doors w/long vertical half-moon molding w/lattice and vine-carved corner sections, each opening to four shelves, a deep stepped & molded flat base, original finish, ca. 1880s, 20 x 72", 6' 6" h. (ILLUS.).......... **7,500**

Victorian country-style secretary-bookcase, cherry, three-part construction: the upper section w/a deep flaring coved cornice above a pair of tall double-paneled doors w/a short panel over a tall panel & opening to an interior fitted w/two rows of pigeonholes w/two dovetailed drawers, the central projecting section w/a hinged slant front opening to an interior fitted w/a row of four drawers over a row of six pigeonholes, the base w/one dovetailed long drawer above the paneled block-and ring-turned legs w/knob feet, attributed to Kentucky, mid-19th c., old finish, 14 3/4 x 41 1/2" top, 85 1/2" h. (replaced brasses, mid-section nailed to base)......... **4,950**

Victorian Country-style Secretary

Victorian country-style secretary-bookcase, walnut, one-piece construction, a rectangular top w/a deep flaring cornice above a pair of tall single-pane glazed doors opening to two shelves above a flat hinged fall-front opening to a writing surface & an interior fitted w/pigeonholes & two small drawers above the lower case w/a pair of paneled cupboard doors, second half 19th c., 19 x 38", 82" h. (ILLUS.)...... **660**

Victorian country-style secretary-bookcase, walnut, two-piece construction: the upper section w/a wide flaring & stepped cornice above a pair of tall single pane glazed cupboard doors w/molded interior edging & rounded top corners opening to three shelves; the lower section w/a wide stepped-out slant-top opening to a fitted interior above a single long drawer w/half-round turned pulls, on ring- and rod-turned legs w/turned feet, old finish, second half 19th c., 19 x 43 1/4", 82 1/4" h. (repaired breaks at hinges) **990**

Victorian "Cylinder-front" Secretary

Victorian Eastlake "cylinder-front"secre-tary-bookcase, walnut & burl walnut, a rectangular top w/flaring cornice above a burled frieze band over a pair of tall glazed cupboard doors opening to shelves above a stepped-out cylinder top w/recessed burl panel opening to a fitted interior above a long drawer above two stepped-back long drawers, flat base, angular brass pulls, ca. 1880 (ILLUS.) **3,400**

Eastlake Walnut Secretary-Bookcase

Victorian Eastlake "cylinder-front" sec-retary-bookcase, walnut & burl walnut, the rectangular top w/a molded flaring

cornice above frieze band over a pair of tall single-pane glazed cupboard doors opening to shelves; the lower section w/a paneled cylinder front opening to an interior w/a pull-out shelf & fitted interior w/two drawers, above a single long burl-veneered drawer projecting over two small burl-veneered drawers w/stamped brass pulls beside a small raised panel burled cupboard door, molded flat base on casters, refinished, ca. 1880, top 14 x 42 1/2", 90 1/4" h. (ILLUS.) **1,705**

Victorian Eastlake "cylinder-front" sec-retary-bookcase, walnut & burl walnut, two-part construction: the upper section w/a high stepped crown crest w/notched edge trim & line-incised diamonds & forked sprigs above a top molding over a pair of tall single-pane glazed cupboard doors trimmed w/forked sprigs & opening to shelves; the lower section w/rectangular back top above the wide cylinder front w/two recessed burl panels opening to an interior fitted w/two drawers & pigeon-holes, the lower case w/a stepped-out long line-incised & stylized leafy branch-decorated drawer flanked by sprigged side blocks above two long matching drawers flanked by curved brackets over blocked stiles all w/incised bands, deep molded flat base on casters, ca. 1890, 15 x 40 1/4", 90" h. **1,870**

Eastlake "Cylinder-front" Secretary

Victorian Eastlake "cylinder-front" sec-retary-bookcase, walnut & burl walnut, two-part construction: the upper section w/a rectangular top & upright front cre-strail w/a low arched center above scroll carving & spaced blocks above a frieze band decorated w/a long narrow raised burl band over a pair of glazed cupboard doors opening to three wooden shelves; the lower section w/a two-panel burled cylinder front opening to a fitted interior above a long line-incised & burl project-ing drawer w/stamped brass pulls above

two smaller drawers beside a small paneled cupboard door, narrow shaped
apron w/pierced panels, refinished, ca.
1880, 22 x 42", 7' 8" h. (ILLUS.)................. **2,600**
**Victorian Eastlake "cylinder-front" sec-
retary-bookcase,** walnut, two-part construction: the upper section w/a rectangular top w/a deep flaring molded cornice
above a frieze band w/incised sprigs
above a pair of tall glazed doors w/in-
cised sprigs around the edges; the lower
section w/a paneled burl-veneered cylinder front opening to an interior fitted w/pi-
geonholes & two drawers above a long
line-incised drawer w/incised leafy vines
slightly overhanging two small drawers
beside a small paneled door all w/line-in-
cised bands & scrolling leafy vines,
blocked & molded edges & base, on
casters, ca. 1890, 22 x 36 1/4", 85" h. **1,870**

Eastlake "Cylinder-front" Secretary

**Victorian Eastlake substyle "cylinder-
front" secretary-bookcase,** walnut &
burl walnut, two-part construction: the upper section w/a high stepped crestrail
carved w/trefoil finials above blocked panels of trefoils & a central arch over a deep
flaring cornice & a sawtooth-cut frieze
band above a pair of tall single-pane
glazed doors opening to shelves; the lower
section w/a narrow notch-cut band above
the burl-paneled cylinder front opening to a
fitted interior w/a pull-out writing surface
above a case w/a long burl-trimmed line-
incised drawer w/stamped brass pulls
above two short drawers beside an arched
burl-paneled cupboard door, blocked &
notched side stiles, deep base band, original hardware, refinished, ca. 1885,
26 x 36", 9' h. (ILLUS.) **2,500**
**Victorian Golden Oak secretary-book-
case,** quarter-sawn oak, the low crestrail
w/an arched scroll-carved center above a
long narrow shelf raised on scroll-carved
supports & a shelf backed by a large oval
beveled mirror, the case w/a tall bow-

Secretary-bookcase in Golden Oak

fronted glazed cupboard door opening to
shelves on the left & a mirror-back small
open compartment on the right above a
small drawer over a hinged flat fall-front
panel w/arched scroll-carving opening to a
fitted interior over a ogee-fronted drawer
over two flat-fronted drawers all w/simple
brass bail pulls, molded base on cabriole
front legs w/paw feet, refinished, ca. 1900,
18 x 42", 6' h. (ILLUS.) **1,600**

Oak Side-by-Side Secretary-Bookcase

**Victorian Golden Oak secretary-book-
case,** side-by-side style, a high top crest
w/scroll-cut sides & a flat crestrail centered
by a scroll-carved finial over a narrow half-
round shelf on slender spindle supports
above an oval beveled mirror above the
rectangular top, the left side of the case
w/a tall glazed cupboard door w/a scroll-
carved top opening to three wood shelves,

the right side w/a rectangular mirrored door w/scroll-carved corner above a wide hinged fall-front w/oval carved detail & opening to a fitted interior above a single drawer w/stamped brass pulls over a small paneled cupboard door, scalloped apron & simple stile feet, refinished, ca. 1900, 18 x 40", 5' 8" h. (ILLUS.)............................. **1,200**

Golden Oak Secretary-Bookcase

Victorian Golden Oak secretary-book-case, the superstructure w/a rounded squared mirror frame w/scroll carving enclosing a matching beveled mirror beside a scroll-carved cornice over two shallow drawers all on a rectangular top above a hinged fall-front w/applied carving opening to a fitted interior above a pair of single-pane glazed cupboard doors opening to shelves over a long drawer at the bottom, scalloped apron & bracket feet on casters, ca. 1900, 14 x 32", 66" h. (ILLUS.)..... **633**

Oak "Side-by-Side" Secretary

Victorian Golden Oak "side-by-side" secretary-bookcase, one side w/a tall single glazed-door bookcase opening to four shelves below a flat crestboard w/scrolled crest all beside an arched & scroll-carved crest & frame enclosing an oval beveled mirror over a small half-round shelf over a narrow rectangular shelf above the wide scroll-carved hinged flat fall-front opening to a fitted interior over three long drawers w/pierced brass

bail pulls, an egg-and-dart-carved apron on bracket feet w/casters, ca. 1900, 13 x 40", 71" h. (ILLUS.)................................. **604**

Golden Oak Secretary-China Cabinet

Victorian Golden Oak "side-by-side" secretary-china cabinet, substyle, quarter-sawn oak, the superstructure w/a high crestrail w/pointed carved central crest & scroll-carved rounded corners flanking a half-round rail over a scroll-fronted shelf backed by an oblong beveled mirror, the lower case w/a curved glass tall door opening to wooden shelves on the left beside a pair of small glazed doors over the hinged slant front w/applied scroll carving opening to a fitted interior above a stack of three block-fronted drawers w/simple wooden knobs, molded apron on paw-carved front feet on casters, some damage, ca. 1900, 16 x 40", 77 3/4" h. (ILLUS.)...................... **1,100**

Two-mirrored Oak Secretary-Bookcase

Victorian Golden-Oak secretary-book-case, the two-part ornate crest w/a long beveled mirror w/a rounded & scroll-carved crest beside an ornate scroll-carved crest over an asymmetrical beveled mirror, the taller left side w/a tall curved-front glazed cupboard door w/a geometrically-leaded top panel opening to bowed shelves, the shorter right side w/an ornately-carved panel & small shelf below the mirror & above a hinged slant-front w/an ornate scroll-carved panel opening to fitted interior all above a round-fronted drawer over two flat-front-ed drawers all w/simple bail pulls, simple short cabriole front legs on casters, original dark finish, ca. 1890s, 18 x 40", 5' 10" h. (ILLUS.)... **2,000**

carved pediment topped by a leaf-carved crest over a diamond panel & flanked by corner scrolls above a wide frieze band above a pair of tall single-pane glazed cupboard doors opening to three shelves above a burl-paneled cylinder front opening to a fitted interior above a long burl-trimmed drawer above an inset small cupboard door beside two small drawers all flanked by reeded edge molding, flat molded base & paneled ends, ca. 1880 (ILLUS. bottom previous column) **2,200**

Victorian Gothic Secretary-Bookcase

Victorian Gothic Revival secretary-bookcase, mahogany & mahogany veneer, two-part construction: the upper section w/a high arched & pierced scroll-carved crestrail w/small turned finials above a plain frieze band over the pair of tall glazed cupboard doors w/quatrefoil & Gothic arch glazing above a pair of thin lower drawers; the lower section w/a stepped-out white marble rectangular top above a single long ogee-front drawer above a pair of Gothic arch-paneled cupboard doors flanked by carved pilasters & ending in heavy block feet, ca. 1840 (ILLUS.) **3,000**

Victorian "Cylinder-front" Secretary

Victorian Renaissance Revival "cylinder-front" secretary-bookcase, walnut & burl walnut, two-part construction: the upper section w/a rectangular top w/deep flaring cornice over frieze band w/narrow raised burl panels & a rondel above a pair of tall arched & glazed cupboard doors opening to shelves; the lower section w/a curved "cylinder-front" w/burl panels opening to a fitted interior & writing surface above a long slightly projecting drawer w/two raised burl panels above two further long drawers w/burl panels & flanked by carved blocks, plinth base, ca. 1875, 13 3/4 x 43 3/4", 92" h. (ILLUS.) **1,870**

Renaissance Revival Secretary

Victorian Renaissance Revival "cylinder-front" secretary-bookcase, walnut & burl walnut, the rectangular top w/a

Burl-trimmed "Cylinder-front" Secretary

Victorian Renaissance Revival "cylinder-front" secretary-bookcase, walnut & burl walnut, two-part construction: the upper section w/a high arched & molded cornice centered by a scroll-carved crown-form crest & flanked by trefoil corner finials above a deep flaring cornice over a pair of tall burl-trimmed glazed cupboard doors opening to three shelves; the lower section w/a thin pull-out drawer over the paneled & burled cylinder front opening to a fitted interior w/pull-out writing surface, the lower case w/a single long burl-paneled drawer w/black teardrop pulls over the set-back raised burl paneled lower doors, deep molded flat base, refinished, ca. 1875, 24 x 42", 8' 2" h. (ILLUS.) **3,800**

Renaissance "Cylinder-front" Secretary

Victorian Renaissance Revival "cylinder-front" secretary-bookcase, walnut & walnut burl veneer, two-part construction: the upper section w/a rectangular top w/a deep flared cornice over a wide frieze band w/two narrow raised burl panels flanking a center button over a pair of two tall single-pane glazed cupboard doors w/arched tops, the tops & sides trimmed w/small raised burl panels, opening to three shelves; the lower section w/a cylinder-front desk w/the two-panel lid trimmed in burl veneer & opening to an interior fitted w/pigeonholes & two small drawers all above a long slightly projecting drawer w/raised burl panels & brass ring pulls above two matching long lower drawers, molded base on casters, ca. 1880, 22 x 43", 87" h. (ILLUS.) **3,136**

Victorian Renaissance Revival secretary-bookcase, country-style, walnut, two-part construction: the upper section w/a rectangular top w/a stepped cornice above a plain frieze band over a pair of arched glazed cupboard doors opening to shelves; the lower section w/a wide flat hinged fall-front opening to a deep compartment w/pigeonholes, drawers & letter slots above a lower case w/three long

Country Renaissance Secretary

drawers w/leaf- and nut-carved pulls, molded base on casters, ca. 1875, 13 1/2 x 43 1/4", 88 3/4" h. (ILLUS.) **1,513**

Renaissance Revival Secretary

Victorian Renaissance Revival secretary-bookcase, parcel-gilt walnut & burl walnut, a rectangular top w/a coved border above a deep cornice above a shallow paneled long drawer w/two large turned wood knobs above a wide paneled hinged fall-front enclosing a writing compartment above three long paneled lower drawers w/knobs all flanked by ring-, knob- and reeded side columns w/top & bottom end blocks, plinth base, third quarter 19th c., 20 1/4 x 38 3/4", 62" h. (ILLUS.) **1,840**

Victorian Renaissance Revival secretary-bookcase, walnut & burl walnut, two-part construction: the upper section w/a rectangular top w/wide stepped-out corners above a deep conforming cornice over a pair of round-topped glazed cupboard doors w/raised burl panels at the top & thin reeded side pilasters; the lower section w/a hinged fall-front opening to pigeonholes & flanked by curved sides above a pair of shallow drawers projecting above a pair of double-paneled lower doors flanked by blocked pilasters, molded

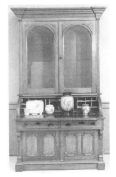

Renaissance Revival Secretary-Bookcase

plinth base, repairs, ca. 1875, 25 1/4 x 52", 91 3/4" h. (ILLUS.) **1,650**

Ornate Rococo Secretary-Bookcase

Victorian Rococo substyle "cylinder-front" secretary-bookcase, carved & laminated rosewood, two-part construction: the upper section w/a high scroll-carved crest w/a central turned urn finial on the molded cornice over a frieze band above a pair of glazed doors w/ornate scroll-carved latticework opening to shelves; the lower section w/a wide solid roll-front opening to a fitted interior above a single long drawer w/wooden knobs, raised on pierced & carved curved end supports joined at the back by arched brackets & a molded rail w/a high pierced scroll-carved crest, slender ring-turned front supports, all on molded rails raised on half-round disk feet, cleaned original finish, attributed to Meeks of New York, ca. 1855-65, 20 x 40", 6' 8" h. (ILLUS.) **3,800**

Victorian Rococo substyle secretary-bookcase, carved mahogany, two-part construction: the upper section w/a high arched scroll-carved cornice centered by a figural bust of Shakespeare above a scroll-carved frieze band above a pair of tall cupboard doors w/large oval mirror panels framed by ornate carved scrolls over a long narrow scroll-carved drawer; the stepped-out lower section w/a white

Elaborate Rococo Secretary-Bookcase

marble top w/a serpentine front above a long scroll-carved fold-down drawer front revealing the writing surface & interior storage, two cupboard doors below w/large round raised panels surrounding large blossom-form panels & w/carved scrolls in each corner w/further scroll-carving down the side stiles, flat blocked base, original finish, possibly by Mitchells and Rammelsberg of Cincinnati, ca. 1850s, 24 x 55", 8' 9" h. (ILLUS.) **8,000**

Secretary in Ornate Converted Case

Victorian Rococo substyle secretary-bookcase, carved rosewood, early conversion from an upright piano or organ, the tall case w/a high peaked & scalloped ornately scroll-carved pediment w/central cartouche, upright end scrolls & a pair of lattice-carved frieze bands over a gadrooned end cornices above spiral-twist turned side columns flanking delicate latticework grill panels flanking a central pair of glazed doors w/Gothic arch muntins, a curved hinged lift-lid opens to a converted desk section w/a row of drawers over a pull-out writing surface between carved rolled ends supported on heavy scroll-carved base supports flanking the central long rectangular base panel, case ca. 1855, probably converted ca. 1900, 26 x 48", 6' 4" h. (ILLUS.) **3,400**

Shelves

Floor shelves, country-style, painted pine, a rectangular board top above board sides on arched cut-out feet, a board back enclosing two shelves, old grey paint, square nail construction, 19th c., 35" w., 35 1/2" h. **$523**

Painted Pine Floor Shelves

Floor shelves, country-style, painted pine, a rectangular top above single-board sides w/arched cut-out feet framing four open mortised shelves, wooden peg construction, old green paint, some old renailing, a bit shaky, open knotholes in one end, 14 3/4 x 33 1/2", 49 1/4" h. (ILLUS.) **550**

Early Painted Floor Shelves

Floor shelves, painted hard pine, the four long graduated open shelves w/two molded rails joining cut-out sides w/arched tops, old blue paint, possibly Pennsylvania, early 19th c., 11 x 60 3/4", 59 1/2" h. (ILLUS.) **2,875**

Floor shelves, painted pine, tall one-board ends tapering sharply toward the top & w/arched base cut-outs, three staggered open shelves, old red finish, 19th c., 12 1/2 x 43", 46" h. **935**

Floor shelves, painted poplar, tall one-board ends w/rounded cut-out feet & curved top front corners, four open shelves, brass braces added to the back, old worn red finish, 9 1/2 x 26", 50" h. **880**

Hanging corner shelf, painted poplar, each half ornately cut w/graduated scallops & spearpoint drops, a single quarter-round shelf above a bin w/slanted baffle, old black paint w/gold edging, 19th c., 16" w., 34" h. **330**

Ornately Carved Rococo Shelves

Hanging corner shelves, Victorian Rococo substyle, carved mahogany, three quarter-round graduated shelves between delicately pierced & carved shaped sides w/tightly scrolling leafy vines w/blossoms & fruit, original finish, ca. 1850-70, 14 x 18", 44" h. (ILLUS.) **2,400**

Hanging shelves, country-style, pine, four narrow open shelves, each joined by slender baluster- and ring-turned spindles joined to blocks at each corner, knob-turned finials & pointed knob bottom corner drops, old worn brown finish, 19th c., 6 5/8 x 28", 31 3/4" h. **1,045**

Hanging shelves, Federal country-style, mahogany, whale-side shaped sides supporting four open shelves, the lower shelf above a pair of short drawers, New England, early 19th c., 24" w., 34" h. **1,000**

Painted Pine Hanging Shelves

Hanging shelves, painted pine, four open graduated shelves between deeply scalloped side boards, square nail construction, old black paint, mid-19th c., some edge damage on back, 8 x 29", 34 1/2" h. (ILLUS.)...................... **1,100**

Hanging shelves, pine, long whale ends supporting two open shelves, old worn finish, found in Lancaster County, Pennsylvania, 10 x 31", 30" h. **660**

Hanging shelves, walnut, four graduated rectangular boards w/rounded front corners joined to each other w/two simple turned corner posts & a flat stick at the back projecting at the top w/a hanging hole, old worn dark patina, possibly Shaker, 7 x 24", 19 1/2" h. (repairs, back post replaced)..................... **495**

Hanging shelves, walnut, four long narrow graduated open shelves w/rounded front corners, joined by slender knob- and baluster-turned spindles & short turned finials at the front, the back w/a slender plain slat at each end & a wider center slat pierced & scroll-carved w/a pinwheel, star & almond shapes, old finish, 19th c., 9 3/4 x 30", 34 1/2" h. (minor edge damage) **330**

Hanging shelves, walnut, whale-end style w/shaped tall sides flanking three shaped & graduated open shelves above a bottom shelf over a pair of small drawers w/small wood knobs, old finish, 7 3/4 x 24 1/8", 35 3/4" h. **2,750**

Wall shelf, painted pine, ogee molded edge on shelf w/extended backboard & box compartment, brown paint, 9 x 20", 29" h. (wear, some wood loss, age crack) **403**

Ornate Victorian Wall Shelf with Mirror

Wall shelf, Victorian Rococo substyle, walnut, a tall scroll-cut top crest w/attached roundels & a small oval mirror above a hinged lid on a shallow box w/raised oval bands enclosing oval ebonzied decal reserves, matching scrolling base bracket & backboard, original finish, ca. 1860-80, 7 x 14", 26" h. (ILLUS.).................... **300**

Wall shelf, walnut, a narrow rectangular shelf above a pair of shallow nailed drawers w/tiny pulls above a lower backboard all joined by scalloped tapering bracket ends, old worn reddish finish, 19th c., 32" l. **550**

Wall shelves, oak, chip-carved through rail joined by shaped sides, centering three graduated shelves, dark finish, late 19th c., 37 x 38".......... **115**

Wall shelves, oak & walnut, ornately pierced & scroll-carved sides w/graduated projections flanking the four open graduated shelves, two narrow back braces, original dark finish, second half 19th c., 24" w., 39" h. (few screws missing, minor hairline)............ **303**

Wall shelves. painted walnut, three-tier, the three graduated tiers w/rounded, chamfered & carved edges, each tier on four vase- and ring-turned baluster-form supports, all joined by two back vertical pierced hangers, old dark paint, New England, 19th c., 8 x 36", 23 1/2" h. (imperfections, medial shelf w/crack on rear right corner)................ **1,265**

Wall shelves, painted wood, the scrolled ends joining three shelves over three short drawers, painted to resemble rosewood w/pinstriped yellow scrolled foliage designs & beige painted backboard, New England, ca. 1836-40, 10 3/4 x 29 1/2", 17" h., pr. (restoration, damage) **2,070**

Wall shelves, painted wood, the shaped sides joining three graduated shelves w/two vertical back supports, old brown grain-painted surface, probably New England, mid-19th c., 9 1/4 x 28 1/2", 30" h. .. **1,035**

Wall shelves, pine, narrow rectangular top & dovetailed frame enclosing three open shelves, old varnish finish, 19th c., 6 1/2 x 38", 30 1/2" h. **330**

Wall shelves, pine, three open shelves between deeply scallop-cut side boards, backed by a central horizontal hanging support board, old dark finish, New England, mid-19th c., 9 x 26", 28" h............... **4,715**

Wall shelves, stained wood, shaped & cut-out sides w/a tall scroll-cut crestboard w/hanging holes above the top shelf, a wide space between the top & bottom shelf, red stain, 6 x 13 1/4", 18 1/2" h. **468**

Sideboards

Art Deco sideboard, mahogany, the long rectangular top w/gently curved front & angled corners above a conforming case w/a pair of large curved doors opening to an interior fitted w/a drawer & shelves, outset blocked corner bands above short curved front legs w/bronze "sabots," France, in the manner of Jules Leleu, ca. 1930, 21 x 63", 33 3/4" h. **$5,462**

Majorelle Art Nouveau Sideboard

Art Nouveau sideboard, carved mahogany, "La Vigne" patt., the superstructure w/a long flat crestrail over a narrow shelf supported by downswept curved supports carved w/grapevines above a paneled back & D-form top over a case w/a pair of paneled drawers above a pair of paneled doors all flanked by boldly carved bands of grapevine & curved side panels, molded serpentine base, Louis Majorelle, France, ca. 1900, 21 3/4 x 102", 72" h. (ILLUS.).................. **14,950**

Art Nouveau sideboard, ormolu-mounted inlaid mahogany & rosewood, "Chicorée" patt., the high superstructure w/a gently arched crestrail centered by a stylized carved floral tapering panel, an upright rectangular glass-doored cabinet at each side of a central open shelf w/floral-carved arched apron above an alcove all on the rectangular top w/molded edges, the case w/a pair of small central drawers w/leafy pulls above a pair of tall paneled cupboard doors inlaid w/leafy vines, each front side w/two open shelves fronted by serpentine floral-carved brackets, molded base, Louis Majorelle, France, ca. 1900, 22 x 66", 75" h. (ILLUS. bottom this page) **14,375**

Fine Art Nouveau Sideboard

Arts & Crafts Oak Server

Arts & Crafts server, oak, the superstructure w/a peaked crestrail over a narrow shelf w/an arched apron & tapering sup- ports above a long rectangular mirror, a rectangular top above slightly canted sides enclosing a pair of drawers w/metal pulls above a pair of cupboard doors w/an arched & fanned glazed panel over a plain panel above a single long drawer at the bottom, short stile feet, in the style of the Shop of the Crafters, unsigned, some damage, ca. 1915, 19 1/4 x 42", 37 1/2" h. (ILLUS.)...................................... **1,265**

Arts & Crafts sideboard, oak, a long rectangular top w/molded edges above a case w/a short drawer w/drop ring pulls beside a long drawer w/matching pulls over a pair of flat cupboard doors w/heavy long strap hinges & square plate & ring pulls centered by a stack of two deep drawers w/matching pulls, flat base, heavy stiles w/short feet on casters, England, early 20th c., wear, 24 x 73", 37" h. (ILLUS. bottom this page)................ **6,612**

Arts & Crafts sideboard, oak, the superstructure w/a long rectangular top above

English Arts & Crafts Sideboard

English Arts & Crafts Sideboard

an arched mirrored back flanked by two shelves & two pedestal supports w/applied copper repoussé floral decorated hardware, the rectangular top over a case w/a pair of drawers flanked by squared cut-out corner brackets above a pair of paneled rectangular cupboard doors w/spearpoint copper & brass hardware, medium brown finish, England, early 20th c., minor wear, 23 1/2 x 60", 66" h. (ILLUS. bottom previous page) **2,415**

Bauhaus style sideboard, oak, flat rectangular top on a case w/three flat cupboard doors w/ball-shaped steel pulls, the interior fitted w/four drawers on one side, shelf & drawer on the other side, short square legs, dark brown finish, Germany, ca. 1927, 23 3/4 x 78 3/4", 45" h. (edge nicks, scratches) **1,150**

Chippendale-Style server, carved mahogany, the long rectangular top w/line inlay, a gadroon-carved edge above an apron w/a row of three drawers w/bail pulls over a gadrooned edge band, raised on acanthus leaf-carved cabriole legs ending in claw-and-ball feet, 20th c., 22 x 59", 30 1/4" h. **770**

Classical country-style server, painted & decorated, a rectangular top above a pair of shallow drawers w/two turned wood knobs each above a deep long drawer w/turned pulls projecting above a pair of paneled cupboard doors flanked by black-painted turned columns continuing to turned tapering feet, overall red & gold graining simulating mahogany, original

paint, most pulls & door hardware changed, Shaftsbury area, Vermont, 1825-40, very minor imperfections, 21 x 46 3/4", 50" h. (ILLUS. bottom this page) **1,840**

Classical country-style sideboard, cherry, rectangular top above a projecting row of drawers w/a long drawer flanked by shorter drawers over tall end doors flanking a pair of central doors each w/double punched-tin panels decorated w/pinwheels in ovals within a looped border, the doors separated by four baluster-, rod- and ring-turned columns on a conforming plinth base raised on ring-turned tapering short legs w/knob & peg feet, further tin panels at the ends, Virginia, ca. 1840 (ILLUS. bottom next page)... **6,250**

Classical Mahogany Server

Classical server, carved mahogany & cherry veneer, rectangular top w/molded edg-

Decorated Country Classical Server

es over a long veneered drawer w/turned wood knobs over a beaded band & a pair of beaded panel recessed tall cupboard doors opening to a shelf, all flanked by veneered squared ogee pilasters on block feet, old refinish, hardware changes, missing top splashboard, minor surface imperfections, Mid-Atlantic States, 1840-45, 18 3/4 x 40", 40 1/8" h. (ILLUS.) **2,530**

Classical server, country-style, cherry & solid curly maple, a high flat-topped crestrail w/shaped sides above the rectangular top on a case w/a row of three small round-fronted drawers w/two wood knobs above a deep long drawer w/beveled edges & two wood pulls overhanging the lower case w/a pair of raised-panel cupboard doors flanked by heavy freestanding turned columns, wide quarterround base molding on heavy ring-turned tapering feet, maple facade & cherry crestrail, ca. 1850, 23 x 44", 60 1/2" h. (one column needs to be reattached, age cracks in feet, chips in burl panels)............. **1,705**

Classical Mahogany Server

Classical server, mahogany & mahogany veneer, a rectangular top above a long ogee-molded drawer projecting above a pair of paneled cupboard doors flanked by S-scroll pilasters ending in blocks on C-scroll feet, minor imperfections, Boston, ca. 1825, 18 1/2 x 40", 34" h. (ILLUS.).. **1,725**

Classical server, mahogany & mahogany veneer, the rectangular top above a case w/a pair of short cockbeaded drawers over a single long cockbeaded drawer w/banded borders flanked by applied Gothic arch panels above the ring-, rod- and spiral-turned legs joined by a medial shelf, all on knob & peg feet on cast brass casters, probably New York, ca. 1825, old refinish, 16 1/4 x 30", 33 1/2" h. (replaced wood pulls, minor imperfections) ... **2,070**

Classical server, mahogany veneer, a rectangular top above a pair of shallow long ogee-front drawers centered by a small flat-fronted drawer over a deep long drawer projecting above a pair of paneled cupboard doors flanked by flattened columns, C-scroll front feet, replaced wood pulls, old surface, New England, 1830s, 18 1/2 x 44", 49" h. (some veneer loss)........ **978**

Classical sideboard, carved mahogany, the pedimented splashboard w/three urn- and pineapple-carved finials over the rectangular top w/a molded edge over a long drawer flanked by short drawers all projecting over a series of four paneled cupboard doors separated by four freestanding columns resting on blocks above heavy paw feet, round brass drawer pulls, Duncan Phyfe or a contempo-

Virginia Classical Sideboard

rary, New York City, ca. 1830, 26 x 79", 58" h. (ILLUS. bottom this page) **6,038**

Classical sideboard, carved & veneered mahogany, the rectangular top w/molded cornice above a rectangular mirror in a frame flanked by two colonettes w/Corinthian capitals flanked by acanthus- and fruit-carved scrolling volutes over a rectangular case w/two short drawers, each above two tall doors flanked by similar colonettes & capitals centering two long drawers over gadrooning above two shorter

paneled doors over a gadrooned band, on foliate-carved & beaded feet on casters, Philadelphia, ca. 1830-40, 23 x 65 1/2", 58" h. (ILLUS. bottom this page) **3,680**

Classical sideboard, mahogany & mahogany veneer, a flat rectangular crestboard flanked by end blocks above the rectangular top over two round-fronted drawers flanking a central flat-fronted drawer all overhanging a row of three paneled cupboard doors flanked by free-standing side columns resting on blocks above the leaf-

Fine New York Classical Sideboard

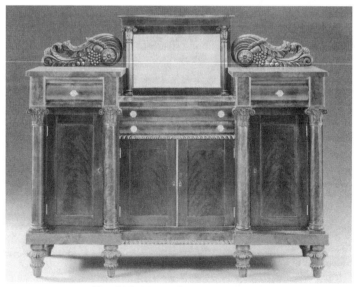

Fine Philadelphia Classical Sideboard

carved front paw feet, ring-turned tapering rear feet, New York, ca. 1825, veneer & other imperfections, 23 3/4 x 60 3/4", 54 3/4" h. (ILLUS. bottom this page) **2,185**

Classical sideboard, mahogany & mahogany veneer, the rectangular top above two short drawers flanking a long central drawer all w/lion mask & ring pulls projecting over a row of four paneled cupboard doors flanked by free-standing end columns w/gilt-metal capitals, raised on heavy double-knob turned front legs, re-placed brasses, old finish, minor imperfections, Boston, ca. 1820, 22 x 59 3/4", 39 1/2" h. (ILLUS. bottom this page) **4,888**

Country-style sideboard, yellow pine, a rectangular top w/molded edges above a pair of three-panel cupboard doors w/a horizontal panel above two vertical panels, turned wood knobs, molded base raised on baluster- and knob-turned legs, old dark varnished finish, attributed to the Carolinas, early 19th c. (ILLUS. following page) **3,630**

Simple Classical Sideboard

Large Classical Sideboard

Southern Country-style Sideboard

Empire Revival Tall Sideboard

Empire Revival sideboard, mahogany & mahogany veneer, a rectangular top w/a narrow cornice above a pair of cupboard doors w/raised geometric molding flanked by narrow paneled sides above a tall open compartment centered by a beveled mirror flanked by wide quarter-round columnar supports, the projecting lower case w/a white marble top over a pair of drawers w/silver metal button pulls over a pair of paneled lower doors flanked by narrow long panels, raised on carved paw front feet, refinished, ca. 1880, 20 x 40", 6' 4" h. (ILLUS. previous page)................................. **1,250**

Empire-Style sideboard, gilt-bronze mounted mahogany & mahogany veneer, the superstructure w/a long low arched crestboard w/gilt-bronze winged lion mounts above a narrow rectangular shelf above the long rectangular mirrored back & four marbleized column supports on the rectangular marble top over a band of three narrow drawers w/pierced scrolling gilt-bronze mounts above three cupboard doors w/figural & wreath gilt-bronze mounts & separated by four flat columns w/gilt-bronze capitals & bases, molded base on short heavy turned feet, France, early 20th c., 24 x 77", 72" h. (ILLUS. below).................... **8,400**

Federal country-style huntboard, walnut, a rectangular top on a deep case w/a pair of deep drawers w/simple turned wood knobs, on slender tall square tapering legs, possibly Tennessee, ca. 1830, 20 x 30", 36" h... **2,464**

Federal country-style huntboard, walnut, rectangular top above a deep apron w/a pair of deep beaded-edge dovetailed drawers flanking a narrow matching center drawer, turned wood knobs, on knob-, ring- and rod-turned legs w/ball-

and-peg feet, refinished, Southern, first half 19th c., 22 1/4 x 49", 43 3/4" h. (repairs, top replaced) **2,475**

Federal country-style sideboard, inlaid walnut & curly maple, rectangular top w/a boldly beaded edge above a case w/a deep bottle drawer at each end flanking two long central drawers, the apron cut w/a band of squared scallops, on eight slender ring- and rod-turned legs w/knob-and-peg feet, a heart inlay at top of one drawer, a second drawer w/replaced inlaid heart & third drawer w/missing heart around keyhole escutcheon, replaced small glass pulls, first quarter 19th c., 21 1/2 x 70 1/2", 43 1/2" h. (wear, edge damage, stains to finish large water stain on top) **5,500**

Federal 'serpentine-front' sideboard, inlaid & veneered mahogany, the rectangular top w/a serpentine front & canted corners above a conforming case w/a center square door w/fan-inlaid corners flanked by a stack of three small drawers w/simple bail pulls on each end, line-inlaid side stiles & square tapering legs ending in spade feet, Maryland, 1790-1810, 21 1/2 x 53", 37 1/4" h. **20,700**

Delicate Federal Server

Empire-Style Mahogany Sideboard

Federal server, brass-mounted figured mahogany, the rectangular top above two short drawers w/lion head & ring pulls on turned swelled supports joined by a platform stretcher over tapering ring-turned legs ending in brass ball feet, pulls appear original, New York City, ca. 1800, 18 x 32", 35" h. (ILLUS.) **4,600**

Inlaid Mahogany Federal Server

Federal server, inlaid mahogany, the rectangular top w/a border of lunette inlay above a single long line-inlaid drawer above a pair of central cupboard doors flanked by tall narrow bottle drawers all flanked by reeded stiles & above another border of lunette inlay, a scalloped apron above the square tapering legs, New England, early 19th c., 22 x 38", 41" h. (ILLUS.).................. **4,025**

Federal sideboard, inlaid mahogany, rectangular top w/bowed front above a conforming case fitted w/line- and quarter-fan-inlaid long drawers w/banded edge centering an inlaid oval reserve over two doors w/line- and quarter-fan inlay & banded edges, each flanked by a bowed line- and quarter-fan-inlaid short drawer w/banded edges above a similar door & flanked by similar stiles, on square line-inlaid tapering legs w/banded cuffs, New York, 1790-1810, 27 1/4 x 71", 41" h. **2,760**

Federal sideboard, inlaid mahogany, rectangular top w/crossbanded veneer outlining the edge which overhangs the case of a stack of two cockbeaded working drawers to the right of a pair of flat central cupboard doors w/a single deep drawer on the left w/a double false-front, all w/outlined stringing w/ovolo corners, on four very slender tapering square legs delicately outlined in stringing & ending in cuff inlays, replaced oval brasses, old refinish, small size, Providence area, Rhode Island, 1790-1825, 21 1/2 x 50", 39" h. (minor imperfections) **20,700**

Federal sideboard, inlaid mahogany, the rectangular top w/incurved front end sections & inlaid edges above a conforming case w/a single central drawer flanked by two small end drawers over four cupboard doors & two sectioned bottle drawers, each of these facades outlined in stringing w/ovolo corners, on six square tapering legs w/cuff inlays, replaced oval brasses, refinished, New England, ca. 1800, 21 x 67 1/2", 41" h. (some restoration) **11,500**

Federal sideboard, inlaid mahogany, the rectangular top w/square corners & banded center above a conforming case w/an inlaid long central drawer flanked by a shorter drawer at each end above single end cupboard doors flanking a pair of central cupboard doors, raised on short inlaid square double tapering legs, replaced butterfly brasses, old finish, Massachusetts, ca. 1790-1800, 27 1/2 x 64", 41" h. (imperfections) **2,990**

Federal Virginia Walnut Sideboard

Federal sideboard, walnut & yellow pine, rectangular top w/molded edges above cockbeaded case w/end drawers, the right drawer visually divided into two drawers & the left w/two working drawers, flanking a central cupboard door w/cockbeading, raised on four tall slender square tapering legs, old oval brass pulls, old refinish, repairs, Virginia, 1790-1810, 22 x 56", 39" h. (ILLUS.) **5,520**

Federal sideboard & butler's desk, inlaid mahogany, the elliptical top w/an inlaid edge overhanging a case of veneered cockbeaded drawers & end cupboards outlined w/stringing & having central bone-inlaid keyhole escutcheons as well as a central hinged drawer opening to an interior of small drawers & open compartments w/a felt-lined writing surface, above a long working drawer & an arched skirt outlined w/patterned inlay, raised on square tapering legs outlined w/stringing & ending in cuff inlays, original surface, replaced oval brasses, Boston area, early 19th c., 24 x 62", 41" h. (imperfections) **14,950**

George III Inlaid Sideboard

George III sideboard, satinwood-inlaid mahogany, the rectangular top w/serpentine sides & front above a conforming case fitted w/a central drawer above the shaped skirt & flanked by two doors, all w/crossbanding & line inlay, on square tapering legs ending in spade feet, veneer losses,

England, late 18th c., 26 1/2 x 65 1/2", 37" h. (ILLUS.) **5,462**

Mission-style (Arts & Crafts movement) server, oak, long coffin-shaped top overhanging long corbels joining the four tall slender square front legs & two rear legs, a wide apron w/a long single central drawer w/two metal pulls, low flat box stretchers joining the legs, Limbert paper label, 22 x 67", 31" h. (very minor finish wear) **825**

Mission-style (Arts & Crafts movement) server, oak, rectangular top w/narrow backsplash overhanging a narrow apron on four tall slender square legs joined by a framed medial shelf, unsigned Stickley Brothers, 20 x 36", 36" h. (recoated original finish) **880**

Mission-style (Arts & Crafts movement) server, oak, a low backsplash above the rectangular top w/inset legs above a single long apron drawer w/hammered brass hardware, the legs joined by a lower medial shelf & back stretcher, fine original finish, branded Stickley Brothers mark, 19 x 36", 37" h. **1,760**

Mission-style (Arts & Crafts movement) server, a double-rail plate rack on the rectangular top overhanging a case w/a row of three small drawers above a single long drawer, all w/cast copper oval pulls, square stile legs & rectangular medial shelf, fine new reddish brown finish, branded Gustav Stickley mark, Model

No. 819, 20 x 48", 43" h. (small veneer patches on side) **1,870**

Mission-style (Arts & Crafts movement) sideboard, oak, a raised plate rail above the rectangular top overhanging a case w/a pair of long narrow drawers over a single long drawer, square copper pulls, gently arched narrow apron, square stile legs joined by mortised end stretchers joined by a medial shelf, light to medium finish, branded mark of the Charles Limbert Co., similar to Model No. 456, refinished, early 20th c., 19 3/4 x 51", 41 1/4" h. (ILLUS. below) **4,025**

Mission-style (Arts & Crafts movement) sideboard, oak, the superstructure w/a narrow crestrail above a narrow long shelf w/rounded corners above a long rectangular mirror flanked by small end panels over the D-form long top over a conforming case w/quarter-round paneled rolling end cupboard doors flanking a pair of shallow drawers over a long deep drawer above a pair of long rectangular plain cupboard doors, square wood knobs, stile legs, ca. 1920s, 23 x 72", 58" h. **920**

Mission-style (Arts & Crafts movement) sideboard, oak, the superstructure w/a narrow shelf & flat crestrail above brackets flanking a rectangular mirror above the rectangular top over a case w/a stack of three small drawers flanked by paneled cupboard doors all above a single long base drawer, wooden pulls, paneled

Simple Mission-style Sideboard

ends, square stile legs, veneer loss at corner, retailed by Paine Furniture, Boston, Model 5229, ca. 1915, 19 3/4 x 54", 54" h. (ILLUS. bottom this page) **1,265**

Mission-style (Arts & Crafts movement) sideboard, oak, the superstructure w/a rectangular plate rack over a shelf above a central mirror flanked by slats above the rectangular top, the case w/two graduated drawers flanked by square paneled end cupboard doors above long deep bottom drawers, gently arched apron, square stile legs joined by three stretchers, branded mark of the Charles Limbert Furniture Co., Model No. 1453 3/4, ca. 1907, 19 x 48", 52" h. (ILLUS. bottom this page) **2,185**

Mission-style (Arts & Crafts movement) sideboard, oak, a high closed plate rack above the rectangular top overhanging a case w/a pair of tall flat cupboard doors w/long pointed strap hinges flanking a central stack of four long drawers w/bail pulls, on eight square stile legs, new medium finish, paper label of Gustav Stickley, 25 1/2 x 70", 41" h. (ILLUS. next page) **6,050**

Mission-style (Arts & Crafts movement) sideboard, oak, a high two-bar plate rack at the back of the rectangular top overhanging a case w/three small central drawers flanked by flat cupboard doors w/long strap hinges above a long drawer, original copper hardware, recent finish, red decal mark of Gustav Stickley, Model

Mission Oak Sideboard

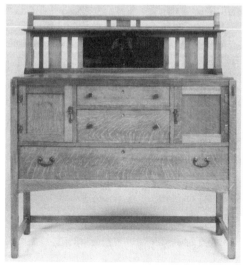

Limbert Mission Oak Sideboard

No. 814 1/2, 22 x 54", 48" h. (height slightly reduced) **3,190**
Mission-style (Arts & Crafts movement) sideboard, oak, a high replaced plate rail above the rectangular top overhanging a case w/a paneled cupboard door w/long strap hinges at each end flanking a central stack of four small drawers w/copper pulls all above a single long drawer across the bottom, square stile legs, cleaned original finish on base, unsigned L. & J.G. Stickley, Model No. 745, 24 x 54", 48" h. (stains on the top) **2,090**

Mission-style (Arts & Crafts movement) sideboard, oak, the superstructure w/a tiered & arched top rail over a setback rectangular mirror on the rectangular top, the case w/a pair of small drawers flanking a long central drawer over an arch-topped central section w/four paneled doors over a single long drawer across the bottom, original copper strap hinges & hardware, arched aprons & paneled ends, through-tenon construction, fine original finish, Charles Limbert Co., Model No. 362, 21 x 51", 52" h. (ILLUS. bottom this page) .. **2,970**

Gustav Stickley Sideboard

Charles Limbert Sideboard

Mission-style (Arts & Crafts movement) sideboard, oak, a high rectangular superstructure w/a single open shelf supported on curved brackets above the rectangular top w/rounded front corners above a case w/long front corbels flanking a case w/a pair of drawers over a pair of square paneled cupboard doors over a single long bottom drawer, on casters, overcoat on original reddish brown finish, Limbert Furniture Co., no visible mark, 20 x 48", 58" h. (some stain on top, one pull replaced w/another early pull) **3,850**

Victorian Aesthetic Movement sideboard, carved mahogany, the superstructure w/a tall rectangular mirror w/a crestrail of short bobbin-turned spindles flanked by corner blocks w/turned finials over bamboo-turned stiles joining the flanking small open shelves w/further spindled crestrails above curved brackets & leaf- and berry-carved panels over a long open shelf w/carved edge supported on two central curved brackets & turned end spindles all backed by floral- or vining

Unique Carved Aesthetic Sideboard

leaf-carved panels over a stepped top w/carved edging, the raised central section w/a boldly carved fern leaf panel above a pair of tall cupboard doors carved w/flying birds, the lower side sections w/two open galleried shelves supported

Aesthetic Movement Cherry Sideboard

by turned corner spindles & the lower w/a spindled front gallery, short notch-cut arched aprons on tapering block feet, by the Cincinnati Women's Wood Carving Movement, 1870s, 16 1/4 x 58", 97" h. (ILLUS. previous page)............................... **10,925**

Victorian Aesthetic Movement sideboard, cherry, the tall superstructure w/a rectangular top w/a three-quarters gallery flanked by low bands of spindles at the sides & front & capped w/two turned finials raised on arched supports w/slender knob-, ring- and baluster-turned spindles above a long open shelf w/low spindled rails at the ends & a spindled arch at the top of each end, the shelf backed by a large rectangular beveled mirror, all raised on plain square supports & a raised paneled back above the long rectangular top w/molded edges, the lower case w/a long drawer beside a shorter drawer over a long carved & paneled door at one end & a shorter matching door at the other end flanking a central stack of three drawers w/a longer drawer at the base, molded base rail on short turned feet, stamped brass pulls, original finish, ca. 1880s, 22 x 54", 6' 4" h. (ILLUS. bottom previous page) **1,600**

Victorian Aesthetic Movement sideboard, walnut & burl walnut, the superstructure w/a high crowned crest w/a central raised panel w/fan-carved finials over four small leaf-carved panels flanked by line-incised side panels w/fan corner fini-

Fine Aesthetic Movement Sideboard

als above a long narrow shelf supported by front slender turned colonettes & overhanging a large beveled rectangular back mirror flanked by panels w/leaf-carved blocks over the long rectangular marble top over a case w/a row of three burl-paneled drawers over a pair of burl-paneled drawers all projecting above a pair of recessed burl panel doors centered by a carved tall panel of flowers & leaves, carved side rails, molded flat base on casters, ca. 1885 (ILLUS. above) **2,200**

Ornate Baroque-Style Sideboard

Victorian Baroque Revival sideboard,
carved oak, two-part construction: the upper section w/a rectangular blocked top fitted w/a high arched & scrolling pierce-
carved crest w/a central cartouche flanked
by small turned corner finials above the
deep flaring cornice w/a scroll-carved
frieze band over a pair of tall cupboard
doors w/rounded panels w/raised molding
enclosing ornately carved game trophies
flanked by pierce-carved scrolling brackets
& two small shelves above a recessed
paneled compartment flanked by ornately
carved brackets; the lower section w/a
wide rectangular top w/a molded edge
over a pair of narrow paneled drawers
carved w/grapevines above a pair of paneled cupboard doors w/raised molding enclosing finely carved clusters of fruits,
three slender turned columns resting on
projecting blocks separate & flank the
doors, on compressed bun feet, refinished, Europe, late 19th c., 24 x 60", 9' h.
(ILLUS. bottom previous page) **5,500**
Victorian Baroque Revival sideboard,
oak, the superstructure w/a high wide
crestboard w/a gadroon-carved rail centered by a grotesque mask above a long
open shelf raised on scroll-trimmed lions'
heads over heavy ring- and urn-turned &
leaf-carved posts on heavy open scroll
brackets & backed by a long rectangular
beveled mirror, the rectangular top w/mold-

Ornate Victorian Baroque Sideboard

ed edges over a pair of long ornate scroll-
carved drawers w/shell-form pulls over a
long paneled cupboard door flanked by
shorter doors all w/ornate scroll carving, a
long deep drawer across the bottom w/fur-
ther scroll carving, the back section flanked
at each corner by carved & reeded blocks
& bulbous turnings, on heavy paw feet, late
19th c. (ILLUS. above) **2,300**
Victorian Baroque Revival sideboard,
walnut, the superstructure w/a tall arched
beveled central mirror w/a forked crest
centered by a large urn-form finial, the
scalloped sides w/urn-topped turned
colonettes flanked by two small graduated shelves above two small handkerchief
drawers on the rectangular top inset
w/red marble, the lower case w/a long
paneled drawer centered by a large

European Baroque-Style Sideboard

raised diamond above a pair of arch-paneled cupboard doors w/corner floral carving & enclosing ornate carved scrolls, flanked at the sides by large spiral-turned columns on blocks flanking a long narrow base drawer above the deep stepped & flaring blocked base, on large compressed bun feet, Europe, last quarter 19th c. (ILLUS. bottom previous page) **1,760**

Victorian Eastlake server, walnut & burl walnut, a low flat molded crestrail on the rectangular pink & grey marble top w/molded edges above a case w/a pair of line-incised & burl-veneered drawers w/oblong pierced brass & bail pulls over a pair of cupboard doors w/raised molding around recessed square burl panels over a single long line-incised & burl veneer bottom drawer w/pulls, block-molded & veneered side stiles, molded flat base on casters, ca. 1885, 19 3/4 x 54", 40 1/2" h. (two rosettes missing at top of stiles, inner edge molding missing on doors) **385**

Ornate Eastlake Carved Sideboard

Victorian Eastlake sideboard, oak, the superstructure w/a pierced & scroll-carved crestrail over a narrow carved band & two raised-panel sections centered by a round beveled mirror flanked by small open shelves w/lattice-carved brackets on slender bobbin-turned spindles all backed by panels w/overall incised leafy vine carving, the rectangular stepped-out top w/molded edge over a pair of line-incised drawers over a long line-incised drawer above a pair of paneled cupboard doors w/a carved band above the recessed panel w/an S-scroll line-incised leafy vine centered by a florette, incised side stiles ending in block feet & a flat plinth base, on casters, ca. 1890, 20 x 43", 68" h. (ILLUS.)................................ **920**

Victorian Golden Oak server, quartersawn oak, the superstructure w/a flat rectangular top above a pair of small shelves w/spiral-turned column supports flanking a rectangular beveled mirror above the rectangular top w/a serpentine front above a pair of bowed drawers over a single long flat drawer above a pair of paneled & scroll-decorated cupboard doors, scalloped apron, square stile legs

Small Golden Oak Server

on casters, stamped brass bail pulls, ca. 1900, 18 x 40", 61 3/4" h. (ILLUS.)................ **550**

Victorian Golden Oak server, the superstructure w/a rounded slanted crestrail decorated w/an incised sunburst & small lines & crosses between square corner blocks w/turned urn finials above the narrow molded shelf over a panel enclosing three small squared beveled mirrors w/rounded corners above another open shelf w/urn-form corner finials supported on slender ring-, baluster- and knob-turned spindles connected to the rectangular top backed by a large rectangular beveled mirror, the lower case w/a pair of line-incised small drawers slightly stepped-out over a single long line-incised drawer over two paneled cupboard doors centered by carved, raised sunbursts, line-incised side stiles, molded flat base on casters, ca. 1890, stenciled label on back "From the Shane Furniture Co....Cincinnati, Ohio," 20 1/2 x 44", 78 1/8" h.. **825**

Sideboard with Leaded Glass Door

Victorian Golden Oak sideboard, oak, the superstructure w/a flat crestrail centered by a small carved peaked crest above an oblong mirror w/scroll-carved upper corner panels & flanked by pierced arched sides supporting a small shaped shelf, resting on a rectangular top above a pair of round-fronted drawers w/brass bail pulls & keyhole escutcheons over a central arched leaded glass door w/scroll-carved trim flanked by carved stylized lion pilasters & a curve-fronted door at each end above the long, deep round-fronted bottom drawer, raised on flat legs ending in paw feet, refinished, ca. 1900, 20 x 42", 4' h. (ILLUS.)....................... **1,750-2,000**

Oak Sideboard with Leaded Glass

Victorian Golden Oak sideboard, quarter-sawn oak, the rectangular top w/a wide bowed center section & a long arched crestrail over the conforming case w/small leaded glass windows at the front sides & ends flanking a pair of large bowed & leaded glass doors each centered by a large fleur-de-lis design above a long deep bowed lower drawer all flanked by a short drawer over a deep drawer at each end, gently arched apron, raised on square legs ending in large paw feet on casters, refinished, early 20th c., 20 x 56", 4' h. (ILLUS.) **1,800**

Unique Golden Oak Sideboard

Victorian Golden Oak sideboard, quarter-sawn oak, the superstructure w/a flat cre-strail centered by a scroll-carved crest above a rectangular shelf w/a bowed center section above two small cupboard doors w/clear glass fronts composed of

beveled glass segments flanking a longer bowed door w/a plain glass front, all raised on curved leg-form supports w/paw feet flanking a long narrow beveled mirror above the rectangular top w/molded edges, the lower case w/a pair of narrow rounded drawers w/pairs of ring pulls above a pair of plain bowed cupboard doors flanking a long rectangular bowed door fitted w/a mirror, all above a deep long bottom drawer, raised on cabriole front legs w/paw feet on casters, original finish, ca. 1900, 20 x 45", 6' h. (ILLUS.)....... **2,200**

Nicely Carved Golden Oak Sideboard

Victorian Golden Oak sideboard, quarter-sawn oak, the superstructure w/a long narrow crest w/a deep carved frieze supported on figural griffin-carved supports above a long rectangular beveled mirror, the rectangular top w/molded edges above a case w/a pair of long gadroon-carved drawers w/carved lion mask pulls above a pair of raised panel end doors flanking an ornately scroll-carved center door above a long bottom drawer all flanked by reeded & blocked pilasters at the sides, base molding above short front cabriole legs w/paw feet, refinished, ca. 1895, 20 x 56", 5' 4" h. (ILLUS.) **2,800**

Golden Oak Sideboard with Mirrors

Victorian Golden Oak sideboard, the tall superstructure w/an arched & scalloped cornice w/rounded scroll-carved corners above an oblong mirror framed by large scrolls & a beaded band above the deeply scalloped open shelf supported by flat uprights w/bold scroll-carved tops & bases & centered by narrow upright beveled mirrors, also supporting a narrow lower shelf below a large scalloped rectangular beveled mirror, all resting on a rectangular top w/a bowed front above a conforming case w/a pair of drawers over a single long drawer flanked by serpentine side rails above a pair of cupboard doors carved w/a large central oval w/beaded border & flanked by large & small scrolls, narrow rounded base rail flanked by small scrolls, raised on short shaped front feet, refinished, ca. 1900, 20 1/2 x 44", 6' 8" h. (ILLUS.) **2,000**

Victorian Renaissance Revival sideboard, carved mahogany, the superstructure w/a long shelf w/rounded ends raised on scroll-carved end brackets & lions' head-carved front supports flanking a long low oblong mirror, the rectangular top w/wide rounded front corners above a conforming case, the curved panels carved in bold relief w/pendent fruit clusters, the front case w/three small raised panel drawers w/scroll-carved pulls above three shaped raised paneled cupboard doors each centered by a large carved bunch of pendent game, on a wide molded base, 24 1/2 x 82", 64" h....... **2,300**

Fine Renaissance Revival Sideboard

Victorian Renaissance Revival sideboard, chestnut & walnut, the very tall superstructure w/a large arched & rounded central section w/a scroll-cut & fruit-carved crest on the molded crestrail terminating in upturned ring-turned finials above a long narrow shelf flanked by raised round candle shelves above the wide scroll-cut rounded side panels w/half-round small shelves flanking a long beveled oval mirror, the rectangular white marble top over a case w/two long drawers flanking a small center drawer all

w/fruit- and leaf-carved pulls above a pair of large paneled cupboard doors w/oval panels centered by large carved fruit mounts & flanking a narrow rectangular recessed panel decorated w/a carved wild game mount, canted front corners & deep molded base on thin corner feet, ca. 1870, 68" w., 95" h. (ILLUS.)........ **3,080**

Victorian Renaissance Revival sideboard, walnut & burl walnut, the long rectangular white marble top w/molded edges & rounded front corners above a conforming case w/a row of three drawers across the top, two longer drawers w/recessed oval burl panels & cartouche-carved pulls & round keyhole escutcheons flanking a shorter central drawer w/recessed oval burl panel & round keyhole escutcheon all above a pair of large cupboard doors w/recessed large oval burl panels w/raised molding, one w/a relief-carved pair of hanging fish & the other w/a hanging gamebird, a narrow central door w/a plain oval burl panel w/raised molding, on a conforming molded flat plinth base, ca. 1870, 21 1/2 x 59 1/2', 36 3/4" h. **2,310**

Outstanding Victorian Sideboard

Victorian Renaissance Revival sideboard, walnut & burl walnut, the superstructure w/a high arched crestrail centered by a large fanned cartouche-carved crest flanked by carved grapevines above an incised band & burl panels above a molded rail over a scroll-trimmed burl framework enclosing a large arch-topped mirror flanked by carved colonettes & scroll-trimmed small candle shelves over carved block panels, the half-round white marble top w/molded edge & two front projections above a conforming case w/a pair of center drawers w/raised burl panels flanked by rounded side drawers above a pair of flat central cupboard doors w/arched raised panels enclosing burl & large carved grape clusters, matching curved end doors, deep molded base, original finish, ca. 1865, 24 x 74", 8' 2" h. (ILLUS.)............................ **8,500**

Renaissance Revival Tall Sideboard

Victorian Renaissance Revival sideboard, walnut & burl walnut, the superstructure w/a high paneled & crown-form crestrail over a narrow shelf above a tall rectangular mirror flanked by wide burl-paneled sides fitted w/two pairs of small open shelves w/blocked support brackets above the rectangular white marble top, the lower case w/a pair of oblong-paneled drawers over a pair of cupboard doors w/large oval panels, plinth base, ca. 1875, 18 x 41", 83" h,. (ILLUS.).. **2,800**

Renaissance Revival Sideboard

Victorian Renaissance Revival sideboard, walnut & burl walnut, the superstructure w/a pedimental crest w/burl panels centered by a carved life-like stag head above a pair of small half-round end shelves above a narrow rectangular beveled mirror above a long narrow shelf above a large rectangular beveled mirror, scroll-cut side braces, all above the rectangular top w/ovolo corners over a case w/a pair of long drawers above a pair of raised burl panel lower cupboard doors all flanked by quarter-turned & carved corner pilasters, molded base, ca. 1875 (ILLUS.) **3,900**

Renaissance Revival Sideboard

Victorian Renaissance Revival sideboard, walnut, the tall superstructure w/a high arched crest boldly carved w/leafy fruits & nuts above scroll-cut sides flanking a central panel w/an arched molding above a ring & roundel all above a narrow shaped shelf on scroll-cut brackets above a large oval mirror, the rectangular white marble top w/molded edges above a case w/a pair of drawers w/leaf-carved pulls over a pair of doors w/oval panels centered by carved fruit clusters & w/raised triangular panels in each corner, scroll-cut apron & bracket feet on casters, refinished, ca. 1860, 22 x 42", 6' 8" h. (ILLUS.) **2,400**

Renaissance-Style Walnut Sideboard

Victorian Renaissance-Style sideboard, walnut, the superstructure w/a narrow rectangular top over a deep flaring cornice supported on tall ring-, rod- and bulbous knob-turned front columns flanking the large rectangular beveled mirror w/curved bottom corner brackets over the stepped-out bow-fronted rectangular top, the bowed center section over a pair of large projecting drawers w/rectangular brasses over a pair of set-back square paneled cupboard doors w/ornate carving & notched panel corners, wide front side stiles, paneled ends, deep plinth base, late-19th c., 20 x 59", 79" h. (ILLUS.)............... **834**

Ornate Victorian Rococo Sideboard

Victorian Rococo substyle sideboard, carved walnut, the high superstructure w/an arched & molded crest centered by a shield medallion above a large relief-carved wild game & fish mount, outswept leafy scroll-carved sides over a narrow rectangular shelf above an oval mirror flanked by pierced scroll-carved brackets over the rectangular white marble top w/cut front corners over a conforming case w/a pair of drawers w/recessed oval burl panels w/leaf-carved pulls above a pair of cupboard doors w/large oval burl recessed panels centered by hanging game & fish carved mounts, molded plinth base, ca. 1860-70, 20 3/4 x 54 1/2", 88" h. (ILLUS.) **5,170**

Finely Carved Rococo Sideboard

Victorian Rococo substyle sideboard, chestnut, the tall superstructure w/an arched & stepped crestrail over a panel centered by a large relief-carved cluster of fruits & nuts above two long narrow tiered half-round open shelves supported by fruit-carved scrolling uprights, the shaped outside edges carved w/bold C-scrolls & fruit, all resting on a half-round white marble top w/a flat projecting center section above a conforming case w/a pair of paneled central drawers flanked by curved end drawers, two flat paneled front doors w/carved fruit clusters & corner roundels w/plain curved & paneled

end doors, conforming molded flat base, attributed to Alexander Roux, New York City, ca. 1855-60, original finish, 22 x 70", 6' 2" h. (ILLUS.) **5,500**

Ornate Victorian Rococo Sideboard

Victorian Rococo substyle sideboard, oak & burl oak, the high superstructure w/a very tall arched scrolling pierce-carved crest above an arched crestrail over raised burl panels above an arched mirror w/molded frame flanked by two graduated small open shelves w/brackets & cut-outs on each side above the rectangular white marble top above a case w/a pair of raised panel drawers w/scroll-carved pulls over a pair of cupboard doors w/oval recessed panels centered by relief-carved fruit clusters & w/carved scrolls at each corner, lightly scalloped apron on bracket feet, mirror worn, hardware replaced, ca. 1850-60, 18 1/2 x 54", 96 1/2" h. (ILLUS.) **2,695**

Victorian-transitional Small Server

Victorian transitional-style server, mahogany & mahogany veneer, a high shaped splashback w/central carved scrolls above the rectangular top above a pair of deep ogee-front drawers w/leaf-carved pulls above a pair of inset arch-paneled cupboard doors w/scrolls at the top & in the center of the panel & flanked by cyma-curved side stiles, S-scroll bracket front feet, ca. 1845-50, 20 x 38", 44" h. (ILLUS.) **650**

Stands

Stickley Bros. Mission Bookstand

Bookstand, Mission-style (Arts & Crafts movement), oak, rectangular top w/three-quarters gallery above three open shelves flanked by three narrow side slats, square stile legs, Stickley Bros., Grand Rapids, Michigan, Model No. 4708, refinished, wear, medium brown finish, 12 x 26 3/4", 38 1/2" h. (ILLUS.) **$1,035**

Mission Oak Bookstand

Bookstand, Mission-style (Arts & Crafts movement), oak, tall narrow board sides w/rounded tops flanking a slanted top shelf over two lower open shelves w/keyed mortise & tenon joinery, medium brown finish, wear, ca. 1910, 7 3/4 x 17", 40 3/4" h. (ILLUS.) **201**

Gustav Stickley Bookstand

Bookstand, Mission-style (Arts & Crafts movement), oak, V-shaped upper shelf w/through-pegged tenons above a flat lower shelf w/through-pegged tenons, solid sides w/D-shaped cut-out at top & low arched base cut-outs, medium brown finish, paper Craftsman label of Gustav Stickley, early 20th c., some wear & staining, 10 x 29 3/4", 30 1/2" h. (ILLUS.).. **1,840**

Unusual Mission-style Bookstand

Bookstand, Mission-style (Arts & Crafts movement), quarter-sawn oak, the tall rectangular framework w/four open shelves topped by four curved supports below a center post supporting an electric light socket w/curved braces supporting an oak-framed pyramidal shade w/leaded glass paneled sides w/floral designs in red & green on a caramel slag ground, ca. 1915-20, 14 x 22", 60" h. (ILLUS.) **1,200**

Victorian Stick-and-Ball Bookstand

Bookstand, Victorian stick-and-ball-style, oak & maple, the high arched & shaped bentwood crest accented w/a pinwheel design of slender spindles centering a small round mirror, bentwood side framing w/flaring spindles flanking the two upper shelves & shaped board sides & backs on the two lower shelves, refinished, late 19th c., 16 x 21", 44" h. (ILLUS.) **450**

Bookstand, Mission-style (Arts & Crafts movement), ash, rectangular board sides w/half-round hand holes near the top flanking the V-shaped top trough over a lower open shelf, keyed through-tenon construction, original green finish, attributed to Gustav Stickley, Model No. 74, 10 x 30", 31" h. **770**

Early Candle Dipping Stand

Candle dipping stand, turned wood, a slender turned upright post w/a bulbous ball top fitted w/ten radiating turned arms each suspending a pierced disk, the post raised on a X-form base, 19th c., 46" d., 34" h. (ILLUS.) **1,495**

Fine Chippendale Candlestand

Candlestand, Chippendale, carved & figured mahogany & walnut, the round top tilting above a slender flaring standard & urn-form support on a tripod base w/cabriole legs ending in claw-and-ball feet, chips to feet, New York City, ca. 1770, 20 1/2" d., 27 1/2" h. (ILLUS.) **5,175**

Candlestand, Chippendale country-style, birch, the square top w/shaped corners tilting on a baluster- and ring-turned pedestal on a tripod base w/cabriole legs ending in carved arris pad feet, probably Massachusetts, refinished, ca. 1780, 17 1/2 x 18", 28" h. **1,495**

Candlestand, Chippendale country-style, cherry, the square top w/ovolo corners &

serpentine sides on a baluster- and ring-turned pedestal on a tripod base w/cabriole legs ending in pad feet, possibly Connecticut River Valley, ca. 1770-90, 18 3/4 x 19", 27 1/2" h. (refinished) **1,035**

Candlestand, Chippendale, mahogany, round dished top on a columnar pedestal w/a ring-turned ball at the bottom above the tripod base w/cabriole legs ending in pad feet on platforms, old finish, probably Pennsylvania, ca. 1760-80, 16" d., 29" h. (imperfections) **8,050**

Chippendale Candlestand

Candlestand, Chippendale, mahogany, square top w/serpentine edges tilting above a block raised on a baluster-turned pedestal over a tripod base w/cabriole legs ending in arris pad feet, incised "I. Young," old surface, Boston or coastal Essex County, Massachusetts, 1775-1800, imperfections, 21 3/4 x 22", 29 1/2" h. (ILLUS.) **2,185**

Classical Country Candlestand

Candlestand, Classical country-style, tiger stripe maple, a rectangular top w/canted corners on a baluster-, urn- and ring-turned pedestal on a tripod base w/flat outswept S-scroll legs, old finish, New England, ca. 1825, 16 3/4 x 21 3/4", 28 1/2" h. (ILLUS.) **1,390**

Candlestand, country-style, cherry & maple, a rounded top on a ringed columnar-turned pedestal on a tripod base w/three tapering flat canted legs ending in button feet, remnants of old dark green paint, southeastern New England, late 18th c., 12" d., 25" h. (imperfections) **1,035**

Candlestand, country-style, painted cherry, a round small top mounted on a rectangular post & triangular chamfered platform & three short splayed turned feet, old bluish grey paint over earlier red wash, probably New England, late 18th - early 19th c., 12 1/4" d., 24 3/4" h. (imperfections) 1,150

Candlestand, country-style, painted wood, a round top on a baluster- and ring-turned pedestal on a tapering cross-form base, original red paint, possibly Connecticut River Valley, late 18th c., 16 3/4" d., 23 1/2" h. (minor imperfections) 3,738

Federal Cherry Candlestand

Candlestand, Federal, cherry, the square top w/ovolo corners on a vase- and ring-turned pedestal on a tripod base w/cabriole legs ending in pad feet w/platforms, probably Connecticut, ca. 1790, minor imperfections, 16 1/2" sq., 28" h. (ILLUS.) 1,495

Federal Country-style Candlestand

Candlestand, Federal country-style, birch, the square top above a slender slightly flaring standard on an urn-form support on a tripod base w/spider legs, top stained, slightly warped, northern New England, ca. 1800, 14 1/2 x 15 1/4", 28 1/4" h. (ILLUS.) 1,150

Candlestand, Federal country-style, cherry, rectangular one-board top w/applied gallery edge on a ring- and baluster-turned birch pedestal on a tripod base w/flattened cabriole legs, good old finish, early 19th c., 16 3/8 x 19 1/8", 25 1/4" h. (repair at base of pedestal, top reattached)... 770

Federal Country-style Candlestand

Candlestand, Federal country-style, cherry, the round fixed top raised on a vase-turned pedestal on a tripod base w/spider legs, old refinish, ca. 1820, 14" d., 31" h. (ILLUS.)... 350

Candlestand, Federal country-style, cherry & tiger stripe maple, a square top w/ovolo corners raised on a vase- and ring-turned pedestal on a tripod base w/spider legs, old refinish, labeled "Jeremiah Gooden Cabinetmaker Milford," New Hampshire, ca. 1800, 16 1/4" w., 28 1/4" h. 4,600

Candlestand, Federal country-style, mahogany & curly maple, the oblong top w/notched corners in mahogany & tilting above a ring- and baluster-turned curly maple column raised on a tripod base w/three outswept mahogany legs on small ball feet, refinished, attributed to New York, early 19th c., 17 x 23", 26" h. 715

Candlestand, Federal country-style, painted birch, rectangular top w/deeply chamfered corners tilting above a baluster- and ring-turned pedestal on the tripod base w/spider legs, painted red, Massachusetts, ca. 1810, 16 x 23", 30" h. 4,025

Candlestand, Federal country-style, painted hardwood, a rectangular one-board top w/cut corners tilting above a tapering rod-turned pedestal on a tripod base w/spider legs, old black paint, early 19th c., 14 x 19", 29 1/2" h. (old nailed repair at base of pedestal, top slightly warped) 715

Candlestand, Federal country-style, painted hardwood, one-board rectangular top w/chamfered corners above an urn-form turned pedestal on a tripod base w/cabriole legs ending in snake feet, old black repaint w/yellow striping, earlier red shows through, late 18th - early 19th c., 15 3/4 x 22", 26 1/2" h. (age cracks in top)... 1,320

Candlestand, Federal country-style, rectangular top w/notched & rounded corners above a boldly turned pedestal w/heavy ring-turnings above & below a central baluster-turned section, on a tripod base w/spider legs, old mellow finish, 16 1/4 x 19 1/2", 27 1/2" h. (one leg w/glued repair at pedestal) 935

Candlestand, Federal, inlaid & carved mahogany, the molded octagonal top

w/geometric stringing & banded edges
tilting above a fluted & leaf-carved urn-
turned pedestal on a tripod base w/mold-
ed spider legs ending in spade feet, Massachusetts, 1800-15, 18 3/4 x 26 1/2",
30" h. (feet replaced)..................................... **1,725**

Fine Federal Candlestand

Candlestand, Federal, inlaid cherry, the
long octagonal cockbeaded top w/a central oval inlaid in mahogany veneer panel
framed by stringing & set in bird's-eye
maple w/crossbanded mahogany border,
on a slender vase- and ring-turned post
on a tripod base w/widely canted simple
cabriole legs w/pad feet, refinished, minor imperfections, possibly New
Hampshire, ca. 1810-20, 13 x 18 1/8",
28" h. (ILLUS.)... **1,955**

Federal Mahogany Candlestand

Candlestand, Federal, mahogany, the wide
serpentine top w/pointed squared corners tilting above a baluster- and ring-
turned pedestal on a tripod base w/cabri-
ole legs ending in pad feet on platforms,
probably Massachusetts, ca. 1800, refinished, minor imperfections, 19 1/2" sq.,
25 1/2" h. (ILLUS.)... **2,300**

Queen Anne Candlestand

Candlestand, Queen Anne, cherry, the
round top on a baluster- and ring-turned
standard on a tripod base w/flattened cabriole legs ending in arris pad feet on
platforms, old refinish, possibly Vermont,
18th c., 15 1/4" d., 25 3/4" h. (ILLUS.)....... **1,035**
Candlestand, Queen Anne, mahogany, the
square top w/scalloped sides & rounded
corners above a ring- and urn-turned
pedestal on a tripod base w/cabriole legs
ending in padded snake feet, Salem,
Massachusetts, 1750-80,
14 1/2 x 15 1/4", 26 3/4" h. **5,750**
Candlestand, Queen Anne, maple, round
molded top on a ring- and vase-turned
pedestal on a tripod base w/cabriole legs
ending in snake feet, old refinish, probably New England, ca. 1740-60, 14" d.,
27 1/2" h.. **1,725**

Early Turned Candlestand

Candlestand, turned wood, the baluster-
turned cross bar supporting two removable candle sockets, raised on a threaded & baluster-turned standard continuing
to an X-form base ending in turned feet,
probably New England, early 18th c.,
28 3/4" h. (ILLUS.).. **2,070**
Candlestand, Wallace Nutting-signed
Windsor-style, Model No. 17 .... **495**

Early Windsor Candlestand

Candlestand, Windsor, a central candle-arm w/a socket at each end adjusting on a screw-turned central post above a round dished platform on a simple turned post on a small thick disk on three tall canted turned legs, old dark finish, candle cups later, New Hampshire, late 18th c., 13" d., 36" h. (ILLUS.)............................. **1,840**

Federal Mahogany Canterbury

Canterbury (music stand), Federal style, mahogany, the curved crestrails form three slots divided by flat column-like inner supports & ring- and baluster-turned corner supports above an apron w/a long cock-beaded drawer w/original turned wood pulls, raised on ring-, rod- & knob turned legs on brass casters, old refinish, minor imperfections, probably Boston, 1815-25, 12 1/2 x 18 1/8", 20 1/8" h. (ILLUS.)............. **4,600**

Crock stand, painted, a three-tiered half-round form w/wide stepped back & a single front brace supporting the rounded shelves, square nail construction, old mustard yellow paint, found in Pennsylvania, 19th c., 25 1/2 x 49 1/2", 36" h. (wear, age splits) **660**

Crock stand, painted hardwood, graduated right angle board shelves forming seven tiers on three notched board supports, old worn dark red paint, 19th c., 57" w., 41" h.. **523**

Crock stand, painted pine, four rectangular tiers, the three upper tiers w/open fronts & backed by an angled frame board, the bottom tier w/a deep apron & raised on heavy square chamfered legs on porcelain casters, old worn green paint, 24 x 48", 35 1/4" h.. **578**

Crock stand, painted poplar, rectangular narrow top shelf above narrow flat canted front legs w/notched brackets supporting two open lower shelves, slender knob- and rod-turned canted rear legs, worn red paint, 32 x 41", 49 1/2" h. **1,210**

Display stand, Arts & Crafts style, oak, a rectangular top raised on four square upright stiles above a narrow arched apron, a medial shelf above a lower case w/a pair of small drawers over two deep drawers all w/rectangular hammered copper pulls, Limbert paper label, Model No. 260, original finish, 15 1/2 x 17", 36" h. (minor buckling to veneer on sides) **3,190**

Rare Mission Oak Drink Stand

Drink stand, Mission-style (Arts & Crafts movement), oak, a round copper-clad top overhanging a conforming apron on four heavy square canted legs joined by wide cross stretchers, L. & J.G. Stickley (ILLUS.) **17,680**

Drink stand, Mission-style (Arts & Crafts movement), oak, a round top above cross braces on four tall square legs joined by lower cross stretchers & a small round shelf, new finish on top, original finish on the base, "Handcraft" label of L. & J.G. Stickley, 18" d., 29" h. **990**

Onyx & Brass Victorian Fern Stand

Fern stand, late Victorian, brass & onyx, an onyx diamond-form top shelf set in a pierced brass frame raised on four spiral-twist supports w/onyx disk finials above a matching lower onyx shelf raised on slender outswept tapering legs w/scroll tips on flat disks, original finish, ca. 1890, 16 x 20", 32" h. (ILLUS.) **450**

Decorative Victorian Fern Stand

Fern stand, Victorian Renaissance Revival substyle, carved walnut, a small rounded molded top w/a marble insert supported on three slender ring- and baluster-turned supports centered by a round shelf w/a carved full-figure standing stag, a central post connecting the supports & raised on a tripod base w/leaf-carved cabriole legs ending in scroll feet, brass chain swags w/four drops around the top, old varnish finish, ca. 1875, two brass drops missing, one support w/damage, 36" h. (ILLUS.) **1,045**

Federal-Style Fern Stands

Fern stands, Federal-Style, mahogany-stained hardwood, an octagonal open top w/molded edges above the basket holder w/caned panel sides, raised on square blocks atop tall slender reeded tapering legs joined by an arched cross-stretcher w/center button finial, small button feet, worn original finish, early 20th c., 12" w., 34" h., pr. (ILLUS.) **750**

Figural Hall Stand with Putti

Hall stands, Renaissance-Style, decorated pine, each carved as two putti, one sitting on the shoulders of the other & holding onto a twist-turned flaring pedestal supporting the round top w/a deep scalloped & shell-carved apron, the lower putto climbing on a large seashell above a ringed round base w/projecting paw feet, faux grained to resemble mahogany, original finish, Europe, ca. 1860-70, 18" d., 38" h., pr. (ILLUS. of one) **6,200**

Arts & Crafts Magazine Stand

Magazine stand, Arts & Crafts style, oak, narrow upright form w/three vertical slots under a back containing five small square cut-outs w/arched & cut-out sides, recent finish, unsigned Lakeside Craftshop, early 20th c., 10 x 14", 38" h. (ILLUS.) **1,210**
Magazine stand, bentwood, the two upright sides composed of three entwined bentwood flaring loops joined by curved bentwood panel forming sides & bottom, small ball feet, attributed to Koloman Moser, made by J. & J. Kohn, Vienna, Austria, early 20th c., 18 x 18", 16 1/2" h. .. **2,185**
Magazine stand, Mission-style (Arts & Crafts movement), oak, a rectangular top w/three-quarters low gallery above slatted sides & back enclosing two lower

shelves, square stile legs, original finish, unmarked Stickley Brothers, early 20th c., 12 1/4 x 16", 31 1/2" h. **880**

Magazine stand, Mission-style (Arts & Crafts movement), oak, a thin square top overhanging a front & back apron above four open rectangular shelves flanked by slender square legs & applied double slats on each side, keyed through-tenons on bottom shelf, tops of shelves refinished, Lifetime Furniture Co., Model No. 6002, 16 1/2" sq., 33" h. **825**

Gustav Stickley Magazine Stand

Magazine stand, Mission-style (Arts & Crafts movement), oak, a square top above paneled solid sides w/cut-out feet flanking three deep open shelves w/a narrow apron at the bottom, flush tenon construction, good recent finish, retailer's tag, box mark of Gustav Stickley, Model No. 547, 15" sq., 36" h. (ILLUS.) **4,675**

Magazine stand, Mission-style (Arts & Crafts movement), oak, rectangular tapering sides w/cut-out half-spheres at the base, four graduated open shelves, original dark finish, five missing screw plugs, branded Charles Limbert Furniture Co. mark, 14 x 20 1/4", 36 3/4" h. **880**

Magazine stand, Mission-style (Arts & Crafts movement), oak, tapered side panels w/cut-outs at top & bottom & set w/four shelves w/through-tenon construction, early 20th o., 12 x 15 7/8", 40" h. **748**

Magazine stand, Mission-style (Arts & Crafts movement), oak, four open shelves above a narrow arched toe board between four square stiles & crestrails over three vertical slats on each side, refinished, minor repair to top, unsigned L. & J.G. Stickley, Model No. 46, 13 x 21", 42" h. **1,320**

Magazine stand, Mission-style (Arts & Crafts movement), oak, rectangular top overhanging a narrow arched apron above three open shelves w/closed sides over the open stile legs joined by base stretchers, original medium brown finish, original Gustav Stickley paper label, Model No. 72, 13 x 21 1/2", 42" h. (minor top stain) **2,875**

Mission-style Magazine Stand

Magazine stand, Mission-style (Arts & Crafts movement), oak, a gently arched crest above four open shelves supported by curved side supports & front stiles, short stile legs, curved aprons, recent finish, unsigned L. & J.G. Stickley, Model No. 45, 12 x 21", 45" h. (ILLUS.) **1,980**

Fine Mahogany Music Stand

Music stand, Federal, mahogany, the square top w/molded edge tilting open on a support bar & shaped rachet mechanism over a single drawer, tall slender square supports enclosing the four open lower shelves each w/a low three-quarters gallery, on casters, appears to retain original brasses, old refinish, England or America, 1800-10, repairs, imperfections, 16 x 17 3/4", 45 1/2" h. (ILLUS.) **2,875**

Night stands, Danish Modern, walnut & cherry, a rectangular top w/concave front above a conforming case w/two drawers within a framework raised on four outset ovoid tapering legs w/incurved rails between the drawers, retailer's metal tag, Scandinavia, ca. 1960, 17 1/2 x 26 1/2", 23" h., pr. **575**

Classical Mahogany Nightstand

Nightstand, Classical, carved mahogany & mahogany veneer, the rectangular top w/gadrooned edges above a single long curved-front drawer w/pressed glass pulls flanked by leaf-carved panels & above a gadrooned apron band, raised on ring- and knob-turned leaf-carved supports over a medial shelf w/shaped front, on carved blocks over short turned legs w/knob feet, probably Philadelphia, ca. 1825, minor imperfections, refinished, 17 x 25", 29" h. (ILLUS.) **978**

Nightstand, Mission-style (Arts & Crafts movement), oak, a square top w/inset stile legs enclosing a case w/a pair of small drawers over two longer drawers all w/square wood knobs, a lower medial shelf, new finish, unmarked, early 20th c., 18" sq., 28 1/2" h. **1,210**

Nightstand, Mission-style (Arts & Crafts movement), oak, rectangular top above two narrow drawers w/ring pulls, on square slender legs, red decal mark & paper label of Gustav Stickley, 17 3/4 x 20", 30 1/2" h. **3,450**

Renaissance Revival Nightstand

Nightstand, Victorian Renaissance Revival substyle, a rectangular white marble top w/molded edges above a case w/rounded corners w/a small drawer w/a raised oval band & carved leaf & nut pull over a mid-molding & a paneled door w/a raised arched band centered by a carved leaf sprig & a turned wood pull, molded base on thin bun feet on casters, refinished, ca. 1865-70, 16 x 18", 30" h. (ILLUS.) **800**

Renaissance Revival Nightstand

Nightstand, Victorian Renaissance Revival substyle, walnut & burl walnut, the rectangular white marble top w/molded edges above a case w/rounded front corners flanking a single drawer w/burl panels flanking a roundel w/wooden knob, a medial molding above the conforming lower case w/a paneled door centered by a raised burl panel w/a carved floral cluster & wooden knob, deep molded base on rounded thin block feet, refinished, ca. 1875, 16 x 18", 30" h. (ILLUS.) **900**

Fine French Art Nouveau Nightstand

Nightstands, Art Nouveau, carved mahogany & rosewood, an arched & paneled crestboard w/pierced loops & floral-carved crest above the brown marble-inset top above a small drawer raised on molded & forked open brackets continuing to the slender square molded front supports joined by a medial shelf, solid back panels above the base shelf on a scroll-carved apron on short curved feet, possibly by Louis Majorelle, France, one w/a lower door, ca. 1900, 11 1/2 x 15", 41" h., pr. (ILLUS. of one) **8,050**

Nightstands, Louis XV-Style, inlaid mahogany, the rectangular top w/a serpentine front & low carved gallery above a deep case w/two drawers w/small ring pulls & veneered in a continuous design form a central oval w/flowers within a larger shield-form inlaid panel, side stiles w/carved flowers & ribbon-tied reeds

Louis XV-Style Inlaid Nightstands

above the simple cabriole legs w/scroll feet flanking the deep serpentine apron, original finish, early 20th c., 15 x 20", 28" h., pr. (ILLUS.).. **900**

Modern Style Nightstand

Nightstands, Modern style, enamel-mounted limed oak, a flat rectangular top above a case w/two deep blocked drawers mounted w/green enameled pulls, raised on short round tapering feet, labeled "Karpen - Guaranteed - Furniture," ca. 1950, finish distressed, 18 x 21", 23 1/2" h., pr. (ILLUS. of one)........................ **805**

European Renaissance-Style Stands

Nightstands, Renaissance-Style, walnut, the superstructure w/a small scroll-carved crest flanked by turned finial on the narrow flared cornice above a narrow scroll-carved panel above a large square panel centered by a small shaped shelf & bracket flanked by slender colonettes at the sides, resting on a rectangular black marble top above a single paneled & scroll-

carved drawer over a tall paneled & scroll-carved door flanked by slender turned colonettes, molded & blocked base on bun feet, original finish, Europe, last quarter 19th c., 16 x 20", 46" h., pair (ILLUS.)......... **1,800**

Victorian Neoclassical Stands

Pedestal stands, Victorian Neoclassical style, giltwood, round marble-inset top w/a molded edge above a beaded apron supported on four slender incurved legs topped w/ scroll medallions joined by open swags surrounding a central reeded post, the legs joined by a medial ring stretcher & ending in hoof feet, on a round molded platform base, ca. 1870, 15" d., 42" h., pr. (ILLUS.)............................ **3,500**

Aesthetic Movement Picture Stand

Picture easel-stand, Victorian Aesthetic Movement, ebonized cherry, the tall back decorated w/a crestrail carved w/small scallops between a center palmette & upright carved corner ears over a pierced & carved square panel w/a wide carved arch over a pierce-carved urn of delicate flowers above a lower rail carved w/tiny spindles, all raised on three square uprights above a lower rail over a hinge-fronted folio compartment carved w/square panels carved w/geometric designs, ring-turned front legs & hinged slender rear support legs, the front legs joined by small turned & angled spindles joining a rectangular center drop panel carved w/large quatrefoils, original finish, ca. 1880, 24" w., 6' h. (ILLUS.)........ **2,600**

Late Victorian Picture Easel-stand

Picture easel-stand, Victorian Aesthetic Movement substyle, cherry, the arched crest carved w/a grotesque face above open quarter-round panels w/three turned spindles each, all atop slender reeded slightly tapering stiles & a center support stile, the lower narrow support shelf w/a scroll-cut border, a flat carved cross stretcher near the bottom, hinged rear support leg, refinished, ca. 1890, 22" w., 62" h. (ILLUS.) **375**

Gallé Inlaid Plant Stand

Plant stand, Art Nouveau, fruitwood marquetry, a small squared top w/molded serpentine edges above narrow arched apron on slender molded & outswept legs joined by a medial shelf on curved & scrolled molded brackets, foliate inlay on the top & shelf, signed by Gallé, France, ca. 1900 (ILLUS.) **2,300**

Art Nouveau Figural Plant Stand

Plant stand, Art Nouveau style, carved mahogany, a round top w/a carved & molded border raised on a figural pedestal carved as a standing Art Nouveau maiden w/her arms up supporting a flower bud on her head, her body entwined by a vine, on a quadripartite platform w/reeded feet, original finish, early 20th c., 12" d., 28" h. (ILLUS.) **650**

Well-carved Figural Stand

Plant stand, Baroque Revival-style, pine, a round top supported by a large carved figure of a bearded man (Atlas?) nude except for a swagged drapery, the body twisted w/arms up & out straining to support the top, standing on a rockwork base, original finish, Europe, late 19th c., 16" d., 34" h. (ILLUS.) **3,500**

Carved Oriental Plant Stand

Plant stand, carved hardwood, a round top w/egg-and-dart border above waisted cylindrical sides carved w/vertical bands & panels w/carved fruit above a pierce-carved rounded shoulder w/blossoms & scrolls tapering to four serpentine legs w/ornate carved band & stepped feet, joined by a small arched cross-stretcher, probably China, ca. 1900, 16" d., 36" h. (ILLUS.) **450**

Chinese Carved Teak Plant Stand

Plant stand, carved teak, the round top inset w/red soapstone above a rounded apron ornately pierce-carved w/flowering vines & continuing down to four carved cabriole legs joined near the bottom by a small cross-stretcher, old finish, China, late 19th to early 20th c., some damage, 36 1/4" h. (ILLUS.) **300**

Painted Country Plant Stand

Plant stand, country-style, painted wood, three graduated demi-lune shelves on baluster- and ring-turned supports joined by square rail, old green paint, on casters, probably New England, 19th c., 20 x 40", 39" h. (ILLUS.) **1,610**

Early 20th Century Plant Stand

Plant stand, early 20th century, mahogany, a rounded top raised on a short baluster-

turned support on a small round disk raised on a tall flaring turned central pedestal flanked by four long C-scroll brackets all on a cross-form base raised on flared block feet, refinished, first quarter 20th c., 15" d., 40" h. (ILLUS.) **450**

Fine Carved Figural Plant Stand

Plant stand, figural, carved mahogany, the round top w/a molded edge & tapering base resting atop the head of a scantily clad classical maiden w/one hand at the top of her head & the other at her side, standing on a domed lobe-carved base w/a round border, refinished, ca. 1900, 14" d., 36" h. (ILLUS.) **1,250**

Golden Oak Turned Plant Stand

Plant stand, Golden Oak, a bulbous baluster-turned pedestal supporting a stepped round top, on a round platform base raised on four paw-and-bun feet, refinished, ca. 1900, 14" d., 32" h. (ILLUS.) **550**

Plant stand, mahogany, a tapering open spiral-twist pedestal supporting a round top w/a rope twist border, raised on a small round platform w/rope twist border & three scroll feet, refinished, ca. 1900, 12" d., 34" h. (ILLUS. top next page) **700**

Plant stand, Victorian Aesthetic Movement substyle, mahogany, the square top w/a scroll-carved narrow apron, raised on a ring- and rod-turned pedestal w/carved bands of flowerheads, on a square platform w/narrow shaped apron raised on cast-metal paw feet, refinished, late 19th c., 14" w., 38" h. (ILLUS.).............................. **650**

Decorative Mahogany Plant Stand

Plant stand, Modern style, stained wood, of cruciform, composed of four rectangular section holders w/pierced slatted panels & metal liners, on four post legs, Austria, early 20th c., 10 1/4 x 31 3/4", 37 3/4" h....... **329**

Plant stand, painted pine, three graduated demi-lune tiers on turned supports over a base of turned posts on arched feet joined by turned stretchers, old green paint, New England, late 19th c., 18 1/2 x 37 3/4", 36" h. **748**

Ornate Victorian Plant Stand

Plant stand, Victorian, gilded brass & onyx, a square white onyx top set onto an ornately pierced flaring apron raised on ornately pierced & leaf-cast slender cabriole legs w/scroll feet all joined by a pierced brass lower medial shelf w/a turned onyx & brass finial, ca. 1890, 18" w., 30 1/2" h. (ILLUS.) **633**

Ornately-carved Chinese Plant Stand

Plant stand, pierce-carved teak or rosewood, the round marble-inset top w/a flat pierce-carved border above the deep floral-carved apron raised on ornately carved legs joined by a round medial shelf & ending in paw feet, original finish, China, late 19th c., 18" d., 30" h. (ILLUS.)..... **450**

Renaissance Marble-top Plant Stand

Plant stand, Victorian Renaissance Revival substyle, carved walnut, the round white marble top w/molded edge on a deep ringed apron raised on a slender columnar pedestal flanked by tall pierced S-scrolls continuing to the scrolled & outswept lower legs, refinished, ca. 1865, 13" d., 32" h. (ILLUS.)..................................... **650**

Plant stand, Victorian Renaissance Revival substyle, cherry, square top w/cut corners on the molded edges above crenulated apron edges & fanned leaf carving at each corner at the top of the molded &

Aesthetic Movement Plant Stand

incurved flat legs joining at a central post w/reeded pointed finial & a bottom ball drop, the lower legs curving outward & each carved along the top w/a long stylized fish, ca. 1880, refinished, 16 3/4" sq., 31 3/4" h. (top replaced).......................... **413**

Fine Renaissance Revival Plant Stand

Plant stand, Victorian Renaissance Revival substyle, figured walnut & maple, the hexagonal top w/molded edges above a deep conforming apron w/burl panels alternating w/incised bands all above a gently tapering paneled pedestal w/a rosette above a long light burl incised panel on the wider sides & resting on a conforming flared line-incised foot on a deep plinth base, refinished, ca. 1880, 14" w., 40" h. (ILLUS.)... **750**

Renaissance Revival Plant Stand

Plant stand, Victorian Renaissance Revival substyle, walnut, the round dished top inset w/marble above a molded apron w/carved rounded drops, raised on a ring-turned pedestal centering four square-carved uprights w/flame-form carved finials & carved tassels all above four arched legs ending in hoof feet, ca. 1870s, 15" d., 30" h. (ILLUS.)......................... **900**

Plant stand, wirework, composed of two stepped & rounded tiers w/scrolling decorated sides above scrolled skirt, on four supports & casters, painted black, late 19th c., 16 1/4 x 35", 32 1/2" h. (minor imperfections) **546**

Plant stand, Mission-style (Arts & Crafts movement), oak, a small square top raised on a heavy tapering pedestal on a square base raised on four faceted square low blocks, original finish, branded mark of the Stickley Brothers, 13" sq., 34" h. **1,100**

Plant stand, Mission-style (Arts & Crafts movement), oak, a square top overhanging a deep flaring apron w/rectangular caned panels & arched bottoms, shaped brackets at each corner under the top, slender square canted legs joined by a cross stretcher supporting a square medial shelf, Ebon Oak line, recent finish, branded signature of the Charles Limbert Furniture Co., 14" sq., 34" h. **2,310**

Plant stand, Mission-style (Arts & Crafts movement), oak, a square top raised on a square slightly tapering tall pedestal w/four corbel brackets, cross-form shoe feet, cleaned original reddish brown finish, minor top edge roughness, branded "The Work of..." mark of L. & J.G. Stickley, 13 1/4" sq., 42" h.................................... **2,860**

Federal Reading Stand & Canterbury

Reading stand w/canterbury, Federal, mahogany, the rectangular lattice stand above a baluster- and ring-turned post on a rectangular canterbury base w/pairs of slender turned spindles forming six slots, on casters, labeled "Blanchard and Parson No. 294 North Market Street, Albany," Albany, New York, early 19th c., 14 x 22 1/4", 47 1/2" h. (ILLUS.) **3,105**

Sewing stand, Federal, inlaid mahogany, the figured mahogany rectangular top w/four turret corners topped by turned disks above colonnettes flanking two graduated cockbeaded drawers raised on a heavy ring-turned pedestal on four scrolled & curving legs ending in brass paw feet on casters, North Shore, Massachusetts, early 19th c., 17 1/4 x 19 1/2", 30 1/2" h. (replaced pulls, sun fading, minor repair)... **1,610**

Sewing stand, Federal, mahogany, bird's-eye & tiger maple veneer, the rectangular bird's-eye veneered top outlined w/mahogany veneer & half-round molding above a case w/two bird's-eye maple veneered drawers w/diamond-shaped inlaid bone keyhole escutcheons, on slender ring- and swelled rod-turned tiger maple tapering legs ending in small ball feet, old refinish, Massachusetts, ca. 1790, 16 3/4 x 20 1/2", 30 1/4" h. (small round brass pulls replaced, minor imperfections).......................... **2,990**

Victorian Rococo Shaving Stand

Shaving stand, Victorian Rococo substyle, walnut, the rectangular top set w/a small oval-framed mirror w/scroll-carved crest swiveling between scroll- and leaf-carved uprights, the shallow case w/two narrow drawers w/line-incised decoration & small knobs & turned corner drops, raised on a slender reeded columnar pedestal on a tripod base w/flared serpentine legs set w/tiny urn finials, on small brass casters, ca. 1860, 16" w., 5' 8" h. (ILLUS.).. **1,650**

Mission Oak Smoker's Stand

Smoking stand, Mission-style (Arts & Crafts movement), oak, a rectangular top overhanging a case w/a small drawer above a tall paneled door, both w/hammered copper pulls, slightly arched aprons, short square stile feet, medium brown finish, red decal mark of L. & J. G. Stickley, Model No. 26, ca. 1907, wear, 15 x 20", 29 1/4" h. (ILLUS.) **4,888**

Smoking stand, Mission-style (Arts & Crafts movement), oak, nearly square top on an upright cabinet w/chamfered case construction, through-tenon corners, a single tall paneled door opening to an interior drawer over a divided storage area w/shelf, original dark finish, unmarked Gustav Stickley, 15 x 17", 27" h. (top & front refinished) **6,050**

Smoking stand, Mission-style (Arts & Crafts movement), oak, a rectangular top above a small drawer over a tall paneled door opening to short shelves, rounded wood knobs, added varnish to dark finish, one shelf missing, possibly by J.M. Young, 7 x 14 3/4", 29" h. **1,430**

Telephone stand, Louis XV Revival, walnut, the rectangular top w/serpentined molded edges centered by an upright compartment w/an arched scroll-carved crest over the molded arched cornice & a conforming door w/ornate leafy scroll carving centered by a cupid face, door opens to telephone compartment, the stand top above a conforming apron w/a single drawer carved w/a latticework design flanking a central scroll-carved cartouche, on tall slender cabriole legs w/leaf-carved knees & ending in scroll-and-peg feet, old finish ca. 1920s, overall 48 3/4" h. **550**

Telephone stand, Mission-style (Arts & Crafts movement), oak, a square top above a single drawer w/square copper knob over an open compartment above a single rectangular door w/square copper knob, paneled sides, new finish, unmarked, early 20th c., 17 1/2" sq., 36" h. .. **1,430**

Umbrella stand, Gothic-style, oak, rectangular grid top supported by four arched-top columnar legs w/recessed arch design, over rectangular base w/fitted metal tray, medium brown finish, 12 1/2 x 34", 29 1/2" h. (splitting) **518**

Umbrella stand, Mission-style (Arts & Crafts movement), oak, a slightly tapering cylindrical container w/slatted sides riveted to interior iron hoops, cleaned original finish, drip-pan missing, unsigned Gustav Stickley, Model No. 100, 12" d., 24" h. **1,760**

Classical Corner-style Washstand

Washstand, Classical country-style, corner-style, maple & bird's-eye maple veneer, a high rounded gallery over the quarter-round white marble top above a conforming deep apron w/a single drawer, on three slender ring- and baluster-turned supports to the lower section on four baluster-turned legs w/knob feet, old refinish, New England, ca. 1820s, imperfections, 19 x 27", 35 3/4" h. (ILLUS.) **1,380**

English Classical Washstand

Washstand, Classical country-style, painted & decorated, the high arched splashback w/lower scroll-cut sides over a rectangular top over an apron w/two drawers w/simple turned wood knobs, on ring-, knob- & rod-turned tapering legs w/peg feet, grain-painted to simulate mahogany except the top which simulates grey marble, minor imperfections, England, ca. 1830, 19 x 36", 40" h. (ILLUS.) **863**

Washstand, Classical country-style, painted & decorated, the shaped splashboard centering a gilt-stenciled eagle & shield design w/flanking quarter-round shelves above the pierced rectangular top on ring-turned tapering supports continuing to legs & joined by a medial shelf over a drawer decorated w/stenciled fruit, overall beige & burnt sienna painted surface, New England, ca. 1825, 16 x 19", 39" h. (imperfections) **374**

Tiger Stripe & Bird's-eye Maple Stand

Washstand, Classical country-style, tiger stripe & bird's-eye maple, the high scrolled backsplash & scrolled lower sides on the rectangular top over a single long drawer w/a simple turned wood knob raised on rod- and ring-turned supports to the rectangular medial shelf w/block corners on ring-turned short legs w/knob feet, refinished, imperfections, probably Pennsylvania, ca. 1825, 17 x 21 3/4", 29" h. (ILLUS.) **1,150**

Classical Marble-topped Washstand

Washstand, Classical, mahogany & mahogany veneer, a molded three-quarters gallery above the rectangular white marble top over a single long drawer w/large round brass pulls, raised on four simple columnar supports over a deep lower shelf w/incurved front, raised on knob-turned feet, refinished, Maryland, ca. 1825, imperfections, 21 1/4 x 29 5/8", 33 1/2" h. (ILLUS.) **1,495**

Massachusetts Classical Washstand

Washstand, Classical, mahogany & mahogany veneer, the top w/a high three-quarters gallery w/a raised scroll-cut center crest above the rectangular bow-fronted top w/a large bowl cut-out, the bowed apron flanked by two small square drawers, the incurved sides above a lower shelf over a single drawer w/replaced brass pulls, raised on spiral-turned legs w/knob feet, refinished, probably North Shore, Massachusetts, ca. 1825, minor imperfections, 14 1/2 x 20 1/2", 51 1/4" h. (ILLUS.)... **1,150**

Washstand, Classical, painted & decorated, the high scrolled splashboard above a pierced top w/bowfront & square corners on a conforming skirt of two flanking small square drawers, the scroll-cut lower sides joined by a medial shelf over a drawer above baluster- and ring-turned legs w/knob feet, light bluish green background paint w/apple green striped borders, the crest stenciled w/a compote of fruit flanked by long scrolling leaves, the upper & lower apron & drawers in black w/gilt cornucopia & Greek key designs, possibly Vermont, ca. 1825-35, 15 x 18 1/2", 37 1/4" h. **2,300**

Washstand, Classical, stenciled mahogany, the rectangular hinged top w/stenciled border & edges & mirrored underside opening to a basin interior above a conforming case fitted w/a short drawer w/stenciled surround over cupboard doors above a short drawer w/stenciled surround, all flanked by stenciled columns on stenciled ring-, baluster- and ball-turned feet, probably New York, ca. 1825-35, 21 x 36 1/4", 34" h. **2,070**

Fine Inlaid Federal Corner Washstand

Washstand, Federal, corner-style, inlaid mahogany, the quarter-round top w/a large round bowl cut-out & two small round cut-outs above a narrow banded inlay apron raised on three square supports to the medial shelf over an inlaid apron fitted w/three small drawers outlined w/stringing, on four square tapering legs w/banded inlay, old refinish, Charleston, South Carolina, 1790-1800, repairs, height loss, 15 x 21 1/2", 29 1/8" h. (ILLUS.)...................................... **2,990**

Washstand, Federal, carved mahogany veneer, a three-quarter shaped low splashboard on the rectangular top above a ve-

neered cabinet door flanked by ovolo top corners & carved columns of leaves & grapes on a punchwork ground continuing to slender ring-turned tapering legs ending in brass casters, paneled sides, narrow cockbeaded drawer below the door w/round pulls, North Shore Massachusetts, ca. 1815-25, 16 x 21 1/2", 35 5/8" h. (old replaced brasses, old refinish, minor imperfections)... **2,300**

Fine Portsmouth Area Washstand

Washstand, Federal, corner-style, inlaid mahogany, the pointed arch & shaped splashboard centered by a quarter-round shelf above a round-fronted top w/a pierced basin hole, the edge w/square string inlay, raised on three square supports continuing to an open shelf over a satinwood veneered apron centered by a small drawer, string inlay on the supports & the three outswept lower legs joined by three slender tapering stretchers centered by an inlaid patera, patterned inlay trim, old finish, minor imperfections, Portsmouth, New Hampshire area, ca. 1800, 16 1/2 x 23", 41" h. (ILLUS.)............ **5,750**

Washstand, Federal corner-style, mahogany, the arched, shelved superstructure above two tiers, one fitted w/a drawer, on square tapering supports w/French feet joined by a shaped undertier, 19th c., 16 x 24", 39 1/4" h. **1,035**

Federal Mahogany & Tiger Stripe Stand

Washstand, Federal, corner-style, mahogany & tiger stripe maple, the high pointed arch & serpentine-sided splashboard above a quarter-round top w/a round basin cut-out & scalloped shallow apron raised on three square supports to the medial shelf above a row of three small tiger stripe maple-veneered drawers over the three square tapering legs & a central turned & reeded front leg, Massachusetts, early 19th c., 23" w., 39" h. (ILLUS.) **1,840**

Washstand, Federal country-style, cherry, a high serpentine splashback on the rectangular top w/a serpentine front above a conforming apron w/a single long drawer w/replaced embossed round brass pulls, ring- and rod-turned columnar supports to the wide medial shelf w/a serpentine front raised on tapering ring- and rod-turned legs w/knob feet, refinished, first half 19th c., 18 7/8 x 34 3/4", 34 1/4" h. (splashback replaced, veneer on drawer painted) **330**

Washstand, Federal country-style, cherry, a high splashback w/down-curved galleried sides on the rectangular top, apron w/a single lower dovetailed drawer w/small original brass button pulls, on double-baluster turned supports to a medial shelf w/incurved front, raised on block- and double-baluster turned legs w/peg feet, refinished, 17 1/4 x 22 1/8", 32 1/2" h. (restorations) **523**

Washstand, Federal country-style, cherry, a high three-quarters gallery w/quarter-round corner shelves above the rectangular top w/a large central hole & two smaller rear holes raised on slender square tapering legs joined by a medial shelf above a narrow dovetailed drawer w/round brass knob, early 19th c., refinished, 17 3/4 x 19 1/2", overall 40 1/2" h. (pull replaced, age cracks & old repair in top, repair in shelf) **495**

Washstand, Federal country-style, cherry, rectangular top w/three-quarters dovetailed gallery over a single drawer in the apron, on turned legs joined by a medial shelf, Pennsylvania, ca. 1820-35, 15 x 28", 34" h. (replaced hardware) **1,760**

Rare Curly Maple Federal Washstand

Washstand, Federal country-style, curly maple, a high shaped backsplash flanked by stepped sides on the rectangular top w/a large central bowl cut-out, raised on ring- and baluster-turned supports above a medial shelf over a single drawer w/early pressed glass knob, on baluster- and ring-turned legs, refinished, early 19th c., 17 x 20", 33" h. (ILLUS.) **3,410**

Washstand, Federal country-style, painted & decorated, a high scroll-cut splashback & low & short scroll-cut gallery sides on the rectangular top w/a large center cut-out round hole raised on ring- and rod-turned supports to the medial shelf above a single drawer, ring- and baluster-turned legs w/knob feet, overall smoke decoration on a creamy white ground bordered w/green striping, early 19th c., 16 x 18 3/4", 28 1/2" h. (minor paint wear)... **770**

Washstand, Federal country-style, painted pine, a rectangular top overhanging a narrow apron raised on four tall simple turned supports to a medial shelf over a single drawer w/porcelain knob, block- and baluster-turned legs, old red paint over earlier mustard yellow, first half 19th c., 18 1/2 x 20", 31" h. (hairline in rear leg, chips in feet) **385**

Federal Country-style Washstand

Washstand, Federal country-style, pine, the square top w/a high three-quarters gallery w/shaped sides & a cut-out bowl hole in the center above a narrow apron raised on ring- and baluster-turned supports on blocks flanking a medial shelf raised on baluster- and ring-turned legs w/knob feet, refinished, first half 19th c., 18" sq., 38" h. (ILLUS.).................................... **450**

Washstand, Federal country-style, stained hardwood, a tall three-quarters splashback w/arched back panel & rolled sides above the rectangular top, raised on simple turned supports on a medial shelf over a single drawer, raised on ring- and

Federal Country-style Washstand

baluster-turned legs w/peg feet, stained, lightly cleaned old surface, New England, early 19th c., minor imperfections, 13 3/4 x 20 1/2", 35" h. (ILLUS.) **460**

Delicate Federal Washstand

Washstand, Federal, mahogany, a high three-quarters gallery w/small quarter-round corner shelves & shaped sides on the rectangular top w/a pierced hole over narrow serpentine aprons & slender supports above a medial shelf & drawer raised on slender tapering ring- and rod-turned legs w/peg feet, old brass pull, refinished, New England, ca. 1815-25, 16 x 20 1/2", 42" h. (ILLUS.) **2,070**

Washstand, Federal, mahogany, a tall shaped splashboard w/a narrow shelf above the rectangular top w/a round cut-out basin hole raised on ring-turned & reeded supports to a medial shelf over a shallow drawer w/wooden pulls raised on ring-turned & reeded tapering legs ending in knob feet, school of John & Thomas Seymour, Boston, early 19th c., 22" w., 41" h. **2,070**

Federal Rectangular Washstand

Washstand, Federal, mahogany, a tall three-quarters gallery w/sloping sides & a small quarter-round shelf in each corner above the rectangular top w/a central large pierced basin hole flanked by two small cup holes over a scalloped front apron, raised on four ring-turned posts on a medial shelf over a single long cock-beaded drawer w/a round brass knob all raised on slender ring-, knob- & baluster-turned tapering legs w/peg feet, old finish, replaced brass, minor imperfections, probably Massachusetts, ca. 1815, 14 1/2 x 20", 41 1/2" h. (ILLUS.) **690**

Washstand, Federal, mahogany & mahogany veneer, a high scroll-cut three-quarters gallery on the rectangular top w/a large round center cut-out framed by four small cut-outs, on columnar turned supports to the medial shelf above a narrow veneered drawer w/original round gilt-brass pulls w/rings, raised on ring-, rod- and knob-turned legs w/knob feet, early 19th c., 15 1/4 x 20", overall 37 1/2" h. (age cracks in top & shelf) **935**

Early Federal Corner Washstand

Washstand, Federal, mahogany & mahogany veneer, corner-style, the high arched & shaped splashboard centered by a small quarter-round shelf over the conforming top w/a cut-out round basin hole over the conforming case w/a pair of cockbeaded cupboard doors over a narrow central drawer w/oval brass flanked by two small cockbeaded panels, on square outward flaring legs joined by the loop-pierced stretchers centered by a molded round medallion, replaced brass, old finish, minor imperfections, probably Massachusetts, ca.   1810, 15 3/4 x 22 3/4", 40 3/4" h. (ILLUS.).............. **690**

Federal Corner-style Washstand

Washstand, Federal, mahogany & mahogany veneer, corner-style, the high scalloped splashback above a quarter-round top w/a large center bowl cut-out flanked by small cut-outs above a narrow scalloped apron, raised on slender square supports above a medial shelf over a curve-fronted drawer w/a scalloped apron, raised on three outswept legs joined by a flattened T-form stretcher, old refinish, ca. 1810, 16 x 22", 40" h. (ILLUS.)...................................... **450**

Federal Mahogany Washstand

Washstand, Federal, mahogany, the square top w/a round molded central opening surrounded by an applied scroll decorative design above the four square supports continuing to beaded edges & square tapering legs joined by a beaded medial shelf over a drawer & lower shaped cross-stretchers w/a central molded platform, old finish, imperfections, possibly Connecticut, ca. 1800, 15 3/4 x 16", 30 1/4" h. (ILLUS.) **690**

Federal "Tambour-front" Washstand

Washstand, Federal "tambour-front" style, mahogany, the top arched & reeded sides centering a retracting tambour top on paneled dies centering a drawer over a cupboard door on turned & reeded legs w/baluster-turned legs on casters, appears to retain original cast-brass hardware, losses to veneer, missing fitted interior, New York City, ca. 1810, 20" sq., 36 1/2" h. (ILLUS.)...................................... **1,495**

Washstand, Modern style, blue-painted wood, the rectangular superstructure w/graduated planes, a high rectangular backsplash w/clipped corners & ceramic tile insets decorated w/a royal blue Secessionist design, side drawer, towel rack & an open bay above a small cabinet door, together w/a matching ceramic water pitcher, wash bowl & cov. bucket, each w/matching Secessionist design, Austria, early 20th c., stand 24 1/8 x 26", 44" h., the set............................... **2,233**

Painted Victorian Cottage Washstand

Washstand, Victorian cottage-style, painted & decorated pine, the tall splashback w/beveled corners fitted w/two small shelves w/brackets above the rectangular top over a case w/a long drawer w/two narrow oblong brass pulls over a pair of cupboard doors on a molded base, original painted decoration of outlined panels & stylized florals w/brown & grey flowers, black striping, etc., wear, some edge damage, ca.   1880,   14 3/4 x 29 1/4", 35 1/2" h. (ILLUS.).. **248**

Washstand, Victorian country-style, curly maple, a rectangular top w/three-quarters gallery over a convex frieze drawer over a pair of paneled cupboard doors flanked by turned pilasters, raised on turned feet, mid-19th c., 18 1/2 x 29", 35" h. **805**

Decorated Victorian Washstand

Washstand, Victorian country-style, painted & decorated pine, a rectangular
hinged top w/molded edges opening to a
deep well above a small working drawer
beside a faux drawer over a heavy mid-
molding & a lower rectangular door, serpentine apron, grain-painted ground
w/painted panels simulating bird's-eye
maple & dark wood, fine finish, second
half 19th c., 18 x 29", 31" h. (ILLUS.)............ **303**

Washstand, Victorian country-style, painted & decorated poplar, a splashback w/a
high arched center above the rectangular
top overhanging a cabinet w/a single
drawer over a flat cupboard door w/origi-
nal cast-iron thumb latch w/porcelain
knob, overall old brown graining, mid-
19th c., 14 1/4 x 24", overall 36 1/2" h.
(drawer pull replaced w/thread spool).......... **605**

Washstand, Victorian Renaissance Revival
substyle, a high white marble backsplash
w/a high arched center above rounded
corners over two half-round shelves over
the rectangular marble top w/molded
edges, the walnut case w/a single long
paneled drawer w/two leaf- and fruit-
carved pulls above a pair of arch-topped
paneled doors w/carved central leaf- and
fruit-carved clusters, molded base on
short bracket feet, ca. 1870 .... **495**

Washstand, Victorian Renaissance Revival
substyle, walnut, a high double-arched
splashboard w/two half-round candle
shelves above the rectangular top over a
long drawer w/an incised long band & two
round wood pulls over a pair of paneled
cupboard doors each w/an incised rectangular panel, thin block feet, ca. 1870,
18 x 41", 30" h. **403**

Washstand, Victorian Renaissance Revival
substyle, walnut, a high rounded & scroll-
cut splashback above the rectangular top
w/rounded front corners above a case
w/a single long drawer w/raised oval
molding & two carved fruit & leaf pulls
over a pair of cupboard doors w/arched
panels, paneled sides, wide molded base
on casters, side pull-out narrow shelf on
top right side, 17 x 31", overall 31 1/4" h. **523**

Washstand, Victorian Renaissance Revival
substyle, walnut, a serpentine molded
splashback connected to outswept end
towel bars flanking the rectangular top
w/molded edges above the case w/a pair of
small drawers w/oval molding & carved leaf

Victorian Walnut Washstand

pulls above two long matching drawers,
low arched & cut-out apron, on casters, ca.
1870, 18 x 35", 35" h. (ILLUS.)......................... **358**

Washstand, Victorian Renaissance Revival
substyle, walnut & burl walnut, a high
scroll-carved & molded backsplash on
the rectangular top w/molded edges &
rounded front corners over a case of
three long drawers w/burl walnut & raised
oval banding, leaf- & fruit-carved pulls,
pull-out towel bar on side, chamfered
front corners w/short knob-turned quarter
drops at the top, scalloped apron &
bracket feet, old worn finish, ca. 1870,
16 1/4 x 30 1/4", 29" h. plus crest (some
edge damage).. **248**

Washstand, Victorian Renaissance Revival
substyle, walnut & burl walnut, a tall white
marble backsplash w/a pointed crest &
rounded corners over two small half-
round shelves above the rectangular
white marble top w/molded edges, the
case w/a long upper drawer w/two
shaped rectangular raised burl panels
w/pear-shaped drops flanking a large
carved keyhole escutcheon & flanked by
chamfered corners w/raised burl panels,
a mid-molding over a pair of raised panel
cupboard doors flanked by beveled front
corners w/scrolled blocking, lower molding above the deep conforming flat apron
on   porcelain   casters, ca.   1875,
15 1/2 x 29 1/4", overall 41" h. (crack in
top & damage to one shelf)............................. **550**

Victorian Marble Top Washstand

Washstand, Victorian Renaissance Revival substyle, walnut & burl walnut, the white marble top w/a high arched backsplash w/two small shelves above the rectangular top over a case w/a deep long drawer w/geometric raised burl panels & hinged metal pulls projecting above two matching long lower drawers, molded side stiles, base molding over flat apron flanked by blocked feet, some missing pulls, small edge chips on marble, ca. 1880, 17 1/2 x 31 5/8", overall 38 3/4" h. (ILLUS.).. **495**

Signed Victorian Walnut Washstand

Washstand, Victorian Renaissance Revival substyle, walnut & burl walnut, the rectangular white marble top w/a serpentine splashback & molded edges, on a case w/a single drawer w/raised burl panels & T-form drop pulls flanked by ring-turned quarter-round corners above blocked & carved edges flanking the single door w/an arched central panel w/a raised fruit-carved central reserve & shaped burl panels at the top corners, deep molded base w/rounded corners, stenciled label in drawer for Mitchell & Rammelsberg Co., Cincinnati, Ohio, refinished, ca. 1875, 16 x 20", 36" h. (ILLUS.).................... **1,900**

Fine Victorian Mahogany Washstand

Washstand, Victorian Rococo substyle, mahogany & mahogany veneer, the rectangular white marble top w/a serpentine front & a three-quarters marble splashback w/small corner shelves above a conforming case w/a single long drawer w/carved acanthus leaf lock plate & corner brackets above a pair of paneled cupboard doors w/scroll-carved corner brackets above the scroll-carved apron w/simple bracket feet on casters, attributed to Prudent Mallard, New Orleans, Louisiana, mid-19th c., 18 x 40", 36" h. (ILLUS.).. **1,344**

Weaver's stand, painted pine, the octagonal top on turned supports & chamfered T-form tripod base, overall old red paint, New England, early 19th c., 14 1/4 x 14 1/2", 23" h. (restored).................. **920**

Classical Tiger Stripe Maple Stand

Classical country-style one-drawer stand, tiger stripe maple, a square top overhanging an apron w/a single drawer raised on ring- and baluster-turned legs ending in knob feet, old refinish, New England, ca. 1830, imperfections, 19 x 20", 29" h. (ILLUS.) **2,070**

Classical Country Two-drawer Stand

Classical country-style two-drawer stand, bird's-eye maple, tiger stripe maple & cherry, the nearly square thick top slightly overhanging the deep apron w/two drawers each w/two large turned wood pulls, raised on baluster-, rod- and ring-turned legs ending in knob feet, old refinish, imperfections, possibly Pennsylvania, ca. 1825, 19 x 21 1/2", 29" h. (ILLUS.) **1,610**

Classical country-style two-drawer stand, cherry & curly maple, a rectangular top above a deep case w/a curved-front drawer over a flat drawer each w/a replaced curly maple knob, raised on baluster-, ring and knob-turned legs w/peg feet, ca. 1850, 17 3/4 x 20 1/2", 29 1/2" h. (wafers added to bottom of feet, age cracks in top) **605**

Classical two-drawer stand, curly maple, a rectangular two-board drop above a deep apron w/two round-fronted drawers each w/two small turned wood knobs, raised on heavy rope-twist-turned legs w/ring-turned top & bottom segments & baluster-turned feet, refinished, ca. 1840, 18 1/4 x 23", 28 1/2" h. (top replaced) **825**

Federal country-style one-drawer stand, cherry, a rectangular one-board top over an apron w/a single drawer w/turned wood knob, raised on slender ring- and rod-turned tapering legs ending in baluster- and knob-turned feet, first half 19th c., 20 1/2 x 22 1/2" h. (top reattached & w/plugged holes) **523**

Federal country-style one-drawer stand, cherry, a rectangular one-board top slightly overhanging an apron w/a single drawer w/a turned wood knob, raised on ring-, ball- and tapering rod-turned legs ending in ball feet, good old finish, early 19th c., 17 1/2 x 19 3/4", 28" h. **440**

Federal country-style one-drawer stand, cherry & curly maple, one-board square top above a cherry frame w/a single curly maple dovetailed drawer w/turned wooden pull, ring- and baluster-turned legs w/a long octagonal central section, knob feet, original finish w/varnish overcoat, early 19th c., 19 1/2" w., 28 1/2" h. **468**

Federal country-style one-drawer stand, cherry & curly maple, the nearly square cherry top overhanging a cherry frame w/a single narrow curly maple drawer w/clear lacy glass knob, raised on very slender rod- and ring-turned legs w/tapering peg feet, early 19th c., 17 1/2 x 18", 29 1/8" h. (minor warp in top) **935**

Federal country-style one-drawer stand, cherry, pegged construction, rectangular one-board top slightly overhanging an apron w/a single dovetailed drawer w/replaced brass bail pull, refinished, early 19th c., 18 3/4 x 24 1/4" **715**

Federal country-style one-drawer stand, cherry, rectangular top overhanging an apron w/a single drawer w/two small turned wood knobs, square tapering legs, old finish, early 19th c., 17 1/4 x 20 1/2", 29" h. (top reworked) **550**

Federal country-style one-drawer stand, cherry, square top w/ovolo corners overhanging an apron w/a single dovetailed drawer w/replaced brass knob, slender square tapering legs, old refinishing, early 19th c., 17 1/2 x 17 3/4", 27" h. **1,073**

Federal country-style one-drawer stand, child's, tiger stripe maple, square top overhangs an apron w/a single drawer, raised on ring- and baluster-turned tapering legs w/knob feet, early surface, New Hampshire, early 19th c.,

14 3/4 x 16 3/4", 19 1/4" h. (replaced drawer pull, minor imperfections) **4,888**

Federal country-style one-drawer stand, curly maple, a rectangular one-board top above an apron w/a single drawer w/an opalescent lacy glass pull, slender ring-, knob and baluster-turned legs w/peg feet, refinished, good wood figure, first half 19th c., 18 1/2 x 21", 30" h. (few chips) **2,090**

Federal country-style one-drawer stand, hardwood, a square top w/ovolo corners widely overhanging an apron w/a single drawer, mortised & pinned apron on tall slender square tapering legs, old dark worn finish, early 19th c., 18 x 18 1/2", 26" h. (top reattached) **1,100**

Federal Country One-Drawer Stand

Federal country-style one-drawer stand, maple & tiger stripe maple, rectangular top overhanging an apron w/a single drawer w/a porcelain pull, on slender ring-, knob- and baluster-turned legs w/knob feet, old refinish, first half 19th c., 18 x 22", 30" h. (ILLUS.) **400**

Federal country-style one-drawer stand, painted & decorated cherry, a rectangular two-board top widely overhanging a deep apron w/a single drawer w/a porcelain knob, on slender knob- and rod-turned legs w/knob feet, original brown sponged vinegar graining w/gold striping & old brown overvarnish, two decal designs on the drawer, Pennsylvania, first half 19th c., 22 x 23 1/2", 30" h. **2,200**

Federal country-style one-drawer stand, painted & decorated cherry & poplar, the nearly square top overhanging an apron w/a single drawer, raised on slightly tapering turned legs w/ring-turned segments at the top & knobbed ankles on the peg feet, later yellow paint w/orangish red striped graining, first half 19th c., 22 1/4 x 22 1/2", 31 1/4" h. (wear, pull & drawer lock missing) **1,100**

Federal country-style one-drawer stand, painted & decorated poplar, a rectangular top overhanging an apron w/a single drawer raised on tapering ring- and knob-turned legs w/peg feet, original red graining w/yellow striping & gold stenciled detail around porcelain knob, drawer bottom w/inscription "Barbara Kaufman Yoder, married to Daniel Yoder," attributed to J. Stahl, Soap Hollow, Pennsylvania, mid-19th c., 20 3/4 x 22", 29 1/2" h. (filled age crack in top, some wear)............ **4,070**

Federal country-style one-drawer stand, painted pine & maple, nearly square top w/ovolu corners above a deep slightly canted apron w/a single conforming drawer, on splayed tapering square legs, yellow paint & scrubbed top, Pennsylvania, early 19th c., 18 1/4 x 20", 28" h. (missing drawer pull, repainted) **690**

Painted Federal One-drawer Stand

Federal country-style one-drawer stand, painted poplar & pine, a square top overhanging a deep apron w/a single drawer raised on ring-, knob- and rod-turned slightly canted legs w/ball feet, painted red & black, Pennsylvania, ca. 1830, 21 1/2" sq., 28 1/2" h. (ILLUS.)................... **1,955**

Federal country-style two-drawer stand, birch & bird's-eye maple veneer, rectangular thin top above a deep apron w/two dovetailed drawers w/veneer & mahogany banded inlay & diamond-shaped escutcheon inlays, on ring- and baluster-turned slender figured wood legs w/tall peg feet, early 19th c., 15 1/4 x 20", 28" h. (slight warp at back of top, chips on banded inlay).. **1,210**

Federal country-style two-drawer stand, cherry & bird's-eye maple, the rectangular top above a deep case w/two graduated drawers w/bird's-eye maple fronts, on spiraled leaf-carved round legs on baluster-form feet on casters, clear lacy glass pulls on one drawer, pressed ribbed knobs on others, refinished, first half 19th c., 17 5/8 x 22", 28" h.................................. **1,100**

Federal country-style two-drawer stand, curly maple, square top overhanging an apron w/two narrow drawers w/pairs of small round brass replaced pulls, on ring- and rod-turned slender legs w/knob-and-peg feet, old mellow refinishing, early 19th c., 18 3/4" sq., 29" h. (top reattached, some plugged holes, one drawer bottom partially replaced) **1,183**

Federal country-style two-drawer stand, walnut, a rectangular top flanked by two wide hinged drop leaves over the deep case w/two drawers w/Rockingham-glazed pottery knobs, raised on simple

sausage-turned legs, old soft finish, mid-19th c., 18 x 24" plus 11 3/4" w. leaves, 28 3/4" h.. **330**

Federal one-drawer stand, cherry, a rectangular two-board top above a narrow apron w/one dovetailed drawer w/old round brass pull, on tall slender tapering square legs, old varnish finish, early 19th c., 16 3/4 x 19 1/4", 27" h. **770**

Federal one-drawer stand, cherry, rectangular top over a single drawer & straight apron on vase- and ring-turned legs ending in ball feet, brass pulls appear to be original, old refinish, southern New England, ca. 1825, 16 1/2 x 21 1/2", 28" h. **578**

Federal Grain-Painted Stand

Federal one-drawer stand, country-style, painted & decorated pine, the nearly square top w/shaped corners overhanging an apron w/a single drawer w/a small turned knob, raised on tall square tapering legs, grain-painted in old burnt sienna & ochre, heavy graining wear to top, replaced pull, New England, early 19th c., 18 x 18 1/2", 27" h. (ILLUS.)...................... **1,725**

Pine & Butternut Country Stand

Federal one-drawer stand, country-style, pine & butternut, rectangular two-board pine top above an apron w/a single drawer, on turned & tapering legs w/bulbous ankles & tall peg feet, imperfections, early 19th c., 19 x 20 1/2", 30" h. (ILLUS.).......... **805**

Federal one-drawer stand, fruitwood, square top w/inset ovolo corners above a conforming apron w/a long drawer, on turned & reeded tapering legs w/ball feet, 19th c., 18 1/4" sq., 27" h. **1,035**

Federal Inlaid-Cherry Stand

Federal one-drawer stand, inlaid cherry, the nearly square top w/line inlay including a center diamond enclosing a pinwheel design & edge banding overhanging the apron w/a single line-inlaid drawer w/round brass pulls, line-inlaid apron & slender tall tapering square legs, crack repair under top, appears to retain original drawer pull, Connecticut, ca. 1800, 19 3/4 x 20 1/4", 28" h. (ILLUS.) **2,300**

Federal Mahogany One-drawer Stand

Federal one-drawer stand, mahogany, a square top overhanging an apron w/a single drawer above ring-turned & reeded legs ending in peg feet in brass casters, refinished, Massachusetts, ca. 1810-15, minor restoration, 19 x 19 1/4", 27 1/2" h. (ILLUS.) **1,840**

Federal one-drawer stand, mahogany & birch, a nearly square top in mahogany above a figured birch apron drawer raised on slender square tapering legs, old refinish, New England, ca. 1790-1800, 17 x 17 1/2", 27 3/4" h. (minor imperfections) **2,875**

Federal one-drawer stand, mahogany & cherry, a rectangular top w/serpentine edges & canted corners widely overhanging an apron w/a single narrow drawer w/a round brass pull, raised on tall slender square tapering legs, refinished, probably Massachusetts, ca. 1800, 15 x 20 1/4", 28 1/2" h. (minor imperfections) **2,070**

Federal one-drawer stand, mahogany, diminutive size w/an oval top above a small drawer w/turned pull, raised on slender square tapering legs, New England, early 19th c., 13 1/4 x 19 1/2", 27" h. **4,250**

Federal one-drawer stand, maple & birch, a nearly square top w/ovolo corners overhanging an apron w/a single drawer w/two brass knobs, raised on swelled ring- and rod-turned legs w/long peg feet, refinished, probably New Hampshire, ca. 1820, 18 1/2 x 20 1/2", 29 1/2" h. (replaced knobs)... **690**

Federal one-drawer stand, painted pine & ash, a nearly square top overhanging a thumb-molded apron w/a single drawer, raised on square chamfered tapering legs, old green paint, possibly New England, early 19th c., 18 3/4 x 19 1/2", 27 3/4" h.. **1,035**

Federal Tiger Stripe Maple Stand

Federal one-drawer stand, tiger stripe maple, square top w/ovolo corners overhanging the apron w/a single drawer w/a tiny replaced brass knob, on square tapering legs, old refinish, very minor imperfections, New England, ca. 1800-10, 19 1/2 x 19 3/4", 28" h. (ILLUS.) **4,313**

Federal two-drawer stand, cherry & mahogany veneer, rectangular top flanked by wide hinged drop leaves above a deep apron w/two paneled drawers w/mahogany veneering & beaded inner edges, raised on ring-, rod- and baluster-turned legs w/knob feet, old finish, 19 1/4 x 22" plus 9 1/4" leaves, 28 1/2" h. (replaced hinges)................. **468**

Federal two-drawer stand, cherry & mahogany veneer, square cherry top above a deep case w/a serpentine front w/two conforming dovetailed drawers w/applied beading & a large lacy glass pull, slender ring-, rod- and knob-turned legs w/knob & peg feet, old finish, early 19th c., 20 x 20 1/2", 28" h. (minor age cracks in top, top reattached, lock removed, one pull chipped)... **1,100**

Federal Country Two-Drawer Stand

Federal two-drawer stand, country-style, tiger stripe maple & mahogany veneer, rectangular top flanked by two wide drop leaves w/rounded corners over a deep apron w/two mahogany-veneered drawers w/simple turned wood knobs, raised on ring- and baluster-turned tapering legs w/knob feet, imperfections, New England, ca. 1825, 17 x 20", 28 1/2" h. (ILLUS.).. **2,990**

Federal two-drawer stand, mahogany & mahogany veneer, a nearly square one-board top flanked by D-form hinged drop leaves flanking the deep apron w/two narrow drawers w/crotch grain veneer & pairs of small round brass pulls, ropetwist-turned legs w/knob- and ring-turning at the top & ending in peg feet, mellow refinish, ca. 1830, 16 x 17" plus leaves, 29" h. (few hairline cracks in legs)..... **880**

Federal two-drawer stand, painted birch & bird's-eye maple, the rectangular top overhanging a deep apron w/two cock-beaded graduated drawers w/bird's-eye maple fronts, the borders stained to imitate inlay, on slender square tapering legs, simple bail pulls & oval keyhole escutcheon appear to be original, New England, ca. 1810, 13 1/2 x 17 1/8", 28 3/4" h. (minor imperfections) **2,990**

Federal two-drawer stand, pine, rectangular one-board top overhanging a case w/two drawers w/turned wood knobs, on tall slender square tapering legs, refinished w/good color, 19th c., 16 1/2 x 20",. 28 5/8" h. **330**

Federal-Style Two-Drawer Stand

Federal work stand, mahogany & mahogany veneer, rectangular top above two narrow cockbeaded graduated drawers w/simple turned wood knobs, straight cockbeaded skirt raised on long ring- and baluster-turned tapering legs w/ball feet, old refinish, New England, ca. 1820, 15 1/2 x 18", 28 1/4" h. (minor imperfections) **2,070**

Federal-Style two-drawer stand, mahogany, a rectangular top w/ovolo corners above ring-turned stiles flanking two narrow drawers w/small metal pulls, raised on slender tapering reeded legs ending in knob- and peg-feet, refinished, ca. 1920, 16 x 20", 30" h. (ILLUS. bottom previous column)... **500**

Gustav Stickley One-Drawer Stand

Mission-style (Arts & Crafts movement) one-drawer stand, oak, a square top above a single narrow drawer w/turned wood pulls raised on tall square legs joined by a medial shelf, branded mark of Gustav Stickley, ca. 1912, 16" sq., 28 1/2" h. (ILLUS.)..................................... **90,576**

Unusual Eastlake Magazine Stand

Magazine stand, Victorian Eastlake substyle, walnut, the top composed of three deeply scalloped upright panels forming deep storage slots, the outside faces ornately incised w/scrolling band w/ebonized trim & a center roundel, raised on a U-form support joining a central post w/urn finial raised on four flat S-scroll legs w/line-incised decoration & ebonized trim, original finish, ca. 1880s, 12 x 18", 28" h. (ILLUS.) **450**

Unique 1920s Figural Magazine Stand

Magazine stand, walnut, the ends carved as a standing bird w/the spread wings forming the ends of the two compartments & the curved neck & head flanking the high arched & scroll-carved central handle panel, the side panels pierced & carved w/scrolls & a central rim shell design, original finish, ca. 1920s, 14 x 18", 20" h. (ILLUS.) **400**

Stools

Art Deco Cone-shaped Stool

Art Deco stool, upholstered bird's-eye maple, the inverted cone-form upholstered seat on a round maple base, 1930s, 17" d., 23" h. (ILLUS.) **$300**

Fine French Art Deco Stool

Art Deco stool, upholstered mahogany, a deep round cushion top on an upholstered apron & round wood frame w/beaded edge & scroll-carved turned legs, Sue et Mare, France, ca. 1925, 27" d., 18 1/2" h. (ILLUS.) **6,325**

Frank Lloyd Wright Bank Stools

Bank teller stools, Modern style, oak, a rectangular top raised on four pairs of slender square supports joined by a narrow medial rail above the squared outswept lower legs w/square feet, one w/paper label "First National Bank of Dwight," designed by Frank Lloyd Wright for Frank L. Smith Bank, Dwight, Illinois, 1908, 12 14 x 18 1/2", 27 & 28" h., pr. (ILLUS.) **7,475**

Bentwood stool, round seat & stretcher joined by pairs of bentwood upright supports each centering a spherical element, the padded seat upholstered in pale green suede, design attributed to Josef Hoffmann, Austria, early 20th c., 14" d., 18 1/8" h. **999**

Classical Carved Footstool

Classical footstool, carved mahogany, the deep rectangular upholstered top above a deep cove-molded & bead-trimmed apron on a half-round band centered by a carved spread-winged eagle w/shield, leafy scroll-carved paw feet, ca. 1830, 24" l. (ILLUS.) **2,185**

Boston Classical Footstool

Classical footstool, carved mahogany, the rectangular overupholstered top on a curule base w/leaf carvings & C-scroll feet & central concentric circles & a ring-turned medial stretcher, old surface, imperfections, Boston, 1825-35, 15 1/2 x 22 1/2", 15" h. (ILLUS.) **1,265**

Classical footstool, mahogany & mahogany veneer, a rectangular deep upholstered concave top on a conforming frame & Grecian cross legs joined by a vase- and ring-turned cross stretcher, probably New York, ca. 1830-35, 14 1/2 x 19", 17" h. **748**

Fine Classical Footstool

Classical footstool, mahogany & mahogany veneer, the rectangular concave overupholstered top on a conforming veneered frame on forked scrolled supports & legs terminating in applied bosses & joined by a baluster- and ring-turned stretcher, old refinish, probably Boston, ca. 1835, 17 x 25", 16" h. (ILLUS.) **1,380**

Classical footstool, mahogany veneer, the high square rounded floral needlepoint top above a deep serpentine apron w/a scalloped & scroll-bordered apron on round bracket feet on casters, ca. 1840, 18 1/2" sq., 16" h. (some edge damage) **220**

Classical footstools, painted & decorated, pillar & scroll style w/pierced seatrails, grain-painted in raw & burnt umber, possibly New York or Pennsylvania, ca. 1830-40, 15 1/2" l., 6" h., pr. (imperfections) **230**

Classical piano stool, mahogany & mahogany veneer, the circular overupholstered top on a conforming veneered base bordered in brass beading on a baluster-turned shaft & three scrolled brass-inlaid legs, resting on brass ball feet, possibly Boston, ca. 1825, 11 1/2" d., 20 1/2" h. (imperfections) **633**

Country-style Stools with Round Tops

Federal footstools, mahogany, the upholstered rectangular seat on horizontally reeded rails joining swelled ring-turned legs on ball feet, old finish, possibly New York City, ca. 1815-25, 9 x 13", 8 1/2" h., pr. (minor imperfections) **920**

Federal Curly Maple Stool

Federal stool, curly maple, the oblong woven rush seat enclosed w/a wooden framework & raised on four ring-, knob- and rod-turned tapering canted legs joined by slender double stretchers separated by three spheres, early 19th c., 11 1/2 x 15", 16 1/4" h. (ILLUS.) **1,980**

Footstool, cherry, small rectangular top w/board edges angled at the ends, on scroll-cut board feet mortised through the top, old & probably original finish, 7 x 12 3/4", 7 1/4" h. **193**

Footstool, country-style, painted pine, rectangular board top once upholstered above long cut-out sides forming legs, old olive grey paint, 19th c., 7 x 17 1/2", 5" h. (wear, some damage) **220**

Footstool, country-style, painted pine, rectangular top over scallop-cut apron, on canted supports w/cut-out feet, worn original black & red graining, 6 x 14", 6" h. **330**

Footstool, country-style, walnut, a small rectangular board top on mortised bootjack legs, scrubbed top, lower original fin-

American Classical Mahogany Stool

Classical stool, upholstered mahogany, the gently bowed rectangular upholstered top on a deep conforming apron raised on two scrolled X-form supports trimmed w/roundels & joined by a turned stretcher, American, second quarter 19th c., 26" l. (ILLUS.) **1,495**

Country-style stool, burl wood, oval top on four turned legs w/double bands, old finish, late 19th c., 10 x 18", 6 3/4" h. (very minor imperfections) **288**

Country-style stool, poplar & hardwood, a round seat on four slender tapering ring-turned canted legs joined by plain double stretchers on each side, red stain, late 19th - early 20th c., 16" h. **193**

Country-style stools, stained wood, a round upholstered top raised on a canted apron raised on ring- and knob-turned reeded & canted legs, stained red, 19th c., pr. (ILLUS. top next column) **1,840**

ish, serpentine pierced in the top, 19th c.,
8 3/4 x 16", 6 5/8" h. **165**

Footstool, inlaid pine, a rectangular top
w/deep aprons inlaid w/a band of stars,
stylized leaves, wreath & stars, old worn
varnish finish, late 19th - early 20th c.,
8 x 16"... **165**

Footstool, painted & decorated, narrow
rectangular top above narrow ornately
scallop-cut aprons, scalloped flat legs
w/arched feet, alligatored red, yellow &
green paint w/gold & black stenciled
buildings, flowers & "E.H." on the top,
19th c., 6 x 14", 6 7/8" h. (minor edge
wear, two scallop points missing on
apron) **770**

Footstool, painted oak, 'rolling pin'-type on
four ring-turned legs, painted yellow,
19th c., 8 1/2 x 19" (paint loss) **144**

Footstool, painted poplar, rectangular top
on slightly splayed turned legs w/old added dowel rod rungs, old worn brown paint
w/gold striping, 9 x 13 3/4", 9" h. **275**

Gout stool, Victorian, mahogany, a rectangular upholstered top, adjustable ratchet
base, on turned feet, England, mid-19th
c., 12 x 19" **173**

Ornate Italian Carved Stool

Italian Renaissance-Style stool, carved
walnut, the lower back w/a central carved
shell flanked by scroll-carved braces
above the upholstered adjustable round
seat w/carved bead border, over a round
platform supported by a realistically-
carved three-quarters figure of a nearly
nude putto supporting the seat & standing among rocks on the stepped & molded round base w/flattened disk feet, 19th
c. (ILLUS.)... **1,000**

Jacobean-Style stool, oak, a rectangular
expanding top & cubbyhole above a deep
canted apron w/panels carved w/double
S-scrolls, one side forming a hinged
door, on short baluster-, ring- and block-
turned legs joined by box stretchers, metal label for Kittinger, 20th c.,
14 1/2 x 22 1/2", 20" h. **110**

Italian Gilt-bronze Rope Stool

Modern style stool, gilt-bronze, the rounded mesh seat enclosed w/a rope-form gilt
frame continuing to four legs conjoined
by a knotted rope stretcher, stamped
twice "Made In Italy," second quarter 20th
c., 26" d., 14" h. (ILLUS.) **1,560**

Modern style stool, wire & upholstery, the
tall waisted cylindrical base w/flaring top
composed of fine vertical bronze wires
w/a round upholstered seat & cushion in
peach fabric, designed by Warren Plat-
ner, manufactured by Knoll, ca. 1950s,
17" d., 21" h... **358**

Modern style stools, molded birch, four flat
tall legs curved at the top supporting a
round seat frame w/laminate seats in red,
blue or yellow, a low open square back &
low footrest near front base, designed by
Alvar Aalto, manufactured by Artek, ca.
1950s, 15" d., 29" h., set of 4 .... **413**

Golden Oak Adjustable Piano Stool

Piano stool, Victorian Golden Oak style,
the tall gently flared back w/a wide
shaped crestrail w/corner scrolls on ring-
turned stiles flanking five slender spindles all above the round adjustable seat,

the seat platform raised on four ring- and knob-turned canted legs joined by ring-turned stretchers to a center ring-turned post, the legs ending in brass paws w/glass balls, original finish, ca. 1890s, seat 14" d., 36" h. (ILLUS.) **300**

Patented Victorian Piano Stool

Piano stool, Victorian Renaissance Revival substyle, carved walnut, Roman-style design w/a rectangular upholstered top on a narrow burl-paneled apron raised on a four-legged scissor-action base w/a threaded mechanism w/large carved rosette handles for controlling the seat height, paper label reads "The X Piano Taboret L. Postawka Co., Cambridge-port, Mass. Pat. April 4, 1871," axle caps appear absent, 16 x 20", 26" h. (ILLUS.) **392**

Queen Anne footstool, carved mahogany, the rectangular slip seat above a conforming frame, on cabriole legs w/shell-carved knees & stocking trifid feet, 18th c., 21" l., 16 1/2" h. **1,725**

Renaissance Revival Ebonized Stool

Victorian stool, Renaissance Revival substyle, ebonized & parcel-gilt wood, the squared upholstered seat w/serpentine ends above a conforming scalloped apron w/gilt-incised line designs, raised on a heavy center post w/four radiating blocked & angled legs curving out at the bottom to form snake feet, American, ca. 1870, 18 1/2" h. (ILLUS.) **805**

Weaver's work stool, painted wood, tall w/a round hollowed seat frame w/woven leather seat on four reverse-tapering legs joined by turned stretchers, worn old red paint, New England, early 19th c., top 13 1/4 x 13 1/2", 28" h. **920**

Early William & Mary Joint Stool

William & Mary joint stool, maple, the rectangular molded top overhanging an apron w/splayed block-, vase- and ring-turned legs on knob feet, joined by flat box stretchers, old refinish, probably Massachusetts, early 18th c., minor imperfections, 16 x 24", 23" h. (ILLUS.) **8,050**

Windsor Painted Footstool

Windsor footstool, painted pine, the oval top w/incised edge raised on widely splayed bamboo-turned legs joined by turned box stretchers, painted white w/red trim, early-19th c., 9 1/2 x 15", 10 1/4" h. (ILLUS.) **287**

Windsor stool, painted, a triangular top on three canted baluster- and ring-turned legs joined by swelled stretchers, old black paint, the top recovered w/worn hooked rug fragment, early 19th c., 13" h. **550**

Tables

Art Deco Bedside Table

Art Deco bedside tables, pale maple w/mirrors, each of cylindrical form w/a flattened back & mounted w/two projecting rounded mirrored shelves, raised on a conforming plinth, losses to veneer, England, probably by Hille, ca. 1930, 14 1/2" d., 35" h., pr. (ILLUS. of one) **$1,092**

Leleu Art Deco Center Table

Art Deco center table, mahogany, a rounded top above a heavy squared cross-form pedestal on four cross-form downswept feet, designed by Jules Leleu, France, ca. 1925, 40" d., 29" h. (ILLUS.)... **8,050**

Art Deco Glass-topped Table

Art Deco center table, the round glass top above a framework of wrought-iron calli-

graphic devices raised on four scrolling legs joined by an X-form looped stretcher, France, ca. 1930, 26 3/4" d., 20 3/4" h. (ILLUS.).. **1,800**

Fine Art Deco Coffee Table

Art Deco coffee table, ormolu-mounted mahogany, a rectangular dished top w/beaded edge raised on an inset frieze above the rectangular frame w/thin ormolu angular mounts at the center apron & raised on tapering curved squared legs ending in brass feet, Jules Leleu, France, ca. 1935, 18 x 30", 15" h. (ILLUS.)................................ **7,475**

Art Deco console table, Macassar ebony, rectangular top w/rounded front corners above downswept side supports & a central reeded flat post on a serpentine, stepped plinth, France, ca. 1925, 16 x 42 1/2", 30" h. (finish uneven) **2,300**

Paul Kiss Art Deco Console Table

Art Deco console table, wrought iron & marble, a half-round top w/flat & angled front edges above a narrow dentil-carved apron raised on wide central S-scroll upright brackets w/a central dentil band, set on a small stepped rectangular foot w/dentil-carved band, antiqued patina,

designed by Paul Kiss, ca. 1925,
9 3/4 x 24 1/2", 34" h. (ILLUS.)................... **4,140**

Fine Art Deco Dining Table

Art Deco dining table, figured mahogany,
the round top w/a rayed mahogany design raised on a heavy wood column on a
nickel band raised on three low arched
splayed legs w/nickeled feet, attributed to
Jules Leleu, France, ca. 1930, 42" d.,
22" h. (ILLUS.).. **14,950**
Art Deco dining table, rosewood, the rect-
angular top w/two draw-leaf extensions
above downswept supports on a flaring
plinth, France, ca. 1925, 36 x 61", 30" h.
(missing leaves, uneven finish) **1,955**
Art Deco dining table, walnut, the round
top w/a sunburst pattern overhanging a
narrow apron raised on five slender
turned & tapering legs w/wide disks near
the top, France, ca. 1935, 63" d., 30" h. **5,750**

French Art Deco Dressing Table

Art Deco dressing table, African Bubinga
wood & rosewood, a stepped form w/an
upright square cabinet at one end fitted
w/a tall burled door w/rosewood trim &
ebonized handle beside a rectangular
top w/low rosewood crestrail & rounded
end enclosing a narrow drawer w/ebon-
ized pull above the kneehole opening & a
smaller upright cabinet door at the other
side, square curved front legs,
France, ca. 1930, 15 3/4 x 50", 36 1/2" h.
(ILLUS.) **1,150**
Art Deco dressing table, burled walnut, the
large circular mirror plate suspended
within the case above a lower shelf on
the right & a projecting rounded section
w/four drawers on the left, American-
made, chips & losses, ca. 1930, 27 x 70",
54" h. (ILLUS. top next column) **345**

American Art Deco Dressing Table

Art Deco side table, black lacquer, thick
round top widely overhanging a cylindrical accordian-pleat standard & spreading
round foot, France, ca. 1925, 29 1/2" d.,
22" h. (wear).. **2,185**

Art Deco Typewriter Table

Art Deco typewriter table, bird's-eye maple veneer & lacquer, an oval top formed
w/a half-round drop leaf at one end
above an upright center board w/two half-
round open shelves below the fixed half
of the top, top & shelves w/black lacquered edges, on three heavy casters,
America, ca. 1930, minor veneer cracks,
small repair, 21 x 36", 31 1/4" h. (ILLUS.)...... **978**

Majorelle Art Nouveau Dressing Table

Art Nouveau dressing table, carved mahogany, "Les Lilas" patt., the large
squared upright mirror within a foliate-
carved frame flanked by flaring stained
side panels, above a central plateau
w/raised ends over two pairs of small

drawers flanking an arched kneehole, gilt-bronze mounts, raised on slender & slightly curved foliate-carved legs, Louis Majorelle, France, ca. 1900, 22 1/2 x 49", 62 1/2" h. (ILLUS.) **4,140**

Gallé-signed Art Nouveau Table

Art Nouveau side table, fruitwood marquetry, a two-tiered form w/each rectangular tier outlined w/an undulating molding enclosing the ornate floral marquetry design, loop-carved S-scroll supports below the upper tier, the lower tier w/ormolu loop edge handles, raised on simple molded cabriole legs w/carved cuffs, by Gallé, designed for the Exposition Universelle, Paris, 1900, marquetry inscription "Sicut Lotus Semer Suum germinal sic Deus germinalit Jus Ti Tiam - Gallé Exposé 1900 - IS," 26 x 37", 34" h. (ILLUS.).......... **10,925**

Art Nouveau side table, fruitwood marquetry, two-tier, a shaped & molded rectangular top w/rounded corners w/foliage marquetry above a conforming lower open shelf, all joined by slender molded shaped legs, signed by Gallé, ca. 1900, 14 x 25", 30" h. (veneer lifting, refinished) **1,955**

Arts & Crafts Round Dining Table

Arts & Crafts dining table, oak, an expandable round top above a conforming apron, supported on a square tapering pedestal pierce-carved w/stylized fleur-de-lis cut-outs, raised on a curve-sided platform base w/curved corbels on casters, late 19th - early 20th c., minor stains & scratches, 48" d., 30 3/4" h. (ILLUS.) **805**

Arts & Crafts library table, oak, rectangular top over an apron w/a single long drawer w/hammered copper pulls, lower median shelf w/through-tenons, arched side stretchers, ca. 1912, 30 1/4 x 48", 30" h. (stains, wear) **518**

Arts & Crafts library table, quarter-sawn oak, a rectangular top slightly overhanging an apron w/a long flush drawer, raised on two square end posts w/scroll-ended flat shoe feet joined by a flat medial stretcher, ca. 1910,. 26 1/4 x 44", 30" h. **248**

Arts & Crafts Oak Tabouret

Arts & Crafts tabouret, octagonal top w/corbel supports above four canted sides w/curved cut-outs & medial shelf w/deep aprons, dark brown finish, ca. 1912, minor scratches & imperfections, 17" w., 23 1/2" h. (ILLUS.) **978**

Baroque Revival Parlor Table

Baroque Revival parlor table, walnut veneer, the octagonal top w/fanned veneering centered by an inlaid floral medallion over a deep carved apron raised on four legs w/ornate scroll carving at the top & feet & joined by a quatrefoil-form stretcher w/central rosette, early 20th c., 30" d., 29" h. (ILLUS.) **345**

Unique Baroque Revival Side Table

Baroque Revival side table, walnut, the octagonal top w/a line-inlaid border raised on four tall finely-carved standing egrets resting on figural carved rams' heads on a scalloped cross-form platform w/center finial & raised on curved blocked & reeded feet, original finish, ca. 1920, 20" w., 30" h. (ILLUS.) **2,400**

Early Bentwood Library Table

Bentwood library table, mahogany, rectangular w/reeded edges above a bentwood double-loop trestle base w/top scrolls & flaring leg bases on arched stretchers on bun feet, by J. & J. Kohn, Austria, ca. 1910, wear, 24 x 40", 29 1/2" h. (ILLUS.) **690**

Chippendale card table, carved mahogany, the rectangular hinged top w/rounded corners above a deep apron w/a pair of cockbeaded drawers w/butterfly brasses, cabriole legs w/leaf-carved knees & ending in claw-and-ball feet, New York or Philadelphia, 18th c., 36" l. **3,500**

Chippendale card table, mahogany, the folding hinged overhanging top w/serpentine edges above a conforming apron w/a serpentine cockbeaded border centering a carved fan joining four square molded slightly tapering legs w/inside chamfering, old finish, probably coastal northern Massachusetts, ca. 1780, 17 3/4 x 35 1/4", 28 1/4" h. (minor imperfections) **18,400**

Chippendale card table, mahogany, the rectangular hinged top w/molded edges above a straight beaded apron on four square Marlborough legs, original surface, Massachusetts, 1760-75, 16 x 33 1/2", 29 1/4" h. (repairs) **1,265**

Chippendale country-style tea table, cherry, a large square top tilting diagonally above a baluster- and ring-turned pedestal on a tripod base w/cabriole legs ending in pad feet on platforms, New England, ca. 1780, 30 x 31 1/2", 28" h. (minor imperfections) **1,265**

Chippendale country-style work table, maple, birch & pine, scrubbed one-board rectangular top w/breadboard ends widely overhanging the deep apron w/a single long dovetailed drawer w/brass pulls, square stile legs joined by box stretchers, original red finish, attributed to Maine, 29 3/4 x 50 1/4", 26" h. **3,300**

Chippendale dining table, carved walnut, a rectangular top flanked by a pair of deep drop leaves, scroll-cut apron above four cabriole legs ending in claw-and-ball feet, refinished, Massachusetts, ca.

1780, open 47 x 47 1/2", 28" h. (imperfections) **2,070**

Chippendale dining table, mahogany, a rectangular top flanked by wide drop leaves, scalloped end skirts joining four molded straight legs, old refinish, New England ca. 1780, open 47 x 47 1/4", 27 3/4" h. (minor imperfections) **1,150**

Chippendale Walnut Dressing Table

Chippendale dressing table, walnut, the rectangular top w/molded edge & shaped front corners overhanging a case w/a long drawer over three small lip-molded drawers, deeply scalloped apron, raised on cabriole legs ending in trifid feet, butterfly brasses, Delaware Valley, 18th c., 21 1/4 x 35 1/4", 29 1/2" h. (ILLUS.) **5,175**

Chippendale Games Table

Chippendale games table, mahogany & mahogany veneer, folding turret-top style w/deep rounded corners & scalloped aprons w/fan-carved drops, raised on cabriole legs w/shell-carved knees & ending in paw feet (ILLUS.) **3,750**

Fine Chippendale Pembroke Table

Chippendale Pembroke table, figured mahogany, the rectangular top w/rounded ends flanked by serpentine-edged drop leaves, a cockbeaded apron drawer at one end w/simple bail pull, on square tapering stop-fluted legs ending in spade feet, appears to retain original brass, minor patches to veneer, sunbleached, Mid-Atlantic States, ca. 1780, closed 20 1/2 x 32", 27 1/2" h. (ILLUS.) **8,050**

Chippendale Pembroke table, mahogany, a boldly grained wide rectangular top flanked by two narrow hinged drop leaves above an apron w/an end drawer w/a butterfly brass, square legs w/inside chamfered corners joined by shaped flat cross-stretchers, old finish, original brass, Connecticut River Valley, ca. 1780, 34 3/4 x 35", 27" h. (top slightly warped) **2,875**

Chippendale Pembroke table, mahogany, rectangular top flanked by hinged rectangular drop leaves, apron w/one dovetailed end drawer w/cockbeading & original brass, square molded legs w/inside chamfer & cross-stretcher, found on Cape Cod, Massachusetts, 20 1/4 x 31 3/4" plus 10 3/4" leaves, 28 3/4" h. (added steel angle braces on underside, minor stains in top) **3,575**

Chippendale Pembroke table, mahogany, a rectangular top flanked by two rectangular drop leaves above an apron w/one end drawer w/replaced brass, raised on four square tapering legs w/inside chamfer joined by a cross-stretcher, old finish, late 18th to early 19th c., 20 x 33" w/9 1/2" leaves, 29" h. (repair to stretcher) **1,540**

Chippendale tea table, carved & figured mahogany, round dished top tilting on a birdcage mechanism above a ring-, rod- and ball-turned pedestal on a tripod base w/cabriole legs ending in claw-and-ball feet, Philadelphia, ca. 1770, 33" d., 28 1/2" h. **14,950**

Chippendale Tilt-top Tea Table

Chippendale tea table, carved mahogany, a round dished top tilting on a columnar pedestal w/a spiral-carved urn & knob at the base above the tripod base w/cabriole legs ending in pad feet on platforms, old refinish, imperfections, England or America, ca. 1780, 27" d., 21" h. (ILLUS.)... **1,380**

English Chippendale Tea Table

Chippendale tea table, carved mahogany, a round top supported on a dovetailed mahogany box open at both ends rotating above a baluster-form pedestal carved w/diamonds enclosing scratch-carved details on a tripod base w/cabriole legs carved at the knees w/acanthus leaves & ending in ball-and-claw feet, old surface, repairs, England, late 18th c., 32 1/4" d., 29" h. (ILLUS.) **2,415**

Chippendale tea table, figured mahogany, a round top tilting above a birdcage support & ring- and baluster-turned pedestal on a tripod base w/three cabriole legs ending in claw-and-ball feet, New York City, ca. 1780, 31 1/2" d., 27 1/2" h. (feet worn & chewed) **3,450**

Chippendale tea table, mahogany, round one-board dished top above a pedestal w/a turned columnar section above a baluster-turned lower section, on a tripod base w/cabriole legs ending in snake feet, old mellow finish, attributed to Newport, Rhode Island, 18th c., 23 1/2" d., 27 5/8" h. (restoration, pieced repairs, filled holes in top from a larger cleat) **8,575**

Chippendale-Style Coffee Table

Chippendale-Style coffee table, carved mahogany, the rectangular white marble top w/molded serpentine edges above the leafy scroll-carved apron, raised on cabriole legs w/leaf-carved knees & ending in claw-and-ball feet, original finish, ca. 1920-40, 18 x 32", 18" h. (ILLUS.) **450**

Chippendale-Style Oak Side Table

Chippendale-Style side table, oak, the large round top w/a molded edge raised on a baluster-turned & acanthus leaf-carved pedestal on four splayed cabriole legs ending in bold paw feet, refinished, ca. 1900, 22" d., 30" h. (ILLUS.) **450**

Chippendale-Style Tea Table

Chippendale-Style tea table, mahogany, stationary octagonal top w/a scalloped & curved low pierced gallery above a curved & scalloped leaf-carved apron, raised on a leaf-carved pedestal on a tripod base w/cabriole legs w/carved knees & ending in raised pad feet, original finish, ca. 1920s, 24" w., 30" h. (ILLUS.) **450**

Chippendale-Style tea table, mahogany, the scalloped round top w/carved fans & rings for plates, raised on a turned columnar support above a spiral-twist knob over the tripod base w/cabriole legs leaf-carved at the knees & ending in elongated claw-and-ball feet, old finish, England, late 19th c., 31 1/2" d., 28 1/2" h. **1,045**

Chippendale-Style tea table, mahogany, wide round top tilting on a birdcage mechanism above a ring- and knob-turned column w/gadrooned & reeded sections above the squatty tripod base w/cabriole legs ending in snake feet, re-finished, 20th c., 35 " d., 27 3/4" h. (two-board top & birdcage old replacements, top wobbles) **275**

Chippendale-Style tea table, rosewood & walnut veneer, a round piecrust top w/molded edges tilting above a leaf-carved pedestal on a tripod base w/three

cabriole legs w/leaf-carved knees & ending in paw feet, ca. 1900, 28" d., 42" h. **1,064**

Classical Mahogany Breakfast Table

Classical breakfast table, carved & inlaid mahogany, the rectangular top w/brass inlay in outline & stamped brass on the edges of the flanking, shaped drop leaves above one working & one faux end apron drawer, drop pendants at the corners, raised on four ring-turned columns on a rectangular curve-edged platform raised on outswept leaf-carved legs ending in paw feet on casters, replaced pulls, old refinish, repairs, losses, New York City, ca. 1820-30, 24 x 39", 28" h. (ILLUS.)....................................... **2,415**

Classical breakfast table, carved mahogany, the wide rectangular top flanked by wide drop leaves w/notched corners above the convex apron flanked by small rosewood panels w/brass inlaid stringing & turned pendants, raised on a heavy turned acanthus leaf-carved pedestal on four scrolled acanthus leaf-carved legs ending in hairy paw feet, old refinish, probably New York, ca. 1825, 24 3/4 x 39 1/2", 29 1/4" h. (minor imperfections) **920**

Classical card table, carved mahogany & mahogany veneer, the fold-over rectangular top w/rounded front corners above a paneled veneered apron flanked by scrolled end panels, raised on a square molded tapering pedestal resting on a quadripartite platform on four scroll- and acanthus-carved feet, attributed to Isaac Vose & Son, Boston, ca. 1825, 18 x 36 1/2", 30" h. (refinished).................. **3,105**

Fine Classical Card Table

Classical card table, carved mahogany & mahogany veneer, the rectangular folding top above a conforming frieze w/beaded edge on a tapering pedestal carved around the lower half w/bold acanthus leaves & basket of fruit on a shaped concave platform w/acanthus leaf-carved paw feet on casters, Philadelphia area, ca. 1825, refinished, 18 1/2 x 38", 30 1/4" h. (ILLUS.) **4,888**

Classical card table, carved mahogany, the hinged rectangular top w/rounded corners above a conforming frame w/applied skirt on foliate-carved & ring- and ball-turned pedestal surrounded by a stylized leaf-carved ring over a square base on downswept legs w/leaf-carved knees fitted w/brass casters, probably Boston, 1810-30, closed 17 3/4 x 35 3/4", 28 1/2" h. **2,300**

Classical Mahogany Card Table

Classical card table, carved mahogany, the rectangular hinged top w/rounded corners above a conforming apron w/horizontally reeded corners above a leaf-turned & leaf-carved & reeded pedestal on outswept beaded legs ending in brass paw feet on casters, old refinish, imperfections, New England, 1825, 17 3/4 x 36", 29 5/8" h. (ILLUS.) **805**

Classical card table, carved mahogany veneer, rectangular top swivels above the ckirt w/ocrolled cndɔ rɑiɔed on ɑ tapering rectangular pedestal w/acanthus leaf carving around the bottom raised on a long cross-form platform raised on carved paw feet on casters, old refinish, attributed to Isaac Vose and Son, Boston, ca. 1825, 17 3/4 x 36", 29" h. **3,738**

Grain-painted Classical Game Table

Classical card table, grain-painted, rectangular hinged top w/rounded corners

opening above a simple ogee apron raised on a heavy slightly tapering square pedestal on a cross-form platform base above flattened ball feet, original red & gold graining simulates mahogany, imperfections, Maine, 1830s, 18 x 36", 28 3/4" h. (ILLUS.) **1,093**

Classical card table, mahogany & mahogany crotch grain veneer, a rectangular fold-over top above a deep ogee apron raised on a heavy pedestal w/a beehive ring-turned section above a wide baluster-turned & acanthus-leaf carved lower section, raised on a long heavy rectangular plinth w/concave sides raised on four carved wing & paw feet on brass casters, old dark finish, ca. 1840, 17 1/2 x 36", 29 3/4" h. (veneer repairs, well done column repair) **1,045**

One of a Pair of Classical Card Tables

Classical card tables, carved mahogany & mahogany veneer, the rectangular hinged top w/rounded front corners above a narrow rounded skirt w/anthemion carved corners, raised on a ring-turned & acanthus leaf-carved pedestal on a shaped veneered platform above leaf-carved paw feet, old refinish, Philadelphia, 1830s, casters missing, other imperfections, 17 3/4 x 36", 28 1/4" h., pr. (ILLUS. of one) **6,325**

Classical Tilt-top Center Table

Classical center table, carved mahogany & mahogany veneer, the round veneered top tilting & overhanging a veneered apron above the central heavy round tapering pedestal w/a molded collar above the egg-and-dart carved base band, centered on the tripartite base above carved paw feet on casters, old refinish, Philadelphia, ca. 1830, imperfections, 44 3/4" d., 28 1/2" h. (ILLUS.) **4,370**

Classical Center Table on Ball Feet

Classical center table, carved mahogany veneer, the round top w/rounded edge on a conforming veneered apron w/banded lower edge, raised on a heavy ring- and knob-turned & acanthus-carved pedestal on a tripartite platform on incised ball feet, imperfections, possibly Boston, ca. 1840, 40 1/2" d., 30 3/4" h. (ILLUS.) **1,955**

Classical Center Table on Casters

Classical center table, carved & veneered mahogany, the round top w/rounded edge above a conforming apron w/applied panels & cast-brass beaded edge, raised on a ring-turned & acanthus leaf-carved post on four outswept scrolled & acanthus-carved legs ending in cast-brass cap caster feet, refinished, minor imperfections, probably Massachusetts, ca. 1825, 36" d., 27 1/2" h. (ILLUS.) **8,050**

Classical center table, japanned wood, the rounded top painted w/chinoiserie decoration in gold on black, tilting above a heavy ring-turned columnar standard, on a cross-form plinth raised on tapered turned feet, New York State, ca. 1830,

Classical Japanned Center Table

some losses & restoration to decoration, 34" d., 27" h. (ILLUS.) **2,760**

Fine Classical Center Table

Classical center table, parcel-gilt & carved mahogany, the round white marble top on a conforming apron w/brass & mother-of-pearl-inlaid edge raised on three white marble columns w/gilt carved scroll capitals on gilt carved winged paw feet joined by a tripartite platform w/central rondel, New York City, ca. 1830, 39" d., 31 1/2" h. (ILLUS.) **8,338**

Rare Small Classical Center Table

Classical center table, part-ebonized mahogany, figured round top above a conforming apron fitted w/a drawer, the turned flaring heavy pedestal on a tripartite platform on leaf-carved scrolling feet on casters, patches & veneer losses, Boston, Massachusetts, possibly by

Vose or one of its comtemporaries, ca. 1825, rare small size, 24" d., 26 1/4" h. (ILLUS.) **3,737**

Classical console table, bird's-eye maple & mahogany, the rectangular white marble top w/a molded edge above a straight apron centering a mahogany inlaid panel w/ovolo corners, repeated on the side, flanked by square mahogany corner blocks ending in turned acorn pendants, on a heavy square tapering pedestal & concave-shaped cross-form platform on double-ball turned feet, old finish, probably Vermont, ca. 1825-30, 20 x 40", 32" h. **2,875**

Classical Mahogany Console Table

Classical console table, mahogany & mahogany veneer, a rectangular black marble top above a deep ogee apron raised on heavy C-scroll forked supports on a serpentine-fronted platform backed by a rectangular mirror, raised on heavy C-scroll front feet, original finish, ca. 1840, 20 x 38", 34" h. (ILLUS.) **1,600**

Classical console table, mahogany & mahogany veneer, the long white marble top w/canted front corners above a conforming ogee apron w/crotch grain veneering raised on two heavy S-scroll front legs w/veneering resting on a rectangular plinth w/concave front, the back framework enclosing a rectangular mirror, ca. 1840, 19 1/2 x 42 1/2", 32" h. **2,990**

Maine Classical Breakfast Table

Classical country-style breakfast table, painted & decorated, a rectangular top flanked by deep rectangular drop leaves w/rounded corners above a straight apron raised on a heavy square pedestal

above a shaped platform on ball feet w/casters, old red & brown graining simulates mahogany, original surface, minor imperfections, Maine, 1830-40, open, 41 1/2 x 42", 28" h. (ILLUS.) **690**

Classical country-style card table, grain-painted, a fold-over rectangular top on a tapering square support & concave platform on turned feet on casters, painted reddish brown to resemble mahogany, New England, ca. 1825-30, 17 x 34", 29 3/4" h. (imperfections) **316**

Classical country-style dressing table, bird's-eye & tiger stripe maple, a narrow rectangular top supporting a pair of tall S-scroll uprights flanking a tall rectangular beveled mirror frame, above a pair of narrow drawers w/large round brass pulls over the stepped-out rectangular top above a single long drawer w/matching pulls, raised on block-form legs w/ring- and knob-turned tops & tapering turned feet, replaced pulls, refinished, imperfections, Vermont, 1835-45, 19 x 36 3/4", overall 58" h. **1,093**

Classical Country Dressing Table

Classical country-style dressing table, painted & decorated, the scroll-cut crestboard behind a small rectangular drawer on the rectangular top overhanging an apron w/a single long drawer, raised on slender ring- and rod-turned tapering legs w/peg feet, original red & brown graining simulating rosewood w/yellow foliate designs on the leg corner blocks & overall yellow-painted bordering to simulate inlay, Maine, early 19th c., 17 3/4 x 34", 34 1/2" h. (ILLUS.) **1,150**

Classical Country-style Work Table

Classical country-style work table, bird's-eye maple, tiger stripe maple & cherry, the rectangular top above a deep case w/two drawers w/turned wood knobs, raised on knob-, ring- and rod-turned legs w/double-knob feet, old refinish, possibly Pennsylvania, ca. 1825, imperfections, 19 x 21 1/2", 29"h. (ILLUS.) **1,610**

Classical Country Work Table

Classical country-style work table, tiger stripe maple, a nearly square top flanked by hinged drop leaves w/rounded corners above a case w/two round-fronted drawers w/pairs of turned wood knobs, raised on a heavy square tapering pedestal on a stepped square base on four belted bun feet on thick short pegs, old finish, minor imperfections, New England, ca. 1820-30, 16 1/2 x 17", 30 1/2" h. (ILLUS.)....................................... **1,495**

Classical dining table, carved & veneered mahogany, a rectangular overhanging top flanked by deep rounded leaves over a straight beaded apron w/a small drawer at each end, raised on two lyre-form supports centering a carved fan w/applied brass rosettes on molded arched & outswept molded legs ending in cast-brass hairy paw feet, ring-turned & beaded square medial stretchers, old refinish, probably New England, ca. 1820, open 50 x 51 1/2", 28 3/4" h. **2,990**

Fine Classical Dining Table

Classical dining table, carved & veneered mahogany, extension-type, round top w/molded edge over a smooth apron w/thin gadrooned base band raised on a clustered column-form split pedestal ending in four downswept foliate-carved legs ending in paw feet on casters, together w/seven leaves, New York City, ca. 1840, closed 48" d., 29 1/2" h. (ILLUS.).. **7,475**

Classical Dressing Table with Mirror

Classical dressing table, mahogany & mahogany veneer, the top fitted w/tall S-scroll brass-mounted supports flanking a rectangular tilting mirror frame, a narrow rectangular top above a pair of drawers w/oval pulls above a stepped-out rectangular top above an apron w/a single long drawer w/oval pulls, raised on ring- and rod-turned legs ending in peg feet, restoration, New England, 1825-35, 19 1/4 x 36 1/2", overall 63 1/2" h. (ILLUS.)............................ **2,645**

Classical library table, mahogany, the wide rectangular top flanked by two hinged drop leaves w/notched & rounded corners above an apron w/a single long drawer w/round brass pulls & turned corner drops, raised on a short bulbous pedestal over four outswept leaf-carved legs ending in brass eagle caps on casters, appears to retain original hardware, New York City, ca. 1830, 39 x 52", 28 1/4" h..... **2,875**

Classical Mahogany Pier Table

Classical pier table, carved mahogany & mahogany veneer, a rectangular black marble top w/rounded edges above a veneered frieze w/banded edges above a pier mirror flanked by heavy scrolled & fan-carved supports on a conformingly shaped platform joined by an incurved shelf, on four turned feet, original finish, Boston, ca. 1825, imperfections, 19 1/4 x 38", 33 3/4" h. (ILLUS.)............... **2,760**

Classical pier table, mahogany & mahogany veneer, a rectangular white marble top w/molded edges above the ogee molded apron on two heavy S-scroll supports & a shaped concave platform w/scrolled front

Classical Marble-topped Pier Table

feet & turned rear feet, a recessed molded base panel flanked by tapering pilasters, old refinish, imperfections, probably Boston, ca. 1825, 19 1/4 x 40 1/4", 37" h. (ILLUS.) **2,070**

Classical Revival Oak Lamp Table

Classical Revival lamp table, oak & quarter-sawn oak veneer, the round top raised on a heavy squared baluster-form pedestal w/a stepped square base resting on a squared platform on C-scroll feet, refinished, ca. 1910, 20" d., 30" h. (ILLUS.) 350

Classical side table, mahogany, rectangular molded top w/a scrolled gallery above two short drawers & a base of two vase- and ring-turned front legs & two rear square tapering legs, old refinish, possibly New England, first quarter 19th c., 19 1/2 x 44", 35 1/2" h. (minor imperfections) 748

Classical sofa table, carved mahogany & mahogany veneer, the long rectangular top flanked by wide drop leaves w/reeded edges above a long ogee-molded frame w/two short drawers, raised on shaped end supports w/Ionic capitals & applied banded panels on molded plinths & outswept square tapering legs ending in brass hairy paw feet joined by a square molded

Classical Sofa Table

tapering stretcher, old refinish, some imperfections, probably New York, ca. 1820-25, 19 1/2 x 41", 30" h. (ILLUS.) **2,990**

Fine Classical Sofa Table

Classical sofa table, mahogany & mahogany inlaid veneer, the rectangular overhanging reeded top w/two rounded end drop leaves above an apron w/one faux & one working cockbeaded string-inlaid drawer on each side, raised on a ring-turned pedestal & concave platform above outswept curving legs ending in cast foliate brass casters, appears to retain original ivory pulls, Rhode Island, ca. 1810-15, imperfections, open 35 1/2 x 55 1/2", 29 1/4" h. (ILLUS.) **6,900**

Classical Work Table

Classical work table, carved mahogany & mahogany veneer, the rectangular top flanked by two wide D-form drop leaves above the deep apron w/two round-fronted drawers w/simple turned wood pulls, on a heavy square tapering pedestal w/a stepped base on the cross-form platform raised on scrolled leaf carving & paw feet on casters, refinished, attributed to Isaac Vose and Son, Boston, ca. 1825, closed 21 x 22", 30 1/2" h. (ILLUS.) **2,875**

Classical Lyre-based Work Table

Classical work table, carved & veneered mahogany, the rectangular top flanked by wide drop leaves w/rounded corners over an apron w/two round-fronted veneered drawers w/early pressed-glass pulls raised on a leaf- and floral-carved lyre-form pedestal on a square platform w/beveled top edge all raised on S-scroll carved feet on casters, probably Massachusetts, ca. 1825, 18 x 19", 28 1/2" h. (ILLUS.) **1,610**

Classical Mahogany Work Table

Classical work table, mahogany & mahogany veneer, a nearly square top flanked by half-round hinged drop leaves above a deep apron w/two small drawers w/original turned wood pulls, raised on a rectangular tapering pedestal w/four concave sides above the conforming platform base on bulbous baluster-turned feet on casters, old refinish, imperfections, Boston, 1830s, 18 1/8 x 19" plus leaves, 29 3/4" h. (ILLUS.) **1,300**

Classical Mahogany Work Table

Classical work table, mahogany & mahogany veneer, the rectangular top inlaid w/sections centering a circular panel w/ovolo corners above quarter-engaged ring-turned posts ending in acorn pendants flanking the two graduated drawers on a vase- and ring-turned spiral-carved pedestal on a rectangular platform w/outset corners above outward flaring beaded legs & applied brass rosettes & ending in brass casters, old round brass pulls, refinished, imperfections, possibly New York, ca. 1815-25, 14 x 20", 29 1/2" (ILLUS.) **1,265**

Classical-Style games table, mahogany, the demi-lune top w/hinged leaf & beaded edge above a conforming apron w/three blocks above the three front legs w/a ring- and compressed knob-turned section above a reeded tapering section ending in a brass claw w/glass ball foot, fourth matching swing-out support leg, old finish, early 20th c., closed 18 1/4 x 36", 29 1/4" h. **633**

Classical-Style Work Table

Classical-Style work table, mahogany & mahogany veneer, the square top w/gadroon-carved edges flanked by wide drop leaves w/similarly carved edges above a case w/a pair of slightly rounded drawers w/small brass knobs flanked by leaf-carved panels, raised on a turned, tapering leaf-carved pedestal raised on four outswept legs w/leaf-carved inner tips & paw-carved feet, original finish, ca. 1890s, 16" w. closed, 30" h. (ILLUS.)............ **750**

Classical-Style Work Table

Classical-Style work table, mahogany, the square top flanked by wide hinged drop leaves above the deep case w/three drawers w/floral-carved pulls flanked by acanthus leaf & rod-turned pilasters, raised on an acanthus leaf-carved pedestal on a cross-form platform raised on paw feet, original finish, ca. 1920s, 16" sq. plus leaves, 30" h. (ILLUS.)..................... **850**

Colonial Revival Mahogany End Table

Colonial Revival end table, mahogany & mahogany veneer, a rectangular top

w/molded edges & carved projecting corner stiles flanking a bow-front case w/three narrow graduated drawers w/ornate brass pulls, raised on simple cabriole legs w/leaf-carved knees ending in peg feet, early 20th c., 15 x 22", 30" h. (ILLUS.).. **800**

Colonial Revival Oak Lamp Table

Colonial Revival lamp table, oak, a four-lobed top overhanging a deep apron w/arched base raised on four ring-turned reeded legs joined by a medial four-lobed shelf, on baluster- and knob-turned feet, original finish, ca. 1890s, 20" w., 30" h. (ILLUS.).. **400**

Country-style tavern table, maple, birch & pine, a rectangular one-board pine scrubbed top w/breadboard ends, on an apron w/a single dovetailed drawer w/beaded edge & brass pull, on knob-and rod-turned legs w/blocks on button feet joined by flat box stretchers, old worn red finish, New England, late 18th c., 18 1/2 x 22 1/2", 25" h. (two posts w/top age cracks w/square nails added)............. **4,675**

Country-style work table, maple, a long rectangular overhanging top w/thumb-molded edges above an apron w/a single long drawer w/two small turned wood knobs raised on baluster- and ring-turned supports on blocks w/knob feet joined by square box stretchers, old refinish, New England, ca. 1740, 19 x 40", 29" h. (replaced pulls, very minor imperfections) **6,900**

Country-style work table, painted pine, a rectangular overhanging top w/a single drop leaf along one side, straight apron joining four square tapering splayed legs, old red paint, New England, early 19th c., open 28 1/2 x 30", 28 1/2" h. **1,150**

Country-style work table, painted pine, a rectangular three-board removable top overhanging a deep apron w/a pair of deep drawers w/turned wooden knobs, on ring-, knob- and baluster-turned legs w/peg feet, old worn brown paint over

red, Pennsylvania, 19th c., 36 x 54",
30 1/2" h. (age cracks, chips on legs, re-
placed pegs in the top) **1,760**

Country-style work table, turned walnut,
heavy rectangular top w/molded edges
overhanging a deep apron w/a single
long drawer w/molded lip, on four balus-
ter- and ring-turned legs joined by ring-,
block- and baluster-turned H-stretcher,
on squat turned ball feet, appears to retain original decorated iron bail drawer
pull, Pennsylvania, mid- to late 18th c.,
25 1/2 x 45 1/4", 27 1/2" h. **6,900**

Danish Modern coffee table, walnut, long
narrow rectangular top w/rounded corners raised on four tapering cylindrical
legs, signed w/metal tag "Illums Boli-
ghus," Copenhagen, Denmark, ca. 1950,
19 3/4 x 60", 16" h. **201**

Danish Modern Dining Table

Danish Modern dining table, walnut, a
wide rectangular top flanked by wide half-
round drop leaves, raised on four plain
turned & slightly tapering legs, w/one leaf
insert, designed by Hans Wegner,
Denmark, ca. 1950 (ILLUS.) **863**

Square Oak Extension Dining Table

Early 20th century dining table, oak, ex-
pandable-type, the wide square top divided at the center & raised on a heavy ring-
turned divided column surrounded by
four smaller ring- and baluster-turned columns resting on knobs & issuing heavy
outswept legs ending in paw feet on casters, w/four leaves, original finish, ca.
1900, 48" w., 30" h. (ILLUS.) **1,200**

Early 20th century dining table, quarter-
sawn oak, round top above a plain
apron, raised on a heavy turned pedestal w/four projecting heavy scroll legs,
on casters, refinished, ca. 1910, 48" d.,
30" h. (ILLUS. top next column) **1,200**

Early 20th Century Oak Dining Table

Early American tavern table, painted
wood, long rectangular two-board top
widely overhanging a deep apron w/a
single deep drawer w/wooden knob,
raised on baluster- and ring-turned supports on tall block feet joined by box
stretchers, old red paint, New England,
mid-18th c., 20 x 32", 26" h. (replaced
drawer pull, some height loss) **3,105**

Edwardian center table, satinwood-inlaid
rosewood, the shield-shaped top raised
on scrolling legs joined by a shelf stretcher, England, early 20th c., 23 1/2" w.,
28" h. **1,092**

Federal card table, carved & figured mahogany, the hinged serpentine-fronted
top w/edge reeding & outset corners
above a conforming apron w/a molded
edge flanked by leaf-carved & punch-
work-decorated dies on ring-turned reeded tapering legs ending in brass cups &
casters, Salem area, Massachusetts, ca.
1815, open 34 3/4 x 35", 29 1/2" h. **2,875**

Fine Federal Mahogany Card Table

Federal card table, carved mahogany &
mahogany veneer, the hinged fold-over
top w/serpentine edges & ovolo corners
above a conforming apron, the rounded
corners carved w/acanthus leaves above
turned, reeded & leaf-carved legs ending
in turned peg feet on casters, attributed
to Salem, Massachusetts, early 19th c.
(ILLUS.) **1,800**

Federal card table, inlaid mahogany, a
folding half-round serpentine top w/ellip-
tic front & cross-banded edge above a

conforming apron w/an inlaid oval panel bordered by geometric band within a mitered rectangle, the cross-banded skirt joining four square double-tapering legs w/stringing & inlaid cuffs, old finish, Massachusetts, ca. 1790-1800, 17 x 36 1/4", 28 7/8" h. (some imperfections) **6,325**

Federal card table, inlaid mahogany, rectangular fold-over top w/ovolo corners & inlaid edges above a conformingly shaped apron centering an inlaid shaped contrasting panel, bordered by stringing w/geometric banding on the lower edge joining four square double tapering legs, the dies inlaid w/panels & stringing continuing to banded cuffs, old finish, probably Massachusetts, ca. 1790, 17 x 35 3/4", 30 3/4" h. (minor imperfections)................... **5,175**

Federal card table, inlaid mahogany & satinwood, the hinged top w/elliptical front half w/serpentine ends & dart inlaid edges above a conforming apron of satinwood panels w/edge of crossbanding & geometric inlay, inlaid dies top the reeded turned & tapering legs ending in swelled peg feet, old finish, Boston, ca. 1810, 36 1/2" w., 29" h. (minor imperfections) **17,250**

Federal card table, inlaid mahogany, the hinged top w/elliptical front & square corners & crossbanded edge above a conforming apron w/a central inlaid oval panel flanked by shaped panels defined by stringing joining four square tapering legs, the dies w/contrasting panels above banding, a leaf device & stringing, old refinish, probably Rhode Island, ca. 1800, 17 1/2 x 34 3/4", 28 3/8" h. (restoration) **2,800**

Massachusetts Federal Card Table

Federal card table, mahogany & flame birch veneer inlay, the rectangular serpentine-edged hinged top w/banded inlay edges & ovolo corners above a conforming top & apron centered by an inlaid birch veneer oval reserve in a rectangular panel, raised on ring-turned & reeded tapering legs w/knobbed ankles & peg feet, imperfections, North Shore, Massachusetts, early 19th c., 17 1/2 x 34 3/4", 29 3/8" h. (ILLUS.)...................................... **4,600**

Federal card table, tiger stripe maple, birch & bird's-eye maple veneer, the rectangu-

lar fold-over top w/a serpentine front & half-serpentine sides & ovolo corners above a conforming apron w/bird's-eye maple veneer joining quarter engaged ring-turned legs ending in swelled peg feet, old refinish, New Hampshire or Massachusetts, ca. 1820, 18 x 36", 28 1/2" h. (imperfections) **1,495**

Federal Inlaid Mahogany Card Table

Federal card tables, inlaid mahogany, the half-round hinged top w/flattened slightly projecting front section above a conforming apron w/a long oval inlaid reserve at the front flanked by line-inlaid blocks, raised on four square tapering slender legs, early 19th c., pr. (ILLUS. of one) **12,100**

Federal country-style breakfast table, tiger stripe maple, a rectangular top flanked by drop leaves w/ovolo corners above a straight apron on four slender square tapering legs, old finish, New England, ca. 1810, 18 x 36 1/4" closed, 27 1/2" h. **3,738**

Federal country-style card table, inlaid cherry, rectangular hinged top above a deep plain apron, on tall square tapering legs, stringed inlay on legs & apron defined in rectangles & bands, stringing on both sides of top forming an oval on each surface, old finish, early 19th c., open 35 x 36", 29 1/4" h. **2,860**

Federal country-style dining table, birch, a rectangular two-board top flanked by deep hinged drop leaves w/rounded corners, the apron raised on swelled turned round legs ending in ring-turned ankles & peg & ball feet, first half 19th c., old red finish, 16 1/2 x 41 1/2" plus 11 3/4" w. leaves, 29 1/4" h. (age crack & edge repair in top, age crack & repair to one leg)...... **330**

Federal country-style dining table, cherry, a rectangular top flanked by wide hinged drop leaf w/rounded cut corners, one dovetailed drawer in the apron at one end, raised on turned cylindrical legs w/double-knob feet, refinished, first half 19th c., 20 x 42" plus 16 3/4" leaves, 28 1/2" h. (age cracks in top)........................... **550**

Federal country-style dining table, curly maple & cherry, the rectangular maple top flanked by wide maple drop leaves above a maple apron, on six baluster-

and ring-turned cherry legs w/knob feet, refinished, first half 19th c., 19 3/8 x 48" plus 18" leaves, 29" h. (age cracks in top, some warp) **715**

Federal country-style dining table, painted pine, rectangular top w/rounded ends flanked by two hinged half-round drop leaves, apron w/a single dovetailed end drawer, on square tapering legs, old brown graining, 19th c., found in Maine, 19 1/4 x 40 3/4" plus 10 3/4" w. leaves, 29 1/4" h. (worm holes, wear, some paint touch-up) **1,320**

Federal Country Dining Table

Federal country-style dining table, tiger stripe maple, a narrow rectangular top w/rounded ends flanked by deep D-form drop leaves above a deep flat apron raised on tall square tapering legs, old refinish, New England, ca. 1800-10, open 41 1/2 x 41 3/4", 28 1/2" h. (ILLUS.) **2,645**

Federal country-style dining table, tiger stripe maple, a rectangular top flanked by wide drop leaves w/rounded corners, on plain turned legs ending in baluster-turned & peg feet, old refinish, New England, ca. 1820, open 20 x 47", 29 1/2" h. (imperfections) **1,150**

Country Federal Dining Table

Federal country-style dining table, tiger stripe maple, the rectangular top flanked by wide hinged drop leaves over a plain apron & six ring- and rod-turned legs w/small bun feet, old refinish, no casters, New England, ca. 1825, 29 x 56 1/2", 28" h. (ILLUS.) **3,335**

Federal country-style dressing table, grain-painted, the high scroll-cut splashboard above a narrow rectangular top over a pair of drawers set-back on the rectangular top w/rounded edges, the apron w/a single long drawer, simple turned-wood knobs, baluster- and ring-turned legs w/peg feet, labeled "J.G. Briggs, Charlestown, New Hampshire," original black & gold graining to similuate rosewood, ca. 1830-33, 16 x 36 3/8", 39" h. (minor imperfections) **920**

Federal country-style dressing table, painted & decorated, an upright flat rectangular backsplash flanked by blocked uprights above a narrow rectangular top over a pair of small drawers on a stepped-out rectangular top w/rounded edges above an apron w/a single long narrow drawer painted to resemble two small drawers, multi-ring turned legs w/knob feet, old yellow ground w/olive green & gold highlights, banding & fruit & foliage stenciled decoration on the backsplash & drawers, original round brass pulls, Newburyport, Massachusetts, ca. 1820-30, 17 1/2 x 35 3/4", 40 1/2" h. (minor surface imperfections) **4,600**

Federal country-style dressing table, painted & decorated, the scroll-cut backsplash w/shaped ends above the rectangular top over a long narrow drawer in the apron, raised on ring-, knob- and tapering rod-turned legs w/knob feet, the backsplash painted w/a stylized stenciled fruit & leaf cluster in gold & green, the table w/a green & mustard gold grained surface & banding, old replaced opalescent glass drawer pulls, New England, early 19th c., 15 x 32 1/4", 34" h. (some old repaint) **1,380**

Federal country-style dressing table, painted pine, a long flat-topped splashboard w/scroll-cut ends above the wide D-form top overhanging an apron w/a single long dovetailed drawer w/two replaced brass pulls, on slender square tapering legs, old red repaint, early 19th c., 14 x 28", overall 33" h. (top renailed) **660**

Federal country-style side table, cherry & maple, the long octagonal top tilting over a baluster- and ring-turned pedestal on a tripod base w/spider legs, New England, ca. 1790, 14 3/4 x 22", 28" h. (old finish) **4,025**

Federal Country-style Tavern Table

Federal country-style tavern table, maple, the rectangular breadboard top widely overhanging an apron w/a single long drawer raised on slender square tapering legs, old surface w/vestiges of dark brown paint, possibly southeastern New England, ca. 1800, 25 x 36", 27 3/4" h. (ILLUS.) **2,875**

Federal country-style tavern table, painted pine & maple, a long rectangular top w/breadboard ends overhanging a deep apron joining four square tapering legs, old red paint on base, New England, ca. 1790-1810, 28 x 46", 28" h. (imperfections) **2,530**

Federal country-style tavern table, pine, rectangular two-board removable top above a slightly canted apron on four canted square tapering legs, old red finish, Pennsylvania, early 19th c., 22 1/2 x 26 1/2", 28 3/4" h. (pins for top missing, top cleaned) **990**

Federal country-style work table, birch & pine, wide one-board rectangular top overhanging the apron w/a single long dovetailed drawer w/replaced small wood turned pulls, square tapering legs, cleaned down to old red wash, pegged construction w/square nails, first half 19th c., 27 1/8 x 41 3/4", 29" h. (chips on top, areas of touch up) **550**

Federal country-style work table, cherry & walnut, scrubbed one-board rectangular top widely overhanging a deep apron, on square tapered legs w/corner bead, old worn finish, first half 19th c., 26 x 41 3/4", 28 1/4" h. (minor edge wear, age cracks, minor top warp) **825**

Federal Country-style Work Table

Federal country-style work table, maple, the square top overhanging a deep apron w/two deep drawers w/original fiery opalescent lacy glass pulls, paneled sides, raised on ring-, knob- and spiral-turned legs w/knob & peg feet, old refinish, ca. 1840, 18" sq., 30" h. (ILLUS.) **450**

Federal country-style work table, poplar, wide rectangular three-board top widely overhanging the deep apron w/mortised

& pinned square tapering legs, refinished, 19th c., 37 x 71", 30" h. (stains on top, repairs to legs, apron braced) **495**

Federal Maple Work Table

Federal country-style work table, tiger stripe & bird's-eye maple, a rectangular top flanked by rounded wide drop leaves above a deep apron w/two drawers w/small brass knobs, on ring-, baluster- and rod-turned legs ending in knob feet, replaced brasses, refinished, probably New York, ca. 1825, 17 x 24", 28" h. (ILLUS.) **805**

Federal country-style work table, walnut, rectangular three-board removable top w/underside cleats dovetailed into the top, on a deep apron w/a pair of deep dovetailed drawers w/turned wood knobs, ring- and knob-turned legs w/a long central octagonal section, knob feet, probably original finish, early 19th c., 33 3/4 x 48", 30" h. (one cleat cracked) **1,320**

Federal country-style work table, walnut, wide rectangular two-board removable top widely overhanging the deep apron w/two drawers, one longer than the other, raised on well done ring-, rod- and knob-turned legs w/peg feet, old mellow refinishing, Pennsylvania, 19th c., 33 x 50 1/2", 30" h. (age crack in top) **1,705**

Phyfe-style Federal Dining Table

Federal dining table, carved & veneered mahogany, two-pedestal form, the oblong reeded top w/reeded corners opening to accept one leaf, raised on two urn-form pedestals above a tripod base w/outswept acanthus-carved legs ending in brass paw caps & casters, in the manner of Duncan Phyfe or one of his contemporaries, repairs to some legs, open 45 x 84", 29" h. (ILLUS.) **2,875**

Federal dining table, mahogany, a long rectangular top flanked by wide rectangular drop leaves, raised on four square double tapering legs, two swinging out for support, joined by a straight apron w/crossbanded & string inlaid edge, cuff inlaid legs, original finish, New England, ca. 1790-1800, 17 x 47", 28 1/2" h. (very minor imperfections).......... **2,990**

Federal dining table, mahogany & bird's-eye maple, long rectangular top flanked by D-form hinged drop leaves above a dovetailed drawer at each end w/maple veneer drawer fronts w/old brass rosette & bail pulls, on slender square tapering legs w/double line inlay, early 19th c., 18 7/8 x 44" plus 9 1/2" leaves, 27 1/2" h. (restorations).. **1,100**

Federal dining table, mahogany & mahogany veneer, three-part, D-form end sections on conforming aprons w/cock-beaded edges joining four vase- and ring-turned slightly swelled reeded legs topped by veneered dies & ending in applied brass ball feet, flanking a central rectangular top w/deep hinged drop leaves on a deeply recessed straight apron joining six tapering square legs, two of which swing out, old surface, Philadelphia, ca. 1810-15, open 54 x 122", 28 3/4" h. (minor repairs)........... **9,200**

Federal dining table, mahogany & mahogany veneer, two-part, each section w/a D-shaped top above a conforming straight apron w/cross-banded lower edges continuing around the square tapering legs, each half w/a single wide hinged rectangular drop leaf, old refinish, New England, ca. 1800, 43 x 84", 29" h. (imperfections)... **2,645**

Federal dining table, mahogany, two-part, each half of demi-lune form w/a molded edge & a wide hinged drop leaf, wide plain conforming apron, each half w/four reeded & ring-turned legs w/ball feet, one leg a swing-out support for the leaf, Massachusetts, probably Newburyport, late 18th to early 19th c., open 48 x 90", 30" h.. **7,188**

Federal dining table, mahogany veneer, three-part, the two D-form ends flanking a rectangular center section w/two hinged drop leaves, raised on square tapering legs, old surface, Virginia, early 19th c., extended 48 x 85 1/2", 28 3/4" h. (imperfections)... **12,650**

Federal dining table, mahogany veneer, two-part, the two ends each rounded & w/a hinged leaf supported from beneath, above a skirt on ring-turned spiral-carved legs ending in ring-turned feet on casters, Massachusetts, 1820s, 46 x 78 3/4", 28 3/4" h. (minor surface blemishes).......... **1,840**

Federal games table, carved mahogany, the rectangular top w/serpentine sides & front w/a hinged leaf over a conforming apron w/flowerhead-carved corner dies on waterleaf-carved reeded tapering legs ending in peg feet, appears to retain old & possibly original finish, attributed to the Haines-Connelly School, Philadelphia, ca. 1810, closed 18 x 35 3/4", 29 1/2" h. (top warp repairs, repairs to top left rear leg)...... **2,587**

Federal games table, inlaid cherry, the rectangular string-inlaid top w/ovolu corners, the apron w/a central long drawer w/round brass pull flanked by oval inlaid dies atop six square tapering legs, appears to have original brass, New York or Connecticut, ca. 1800, closed 17 x 34 1/4", 29 3/4" h. **4,887**

Federal library table, carved & figured mahogany, the rectangular top flanked by trefoil hinged leaves above a paneled apron w/turned corner drop finials on four leaf- and baluster-turned columnar supports above a block raised on downswept acanthus-carved legs ending in brass paw caps & casters, in the manner of Duncan Phyfe, New York, ca. 1815, open 39 x 51", 28 1/4" h. (repairs to two legs)...................... **2,875**

Federal Pembroke Table

Federal Pembroke table, cherry, rectangular top flanked by rectangular drop leaves above an apron w/a single end drawer w/wooden knob, raised on slender square tapering legs joined by arched cross-stretchers, old refinish, New England, ca. 1810, open 34 x 38", 29" h. (ILLUS.)........... **1,495**

Inlaid Cherry Pembroke Table

Federal Pembroke table, inlaid cherry, rectangular top w/rounded ends flanked by half-round drop leaves w/incised beaded edges above a conforming skirt w/an end drawer, the lower edge inlaid w/contrasting stringing, on four square tapering legs w/icicle inlay, stringing & banded cuffs, original drawer handle, old refinish, minor imperfections, probably Rhode Island, ca. 1800, 32 3/4 x 36 3/4", 27 3/4" h. (ILLUS.).. **7,475**

Federal Pembroke table, inlaid mahogany, a rectangular top flanked by elliptically edged leaves w/square corners & stringing above a crossbanded apron of working & faux birch-veneered end drawers, bordered by stringing joining four square tapering legs inlaid w/wavy birch panels in the dies above stringing & inlaid legs, New York, ca. 1790-1800, 20 1/2 x 30 1/2", 28 1/2" h. (refinishing, some sun fading) **2,300**

Federal Pembroke table, inlaid mahogany, a rectangular top flanked by hinged drop leaves w/notched & rounded corners bordered by inlaid stringing, the apron w/a working drawer at one end & a false drawer at the other, each w/stringed inlay & flanked by shaped satinwood corner panels above the square tapering legs, old oval brasses, old finish, probably New York, 1790-1800, closed 19 x 32", 28 1/2" h. (imperfections) **2,990**

Federal Pembroke table, inlaid mahogany, a rectangular top w/gently bowed ends flanked by D-form drop leaves above a conforming apron w/a single line-inlaid drawer at one end, on square tapering legs w/inlaid cuffs, New York, early 19th c., 32" l., 28" h. **5,175**

Federal Pembroke table, mahogany & mahogany veneer, rectangular top flanked by two half-round scalloped drop leaves above an apron w/a working beaded drawer at one end & a false drawer at the other, on slender reeded turned & tapering legs w/peg feet, attributed to Newburyport, Massachusetts, early 19th c., refinished top, old finish on base, closed 19 x 30 1/2", 28 1/2" h. (replaced brasses, break in one rule joint, minor restoration) **2,090**

Federal Pembroke table, mahogany veneer, a rectangular top flanked by wide D-form drop leaves w/notched corners above an apron w/a working drawer at one end & a faux drawer at the other, raised on turned tapering reeded legs w/baluster- and knob-turned feet, old refinish, New York, early 19th c., 22 1/2 x 36", 28 1/8" h. (replaced drawer pull, very minor imperfections).................... **1,380**

Federal Pembroke table, mahogany veneer, rectangular top flanked by shaped drop leaves & two end drawers, one working, one faux, above a cockbeaded skirt & turned & reeded tapering legs on casters, old refinish, replaced brass, New York, New York, ca. 1815, 22 1/4 x 34", 29" h. (very minor imperfections) **3,105**

Federal Pembroke table, mahogany veneer, rectangular top flanked by wide half-round hinged leaves above an apron w/a working drawer at one end & a faux drawer at the other, cockbeaded skirt raised above spiral-turned tapering legs ending in ring-turned peg feet, old refinish, New York, ca. 1815, 23 x 36", 27 1/2" h. (replaced brass).......................... **1,150**

Federal side table, inlaid cherry, a rectangular top w/tiger maple inlaid edging above an apron w/a single long drawer w/line inlay above a serpentine front apron, raised on square tapering legs w/arched line & geometric inlay, Newburyport, Massachusetts, early 19th c., 21 x 33", 30 1/2" h...................................... **8,050**

Federal side table, mahogany, a rectangular top w/molded edges flanked by D-form drop leaves flanking an apron w/a single long drawer w/replaced lion head brass pulls, raised on a tapering octagonal column over four outswept sabre legs ending in brass paw feet on casters, refinished, early 19th c., 29 1/4 x 79 1/4" plus 9 1/2" leaves, 27 1/2" h. **605**

Unusual Federal Sofa Table

Federal sofa table, figured maple, the rectangular long top w/reeded edges flanked by D-form drop leaves above an apron w/a long cockbeaded drawer w/two oval brass pulls, on slender ring- and rod-turned legs w/knob ankles & peg feet, appears to retain original hardware, probably New England, early 19th c., 29 3/4 x 44 3/4", 29" h. (ILLUS.) **4,887**

Federal tea table, inlaid mahogany, a rectangular top w/cut corners bordered w/inlaid geometric stringing & crossbanding tilting on a vase- and ring-turned post on a tripod base w/spider legs inlaid w/geometric banding, old refinish, probably Massachusetts, 16 1/4 x 23 1/4", 29" h. (imperfections) **2,990**

Federal New England Work Table

Federal work table, birch & mahogany veneer, rectangular top flanked by D-form drop leaves over an apron w/two drawers each w/two large round brass pulls, raised on bobbin-, baluster- and ring-turned tapering legs w/knob feet on casters, old finish, imperfections, New England, ca. 1830, 16 3/4 x 19 3/4", 28 3/4" h. (ILLUS.) **748**

Fine Federal Work Table

Federal work table, figured mahogany, the hinged rectangular top opening to a fitted interior w/adjustable writing surface flanked by compartments, the deep case w/two flush drawers w/pairs of round brass pulls raised on slender ring- and baluster-turned supports to a medial shelf w/concave front over short ring- and baluster-turned legs on casters, appears to retain original drawer pulls, patches to veneer, New York City, ca. 1810, 16 3/4 x 20 1/2", 31" h. (ILLUS.) **4,312**

Federal work table, mahogany & figured mahogany veneer, a rectangular top above a deep case w/figured veneer on the front including two drawers w/original florette & ring gilded brasses, a shallow small writing drawer under the top to the right side, raised on turned reeded legs w/ring-turned sections at the top & bottom w/peg feet on casters, refinished, ca. 1810-20, 16 1/2 x 21", 30" h. (minor veneer repair, writing drawer missing hinged shelf, age cracks) **1,540**

Federal-Style card table, inlaid mahogany, a fold-over D-form top w/two pointed rim sections above the conforming lower top on a deep apron w/line-inlaid panels & diamonds at the top of the four square tapering legs, rear spring legs, old dark finish, early 20th c., 18 x 35", 28 3/4" h. (veneer chips on inside of apron) **550**

Federal-Style card table, inlaid mahogany, a rectangular hinged top w/rounded inset corners above a conforming apron w/line-inlaid reserves, the center w/an inlaid shell, flanked by two inlaid urns over a banded edge, on square tapering legs w/bellflower & line inlay & banded cuffs headed by inlaid rosettes, 20th c., open 34 x 36", 29" h. **460**

Federal-Style side table, mahogany & mahogany veneer, the delicate superstructure w/a narrow rectangular top w/low serpentine gallery raised on end crossform supports & a solid back w/fine crock-grain veneer above the small rectangular top w/molded edges above a case w/a pair of cross-banded drawers over a long drawer all w/small round

Delicate Federal-Style Side Table

brass pulls, the case w/bail end handles, raised on ring-turned & reeded slender legs w/tapering outswept feet, original finish, ca. 1910, 15 x 22", 42" h. (ILLUS.) **650**

George II-Style Console Table

George II-Style console table, carved giltwood, the rectangular thick marble top above a carved frieze band centering a large scroll-carved cartouche, raised on fully carved spread-winged giltwood eagles on rockwork raised on a conforming plinth base, England, 19th c., 27 x 73", 35" h. (ILLUS.) **8,625**

Harvest table, country-style, pine, a large rectangular two-board 'pumpkin pine' top raised on a quilt frame base w/braced upright end legs on cross-form feet w/curved toes, worn old red, 19th c., 38 3/4 x 78", 28 3/4" h. (leg repairs) **688**

Harvest table, painted pine, a very long scrubbed top flanked by hinged drop leaves, painted base w/ring- and rod-turned legs w/knob feet, early surface w/old natural color top & early olive green paint on base, New England, late 18th - early 19th c., open 39 3/4 x 102 3/4", 20 1/2" h. (imperfections) **11,500**

Harvest table, painted pine, long rectangular two-board top w/breadboard ends widely overhanging a straight skirt & ring- and baluster-turned tapering legs w/ball feet, original red paint, central Massachusetts, 1820-30, 32 x 96", 29 1/4" h. (very minor imperfections)..................................... **9,775**

Hutch (or chair) table, cherry, round three-board scrubbed top on scalloped braces tilting above a nearly square hinged seat lid w/a deep scalloped apron, on wide board legs w/scalloped edges on shaped shoe feet, underside of top in old black paint, late 18th - early 19th c., 43 x 45 1/2", 28 1/2" h. (some edge damage to feet, repair at hinge of seat, age cracks on seat lid).. **9,350**

Early Painted Hutch Table

Hutch (or chair) table, painted & decorated pine, the rectangular overhanging top lifting above a bench seat joining cut-out ends w/recessed panels on cut-out feet, old yellow paint w/grain-painted oblong panels & black accents, possibly Upstate New York, early 19th c., imperfections, 35 3/4 x 52 1/4", 30" h. (ILLUS.) **3,335**

Hutch (or chair) table, painted maple & pine, wide square breadboard top widely overhanging & tilting above four square chamfered tapering posts joined by two horizontal rails & continuing to form square legs joined by a medial square seat & box stretchers, old red paint, New England, late 18th c., 44 1/2 x 46 3/4", 27 1/2" h. (loss of height)............................ **5,175**

Hutch (or chair) table, painted pine, a long wide rectangular three-board top tilting on mortised braces above wide bootjack ends flanking the wide two-board seat w/apron, old worn green repaint, 35 x 72", 28" h. (chips, age cracks) **3,300**

Hutch (or chair) table, painted pine, the long rectangular top lifting above a reeded bench seat joining double-demi-lune cut-out ends w/exposed tenons, old red paint, New Jersey, early 19th c., 35 3/4 x 76", 27" h. (minor imperfections).. **9,775**

Hutch (or chair) table, painted pine, the oblong scrubbed top tilts above the base on shoe feet, lift seat over deep box compartment, old red paint, New England, 18th c., 42 1/2 x 43 1/4", 26 1/2" h. (top squared at the ends, other minor imperfections).. **1,380**

Rectangular Hutch Table

Hutch (or chair) table, painted pine, the rectangular cleated top w/old red paint tilting above wide sides & closed back over seat w/narrow apron, low cut-out feet, original red surface, minor surface imperfections, New England, early 19th c., 36 x 43", 27 1/2" h. (ILLUS.) **3,220**

Hutch (or chair) table, painted pine, the round top attached w/dowels & tilting above the shaped arms & plank seat over shoe feet, early red paint, New England, 18th c., 48 3/4 x 54 1/4", 27 1/2" h. **6,900**

Early Painted Pine Hutch Table

Hutch (or chair) table, painted pine, the round top tilting on two cut-out ends joined by a beaded frontal panel continuing to molded shoe feet, red paint over earlier paint, probably New England, 18th c., 31" d., 26 1/4" h. (ILLUS.)............. **6,900**

Hutch (or chair) table, pine, birch & poplar, two-board rectangular top w/breadboard ends & scrubbed finish, tilting above a mortised & pinned base w/a single drawer under the seat & raised on shoe feet, traces of old red finish, found in Vermont, 19th c., 37 3/4 x 41 3/4", 28 3/4" h. (age cracks in top)... **4,180**

Hutch (or chair) table, pine, long rectangular top hinged on two sides w/demi-lune tops & cut-out feet joined w/a medial shelf w/exposed tenons, old surface, possibly Pennsylvania, early 19th c., 35 3/4 x 55", 29 3/4" h. **1,380**

Hutch (or chair) table, pine & maple, round top overhanging & tilting above a seat between square leg stiles & box stretchers, old refinish, New England, early 19th, 44" d., 29" h. **805**

Jacobean-Style Dining Table

Jacobean-Style dining table, inlaid walnut, draw-leaf extension-type, the rectangular top w/draw-leaf extensions above an S-scroll-carved apron w/scroll-carved brackets above the bulbous carved cup-and-cover design legs on shaped shoe feet joined by a half-round stretcher, some wear, ca. 1900, 35 x 71 1/2", 31" h. (ILLUS.).. **8,625**

Late Victorian Oak Parlor Table

Late Victorian parlor table, quarter-sawn oak, a square top w/carved corners raised on four canted ring-turned & reeded legs w/bulbous center knobs joined by aprons w/a central palmette leaf carved panel flanked by ring-turned rails & a squared, shaped medial shelf joined to the legs w/iron scrolled mounts, the legs ending in brass claw-and-ball feet w/glass balls, original finish, ca. 1900, 20" w., 30" h. (ILLUS.) **400**

Fine Louis XV-Style Side Table

Louis XV-Style bouilllotte side table, bronze-mounted veneer, the rounded shaped inset marble top w/gilt-bronze edge banding over a veneered apron w/gilt-bronze banding & simple slender cabriole legs w/long leafy scroll gilt-bronze mounts & banding ending in leaf-form "sabots," France, late 19th cf., 23" d., 29 3/4" h. (ILLUS.)........................... **5,175**

Louis XV-Style French Console Table

Louis XV-Style console table, giltwood, the half-round marble top w/serpentine molded edges above a deep pierced trellis-carved apron centered by a foliate-carved cartouche, raised on shell-, berry- and foliate-carved incurved scrolled legs joined by a floral-carved X-form stretcher centered by a shell, stamped four times "Sormani," by Paul Sormani, Paris, France, late 19th c., 55" w., 37" h. (ILLUS.).................................. **8,625**

Louis XV-Style Marquetry Side Table

Louis XV-Style side table, gilt-bronze mounted tulipwood marquetry, the shaped rectangular top veneered w/a flower-filled basket & sprays of flowers within a brass banding, above a single frieze drawer, the drawer & apron sides similarly inlaid w/flowers, raised on simple cabriole legs w/gilt-bronze knee mounts & sabots, France, late 19th c., 16 x 27", 28" h. (ILLUS.) **6,600**

Louis XVI-Style center table, carved giltwood, the shaped rectangular top above an apron w/floral sprays, raised on fluted tapering round legs joined by an H-stretcher, France, late 19th c., 27 x 35", 31" h. **632**

Mission-style (Arts & Crafts movement) dining table, a narrow rectangular top w/rounded ends flanked by wide half-round drop leaves, raised on double square legs forming a trestle base & w/two swing-out support legs, branded mark of L. & J.G. Stickley, Model No. 553, ca. 1915, 42" d., 30" h. **4,935**

Mission-style (Arts & Crafts movement) dining table, oak, the wide rectangular top w/rounded ends flanked by narrow D-form drop leaves, over a round split apron supported on a heavy square central post issuing cross stretchers to the four heavy square outside legs, new reddish brown finish, red decal mark of Gustav Stickley, open 54" d., 28 1/2" h. **4,675**

Mission-style (Arts & Crafts movement) dining table, oak, divided round top w/molded edge above a square pedestal w/four square extended feet, fine original finish, branded marks of the Charles Limbert Furniture Co., w/two original leaves, veneer chip to apron, 48" d., 30" h. **2,090**

Mission-style (Arts & Crafts movement) lamp table, oak, a round top over a narrow conforming apron w/four inset square slender legs joined by a round medial shelf, refinished top, remnant of Gustav Stickley paper label, 24" d., 29" h. **2,310**

Mission-style (Arts & Crafts movement) library table, oak, a rectangular top slightly overhanging an apron w/a pair of drawers w/rectangular copper pulls over long corbels on the heavy square legs joined by a lower medial shelf w/through-tenons joining the end stretchers, Handcraft decal of L. & J.G. Stickley, Model No. 522, 1906-10, 30 x 48", 30" h. **1,840**

Limbert Mission Oak Library Table

Mission-style (Arts & Crafts movement) library table, oak, a wide rectangular top overhanging a case w/two-tiered end open shelves w/vertical slats at each end & joined by a single long drawer over a lower medial stretcher shelf, original finish, branded Charles Limbert mark, Model No. 106, ca. 1907, 29 1/2 x 48", 29 1/2" h. (ILLUS.) **1,380**

Mission-style (Arts & Crafts movement) library table, oak, rectangular top above

an apron w/a row of three drawers w/metal plates & looped pulls, square stile legs joined by a cross stretcher w/wide upright splat & a medial wide shelf, red decal & paper label of Gustav Stickley, Model No. 659, ca. 1909, 31 3/4 x 53 7/8", 29 3/4" h. **7,475**

Mission-style (Arts & Crafts movement) library table, oak, rectangular top overhanging an apron w/a pair of drawers w/rectangular copper pulls, heavy square legs joined by medial shelf w/pegged through-tenons, medium brown finish, red decal mark of Gustav Stickley, Model No. 675, 29 3/4 x 47 1/2", 30" h. (stains, scratches, joint separation) **1,840**

Fine Gustav Stickley Library Table

Mission-style (Arts & Crafts movement) library table, oak, the round leather-covered top trimmed w/large brass edge tacks overhanging the canted & arched apron joining the heavy canted rectangular legs w/through-tenon cross stretchers, Gustav Stickley Model No. 636, early 20th c. (ILLUS.) **24,750**

Mission-style (Arts & Crafts movement) library table, oak, spindle-style, the rectangular top above a narrow apron on slender square legs joined by end stretchers w/13 small slender close spindles joining them to the top at each end, medial shelf below, fine new finish, unsigned Gustav Stickley, Model No. 655, 24 x 36", 29" h. **4,125**

Mission-style (Arts & Crafts movement) library table, oak, rectangular top over an apron w/a single drawer w/original brass pulls flanked by book shelves opening at the sides, fine original reddish brown finish, branded mark of Charles Limbert Co., Model No. 132, 28 x 45", 29" h. **935**

Mission-style (Arts & Crafts movement) library table, rectangular top overhanging an apron w/two drawers w/original copper hardware, double- keyed lower stretcher, refinished, unsigned L. & J.G. Stickley, Model No. 531, 30 x 48", 29" h. (extensive restoration) **413**

Mission-style (Arts & Crafts movement) library table, oak, rectangular top above a deep apron w/gently arched ends & two long drawers w/original hardware along one side, long corbels at the outside top

Lifetime Mission-style Library Table

of the four square legs, six wide slats on the lower ends on rails joined by a narrow medial stretcher shelf, original finish, some veneer restoration, paper label of the Lifetime Furniture Co., Model No. 999, 30 x 54", 30" h. (ILLUS.) **990**

Lifetime Company Library Table

Mission-style (Arts & Crafts movement) library table, oak, a thick wide rectangular top overhanging a deep apron w/two long drawers on the long sides w/original copper hardware, on heavy square legs w/through-tenon end stretchers & a medial shelf stretcher, recent finish, paper label of the Lifetime Furniture Company, Model No. 911, 32 x 54", 30" h. (ILLUS.)... **1,870**

Mission-style (Arts & Crafts movement) library table, oak, a wide rectangular top overhanging an apron w/a pair of drawers w/original copper bail pulls, heavy square legs w/upper corbels & through-tenon end stretchers joined by a wide medial shelf, fine original reddish brown finish w/some color added to stretcher, branded signature of Gustav Stickley, Model No. 617, 32 x 54", 30" h. **3,850**

Mission-style (Arts & Crafts movement) parlor table, round top overhanging an apron w/inset square legs joined by cross stretchers below a round medial shelf, original finish w/some stains, "Handcraft" decal of L. & J.G. Stickley, Model No. 541, 30" d., 29" h. **1,760**

Mission-style (Arts & Crafts movement) parlor table, oak, round top above a deep apron w/molded rim, four inset square legs joined by a cross stretcher,

fine original finish, orb mark of The Roycroft Shop, Model No. 073, 36" d., 30" h. ... **7,700**

Mission-style (Arts & Crafts movement) side table, oak, a round top raised on heavy square legs joined by an arched cross-stretcher w/through-tenon construction, cleaned original finish, signed w/faint box mark of Gustav Stickley, Model No. 603, 18" d., 20" h. (minor splits) **1,440**

Mission-style (Arts & Crafts movement) side table, oak, octagonal top w/through-tenon square legs joined by arched cross stretchers, top w/a recent finish, base w/original finish, branded mark of L. & J.G. Stickley, Model No. 558, 18" w., 20" h. **1,320**

Mission-style (Arts & Crafts movement) side table, oak, a rectangular top raised on four slender square legs joined by a rectangular medial shelf, legs mortised through the top w/flush tenons, some wear to top, otherwise good original finish, L. & J.G. Stickley, Model No. 509, 17 x 26", 24" h. **2,420**

Mission-style (Arts & Crafts movement) side table, round top w/inset heavy square legs joined by a flared cross-stretcher base, cleaned original finish, unsigned Gustav Stickley, Model No. 440, 30" d., 29" h. **2,200**

Stickley Brothers "Quaint" Side Table

Mission-style (Arts & Crafts movement) side table, oak, a round top above a square narrow apron on four slender square legs w/through-tenon cross stretchers, original finish, Quaint metal tag of the Stickley Brothers, Model No. 2500, 24" d., 30" h. (ILLUS.) **990**

Mission-style (Arts & Crafts movement) tea table, oak, square top on four square post legs joined by a single lower shelf, paper label of L. & J.G. Stickley, Model No. 587, 1902-16, 15 7/8 x 16", 27" h. **460**

Mission-style (Arts & Crafts movement) trestle table, oak, a rectangular top widely overhanging end aprons w/incurved ends above pairs of wide slats joined by a medial shelf w/through-tenons, flat wide shoe feet below, recoated original finish, branded Gustav Stickley mark, 29 x 48", 30" h. **1,980**

Modern style coffee table, laminated birch, "Surfboard"-style, the top of seven-ply Baltic birch cover, long oval high-pressure laminate top & underside, raised on a wire base w/black power-coated finish, Herman Miller, ca. 1950s, 29 x 89", 10" h... **7,280**

Fine Modern Style Coffee Table

Modern style coffee table, maple, glass & brass, the long tapering oval plate glass top raised on a widely flaring V-shaped maple three-part support w/a pair of forked legs at the front & tiny brackets at the back, an oval plate glass medial shelf, designed by Carlo Mollino, manufactured by Singer and Company, New York, glass shelves acid-etched "Secuisit," ca. 1952, 24 1/2 x 50 1/2", 16" h. (ILLUS.)... **19,550**

Modern Style Bronze Coffee Table

Modern style coffee table, patinated bronze, the round top cast in low-relief w/Chinese figures in a landscape, raised on round-section legs headed by brackets & ending in casters, signed by Philip La Verne, 1950s, 45" d., 17" h. (ILLUS.) ... **2,070**

Modern style dinette table, laminate & aluminum, the round white laminate top w/rubber edge raised on a white enamel slender pedestal & cased aluminum cross-form base, designed by Charles Eames, manufactured by Herman Miller, ca. 1950s, 48" d., 29" h........................ **176**

1950s Dinette Table

Modern style dinette table, laminate & metal, the rectangular top flanked by wide D-form drop leaves all in red laminate w/black edging, raised on forked black tubular metal angled legs, National Chair Company, Whitman, Massachusetts, ca. 1955, minor surface abrasions, closed 21 3/4 x 29 3/4", 29 1/4" h. (ILLUS.).................. **86**

Modern Style Trestle Dining Table

Modern style dining table, golden birch, draw-leaf trestle-style, the rectangular top incised w/a grid flanked by the ends sliding open to accept a leaf at each end, raised on X-form trestle supports joined by a wide stretcher, design attributed to T. H. Robsjohn-Gibbings, ca. 1950s, 40 x 60", 30" h. (ILLUS.) **1,380**

Modern style dining table, rectangular top w/grey laminate resting on a black frame, designed by Charles & Ray Eames, made by Herman Miller, ca. 1952, 34 x 54", 29" h. **862**

Modern style 'dish' table, ash plywood & metal, the wide round dished plywood top raised on four slender black metal legs w/rubber boot feet, designed by Charles Eames, manufactured by Herman Miller, ca. 1950s, 34" d., 16" h. (minor stains in top).. **990**

Haywood-Wakefield Dressing Table

Modern style dressing table, mahogany, a high pointed arch mirror above a tapering rectangular top on conforming open compartment at one end w/a quarter-round rank of three drawers w/long wooden pulls at the opposite end, on tapering bracket feet, champagne finish, mark of Haywood-Wakefield, Model No. M586, ca. 1955, 19 1/4 x 50", 62 3/4" h. (ILLUS.)............ **345**

Unique Stacked Book End Table

Modern-style end table, painted gesso on wood, carved to resemble a stack of colorful large books set at various angles, ca. 1950s-60s, 16" w., 24" h. (ILLUS.) **350**

Fine Napolean III Side Table

Napolean III side table, marquetry & burl, square top w/ornate central marquetry squared panel framed by ornate scrolling above four D-form burl-banded & marquetry scroll-decorated drop leaves, on gilt-metal-mounted turned & tapering legs w/ring-turned peg feet joined by a curved cross stretcher centered by an urn-form finial, France, late 19th c., 21" sq., 30" h. (ILLUS.) **2,300**

Queen Anne country-style tavern table, maple, rectangular two-board top w/notched corners cleaned & w/old finish w/stains, widely overhanging a deep flat mortised & pinned apron on turned tapered legs ending in duck feet, old red on the base, 18th c., 26 1/2 x 36", 27 1/2" h. (minor old age crack in top) **5,500**

Queen Anne country-style tavern table, pine & maple, rectangular top widely overhanging a deep apron w/a single dovetailed drawer w/early peg pull, on ring-, baluster- and block-turned legs w/worn button feet, joined by worn box stretchers, mortise & peg construction, refinished, 18th c., 26 x 39", 27" h. (two glued breaks w/putty repairs in top) **2,640**

Queen Anne Country Tea Table

Queen Anne country-style tea table, maple & pine, the rectangular breadboard top widely overhanging a valanced apron w/a single long drawer, raised on four cabriole legs ending in pad feet, old refinish, top of different origin, other imperfections, New England, 18th c., 26 x 38 1/4", 27" h. (ILLUS.) **2,875**

Early Queen Anne Dining Table

Queen Anne dining table, carved & figured walnut, the rectangular top flanked by deep rectangular drop leaves, arched end aprons on cabriole legs ending in paneled trifid feet, appears to retain an old & possibly original finish, warm nut-brown color, Pennsylvania, ca. 1750, closed 17 1/2 x 50 1/2", 28" h. (ILLUS.) **4,887**

Queen Anne dining table, mahogany, a narrow rectangular top flanked by two wide rectangular drop leaves above a scalloped apron & four cabriole legs w/arris knees continuing to pad feet, old refinish, New England, late 18th c., 46 x 47", 27 3/8" h. (imperfections) **2,760**

Queen Anne dining table, maple, a narrow rectangular top w/rounded ends flanked by wide D-form drop leaves on a straight apron raised on four block-turned tapering legs ending in pad feet, old refinish, Rhode Island, ca. 1750-70, 41 x 42", 26 1/2" h. (imperfections, restorations) **1,610**

Queen Anne dining table, maple, narrow rectangular top w/slightly rounded ends flanked by wide half-round hinged drop leaves above a straight apron on four block-turned tapering legs ending in pad feet, two legs swing-out for support, southeastern New England, 1740-60, refinished, 30 1/2 x 38 1/4", 26" h. (minor imperfections)... **6,325**

Queen Anne dining table, painted maple, a rectangular top w/rounded ends flanked by D-form hinged drop leaves over the deep straight skirt on ring- and baluster-turned legs w/turned tab feet, scrubbed top, original surface, faint greyish green paint, original but rough condition, Rhode Island, late 18th c., 14 1/2 x 42", 26 3/4" h. **5,463**

Queen Anne dining table, Santo Domingo mahogany, rectangular narrow top flanked by deep rectangular hinged leaves overhanging the shaped apron on cabriole legs ending in pad feet on platforms, old finish, Rhode Island, ca. 1750-60, 16 1/2 x 47 3/4", 28 1/2" h. (minor imperfections)... **10,925**

Queen Anne dressing table, carved cherry, rectangular thumb-molded top overhanginig the case w/a single long drawer above a row of three smaller drawers, the central one fan-carved, large ornate butterfly brasses, cyma-curved apron, four cabriole legs w/spurs & arris knees ending in high-pad feet, original brasses, old refinish, coastal Massachusetts, New Hampshire or Maine, 1750-80, 20 x 33", 30" h. (imperfections) **29,900**

Queen Anne Dressing Table

Queen Anne dressing table, maple & pine, rectangular top w/molded edges above an apron w/a pair of deep drawers flanking a small shallow central drawer above a deeply scalloped apron w/two urn-turned drops, simple cabriole legs ending in pad feet, rear knee return missing, formerly painted white, New England, 1740-60, 18 1/2 x 34 1/2", 29 1/2" h. (ILLUS.) **3,737**

Boston Queen Anne Dressing Table

Queen Anne dressing table, walnut, the rectangular top w/a molded edge & notched front corners overhanging a case w/a long thumb-molded drawer over a row of three deep drawers, the central long one w/fan carving, the apron w/flat-headed arches on cabriole legs ending in pad feet, replaced brasses, old surface, Massachusetts, 1730-50, 19 1/2 x 34 1/2", 28 1/2" h. (minor repairs & losses)............ **28,750**

Queen Anne dressing table, walnut, the thumb-molded rectangular top w/shaped front corners overhanging a case w/one long drawer over a row of three deep drawers, the central one w/a lunette, flat arched apron w/drop pendants, on cabriole legs ending in high pad feet, replaced brasses, old finish, repairs, Boston, 1730-50, 21 x 34 1/2", 30 1/2" h. (ILLUS. bottom previous column) **10,350**

Queen Anne mixing table, painted, a rectangular top w/a projecting molded edge enclosing a black marble slab above a deep openwork apron carved w/overlapping circles & diamonds, raised on angular cabriole legs w/scrolled returns & ending in stylized hairy paw feet, painted black, 18th c., 20 x 32 1/2", 28" h. **7,000**

Quality Queen Anne Tavern Table

Queen Anne tavern table, painted pine, oval top widely overhangs a deep apron on splayed ring- and rod-turned tapering legs ending in turned feet, scrubbed top, original red paint on base, minor imperfections, New England, 18th c., 26 3/8 x 35", 26 1/4" h. (ILLUS.) **14,950**

Queen Anne Small Tavern Table

Queen Anne tavern table, poplar & turned maple, rectangular top w/rounded corners above a deep apron on tapering turned legs ending in pad feet, repair to top, top possibly reshaped, New England, 1740-60, 14 x 19 1/2", 25 1/2" h. (ILLUS.)............ **2,875**

Queen Anne tea table, cherry, round dished top tilting & turning on a birdcage mechanism over a ring- and baluster-turned pedestal above a tripod base w/cabriole legs ending in slipper feet, Connecticut River Valley, 1760-90, 23 1/2" d., 28 1/2" h....................... **2,530**

Queen Anne tea table, cherry, the round top tilting above a birdcage platform & a vase- and ring-turned pedestal on a tripod base w/cabriole legs ending in pad feet on platforms, old surface, probably Rhode Island, late 18th c., 33" d., 29 3/4" h. (minor imperfections) **1,610**

Queen Anne Tilt-top Tea Table

Queen Anne tea table, mahogany, wide round top tilting on a vase- and ring-turned pedestal on a tripod base w/cabriole legs ending in pad feet on platforms, refinished, minor imperfections, probably Massachusetts, ca. 1760, 33 1/8" d., 27 3/4" h. (ILLUS.)..................................... **1,840**

Queen Anne tea table, maple, oval overhanging top on a deep apron w/corner blocks continuing into turned tapering legs ending in pad feet, old refinish, 26 x 32 1/2", 25 3/4" h. (minor imperfections)... **3,220**

Queen Anne tea table, maple, oval top overhanging the valanced apron raised on four block-turned tapering round legs ending in raised pad feet, old refinish, New England, late 18th c., 26 1/2 x 32 3/4", 27 1/2" (minor imperfections).. **5,463**

Pennsylvania Queen Anne Tea Table

Queen Anne tea table, turned walnut, the large round dished top hinged & tilting & revolving above a birdcage support, the tapering columnar pedestal w/urn-form compressed-ball bottom on a tripod base w/squatty cabriole legs ending in snake feet, small section of stem at top of pedestal replaced, Pennsylvania, ca. 1750, 25 1/2" d., 26 1/2" h. (ILLUS.) **6,900**

Queen Anne work table, painted black walnut, the removable rectangular plank three-board pine top supported by cleats w/four dowels widely overhanging a deep apron w/a long & shorter drawer on one side each w/a simple turned wood knob, on beaded-edge straight cabriole legs ending in pad feet, original apple green paint, old replaced wood pulls, Pennsylvania, 1760-1800, 32 x 48 1/2", 27" h. (surface imperfections, cracked foot)......... **2,415**

Queen Anne-Style dressing table, mahogany, rectangular top w/molded edges above a conforming case fitted w/one thumb-molded long drawer over three thumb-molded short drawers, above a shaped skirt, on tapering cylindrical legs w/shaped knee returns & padded disk feet, early 20th c., 18 1/2 x 29 1/2", 28" h... **1,380**

Queen Anne-Style Dressing Table

Queen Anne-Style dressing table, painted & decorated, the shaped splashboard above a rectangular top w/black detailing over a conforming case fitted w/one thumb-molded long drawer over three thumb-molded short drawers over a scalloped apron, on cabriole legs ending in padded disk feet, yellow paint w/graining, 19th & 20th centuries, 22 1/2 x 40 1/2", 41 3/4" h. (ILLUS.)...................................... **1,840**

Queen Anne-Style Side Table

Queen Anne-Style side table, walnut, a round tan marble top w/a long pierced brass gallery raised on a reeded turned & tapering pedestal on a tripod base w/simple cabriole legs ending in pad feet on casters, ca. 1920, 24" d., 25" h. (ILLUS.) **300**

Fine Regency Sofa Table

Regency sofa table, rosewood, a rectangular top w/rounded corners & rounded edges slightly overhanging a conforming apron w/a beaded lower edge, raised on ring-, knob & baluster-turned & reeded end legs on blocked cross bars on bun feet, England, early 19th c. (ILLUS.) **4,000**

Regency-Style center table, mahogany, round top above a frieze raised on three monopodia supports carved w/lion's heads at the top & terminating in hairy paw feet joined by a tripartite concave-sided plinth centering a foliate finial, England, late 19th c., 64" d., 30 1/4" h. (wear)... **6,325**

Renaissance-Style refectory table, mahogany, the simple rectangular top raised on a scrolling standard carved w/an armorial medallion, Europe, late 19th c., 39 x 101", 30" h. **2,760**

Ornate European Console Table

Rococo style console table, giltwood, a large squared mirror w/a double-arch top

within a narrow ribbon-twist framework w/high ribbon loop crests, resting on a D-form white marble top w/molded edge resting on a narrow apron supported by a single large winged caryatid tapering to a cabriole leg w/scroll foot, Europe, mid-19th c., 16 x 40", 6' 8" h. (ILLUS.) **2,400**

"Sawbuck" table, country-style, painted pine, rectangular one-board top w/scrubbed & stained finish above the flat cross-legs w/flat stretchers, old yellow & brown ground repaint on base, found in New Hampshire, 26 x 50", 30" h....... **550**

"Sawbuck" table, painted pine, a rectangular one-board scrubbed top on crossed end legs joined by cross stretcher of applied moldings w/beaded edges, old red paint on base w/traces of white, square nail construction, 19th c., 18 3/4 x 31 3/4", 25 1/4" h. **990**

"Sawbuck" table, painted pine, one-board rectangular top w/scrubbed finish on crossed end legs joined by flat board braces w/a removable board top forming a shallow bin, square nail construction, old bluish grey repaint, 19th c., 25 1/2 x 36 1/2", 28" h. (top age cracks, some water damage to feet)....................... **2,420**

Early "Sawbuck" Table

"Sawbuck" table, painted pine, the rectangular overhanging top on a nail-constructed rectangular skirt & chamfered crossed legs joined by a turned medial stretcher w/keyed exposed tenon, old reddish brown paint, New England, mid-19th c., 28 x 50", 30" h. (ILLUS.) **2,070**

"Sawbuck" table, painted pine, wide rectangular four-board top on heavy braces raised on crossed end legs joined by slender crossed brace stretchers, old green repaint, square & wire nail construction, some old added braces, 19th c., 40 1/2 x 60 1/4", 29" h................................ **330**

"Sawbuck" table, pine & painted pine, the rectangular top w/a natural finish raised on a black-painted base w/end cross-legs joined by a flat chamfered stretcher, each section of legs w/chamfered edges, late 19th c. copy of earlier style, 23 x 48 3/4", 30" h.. **880**

"Sawbuck" table, pine, rectangular top on braces over cross-form legs joined by stretchers, enclosing a V-shaped trough, bluish green paint over old red stain, New England, 19th c., 25 1/2 x 42", 30 1/2" h. (imperfections) **805**

Early New England Sawbuck Table

"Sawbuck" table, the rectangular table overhanging a trough above square tapering X-legs, original surface w/a darkened top above a red-stained base, New England, late 18th - early 19th c., minor imperfections, 23 5/8 x 34 1/2", 28 1/2" h. (ILLUS.) **2,645**

Store table, country-style, painted, a very long rectangular top widely overhanging a deep apron w/three large drawers each w/two old iron finger-grip pulls, on square tapering chamfered legs, old beige & brown grain painting, probably New England, first half 19th c. **10,925**

Tavern table, country-style, maple, poplar & pine, a rectangular one-board wide top w/scalloped corners & a single wide drop leaf at one side also w/scalloped corners, pegged apron raised on four baluster- and block-turned legs w/turned feet all joined by flat box stretchers, refinished, late 18th - early 19th c., 23 1/2 x 39 1/2", 29" h. (hinged replaced, top loose & w/age crack, feet ended out) **1,320**

Tavern table, country-style, painted pine, a rectangular top widely overhanging a beaded apron on four square chamfered legs w/molded edges, painted red, early, 27 x 38 1/2", 26 1/2" h. **2,000**

Early Country Tavern Table

Tavern table, country-style, pine & cherry, rectangular overhanging top on four square tapering beaded splayed legs joined by a deep beaded skirt, old refin-ish, imperfections, top stains, some surface loss, two interior 19th c. braces, New England, ca. 1790, 32 x 34 1/4", 25 1/2" h. (ILLUS.) **1,265**

Early Stained Tavern Table

Tavern table, country-style, stained pine & maple, the long rectangular top w/breadboard ends overhanging an apron w/a long single drawer & simple wood knob, raised on baluster-, ring- and block-turned legs joined by a block-, ring & sausage-turned H-stretcher, on turned tapering feet, old surface, alterations, probably Mid-Atlantic States, 18th c., dark stain, 23 1/2 x 37", 26 1/4" h. (ILLUS.) **2,875**

Turn-of-the-century Oak Dining Table

Turn-of-the-century dining table, oak & oak veneer, extension-type, square top w/rounded corners & center split over a conforming apron, raised on an octagonal split pedestal w/four angled block legs on casters, w/leaves, ca. 1900, closed 45" w. (ILLUS.) **345**

Turn-of-the-century dining table, oak, round divided top resting on a columnar pedestal supported by four heavy cabriole legs ending in carved paw feet, ca. 1900, 48" d., 30 1/2" h. **588**

Turn-of-the-century library table, oak, an oblong top above a conforming apron w/a pair of drawers on one side w/bail pulls, each corner carved w/a classical female bust at the top of a cabriole leg ending in a claw-and-ball foot, a rectangular medial shelf w/serpentine sides joined w/C-scroll brackets to each leg, ca. 1890, 28 x 42", 29" h. **1,568**

Old Physician's Examination Table

Turn-of-the-century physician's examination table, quarter-sawn oak, the upholstered rectangular top above a deep apron w/applied leaf carving & hinged fold-down extensions at each end, the lower case w/a small & two larger drawers beside a large cupboard door w/applied wreath carving, all flanked by fluted corner columns, molded base, drawers fitted w/instrument trays (one missing), cast-steel foot rests labeled "The Allison. W.D. Allison Co. Indianapolis, Ind.," top recovered, ca. 1900, 22 x 40", 29" h. (ILLUS.) **550**

Carved Baroque-Style Console Table

Victorian Baroque Revival console table, quarter-sawn oak, the rectangular top w/molded edge raised on an apron w/a long deep drawer w/two leafy scroll-carved rectangular panels flanking a large central shield device w/a rampant lion, raised on four heavy square scale-carved legs on end stretchers joined by a stretcher shelf, front scroll feet, original finish, ca. 1880, 18 x 44", 38" h. (ILLUS.) **950**

Victorian Baroque Dining Table

Victorian Baroque Revival dining table, carved walnut, a rectangular draw-leaf top w/a molded & scallop-carved chamfered edge above a deep scroll-carved apron, raised on large boldly carved angled figural griffin legs joined by a cross-stretcher, late 19th c., 41 x 48", 31" h. (ILLUS.) **1,150**

Late Victorian Round Dining Table

Victorian Baroque Revival dining table, mahogany, the round expandable top w/narrow gadrooned rim band & deep apron raised on a heavy round pedestal w/the ribbed lower section surrounded by four large carved lion's heads over leaf-carved scrolls continuing into extended legs ending in paw feet, old mellow alligatored finish, w/five leaves, minor wear, late 19th c., 59 1/2" d., 29 1/2" h. (ILLUS.) **5,225**

Victorian Baroque Revival Dining Table

Victorian Baroque Revival dining table, oak, expandable, the divided round top w/a deep apron decorated w/applied leaf carving & a beaded lower edge raised on five heavy ring-turned & tapering block supports w/carved leafy scroll decoration raised on a heavy H-form flattened stretcher w/arched & scroll-carved crests, each corner resting on a heavy carved paw foot, original finish, ca. 1895, w/five leaves, 48" d., 30" h. (ILLUS.) **3,000**

Victorian Baroque Revival library table, carved mahogany, rectangular top w/beveled & carved edges above a deep gadroon-carved front apron centered by carved cherub panels, end aprons supported on central round columns flanked by figural scroll-carved winged seated griffins on blocks joined by flat medial rails, on low beaded bun feet, late 19th to early 20th c. (ILLUS.) **3,100**

Baroque Revival Library Table

Victorian Baroque Revival library table, carved oak, the rectangular top w/angled corners & stepped edges above a deep gadroon-carved apron w/the corners carved w/lion masks w/brass rings above drop blocks w/turned drop finials, triple-arch ends on lower apron raised on pairs of heavy turned & tapering legs w/ga-drooned tops, legs resting on a heavy squared leaf-carved trestle base w/out-swept dolphin-carved feet at the ends, late 19th c., original finish, 22 x 42", 30" h. (ILLUS.).................................... **1,000**

Fine English Baroque Revival Table

Victorian Baroque Revival library table, carved walnut, a long rectangular top w/molded edges above a deep apron carved w/scrolled gadrooning raised on heavy shell- and fruit-carved tapering supports on shoe feet ending w/carved recumbent lions, the ends joined by a carved trestle stretcher w/baluster-turned spindles, England, late 19th c. (ILLUS.)..... **3,000**

Elaborately Carved Oak Library Table

Victorian Baroque Revival library table, quarter-sawn oak, the wide rectangular top w/chamfered corners decorated around the border w/a wide leafy scroll band & slash-carved edge above the deep apron w/the long sides carved w/two panels each w/a grotesque mask framed by leafy scrolls, florette-carved corner blocks, raised on large nude figural caryatid supports over lion-form legs ending in paws, the legs joined by end stretchers connected by a wide medial shelf, refinished, attributed to R.S. Horner, New York City, ca. 1880s, 30 x 44", 36" h. (ILLUS.) **10,000**

Victorian Eastlake parlor center table, walnut & burl walnut, a rectangular purplish grey marble top w/rounded corners above a reeded conforming apron w/scalloped trim & central drop panels w/burl veneer trim, raised on a four-part base w/angled, molded & burl-paneled sections joined to a turned central column, on casters, ca. 1885, 20 1/4 x 30", 30" h. **385**

Victorian Eastlake Parlor Table

Victorian Eastlake parlor table, walnut, a rectangular white marble top w/scalloped corners above a line-incised apron w/scallop-cut trim raised on a cluster of four squared legs curving out at the lower section & each w/cut-out bands & scallop-cut trim, the cluster joined at the center by a center ring-turned post, on casters, ca. 1885, 18 x 30", 26" h. (ILLUS.) **252**

Eastlake Marble-topped Parlor Table

Victorian Eastlake parlor table, walnut, the white rectangular molded top w/molded edges above a flat apron w/incised bands of flowerheads & angled carved drop corners, raised on four flat scallop-carved & line-incised outswept legs joined by short flat double stretchers to a ring-turned central post, on casters, refinished, ca. 1880, 20 x 30", 30" h. (ILLUS.) 600

Victorian Eastlake side table, walnut, a rectangular top w/molded edges above a deep apron w/a narrow central burl panel flanked by incised line bands & a scroll-cut edge band on each side, raised on a cluster of four slender flat rectangular line-incised legs flaring out at the bottom & on porcelain casters, the legs centered by a baluster- and ring-turned post joined to them by a short cross stretcher, ca. 1890, 20 1/2 x 28", 31 1/4" h. 358

Victorian Eastlake side table, walnut & burl walnut, the rectangular pinkish brown marble top w/cut corners above a line-incised apron w/rectangular burl panels at the centers w/fan-scalloped designs, raised on four flat rectangular supports joined by line-incised & pierced-cut stretchers joined to a central turned post w/knob drop, raised on downswept legs w/rondels above long burl panels & scroll-incised feet raised on casters, ca. 1880, 20 x 30", 30" h. 358

Oak Dining Table with Dolphins

Victorian Golden Oak dining table, quarter-sawn oak, expandable, the divided square top over a deep flat apron w/incised bands & carved scrolls at each corner, raised on four heavy ring-, reeded baluster- and block-turned legs & a pair of slender ring- and baluster-turned inner supports, the legs joined by heavy carved stretchers topped by a high rounded panel flanked by carved figural dolphins, refinished, w/six leaves, ca. 1910, 54" w. closed, 30" h. (ILLUS.) 3,300

Victorian Golden Oak dining table, rounded divided top slightly overhanging the apron, raised on a heavy round pedestal above four large outstretched downcurved legs w/pleat-carved knees & ending in large paw feet on casters, ca. 1900, 42" d., 29 1/2" h. 413

Victorian Golden Oak side table, the square top w/a slightly serpentine edge above a narrow apron, raised on four slightly canted sausage-turned legs joined by a squared serpentine medial rail & ending in brass claw & glass ball

Golden Oak Square Side Table

feet, original finish, ca. 1900, 22" w., 30" h. (ILLUS.) 300

Victorian Renaissance Revival card tables, carved & grain-painted, each w/a D-shaped hinged top w/tongue & groove molded edge above a conforming frame fitted w/one drawer & a cartouche w/C-scrolls flanked by volutes over ring- and vasiform-turned paneled base enclosed by C-scrolled supports w/foliate carving above a tripartite base surmounted by a line-incised embellishment, on casters, ca. 1870, open 35 1/2 x 36", 30 1/2" h., pr................................. 2,070

Victorian Renaissance Revival center table, walnut marquetry, part-ebonized & parcel-gilt, the rectangular top w/rounded ends & blocked corners decorated w/inlay above a deep conforming apron w/raised burl panels w/incised gilt line decoration, on four square legs w/large square knobby blocks above the reeded tapering lower legs ending in tapering knob feet & joined by a pierced scroll-carved fan-end H-stretcher w/a turned central urn finial, ca. 1865-75, 28 1/2 x 54", 28 1/2" h. (shrinkage) 3,738

Victorian Dining Table with Ornate Legs

Victorian Renaissance Revival dining table, mahogany, expandable, the round divided top w/a deep apron carved w/scroll trim, raised on a heavy octagonal split pedestal w/half-round knob-turned spindles on panels alternating w/heavy S-scroll outswept legs carved w/beads, panels & roundels, on casters, original finish, w/six leaves, ca. 1875, 48" d., 30" h. (ILLUS.) 1,800-2,000

Renaissance Revival Dining Table

Victorian Renaissance Revival dining table, walnut & burl walnut, expandable, the divided square top w/rounded corners above a deep apron w/burl trim & burl end panels, raised on a heavy octagonal central post w/burl trim surrounded by four heavy scroll-cut outswept legs w/burl roundels & panels, on casters, refinished, closed 50" w., 30" h. (ILLUS.)...... **3,500**

Victorian Renaissance Revival dining table, walnut, round extension top w/molded edges & a molded apron, raised on a heavy octagonal split pedestal w/four ornate molded & S-scroll legs on casters alternating w/slender tall oblong raised panels, w/three leaves, ca. 1870, 45" d..... **2,520**

Victorian Tilt-top Games Table

Victorian Renaissance Revival games table, walnut, burl walnut & maple, the rounded dished top w/a wide molded border around walnut burl panels centered by a diamond-shaped inlaid checkerboard, tilting & pivoting above a slender turned pedestal on a tripod base w/outswept scroll-cut legs mounted w/roundels, ca. 1875, refinished, 22" d., 30" h. (ILLUS.) **450**

Round Renaissance Revival Table

Victorian Renaissance Revival parlor center table, rosewood, a round white marble top w/molded edge above a conforming apron carved w/scrolls flanking raised cartouches, raised on serpentine inwardly tapering supports resting upon heavy outswept S-scroll legs joined at a central turned post & resting upon a flattened carved cross stretcher resting on bun feet, ca. 1860 (ILLUS.)......................... **1,400**

Fine "Turtle-top" Parlor Table

Victorian Renaissance Revival parlor center table, rosewood, oblong white marble "turtle-top" above a conforming panel-carved serpentine apron raised on four S-scroll-carved legs joined by double S-scroll-carved cross stretchers joined in the center by a post w/a large urn-carved finial, ca. 1850-60 (ILLUS.) **3,000**

Victorian Renaissance Revival parlor center table, walnut, a rectangular white marble top w/notched & rounded corners above a conforming molded & flaring apron w/angular line-incised central drops, raised on a four-part base w/molded S-scroll supports continuing to outswept molded legs & joined to a central block topped by a columnar ring-turned post, refinished, ca. 1870, 22 1/2 x 33", 28" h. (hairline in one corner of marble) **660**

Victorian Renaissance Revival parlor center table, walnut, a shaped wood-framed brown marble top resting on a center urn pedestal surrounded by four shaped legs w/acanthus leaf- and medallion-carvings, w/burl wood veneer panels & incised gilt carvings overall, ca. 1875, 23 1/2 x 33", 30 1/2" h. **990**

Ornate Renaissance Revival Table

Victorian Renaissance Revival parlor center table, walnut, burl walnut, marquetry, part-ebonized & gilt-incised, the rectangular top w/wide rounded ends ornately inlaid w/marquetry swag & scroll designs & a central trophy panel, on a conforming apron w/raised burl & gilt-incised panels & drops, raised on scrolled end supports flanking a block-, urn- and knob-turned central column on flat stretchers w/shoe feet, joined by a ring-turned & reeded cross-stretcher w/central knob & turned finial, all w/gilt-incised decoration, third quarter 19th c., 26 x 45", 28 1/2" h. (ILLUS.) **3,738**

Renaissance Revival Parlor Table

Victorian Renaissance Revival parlor center table, walnut & burl walnut, the rectangular top w/a wide molded edge w/chamfered corners & an inset white marble top above the deep apron w/raised burl panels & molded lower edge, raised on four slender trumpet-turned legs w/baluster-turned feet & a serpentine cross-stretcher centered by a turned urn finial, ca. 1875, 22 x 28", 35" h. (ILLUS.)... **1,064**

Victorian Renaissance Revival parlor center table, walnut, the rectangular top w/wide rounded ends & molded edges above a conforming apron w/panels & incised decoration flanked at each corner by a block w/a small square carved lion head, knob-, block & tapering cylindrical-turned legs w/peg feet joined by a knob- and ring-turned cross-stretcher joining incurved end stretchers, ca. 1875, 24 1/2 x 41", 29" h. **633**

Inlaid Renaissance Revival Table

Victorian Renaissance Revival parlor table, inlaid & burl walnut, the rectangular top w/pointed ends formed by a wide raised molding enclosing a top surface ornately inlaid w/a central rectangular panel w/flowers flanked by ornate scroll clusters, the deep apron w/raised burl panels & corner blocks raised on forked side supports on reeded, turned & tapering legs & angular, incurved end supports all joined by a cross-stretcher centered by a turned finial, on original porcelain casters, original finish, ca. 1875, 22 x 36", 30" h. (ILLUS.) **1,500**

Ornate Renaissance Revival Table

Victorian Renaissance Revival parlor table, inlaid, gilt-incised & ebonized rosewood, the rectangular top w/wide rounded ends centered by an oblong satinwood-inlaid floral reserve surrounded by a wide band of inlaid burl, the raised molded edges w/an ebonized band raised on a conforming apron w/gilt line-incised central panels, raised on four knob- and ring-turned reeded & ebonized tapering legs joined by a flattened trestle-form stretcher w/gilt line incising & centered by an ebonized & gilt-trimmed carved central urn finial, original brass casters, original finish, ca. 1875, 22 x 36", 30" h. (ILLUS.) **2,500**

Victorian Marble Top Parlor Table

Victorian Renaissance Revival parlor table, walnut, an oval white marble top w/molded edge above a conforming molded apron w/thin scroll-carved drops, raised on four molded S-scroll supports centered by a ring- and knob-turned posts & raised on four molded outscrolled legs, ca. 1870, 24 x 32", 27 1/2" h. (ILLUS.)... **450**

Renaissance Revival Parlor Table

Victorian Renaissance Revival parlor table, walnut, rectangular white marble top w/molded serpentine edges on a conforming molded apron w/central arched panels, raised on a scroll-carved & molded four-leg base centered by a ring-turned column & drop, on casters, refinished, ca. 1870, 20 x 28 1/4", 29" h. (ILLUS.) **578**

Round Marble-topped Parlor Table

Victorian Renaissance Revival parlor table, walnut, the round white marble top w/molded edge on a deep serpentine apron carved w/raised burl panels & central oval medallions w/half-round spindle drops at each corner, raised on four inset columnar turned supports joined to a center post flanked by long projecting S-scroll legs ending in paw feet on casters, a large urn-form finial at the center of the base, attributed to Thomas Brooks, New York City, ca. 1870 (ILLUS.) **2,296**

Renaissance Revival Oval Side Table

Victorian Renaissance Revival side table, walnut & burl walnut, the oval white marble top w/molded edges above a deep molded apron, raised on a short heavy baluster-turned post w/a beaded band above four scroll-carved supports above arched & flaring flat legs w/curved raised burl panels & centering a turned bowl-form finial, original casters, original finish, ca. 1870, 16 x 22", 30" h. (ILLUS.)...... **500**

Inlaid Renaissance Revival Side Table

Victorian Renaissance Revival side table, walnut, the oval top w/a wide beveled rim decorated w/an ebonized background centering a large ornate inlaid scrolling cartouche, raised on four inset carved angular supports around a turned central post, squared angled legs w/turned finials, original finish, ca. 1870s, 15 x 20", 30" h. (ILLUS.) **1,200**

Victorian Rococo card table, walnut, serpentine hinged molded top over a carved apron, raised on foliate-carved cabriole legs ending in scrolled toes on casters, third quarter 19th c., 19 1/4 x 35 1/2", 31 3/8" **546**

Fine Victorian Rococo Console Table

Victorian Rococo console table, rosewood marquetry, the bow-front white marble top w/rounded outset corners above a conforming apron w/floral marquetry above an applied scroll skirt centered w/an ormolu rosette on two scroll-carved legs headed w/stylized flower and scroll ormolu mounts & joined by a shaped arched stretcher w/a central cartouche decorated w/a rocaille mount, New York, ca. 1860, 21 3/4 x 35 1/2", 35 5/8" h. (ILLUS.) **3,680**

Victorian Rococo Dining Table

Victorian Rococo dining table, carved walnut, divided expandable top, the round top w/molded edges & deep apron raised on four baluster-turned & scroll-carved legs & long carved scrolling supports tapering toward the top center & joined by a heavy leaf-carved cross-stretcher centered by a heavy center post w/an acanthus leaf-carved band, five original leaves w/case, original dark finish, ca. 1860, 60" d. closed, 30" h. (ILLUS.) **7,000**

Victorian Rococo Parlor Center Table

Victorian Rococo parlor center table, carved rosewood, a white marble 'turtle-top' above a serpentine molded apron deeply carved on all sides w/a spray of flowers & fruit, raised on four incurved cabriole legs carved to match & joined by a pierced foliate-carved X-form stretcher centered by an urn filled w/nuts & w/a turned finial, on casters, ca. 1850, 30 1/2 x 42 3/4", 30" h. (ILLUS.) **2,880**

Victorian Rococo parlor center table, carved rosewood, the shaped "turtle-top" inset w/conforming white marble, the shaped apron w/carved floral clusters at the center of each side, molded edging & pointed long drops at each corner, raised on a four-part base w/scroll-carved & molded flaring legs joined to a central paneled post w/drop finial, each leg w/carved acanthus leaf trim, on casters, ca. 1855,

25 x 43", 30" h. (age cracks, repair, old metal brace holding legs) **1,760**

Victorian Rococo parlor center table, rosewood, a white marble "turtle-top" above a deep conforming serpentine apron carved w/banded panels centered by a large fruit cluster on each side, raised on incurved cabriole legs w/carved knees & joined by cross-form S-scroll stretchers centered by a small turned urn, on casters, ca. 1860, 42" l., 29" h. **1,120**

Victorian Rococo parlor center table, walnut, a white marble "turtle-top" above a narrow conforming molded apron w/scalloped center panels, raised on four heavy molded & scroll-carved S-scroll legs joined by a lower platform stretcher topped by the carved figure of a small reclining dog, old dark finish, ca. 1860, 23 x 37", 29" h. (marble cracked & repaired) **770**

Rococo Ornate "Turtle-top" Table

Victorian Rococo parlor table, carved rosewood, the long white marble "turtle-top" above a deep scroll-carved conforming apron, raised on four slender ring-turned posts over outswept pierce-carved figural griffin legs centered by an ornately carved central post, on casters, attributed to George Henkel, ca. 1850s (ILLUS.) **11,550**

Rare & Fine Meeks Parlor Table

Victorian Rococo parlor table, laminated carved rosewood, white marble "turtle-top" on a molded conforming frame w/a deep arched floral- and fruit-carved pierced apron raised on four flower- and leaf-carved cabriole legs w/scroll & peg feet on brass casters, arched pierced-carved cross stretcher centered by a large carved urn of fruit over gadroon-carved bands & pierced scroll carving, J. & J. W. Meeks, New York City, ca. 1855 (ILLUS.) **31,350**

Victorian Rococo Mahogany Table

Victorian Rococo parlor table, mahogany, the oblong top w/serpentine molded edges above a conforming deep apron w/large shell-carved design flanked by C-scrolls at the center sides, raised on incurved cabriole legs w/ornate scroll carving, joined by serpentined cross stretchers w/a floral-carved center finial, old refinish, ca. 1850-60, 18 x 45", 34" h. (ILLUS.) **1,500**

Rococo Parlor Table with Carved Dog

Victorian Rococo parlor table, walnut, white marble "turtle-top" above a molded conforming apron w/central arched panels w/scrolls, raised on four bold tapering S-scroll supports tapering to an oblong platform centered by a carved reclining dog, raised on outswept scroll-carved legs on casters, 22 x 36", 28" h. (ILLUS.) **805**
Wallace Nutting-signed Pembroke table, mahogany, rectangular top flanked by drop leaves, Model No. 628b....................... **1,485**

Round Wicker Table with Shelf

Wicker side table, round oak top w/wicker banding on four tightly woven wicker panels framing a lower oak shelf over a tightly woven conforming apron, pointed flaring woven legs, painted white, ca. 1910, 30" d. (ILLUS.)... **201**
Wicker tea cart, rectangular top w/deep slightly rounded tightly woven apron supporting a wicker-trimmed lift-off glass tray top, wrapped corner supports

joined by a lower oak shelf w/flat braided wicker edging, front wooden-spoked wheels, upright tall S-scroll wrapped handle at the back, old brown-stained finish, early 20th c., 20 x 33 3/4", 33 1/2" h. (minor damage & small repaired break on one side of handle) **385**

Rare William & Mary Dining Table

William & Mary dining table, figured walnut, a rectangular top w/rounded molded ends flanked by D-form matching drop leaves over an apron w/a deep drawer at each end, on square chamfered legs & swing-out gate-leg supports, joined by box stretchers, repairs to drawer fronts, possibly southern U.S., 1700-30, closed 16 x 44", 31 1/2" h. (ILLUS.)..................... **10,925**

Early William & Mary Dining Table

William & Mary dining table, maple, gate-leg type, a rectangular top w/rounded ends flanked by wide rounded drop leaves forming an oval top above an apron on six block-, ring- and baluster-turned legs joined by block-, ring- and baluster-turned stretchers, flattened knob feet, refinished, imperfections, Massachusetts, early 18th c., open 41 1/2 x 52 1/4", 22" h. (ILLUS.) **9,775**

Early William & Mary Dining Table

William & Mary dining table, turned & figured maple, the rectangular top w/gently rounded ends flanked by two wide D-form drop leaves above an apron w/a drawer at one end, swing-out gate-leg supports, baluster- and ring-turned legs joined by block-, ring- and baluster-turned stretchers, on ball feet, restoration, New England, 1730-50, closed 19 x 49", 28" h. (ILLUS.)............................... **3,737**

William & Mary "hutch" or chair table, painted maple & pine, the oval two-board top tilting on a base of two horizontal supports ending in scrolled handholds joining four block- and baluster-turned legs w/a medial seat & box stretchers all resting on turned feet, original Spanish brown paint, southeastern New England, early 18th c., 47 1/4 x 51 1/4", 26" h. (minor imperfections)....................................... **20,700**

William & Mary tavern table, a long rectangular top widely overhanging a deep apron w/a single long drawer, raised on rod- and block-turned legs joined by box stretchers & on small turned feet, old finish, southeastern New England, 18th c., 28 x 41 3/4", 27 1/2" h. (minor imperfections) **2,990**

William & Mary tavern table, maple & pine, the rectangular breadboard top overhanging an apron on block-, baluster- and ring-turned splayed legs joined by box stretchers on small knob feet, old surface, 15 x 21 3/4", 25" h. (imperfections) **2,530**

William & Mary tavern table, maple & pine, the wide rectangular breadboard top overhanging the apron w/a single long drawer w/wooden knob, on ring-, baluster- and block-turned legs joined by square stretchers & ending in button feet, old refinish, New England, 18th c., 21 x 33", 27" h. (minor imperfections) **1,610**

William & Mary tavern table, painted, a wide rectangular top w/breadboard ends above an apron w/a single long drawer w/simple turned pull, on baluster-, ring- and block-turned legs joined by box stretchers, worn red paint, Massachusetts, 18th c., 28 x 38", 28 1/2" h. **3,000**

William & Mary Tavern Table

William & Mary tavern table, painted birch & pine, the oval overhanging top rests on four splayed slender baluster- and ring-turned legs continuing to turned feet & joined by a straight apron & box stretchers, painted black, probably New England, mid-18th c., imperfections, 24 x 33", 17" h. (ILLUS.)............................... **8,050**

Small William & Mary Tavern Table

William & Mary tavern table, pine & birch, the oval top above a deep canted apron w/a single drawer raised on canted baluster- and ring-turned legs ending in blocks joined by box stretchers & raised on waisted knob feet, retains traces of red wash, New England, 1700-30, diminutive size, 17 1/4 x 25 1/2", 25" h. (ILLUS.) **12,650**

William & Mary Tavern Table

William & Mary tavern table, the rectangular top widely overhanging a flat apron w/a single long thumb-molded drawer joining four block-, baluster- and ring-turned legs continuing to turned feet joined by box stretchers, old refinish, some imperfections, New England, 18th c., 26 x 37 1/2", 26 1/2" h. (ILLUS.)............ **2,070**

William & Mary-Style games table, inlaid wood, the shaped rectangular top w/bone & ebony geometric designs, above an apron w/a single drawer, raised on turned legs joined by a cross stretcher, England, late 19th c., 32 x 45", 29" h. ... **3,737**

Early Windsor Side Table

Windsor side table, painted pine, a scrubbed rectangular top w/breadboard ends widely overhanging four slightly canted rod- and baluster-turned legs joined by upper & lower box stretchers, legs w/red staining, top w/old natural finish, New England, early 19th c., 20 1/4 x 29 1/2", 26 1/2" h. (ILLUS.) **2,415**

Wardrobes & Armoires

French Art Deco Armoire

Armoire, Art Deco, mahogany & bird's-eye maple, the shaped rectangular top above a pair of wide doors set w/copper looping handles & opening to an interior w/mirror, shelves & drawers, all raised on a shaped, stepped plinth, in the manner of Dominique, France, ca. 1935, 19 x 62", 78" h. (ILLUS.)... **$2,875**

Early Biedermeier Armoire

Armoire, Biedermeier, mahogany, the stepped rectangular top over a flaring graduated cornice over a pair of tall three-panel cupboard doors opening to later shelves, restoration, Europe, early 19th c., 21 x 49", 76" h. (ILLUS.) **3,450**

French Art Deco Armoire

Armoire, Art Deco, mahogany veneer, a three-section curvilinear form composed of a center section w/two short open shelves above a cupboard w/hinged drop door opening to a compartment w/two drawers in shades of blond wood & three drawers below, the whole flanked by two tall flat cupboard doors w/rounded corners, one opening to three shelves, France, ca. 1930, 22 x 71", 71" h. (ILLUS.)............................. **1,955**

Elegant Classical Armoire

Armoire, Classical, mahogany & mahogany veneer, the rectangular top w/a widely flaring deep ogee cornice above a frieze band w/ormolu figural swan mounts above a pair of tall paneled doors flanked by half-round columns w/acanthus leaf & scroll carvings & ormolu mounts, flat rounded front feet w/mounts, early 19th c., 19 x 60", 90" h. (ILLUS.) **2,200**

French Provincial Carved Armoire

Armoire, French Provincial, oak, a rectangular top w/a widely flaring deep stepped cornice w/carved geometric frieze bands centered by pierce-carved central blocks, birds & grapevines above a pair of tall paneled doors w/grapevine carved panels at the top & base of each & long narrow brass strap hardware, a long carved pilaster between the doors, the deep scalloped apron carved w/further grapevines & a central floral medallion, short scroll front feet, France, 19th c., 18 x 72", 88" h. (ILLUS.).. **2,415**

Fancy Burled Victorian Armoire

Armoire, late Victorian, walnut & Circassian walnut veneer, the high serpentine crestrail carved w/bold leafy scrolls at the top & rounded ends w/further carved leafy band in the frieze above a pair of tall paneled cupboard doors featuring fancy burl veneer & flanked by burl ve-

neer side bands, the base w/a pair of raised panel burled drawers w/pierced brass pulls, deep molded base, demountable, refinished, ca. 1875-95, 20 x 48", 8' h. (ILLUS.) **2,400**

Armoire, Louis XV Provincial-style, fruitwood, the arched molded wide cornice above a pair of paneled & scroll-carved doors, raised on short cabriole legs ending in scrolled toes, France, late 18th - early 19th c., 24 1/2 x 56", 95" h. (worming, restoration).. **1,725**

French Provincial Carved Armoire

Armoire, Louis XV Provincial-Style, hardwood w/walnut finish, the arched & molded cornice above a frieze band carved w/a fruit basket flanked by leafy vines above the cupboard door w/a beveled mirror flanked by pairs of raised panels & floral-carved reserves above the serpentine apron w/a central low-relief carved urn & leafy scrolls, on short scroll-carved front legs, demountable, Europe, late 19th - early 20th c., top 20 x 60", 90" h. (ILLUS.) **1,980**

Louis XV-Style Veneered Armoire

Armoire, Louis XV-Style, mahogany veneer, the arched & molded crestrail centered by a carved flute & shell crest above a raised veneered frieze panel above the pair of tall mirrored doors w/narrow serpentine molded top & bottom rails & decorated w/herringbone veneering, above a pair of veneered bottom drawers w/raised panels over the serpentine apron w/a scroll-carved central cartouche, raised on short scroll-carved front cabriole legs, demountable, Europe, late 19th c., 24 x 60", 94 1/2" h. (ILLUS.)...................................... **1,870**

Louis XV-Style Oak Armoire

Armoire, Louis XV-Style, oak, a rectangular top w/rounded corners on the deep, widely flaring stepped cornice above a leaf-carved frieze band centered by a carved basket above a pair of tall doors w/scroll and floral vine top border over an asymmetrical glazed panel above a medial band of leafy scroll carving above the lower solid panel, the sides w/three square panels, raised on a molded plinth on square feet, w/the original oak panels for the glazed door sections, France, 19th c., 24 x 60", 87" h. (ILLUS.)................. **3,450**

French Provincial Hardwood Armoire

Armoire, Louis XV-Style Provincial style, hardwood, a rectangular top above a deep rounded & curved cornice above a pair of tall paneled cupboard doors w/long scroll-tipped keyhole escutcheons opening to shelves & a drawer, a deep scallop-edged front apron joining tall scrolled feet, France, 19th c., 23 x 50", 7' 6" h. (ILLUS.) **690**

Armoire, Louis XV-Style, the arched crestrail w/a high scroll- and cartouche-carved center crest above a conforming molded frieze band over the tall arched mirrored door, scroll-molded apron on short scrolled cabriole legs, overall marquetry veneer work, France, late 19th - early 20th c., 19 x 39", 99" h. .. **1,100**

Armoire, Louis XV-XVI Provincial-style, cherry & elm, a later rectangular molded cornice above a pair of tall paneled doors, shaped skirt, raised on short cabriole legs w/scroll feet, late 18th c., 24 1/2 x 55", 80" h. (restorations, worming) **1,150**

Provincial Louis XVI Armoire

Armoire, Louis XVI Provincial-style, oak, the rectangular top w/a widely flaring curved cornice w/round corners over a pair of tall cupboard doors each w/three matching molded serpentine panels, rounded paneled front stiles, on plain feet, France, late 18th to early 19th c., 22 x 44 1/2", 86 1/2" h. (ILLUS.) **4,025**

Fine Aesthetic Movement Armoire

Armoire, Victorian Aesthetic Movement substyle, walnut & burl walnut, a high upright crestrail composed of roundels over carved points w/roundel-topped corner blocks, a deep stepped & flaring cornice above a single tall burl paneled door flanked by reeded pilasters w/small florette-carved panels, a narrow burl veneered bottom drawer w/brass bar & ring pulls, deep molded front molding, paneled sides, opens to a single top shelf, refinished, original hardware, last quarter 19th c., 20 x 38", 7' 6" h. (ILLUS.)............... **2,800**

Victorian Rococo Armoire

Armoire, Victorian Rococo substyle, walnut w/faux rosewood graining, the rectangular top w/a wide arched front & deep ogee cornice over a large central frieze panel w/ornate carved leafy scrolls over a pair of tall arch-paneled doors w/brass pulls above a pair of bottom drawers w/carved trim, scallop-carved apron, bracket feet, refinished, demountable, ca. 1860, 16 x 45", 7' 6" h. (ILLUS.)........................... **2,400**

Large Baroque-Style Rosewood Kas

Kas (a version of the Netherlands Kast or wardrobe), Baroque-Style, rosewood, the large rectangular top w/a widely flaring & stepped cornice overhanging the case w/a wide frieze band centered by a carved figural tablet above the pair of tall paneled cupboard doors opening to shelves, on a molded plinth raised on heavy turned bun front feet, Europe, 19th c., 32 1/2 x 87", 88" h. (ILLUS.) **1,440**

Early Pennsylvania Kas

Kas (a version of the Netherlands Kast or wardrobe), butternut, poplar & cherry, made to disassemble, the rectangular top w/a deep stepped & coved cornice above a wide frieze band w/thin molding above a pair of tall three-panel doors w/two large square raised-panel segments centered by a rectangular chamfered panel, a narrow molding above the wide base band & coved molded flat base, old soft finish, one side of interior w/wooden garment hooks on swivel arms, other side w/shelves, modern metal latches added, Pennsylvania, late 18th - early 19th c., top 25 x 75 1/2", 83" h. (ILLUS.).. **2,035**

Fine Early New York Kas

Kas (a version of the Netherlands Kast or wardrobe), cherry, a rectangular top w/a very deep & widely flaring stepped cornice above a molded frieze band over a pair of tall doors w/stepped raised panels, flanked & centered by wide vertical two-panel raised above a lower molding over a pair of deep drawers w/wooden knobs separated by three raised diamond devices, flared molded base raised on heavy turned turnip feet, top part of crown of later date, New York state, ca. 1750 (ILLUS.) **3,360**

Chippendale Gumwood Kas

Kas (a version of the Netherlands Kast or wardrobe), Chippendale, gumwood, the rectangular top w/a widely flaring deep stepped cornice above a pair of tall raised panel cupboard doors opening to three shelves, a mid-molding over a long bottom drawer on the molded base w/ogee bracket feet, cast brass hardware, New York or New Jersey, ca. 1780 (ILLUS.) **8,400**

Country Kas with Original Paint

Kas (a version of the Netherlands Kast or wardrobe), painted pine, rectangular top w/flared cornice above a pair of tall double raised-panel doors w/a long panel over a shorter panel, a pair of false drawer fronts at the bottom above the molded base w/scroll-cut bracket feet, original salmon red paint w/black trim, pegged construction, mid-19th c., 19 1/2 x 46", 6' 4" h. (ILLUS.) **1,200**

Early William & Mary Kas

Kas (a version of the Netherlands Kast or wardrobe), William & Mary style, cherry, pine & poplar, the rectangular top w/a high flaring architectural cornice molding over a pair of two arch-paneled cupboard doors flanked by reeded pilasters over applied mid-molding over a single long bottom drawer flanked by raised panels, molded base on painted detachable disc & stretcher turnip-form feet, replaced hardware, refinished, restored, Long Island, New York area, 1730-80, 26 1/4 x 65 1/2", 77 1/4" h. (ILLUS.) **4,025**

William & Mary New York Kas

Kas (a version of the Netherlands Kast or wardrobe), William & Mary style, gumwood & poplar, the rectangular top w/a widely flaring deep stepped cornice above a frieze band over a pair of tall raised panel doors separated by three sections of rectangular applied molding, the interior w/two shelves, a mid-molding over a single long drawer w/the face divided w/moldings to resemble two drawers & flanked by raised diamonds, molded base on tall turnip front feet, refinished, New York, ca. 1740, imperfections, 55 1/2" w., 78" h. (ILLUS.).......... **13,800**

New York Stained Poplar Kas

Kas (a version of the Netherlands Kast or wardrobe), William & Mary style, stained poplar, the rectangular top w/a widely flaring deep stepped cornice above a paneled frieze band over a pair of doors each w/two raised panels, the upper panel w/an arched top, exterior-mounted butterfly hinges, narrow vertical panels flanking the doors, a single long drawer across the bottom, deep molded base raised on large ball feet, New York state, mid-18th c., feet replaced, wear, 23 x 59", 78 3/4" h. (ILLUS.) **5,175**

Art Deco Style Wardrobe

Wardrobe, Art Deco, oak, a flat rectangular top above a plain case w/a large tall flat door on the left & two shorter flat doors on the right, one side opens to a clothes rack, the two doors fitted w/four slide-out shelves, light finish, Bauhaus influenced design, Germany, ca. 1930, wear, scratches, 23 3/4 x 53", 71 1/2" h. (ILLUS.) **460**

Wardrobe, Chippendale, painted poplar, a rectangular top w/cove-molded cornice above a pair of tall cupboard doors w/two raised panels, the upper panels w/arched tops, a single long deep drawer w/molded edging at the bottom, molded base on scroll-cut bracket feet, mustard yellow repaint, old round brasses on the drawer, late 18th - early 19th c., 20 x 45", 67" h. (replaced brass escutcheon, repaired breaks in feet) **2,750**

Fine Classical Wardrobe

Wardrobe, Classical, mahogany veneer, the wide rectangular top w/a deep stepped & flaring cornice above a pair of large tall two-panel doors opening to an interior w/veneered drawers, molded base on simple bracket feet, paneled sides, some small interior drawers added, other minor imperfections, mid-Atlantic states, ca. 1840, 26 x 65", 79 1/2" h. (ILLUS.).. **3,105**

Painted Country-style Wardrobe

Wardrobe, country-style, painted pine & poplar, a rectangular thick top above a tall two-panel off-center door above a single bottom drawer, molded flat base, pottery knob on door, wood knobs on drawer, interior fitted w/14 small cast-iron hooks & replaced shelf, old brown repaint, 19th c., age crack in door, top 19 x 39 3/4", 83 1/2" h. (ILLUS.) **523**

Wardrobe, country-style, painted pine, rectangular top over a single tall door opening to an interior of nine coat pegs & four short shelves, on a cut-out base joined by shaped skirt, overall original red paint, New England, early 19th c., 13 x 46 3/4", 67 1/2" h. (paint wear) **4,140**

Early Canadian Wardrobe

Wardrobe, country-style, painted pine, rectangular top w/low cornice overhanging a pair of tall six-panel cupboard doors & paneled sides opening to an interior of four shelves, molded scroll-cut apron & simple bracket feet, old green paint, some hardware loss & changes, shelves added later, some paint retouched, Canada, 19th c., 16 x 57", 87 1/2" h. (ILLUS.) .. **1,495**

Painted Break-down-style Wardrobe

Wardrobe, country-style, painted poplar, a rectangular top w/a deep coved cornice above a pair of tall two-panel cupboard doors opening to four added shelves & a peg rack, four wide boards across the back, well done brown over mustard yellow grained repaint, breaks down into three sections, 19th c., 17 x 59", 80" h. (ILLUS.) **440**

Ohio Amish Painted Wardrobe

Wardrobe, country-style, painted poplar, a rectangular top w/a flat flaring cornice above a pair of tall narrow double panel doors opening to eight adjustable shelves & fixed center shelf, simple low bracket feet, original brown over tan wood graining, Amish, Ohio, 19th c., 20 1/4 x 64", 93 1/4" h. (ILLUS.) **990**

Wardrobe, country-style, walnut, a rectangular removable top w/upright border boards centered at the front w/a long triangular pediment w/a large fan carving above a molded coved cornice above a wide frieze centered by a raised diamond above a pair of tall two-panel cupboard doors w/a small rectangular panel above a tall raised rectangular lower panel, a mid-molding above the deep lower case w/molded bottom on blocked feet, original dark brown alligatored finish & black-painted detail, Zoar, Ohio, mid-19th c., 19 x 56 1/2", 83" h. (minor chips on cornice, narrow section of side molding missing) **2,750**

Wardrobe, Mission-style (Arts & Crafts movement), oak, a rectangular top above a pair of tall double-paneled doors w/a small panel over a tall panel, copper V-pulls, interior fitted w/two open compartments over four long drawers above two open shelves, gently arched apron, red decal & paper Craftsman label of Gustav Stickley, Model No. 920, ca. 1910, some

Gustav Stickley Mission Wardrobe

wear, small losses to wood at top, 16 1/2 x 34", 59 3/4" h. (ILLUS.) **14,950**

Fine Aesthetic Movement Wardrobe

Wardrobe, Victorian Aesthetic Movement style, walnut & burl walnut, the rectangular top w/a high stepped front crest w/a geometric band above panels of bold scroll & leaf carving above a frieze band w/burl panels & leaf-carved blocks over a pair of tall panels & finely burled doors flanked by narrow side burl bands, two burled drawers at the bottom w/stamped brass pulls, molded flat base on thin block feet, refinished, demountable, ca. 1880s, 20 x 46", 8' h. (ILLUS.)..................... **2,800**

Wardrobe, Victorian country-style, painted pine, five-board construction, a flat rectangular top above a tall case w/wide front side boards flanking the central beaded board tall door w/wooden thumb latch & white porcelain knob, original blue paint, late 19th c., 17 x 41", 71" h. **518**

Simple Country Victorian Wardrobe

Wardrobe, Victorian country-style, walnut, a rectangular top w/a narrow molded cornice over a single tall double-panel door opening to a fitted rod above a single deep bottom drawer, simple bracket feet, one-board sides, door edge strip w/pieced repairs, found in Missouri, mid-19th c., 17 3/4 x 32", 73" h. (ILLUS.).......... **1,650**

Victorian Faux Bamboo Wardrobe

Wardrobe, Victorian faux bamboo-style, bird's-eye maple, the pedimented top outlined w/bamboo-turned trim forming a forked finial above a deep frieze band w/applied bamboo-turned panels over the tall mirrored door framed w/bamboo turnings & opening to shelves, flanked by bamboo-turned stiles, a bamboo-turned medial rail over the single bottom drawer w/further applied bamboo turnings, side stiles continue down to form round feet, America, second half 19th c., 17 3/4 x 40", 92" h. (ILLUS.)` **3,162**

Elaborate Golden Oak Wardrobe

Wardrobe, Victorian Golden Oak style, the high arched top crestrail decorated w/ornate scroll carving & a central flower head & rounded corners above a pair of tall paneled cupboard doors w/scroll-carved trim flanked by corner columns & centered by a small vertical rectangular beveled mirror above a flat serpentine panel, a bow-fronted base w/two drawers w/pierced-brass pulls flanked by leaf-carved feet, original dark finish, ca. 1900, 22 x 48", 7' 10" h. (ILLUS.)............................ **2,800**

Fine Victorian Golden Oak Wardrobe

Wardrobe, Victorian Golden Oak style, the high front crest w/a scalloped, scroll-carved top centered by a large shell carving over a frieze band w/further scroll carving over a flared cornice above a frieze band trimmed in scroll carving over a pair of tall cupboard doors w/rectangular panels w/rounded corners & scroll-carved trim, a pair of drawers w/stamped brass pulls at the base above the serpentine apron & scroll-carved feet, refinished, demountable, ca., 1900, 20 x 48", 8' h. (ILLUS.) **2,500**

High-crested Golden Oak Wardrobe

Wardrobe, Victorian Golden Oak style, the high crestrail w/a scroll-carved top over a plain bar, a wide frieze w/serpentined scrolls above a flaring stepped cornice over a long low rounded bar frieze above a pair of tall doors w/long leafy scrolls above tall beveled mirrors w/shaped tops flanked by spiral-twist bars w/knob ends down the sides, a pair of line-incised drawers w/simple bail pulls, serpentine apron & bracket feet on casters, demountable, original finish, ca. 1890s, 21 x 42", 8' 2" h. (ILLUS.) **2,000**

Single-door Golden Oak Wardrobe

Wardrobe, Victorian Golden Oak substyle, a rectangular top w/a high arched & scroll-carved crest on a rounded rail flanked by scrolls & above an arched frieze panel, a tall single door w/carved scrolls above the beveled mirror front, wide side stiles w/scroll-carved drops at the tops, a small projecting shelf below the door & over a long round-fronted bottom drawer w/bail pulls & carved scrolls at each end, beaded base band above the narrow serpentine apron w/shaped block feet on casters, refinished, ca. 1900, 22 x 36", 7' 4" h. (ILLUS.) **1,800**

Oak Wardrobe with a High Crest

Wardrobe, Victorian Golden Oak substyle, a tall scalloped & scroll-carved front crest above a bead-carved flaring cornice above a scroll-carved frieze band over a pair of tall paneled cupboard doors w/carved scrolls across the top, a pair of flat drawers at the base w/original stamped brass hardware, refinished, ca. 1900, 18 x 48", 7' 10" h. (ILLUS.)............... **1,800**

Victorian Gothic Revival Wardrobe

Wardrobe, Victorian Gothic Revival substyle, walnut, the rectangular top w/a deep flaring cornice over a pair of tall cupboard doors w/Gothic Arch panels over a single long drawer at the bottom, scalloped front apron, ca. 1865, 16 x 42", 73" h. (ILLUS.).. **690**

English Victorian Mahogany Wardrobe

Wardrobe, Victorian, mahogany & mahogany veneer, the rectangular top w/a narrow undulating cornice band w/rounded corners above a matching frieze band over a pair of tall arch-paneled doors w/carved scrolls at the top & further undulating molding outlining the panels, a matching base molding on the flat plinth base, brass pulls, refinished, England, mid-19th c., minor damage, 21 1/2 x 57", 82 3/4" h. (ILLUS.)... **1,375**

Victorian Rococo Walnut Wardrobe

Wardrobe, Victorian Rococo substyle, walnut, the high arched & scroll-carved front cornice w/a pair of lobed center cut-outs over a molded cornice above a pair of tall arch-paneled doors w/scroll-carved top corners, narrow beveled front corners w/small carved scrolls, two drawers at the bottom w/leaf-carved pulls, serpentine apron & bracket feet, paneled sides, demountable, original finish, ca. 1850-70, 20 x 54", 8' h. (ILLUS.)............ .... **3,500**

L. & J.G. Stickley Wardrobe

Wardrobe, Mission-style (Arts & Crafts movement), oak, a low arched crestrail above the rectangular top over a pair of tall paneled doors opening to a group of four small drawers w/copper pulls above four long drawers, flat apron, square stile legs, fine original finish, "The Work of..." decal of L. & J. G. Stickley, Model No. 111, 19 x 40", 48" h. (ILLUS.)..................... **8,250**

Whatnots & Etageres

Rare Gallé Etagere

Etagere, Federal-Style, mahogany & oak, a three-quarters gallery on the rectangular top above four tiered open rectangular shelves each w/an X-form back brace & three baluster-turned supports on each side, the bottom shelf above a single long drawer w/brass ring pulls, baluster- and ring-turned legs, turned acorn finials at the front of the two middle shelves, dark varnished finish, signed "Sahon, New York," early 20th c., 15 1/2 x 24", 64" h. (ILLUS.).. **1,705**

Etagere, Art Nouveau, fruitwood marquetry, *Ombellière* patt., the pierce-carved gallery top w/leafage above a flat door w/foliate-cast hinges inlaid on one side w/a tableau of thistles beneath rays of sun & on the other w/a scrolling ribbon inlaid *"L'INSTANTEST SI BLAU LUMIERE DE NOTRE COEUR AUX FOND DE NOUS,"* opening to storage, above a center support carved as an open blossom & molded supports, above open shelving & back panel inlaid w/thistles, crown & stars w/a pierce-cut crest, all raised on molded gently outswept legs joined by a pierce-carved blossom apron, inlaid in marquetry "Gallé," ca. 1900, 18 x 26", 59" h. (ILLUS.)........ **$23,000**

English Regency-Style Etagere

Etagere, Regency-Style, mahogany, composed of four open graduated square shelves supported on slender ring-turned supports, the bottom shelf over a shallow drawer, slender turned legs on casters, marked by Edwards & Roberts, England, late 19th c., restorations, 21" sq., 54 1/2" h. (ILLUS.).................................... **4,025**

Federal-Style Mahogany Etagere

Elaborate Brass & Onyx Etagere

Etagere, Rococo Revival style, brass & onyx, the delicate brass framework topped by a high pierced scrolling brass crest above a narrow white onyx shelf above incurved leafy scroll sides flanking a large half-round beveled mirror above a serpentine onyx shelf raised on slender ornate figural griffin-shaped front supports continuing to slender curved brass legs, the side stiles composed of rods mounted w/cylindrical sections of onyx, a pair of small quarter-round onyx medial shelves above a lower serpentine shelf composed of quarter-round end sections flanking a central mirror section, ca. 1885, 38" w., 4' 6" h. (ILLUS.) **3,080**

Aesthetic Movement Etagere

Etagere, Victorian Aesthetic Movement substyle, brass-mounted rosewood, rectangular top w/upturned ends w/pierced metal rails raised on four simple round tapering legs joined by three staggered open shelves over a fretwork front apron, splayed brass feet, possibly by Lejambe, Philadelphia, last quarter 19th c., 19 x 24 1/4", 23" h. (ILLUS.) **1,265**

Victorian Aesthetic Corner Etagere

Etagere, Victorian Aesthetic Movement substyle, corner-style, fruitwood w/ivory inlay, the superstructure w/a scroll-cut & pierced pediment above a swag- and dentil-inlaid cornice over a scroll & floral triangular panel flanked by mirrored triangular panels over two rectangular mirrored panels above a galleried shelf

above a pair of rectangular mirrors flanked by narrow inlaid side panels, the lower case w/a three-sided front above a conforming case w/a rectangular ribbon-, scroll & grotesque face panel flanked by two side shelves over a deep open lower compartment w/slender turned front supports, ca. 1870, 17 x 27 1/2", 6'10" h. (ILLUS.) **2,300**

Ornate Renaissance Revival Etagere

Etagere, Victorian Renaissance Revival substyle, carved rosewood, the arched & molded crestrail w/an ornate pierce-carved crest centered by an arched crest over an oval floral-carved panel above the arched scroll-carved frieze panel over an arched tall mirror plate w/outset corners above a narrow shaped shelf & bracket above a similar smaller lower mirror, flanked by scroll-carved sides w/four quarter-round graduated shelves alternating w/rounded rectangular veneer panels & cut-outs, the bottom sides w/ornate pierce-carved panels flanking a pair of slender turned spindles on a white marble rectangular shelf w/serpentine front above a conforming drawer w/scroll-carved pull, serpentine scalloped apron on short turned legs, ca. 1875 (ILLUS.) **3,105**

Ornate Renaissance Revival Etagere

Etagere, Victorian Renaissance Revival substyle, carved walnut, the very high crest topped by a small arched & scroll-carved finial over a scroll-carved cartouche flanked by angled rails over raised burl panels & an arched molding w/a bold carved center cartouche flanked by turned finials, further raised burl panels above a tall arched mirror flanked by shaped sides w/three graduated quarter-round shelves on each side w/two oblong mirror panels on each side, the stepped-out base w/a shaped white marble top above a conforming plinth centered by a single drawer w/a carved ram's head pull, base molding on small block feet, two side scrolls missing, minor backboard replacements, ca. 1875, 17 x 43 1/4", 95 1/2" h. (ILLUS.) **3,850**

Fine Renaissance Revival Etagere

white marble shelf w/block projections above a deep comforming plinth base w/a center drawer, refinished, ca. 1865-75, 18 x 46", 8' 2" h. (ILLUS.) **4,500**

Renaissance Revival Etagere

Etagere, Victorian Renaissance Revival substyle, walnut & burl walnut, the tall back w/a large boldly scroll-carved pediment center w/a large cartouche finial over a smaller cartouche flanked by pierced leaf-carved panels & small pointed raised burl panels, above a tall round-topped mirror flanked by wide scalloped sides set on each side w/quarter-round graduated shelves backed by oblong mirrors, the lowest shelves on carved & curved brackets flanked by raised burl panels above the half-round white marble shelf w/a flat projecting center section above a conforming apron trimmed w/raised burl panels & a central roundel, molded base on short turned front legs, ca. 1870, 50" w., 7' 10" h. (ILLUS.) ... **3,920**

Ornate Rosewood Etagere

Etagere, Victorian Rococo substyle, carved rosewood, composed of three upper graduated open serpentine shelves supported by ornate S- and C-scroll brackets w/a leaf-carved top finial over looping scrolls w/pierced looping scrolls backing the lower two shelves & the large bottom shelf, a scroll-carved apron at the front, mid-19th c., 36" w., 68" h. (ILLUS.) **476**

Etagere, Victorian Renaissance Revival substyle, walnut & burl walnut, the top w/a high arched crestrail centered by a tall carved & pointed crest w/the carved head of Robin Hood above pierced open scrolls above a flat crestrail over a frieze band centered by a palmette carving & raised burl panels w/leafy C-scrolls at each side above the tall oblong mirror flanked by wide tapering sides w/cut-out oblong openings & three shaped graduated shelves on each side above closed side panels & a band w/raised burl panels above a serpentine

Fabulous Rococo Rosewood Etagere

Etagere, Victorian Rococo substyle, carved rosewood, the shaped top w/a high arch-centered rail w/a shell-carved recess topped by three urn-turned finials & pierced scrolling bands all raised on very slender ring-turned supports backed by a large arched central mirror flanked by narrow arched side mirrors behind the shaped open shelves & projecting turned side posts enclosing small mirrors, all above the wide serpentine-topped lower section w/a wide shell-carved apron supported on four leafy scroll-carved C-scrolls on turned columnar supports flanking raised side shelves & a mirrored back, inset serpentine lower shelf w/scroll-carved trim, on button feet, original finish, attributed to Thomas Brooks of New York, ca. 1850-60, 24 x 62", 9' 6" h. (ILLUS.) **17,000**

Etagere, Victorian Rococo substyle, rosewood, a fretwork-carved pediment surmounting a triptych mirror w/tiered shelves, over a demi-lune marble top base w/mirrored back & tiered shelves, supported by acanthus leaf-carved cabriole legs, mid-19th c., 23 x 55", 94" h. **2,200**

Unusual Victorian Etagere

Etagere, Victorian Rococo substyle, walnut, an arched & pierced scroll-cut crest above an open shelf above five graduated open shelves supported between scroll-cut sides & each backed by scroll-cut trim, a central two-panel fold-down writing surface opening to a fitted interior, ca. 1850-60 (ILLUS.) **2,300**

Etagere, Victorian Rococo substyle, walnut, the very tall superstructure w/a high arched molded crestrail w/pierced scrolls & a turned center finial along the top & enclosing an arched pierced-carved panel trimmed w/small raised burl panels all above the tall rectangular mirror w/rounded top corners flanked by pierced scroll-carved sides w/slender turned spindles & two small open shelves on each side, the lower shelves w/slender turned spindle supports above small oblong mirrors, all on a half-round white marble top over a

Very Tall Rococo Etagere

conforming deep apron w/a central drawer w/leaf-carved pull raised on turned & tapering front supports & S-scroll side supports above a medial shelf w/incurved sides backed by an arched pierce-carved crest, on small peg feet, ca. 1855-70, 38" w., 7' 1" h. (ILLUS.) **2,520**

Victorian Walnut Whatnot Shelf

Whatnot, Victorian corner-style, walnut, six graduated quarter-round open shelves each backed w/pierced scrollwork & joined by three ring- and baluster-turned spindles w/finials, some damage to scrollwork & some missing, refinished, joints loose, ca. 1870, 67 1/2" h. (ILLUS.)...... **160**

Whatnot, Victorian Rococo substyle, walnut, six-shelf, the upper three open shelves w/molded serpentine front & joined by slender baluster- and ring-turned spindles & turned pointed corner finials, the upper three shelves stepped back from top of the conforming lower section w/a shallow drawer at the top & bottom shelf, each shelf backed by an arched & scroll-pierced backrail, on short double-knob feet on casters, refinished, mid-19th c., 12 1/2 x 34", 66" h. **440**

SELECT BIBLIOGRAPHY

Bivins, John, Jr. The Furniture of Coastal North Carolina, 1700-1820. Winston-Salem, N.C.: Museum of Early Southern Decorative Arts, 1988.

Bjerkoe, Ethel Hall. The Cabinetmakers of America. New York: Doubleday and Co., 1957.

Bowman, John S. American Furniture. New York: Exeter Books, 1985.

Butler, Joseph T. Field Guide to American Antique Furniture. New York: Facts on File Publications, 1985.

Carpenter, Ralph E., Jr. The Arts and Crafts of Newport, Rhode Island, 1640-1820. Newport: Preservation Society of Newport County, 1954.

Cathers, David M. Furniture of the American Arts & Crafts Movement. New York: New American Library, 1981.

Cescinsky, Herbert. English Furniture from Gothic to Sheraton. New York: Dover, 1968, rpt.

Comstock, Helen. American Furniture, Seventeenth, Eighteenth, and Nineteenth Century Styles. New York: The Viking Press, 1962.

Cooper, Wendy A. Classical Taste in America, 1800-1840. New York: Abbeville Press, 1993.

Downs, Joseph. American Furniture, Queen Anne and Chippendale Periods in the Henry Francis du Pont Winterthur Museum. New York: Macmillan Co., 1952.

Dubrow, Eileen and Richard. American Furniture of the 19th Century, 1840-1880. Exton, PA.: Schiffer Publishing, Ltd., 1983.

Dubrow, Eileen and Richard. Furniture Made in America, 1875-1905. Exton, PA.: Schiffer Publishing, Ltd., 1982.

Duncan, Alastair. Art Nouveau Furniture. New York: Clarkson N. Potter, Inc., 1982.

Fairbanks, Jonathan L. and Elizabeth Bidwell Bates. American Furniture, 1620 to the Present. New York: Richard Marek Publishers, 1981.

Fales, Dean A., Jr. American Painted Furniture, 1660-1880. New York: Crown Publishers, 1986.

Fitzgerald, Oscar. Three Centuries of American Furniture. Englewood Cliffs, N. J.: Prentice-Hall, 1982.

Forman, Benno M. American Seating Furniture, 1630-1730. New York: W.W. Norton & Co., 1988.

Fredgant, Don. American Manufactured Furniture. Atglen, PA: Schiffer Publishing, Ltd., 1988.

Gilborn, Craig. Adirondack Furniture and the Rustic Tradition. New York: Harry N. Abrams, 1987.

Gusler, Wallace B. Furniture of Williamsburg and Eastern Virginia, 1710-1790. Richmond, VA: Virginia Museum, 1979.

Heckscher, Morrison H. American Furniture in the Metropolitan Museum of Art, II, Late Colonial Period: The Queen Anne and Chippendale Styles. New York: The Metropolitan Museum of Art and Random House, 1986.

Jobe, Brock, and Myrna Kaye. New England Furniture: The Colonial Era. Boston: Houghton Mifflin Co., 1984.

Kane, Patricia E. 300 Years of American Seating Furniture. Boston: New York Graphic Society, 1976.

Kaplan, Wendy. The Art That Is Life. Boston: Little, Brown & Company, 1987.

Kaye, Myrna. Fake, Fraud or Genuine? Identifying Authentic American Antique Furniture. Boston: Little, Brown & Company, 1987.

Kettell, Russell Hawes. The Pine Furniture of Early New England. New York: Dover, 1949, rpt.

Kirk, John T. American Furniture and The British Tradition to 1830. New York: Alfred A. Knopf, 1982.

Kirk, John T. The Impecunious Collector's Guide to American Antiques. New York: Alfred A. Knopf, 1982.

Knell, David. English Country Furniture: The National & Regional Vernacular, 1500-1900. London: Barrie & Jenkins, 1992.

Kovel, Ralph and Terry Kovel. American Country Furniture, 1780-1875. New York: Crown Publishers, 1965.

Lockwood, Luke Vincent. Colonial Furniture in America, 2 vols. New York: Castle Books, 1951, rpt.

Madigan, Mary Jean. Nineteenth Century Furniture. New York: Art & Antiques, 1982.

Marsh, Moreton. The Easy Expert in American Antiques. Philadelphia: J.B. Lippincott, 1978.

McNerney, Kathryn. Pine Furniture — Our American Heritage. Paducah, KY: Collector Books, 1989.

Miller, Edgar G., Jr. American Antique Furniture, A Book for Amateurs, 2 vols. New York: Dover, 1966, rpt.

Montgomery, Charles F. American Furniture, The Federal Period in the Henry Francis du Pont Winterthur Museum. New York: The Viking Press, 1966.

Morningstar, Connie. American Furniture Classics. Des Moines, IA: Wallace-Homestead Book Co., 1976.

Morningstar, Connie. Early Utah Furniture. Logan, UT: Utah State University Press, 1976.

Neat Pieces: The Plain-Style Furniture of 19th Century Georgia. Atlanta: Atlanta Historical Society, 1983.

Nutting, Wallace. Furniture Treasury, vols. I, II. New York: Macmillan, 1928.

Nutting, Wallace. Furniture Treasury, vol. III. New York: Macmillan, 1933.

Sack, Albert. The New Fine Points of Furniture. New York: Crown Publishing, 1993.

Santore, Charles. The Windsor Style in America. Philadelphia: Running Press, 1981.

Santore, Charles. The Windsor Style in America, Vol. II. Philadelphia: Running Press, 1987.

Schiffer, Herbert F. The Mirror Book, English, American & European. Exton, PA: Schiffer Publishing, 1983.

Stillinger, Elizabeth. The Antiquers. New York: Alfred A. Knopf, 1980.

Symonds, R.W. and B.B. Whineray. Victorian Furniture. London: Studio Editions, 1987.

Ward, Gerald R. American Case Furniture in the Mabel Brady Garvan and Other Collections at Yale University. New Haven, CT: Yale University Art Gallery, 1988.

Warner, Velma Susanne. Golden Oak Furniture. Atglen, PA: Schiffer Publishing, Ltd., 1992.

APPENDIX I

AUCTION SERVICES

The following is a select listing of larger regional auction houses which often feature antique furniture in their sales. There are, of course, many fine local auction services that also feature furniture from time to time.

East Coast:

Christie's
502 Park Ave.
New York, NY 10022
Phone: (212) 546-1000

Douglas Auctioneers
Route 5
South Deerfield, MA 01373
Phone: (413) 665-3530

William Doyle Galleries
175 E. 87th St.
New York, NY 10128
Phone: (212) 427-2730

Willis Henry Auctions
22 Main St.
Marshfield, MA 02059
Phone: (617) 834-7774

Dave Rago
9 So. Main St.
Lambertville, NJ 08530
Phone: (609) 397-9374

Skinner Inc.
357 Main St.
Bolton, MA 01740
Phone: (508) 779-6241

Sotheby's
1334 York Ave.
New York, NY 10021
Phone: (212) 606-7000

Withington, Inc.
R. D. 2, Box 440
Hillsboro, NH 03244
Phone: (603) 464-3232

Midwest:

DuMochelles Galleries
409 East Jefferson Ave.
Detroit, MI 48226
Phone: (313) 963-6255

Garth's Auctions
P.O. Box 369
Delaware, OH 43015
Phone: (614) 362-4771

Gene Harris Antique Auction Center
P.O. Box 476
Marshalltown, IA 50158
Phone: (515) 752-0600

Jackson's Auctioneers & Appraisers
2229 Lincoln St.
Cedar Falls, IA 50613
Phone: (319) 277-2256

Treadway Gallery
P.O. Box 8924
Cincinnati, OH 45208
Phone: (513) 321-6742

Far West:

Butterfield & Butterfield
7601 Sunset Blvd.
Los Angeles, CA 90046
Phone: (213) 850-7500

Pettigrew Auction Company
1645 So. Tejon St.
Colorado Springs, CO 80906
Phone: (719) 633-7963

South:

Neal Auction Company
4038 Magazine St.
New Orleans, LA 70115
Phone: (504) 899-5329

New Orleans Auction Galleries
801 Magazine St.
New Orleans, LA 70130
Phone: (504) 566-1849

APPENDIX II
Stylistic Guidelines: American & English Furniture

AMERICAN

Style: Pilgrim Century
Dating: 1620-1700
Major Wood(s): Oak
General Characteristics:
Case pieces: rectilinear low-relief
     carved panels
     blocky & bulbous turnings
     splint-spindle trim
Seating pieces: shallow carved panels
     spindle turnings

Style: William & Mary
Dating: 1685-1720
Major Wood(s): Maple & walnut
General Characteristics:
Case pieces: paint decoration
     chests on ball feet
     chests on frame, chests
      with two-part construction
     trumpet-turned legs
     slant-front desks
Seating pieces: molded, carved crestrails
     banister backs
     cane, rush (leather) seats
     baluster, ball &
      block turnings
     ball & Spanish feet

Style: Queen Anne
Dating: 1720-50
Major Wood(s): Walnut
General Characteristics:
Case pieces: mathematical proportions
     of elements
     use of the cyma or S-curve
     broken-arch pediments
     arched panels, shell carving,
      star inlay
     blocked fronts
     cabriole legs & pad feet
Seating pieces: molded yoke-shaped
     crestrails
     solid vase-shaped splats
     rush or upholstered seats
     cabriole legs
     baluster, ring, ball &
      block-turned stretchers
     pad & slipper feet

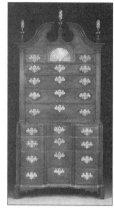

Style: Chippendale
Dating: 1750-85
Major Wood(s): Mahogany & walnut
General Characteristics:
Case pieces: relief-carved
      broken-arch pediments
      foliate, scroll, shell,
        fretwork carving
      straight, bow or
        serpentine fronts
      carved cabriole legs
      claw & ball, bracket
        or ogee feet
Seating pieces: carved, shaped crestrails
      with out-turned ears
      pierced, shaped splats
      ladder (ribbon) backs
      upholstered seats
      scrolled arms
      carved cabriole legs or
      straight (Marlboro) legs
      claw & ball feet

Style: Federal (Hepplewhite)
Dating: 1785-1800
Major Wood(s): Mahogany & light inlays
General Characteristics:
Case pieces: more delicate
      rectilinear forms
      inlay with eagle &
        classical motifs
      bow, serpentine or
        tambour fronts
      reeded quarter columns
        at sides
      flared bracket feet
Seating pieces: shield backs
      upholstered seats
      tapered square legs

Style: Federal (Sheraton)
Dating: 1800-20
Major Wood(s): Mahogany & mahogany
      veneer & maple
General Characteristics:
Case pieces: architectural pediments
      acanthus carving
      outset (cookie or ovolu)
        corners & reeded columns
      paneled sides
      tapered, turned, reeded or
        spiral turned legs
      bow or tambour fronts
      mirrors on dressing tables

Style: Federal (Sheraton) continued
Seating pieces: rectangular or square backs
     slender carved banisters
     tapered, turned or
      reeded legs

Style: Classical (American Empire)
Dating: 1815-50
Major Wood(s): Mahogany & mahogany
     veneer & rosewood
General Characteristics:
Case pieces: increasingly heavy
     proportions
     pillar & scroll construction
     lyre, eagle, Greco-Roman &
      Egyptian motifs
     marble tops
     projecting top drawer
     large ball feet, tapered fluted
      feet or hairy paw feet
     brass, ormolu decoration
Seating pieces: high-relief carving
     curved backs
     out-scrolled arms
     ring turnings
     sabre legs, curule
      (scrolled-S) legs
     brass-capped feet, casters

Style: Victorian – Early Victorian
Dating: 1840-50
Major Wood(s): Mahogany veneer, black
     walnut & rosewood
General Characteristics:
Case pieces: Pieces tend to carry over the
     Classical style with the
     beginnings of the Rococo
     substyle, especially in
     seating pieces.

Style: Victorian – Gothic Revival
Dating: 1840-90
Major Wood(s): Black walnut, mahogany
     & rosewood
General Characteristics:
Case pieces: architectural motifs
     triangular arched pediments
     arched panels
     marble tops
     paneled or molded
      drawer fronts
     cluster columns
     bracket feet, block feet or
      plinth bases

Style: Victorian – Gothic Revival continued
Seating pieces: tall backs
      pierced arabesque backs
        with trefoils or quatrefoils
      spool turning
      drop pendants

Style: Victorian – Rococo (Louis XV)
Dating: 1845-70
Major Wood(s): Black walnut, mahogany
    & rosewood
General Characteristics:
Case pieces: arched carved pediments
    high-relief carving, S- &
      C-scrolls, floral, fruit
      motifs, busts & cartouches
    mirror panels
    carved slender cabriole legs
    scroll feet
    bedroom suites (bed,
      dresser, commode)
Seating pieces: high-relief carved crestrails
    balloon-shaped backs
    urn-shaped splats
    upholstery (tufting)
    demi-cabriole legs
    laminated, pierced &
      carved construction
      (Belter & Meeks)
    parlor suites (sets of chairs,
      love seats, sofas)

Style: Victorian – Renaissance Revival
Dating: 1860-85
Major Wood(s): Black walnut, burl veneer,
    painted & grained pine
General Characteristics:
Case pieces: rectilinear arched pediments
    arched panels, burl veneer
    applied moldings
    bracket feet, block feet,
      plinth bases
    medium & high-relief
      carving, floral & fruit,
      cartouches, masks &
      animal heads
    cyma-curve brackets
    Wooton patent desks
Seating pieces: oval or rectangular
    backs with floral or
    figural cresting
    upholstery outlined
      with brass tacks
    padded armrests
    tapered turned front legs,
      flared square rear legs

Style: Victorian – Louis XVI
Dating: 1865-75
Major Wood(s): Black walnut &
ebonized maple
General Characteristics:
Case pieces: gilt decoration,
marquetry, inlay
egg & dart carving
tapered turned legs, fluted
Seating pieces: molded, slightly
arched crestrails
keystone-shaped backs
circular seats
fluted tapered legs

Style: Victorian – Eastlake
Dating: 1870-95
Major Wood(s): Black walnut, burl veneer,
cherry & oak
General Characteristics:
Case pieces: flat cornices
stile & rail construction
burl veneer panels
low-relief geometric &
floral machine-carving
incised horizontal lines
Seating pieces: rectilinear
spindles
tapered, turned legs,
trumpet-shaped legs

Style: Victorian
Jacobean & Turkish Revival
Dating: 1870-90
Major Wood(s): Black walnut & maple
General Characteristics:
Case pieces: A revival of some heavy
17th century forms,
most commonly in dining
room pieces
Seating pieces:
Turkish Revival style features:
oversized, low forms
overstuffed upholstery
padded arms
short baluster,
vase-turned legs
ottomans, circular sofas
Jacobean Revival style features:
heavy bold carving
spool & spiral turnings

Style: Victorian – Aesthetic Movement
Dating: 1880-1900
Major Wood(s): Painted hardwoods, black
      walnut, ebonized finishes
General Characteristics:
Case pieces: rectilinear forms
      bamboo turnings, spaced
        ball turnings
      incised stylized geometric &
        floral designs, sometimes
        highlighted with gilt
Seating pieces: bamboo turnings
      rectangular backs
      patented folding chairs

Style: Art Nouveau
Dating: 1895-1918
Major Wood(s): Ebonized hardwoods,
      fruitwoods
General Characteristics:
Case pieces: curvilinear shapes
      floral marquetry
      carved whiplash curves
Seating pieces: elongated forms
      relief-carved
        floral decoration
      spindle backs, pierced
        floral backs
      cabriole legs

Style: Turn-of-the-Century
    (Early 20th Century)
Dating: 1895-1910
Major Wood(s): Golden (quarter-sawn)
      oak, mahogany
      hardwood stained to
      resemble mahogany
General Characteristics:
Case pieces: rectilinear & bulky forms
      applied scroll carving or
        machine-pressed designs
      some Colonial & Classical
        Revival detailing
Seating pieces: heavy framing or high
        spindle-trimmed backs
      applied carved or machine-
        pressed back designs
      heavy scrolled or
        slender turned legs
      often feature some Colonial
        Revival or Classical
        Revival detailing such as
        claw & ball feet

tyle: Mission (Arts & Crafts movement)
ating: 1900-1915
Major Wood(s): Oak
General Characteristics:
'ase pieces: rectilinear through-tenon
                 construction
                 copper decoration,
                 hand-hammered hardware
                 square legs
eating pieces: rectangular splats
                 medial & side stretchers
                 exposed pegs
                 corbel supports

tyle: Wicker
ating: mid-19th century - 1930
Major Wood(s): Natural woven wicker or
                   synthetic fibers
General Characteristics:
'ase &   Earlier examples feature tall
eating pieces: backs with ornate lacy
                  scrolling designs
                  continuing down to the
                  arms & aprons
                  tables & desks often feature
                  hardwood (often oak) tops
                  after about 1910 designs
                  were much simpler with
                  plain tightly woven backs,
                  arms & aprons
                  pieces were often given a
                  natural finish but painted
                  finishes in white or dark
                  green became popular
                  after 1900

tyle: Colonial Revival
ating: 1890-1930
Major Wood(s): Oak, walnut & walnut
                   veneer, mahogany veneer
General Characteristics:
'ase pieces: forms generally following
                  designs of the 17th, 18th
                  & early 19th centuries
                  details for the styles such as
                    William & Mary, Federal,
                    Queen Anne, Chippendale
                    or early Classical were
                    used but often in a
                    simplified or stylized form
                  mass-production in the early
                    20th century flooded the
                    market with pieces which
                    often mixed & matched
                    design details & used a
                    great deal of thin
                    veneering to dress
                    up designs

Style: Colonial Revival continued
Case pieces: dining room & bedroom
                 suites were especially
                 popular
Seating pieces: designs again generally
                 followed early period
                 designs with some mixing o1
                 design elements.

Style: Art Deco
Dating: 1925-40
Major Wood(s): Bleached woods, exotic
                   woods, steel & chrome
General Characteristics:
Case pieces: heavy geometric forms
Seating pieces: streamlined, attenuated
                 geometric forms
                 overstuffed upholstery

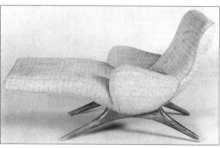

Style: Modernist or Mid-Century
Dating: 1945-70
Major Wood(s): Plywood, hardwood or
                   metal frames
General Characteristics:
Modernistic designers such as the
Eames, Vladimir Kagan, George Nelson
& Isamu Noguchi lead the way in post-
War design. Carrying on the tradition of
Modernist designers of the 1920s &
1930s, they focused on designs for the
machine age, which could be mass-
produced for the popular market. By the
late 1950s many of their pieces were
used in commercial office spaces &
schools as well as in private homes.
Case pieces: streamlined or curvilinear
                 abstract designs with
                 simple
                 detailing
                 plain round or flattened legs
                 & arms commonly used
                 mixed materials including
                 wood, plywood, metal,
                 glass & molded plastics
Seating pieces: streamlined & abstract
                 curvilinear designs
                 generally using newer
                 materials such as plywood
                 or simple hardwood
                 framing

Style: Modernist or Mid-Century continued
Seating pieces: Fabric & synthetics such as
vinyl were widely used for
upholstery with finer
fabrics & real leather
featured on more
expensive pieces.
seating made of molded
plastic shells on metal
frames & legs used on
many mass-produced
designs

Style: Danish Modern
Dating: 1950-70
Major Wood(s): Teak
General Characteristics:
Case &   This variation of Modernistic
Seating pieces: post-war design originated
in Scandinavia, hence the
name.
designs were simple &
restrained with case pieces
often having simple boxy
forms with short rounded
tapering legs
seating pieces have a simple
teak framework with lines
coordinating with case
pieces
vinyl or natural fabric were
most often used for
upholstery
in the United States dining
room suites were the most
popular use for this style
although some bedroom
suites & general seating
pieces were available

ENGLISH

Style: Jacobean
Dating: Mid-17th century
Major Wood(s): Oak, walnut
General Characteristics:
Case pieces: low-relief carving,
geometrics & florals
panel, rail & stile
construction
applied split balusters
Seating pieces: rectangular backs
carved & pierced crests
spiral turnings
ball feet

Style: William & Mary
Dating: 1689-1702
Major Wood(s): Walnut, burl walnut veneer
General Characteristics:
Case pieces: marquetry, veneering
               shaped aprons
               6-8 trumpet-form legs
               curved flat stretchers
Seating pieces: carved, pierced crests
               tall caned backs & seats
               trumpet-form legs
               Spanish feet

Style: Queen Anne
Dating: 1702-14
Major Wood(s): Walnut, mahogany, veneers
General Characteristics:
Case pieces: cyma curves
               broken arch pediments &
                   finials
               bracket feet
Seating pieces: carved crestrails
               high, rounded backs
               solid vase-shaped splats
               cabriole legs
               pad feet

Style: George I
Dating: 1714-27
Major Wood(s): Walnut, mahogany, veneer
                      & yewwood
General Characteristics:
Case pieces: broken arch pediments
               gilt decoration, japanning
               bracket feet
Seating pieces: curvilinear forms
               yoke-shaped crests
               shaped solid splats
               shell carving
               upholstered seats
               carved cabriole legs
               claw & ball feet, pad feet

Style: George II
Dating: 1727-60
Major Wood(s): Mahogany
General Characteristics:
Case pieces: broken arch pediments
               relief-carved foliate, scroll &
                   shell carving
               carved cabriole legs
               claw & ball feet,
                   bracket feet, ogee
                   bracket feet

Style: George II continued
Seating pieces: carved, shaped crestrails,
          out-turned ears
          pierced shaped splats
          ladder (ribbon) backs
          upholstered seats
          scrolled arms
          carved cabriole legs or
            straight (Marlboro) legs
          claw & ball feet

Style: George III
Dating: 1760-1820
Major Wood(s): Mahogany, veneer,
          satinwood
General Characteristics:
Case pieces: rectilinear forms
          parcel gilt decoration
          inlaid ovals, circles, banding
            or marquetry
          carved columns, urns
          tambour fronts or bow fronts
          plinth bases
Seating pieces: shield backs
          upholstered seats
          tapered square legs,
            square legs

Style: Regency
Dating: 1811-20
Major Wood(s): Mahogany, mahogany
          veneer, satinwood &
          rosewood
General Characteristics:
Case pieces: Greco-Roman &
            Egyptian motifs
          inlay, ormolu mounts
          marble tops
          round columns, pilasters
          mirrored backs
          scroll feet
Seating pieces: straight backs, latticework
          caned seats
          sabre legs, tapered turned
            legs, flared turned legs
          parcel gilt, ebonizing

Style: George IV
Dating: 1820-30
Major Wood(s): Mahogany, mahogany
          veneer & rosewood
General Characteristics:
    Continuation of Regency designs

Style: William IV
Dating: 1830-37
Major Wood(s): Mahogany, mahogany
veneer
General Characteristics:
Case pieces: rectilinear
brass mounts, grillwork
carved moldings
plinth bases
Seating pieces: rectangular backs
carved straight crestrails
acanthus, animal carving
carved cabriole legs
paw feet

Style: Victorian
Dating: 1837-1901
Major Wood(s): Black walnut, mahogany,
veneers & rosewood
General Characteristics:
Case pieces: applied floral carving
surmounting mirrors,
drawers, candle shelves
marble tops
Seating pieces: high-relief carved crestrails
floral & fruit carving
balloon backs, oval backs
upholstered seats, backs
spool, spiral turnings
cabriole legs, fluted
tapered legs
scrolled feet

Style: Edwardian
Dating: 1901-10
Major Wood(s): Mahogany, mahogany
veneer & satinwood
General Characteristics:
Neo-Classical motifs & revivals of
earlier 18th century & early
19th century styles.